# PHOTOSHOP 7

SAVVY™

# PHOTOSHOP® 7

STEVE ROMANIELLO

SAN FRANCISCO | LONDON

SYBEX®

**Associate Publisher:** DAN BRODNITZ

**Acquisitions and Developmental Editor:** BONNIE BILLS

**Editors:** DONNA CROSSMAN, JIM COMPTON, BRIANNE AGATEP, CAROL HENRY, PETE GAUGHAN

**Production Editor:** DENNIS FITZGERALD

**Technical Editor:** STEPHEN MARSH

**Production Manager:** AMY CHANGAR

**Cover, Interior, and Technical Illustration Designer:** CARYL GORSKA

**Icon Illustrator:** TINA HEALEY ILLUSTRATIONS

**Compositors:** MAUREEN FORYS, KATE KAMINSKI, HAPPENSTANCE TYPE-O-RAMA

**Proofreaders:** AMEY GARBER, NELSON KIM, DAVE NASH, LAURIE O'CONNELL, NANCY RIDDIOUGH

**Indexer:** TED LAUX

**CD Coordinator:** DAN MUMMERT

**CD Technician:** KEVIN LY

**Cover Illustrator/Photographer:** ALFRED GESCHEIDT, THE IMAGE BANK

LIBRARY OF CONGRESS CARD NUMBER: 2002101988

ISBN: 0-7821-4110-2

Dear Reader,

Thank you for choosing *Photoshop 7 Savvy*. This book is part of a new wave of Sybex graphics books, all written by outstanding authors who know their stuff — and know you, their audience. Steve Romaniello is an educator and Photoshop guru who has crafted a book that will guide you toward Photoshop 7 mastery. Its expressiveness, clarity, and depth are the best recipe for Photoshop savvy we've seen.

With each title we publish, we're working hard to set a new standard, both for the industry and for ourselves. From the paper we print on, to the designers we work with, to the visual examples our authors provide, our goal is to bring you the best graphics and Web design books available.

I hope you see all that reflected in this title. I'd be very interested in hearing your feedback on how we're doing. To let us know what you think about *Photoshop 7 Savvy*, please visit us at www.sybex.com. Once there, go to the product page, click on Submit a Review, and fill out the questionnaire. Your input is greatly appreciated.

Best regards,

Daniel A. Brodnitz
Associate Publisher—Graphics
Sybex Inc.

*For Rebecca*

# Acknowledgments

*Writing a book* of this kind is by no means a solitary venture. It would have been impossible to produce *Photoshop 7 Savvy* without the efforts and support of many friends who gave freely of their time and expertise. ■ First of all, thanks are owed to my agent, David Fugate at Waterside Productions Inc., for representing me with integrity and finesse. Much gratitude to the editorial and production team at Sybex: particularly acquisitions and development editor Bonnie Bills, whose encouragement and drive kept me on track; Dennis Fitzgerald, production editor, who carefully inventoried and organized the book's contents; and editors Donna Crossman, Jim Compton, Brianne Agatep, Carol Henry, and Pete Gaughan, whose ample experience helped me craft ideas and images into a real manuscript. My thanks to my technical editor, Stephen Marsh, for his vast knowledge and insistence on precision and attention to detail. I'm grateful to Amy Changar, Caryl Gorska, and Maureen Forys for their aesthetic vision in designing this book and laying out its pages, and to Dan Mummert and Kevin Ly for helping to compile the CD. ■ I am extremely grateful to those who contributed material to the book, including Photoshop masters Imo Baird, Rich Morgan, Ramona Pruitt, and Cyndee Wing. All shared their experience and expertise in several of the chapters. Thanks to Peter Bradshaw of ColorVision for providing calibration hardware and software. Thanks to my artist friends—Liisa Phillips, who provided inspiration; Andrew Rush, Chris Mooney, and my daughter Leah, who provided images for the book; and Seth Schindler and Carol Peterson Beech, whose encouragement helped me through some tough moments. ■ Thanks to all of my colleagues at Pima Community College, but particularly Frank Pickard, Dennis Landry, and Dave Wing, who provided continual moral support, and Mary Leffler, who provided technical support. I also want to thank the many students I've taught over the years. I'm sure that I have learned as much or more from them as they have from me. ■ My gratitude to Adobe Systems and the beta support team, who helped me leap over some of the hurdles by providing the Windows and Macintosh beta versions of the software early in the process. Thanks to Image Stock, Corel, PhotoDisk, ImageIdeas, and Eclectic Collections for providing images from their CD libraries. And thanks to Alien Skin Software for providing the cool Eye Candy plug-ins on the CD. ■ Thanks especially to my wife Rebecca and daughter Leah for their unwavering patience and support.

# CONTENTS AT A GLANCE

# Contents

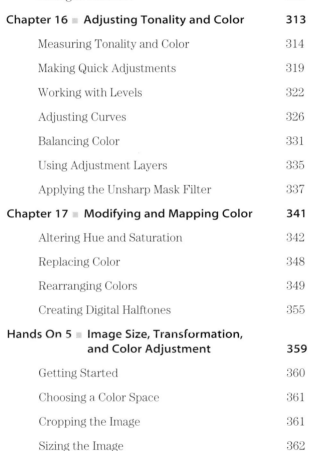

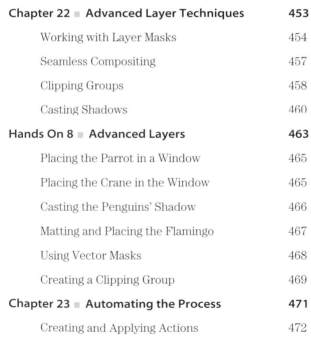

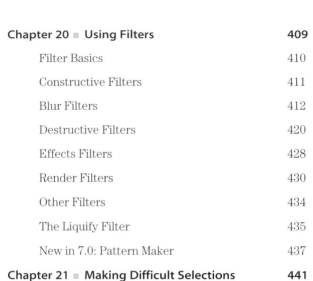

# Introduction

## The Image Transformed

I introduced my last book, *Mastering Photoshop 6*, which this book is based upon, by presenting a brief chronology of the development of photography and its importance to modern culture. It has been 18 months since the release of Photoshop 6 and here I am again looking for the words to describe a profound technological phenomenon.

The photographer has been the primary recorder of events since the early 19th century. A photograph captures fleeting moments of time and commits them to film, paper, or pixels. Photographic images have been altered for many reasons: to conceal or fabricate evidence, to discredit or accuse, to promote a political agenda. Let's not forget that images have also been altered for less sinister ends. Like the cosmetic surgeon, the airbrush artist routinely removed unwanted wrinkles and hair, photos were optically enhanced in the darkroom in the process of preparing them for publication, and of course, artists have found the photograph fertile ground for fantasy and experimentation.

From the introduction of computer graphics in the 1960s and the evolution of imaging software in the '70s and '80s, to the release of a powerful, personal, mainstream image-editing package called Adobe Photoshop in the early '90s, the image has become a far more fluid reality accessible to anyone with a personal computer. In *Photoshop 7 Savvy*, you will find everything you need to know to use this powerful program to create and alter images for print, multimedia, and the World Wide Web.

## *Photoshop 7 Savvy*: Who Should Use This Book

The immense popularity of Adobe Photoshop is in part attributable to the fact that it enables us to alter the reality of images. And who, after all, can resist the temptation to change the nature of what we see? *Photoshop 7 Savvy* is for anyone who has ever unconsciously scribbled a mustache on a face in a magazine while talking on the telephone. It's for those of us who take photographs, draw, paint, and cut and paste pictures. It's for computer artists, graphic designers, Web designers, and printers. It is intended to help master the software, at whatever level you may be in the learning curve.

## A Systematic, Comprehensive Approach

The focus of *Photoshop 7 Savvy* is to present a complete and organized guide to the tools and operations of Adobe's amazing image-editing software. It is intended to offer descriptions, explanations, and techniques that will make all aspects of the software more accessible and familiar to you without oversimplifying or "dumbizing" the information. How you work in Photoshop will be defined by your specific output goals. The book explores the basic concepts that are fundamental to your understanding of the digital image. Each chapter contains information to help you master the Photoshop skills you need. Most chapters contain step-by-step modules, and are interspersed with Hands On projects, which will further enhance your capabilities so that you can ultimately apply the techniques to your own images.

Photoshop is an enormous software package with the capability to perform almost any imaging operation. When you consider the number of operations that Photoshop can execute, and how they might be combined, the image-editing possibilities become infinite. Making this information understandable and, above all, interesting to you, is the intent of *Photoshop 7 Savvy*.

## How to Become Photoshop Savvy

*The Master in the art of living makes little distinction between work and play, labor and leisure, mind and body, education and recreation, love and religion. He simply pursues his vision of excellence in whatever he does, leaving others to decide whether he is working or playing. To him he is always doing both.*

—*ZEN APHORISM*

Becoming Photoshop savvy is more than learning where the tools and operations are and how to use them. The real knowledge comes from being able to creatively apply what you know. Although Photoshop is used by scientists and engineers for image manipulation and color correction, the majority of end users are interested in expressing visual ideas. Photoshop gives them the power to paint, color, synthesize, collage, composite, manipulate, and distort the reality of their pictures and fulfill the potential of their artistic vision.

Photoshop is like all visual art forms, in that the best work is created with love, passion, focus, and skill. The fundamentals of design, composition, and color apply to digital images just as they do to traditional drawings, paintings, and graphics. The basic principles of design are balance, proportion, unity, direction, and emphasis. Great images are *balanced* in that they carry an appropriate weight within a given space. The viewer's eye can move from one element to another with fluid ease. The *proportional* relations of elements create an optical rhythm throughout the composition that the viewer can sense, which effectively communicates the content of the image. The image is *unified* by a strong cohesive force that holds it together. The eye moves in a determined *direction* and does not wander aimlessly around looking for a place to rest. Elements are structured in a visual hierarchy, which *emphasizes* them in the order of their importance. The mood, color scheme, and ambiance are relevant to the content and message of the image.

Along with a cognizance of the importance of design, an innate sensitivity to the formal elements of the image—color, light, shadow, form, and perspective—is imperative. The knowledge of the potential and the limitations of the tools that are needed to produce the desired results are also critical. Pay attention to the minutest of details with the realization that the photographic image is relentless in its seamless portrayal of reality.

Finally, becoming Photoshop savvy means a commitment to the attainment of absolute perfection, but also an awareness of its elusiveness. Each new project presents a fresh opportunity to apply your knowledge, skills, and insights to the fulfillment of this exalted goal.

*Photoshop 7 Savvy* takes the sting out of learning the program and makes the experience pleasant and interesting. It will be your tour guide and point out some of the remarkable landmarks and points of interest along the way, helping to make your journey absorbing and entertaining. Of course, merely reading this book is not enough. You must work through the step-by-step operations and Hands On tutorials until you understand the concepts, and then apply what you've learned to your images. From time to time you will need specific questions answered, and I hope *Photoshop 7 Savvy* will provide all the answers you need.

## Making the Most of *Photoshop 7 Savvy*: What's Inside

*Photoshop 7 Savvy* thoroughly covers the latest and greatest features in Photoshop 7—from the File Browser to new tools and features to Web enhancements. Throughout the text I've identified features that are new to Photoshop 7 with a "New" margin flag. If you're familiar with previous versions of Photoshop and want to skim a topic for the latest changes, look for this marker. Photoshop's new features and operations are also summarized in Chapter 2.

*Photoshop 7 Savvy* is for users on both the Mac and Windows platforms. Differences between the Mac and Windows versions of Photoshop are slight. One obvious difference is key commands, which vary in some cases due to differences between keyboards for the two platforms. When keys differ, both are given, with the Mac key first: ⌘/Ctrl, Option/Alt, Return/Enter, Delete/Backspace. When keys need to be pressed in combination, they are separated by a hyphen. For example, ⌘/Ctrl-S indicates that you should press ⌘ and S (Mac) or Ctrl and S (Win).

The primary content of *Photoshop 7 Savvy* is distributed into several parts. There is also a special color section that provides the material you need to see in color, as well as a supporting CD-ROM containing the documents and images used in this book.

## Part I: Photoshop Core

To put the phenomenon of Adobe Photoshop into a historical perspective, the introductory chapter presents the artistic foundations and technical innovations that have led to its emergence as the leading image-editing methodology in the world today. The sources are as diverse as the Impressionist movement and the development of the World Wide Web. In Chapter 2, I cover all of the new features that make version 7 a formidable upgrade.

The rest of Part I, which is by far the largest section of the book, explores the nuts and bolts of Photoshop. The fundamentals of digital imaging are explained to provide insight as to how Photoshop documents are created and structured. With this basic information under your belt, you will gain a working, hands-on knowledge of Photoshop's core tools and operations, knowledge enough to begin to apply them to real-world projects.

## Part II: Photoshop Color

Part II presents techniques for managing and manipulating color. This is the section where you will learn how to manage color throughout the entire imaging process to assure predictable results. Part II also delves into tonal adjustment and color correction. A variety of creative color-mapping and correction possibilities are explored, along with techniques for image enhancement and photo retouching.

### Part III: Photoshop Savvy

You'll really flex your Photoshop muscles in Part III. Featured are advanced techniques to retouch photos, manage layers, make complex selections, apply creative enhancement filters, superimpose images, and automate the program.

### Part IV: Photoshop, WWW, and DV

The Internet, being a fundamental aspect of communication in the 21st century, deserves an exclusive section of the book. Photoshop is universally used to create and edit images for the Web. We will explore techniques for Web page design in Photoshop and methods for optimizing and saving images for use on the Internet. You'll explore ImageReady, Adobe's Web image–preparation software that is bundled with Photoshop, and you'll learn to create spliced images, rollovers, and animations.

This part of the book also covers some of the aspects of digital video and the integration of Photoshop images with nonlinear editing software like Adobe Premiere.

### Hands On: Comprehensive Tutorials

Among the chapters, you'll find in-depth tutorials called "Hands On." In these sections you get your hands dirty in complex, real-world projects that utilize a combination of the techniques discussed in previous chapters. Follow along using the image files on the CD.

### Appendices

The appendices provide a reference to Photoshop 7. They include a description of Photoshop 7's tools, file format information, explanations of blending modes, and a list of key commands.

### Glossary

The purpose of *Photoshop 7 Savvy* is to demystify the software and make it more user-friendly and understandable to you. I have deliberately taken pains to avoid computerese wherever possible; however, in many instances it is not possible to explain certain concepts without using a specialized vocabulary. For this reason, I have included a comprehensive glossary for common (and uncommon) terminology that you may not be familiar with or that is needed to clarify a concept.

## Color Material

The 32-page color section showcases color-oriented material from the chapters and Hands On sections. When you see a figure numbered C12, for example, within a chapter or tutorial, turn to the color section to see that image in full color.

## The *Photoshop 7 Savvy* CD

The CD that accompanies this book features the images and documents used in the book's step-by-step operations and Hands On sections. Images are contained within labeled folders for each chapter or Hands On tutorial. The CD also contains demo versions of some powerful Photoshop plug-ins.

 Throughout the book, we've flagged the places where you can take advantage of files on the CD. Look for the CD margin icon to quickly spot hands-on practice and demonstration files.

# How to Reach the Author

It gives me great pleasure to make the information I've gathered over the past 10 years available to you. I truly hope that *Photoshop 7 Savvy* meets your needs and answers your questions. When I coauthored *Mastering Adobe GoLive 4* with Molly Holzschlag, and wrote *Mastering Photoshop 6* a year later, I was amazed at the incredible feedback for the book I received from all over the world. I appreciate your comments and would like to hear from you. You can reach me at www.sybex.com.

Steve Romaniello

Tucson, Arizona

# Photoshop Core

**The first part** *of Photoshop 7 Savvy introduces you to the fundamental concepts of digital imaging. You'll see how Photoshop and digital image manipulation fit into the evolution of image technology. You'll explore Photoshop's newest features, its interface, and its logic and organization.*

*Part I also covers the key techniques of selections, layers, painting, and transforming images. You'll work with Photoshop's new paint engine, learn about digital color, and address resolution issues. Three Hands On projects allow you to apply your new skills.*

# CHAPTER 1

# The Foundations of Photoshop

*To understand how Photoshop* works, it's helpful to be familiar with the artistic and technical traditions from which it evolved. Techniques such as painting, mosaic, photography, and printing remained the primary methods of producing two-dimensional images for centuries, and are the source of most of what we can do on a computer today. The 20th century has seen the rapid development of new hybrid image technologies that extend and amplify these traditional ones. Photoshop embraces a myriad of technologies, uniting them into a single interface that allows the user to work with any conceivable combination. Putting Photoshop into a historical context and learning how its many features are related to traditional methods of working with images will give you a perspective on its potential.

This chapter covers these topics:

- **What is image technology?**
- **The history of imaging, from prehistory to today**
- **Painting, printing, collage, and photography**
- **The world of Photoshop and the Web**

## Image Technology

Image technology is the method with which pictures are produced. Since the first images were painted on the stone walls of caves with pigment extracted from natural materials, humans have invented new image technologies to visually express their ideas and experiences. The process of technical evolution was slow in preindustrial societies, so for thousands of years, techniques for creating images were primarily done by the skilled hands of artists and artisans. During and after the industrial revolution, however, image technology accelerated to the point that, today, we see new innovations on an almost daily basis.

The evolution of the visual image is due, in part, to the methods available to the artist. Artistic styles are an expression of the zeitgeist of the periods that produce them. As technology evolves, new ideas and visual idioms emerge that reflect the cultural ambiance of their times.

This idea was quite apparent in the 20th century from the speed in which new technologies emerged. The obvious changes in aesthetic values can be observed decade by decade as cultural, political, and technological influences affected visual expression. Each decade of the 20th century can be associated with distinct aesthetic styles that are part of the ongoing development of culture.

## Mosaics

One significant milestone in the history of visual art was the ability to portray tonality. *Tonality* is the effect of changing light or color on an image. In the real world, we see a seamless continuum of blended color that defines our visual world in light and shadow, and produces a tangible, three-dimensional reality of color and form. Primitive artists made no attempt to express tonal differences, in part because the technology was unavailable to them.

If you think that tonal variations in digital images is a new phenomenon, however, think again. One of the first methods of simulating the effect of tonal variation was to place tiny individual units of slightly varied color next to each other. We see this tech-

Figure 1.1

A mosaic from first-century B.C.E. Pompeii, *The Defeated Persians under Darius* (detail)

nique commonly employed in mosaics from imperial Rome, like the one in Figure 1.1. Each element of color is a separate glass or ceramic tile. The tiles, placed next to each other in a graduated sequence, produce the effect of varied tonality.

The mosaics of two thousand years ago are the predecessors of today's Photoshop images. Instead of tiles of glass, the digital artist uses squares of colored light called *pixels* (see Figure 1.2). Today's scanners can "see" and interpret color information from a continuous-tone image into these tiny units. When the image has been captured, we can, in Adobe Photoshop, select and change the color of pixels individually or in groups.

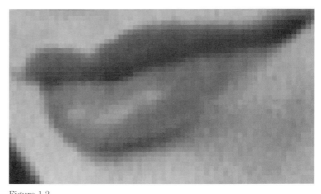

Figure 1.2

**A close-up of a digital image displaying its pixels**

## Painting

Creating images by applying color to a surface is one of the most basic forms of artistic expression; indeed, the history of the world can be viewed in the legacy of paintings that have been left behind by our talented predecessors. Throughout history, the technical and aesthetic qualities of painting have changed, various styles have emerged, and pictorial content has evolved.

Representational painting dominated the world for centuries. Paintings contained content that could be easily recognized, whether the subject matter was religious, historical, or descriptive. Then in the late 19th century, artists began to abstract the tangible realities that they observed to produce art filtered through their personal experiences. Within 50 years, abstraction led to the creation of a totally nonobjective idiom in styles like the Abstract Expressionism of the 1950s and the Minimalism of the 1960s.

Still, the tradition of representation coexisted with abstract painterly forms, but it was reinvented time and again as it reflected the zeitgeist in which it was created. Pop Art of the 1960s, for example, introduced us to the idea that the objects and icons of popular culture could be assimilated and even elevated into the realm of "pure art." This concept was revolutionary because it changed the way we viewed the commonplace.

Though the imagery has changed, the painter's tools have remained pretty much the same over the centuries. Paint, palette, knife, brushes, solvent, paper, canvas, panel, and easel have been around for quite some time, having seen few refinements throughout history. (Even the airbrush evolved from an air-driven breath atomizer that has been in use since the 18th century.) The concept remains the same: mix colors on the palette, adding solvent if desired, and apply them to the painting surface with a brush or knife. Only recently have methods of applying color to a surface been substantially transformed.

Photoshop is a virtual art studio. Through Photoshop's graphical user interface, you can apply color to an image as if you were painting. Instead of pigment, however, you are mixing colors and painting with light. Photoshop has numerous tools, operations, and filters that enable you to make a photographic image appear as if it had been painted in virtually any style and with any paint medium (see Figure 1.3). You have 16,777,216 colors to choose from and brushes of almost any size or shape with which to apply the color. For a full view of this image, see Figure C1 in the color section of this book.

Figure 1.3

**A photograph altered to look like a painting using Photoshop's brushes and filters**

CHRIS MOONEY ILLUSTRATION, 1996

## Impressionism

In the 19th century, in an attempt to revive what was perceived to be the glories of the classical civilization of the Greeks and Romans, much of what was being produced in the art world consisted of the representational, idealized images of the Neoclassic style. In the latter part of the century, the nature of European art shifted. The Impressionist movement emerged with a fresh new approach to painting. Artists like Claude Monet, Paul Cézanne, and Mary Cassatt produced paintings that were explorations of the quality and nature of light and color.

The importance of the Impressionists' contribution to the way we perceive color cannot be overstated. One particular group of Impressionists, the Pointillists—and particularly Georges Seurat and Paul Signac (see Figure 1.4, which is also Figure C3 in the color section)—most influenced the digital art we practice today. The Pointillists worked extensively with color theory and how one color affects the colors around it. They applied paint to the canvas in units, or little dots, not unlike the pixels on a Photoshop document or the halftone dots on a color separation. They experimented with how the eye mixes adjacent colors. Placing dots of two opposite colors—red and green, for example—next to each other will produce gray when seen from a distance. The relative density of the dots affects the darkness and lightness of the perceived color and its tint.

Pointillism influenced the development of process printing, which uses four colors to produce full-color images. Figure 1.5 presents a close-up view of such a four-color picture (for a color view of this image, see Figure C4 in color section). In process printing, each color plate contains tiny dots of cyan, magenta, yellow, or black (CMYK). Like Pointillist painting, the densities of the colored dots on each plate influence the surrounding colors when the eye mixes them together.

Photoshop is the ultimate color separator. It can configure and generate process-color separations, and separate duotones, tritones, and quadtones. In addition, Photoshop has filters that allow you to simulate Impressionist and other painterly effects.

Figure 1.4

**Paul Signac, *The Port at Sunset, Saint-Tropez, Opus 236*, 1892**

Figure 1.5

**Detail of a four-color process image**

# Printing

Another significant change in the ability to produce images came about a thousand years ago with the emergence of woodcuts, which were used to print textiles. In the early 15th century, the use of woodcuts and wood engraving began to take hold in Europe as a method of producing pictures (see Figure 1.6). At about the same time, Gutenberg introduced the concept of movable type technology. Printing gave us the capability of producing multiples of the same image—the first big step in mass communication.

Of course, the printed image has evolved over the past 500 years; we've invented numerous methods of imprinting ink on paper, monochromatically or in full color. In the case of traditional offset printing, the process involves separating colors into their ink components, transferring the information to a piece of film and then to a metal plate. Ink is applied to the plate, and the color is imprinted onto paper.

Photoshop software is used to prepare images for almost any commercial printing technique, including offset lithography, silk screen, and digital press. Artists even use Photoshop to create and transfer images for traditional copper or zinc intaglio printing.

The most direct method of printing a Photoshop image is to a laser or ink-jet printer, but Photoshop files can also be output to film recorders to generate color slides, to imagesetters to produce high-resolution color separations on film, or directly to the printing plate. Exciting new output technologies have appeared within the last few years to print super-sized ink-jet images and continuous-tone photographic prints.

Figure 1.6

**A woodcut from a Venetian edition of the fables of Aesop, published in 1491**

# Photography

When you think of how many centuries passed in which images were created exclusively by hand, you can appreciate how revolutionary the photograph was. A crude type of camera called a camera obscura, which was developed in the beginning of the 14th century, captured and projected light on a surface. However, it wasn't until 1826 that the first true photograph was taken. Early photographers needed special equipment and a broad knowledge of chemistry to produce photographs (see Figure 1.7). As a result of the scientific and technical discoveries of the 19th and 20th centuries, cameras became more efficient and easier to operate. Now, millions of still photographs are taken and processed everyday.

A camera is very much like the human eye. Light rays enter a camera and are focused on a surface into an image. Film rests on the surface and is exposed, causing a chemical reaction. The exposed film is then bathed in certain chemicals in a process called developing. If the film is a negative, light passes through it onto a piece of photosensitive paper. The paper is developed, stopped, and fixed, producing a positive photographic image.

Several tools, filters, and operations are specially designed to make the photographer feel right at home in the digital Photoshop environment. In fact, Photoshop is a virtual darkroom that includes tools to dodge, burn, saturate, enlarge, crop, mask, and, of course, correct and adjust color. New digital printers are available that focus laser light on photosensitive materials to produce continuous-tone color prints and transparencies.

Figure 1.7

**Lady Clemintina Hawarden, photograph of a model, 1860**

As a result of the popularity of computer programs like Adobe Photoshop, digital cameras have become a recent addition to photo technology. Digital cameras create pictures that can be transferred to a computer or television set. The digital camera's lens focuses light on a light-sensitive mechanism called a charge-coupled device (CCD), which changes the light into electrical signals. The electronic pictures can then be stored on disks or opened in a computer graphics program. With additional equipment, electronic images can also be sent over telephone lines or printed on paper.

## Collage

In the early part of the 20th century, the artistic revolution in Europe was shocking the world with images that had never before been seen. Instead of representational content, the pictorial sources came from an abstraction of physical reality or the realization of a personal, inner reality. Cubists, Dadaists, and Surrealists changed the face and meaning of art.

Before World War I, the Dada movement produced works of anti-art that deliberately defied reason. Growing principally out of Dada, Surrealism flourished in Europe between the world wars as a visual art and literary movement. Surrealist images had a dreamlike quality where time, space, and matter were completely malleable. Compelled by the idea that rational thought and behavior had brought the world close to the brink of annihilation, the

Figure 1.8

**An engraving from Max Ernst's *Une semaine de bonté***

Surrealists created images that were anti-rational and anti-bourgeois. Surrealist painters like Jean Arp, Max Ernst, Salvador Dalí, Paul Delvaux, René Magritte, André Masson, Joan Miró, and Yves Tanguy created new worlds where the nature of reality depended only on the artist's unlimited imagination.

Hand in hand with this new aesthetic freedom came new image technologies. For artists concerned with the free association of images and the meaningful relation of unrelated objects, collage was the technique of choice. The recycling of printed graphics and text in the form of collage was developed to accommodate the Surrealists' need to create the visual non sequitur. For the first time, printed images from multiple sources were combined to produce a new pictorial reality. The Surrealist Max Ernst created a book called *Une semaine de bonté* (*A Week of Kindness*), a pictorial novel consisting entirely of recycled engravings from newspapers, magazines, and catalogs (see Figure 1.8). This novel was a technical and aesthetic tour de force when it was published in 1933. It epitomized and refined the absurdist viewpoint of the Surrealists and the freedom and creativity in which they pursued their artistic vision.

## Photomontage

New movements in art and graphic design blossomed in Europe in the 1920s and 1930s as a result of the instability brought about by the aftermath of World War I, the Great Depression, and the Russian Revolution. Constructivism, New Typography, Streamline, and Dada recycled photographic images, typography, and graphics as collage elements in a new process called photomontage.

Radical magazines and newspapers from the period, like *Simplicicimus* and *Arbeiter-Illustrierte Zeitung* (*AIZ*, or *Worker's Illustrated Times*), published photomontage images as satirical cartoons to promote a socialist or anti-fascist political agenda. Photomontage is a collage of photographs that are carefully cut and pasted together to create a new visual reality. Often, type and other graphic elements are incorporated into the composition. These images synthesized the seamless pictorial realities of multiple photographic images into biting political metaphors (as in Figure 1.9) and clever visual puns. Traditional cut-and-paste photomontage was an art form derived from the Cubist, Dadaist, and Surrealist movements, but was displayed in the commercial venue of magazine publications. It was the predecessor of the digital composite images we see in many of today's advertisements.

The ability to combine photographs, text, and graphics from multiple sources is one of Photoshop's strongest features. Images can be collected from a scanner, digital camera, or PhotoCD, and be composited, superimposed, positioned, scaled, flipped, rotated, and distorted. In Photoshop, almost any effect is possible; the only limitation is your imagination.

## The Web

Recently, the world has been transformed by a powerful new invention. This new communication technology is as revolutionary as the telephone and as ubiquitous as the automobile. Within a few years, it has embedded itself deeply in our lives and has affected how we communicate

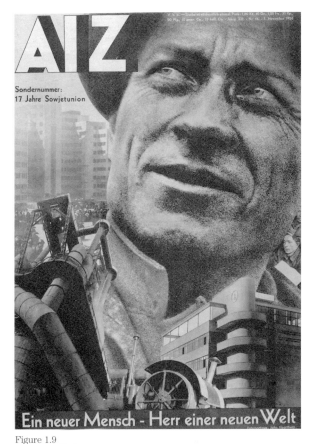

Figure 1.9

*A New Man, Master of the World.* **Photomontage by John Heartfield, published in** *Arbeiter-Illustrierte Zeitung,* **1934. Reproduced with permission of Artists Rights Society (ARS), New York.**

and how we do business. The World Wide Web (Figure 1.10) is by far the most accessible communication medium in which to publish images or text. As a research tool, the Web gives us instant access to every conceivable form of information. The Web is the ultimate technical manifestation of democracy in that it embodies the essence of free speech and freedom of the press. Being the most unregulated of all publishing mediums, anyone can publish anything at any time.

The Web has changed the nature of how we handle pictures. Images can be transmitted electronically and downloaded, making access to them almost instantaneous, even at a distance. Many art museums and libraries have placed digital files of their entire archives online, making them accessible to everyone. If you need a picture of a particular subject, the first and last place to look is now the Web.

Figure 1.10

**An Adobe Web page**

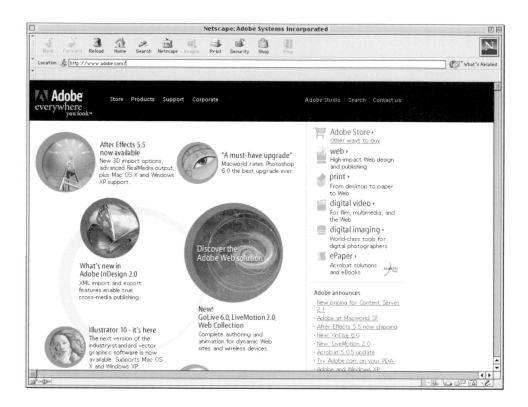

The tools and functions introduced with Photoshop 5.5 were almost exclusively devoted to Web publishing. Methods for choosing, optimizing, and saving files in the appropriate format have been seamlessly integrated into the program, eliminating all guesswork. A new color picker offers the choice of Web-compatible hexadecimal colors. ImageReady, software used for creating slices, animations, and rollovers, is now bundled with Photoshop to further extend Photoshop's capabilities and to work in a fully integrated environment.

## Photoshop

The introduction of new artistic idioms into our culture not only affects the world of art galleries and museums; it influences advertising, architecture, industrial design, and fashion. As new styles appear on the scene through commercial vehicles, they become an integral part of our everyday lives. The same is true of new image technologies: as new ones are introduced, they become embedded into the production cycle of our economy.

In our contemporary culture, images are everywhere. Pick up a book, magazine, or newspaper, and images dominate the layout. Take a walk or drive, and you'll see images on billboards, signs, and the sides of buildings. These pictures are the result of the work performed by artists, designers, illustrators, and photographers. The legacy of image technology is the primary influence on the images we see today. Its evolution has given us the foundation to create and manipulate images to visually communicate ideas in personal, commercial, or artistic venues.

Never in the history of art have we seen anything quite like Adobe Photoshop. Never has one single tool, studio, or machine combined so many powerful methods of working with images. Photoshop is the culmination of the development of image technology over thousands of years. It is a revolutionary new way of visually communicating ideas. It unites the vision of the artist with the technology of the moment. Since its first release, it has been the world's most popular imaging software, because it endows its users with so many possibilities for the creation and development of images for any form of publication. Photoshop presents those possibilities in the elegant, user-friendly environment of the virtual art studio, darkroom, or print shop, where images can be created and edited in almost any conceivable size, content, or configuration.

# CHAPTER 2

# What's New in Photoshop 7

*While Photoshop 6* saw a complete interfacelift, the alterations to version 7 are less visible but equally as powerful. Photoshop 7 is full of new surprises that make image editing a breeze.

From the ground up, a revised architecture, new control windows, and an overhauled paint engine enhance the power of the program. New retouching tools and enhanced Web features round out Photoshop's capabilities to meet any creative or production demand and handle any image-editing task.

Some of the new components of the upgrade have revitalized dialog boxes and enhanced workflow capabilities. The centerpieces include the File Browser to visually identify and open images; the Healing Brush and Patch tool to restore distressed images; the Auto Color command for instant, reliable color correction; a customizable and savable workspace; and a spell checker and Search and Replace features.

This chapter will cover new features such as:

- **Viewing and accessing additions**

- **Tool improvements**

- **Workspace operations**

- **New text functions**

- **Web authoring enhancements**

# System Requirements

The following sections list the hardware and operating system requirements for Windows and Macintosh.

## Windows

Windows requirements include:

- Intel Pentium–class processor
- Microsoft Windows 98, Windows ME, Windows 2000, Windows NT 4 (service pack 6), or Windows XP
- A minimum of 128 MB of RAM
- A color monitor capable of displaying a minimum of 256 colors
- An 8-bit or greater video card
- An 800×600 or greater monitor resolution
- A CD-ROM drive

## Macintosh

Mac requirements include:

- PowerPC processor
- MacOS software version 9.1 or OS X
- A minimum 128 MB of RAM
- A color monitor capable of displaying a minimum of 256 colors
- An 8-bit or greater video card
- 800×600 or greater monitor resolution
- A CD-ROM drive

# Accessing and Viewing

The File Browser, which is the centerpiece of the upgrade, provides visual access to image thumbnails that you can quickly identify and open whether they are on your hard disk, external drive, CD, DVD, or network. The File Browser displays image history such as the date created and the date modified, and EXIF information from digital cameras. Files can be rotated, renamed, ranked, and reorganized.

The File Browser presents four different fields for accessing images:

- A tree hierarchy field, similar to desktop lists, shows the folders from which you choose your images.
- The thumbnail field displays thumbnails of image files within a selected folder or disk. You can choose from three thumbnail sizes. The thumbnail field also displays image data such

as the filename, the date it was created and last modified, its file format, image size, rank, and a copyright.

- The preview field presents a larger view of a selected thumbnail.
- The metadata pane displays additional information about a selected image.

# Tools

Photoshop 7 introduces a few new tools and a reorganized Tool palette. You can customize and save tool settings:

**Tool Presets**  The new Tool Preset Manager, which sits on the left side of the Options bar, allows you to save and load specific tool configurations.

**Healing Brush Tool**  Restores images by sampling and replacing pixels. It preserves attributes like texture, highlight, and shadow when sampling on or between layers that contain pixels.

**The Patch Tool**  Lets you select an area of the image, copy it, and move it to repair larger areas. It then samples the areas around the patch for perfect blending.

**Paint Tools**  You can reproduce a myriad of traditional painting techniques with new dynamic brush options. In addition, you have more precise control over the quality of your brush strokes. You can take full advantage of your Wacom graphics tablet's tilt and airbrush thumbwheel features, giving you even greater control over brush strokes.

# Dialog Boxes

In version 7, some of the dialog boxes are easier to use:

**Filters**  The Filter dialog boxes now display bigger preview windows, making it much easier to foresee the results when applying your settings.

**Curves**  The Curves dialog box can be enlarged for precise control.

# Workspace

Photoshop 7 empowers you to save and load custom workspaces. The workspace lets you save custom palette configurations that you can use for a task-specific, efficient workflow. For example, you can save a custom workspace specifically for color correction with pallet positions, options, and presets ready to go.

# Text

Version 7 offers these improvements in working with text:

**Spell Checker**  The new spell checker ensures accuracy. You can check text on a single layer or across the entire document in multiple languages.

**Search and Replace**  You can find and replace words, and change their content or case.

## Liquify

The Image → Liquify command has been moved to the Filter menu along with the Extract feature. Its enhanced interface gives you greater control over image warping with zoom, pan, and multiple undos. You can save your meshes and apply them to the same image at a later time or to a different image. The meshes can be automatically resized to fit new images at any resolution.

The new Turbulence Brush tool mixes up the pixels for easy distortion and applies interesting multiple effects. The Backdrop option lets you view individual layers or the flattened version of your document, enabling you to compare layers as you work.

## Color Correction

The Auto Color command creates reliable color correction with the click of a mouse. This auto function provides more reliable color correction than Auto Levels or Auto Contrast, depending on the image, and is easily applied with a click of your mouse.

## Patterns

The new Pattern Maker lets you create patterns simply by selecting a section of an image. It randomly creates new patterns and seamlessly tiles them. You can generate realistic and abstract patterns from image textures such as grass, rocks, bark, and sand. And you can determine the scale of the generated pattern, and create multiple larger tiles from a smaller one. The random option generates unlimited versions of the pattern and lets you choose the best option from a list.

## Automations

Two of the automated features have been substantially improved:

**Picture Package** A more interactive interface with previews and custom settings has been added to this feature. You can print multiple images on one page, saving time and materials. Enhancements to Photoshop 7 let you print to different page sizes and add labels or text to each image for printing.

**Web Photo Gallery** The Web Photo Gallery creates an instant Web site of your work. It has been improved to offer sophisticated new templates that give you more choices for layout and a new security option that lets you enter text or place the filename, caption, or copyright information on the image as a watermark.

## Web Tools

In both Photoshop and ImageReady, you can preview images to see how they'll look as JPEGs, GIFs, or PNGs. You can compare the quality and file size of the image before optimizing them.

New Web enhancements in Photoshop and ImageReady include:

**Knockout Color**  Click on a color to knock it out. You can remap more than one color at a time and restore colors to their original settings.

**Dithered Transparency**  With the new Dithered Transparency option in Photoshop and ImageReady, you can create degrees of transparency. Using this option, Web graphics can be seamlessly blended onto a background—even patterned backgrounds—without having to first choose a matte color.

**Vector Art**  When optimizing images for the Web, you can keep vector art and text looking crisp by assigning a higher priority to it.

**Rollovers**  New preview options enable you to see slices, rollovers, image maps, and animations of a document in the new Rollover palette.

## Security

Photoshop 7 supports Adobe Acrobat 5 security settings, allowing you to create more tightly protected Photoshop PDF files before sharing them with others. The new security features protect copyrighted art and photography, and place the usage options firmly in your hands.

## XMP

XMP (Extensible Metadata Platform), is a format used to make workflows more efficient so that their content can be transparently applied to print and Web documents, e-books, and other media. XMP uses XML, Extensible Markup Language framework that can be applied to Adobe applications such as Photoshop 7, Acrobat 5, Adobe InDesign 2, and Adobe Illustrator 10 that standardizes the creation, and exchange of metadata across publishing workflows. For example, the keywords you add to your Photoshop 7 files can be indexed by Web search engines giving potential clients greater ability to access them. For more information about XMP, go to `www.adobe.com/products/xmp/main.html`.

# CHAPTER 3

# The Nature of the Beast

*Every 18 months or so,* Adobe releases a new version of Photoshop, which is currently in its seventh iteration. Some users are frustrated by the new release, saying that they barely had time to learn version 6, and now they have to learn an entirely new program. But let's consider the strategy of the new release. First of all, most of the components of Photoshop 6 remain intact. The upgrade has either added to or improved the features. Users who are comfortable in 6 will feel even more at home in 7. Just as importantly, in order for Photoshop to continually remain on the cutting edge of digital-imaging technology, it needs frequent upgrades. The architecture of this current version of Photoshop has been changed to run seamlessly on MacOS X and Windows XP. In addition, there are many new whistles and bells that make the upgrade worthwhile (refer to Chapter 2, "What's New, Briefly," for the full list).

There are few software programs that end users love as much as Adobe Photoshop! Organizations of PS aficionados exist throughout the world. The National Association of Photoshop Professionals (NAPP) boasts thousands of members from 64 countries and is one of the largest graphics related organizations in the world. NAPP holds annual conferences and training seminars in the U.S., the U.K., and Europe. See `www.photoshopusers.com` for more information.

Photoshop is not a soft and fuzzy program, however. It's big, it's powerful, and it will do almost anything for you if you ask it nicely. Before you jump into the world of Photoshop headfirst, you need to understand its temperament. In this chapter, you'll learn about:

- **The anatomy of a digital image: vector and raster images**

- **Color channels**

- **Working wisely in Photoshop**

- **Opening, saving, and duplicating documents**

- **File formats and compatibility**

# The Anatomy of a Digital Image

Graphics software uses two fundamentally different methods to construct images. First, vector graphics consist of objects constructed by mathematically defined points and curves. And second, raster images use a grid of squares, or pixels, to determine color variations.

## Understanding Vector Graphics

*Vector graphics* are composed of lines and objects that define their shapes. On a computer, you can draw hard-edged graphics that, when printed, produce clean, sharp lines and edges. This is particularly valuable for illustrators who want to create crisp, well-defined artwork. Vector software is also ideal for graphic designers who work with type, because type characters need razor-sharp edges with no "jaggies" (stair-step edges caused by a series of right angles trying to represent a curve).

Vector-based illustration software like Adobe Illustrator, Macromedia FreeHand, and Corel-DRAW, or page-layout programs like QuarkXPress, Adobe PageMaker, and Adobe InDesign, are sometimes referred to as *object-oriented* software, because the primary technique requires building independent graphic lines or shapes ("objects") point by point, segment by segment, and stacking and arranging them until your drawing or page is complete.

To draw these objects, the artist uses a method of clicking and dragging the mouse, which deposits points, line segments, or shapes. The objects created in vector-based software are made from *Bezier curves*, like the ones in Figure 3.1. Bezier curves can even be straight lines, but what makes them different from the pixels used by raster images is that that they are composed of mathematically defined points and segments.

One advantage of using vectors is that the images are *resolution-independent*, which means that they automatically conform to the highest resolution of the output device on which they are printed, whether it's a desktop ink-jet, a laser printer, or a high-resolution imagesetter.

Because the data of vector-based images involves mathematical equations, a printer can read the formulas of each object transmitted in a printer language and convert the information into tiny dots. An image that is created at the size of a postage stamp can be resized and printed at the size of a billboard with no loss of quality. The complexity of a vector image, not its physical size, is what determines the file size; therefore, vector images take up much less space on a disk than raster images of comparable dimensions. Figure 3.2 shows raster and vector versions of the same image. The image on the left is composed of pixels; the image on the right is composed of objects surrounded by anchor points and line segments that define Bezier curves. The Bezier curves do not print. (See a color version of this image, Figure C2, in the color section.)

Figure 3.1

**Bezier curves**

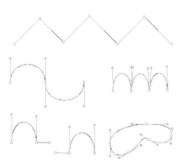

Figure 3.2

A raster image composed of pixels (left) and a vector version of the same image, composed of shapes constructed from Bezier curves (right)

Object-oriented software extends your capability to produce high-impact color graphics. Vector-based illustration software is appropriate for the creation of traditional logos, charts, graphs, maps, cartoons, highly detailed technical and architectural plans, and illustrations and images that require hard edges, smooth blends, and sumptuous color. Vector-based page-layout software is ideal for the creation of documents where Images and text are combined, as in books, pamphlets, brochures, and flyers.

## Understanding Raster Images

Although Photoshop 7 uses vector-based graphics in several of its operations (see the sidebar in this chapter titled "Vector Tools in Photoshop"), it is primarily designed to edit *raster images*. Raster images, sometimes called *bitmaps*, are fundamentally different from vector images in that they consist of a grid of little squares called *pixels* (short for *picture elements*). A pixel is an individual square of colored light and is the smallest editable unit in a digital image. The pixels in a digital image are usually so small that, when seen on a monitor, the colors blend into what appears to be a continuous-tone image. Figure 3.3 is enlarged so you see the individual pixels that make up the image's overall effect.

Figure 3.3

A close-up detail of an image composed of pixels

## VECTOR TOOLS IN PHOTOSHOP

Although Photoshop's capabilities are primarily designed to select and edit pixels, it does offer some vector tools. The Pen tool, for example, uses Bezier curves to make accurate selections. Its operation is similar to the Pen tool in Adobe Illustrator. Once you've created a curve or path, you can stroke or fill it, convert it into a selection for raster editing, or export it to a vector-based program. (The Pen tool is discussed in detail in Chapter 9, "Drawing Paths.")

The Photoshop Type tool creates type generated from your installed fonts. The type remains editable until you rasterize it or "flatten" the image. This tool is extremely powerful for creating display text and special text effects, but it is not really designed to produce body copy (usually text is 12 points or smaller) on most documents. It is better to import your Photoshop image into a vector-based illustration or layout program and generate the body copy there. When printed, the image will conform to its specific image resolution, and the text will print at the resolution of your printer. (See Chapter 8, "Working with Type," for more on the Type tool.)

Photoshop's Shape tool (described in Chapter 9) is another vector generator. You can choose from a list of standard shapes, such as rectangles, ellipses, and polygons, and you can construct, edit, and store entirely unique vector-based shapes.

The distinction between Photoshop and vector-based illustration software, like Illustrator, FreeHand, or CorelDRAW, is that Photoshop does not print object-oriented graphics as vectors. Instead, it depends on the resolution information of the document to automatically rasterize them before they are sent to the printer. The vector operations in Photoshop are designed to make the interface more powerful and user-friendly, but they do not affect the image when it is output.

The quality of a raster image and how it prints depend on the number of pixels the image contains, or its *resolution*. If you think of a pixel as the basic building block of an image, you can envision how a larger number of smaller blocks will define an edge or an area more precisely than fewer, larger blocks. The file sizes of raster images are usually quite large compared to other types of computer-generated documents, because information needs to be stored for every pixel in the entire document.

Raster-based software is best suited for editing, manipulating, and compositing scanned images, images from digital cameras and Photo CDs, continuous-tone photographs, realistic illustrations, hyperreal artwork including logos with subtle blends, soft edges, or shadow effects, and artistic filter effects like impressionist or watercolor.

# Color Channels

When you scan an image, the color information the scanner "sees" is separated into red, green, and blue components. Photoshop configures this information into three color channels plus a composite RGB channel, which displays the entire image in full color. Think of each color channel as a separate, transparent color overlay consisting of red, green, or blue pixels. The combination of the three color values, when superimposed over each other, produces full color.

When an image is scanned, each channel can potentially contain a total of 256 possible shades each of red, green, or blue, because each pixel on the channel contains 8 bits of tonal information (see the sidebar titled "Bit Depth"). The computer processes the information in each channel as an independent grayscale image. Each pixel is assigned a specific numerical gray value, where black equals 0 and white equals 255.

By default, individual color channels are displayed in grayscale because it is easier to see the subtle variations in contrast when looking at the channel in black and white. You can, however, see the independent components of an RGB image in color. Follow these steps:

1. Choose Window → Channels.

2. Choose Edit → Preferences → Display & Cursors.

3. Check the Color Channels In Color option.

4. In the Channels palette, click the thumbnail of the red, green, or blue color channel to display that color component of the image on-screen.

# Working in Photoshop

If you think about it, the computer is really a megacalculator that sits on your desktop and crunches numbers at lightning speed. Although the graphical user interface, or GUI (pronounced "gooey"), of a raster software program like Photoshop lets you perform virtual operations that mimic real-world tasks like painting, compositing, or filtering, what is actually happening behind the scenes is that the numeric color values of the red, green, and blue pixels in each color channel are being changed.

Photoshop works as an image editor, color corrector, or photo compositor, but by no means is it limited to these tasks. Its primary purpose is to alter reality, and that is the ultimate reason for its popularity. There is something very compelling and empowering about changing the color of the sky in a landscape or replacing Uncle Herman's scowl with a smile from another photograph.

No matter how you alter an image, the sequence of procedures you employ is quite similar:

1. Capture the image using a device like a scanner or digital camera. These devices "see" the continuous-tone image and divide the information into pixels, which Photoshop can display and edit.

## BIT DEPTH

A computer uses the binary number system to describe pixels. The simplest graphic images are 1 bit "deep." In these files, only 1 binary digit of information describes the pixel: 0 for off, 1 for on. Each pixel is one of two colors, either black or white.

Grayscale and Indexed color images use an 8-bit system, in which any pixel can be one of 256 shades of gray or color, respectively. Each pixel contains 8 bits of information. Each bit can be either on (black) or off (white), which produces 256 possible combinations ($2^8 = 256$).

Full-color images are 24-bit color, using three 8-bit primary color channels—for red, green, and blue—each containing 256 colors. These three channels produce a potential 16.7 million colors ($256^3 = 16,777,216$). Photo-realistic images that consist of smooth gradations and subtle tonal variations require 24-bit color to be properly displayed.

Some scanners can produce images of 48-bit color. In this system, the information is being distributed into 3 16-bit channels, each with 65,536 possible color combinations ($2^6 = 65,536$). These images can produce trillions of possible colors. Some professionals prefer these high-bit images because they offer an extended dynamic range and more subtle tonal variations. Photoshop can read images with 16 bits of information per channel, like a 48-bit RGB or a 64-bit CMYK color image, but the file sizes of these images are much larger and the commands and filters that are available to edit them are quite limited.

Even though images with higher bit depths contain more color information, they are displayed on the monitor at the bit depth capability of your video card, which in most cases is 24 bits. To see an image in 24-bit color depth on a Macintosh, the monitor should be set to Millions Of Colors; in Windows, the setting should be True Color.

The information from the image that you create in Photoshop is transmitted from the computer to the monitor. A color monitor consists of a grid of screen pixels that are capable of displaying three values of color simultaneously. In a CRT (cathode ray tube) monitor, there are three electron guns inside—a red, a green, and a blue—that scan the surface of the screen and fire streams of electrons at it. (LCD monitors use a different system. See Chapter 15, "Color Management and File Preparation.") The more electrons that hit the screen pixel, the brighter it glows. When all three guns are firing at full intensity, the screen pixel appears white; when all three guns are not firing, the pixel appears black. The variation of the intensities of red, green, and blue electrons striking the pixels is what produces the full range of color that we see on-screen. Of course, all of this happens much faster than your eye can perceive, so you see a stable image on your monitor.

2. Save the image to a disk. The image is stored on your disk media as a sequence of numbers that represent its pixel information.

3. Open the image in Photoshop and use one of Photoshop's selection techniques to isolate the part of the image you want to affect. When you make a selection, you are telling Photoshop in advance where you would like to apply an operation.

4. Apply one of Photoshop's numerous tools or operations to the image to implement an edit.

Of course, this sequence can vary and can become extremely complex by the application's specialized selection techniques, multiple operations, or sophisticated layer methods, but, generally speaking, this is how you work in the program.

## Developing Strategies

Because high-resolution images require large amounts of RAM and processing time, the digital artist or designer should develop a strategy for each job. A good production strategy should focus on four areas:

- Configuring and optimizing your system so that it runs smoothly
- Working wisely and efficiently in Photoshop
- Using shortcuts
- Communicating clearly with your client

### Optimizing Your System

These items are discussed in detail in Chapter 5, "Setting Up the Program," and Chapter 15, "Color Management and File Preparation," but here are some tips for optimizing your system:

- Increase the application memory.
- Assign the first scratch disk to your fastest hard drive with the most disk space. For the scratch disk, Photoshop requires three to five times the disk space of your largest open file. You can choose additional scratch disks to increase the amount of virtual memory.
- Keep the Clipboard clear of large amounts of data.
- Use a utilities program regularly to keep your disks optimized.
- Install as much RAM as possible.
- Work on a calibrated system.
- Compress files whenever possible.
- Work on an optimized system by deleting old files, backing up data, and regularly defragmenting your disk with a program like Norton Utilities.

## Working Wisely

You'll want to keep the following items in mind when you are working in Photoshop. These items are discussed in more detail throughout the book:

- Create a low-resolution version of the document. Lay out the image and experiment with operations and effects. Then apply those same operations to a high-resolution version.

- Save your settings when adjusting color.

- Work on a duplicate of your image (Image → Duplicate) so that you can experiment freely.

- Save selections as paths or alpha channels whenever possible.

- Use layers to segregate parts of the image in order to keep the editing process dynamic.

- Apply filters to each channel individually when necessary.

- Learn and use keyboard shortcuts and the Actions and History palettes.

- Save tool and brush presets and your workspace using the new Save Workspace feature.

- Save your document often, and back up your work.

- Archive your images to CD or other media in order to free up hard-disk space.

## Using Shortcuts

While a good production strategy will smooth your workflow, numerous key commands and shortcut techniques can enhance your performance. In Photoshop, there are several ways to execute almost every operation, which can be confusing at first. Many of the same operations can be performed from a menu, by a key command, or from a palette, field, or button. As you develop knowledge of the program, however, you will begin to fashion a way of working that is unique to your personal style, and it will be only a matter of deciding which method suits you.

The quick-key list in Appendix D gives you a list of Photoshop's key commands. It pays to learn as many of them as possible, particularly the ones that you use most frequently. Not only will this save you work time, but it can also be physically beneficial to try a new style of operating your computer. Finally, if you work on more than one operating system, be sure to read the section titled "Platform Compatibility" later in this chapter for more on keyboard shortcuts.

### TAKING ADVANTAGE OF ACTIONS

You can write a Photoshop script, called an Action, that you play by pressing a function key. Actions automate one operation or a sequence of operations, and they enable you to perform multiple tasks quickly. One nice perk is that you can save Actions to a file. When you need a particular Action or Action sequence, you can play it and apply its operations to any image. Photoshop ships with some tasty default Actions that are really convenient to use. You can even run a Batch Action that will be applied to all of the images in a folder while you are sleeping, watching television, or eating a grilled cheese sandwich. For more about Actions, read Chapter 23, "Automating the Process."

### ACCESSING TOOLS

Photoshop's numerous tools are accessible by simply touching a letter key on the keyboard. Of course, you have to remember what tool each letter represents. Sometimes it's quite obvious—for example, M for the Marquee tool—but sometimes it's not, as in K for the Paint Bucket tool. Don't worry if you forget a tool's keyboard equivalent. Simply hold your cursor over any tool, and a little label called a *tool tip* will tell you the name of the tool and the key that represents it. As you can see in Figure 3.4, the shortcut key for the History Brush tool is Y.

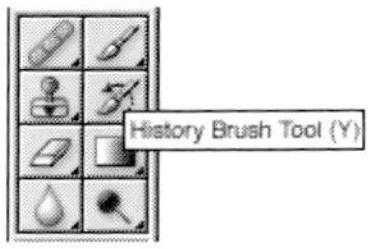

Figure 3.4

**Tool labels**

### SAVING ADJUSTMENTS, COLORS, AND BRUSHES

Color adjustment settings can be saved as a separate file and loaded for application to other documents. You can make a brush of virtually any shape, size, hardness, or angle and save it for use in any Photoshop document. You can create and save special Color palettes and apply the colors to any Photoshop image. These techniques are covered in detail in Chapter 10, "Creating and Applying Color," and Chapter 16, "Adjusting Tonality and Color."

Photoshop's interface is so well designed that the processes of saving and loading adjustments, colors, brushes, or Actions are all the same. When you've learned to save or load one, you've learned to save or load them all.

## Communicating with Your Clients

Whether you're a professional designing for commercial customers or a volunteer producing images for nonprofits, many of you are using Photoshop to create images for clients. When you're working for a client, the creative process becomes a collaboration. Clear and open communication with your client is essential to maintaining a smooth workflow. Here are some keys to keeping your client satisfied:

- Make sure that you and your client have agreed on the job's objectives and specifications. Show your client your work in stages. Start with thumbnails and develop the project over time, getting your client's approval for each iteration before proceeding with the next. Determine how the finished image will be used. If you are going to output to print, determine film and print specifications like paper, ink, and halftone screens. If it's going to be output to CD-ROM or the Web, be sure find out what the size and format specifications are. Put all the job specifications in writing.

- Determine the nature of the job, what work is to be done, and what third-party vendors will be involved. Will you need to purchase high-end scans, or will desktop scans suffice? Are you responsible for output, or will your clients deal directly with the service bureaus, printers, or Internet providers?

- Define each component of the project and build a realistic schedule around this information. You will then be able to structure your time and make consistent progress on the project.

Figure 3.5

**The Open dialog box**

## Opening Documents

Most of your work in Photoshop will be performed on images that have been acquired using some piece of digital technology that converts color information into pixels. After you've captured an image with a scanner or digital camera and stored it to a disk, you can open these files by choosing File → Open, which brings up the dialog box shown in Figure 3.5.

You are presented with a list of files on your disk. Highlight one by clicking it with your mouse. If the Show Preview button is clicked (it then becomes the Hide Preview button), the dialog box displays a thumbnail of the image.

Windows displays a preview at the bottom of the Open window. The Show/Hide Preview option is only available for Mac.

Photoshop
Photoshop 2.0
BMP
CompuServe GIF
Photoshop EPS
Photoshop DCS 1.0
Photoshop DCS 2.0
EPS PICT Preview
EPS TIFF Preview
Filmstrip
JPEG
Generic PDF
Generic EPS
PCX
Photoshop PDF
Acrobat TouchUp Image
Photo CD
PICT File
PICT Resource
Pixar
PNG
Raw
Scitex CT
Targa
TIFF
Wireless Bitmap

Figure 3.6

**The Open dialog's Format list**

What if you swear that you saved an image to a particular disk, but it does not appear in the list? Well, the Photoshop Open window may not display certain files when it doesn't recognize the file's type. On the Macintosh, a file's type code is four characters long and can be seen in its Get Info box. On Windows, the file type is represented by the filename extension, which is usually three characters long. For example, TIFF in MacOS equates to .tif in Windows.

To display files regardless of their type code or extension, Macintosh users should select All Documents from the Show options pop-up list; Photoshop attempts to guess at the format in which it thinks the file has been saved. If you think Photoshop has guessed incorrectly, then click the Format options list and choose the correct format (as shown in Figure 3.6). If you get an error message, keep trying. If you've tried all of the formats and can't open the image, it is either corrupt or incompatible with Photoshop.

Windows users should click the down arrow in File Of Type and select All Formats. If the image won't open, try the Open As feature and assign a format. Once again, if you've tried all of the formats and can't open the image, it is either corrupt or incompatible with Photoshop.

### Finding Files

In Photoshop for MacOS, the Open command has a Find function built into it. If you can't find the file you're looking for, click the Find button. In the next dialog box, enter all or part of the filename, click Find, and the program will take you to the first item on your disk with the same name. If the Find function displays the wrong file, click Find again until you locate what you're looking for.

### Browsing Files

You can preview the images in a folder or on a disk prior to opening them with Photoshop 7's new File Browser. To use this feature, follow these steps:

1. Choose File → Browse. The browser window appears, displaying the contents of the selected folder (see Figure 3. 7).

2. Choose the desired folder or disk from the pull-down menu or from the directory at the upper-left of the screen.

3. Click on a thumbnail of an image in the image list to see a larger version of it in the preview field. The preview area can be expanded or contracted by dragging its top and bottom borders. The field below the preview presents information about the image.

4. Double-click (Mac) or right-click (Win) an image to open it. A few useful features appear at the bottom of the window:

   - Toggle Expanded View expands the window to show more thumbnails.

   - Sort By enables you to reorganize the images by different categories chosen from the menu.

   - View By lets you choose the type and size of thumbnail displayed.

   - Rotate will automatically rotate an image clockwise 90 degrees or, if Option/Alt is pressed, counterclockwise.

   - Delete will discard a file.

Figure 3.7

**The File Browser**

## Importing a Scanned Image

Scanner software often has a plug-in module that will work directly within Photoshop to scan an image. The module must be placed in the `Plug-Ins` folder in the `Adobe Photoshop 7` folder when the scanner software is installed. In most instances, the plug-in will automatically be placed in the `Plug-Ins` folder when it is installed. Choose File → Import to access the module. When the image is scanned, it will automatically appear in a new Photoshop window. (For more on this, see Chapter 14, "Capturing Images.")

# Creating New Documents

You can generate a new, empty document in Photoshop that can be used as a blank canvas on which to paint or paste images from other sources.

To create a new document, follow these steps:

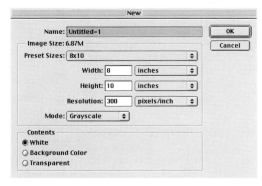

Figure 3.8

**The New dialog box**

1. Choose File → New. The New window (shown in Figure 3.8) appears.

2. In the Name field, enter a name for the document, but remember that naming the document is not the same as saving it. Eventually you will need to save it to your disk.

3. Just under the Name field, the file size in bytes is displayed. This will change depending on the height, width, resolution, and color mode you choose for the document. Enter a width and a height in the appropriate units.

4. Enter the resolution of the document. This will depend on how the document will be output. (See Chapter 13, "Sizing and Transforming Images.")

5. Choose a mode from the Mode list, which indicates how the color information of the new document will be configured. Use Bitmap for line art and Grayscale for black and white images with tonality. RGB (red, green, blue), CMYK (cyan, magenta, yellow, and black), and Lab (Lightness, A, and B) modes will produce full-color images. (See Chapter 10 for more on color modes.)

6. In the Contents field, indicate the color of the background. You can choose White, or choose the current background color in the Tool palette; these settings will produce a flattened image. If you choose Transparent, the background will become a regular layer (with a checkerboard pattern to indicate transparency), because the background cannot be transparent (see Chapter 7, "Layering Your Image").

7. Click OK.

The Photoshop 7 New dialog box displays a new menu (shown in Figure 3.9) with preset sizes, including standard image sizes for letter, legal, and tabloid paper, as well as metric ISO A sizes and typical pixel-size documents for display on monitors and the Web.

Figure 3.9

**The new preset list in the Photoshop 7 New window**

## Creating a Document from the Clipboard

You can create a document window from an image that has been copied to the Clipboard. To perform this operation, follow these steps:

1. Choose Select → All.

2. Choose Edit → Copy to copy an image or the contents of a selection in Photoshop, or a raster image from another software program, to the Clipboard.

3. Choose File → New; Photoshop automatically displays a New Document dialog box with the dimensions of the copied image and color mode.

4. Click OK. The new, empty image window appears.

5. Choose Edit → Paste, and the image is copied into the new document.

# Saving Files

There are five different methods for saving a Photoshop document to a disk—Save As, Save As A Copy, Save, Paths To Illustrator, and Save For Web—which you can find in the File menu. They are affected by the options set under Edit → Preferences → File Handling (see Chapter 5). What follows is a description of each method.

Figure 3.10

**The Save As dialog**

## Saving As

Use File → Save As to save your document to a designated location on your disk. You can name the document and choose a format for it. The newly named file will replace the document in the active window. Version 7 provides these options in the Save As dialog box (Figure 3.10).

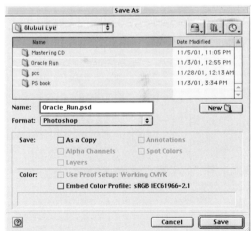

Checking or unchecking the boxes in the Save field of the Save As dialog box allows you to choose options that configure the document to your particular needs.

**As A Copy** When you check As A Copy, the document is saved to a designated location on your disk but does not appear in the image window. Be sure to rename it so as not to replace the current image.

Selecting the As A Copy option creates a new, identical document that is automatically renamed with the current document's name plus the word copy—for example, mydocumentcopy.psd. If you save as a copy with the same name to the same location, you replace the original file, defeating the make-two-versions purpose of the command and essentially just performing a plain save. Proceed with caution, because it is possible to lose the previous document.

**Alpha Channels**  If you're saving an image that contains alpha channels to a format that supports alpha channels, this box will be active. Formats that support alpha channels are Photoshop (PSD), Photoshop 2.0 (Mac format only), Photoshop PDF, PICT, PICT Resource (Mac format only), Pixar, Raw, Targa, TIFF, and Photoshop DCS 2.0. (See Chapter 12, "Using Alpha Channels and Quick Mask.")

**Layers**  If you're saving an image that contains layers to a format that supports layers—TIFF, Photoshop PDF, or Photoshop (PSD)—this box will be active. (See Chapter 7.)

**Annotations**  If you've attached notes to your document with the Notes tool, you can include them in the saved version by checking the Annotation box. Photoshop (PSD), Photoshop PDF, and TIFF are the only formats that support annotations. (See Chapter 4, "Navigation: Know Where to Go.")

**Spot Colors**  Spot color channels can be saved by checking this box. Formats that support spot color are Photoshop (PSD), Photoshop PDF, TIFF, and Photoshop DCS 2.0. (See Chapter 18, "Duotones and Spot Color.")

The boxes in the Color field of the Save As dialog box determine whether color management information will be saved with the document. (See Chapter 15.)

**Use Proof Setup**  A soft proof is an on-screen document that appears as close as possible to what the image will look like if printed to a specific device. If you are saving the image as a Photoshop EPS, Photoshop PDF, or Photoshop DCS 1.0 or 2.0, you can embed in the document the soft proof profile, which you choose from the View → Proof Setup menu. (See Chapter 15.)

**Embed Color Profile (Mac)/ICC Profile (Win)**  Checking this box embeds the RGB, CMYK, or grayscale profile chosen in the Edit → Color Settings dialog box under the Working Spaces field. You can select this option if you're saving to Photoshop PSD, Photoshop PDF, JPEG, TIFF, EPS, DCS, and PICT formats. (See Chapter 15.)

## Saving

Saving a document (File → Save) updates the file that you are working on and saves it to the current document. When working in Photoshop—or any software, for that matter—it is always a good idea to save frequently so you won't lose valuable time and effort should your system crash.

## Saving for the Web

This option (File → Save For Web) was introduced in version 5.5 and serves as a convenient tool for preparing files for Web publication. On the Web, as in life, there is always a compromise between quality and speed. When you choose Save For Web, you choose the best combination of format characteristics for Web images (Figure 3.11). You can compare the appearance and download times of up to four possible configurations for your image at a time. The Save For Web option is covered in detail in Chapter 25, "Photoshop 7 for the Web."

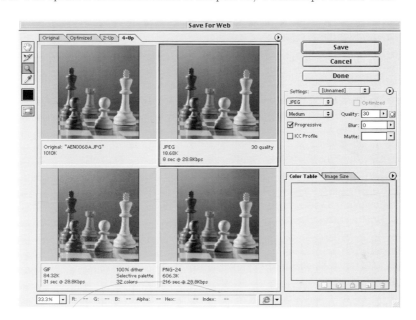

Figure 3.11

**The Save For Web dialog box**

### Exporting Paths to Illustrator

The File → Export → Paths To Illustrator command lets you save paths created with Photoshop's vector tools as an Adobe Illustrator file. You can align and trace paths on an image in Photoshop and export using Paths To Illustrator; when you open them in Illustrator, they will be fully editable as Bezier curves. (See Chapter 8 for more about paths.)

## Duplicating a Photoshop Document

You can duplicate a document on the fly. The Image → Duplicate function will produce an exact copy of the document along with its layers and alpha channels. It is useful for quick experimentation when you don't want to affect the original image. The new file, which by default is given the original filename plus the word *copy*, is unsaved and exists only in memory. If you plan to keep the duplicate file, it is wise to save it immediately. Check the Duplicate Merged Layers Only box if you want to combine the visible layers into one merged layer in the new document.

# Understanding File Formats

Different file formats serve different purposes. Some formats compress data to make the file-size smaller on the disk, while others are used to make a file compatible with another software program or the World Wide Web. The format you choose will depend on how the image will ultimately be used. It is important to know what saving an image to a specific format will do. At worst, saving a file to the wrong format can actually damage it; at the very least, it will inconvenience you by losing the ability to place the document into another program.

Photoshop 7 can open 26 different file formats on the Mac and 23 on Windows and save to 18 different file formats on the Mac and 16 on Windows. With the addition of plug-ins that attach to the Import and Export submenus, Photoshop supports even more, which means it is a great program for converting files to make them compatible with other software programs. A complete list of file formats, what they do, and how they operate can be found in Appendix B.

# Platform Compatibility

In ancient computer times (less than a decade ago), a battle raged between Macintosh and Windows users. Amazingly, the passion and prejudice generated by proponents of one platform or the other bordered on religious fervor. What is it about a computer platform that generates such divisiveness in its adherents? I think it has to do with the fact that a personal computer is, in essence, an auxiliary brain. It stores information and ideas that can't fit into the limited storage capacity of our own gray matter and extends our ability to make calculations and perform complex tasks. A platform simulates the way we think and organize our reality. We can personalize the way each interface behaves and how it looks, to a certain extent, which increases our attachment to it.

The phenomenon of platform prejudice will, I'm sure, be a topic for social theorists to thoroughly investigate in the future. The battle has died down because of the ability of the different computers to read each other's data. The latest Macintosh operating system, MacOS X, has a program called PC Exchange bundled into the system, which gives the computer the ability to read Windows disks. If you install a program like MacOpener by DataViz (www.dataviz.com) on your Windows PC, it will read Macintosh disks. With the same data now readily accessible by both platforms, the barriers have come down.

> The one area of disparity between platforms remains the distinction between Mac and PC fonts, which has graphic designers and computer artists cringing when they have to work on more than one platform.

The platform issue has also diminished because of programs like Photoshop that, for the most part, ignore platform differences. Photoshop is designed to be cross-platform compatible and to perform comparably in Windows and Macintosh environments. Photoshop will open documents from either platform, providing they have been saved in a format that supports cross-platform compatibility. The native Photoshop format is probably your best bet, because it supports layers. TIFF (which also supports layers in version 7), PICT, and EPS are good alternatives for flattened images, providing they are saved with cross-compatibility in mind. You can use JPEG format with its efficient compression scheme to archive images to CD and open them in either platform.

Photoshop performs equally well on Macintosh and Windows computers. For the most part, the Photoshop interface is similar for both versions of the software, with minor differences in appearance. Because Macintosh and Windows keyboards differ slightly, keyboard commands are different. Table 3.1 lists the parallel command keys of the two systems.

| MACINTOSH | WINDOWS |
|-----------|---------|
| ⌘ | Ctrl |
| Option | Alt |
| Delete | Backspace |
| Return | Enter |

Table 3.1

**Macintosh and Windows Keyboard Equivalents**

## Software Compatibility

In the age of information, publishing is indeed a universe unto itself. The process of creating an image for print, multimedia, video, or the Web may involve many steps that require specific tools. It is the task of the designer, image editor, desktop publisher, or computer artist to assemble the tools that best perform the necessary tasks. Photoshop does not exist in a vacuum, but works in concert with other computer programs to integrate the images, text, graphics, animations, digital video, etc. that compose the final publication.

Images created and edited in Photoshop integrate into all mainstream desktop-publishing, illustration, Web-authoring, and video-editing programs. Because of its ability to open and save in so many different file formats, Photoshop is preferred by most design professionals as the essential image-editing software and is the mainstay in a suite of powerful publishing tools.

# CHAPTER 4

# Navigation: Know Where to Go

*A computer-generated image* is not really that complex. In fact, it exists most commonly as a series of positive and negative charges on a piece of magnetic media. Quite unlike a drawing, painting, or photograph for which you need only your eyes and a half-decent light source to see, viewing a digital image requires some very fancy electronic equipment, starting with a computer and a monitor. To seriously edit or manipulate the image, you need a big pixel-pusher program like Adobe Photoshop.

Photoshop is big all right—so big that it's quite possible to get confused or lost trying to determine where all the stuff is and what it means. Use this chapter as your road map, because it explains Photoshop's numerous navigation features that enable you to find your way around the program. In this chapter, you'll travel through the workspace, tour the menus and palettes, and zoom through Photoshop's viewing options. By the end of your journey, you'll be a seasoned Photoshop traveler.

In this chapter, you'll learn about:

- **Launching the program**

- **Using Photoshop's GUI**

- **Accessing menus**

- **Working with palettes, rulers, guides, and grids**

- **Displaying the image**

# Launching the Program

When you install Photoshop 7, you can access the program files from your Macintosh `Applications` folder on the hard disk or in Windows at `C:\Program Files\Adobe\Photoshop 7.0`. The `Adobe Photoshop 7.0` folder (see Figure 4.1 for the Mac version) contains icons that make Photoshop functional, plug-ins that extend its capabilities, and settings that contain Photoshop's preferences. Additional folders and the Install CD contain extras like stock art, additional color palettes, custom brushes, and other freebies. The `Adobe Photoshop 7` folder also contains the Photoshop application (called Adobe Photoshop 7.0 in Mac and Photoshop.exe in Windows). To launch the program, double-click its icon.

## The Splash Screens

When you double-click the Photoshop 7 icon, the splash screen (Figure 4.2) appears, telling you what components of the program are loading. It also displays some of the data you entered when you loaded the program onto your computer, such as your name and the program's serial number. The splash screen contains a few amusing features worth mentioning. It is the signature piece of the designers and software engineers who contributed to the program's development.

As soon as the program finishes loading, the splash screen disappears. You can display it again by choosing About Photoshop from the Apple menu on a Macintosh or from the Help menu in Windows. Wait a moment, and the text starts to scroll. Hold down the Option key (Mac) or the Alt key (Win) to accelerate the scroll rate. If you wait for one complete scrolling cycle and then hover or Ctrl-click your cursor just above the large Adobe Photoshop 7 title, you will see Adobe Transient Witticisms (ATWs), a series of one-liners created by Photoshop's program

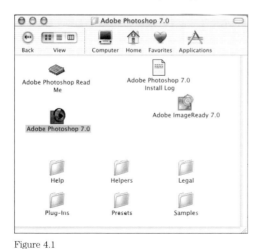

Figure 4.1

**The Photoshop folder (MacOS X version)**

Figure 4.2

**Photoshop's splash screen**

developers and engineers. The ATWs are very amusing—perfect for jaded Photoshop users in need of a chuckle—and provide an insight into the stressful life of the Photoshop development team. There is even a list of the music that the programmers listened to while crafting the beta. To make the splash screen disappear, click it.

The eye icon at the top of the Tool palette accesses the Adobe Online splash screen, which launches your browser and takes you to the Adobe website at `www.adobe.com` for online help.

The Photoshop interface, as shown on MacOS X, looks like Figure 4.3. The Tool palette is displayed on the left side of the screen, and four palette clusters are displayed on the right side. At the top of the screen are the menus. From these three areas, you will access all of Photoshop's image-editing tools and operations.

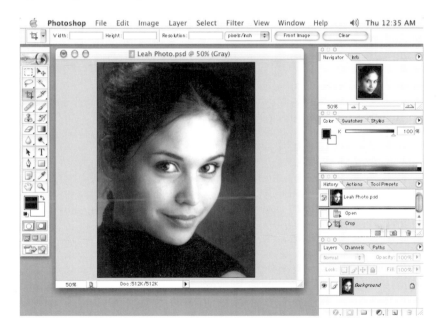

Figure 4.3

**The Photoshop work-space in MacOS X, showing default settings**

## Photoshop's GUI

A GUI is a software program's way of communicating with you. The computer is really not much more than a machine that does really fast math, and each operation is a series of mathematical calculations. Imagine how labor-intensive it would be if you had to perform that math yourself. For example, suppose you had to change the RGB values of the pixels in 1 square inch of an image to be printed in a magazine. You would have to perform 90,000 calculations by hand. Talk about mathaphobia! Fortunately, software designers have set up an environment—the GUI—that makes it easy for you to perform complex calculations quickly and without even having to add 2 + 2. In fact, when you work in a program like Photoshop, the GUI is so seamless that it feels as though you're painting or drawing to change the color of the pixels.

Photoshop's GUI is very easy to use once you learn what the tool icons, menus, and floating palettes represent and how they perform. This can take awhile, because Photoshop can do so much. The Photoshop GUI provides tools and operations that are used by many image-related professionals, including designers, architects, photographers, artists, printers, and scientists. These virtual tools simulate the processes and operations performed by their real-life counterparts, and furnish a comfortable, familiar working environment.

## Touring the Image Window

When you open or create an image, it is displayed in the image window (shown in Figure 4.4). To change the window's size, place your cursor on the lower-right corner, click the mouse button, and drag while holding it down.

In the Windows interface, you can also enlarge or reduce any resizable window or palette by dragging any corner or edge.

To move the window, click the bar at the top of the window and drag. The scroll bars to the right and at the bottom allow you to scroll around images that appear larger than the size of the window.

The image window contains information about the document. The title bar gives the document's name, the percentage of the image's full size in pixels, in which you are viewing it, and the current layer and channel or mask. In the lower-left of the image window (on the Macintosh) or the Photoshop application window (in Windows) is the status bar. The left-most field of the status bar shows, again, the view size as a percentage of the image, but this field is the magnification box where you can enter a specific percentage—to the hundredth of a percent—in which to view the image.

### CALCULATING FILE SIZE

A document's file size is calculated by multiplying its height and width in pixels by its bit depth, or the amount of memory each pixel consumes. For example, a full-color document that is 5" tall by 7" wide and has a resolution of 72 ppi (pixels per inch) is 504 pixels by 360 pixels.

Since the image is in full color, each pixel consumes 24 bits of space on the disk. For this information to be of use to us, we must convert it into bytes; since there are 8 bits in a byte, we divide 24 by 8 and get a factor of 3. We multiply the height by the width by the bit-depth factor, or $504 \times 360 \times 3 = 544{,}320$ bytes. Since there are 1024 bytes in a kilobyte, we divide 544,320 by 1024 to get 531.56, or 532 kilobytes when rounded off to the nearest whole number.

The value derived from this formula is the raw file size. The file size may be further reduced when the image is saved to an image format with a compression scheme like JPEG, TIFF, or PSD.

The second field at the bottom of the window shows,by default, two numbers divided by a slash, which is the document file size. The number to the left of the slash represents the base amount of uncompressed space the file consumes on your disk, or the size of a flattened TIFF image. When you save the image in another format, the file size may shrink, because many formats use a compression scheme to consolidate data. The number to the right of the slash indicates the size of the image with the addition of any alpha channels, paths, spot color channels, or layers you may have created. The second number, of course, better represents the actual size of the image.

Figure 4.4

**The image window labeled**

## Getting Information about Your Documents

Photoshop has options that show you important information about your document, your computer, and the program's current state of operation. All of this information is useful in determining how efficiently your file will process and print.

### Clicking the Status Bar

You can quickly view information about your document when you click the arrow on the right side of the status bar:

**Image Position**  Clicking the information field itself displays a diagram of the image as it will appear on the paper, as specified in File → Page Setup (see Figure 4.5). Use this to assure that the image will fit on your paper before you print it.

Figure 4.5

**Click the information field to show you the position of your image on the paper size designated in Page Setup**

**Size and Mode Info**  Option-click (Mac) or Alt-click (Win) the field to display the image's size, resolution, color mode, and number of channels.

**Tile Info**  ⌘-click/Ctrl-click to display the tile sizes of the document. Photoshop uses tiles to display and process images. When you display an image or when the image refreshes, you can sometimes see the image appear progressively as it tiles on-screen. This window tells you how many tiles comprise the image, and is of little practical use to most users.

### Clicking the Status Bar Pop-Up Menu

The status bar, by default, displays the current size of your document. But if you click the small black arrow at the right end of the bar, a pop-up menu allows you to select other information to be displayed.

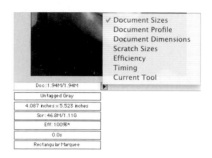

**Document Profile** This option displays the name of the color profile with which the image was saved. The color profile affects how the image appears on-screen (see Chapter 15, "Color Management and Printing"). In the case of untagged images (an image without a profile), the word *Untagged* will appear next to the color mode of the file.

**Document Dimensions** Here, the physical width and height of the document is displayed in the current units specified in the preferences.

**Scratch Sizes** The number to the left of the slash indicates the amount of memory needed to hold all current images open in RAM. The number to the right indicates the amount of memory Photoshop has been allocated (see the section on allocating memory in Chapter 5, "Setting Up the Program"). Because of Photoshop's ability to record events in its History palette, the number on the left grows every time you perform an operation, as RAM is being consumed. (See Chapter 11, "Altered States: History," to learn more about Photoshop's History features.)

**Efficiency** This option indicates what percentage of the last operation was performed in RAM. If this percentage drops below 80%, you may want to consider allocating more memory to Photoshop or installing more physical RAM. (See the section titled "Allocating Memory" in Chapter 5).

**Timing** If you select Timing, the information field tells you how long the last operation took to perform to the tenth of a second.

**Current Tool** This option displays the name of the currently selected tool.

## Accessing Menus

You access the majority of Photoshop's most powerful operations through the pull-down menus at the top of the screen. MacOS X offers 10 menus (as illustrated in Figure 4.6); Windows and MacOS 9 have nine. The menus are quite logical and user-friendly, with related operations accessible from the same menu.

Commands on the menus apply various filters, effects, or operations to an image, directly or through dialog boxes. Some of the menus, such as the View menu or the Window menu, are used to display additional tools or palettes and to change how the image appears on-screen.

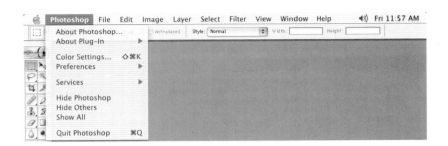

Figure 4.6

**Photoshop's menus, with the new Photoshop menu selected (in MacOS X)**

When applying an operation such as an image adjustment, you will see a dialog box that displays the items for that particular operation. You usually cannot perform any other operations until you implement or cancel the dialog. There are a couple of exceptions: You can still access the Zoom tool while a dialog box is open (see "Navigation Shortcuts" later in this chapter), and you can hide the edges of the selection marquee by pressing ⌘-H/Ctrl-H (see Chapter 6, "Making Selections").

The dialog boxes are similar to each other in the way that they perform. To access options that are in a dialog box, follow these general steps:

1. Choose the desired operation from the menu. The dialog box appears.

2. Choose from the displayed options, or enter values in the dialog box.

3. If there is a preview box, make sure it's checked to preview the result of the operation before closing the dialog box.

4. Make your changes, or abandon them, using these methods:

   - To undo the last operation inside a dialog box, press ⌘-Z/Ctrl-Z.

   - If you've entered values and wish to cancel the operation but keep the dialog box open, press the Option/Alt key, and the word *Cancel* changes to *Reset*. Click the Reset button.

   - Click Cancel to abort the operation and close the dialog without making any changes.

   - Click OK to implement the command.

## Document Viewing

In the Window menu, just above the Workspace submenu you'll read about in the next section, is the Documents menu. The Window → Documents → New Window command displays multiple windows of the same document. Multiple windows give you the ability to observe two or more views of your image simultaneously so that you can see both the close-up detail in which you are working and the global effect on the entire image. When you edit the image, you will see the changes on both views.

Choose Window → Documents → Cascade to display multiple open documents on the desktop stacked and slightly offset. Use Window → Documents → Tile to organize them in rows and columns. This window also displays a list of the current images that are open on the desktop and can be used to quickly navigate to a specific document.

## Organizing Your Workspace

The workspace controls, a new feature under the Window menu in Photoshop 7, give you the ability to organize and save a working environment. Specifically, the Workspace command enables you to save and restore palette locations and tool settings.

To use the new Workspace command, follow these steps:

1. Choose Window → Workspace → Save Workspace to save the current environment.

2. In the box that appears, name the workspace and click Save (see Figure 4.7). Its name will appear on the list in the Workspace dialog.

3. To restore Photoshop to the desired workspace, choose its name from the list.

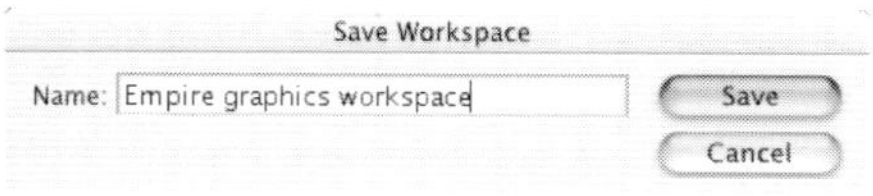

To delete a Workspace, choose Delete Workspace from the list. In the dialog box that appears, choose the workspace you wish to remove from the menu and click OK/Delete.

Figure 4.7

**The Save Workspace dialog**

| Save Workspace |
|---|
| Name: Empire graphics workspace |
| Save |
| Cancel |

## Working with Palettes

Many of Photoshop's tools and operations are displayed in a system of floating palettes, which appear on the desktop when you launch the program. These palettes let you efficiently apply operations directly to the image, thereby saving the time and hassle of following a sequence of windows to accomplish a task.

To display or hide a palette, go to the Window menu and choose the palette's name. To hide or display all of the palettes simultaneously, press the Tab key. Press Shift-Tab to hide all palettes except for the Tool palette.

### Palette Clusters

By default, palettes appear in clusters that can be separated or reconfigured according to how you may want to use them. To place a palette into a cluster, click the palette's tab and drag it into the cluster. When you see a heavy black outline appear around the cluster, release the mouse button. To separate a palette from a cluster, click its tab and drag it away from the cluster. The palette's new position is wherever you release the mouse.

Open palettes can be docked (joined) and moved as a unit. To dock a palette to another palette while keeping both visible, click the palette's tab, drag it, and place it on the bottom of the target palette. When you see a bold double line, release the mouse; the palette should snap to the bottom of the target palette. To move the palettes as a group, click the bar of the topmost palette and drag the set into position.

## Organizing Palettes

Palettes can be organized to use the desktop space more efficiently. You can move a palette or a cluster by placing the cursor on the bar at the top of the palette and dragging it. You can reduce the size of a palette by clicking the Minimize button on the bar at the top of the palette. This method unfortunately conceals the tabs that identify the palette, and you will have to maximize the palette to see its contents. A more efficient method of decreasing a palette's size is to double-click the tab; the palette will collapse, but the name tab will remain visible, as shown in Figure 4.8.

Once you've moved or separated the palettes, or changed the way they function, you may want to reset them to their original positions and reset their values to the original defaults of the program. You can accomplish this quickly and easily by choosing Window → Workspace → Reset Palette Locations.

If desired, you can save your current workspace before you reset the palette locations to their defaults. Choose Window → Workspace → Save Workspace.

Figure 4.8

**The tab remains visible when you collapse the palette.**

### The Palette Dock

The Palette Dock is a neat way to organize your palettes so that you can easily locate them. The dock is at the far right of the Options bar. To place a palette in the Palette Dock, click its tab, drag it to the dock, and release the mouse. You can place as many palettes in the dock as you wish, but their names will become obscured if you place too many. To find a palette, drag over the dock and each palette's name will appear. Click to expand the palette, and click again to collapse it.

> The Palette Dock is visible only at monitor resolutions of 1024 × 768 or greater. If palettes are docked and you decrease monitor resolutions, the palettes will be stacked in the workspace. Returning the monitor to a higher resolution will not redock them.

## The Tool Palette

Photoshop's Tool palette displays the icons for 22 different tools. Some of the tool icons expand to access tools that are not visible, bringing the entire number of tools to 54, plus paint swatches, Quick Mask icons, view modes, and the Jump To command. Figures 4.9 and 4.10 show the Tool palette with all of its pop-up tools and their shortcut keys. If you see a small black arrow next to the tool, click it with your mouse and hold down the mouse button, and the additional related tools will pop up.

Don't be intimidated by the Tool palette! When you place your cursor over a tool, a help-ful label, or tool tip, identifies the tool, and its shortcut key appears within a few seconds. Photoshop 7 extends the use of tool tips to describe the function of many of its operations

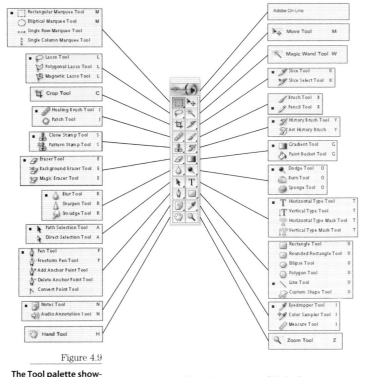

Figure 4.9

**The Tool palette showing the expanded tools**

inside palettes, toolbars, and dialog boxes, which can be an asset to obtaining a quick understanding of the program. To activate a tool tip, "hover" your cursor on the function or operation and wait a few seconds.

The Tool palette is divided into nine general sections. From top to bottom, as very broad categories, are the Adobe On-Line access logo, selection tools, painting tools, editing tools, vector tools, and display tools. Below that are the foreground and background color swatches, Quick Mask options, display options, and (at the very bottom of the palette) the Jump To command.

The Tool palette is designed to place all of the program's manual operations in full view on the desktop for easy access. Each tool is represented by a different cursor icon. To choose a tool, click its button on the Tool palette. Then place the cursor where you want to affect the image. Click the mouse, or click and drag (depending on the tool), to apply the tool's function to the image.

> To access a tool through its shortcut key, press the shortcut letter or Shift plus the letter (depending on your preference settings). For grouped sets of tools (like the three Lassos or Blur/Sharpen/Smudge), type the shortcut repeatedly to cycle through the tools in the group.

## The Options Bar

Photoshop 7, by default, displays an Options bar at the top of the screen when you launch the program. This element is similar to the Options palette in earlier versions of the program, but more convenient because it is easier to locate. When you select a tool, its options become visible in the Options bar, and you can determine the behavioral characteristics of the tool. Figure 4.11 shows the Options bar with the Brush tool selected. A tool's performance can vary considerably with different options, so it's a good idea to check out the settings before you apply the tool to the image.

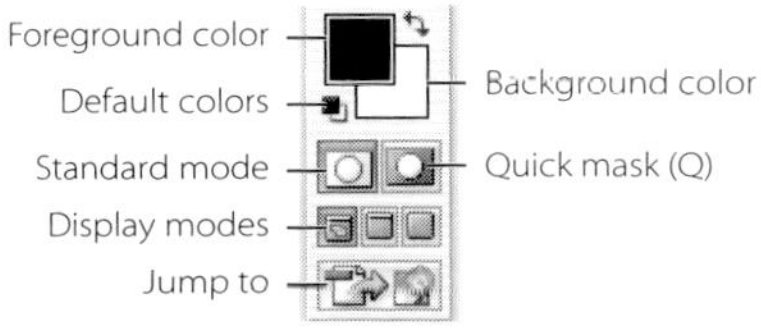

A few new tools have been added to Photoshop 7. See Appendix A for a complete list of tools and descriptions of what they do and how they operate.

Foreground color
Default colors
Standard mode
Display modes
Jump to
Background color
Quick mask (Q)

Figure 4.10

**The Tool palette, bottom portion**

Figure 4.11

**The Options bar (with the Brush tool selected)**

## Tool Presets

The tool icon on the far left side of the Options bar accesses the current Tool Preset menu (Figure 4.12). It provides you with a handy way to save and access tool configurations that you frequently use. To access a tool, click the desired tool in the Tool palette. Place your cursor on the arrow next to the tool icon, and press the mouse button to display the list. Scroll down and choose a preset from the list.

Figure 4.12

**Photoshop's new Tool Preset menu**

To save a new tool preset, follow theses steps:

1. Choose a tool from the Tool palette and set its characteristics in the Options bar.

2. Click the small arrow next to the icon to display the Tool Presets list.

3. Click the New Tool Preset icon in the upper-right of the palette, or click the small arrow at the upper-right side of the palette, to display the pull-down menu. Choose New Tool Preset.

4. In the window that appears (see Figure 4.13), name the tool preset and click OK. It now appears in the Tool Preset list.

When naming a preset, remember that descriptive names help you quickly locate a tool.

## The Notes Tool

Two tools in Photoshop 7 let you conveniently attach reminder notes to the image. You can create an annotation as either a sticky note or an audio recording.

To create a written annotation:

1. Click the Notes tool [⧉] in the Tool palette, or press N on the keyboard.

2. Click the image, and a yellow sticky note appears.

3. Enter the information, as shown in Figure 4.14, and click Close.

4. To access the information on the note, double-click the note icon on the image.

Figure 4.13

**The New Tool Preset dialog box**

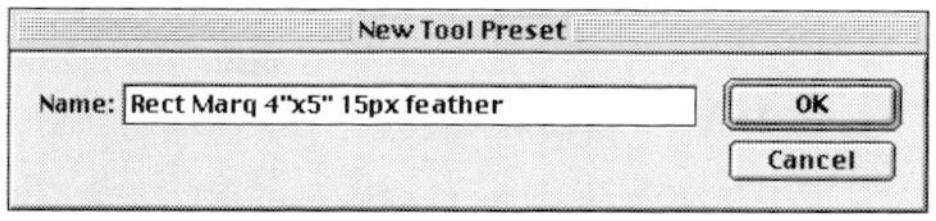

Figure 4.14

**A written notation**

To record an audio annotation, you'll need a microphone and audio input capabilities. Then follow these steps:

1. Click the Notes tool and hold down the mouse to expand the palette. Choose the Audio Annotation tool 🔊 .

2. Click the image, and the Audio Notation dialog box appears.

3. Click the Start button to record; click Stop when you've completed the recording.

4. To play the annotation, double-click the audio icon on the image.

# Displaying the Image

When you open an image in Photoshop, it is displayed to fit in the image window so that you can see the entire image regardless of its size. When working on an image, it's often necessary to vary the view size so that you can see changes to the document as a whole, concentrate on specific areas of the image, or work closely on details. Varying the size of the image display does not affect the physical size of the image. You can choose from several viewing methods in Photoshop 7.

## The Zoom Tool

The Zoom tool 🔍 is a fast way to take a closer look at an image and probably the technique you'll use most frequently for changing the view. Choose the Zoom tool from the Tool palette by clicking it, or type the letter Z on the keyboard. Place your cursor on the area of the image that you want to see close-up; you will see the Zoom tool cursor (a magnifying glass) with a plus sign to indicate that the Zoom tool will enlarge the view. Click your mouse, and continue to click until the image appears at the desired view. Each time you click, the image appears larger, to a maximum view size of 1600%.

You can reduce the size of the displayed image by pressing the Option/Alt key. The Zoom tool displays a minus sign to indicate that it will reduce the view. Each time you click the mouse with the Option/Alt key held down, the image diminishes in size, all the way down to 1 screen pixel.

**DISPLAY SIZE AND IMAGE RESOLUTION**

The percentage at which you see an image in Photoshop depends on the ratio of the image resolution to the monitor's screen resolution. Macintosh monitors have a screen resolution of 72 ppi, while Windows monitors use 96 ppi to display an image.

A document with an image resolution of 72 ppi, when viewed at 100%, will display at a ratio of 1:1 of its actual height and width dimensions on a Mac and 33% larger on Windows. A resolution of 144 ppi will display an image at twice its print size on a Mac and, again, larger on a Windows machine when displayed at 100% viewing size. (See Chapter 13, "Sizing and Transforming Images," for more on monitor and image resolution.)

## Scrolling in Photoshop

Scrolling tools and techniques let you move the image around the window when the image is larger than the image window.

**The Hand Tool**   Click the Hand tool [icon] in the Tool palette or press the H key. Click the image and drag to move the image around.

**Scroll Bars**   Like most software, the scroll bars are to the right and bottom of the image. Click and drag a scroll handle, or click an arrow at the end of a scroll bar, to scroll in the desired direction. Or click in the scroll bar section above or below the scroll handle to jump a full screen view up or down.

**Keyboard**   You can use either a keyboard or an extended keyboard to scroll the image up, down, left, or right. Table 4.1 lists the commands.

| SCROLL ACTION | MACINTOSH KEYBOARD | MAC EXTENDED KEYBOARD | WINDOWS KEYBOARD |
|---|---|---|---|
| Up | Control-K | PgUp | PgUp |
| Up slightly | Shift-Control-K | Shift-PgUp | Shift-PgUp |
| Down | Control-L | PgDn | PgDn |
| Down slightly | Shift-Control-L | Shift-PgDn | Shift-PgDn |
| Left | ⌘-Control-K | ⌘-Control-PgUp | Ctrl-PgUp |
| Left slightly | Shift-⌘-Control-K | Shift-⌘-Control-PgUp | Shift-Ctrl-PgUp |
| Right | ⌘-Control-L | ⌘-Control-PgDn | Ctrl-PgDn |
| Right slightly | Shift-⌘-Control-L | Shift-⌘-Control-PgDn | Shift-Ctrl-PgDn |

Table 4.1

**Keyboard Commands for Scrolling**

## Navigation Shortcuts

Clicking over and over again to display the image can become tiresome and consume precious time. As you become more proficient in Photoshop, you will want to consider alternative methods to speed up the process of viewing your image at the right size. What follows are a few techniques that will enhance your ability to see the image on-screen.

**Centering an Image**   This technique centers and zooms in on an area of the image on-screen. It is the fastest way to closely see a detail of the image you are working on. Choose the Zoom tool, click in the image, drag a marquee around the portion of the image you wish to enlarge, and release the mouse. The selected area enlarges to fill the window.

**Restoring the Display to a 100% View**   Double-click the Zoom tool icon in the Tool palette.

**Toggling to the Zoom Tool**   To toggle directly from any tool or dialog box to the Zoom tool, use one of these shortcuts:

- Hold down the ⌘/Ctrl key and the spacebar, and click the mouse to zoom in. Release the keys to resume using the tool.

- Hold down the Option/Alt key and the spacebar, and click the mouse to zoom out. Release the keys to resume using the tool.

**Toggling to the Hand Tool**  To quickly access the Hand tool from any tool or dialog box, press the spacebar. Click and drag your mouse to scroll. The Hand tool lets you scroll around the image when it exceeds the size of the image window. Release the spacebar to resume using the tool.

## The Navigator

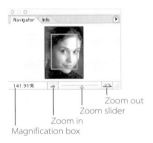

When you are viewing an image close-up, it can be difficult to tell exactly what you are looking at and where you are in the image, especially if the image contains large areas of similar texture. The Navigator (Figure 4.15) is a map of the image, displayed as a thumbnail, showing the exact location of what appears in the image window relative to the entire image.

When you launch Photoshop, the Navigator is displayed by default and offers the following navigational features:

**View Box**  The red rectangle on the thumbnail indicates what is currently displayed in the image window. Place your cursor on the rectangle, click your mouse, and drag to scroll around the image. You can change the color of the View box by clicking the arrow in the upper-right corner of the palette and choosing Palette Options. You can then choose a color from the pull-down menu or click the swatch to choose a color from the Color Picker.

**Zoom Slider**  You can zoom in on the image by moving the slider to the right, or zoom out by moving the slider to the left.

**Zoom In and Zoom Out Buttons**  The button with the small mountains on the left of the slider zooms out, and the button with the large mountains to the right of the slider zooms in. The buttons use the same predefined increments as the Zoom tool.

**Magnification Box**  At the bottom-left of the Navigator palette, you can enter a specific percentage at which to view your image.

**Sizing the Navigator Palette**  On Mac, you can drag the lower-right corner of the Navigator box to increase or decrease the size of the Navigator palette and its image thumbnail. In Windows, you can drag from any resizable edge.

## The View Menu

When you get to know the program a little better, you will discover that many of its operations seem to be redundant, and working effectively becomes a matter of choosing your favorite method for achieving identical end results. For example, the View → Zoom In command achieves the same results as the keyboard shortcut ⌘/Ctrl-plus sign; the Zoom Out command is the same as typing ⌘/Ctrl-minus sign. These techniques are identical to the Zoom tool and, of course, all of these commands are similar to the function of the Navigator and the magnification box, with slight variations.

The other options in the View menu include the following:

- Fit On-Screen displays the image at the maximum horizontal or vertical size the monitor screen will accommodate.
- Actual Pixels displays the image in a 1:1 ratio with the monitor's screen resolution.
- Print Size accurately displays the height and width dimensions of the image.

## Display Modes

Three icons on the Tool palette determine the display modes, or how you see the image on-screen. These modes act like electronic mattes. There are three options:

**Standard Screen Mode**  The default view displays the image up against the operating system's desktop or against the neutral gray Photoshop desktop in Windows, which obscures the operating system's desktop.

**Full Screen Mode with Menu Bars**  The image takes up almost the entire surface of the monitor screen and displays menu bars across the top. When you zoom to a smaller display size, the image appears centered against a neutral gray background.

**Full Screen Mode**  The image takes up the entire surface of the monitor screen. When you zoom to a smaller display size, the image appears centered against a black background.

The Full Screen display modes are ideal for displaying a view of your work unobstructed by other windows. It can be even more helpful to see an image in the Full Screen modes without any distracting palettes. To conceal or reveal all currently visible palettes, press the Tab key.

# Using Rulers, Guides, and Grids

Rulers, guides, and grids are used to align image content. Alignment of visual elements is critical to maintaining a cohesive structure to the composition. A good composition gently guides the viewer's eye across its surface so that important elements are emphasized. Rulers, guides, and grids can assure the precise measurement and placement of image components.

## Setting Preferences for Rulers and Guides

Photoshop can display a horizontal ruler across the top of the screen and a vertical ruler along the left side of the screen; to display them, choose View → Rulers. Rulers give you a visual reminder of the physical size of your image, which you may forget from time to time as you zoom in or out. You can change ruler units by choosing Edit → Preferences → Units & Rulers.

The *zero point*, or point of origin for all measurements, is in the upper-left corner of the image where the rulers intersect. The point of origin can be changed by placing your cursor on the crosshairs, clicking and dragging down and to the right, positioning to the desired location, and releasing the mouse. If you've changed the position of the point of origin, double-click on the origin point to reset the zero point.

Graphic designers use grids and guides to align elements within a layout. Aligning visual elements creates a compositional structure, which helps to control the viewer's eye. The importance of good composition in a Photoshop document cannot be stressed enough. The View menu contains the commands that let you create guides and display a grid, which are superimposed over the image to help you align elements within the composition. Neither guides nor grids print. You can change the color and properties of guides or grids by choosing Edit → Preferences → Guides, Grids, & Slices.

Chapter 5 goes into more detail on preference settings.

## Using Guides

Guides are horizontal or vertical lines that can be positioned anywhere on the image's surface. To create a horizontal or vertical guide, choose View → Rulers. Place your cursor on the ruler, click your mouse, and drag down or to the right, releasing the mouse wherever you want to place a guide (see Figure 4.16).

Figure 4.16

Guides on an image can be used for alignment.

PHOTO: LEAH ROMANIELLO

Use the following operations to position or move guides on your image:

**Display or Conceal Guides**  You can hide or reveal guides with the Show command. Choose View → Show → Guides to toggle them on and off; if the option is checked, they'll be visible, and if it's unchecked they'll be hidden.

**Snap To Guides**  When moving a portion of a layer or a selected area of the image, you can snap it to a guide to assure the accuracy of its position using the Snap To command. Choose View → Snap To → Guides to toggle snapping on and off.

**Move a Guide**  With the Move tool selected, click the guide and drag. If another tool is selected, ⌘-click/Ctrl-click the guide and drag. The Move a Guide ⌘/Ctrl-click shortcut does not work with the Slice tool or the Hand tool.

**Delete a Guide**  Select the guide as if you were going to move it, and drag it out of the image window.

**Delete All Guides**  Choose View → Clear Guides.

**Lock a Guide**  Choose View → Lock Guides. This prevents accidentally moving a guide while you work.

**New Guide**  Another method of generating a new guide is to choose View → New Guide (see Figure 4.17). The advantage of this method is that you can enter a value for the guide's exact location, and you can determine whether the guide is horizontal or vertical.

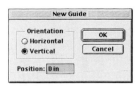

Figure 4.17

**The New Guide dialog box**

**Change the Orientation of a Guide**  You can change a guide from horizontal to vertical or vertical to horizontal. While in the Move tool, place your cursor on the guide. Hold down the Option/Alt key and click the guide.

**Change Guide Characteristics**  The color and style of your guides can be modified by choosing Edit → Preferences → Guides, Grids, & Slices. Choose a color from the pull-down menu, or click the swatch to display the Color Picker. From the Style pull-down menu, choose either a dashed or solid line.

## Using a Grid

A grid helps you see the global relationships between aligned elements on a page (as shown in Figure 4.18). A grid is a series of equally spaced horizontal and vertical lines that create a visual matrix. Like guides, grids do not print.

Use the following operations to work with a grid:

Figure 4.18

**The Photoshop grid**

**Display or Conceal the Grid**  Choose View → Show → Grid.

**Snap To Grid**  When moving a portion of a layer or a selected area of the image, you can snap it to a horizontal or vertical grid line using the Snap To command. Choose View → Snap To → Grid.

**Grid Characteristics**  The color and style of the grid can be modified by choosing Edit → Preferences → Guides, Grids, & Slices. (In Mac OS X, the Preferences submenu is found under the Photoshop menu.) Choose a grid color from the pull-down menu, or click the swatch to display the Color Picker. From the Style pull-down menu, choose either a dashed line, a solid line, or dots. You can also change the grid size by entering values in the Gridline and Subdivisions boxes.

# Setting Up Photoshop

*Before any job,* there is always preparation. Let's say you are going to change the oil in your car. Before you crawl under it and loosen the plug, you'll need to move the car to an appropriate location—certainly not near your newly planted front lawn, and not on the side of a hill. You'll need to find a level spot and gather an oil filter, pan, pouring spout, and rag. A simple job, yes. But consider how difficult the task would be if any of the elements were missing. If you choose the wrong location, you might kill your grass; if you park on a hill, some of the old, dirty oil will stay in the crankcase. The pan is essential, because without it, the oil will spill onto the ground.

The point is, you need to choose the right workspace and prepare it with all of the things you need before you begin the job. In the case of Photoshop 7, that means setting up the program to run at its optimal level, customizing the interface to best suit your needs, and choosing the best color environment.

This chapter will describe:

- **Settings and preferences**
- **Allocating memory**
- **Utilizing the Preset Manager**
- **Monitor calibration, gamma, and choosing a color space**

# Modifying Photoshop's Settings

The settings control how Photoshop appears and behaves. Many settings are stored in files in folders and directories with names like Settings or Preferences or in the Windows Registry. When you modify any setting and quit the program, the information is saved to these files.

When you launch Photoshop for the first time, a set of *preferences* is created. These are the factory default settings. Any changes you make in the appearance or the behavior of the program is recorded in the preferences file. After a work session when you quit the program, these preferences are stored so that the next time you launch the program, the position of the palettes, the tool settings, the color of the guides or grid, and any other changes you made remain the same.

If Photoshop starts behaving unpredictably or bombing frequently, it could indicate that the preferences are damaged. You should restore your preferences to the originally installed default settings. Re-creating your preferences file resets Photoshop to its defaults and may help to troubleshoot problems.

> I recommend that, as you begin each of the Hands On projects in this book, you discard or hide your "prefs" file and restart Photoshop to create a clean set of options. This will make working the exercises easier.

## Restoring Preferences

To restore your preferences, follow these steps:

1. Double-click the Photoshop program icon to launch the program.

2. Immediately after double-clicking, press Shift-Option-⌘ on a Macintosh or Shift-Alt-Ctrl on Windows.

3. A dialog box will ask you if you wish to discard the Photoshop's Settings file, as in Figure 5.1. Click Yes and the program will continue to launch.

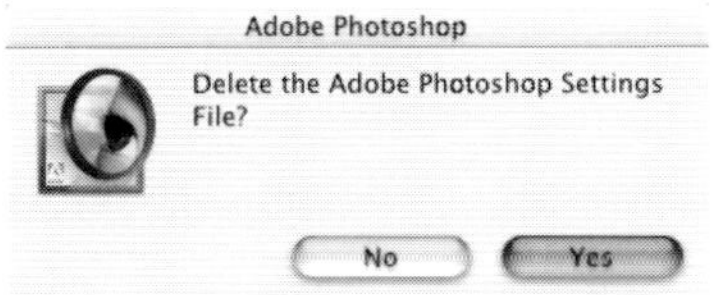

Figure 5.1

**The Discard Photoshop Settings dialog box**

After Photoshop has launched, another dialog box will appear asking if you wish to change Photoshop's color settings. Click Yes or No depending on what you want to do. (See the section "Choosing a Color Working Space" later in this chapter and Chapter 15, "Color Management and Printing," for a comprehensive explanation of color management.)

The disadvantage of restoring your preferences file is that you lose any and all customization you've done in Photoshop, everything from brush definitions to function keys. If you want to try a clean set of preferences—either to debug troublesome Photoshop behavior or to attempt a new technique uncomplicated by settings you've already chosen—you can "hide" your preferences temporarily. Quit Photoshop and drag the preferences file from its current location to an unrelated folder or directory (named something like `temppref` or `hideit`). When you restart Photoshop, the default preferences will be restored. If you want your old settings back, you can always reverse the process, closing the program and dragging the old `Preferences` file back to where Photoshop can find it.

To use this method of restoring the settings to the factory defaults on a Mac:

1. Quit Photoshop.

2. Locate and open the `Adobe Photoshop 7 Settings` folder. It's in the `Preferences` folder inside the `System` folder.

3. Select the file named `Adobe Photoshop 7 Prefs` and drag it to a location outside any `Photoshop` or `System` folder. If you might want to recover these preferences, create a folder named something like `OldPrefs`; if you won't need the current settings again, you can drag the file to the Trash (or Control-click it and choose Move To Trash from the shortcut menu).

4. Launch Photoshop.

Here's the same method for Windows operating systems:

1. Quit Photoshop.

2. Locate and open the directory with the `Preferences` file, which should be the PSP file at the end of this path:

   `C:\WINDOWS\Application Data\Adobe\Photoshop\7.0\Adobe Photoshop 7.0 Settings\Adobe Photoshop 7.0 Prefs.psp`

3. Drag the `Adobe Photoshop 7.0 Prefs.psp` file to a location outside the `WINDOWS` directory. If you might want to recover these preferences, create a directory named something like `OldPrefs`; if you won't need the current settings again, you can drag the file to the Recycle Bin (or right-click it and choose Delete from the shortcut menu).

4. Launch Photoshop.

> The file location will vary from version to version of the Windows operating system. You may have Windows configured to hide system files and other content that could be damaged by accidental deletion. If so, you'll need to change your Windows system settings in order to make the Photoshop preferences file accessible. See your Windows documentation for details.

## Allocating Memory

Processing graphics files requires large amounts of memory. Photoshop is a memory hog, so the often asked question, "How much memory do you need to best operate Photoshop?" is easily answered with another question: "How much memory can you afford?" Adobe's minimum requirement of 128 MB of RAM is enough to launch and run the program, but its performance will be clunky. Purchase and install as much memory as you can. Once you've installed the memory, be sure to allocate it to Photoshop, using one of the following procedures.

## Allocating Memory on Macintosh OS 9.2 and Earlier Versions

Older versions of MacOS allocate RAM from the operating system's Get Info window. Here's how you do it:

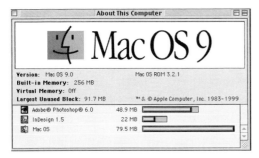

Figure 5.2

**This OS 9 Mac has 91.7 MB of additional available RAM.**

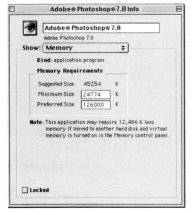

Figure 5.3

**You could add an additional 80 MB of RAM to Photoshop's allocation.**

1. Launch Photoshop and all other programs that you need to run while using Photoshop.

2. Switch to the Finder and, under the Apple menu, choose About This Computer (see Figure 5.2). Add the Largest Unused Block and the memory Photoshop is currently using; this is your available memory.

3. Quit all programs.

4. Highlight the Photoshop application icon and choose File → Get Info → Memory.

5. In the Info dialog (see Figure 5.3), Suggested Size is the amount of memory Photoshop wants in order to operate. In the Preferred Size field, specify the memory dedicated to Photoshop. Allocate as much as possible, but never more than 90% of the available memory. Use this calculation to get the Preferred Size in Figure 5.3: 90% × 256 MB = 230 MB, 230 MB – 150 MB (the allocated RAM) = 80 MB, rounded off to a total of 80 + 46 = 126 MB (126,000 KB) under Preferred Size.

6. Close the Get Info window and relaunch Photoshop.

You can round off RAM allocations to the nearest 100 KB.

## Allocating Memory in MacOS X and Windows

To allocate memory in MacOS X and Windows, follow these steps:

1. With Photoshop running, choose Edit → Preferences → Memory & Image Cache (bringing up the dialog shown in Figure 5.4).

2. In the Used By Photoshop field, enter the proportion of available memory you want to dedicate to Photoshop. The 50% default setting is a good beginning for operating the software.

3. During a Photoshop work session, if the Efficiency setting (in the status bar at bottom of the window) ever drops below 100%, increase the percentage of memory by 10% increments until the efficiency remains at the maximum 100%.

4. After you reset the memory allocation, you must quit and relaunch the program for the change to take effect.

# Setting Preferences

When you change Photoshop's preferences, you affect the behavior or the appearance of the program. By so doing, you can customize the interface to best suit your style of working. In the descriptions throughout this chapter, I recommend (in parentheses within the text) the preference configuration that is most suitable for the majority of working situations.

You find the Preferences dialog box in Mac System 9.2 under the Edit menu. In MacOS X, you access it through the Photoshop menu. In either platform, you can choose Edit → Preferences → General, or type ⌘-K (Mac) or Ctrl-K (Win), to display Photoshop's Preferences dialog box. You also have the option of going directly to the preference category you want under the Edit → Preferences submenu.

From the dialog, you can navigate to any of the preference categories by clicking the pop-up list at the top of the dialog box. You can also jump from category to category by clicking the Next or Prev buttons.

## General Preferences

When you first open the Preferences dialog, you see Photoshop's General preference settings (Figure 5.5), which are global settings that affect most of your working environment.

These settings include:

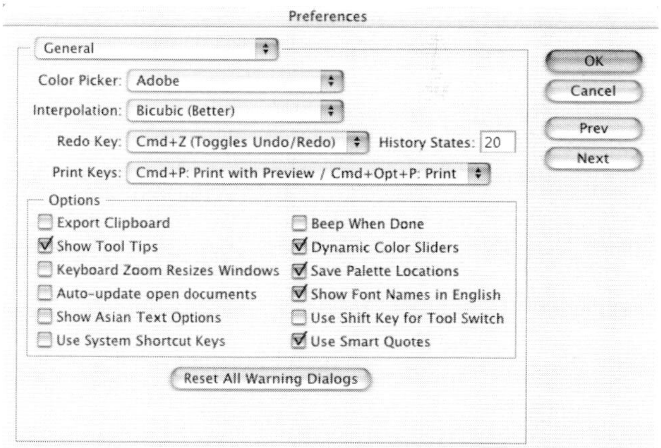

**Color Picker (Adobe)** You can specify which color picker to use when choosing a foreground or background color. The color picker you select is also used throughout the program to define preferences, such as the color of your guides and grids. In both Macintosh and Windows, you can choose between the Adobe Color Picker and the operating system's color picker.

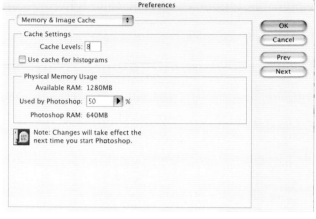

Figure 5.4

**The Memory & Image Cache preferences in MacOS X**

Figure 5.5

**The General preferences**

**Interpolation (Bicubic)** This sets the global default for how Photoshop resamples, or sizes, images. When you resize an image, pixels are either added (if you increase the image size or resolution) or subtracted (if you reduce the image size or resolution). When adding pixels, the Nearest Neighbor setting, which is the fastest, makes an exact copy of the adjacent pixel. Bilinear uses an average of the two pixels above and below and the two pixels on either side to create gradations for smoother transitions. Bicubic produces the best results by averaging the eight closest neighbors and adding a sharpening effect to increase the contrast.

Nearest Neighbor is useful to increase the size of a bitmap or line art image where all the pixels are either black or white. Nearest Neighbor will preserve the absolute values without producing intermediate gray transitions or anti-aliasing. It's also good for maintaining the integrity of some screen captures when resampling up for print, as image quality may be reduced by the anti-aliasing effect of Bicubic interpolation. For virtually every other application, choose Bicubic interpolation.

**Redo Key (⌘/Ctrl-Z)** You can specify which key command will undo or redo the last operation. The three default options include the following:

⌘/Ctrl-Z toggles between undo and redo.

Shift-⌘/Ctrl-Z goes backward in the History palette.

⌘/Ctrl-Y redoes the last operation. Choosing it will disable the ability to toggle in and out of the Proof Colors CMYK preview.

**History States (20)** You can determine the maximum number of states that will appear in the History palette before the earliest one is discarded. History requires RAM to remember stages or "states" in the process of developing an image. Limit the number of states to the default so as not to compromise the efficiency of the program.

**Print Keys (⌘/Ctrl-P)** If you want to see a preview before printing, the Print With Preview dialog box will display the image in relationship to the page. This Preference designates which key commands will print the image with or without the Print With Preview dialog box.

**Export Clipboard (Off)** If you are running more than one program, the content of Photoshop's Clipboard will be transferred to the system's Clipboard. When you switch to another program, those contents can be pasted into a document there. If you copy and paste images within Photoshop only, turn off this option to reduce the amount of time it takes to activate another program.

**Show Tool Tips (On)** The small yellow identification tags on the Tool palette that display each tool's name and keyboard shortcut are turned on and off from this setting. The Tool palette in version 7 also displays the same information when the tool items are expanded, so the information is somewhat redundant. It's not a bad idea, however, to get a double hit of this information until you learn what the tools are and how to access them with shortcut key commands. Another reason to keep this box checked is that the tool tips in version 7 also appear as short descriptions on many of Photoshop's commands, giving you a clear idea of their purpose.

**Keyboard Zoom Resizes Windows (Off)** This preference lets you resize the image window when you use the key commands for zooming in (⌘/Ctrl-plus sign) and zooming out (⌘/Ctrl-minus sign). The window will increase in size until it fills the screen vertically or horizontally.

**Auto-Update Open Documents (Off)** If an image is updated by another program outside of Photoshop, Photoshop will automatically reread and replace the open document with the updated version.

**Show Asian Text Options (Off)** Checking this box displays Chinese, Japanese, and Korean text options in the Paragraph palettes. You need this option only if you are working with Asian characters.

**Use System Shortcut Keys** The Macintosh Operating System's shortcut keys will override any keys designated in Photoshop that perform operations or Actions. (This item is not available in Windows.)

**Beep When Done (Off)** You can instruct Photoshop to emit a warning signal after it has performed an operation that displays a progress window. This can be helpful if you are away from your computer waiting for a long process, like a rotation or resize of a high-resolution image, to be completed.

**Dynamic Color Sliders (On)** When this box is checked, the sliders on the Color palette preview the range of potential colors that can be designated, so that you know exactly where to move them to designate a specific foreground or background color. Leave this box checked to speed up the process of determining your colors.

**Save Palette Locations (On)** If you choose this option, Photoshop will remember the position of your palettes when you quit and then relaunch the program. If the box is unchecked, Photoshop restores the palette locations to the default positions.

**Show Font Names in English (On)** If you have any fonts on your system that do not use Roman characters, such as Asian fonts, their names will be displayed in English in the font list.

**Use Shift Key for Tool Switch (Off)** With this preference off, in order to switch to a tool or switch among grouped tools, you simply type the shortcut key for that group (L for the Lassos, E for the Erasers, etc.). Checking this option adds the Shift key to the process, to prevent you from inadvertently switching while using a tool.

**Use Smart Quotes (On)** The program automatically reverses the closed quotation marks.

## File Handling

The File Handling preferences (Figure 5.6) replace the Saving Files preference of former versions. These settings let you manage files when you save them either to your disk or to a workgroup server and designate whether your saved files will have previews or extensions attached.

These settings include:

**Image Previews (Always Save)** The Macintosh Thumbnail and Windows Thumbnail options create previews that will be displayed in the dialog box that you see when you open the image using File → Open. There are two more options on Photoshop for MacOS: Icon creates a tiny picture that you can view from the desktop for the purpose of identifying an image before you open it, and Full Size creates a preview that can be placed in a desktop-publishing program. The problem with previews is that they produce larger file sizes, so you need to decide whether the convenience of seeing the image prior to opening is worth the memory used.

**Append File Extension (Always, Use Lower Case)** On the Macintosh version, Append File Extension determines when to add an extension to the filename (like .tif, .psd, or .eps); your options are Always, Never, or Ask When Saving. The Windows version automatically adds the three-character extension to the filename, and the extension won't hurt a Mac file, so choose Always. You will be able to readily identify the type of image even if it's in a folder on the desktop, and you don't have to worry about adding the extension when saving for a Windows platform computer or publication to the Web.

This option also allows you to select whether the extension is uppercase or lowercase. (Whichever way you choose here, you have the option to switch the extension's case for each given file as you use the Save dialog boxes.) I recommend that you choose the Use Lower Case option when saving files to the Web because of Unix servers' preference for lowercase extensions.

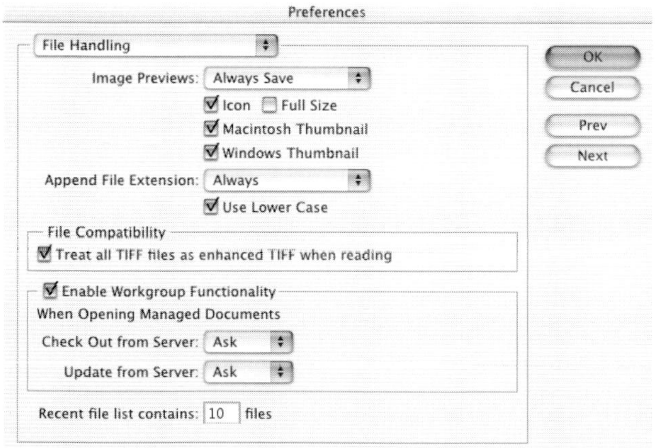

**File Compatibility (On)** Photoshop 7 offers two options for maintaining compatibility with other software:

**Ask when Saving Layered TIFFs (On)** Checking this preference displays a reminder that your TIFFs are layered before you save them. As layers increase file size, it's a good idea to keep this on.

**Always Maximize Compatibility with Photoshop (PSD) files (On)** Checking this preference saves a flattened preview with a PSD file. Turning it off may compromise compatibility with other software programs and future versions of Photoshop.

Figure 5.6

**The File Handling preferences**

**Enable Workgroup Functionality (On, Ask, Ask)** Within this option, you can choose Always, Never, or Ask when opening or updating images that reside on a managed file server. This pertains to workgroups who often use the same source images for publications. Choose Ask in both instances when checking out or updating to be sure that you don't automatically replace a file.

**Recent File List Contains (10)** You can find a list of the most recent files that have been opened under File → Open Recent. Enter a value for how many of the latest documents you would like to see displayed; the maximum is 30.

## Display & Cursors

Use the Display & Cursors preferences (Figure 5.7) to configure the way cursor icons and colors appear on-screen. These preferences do not affect the image data, but they do affect how you see the image.

**Color Channels in Color (Off)** By default, color channels appear in black and white. Each color channel is actually an 8-bit grayscale image that supports 256 shades of gray. Photoshop will display a channel in red, green, or blue, depending on the color information it represents, if this box is checked. The black-and-white information of the default is displayed more clearly and is probably more useful to you, so leave the box unchecked.

Figure 5.7

The Display & Cursors preferences

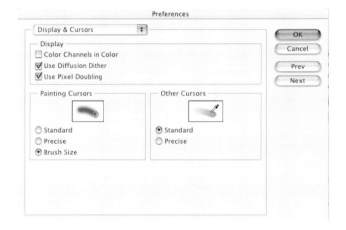

**Use Diffusion Dither (On)** This option is used to control the pattern of pixel blending on low-resolution color monitors, or if you're displaying anything less then Millions Of Colors (Mac) or True Color (Win). Dithering is a method of distributing pixels to extend the visual range of color on-screen.

**Use Pixel Doubling (On)** When moving an image from one file to another, you can speed up the process by reducing the resolution display. When you move an image with this box checked, it will appear jagged and unrefined until it is in position and the operation is complete.

**Painting Cursors (Brush Size)** To change the display of the painting cursor, click the desired radio button. Standard displays the tool icon as the cursor. Precise displays crosshairs. Brush Size, the default, displays a cursor that is the size and shape of the brush for the currently selected tool.

**Other Cursors (Standard)** To change the display of tool cursors that do not use brushes, choose either Standard (the tool icon as the cursor) or Precise (a crosshair icon).

If you use standard or brush size cursors, you can toggle back and forth to the precise cursor with your Caps Lock key.

## Transparency & Gamut

These settings control the appearance of transparency on the Layers palette and the color of the CMYK gamut warning (Figure 5.8).

These settings include:

**Transparency Settings (Default)** With this option, you can set the default preferences for the transparency display on your layers. Sometimes the default gray checkerboard is not visible due to similar colors within the image. Under Grid Size, choose from a small, medium, or large grid. Grid Colors lets you select from a predefined list of color checkerboards. To choose specific grid colors, click either of the color swatches to display the Color Picker.

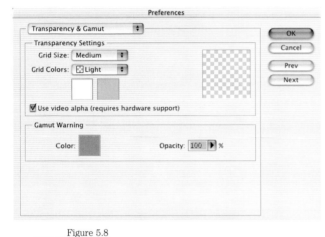

Figure 5.8

**The Transparency & Gamut preferences**

**Use Video Alpha** You can display alpha channels at a predefined opacity if you have the hardware that supports this type of display.

**Gamut Warning (Default)** When working on RGB images intended for four-color process printing, you'll want to preview the files before converting to CMYK. To see which colors are out of the CMYK gamut, choose View → Gamut Warning. The Gamut Warning displays a colored mask over the areas that are out of range. The Gamut Warning preferences let you determine the color of the mask. Click the color swatch to display the Color Picker. Choose an opacity percentage between 1 and 100 to affect the transparency of the mask.

## Units & Rulers

You can establish settings for all measurement systems in Photoshop (Figure 5.9).

These settings include:

**Rulers (Inches)** The Rulers setting allows you to determine which measurement system will appear on the rulers when they are displayed. You can choose among pixels, inches, centimeters, points, picas, and percent.

> A shortcut to this preference is to double-click the rulers within the Photoshop workspace.

**Type (Points)** You can determine how type size, leading and other characteristics are displayed in the Options bar and Character and Paragraph palettes. Choose points, pixels or millimeters.

**Column Size (Default)** If you're importing your image to a desktop-publishing program for publication to a newspaper, newsletter, or magazine, you may want to configure it to a specific column size. You can choose the width of the column and a gutter size so that your image will conform to the column size of the intended publication. You can determine the number of columns on the document when choosing File → New or Image → Image Size.

**New Document Preset Resolution (300 and 72)** This preference allows you to determine the default document and printing resolutions for new documents.

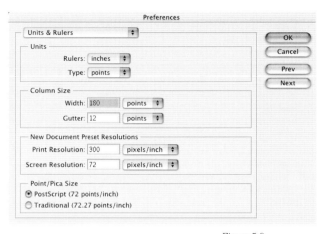

Figure 5.9

**The Units & Rulers preferences**

**Point/Pica Size (PostScript)** This preference determines the size of your type characters. In PostScript type, there are 72 points per inch; in Traditional type, there are 72.27 points per inch. PostScript has clearly become the convention with the advent of desktop publishing and computer typography. Some purists still may prefer the Traditional type option, so it remains available.

## Guides, Grid, & Slices

Graphic designers use guides and grids to align visual elements on a page (as described in Chapter 4, "Navigation: Know Where to Go"). Slices divide an image into pieces for faster display on the Web. The Guides, Grid, & Slices preferences (Figure 5.10) allow you to determine the color and style of your ruler guides and your grid. Under Color, choose from the options list or click the large swatch on the right side of the dialog to select a specific color from the Color Picker. You can determine the matrix of your grid by entering a value in the Gridline Every field and the number of subdivisions in the grid by entering a value in the Subdivisions field.

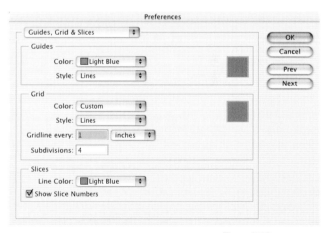

Figure 5.10

**The Guides, Grid, & Slices preferences**

## Plug-Ins & Scratch Disks

Plug-ins are modular mini programs or filters that add functions to Photoshop. You can activate or deactivate third-party plug-ins from the Plug-Ins & Scratch Disks preferences dialog (Figure 5.11).

Figure 5.11

**The Plug-Ins & Scratch Disks preferences**

A scratch disk is hard-disk space used as memory. You can designate one or more hard disks in which to process images to increase the processing capabilities of your computer.

The settings in this dialog box include:

**Additional Plug-Ins Folder/Directory**  Plug-ins extend Photoshop's capabilities; they include the filters, import/export modules, displacement maps, and third-party programs like Kai's Power Tools. You load or unload preferences from the Plug-Ins folder in the Photoshop application folder or any other folder on your disk. You can reorganize and load specific plug-ins into the program by checking this option, clicking the Choose button, and locating the desired folder on your disk.

**Legacy Photoshop Serial Number**  Checking this box allows backward compatibility to older plug-ins. Enter the serial number in this field if you use plug-ins that require an old-style Photoshop serial number.

**Scratch Disks**  When Photoshop exceeds the amount of allocated memory, it uses a scratch disk as a source of virtual memory to process images. In the Scratch Disks field, assign the first scratch disk to your fastest hard drive with the most unused disk space. If you have additional hard drives, you can choose second, third, and fourth disks on which to allocate space. When the primary scratch disk is maxed out, the second one will kick in, then the third, and so on. Built-in memory is considerably faster than virtual memory, so you will experience a significant change in Photoshop's performance when you exceed the RAM allocation. Photoshop requires at least three to five times the file size for the amount of empty hard-disk space, so be sure to keep a block of space on your scratch disk(s) free of data. The disk should be defragmented and optimized regularly using a utility program. Adobe recommends that you avoid working on removable media Zip disks, because they are less stable and much slower than hard drives.

A warning may appear at the bottom of the dialog that says changes to the Plug-Ins & Scratch Disks options kick in only after you've quit and relaunched the program. If you anticipate the need to change the plug-ins, hold down the ⌘-Opt (Mac) or Ctrl-Alt (Win) keys while the program is launching. The Plug-Ins folder will appear, where you can designate the plug-ins for the your work session without having to quit and restart the program.

**PURGE MEMORY**

Let's say you've been working on a file for the past 20 minutes, and you're about to apply the Unsharp Mask filter to give the image that final sparkle before sending it to the printer. You tweak the filter settings to perfection and click the OK button. A dialog box appears that tells you the filter cannot be applied because the scratch disk is full. Before you throw your shoe at the monitor in frustration, try purging the data stored on the scratch disks.

Choose Edit → Purge and choose data you would like to delete from the submenu. You can free up the Undo, Clipboard, and History memories individually, or choose All to dump everything. Be careful, though; you cannot undo this operation.

## Memory & Image Cache

Image caching accelerates the screen redraw during the editing process. Control your use of this feature in the Image Cache (MacOS 9.2 and earlier) or Memory & Image Cache (MacOS X and Windows) preferences (shown in Figure 5.12).

The preference settings include:

**Cache Levels (8)** Specifies how many copies of your image are stored in memory to update the screen more quickly at reduced view sizes. For example, if you do a color adjustment to an image at 50% view, it happens much faster because the program only has to change 25% of the pixels. Experiment with the settings for images larger than 15 MB. Eight is the maximum setting, but high settings will deplete your system resources because the smaller previews are stored in memory. If you are working on large images and have sufficient RAM, as most computers do today, set the image cache to 8 levels. For smaller images with less RAM, use lower settings.

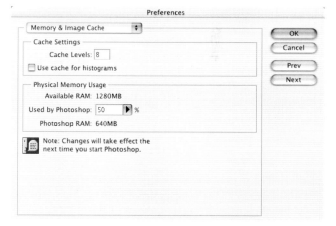

**Use Cache for Histograms (Off)** This preference defines the histogram based on the zoom ratio and the cumulative display of histograms throughout the work session, which compiles a histogram faster but with less accuracy. Uncheck this option. For more on histograms, see Chapter 16, "Adjusting Tonality and Color."

Figure 5.12

**The Memory & Image Cache preferences**

**Physical Memory Usage** This field displays the system's total RAM, the RAM allocated to Photoshop, and the memory used by Photoshop in percentage and in kilobytes. The default setting of 50% is a good beginning to operating the software. During a Photoshop work session, if the Efficiency setting (in the status bar at bottom of the window) ever drops below 100%, increase the percentage of memory by 10% increments until the efficiency remains at the maximum 100%. Never allocate, however, more than 90% of the memory. After you reset the memory allocation, you must quit and relaunch the program for the change to take effect.

## Utilizing the Preset Manager

Photoshop gives you the ability to manage several libraries from a single window. The Preset Manager is the storage unit for all of the elements that you may want to apply to the image,

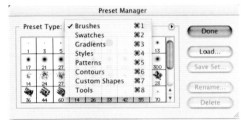

Figure 5.13

**The Preset Manager**

and it's a library of palettes that can be utilized by the program. As you add or delete items from the palettes, the currently loaded palette in the Preset Manager displays the changes. You can save the new palette and load any of the palettes on the system.

Choose Edit → Preset Manager to access its dialog box (Figure 5.13). From the Preset Type option list, choose the type of palette you wish to affect.

The small arrow to the right of the Preset Type list displays a pop-up menu that is divided into three groups of commands. The top group includes a list of display options for the items within the palette, which let you display the items as thumbnails or by their names. The second field lets you restore the current palette to the default or replace it with a previously saved palette. The third group lists additional palettes that can be readily accessed.

> Adobe provides several different palettes with Photoshop 7. If, for example, you are working on a document that will be used exclusively on the Web, you may want to load the Web Safe Swatches palette.

## Calibrating Your Monitor with Adobe Gamma

Part of the initial setup in Photoshop involves assuring that your colors look right on-screen. A calibrated monitor is the foundation from which all other color settings are determined, and is the initial stage of color management that will ultimately provide consistency during each work session and predictable results from your printer. Calibration configures the best possible characteristics for a particular monitor so that the display is optimal. Adobe Gamma software is bundled with Photoshop and will calibrate your monitor and record the resulting data to an ICC (International Color Consortium) profile.

Because Adobe Gamma is a visual calibration system, it is not adequate for precision calibration. If you need precise calibration, use a device called a colorimeter, which sticks on the surface of your monitor's glass, measures the temperature of the phosphors, and records this state into an ICC profile. These devices are more accurate than Adobe Gamma in that they measure the phosphor temperatures to determine the optimal settings for the monitor and don't rely on subjective visual decisions. (For a demonstration of ColorVision's hardware and software calibration system, refer to Chapter 15.)

The Adobe Gamma calibration package—which includes Adobe Gamma software, the Gamma Wizard, and ICC color profiles for some RGB devices—is simple to use. When you install Photoshop, the Adobe Gamma software automatically loads into a control panel on Macintosh and Windows systems. Before calibrating, be sure that the monitor has been on for at least 30 minutes and that the ambient light in the room is set as you will use it during your work sessions – preferably low. Your monitor's bit depth should be set to Millions Of Colors or True Color (but see the accompanying warning note). Turn off any background patterns or screen images, and change the background color to neutral gray. (The sidebar "Creating a Neutral Gray Desktop" shows how to do this.) If your monitor has a white point adjustment, use the monitor's utility and later set Adobe Gamma's white point control to match the monitor's settings.

> Do not attempt to change the screen bit depth of your monitor while running Photoshop on Windows systems. If you need to change the monitor's bit depth from 256 to True Color, for example, quit Photoshop, change the bit depth, and then launch Photoshop again.

## Using Adobe Gamma

A monitor's gamma actually measures the contrast of the mid-tones of images displayed on-screen. You can learn about the Gamma utility in the Photoshop Help menu: choose Help → Help Contents → Search, and in the Search field, type **Adobe Gamma**.

Windows systems default to a higher gamma (2.2) than Macs (1.8), meaning that images will look slightly darker and have more contrast on a computer running Windows than on a Mac. To calibrate your monitor on the Macintosh, choose the Adobe Gamma utility (Figure 5.14) from the control panels. On Windows, choose Start → Settings → Control Panel → Adobe Gamma.

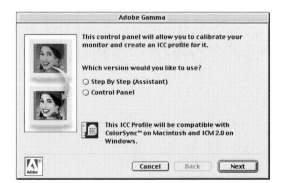

Figure 5.14

**The Adobe Gamma utility**

The first time you calibrate, choose Step By Step (called Assistant in MacOS and Wizard in Windows) by checking its radio button and clicking Next. The Gamma Wizard takes you by the hand and walks you through the calibration process, explaining the hows and whys of brightness and contrast, gamma, white point, and black point. (Once you are familiar with its components, you can access the Control Panel version of Adobe Gamma.) As a starting point, click the Load button and select, as an ICC profile, Adobe Monitor or a manufacturer-supplied profile for your particular monitor. Choose Next and follow the instructions and explanations as detailed by the Gamma Wizard. At the end of the session, compare the results by clicking the Before and After radio buttons and then name and save the new profile.

The Adobe Gamma settings that you specify will automatically load each time your computer starts. Monitors deteriorate over time, so recalibrate weekly. If you find it impossible to calibrate your monitor to the standard settings, then it may be too old and faded and should be replaced.

## Choosing a Color Working Space

The next step in setting up the program is to choose a *color working space* to compensate for variables that occur as a result of different output devices. For example, an image intended for four-color process printing needs to look different on-screen than an image intended for the Web. Photoshop 7 lets you work in RGB spaces other than those defined by your monitor.

To choose a color working space, go to Edit → Color Settings. In the Settings pop-up list, choose Web Graphics Defaults if you're preparing images for the Web or U.S. Prepress Defaults if you're prepping files for four-color printing (see Figure 5.15). See Chapter 15 for a more complete description of the Color Settings dialog box.

Figure 5.15

**The Photoshop 7 Color
Settings dialog box**

## CREATING A NEUTRAL GRAY DESKTOP

Basic color theory teaches us that your perception of a color is affected by the colors surrounding it. To assure that your perception of color is unaltered by any ambient color or patterns, it's best to work with a completely neutral desktop.

### Macintosh System 9.2 and Earlier

To create a neutral gray desktop in MacOS 9.2 or earlier:

1. Choose File → New. In the dialog box that appears, enter the filename **Gray Background.** and the following specifications:

   For the width, choose 640 pixels (choose Pixels from the pull-down menu).

   For the height, choose 480 pixels.

   For the contents, choose White.

2. Click the foreground color swatch in the Tool palette to display the Color Picker.

3. Enter these values in the Hue, Saturation, and Brightness fields: H = 0, S = 0, and B = 50. Click OK. Notice that the foreground color swatch has turned gray.

4. Choose Select → Select All, or type ⌘-A, to select the entire image.

5. Press Option-Delete to fill the selection with the gray color.

6. Choose File → Save As and save the file to a folder on your hard disk as Gray Background. Save it as a PICT document, (the .pct file extension will be added by default.)

7. From the Apple menu, choose Control Panels → Appearance → Desktop.

8. Choose Place Picture and locate the Gray Background.psd image.

9. Click the Set Desktop button.

### Macintosh OS X

To create a neutral gray desktop in MacOS X:

1. From System Preferences, choose Desktop.

2. Choose Collection → Solid Colors.

3. Click the medium-gray swatch.

### Windows

To create a neutral gray desktop in Windows:

1. Choose Start → Settings → Control Panel. Launch the Display applet.

2. Click the Appearance tab.

3. From the Item list, choose Desktop.

4. From the color swatch pop-up list, choose Medium Gray (the color on the far right in the first row).

5. Click Apply to see the result or OK to implement the operation.

# CHAPTER 6

# Making Selections

*Essential to image editing* is the ability to isolate an area of the image so that an effect can be applied exclusively to that area. A selection serves two contradictory purposes: it affects and it protects. When you apply a Photoshop tool or operation, the area within the bounds of the selection marquee will be altered and the area outside the selection marquee will remain unaffected. Think of a selection simply as a hole through which you can alter the reality of your image.

Because there are so many variables to selecting an area, Photoshop provides several tools that facilitate the selection process. You'll encounter a wide range of methods, from the labor-intensive to the fully automatic, that enable you to select pixels for the ultimate purpose of altering their appearance.

This chapter will introduce you to:

- **The power of masking**
- **Using selection tools**
- **Applying selection techniques**

# The Power of Masking

*Masking*, or the process of protecting portions of an image, used to be an entirely manual process. In ancient times—that is, the 1980s—one of the most common methods of altering a photograph was to paint it with an airbrush. Airbrushing required a person with a steady hand and a razor-sharp knife. A piece of transparent frisket film was placed over the entire image. The artist slowly, carefully, and gently (so as not to damage the photo) cut a hole in the frisket to expose the area of the photograph to be painted. The exposed portion of the image was painted, and the areas where the frisket remained were protected. The frisket was then peeled back to reveal the colored shape of the hole.

Photoshop 7 offers an arsenal of tools and operations that give the user versatility and control unimagined in that bygone era. The selection tools range from purely manual, like the Lasso, to semimanual, like the Marquee, to semiautomatic, like the Magnetic Lasso, to fully automatic, like the Magic Wand. Each selection tool is designed to hasten the masking process, depending on the characteristics of the image. Since images vary in contrast, tonality, color, and content, Photoshop provides tools and methods that can be applied to every possible situation. Nevertheless, making selections is undoubtedly the most labor-intensive and time-consuming of all Photoshop operations. There are many situations where one selection method is insufficient and several must be combined to define the target area. Often, other selection techniques will be employed in combination with the tools for greater accuracy or to isolate a tricky area.

# Using Selection Tools

When you make a selection in Photoshop, an animated marquee defines the approximate boundaries of the selected area. This moving, dash-lined border is sometimes referred to as the "marching ants" because of its resemblance to a column of tiny insects on the move.

Figure 6.1

**Photoshop's selection tools**

Three of Photoshop's selection tools are located at the top of the Tool palette (see Figure 6.1). When you press and hold the mouse on the Rectangular Marquee tool, the palette expands to reveal three additional tools. When you expand the Lasso tool, two more tools are revealed, for a total of eight different selection tools.

Other methods can enhance the speed or accuracy of the selection process. The Pen tool, covered in Chapter 9, "Drawing Paths," uses Bezier curves to define edges; Quick Mask (Chapter 12, "Using Alpha Channels and Quick Mask") uses paint tools to select areas; and Color Range (Chapter 21, "Making Difficult Selections") is an industrial-strength Magic Wand tool.

## The Selection Tool Options Bar

The Options bar, as shown in Figure 6.2, displays the characteristics of the current selection tool. You can input values or choose options that will affect the selection tool's behavior.

Figure 6.2

**The Options bar show-ing the default options for the Rectangular Marquee tool**

When you choose a selection tool, the icon that represents it appears on the left end of the Options bar, which is also the Tool Preset menu. The next four icons represent the selection options. The selection options include the following:

**New Selection**  Click this button to create a new selection with the chosen selection tool.

**Add To Selection**  Click this button to add to an existing selection with the chosen selection tool. The addition can either expand a selection's boundaries or be used to select an unconnected area. You can perform the same function by holding down the Shift key as you drag with the selection tool.

**Subtract from Selection**  Click this button to exclude a portion of an existing selection. You can perform the same function by holding down the Option (Macintosh) or Alt (Windows) key as you drag with the selection tool.

**Intersect Selection**  After making an initial selection and choosing this option, make a second selection overlapping the first. Only that portion of the image common to both selections will remain active. You can perform the same operation by pressing Shift-Option (Mac) or Shift-Alt (Win) as you use the second selection tool.

**Feather**  Prior to drawing a selection, you can program a tool to produce a soft-edged selection by specifying a numerical value in the Feather field of the tool's Options bar.

Feathering creates a gradual transition between the inside and the outside of the border. When you apply an effect to a feathered selection, it diminishes and becomes more transparent, producing a softening or blurring effect, as shown in Figure 6.3. Feathering a selection gives you the power to increase the credibility of your image by gradually blending colored pixels into each other and eliminating any evidence of a hard edge. When you choose Select → Feather, a dialog box appears; enter a value in the Feather Radius field. The Feather Radius value extends the specified number of pixels into the selection outline (becoming increasingly more opaque) and outside the selection border (becoming increasingly more transparent). For example, if you enter a value of 10, the distance of the feather will be 20 pixels from the opaque pixels inside the selection border to absolute transparency outside the selection border.

When you apply a feather to an existing selection border, sometimes you will see it decrease in size or slightly change shape. This is because Photoshop displays selection borders only around areas that represent 50% transparency or more. You can select areas less than 50%, and you will notice a change when you apply an effect, but you do not see an outline around them. Feathering can be preprogrammed into a selection by entering a value in the Options bar, or applied to an existing selection outline by choosing Select → Feather.

Figure 6.3

The Feather command softens the edge of a selection border. On the left, an image has been pasted into a selection. On the right, the same image has been pasted into a selection border with a 10-pixel feather radius.

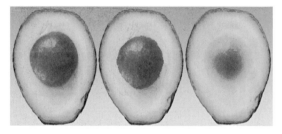

Figure 6.4

(left) Anti-aliased, (center) aliased, and (right) feathered edges

**Anti-Aliased** An anti-alias is a two- or three-pixel border around an edge that blends into the adjacent color to create a small transition zone. It is intended to simulate depth of field in a photograph. Without the anti-alias, an image would look "aliased," or stair-stepped, without smooth transitions between colors. Anti-aliasing is different than feathering because the size of the transition of a feather can be controlled, whereas an anti-aliased edge is automatically applied when the option is chosen and is usually just a few pixels wide, depending on the resolution of the document (see Figure 6.4).

## Shape Selection Tools

You use the Rectangular Marquee tool and its fly-out, the Elliptical Marquee tool, primarily when you need to select a fairly standard shape within your image—a rectangle, square, circle, or ellipse. Don't forget, however, that many more complex shapes can be obtained with just these two tools when they are used in combination with the Add, Subtract, and Intersect options.

Within the Marquee fly-out (but for some reason not included in the Shift-M key shortcut when you cycle through them), you have two more options: the Single Column Marquee and the Single Row Marquee.

## Rectangular Marquee

The Rectangular Marquee tool [⬚] is used to select rectangular or square portions of the image. Click in the image and drag in any direction to select a rectangular area of the image.

The Style menu in the Marquee tools' Options bar enables you to choose from three methods for sizing the Rectangular and Elliptical Marquees:

**Normal** I wish they would rename this "Manual" because that's precisely what it is—the setting for hands-on control of these Marquee tools. By choosing Normal, you determine the size and proportion of the marquee by dragging.

**Fixed Aspect Ratio** Enter numerical values for the proportion of the marquee in the Height and Width fields. Although you can change the *size* of the marquee by dragging, its *proportions* will remain constant.

**Fixed Size** The size of the marquee is determined by the values, in pixels, that you enter in the Height and Width fields. A marquee size is defined by pixels because it can't select anything smaller. If you want Photoshop to accept values in units other than pixels—inches, for example—then Control-click/right-click on the Width and Height fields and drag to your preferred units. Photoshop will create a marquee to the nearest pixel that you specify.

Table 6.1 describes the keyboard modifiers you can use with the Rectangular and Elliptical Marquee tools that allow you to control the behavior of marquees as you draw them.

The Elliptical Marquee tool has the same style options as the Rectangular Marquee. See Table 6.1 for keyboard modifiers you can use to constrain or move the Elliptical Marquee tool.

| TECHNIQUE | HOW TO DO IT |
|---|---|
| Constrain to square or circle | Shift-dragging constrains the Rectangular Marquee selection to a square or the Elliptical Marquee to a circle. |
| Draw from center | By default, a marquee originates from a corner point. To originate the marquee from its center, place your cursor in the center of the area and Option-drag/Alt-drag. |
| Reposition while dragging | While dragging out a marquee, hold down the spacebar and drag at any time to reposition it. |
| Reposition after drawing | While in the Marquee tool, place the cursor inside the marquee and drag to reposition it. |
| Combination techniques | You can combine any of these key command techniques. For example, press the Shift key and the mouse button and drag to constrain the image to a circle or square. Then while dragging, press the Option/Alt key to radiate it from its center point. |

Table 6.1

**Moving and Constraining Marquees**

## Elliptical Marquee

Use the Elliptical Marquee tool [◯] to create ellipses or circles. It performs similarly to the Rectangular Marquee: Click and drag in any direction to produce an elliptical, or circular, selection.

### Single Row Marquee

The Single Row Marquee tool [⊏⊐] selects a single *horizontal* row of pixels. Click anywhere in the image, and a selection marquee appears around a single row of adjacent pixels that runs horizontally across the entire image.

### Single Column Marquee

The Single Column Marquee tool [⫿] selects a single *vertical* column of pixels. Click any-where in the image, and a selection marquee appears around a single column of adjacent pixels that runs vertically from the top to the bottom of the image.

The Single Column Marquee tool selects a single vertical column of pixels, but you can also use this feature to create stripes that can later be colorized to produce wood-grain effects. Here's how:

1. Open an RGB document with a white background.
2. Select a single column of pixels.
3. Choose Filter → Noise → Add Noise → 400, and click OK.
4. Choose Edit → Transform → Scale. Drag the center handle of the left or right edge to the left or right.
5. Press the Return/Enter key to initiate the transformation (or the Esc key to cancel it).
6. Choose Image → Adjustments → Hue/Saturation. Check the Colorize box and move the sliders until the image changes to the desired color.

## Free-Form Selection Tools

Photoshop offers three tools for making irregularly shaped selections. The Lasso tool and its fly-outs, the Polygonal Lasso, and the Magnetic Lasso draw selections based on your mouse movements. Cycle through these tools by pressing Shift-L.

### Lasso

The Lasso tool [�’] draws free-form selections. Click the edge of the area you want to select and drag to surround the area with the selection border. Close the marquee by placing the cursor on the starting point, or release the mouse to close the selection with a straight line.

### Polygonal Lasso

The Polygonal Lasso tool [🔽] is used to create straightedged selection borders. Click and release the mouse. Then reposition the mouse to the next corner of the polygon, and click and release again. You can repeat the process until you return to the point of origin and close the marquee by clicking the starting point, or double-click to close the selection from the most recently established point. By holding down the Shift key, you can lock line segments horizontally, vertically, or at 45-degree angles.

> When using either the Lasso or Polygonal Lasso, you can toggle between the two by pressing the Option/Alt key.

## Magnetic Lasso

The Magnetic Lasso tool [icon] intuitively makes selections based on the contrast values of pixels. As you click and drag, the Magnetic Lasso deposits a path that is attracted to areas of the most contrast. When you release the mouse, the path becomes a selection.

The Magnetic Lasso selection tool takes awhile to get used to. If you find that you've lost control over the path, double-click the mouse to complete the selection, deselect (using Select → Deselect or ⌘/Ctrl-D), and begin again. The Magnetic Lasso tool rarely makes perfect selections, but it's a time-saver if combined with other selection tools.

The tool has three settings in the Options bar that affect its behavior:

**Width** This setting (in pixels) determines the distance from the path of the mouse within which pixels will be evaluated for contrast by the Magnetic Lasso.

**Edge Contrast** This is the minimum percentage of pixel contrast that the Magnetic Lasso will be attracted to. The higher the number, the smaller the range of contrast, hence the more selective the tool will be.

**Frequency** Enter a value for the frequency with which points are automatically deposited. The points create segments along the path that fix the previous segments and better control its behavior. You can always deposit a point manually by clicking your mouse as you drag along the edge to be defined. While these anchors are not editable like vector points, adding them can help guide the Magnetic Lasso when making a selection in an area where a clear outline is not present and your vision and the tool's "intuition" are at odds. (See Chapter 9 for a thorough discussion of editing anchor points while using Photoshop's vector-based tools.)

**Pen Pressure** Check this box to increase the width of the tool with stylus pressure when using a tablet.

### Magic Wand

The Magnetic Wand tool [icon] (shortcut key Shift-W) makes "automatic" selections based on the similarity of pixel brightness. To use the Magic Wand, place your cursor on the area to be selected and click your mouse. Adjacent pixels of similar color will be included in the selection.

You can affect the range of pixels that are selected by adjusting the Tolerance setting in the tool's Options bar. Higher tolerance values include in the selection more pixels of greater color and brightness range. Lower values include fewer pixels in the selection.

The Eyedropper tool's sample size also plays a role in the Magic Wand selection. If the Eyedropper is set to a point sample, the Magic Wand will calculate its selection based on the tolerance of a single pixel. If it's set to a $3 \times 3$ or $5 \times 5$ average, then the tolerance is determined by the average brightness of 9 pixels or 25 pixels, respectively.

In the middle example in Figure 6.5, I entered a tolerance of 32 and clicked a pixel with a value of 128, or mid gray. (I determined its value by looking at the Info palette.) The Magic Wand included all the pixels that are 32 steps lighter and all the pixels that are 32 steps darker than the sampled pixel—that is, all adjacent pixels with brightness values between 96 and 160 were selected.

When selecting RGB color images with the Magic Wand tool, the range is determined by each of the red, green, and blue values of the sampled pixel.

Figure 6.5

**Tolerance determines the range of pixels that the Magic Wand selects.**

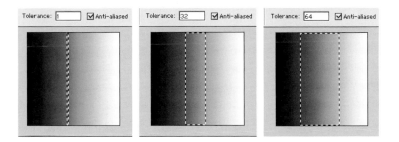

Other choices in the Options bar enhance your ability to control the operation of the Magic Wand tool:

**Contiguous** By default, the Contiguous box is checked, which limits the selection to adjacent pixels. Uncheck this box to select all the pixels in the image within the same tolerance range.

**Use All Layers** If this box is unchecked, you will limit the selection to pixels within the same tolerance range on the same layer. Checking this box includes pixels within the same tolerance range on other layers. (Layers are covered in Chapter 7, "Layering Your Image.")

## Applying Selection Techniques

You can modify a selection outline several ways; among them, you can conceal it, transform it, add to it, subtract from it, soften its edges, and eliminate it. These commands are important because they facilitate the process of masking. For example, if you draw a selection incorrectly, instead of redrawing it from scratch, it might be more efficient to make a few alterations to it. What follows are some outline-altering techniques that you will find indispensable.

## The Select Menu

Some selection adjustments can be automatically applied by accessing them from the Select menu or applying a shortcut key command. You will find that you use these commands quite frequently, so in the interest of working efficiently, I recommend that you learn to use the shortcuts.

**Select All** (⌘/Ctrl-A) This command selects the entire content of an image or a targeted layer. Because you can perform virtually any operation to the entire image in Photoshop when no specific area has been defined by a selection border, this command is used primarily to select the image prior to copying and pasting.

**Deselect** (⌘/Ctrl-D) Use Select → Deselect to deactivate the selection. Another method is to click off the selection anywhere on the image—except when using the Single Column and Single Row Marquee tools or the Magic Wand tool.

**Reselect** (Shift-⌘/Ctrl-D) Choose this command to reactivate the last deselected selection border.

**Inverse** (Shift-⌘/Ctrl-I) To deselect the selected portion of the image and select the masked portion, choose Select → Inverse. This technique can save time when an image has been photographed on a single colored background. The background can be selected quickly with the Magic Wand and inverted to select the desired content, as in Figure 6.6.

Figure 6.6

After selecting the background (left), the Inverse command deselects that portion of the image and selects the masked portion (right).

**Show/Hide Selection Edges** Use View → Show → Selection Edges to conceal (and reveal) the marching ants from view while the selection remains active. You can then choose View → Extras (or ⌘/Ctrl-H) to perform the operation. This command is useful in seeing changes to the image without the distracting selection border.

With the border invisible, you may forget that an area of the image is selected. Photoshop will not perform operations anywhere else on the image until the selection border is deactivated. If you find that the Paintbrush tool is not painting or the Smudge tool not smudging, press ⌘/Ctrl-D to deactivate the invisible selection.

**Modify**  Once a selection has been made, you can alter its dimensions by choosing one of the Select → Modify subcommands. Each command changes the selection marquee and alters its dimensions:

**Border**  frames the selection and deselects the inside area of the outline, producing a selected border of specific thickness (see Figure 6.7). When you choose Select → Modify → Border, you can determine the thickness of the border by entering a value in pixels in the Width field.

Figure 6.7

The Border command selects only the outer-most portion of your selection (here, the pixels immediately inward and outward from the edge of the plant).

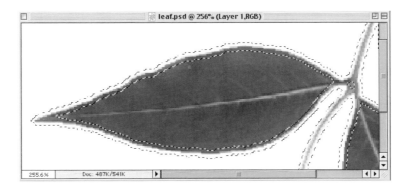

**Smooth**  rounds sharp corners of a selection, eliminating protrusions and stair-stepped areas of the selection border. Choose Select → Modify → Smooth, and then enter a sample radius value (larger values increase the effect). In Figure 6.8, the sample radius results in "cutting off" the left tip of the triangle.

**Expand and Contract**  both perform in the same way to enlarge or reduce the size of the selection by a specified number of pixels. This command is quite useful for trimming off stubborn, unwanted edge pixels (see the section on matting in Chapter 22 "Advanced Layer Techniques") or tightening up your selection a bit. Choose Select → Modify → Expand or Contract, and enter a value between 1 and 100 pixels. Click OK to implement the operation.

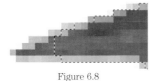

Figure 6.8

The Smooth command rounds off jagged corners, like the tip of this triangle.

**Grow**  The value entered in the Tolerance field of the Magic Wand's Options bar determines how much the selection will grow. When you choose Select → Grow, the selection marquee expands to include adjacent pixels that are lighter or darker by no more than the tolerance range.

**Similar**  In order to use this operation, a selection must be active. When you choose Select → Similar, Photoshop selects all pixels within the image that are the same colors as the pixels within the selected area. The amount selected is controlled by the Tolerance setting in the Magic Wand's Options bar.

## Transforming a Selection

Once you make a selection, you may want to alter its shape before applying one of Photoshop's many powerful operations to its content. Photoshop gives you the ability to scale, rotate, or move a selection border. To transform a selection, choose Select → Transform Selection. A rectangular transformation box appears around the selection border. You can then transform the size, angle, or position of the selection border with the following procedures:

**Move**  To move the selection, place your cursor within the rectangular transformation box; the Move cursor ▶ appears. Press your mouse button and drag the selection into position, then release the mouse.

> The icon in the center of the transformation box represents the point of origin. You can move this icon prior to scaling or rotating the selection to change the point from which the selection will transform. When you want to move the box, however, you place your cursor anywhere in the selection *except* on the icon.

**Scale**  To scale a selection border, place your cursor on one of the square handles on the corners ↖ or sides of the box. The Scale cursor appears. Press your mouse button and drag. To keep the selection border in its current proportion, press your Shift key while dragging.

**Rotate**  To rotate a selection, place your cursor outside the box. The Rotate cursor ↻ appears. Press your mouse button and drag to rotate the selection. Holding down the Shift key enables precise rotation in 15-degree increments.

Scale and Rotate are demonstrated in Figure 6.9. To implement the transformation, click the check mark or press Return/Enter; the transformation box will disappear. To cancel the transformation, click the Cancel box or press the Escape key.

Figure 6.9

**Transform Selection techniques: Scale (left) and Rotate (right)**

After you've chosen Select → Transform Selection and the transformation box is displayed, you can also apply many more transformations to the selection by choosing Edit → Transform. A list of options appears, including Skew, Distort, Perspective, and various precise Rotate commands. You perform these additional functions by repositioning the anchor points of the transformation box. The Flip Horizontal or Flip Vertical commands will mirror the marquee across a horizontal or vertical axis passing through its point of origin icon. See Chapter 13, "Sizing and Transforming Images" for more on this topic.

## Other Selection Techniques

Once a selection has been made, you can reposition the marquee with or without its contents using the following techniques:

**Move Selection Outline**  While in any selection tool, click inside the marquee and drag. When you've relocated the outline, release the mouse.

**Nudge Selection Outline**  While in any selection tool, press the right, left, up, or down arrow keys to move a selection in increments of one pixel. Press Shift plus any of the arrow keys to move the selection outline 10 pixels at a time.

**Move Selection Contents**  Choose the Move tool; click inside the marquee and drag. When you've relocated the marquee, release the mouse. You can also move the contents while in any selection tool: ⌘-click/Ctrl-click inside the marquee and drag.  The icon ➤ₓ displays a symbol that looks like scissors, indicating that you are cutting the contents of the selection outline and moving them. When you've relocated the selection, release the mouse and then the key.

> After you've selected an area and moved it once, it "floats." That is, it can be moved again by placing a selection tool inside the marquee, pressing the mouse button, and dragging. You no longer need to press ⌘/Ctrl. The selection continues to float until you deselect it.

**Nudge Selection Contents**  You can nudge the contents of a selection in one-pixel increments: With the Move tool active, press the left, right, up, or down arrow keys. Press Shift and any of the arrow keys to move the selection contents 10 pixels at a time.

**Duplicate Selection Contents**  With the Move tool active, hold down Option-Alt/⌘-Ctrl while you click and drag. You'll see a double Move cursor ▶, which indicates that you are duplicating the selection. (Or, while any other tool is active, hold down ⌘/Ctrl while you drag.) When you've relocated the copy to the desired position, release the mouse.

# Making Selections

## Fred Photato Head

When I was a kid, Mr. Potato Head was a special toy. It was one of the only objects in my toy chest that let me make real aesthetic choices. I would start with a potato and choose from dozens of plastic facial features that could attach to produce a unique character.

For this first Hands On exercise, Fred Photato Head is the virtual version of the popular toy. In the process of assembling a character from dozens of features, you will learn how to use the selection tools. All of the elements are on this single document. You will choose a feature, select it, and drag it to the character. In this way, you will build your unique version of Fred Photato Head.

Making accurate selections is fundamental to maintaining the credibility of your image. Poorly drawn selections that are rough, inaccurate, or stair-stepped, or that contain unwanted edge pixels, are sure to destroy the illusion of a seamless reality. It's important, then, to familiarize yourself with the masking process and to hone your selection-making skills. That is what I hope this step-by-step section will accomplish.

## Getting Started

Delete or hide your preferences file before beginning this Hands On exercise. The "Modifying Photoshop's Settings" section in Chapter 5, "Setting Up the Program," details how to reset your preferences to Photoshop's defaults. Once you have launched Photoshop with default preferences, here's how to begin the Hands On project:

1. Insert the *Photoshop 7 Savvy* CD in the CD-ROM drive.
2. Choose File → Open; select and open `Fred_Photato_Head_Start.psd` in the `H01` folder on the CD (see Figure H1.1).
3. Save the file to your disk.

   Figure H1.2 shows one possible outcome.

   See the color versions of `Fred_Photato_Head_Start` and `Fred_Photato_Head_End`—Figures C39 and C40—in the color section of this book.

Figure H1.1

**The open Fred Photato Head file**

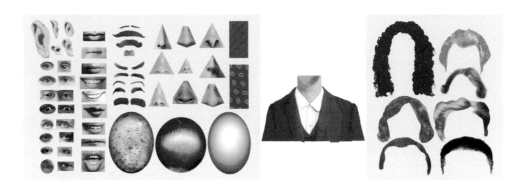

## Moving the Mannequin

We'll use the Rectangular Marquee tool ⬚ to move the mannequin into position.

1. Use the Navigator (Figure H1.3) to zoom in or out so you can see all of the mannequin in the center of the screen.

2. Choose the Rectangular Marquee tool. Place your cursor just below the lower-left corner of the mannequin. Click and drag to the upper-right corner to make your selection, as shown in Figure H1.4.

Figure H1.2

**This is what I made out of the virtual elements, but yours may look quite different.**

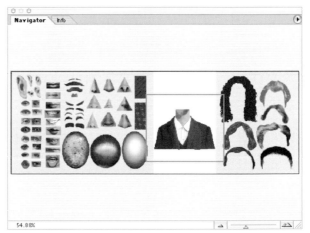

Figure H1.3

**Use the Navigator palette to bring the mannequin into view.**

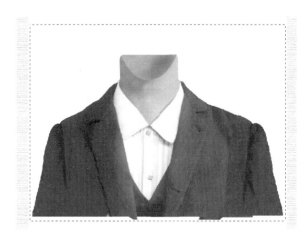

Figure H1.4

**Drag a rectangle around the mannequin.**

Figure H1.5

**The mannequin positioned at the bottom of the background**

3.  Choose the Move tool  . Place your cursor inside the marching ants. Press Shift to constrain the vertical movement of the marquee as you drag down. Drag the mannequin until its ragged bottom edge is just outside the bottom of the white background, as shown in Figure H1.5.

4.  Press ⌘-D (Mac) or Ctrl-D (Win) to deselect.

## Selecting a Head

You can choose between the potato, the onion, or the egg for the head. We'll choose the egg.

1.  With the Navigator, zoom out so that you can see the egg, the onion, and the potato.

2.  Press Shift-M to select the Elliptical Marquee tool ⬭ . Place your cursor in the approximate center of the egg. Press the Option/Alt key as you drag an ellipse from the center. As you near the edge, press the spacebar (but don't release the Option/Alt key!). Drag the marquee to accurately position it so that it just touches the edge. Release the spacebar to resize, and press it again to reposition the marquee until you've centered and positioned the selection outline on the edge of the egg. Release the mouse first and then the keys.

3.  Choose the Move tool. Place the cursor inside the marquee and drag the egg to position it on the mannequin, as in Figure H1.6.

4.  Press ⌘/Ctrl-D to deselect and ⌘/Ctrl-S to save the document.

Figure H1.6

**The egg positioned on the mannequin**

## Selecting the Eyes

With the Elliptical Marquee tool still chosen, we will now select the eyes:

1. In the Options bar, from the Style pop-up list, choose Fixed Aspect Ratio. Enter 1.25 for the width and 1 for the height, as in Figure H1.7.

Figure H1.7

**Choosing a fixed aspect ratio**

Style: [ Fixed Aspect Ratio ▲▼ ]  Width: [1.25]   Height: [1]

2. You'll find a group of eyes to the left of the mannequin. Zoom in on one of the left eyes and place your cursor in the center of it. Press the Option/Alt key and drag outward. Don't drag to the very edge, but stay a few pixels within the oval shape, as seen in Figure H1.8.

3. Choose Select → Feather. Enter a value of 2 pixels. (See Chapter 6, "Making Selections," for more on feathering.)

4. Choose the Move tool. Drag the eye and position it on the egg. Notice the seamless transition between the egg and the eye due to the feathered selection.

5. Choose the Elliptical Marquee. In the Options bar, from the Style pop-up list, choose Fixed Size. Enter 43 px for the width and 30 px for the height. (The fixed size may vary on some of the eyes.)

6. In the Options bar, enter a value of 2 px for the feather. (Entering a value in the Options bar allows you to feather a selection before drawing it.)

7. Place your cursor on a right eye. Click your mouse and drag to position the Fixed Size marquee.

8. Choose the Move tool. Drag the eye and position it on the egg. Once again, there is a seamless transition between the egg and the eye due to the feathered selection, as shown in Figure H1.9.

9. Press ⌘/Ctrl-D to deselect and ⌘/Ctrl-S to save the document.

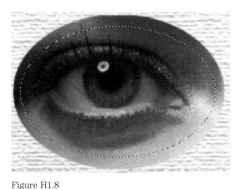

Figure H1.8

**The selection of a left eye**

Figure H1.9

**The eyes positioned on the egg, with a feathered transition**

## Selecting a Nose

You'll use two variations of the Lasso tool 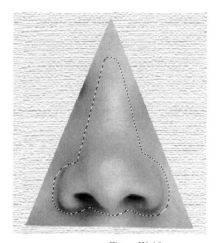 to select the nose.

1. Choose the Lasso tool. In the Options bar, set the feather radius to 2 px.

2. Choose a nose. Start at the lower-left of the nose and drag to the right around the curved shapes.

3. When you reach the side of the nose, press and hold the Option/Alt key. Release the mouse. The tool changes to the Polygonal Lasso. Drag a straight line up the right side of the nose. When you reach the top portion of the nose, press the mouse button, release the keys, and drag the curve with the Lasso tool.

4. Press the Option/Alt key. Release the mouse and drag a straight line down the left side of the nose. When you reach the curved portion of the left nostril, press the mouse button, release the keys again, and drag the lasso to close the selection. The selection should look like Figure H1.10.

Figure H1.10

**The selected nose**

5. Choose the Move tool, drag the nose, and place it on the egg.

6. Press ⌘/Ctrl-D to deselect and ⌘/Ctrl-D to save the document.

## Selecting the Mouth

You also select the mouth with the Lasso tool:

1. Choose the Lasso tool. Encircle one of the mouths as close to its edge as possible.

2. Choose Select → Feather. Enter a value of 2 pixels.

3. Choose the Move tool. In the Options bar, check Show Bounding Box. Place the cursor inside the bounding box. Drag the mouth and place it on the egg.

   Press Shift while dragging to constrain the proportions.

4. To size the mouth, place your cursor on any one of the bounding box handles, and drag inward to decrease or outward to increase the size, as in Figure H1.11.

   Press the ⌘/Ctrl key to independently move the corner points of the bounding box to distort the mouth.

5. To rotate the mouth, place the cursor on the outside corner of the box until the rotate icon appears, then drag.

6. In the Options bar, click the check mark to commit the transformation or the cancel icon to cancel it.

7. Deselect and save the document.

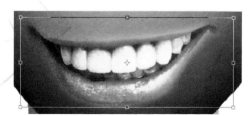

Figure H1.11

**Sizing the mouth**

## Adding a Mustache

Use this fast technique of selecting the mustache by subtracting the area around it from the selection:

1. Choose the Rectangular Marquee tool.

2. Drag a rectangle around the mustache of choice.

3. Choose the Magic Wand tool. In the Options bar, set the tolerance to 24. Set the feather radius to 1 px.

4. Choose the Subtract From Selection icon from the toolbar.

5. Click within the rectangular selection but not on the mustache. The mustache is automatically selected.

6. Choose the Move tool. In the Options bar, check Show Bounding Box. Place the cursor inside the bounding box. Drag the mustache and place it between the mouth and the nose on the egg.

7. Size the mustache to fit the space.

8. Deselect and save.

## Selecting the Eyebrows

To give Fred a little character, let's add eyebrows. There are some real whoppers to choose from.

1. Choose the Magic Wand tool. In the Options bar, set the tolerance to 32.

2. Click a right eyebrow. Only a portion of the eyebrow is selected, as shown in Figure H1.12. Depending on the eyebrow you select, you'll have to readjust the tolerance to make a complete selection, or you can click the Add To Selection icon in the Options bar and continue to click the unselected areas. Select the right and left eyebrow in the same way.

Figure H1.12

**Only a portion of the eyebrows is selected.**

3. Choose the Move tool. In the Options bar, check Show Bounding Box. Place the cursor inside the bounding box. Drag the eyebrows and place them above the eyes on the egg. Resize them if desired.

4. Deselect and save.

## Choosing the Hair

The easiest way to select a complex shape with an irregular edge and a lot of tonal variation is with the Magnetic Lasso tool 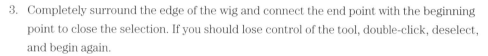 .

1. Choose the Magnetic Lasso tool. Use the default settings in the Options bar to control its performance.

2. Zoom in on one of the wigs. Place your cursor on the edge of one of the wigs and drag slowly around its edge. A path is laid down as you drag, as demonstrated in Figure H1.13.

    For more control, add additional anchors by clicking your mouse as you drag.

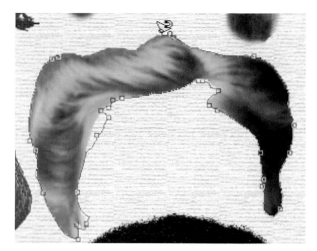

**Figure H1.13**

The wig selected with the Magnetic Lasso tool. Notice where some of the edge was not precisely selected. You can later refine these imperfect areas by subtracting them from the selection with the Lasso tool.

3. Completely surround the edge of the wig and connect the end point with the beginning point to close the selection. If you should lose control of the tool, double-click, deselect, and begin again.

    You may find that this tool does not make a perfect selection. Often it is necessary to refine the selection by adding or subtracting from the selection with the Lasso tool (see Figure H1.13).

1. You'll want to soften the edge of the hair. Once the selection has been made, choose Select → Modify → Contract. Enter 2 pixels for the Contract By value (see Figure H1.14).

2. Choose Select → Feather. Enter 2 pixels for the radius.

3. Zoom out. Choose the Move tool. In the Options bar, check Show Bounding Box. Place the cursor inside the bounding box. Drag the wig and place it on the egg. Resize it for a perfect fit.

4. Deselect and save.

## Selecting and Duplicating the Ears

To choose the ears, you will once again use the Magnetic Lasso tool.

1. Again, use the default settings in the Options bar to control this tool's performance.

2. Carefully drag along the edge of one of the ears to encircle it.

3. When you've entirely surrounded the edges with the magnetic selection outline, place your cursor on the original point and click your mouse to implement the selection.

4. Choose the Move tool. Check Show Bounding Box in the Options bar. Click inside the bounding box and press Option/Alt as you drag to duplicate the ear. Position the ear on the left side of the egg. Size and rotate the ear as desired. In the Options bar, click the check mark to commit the transformation or the cancel icon to cancel it. Release the mouse.

**Figure H1.14**

**The Contract Selection dialog box**

5. Press Option/Alt. Drag a duplicate ear and place it on the right side of the head.

6. Choose → Edit → Transform Flip Horizontal.

7. Reposition the ear.

8. Deselect and save.

## Creating the Tie

First, you'll make a selection of the area where we want the tie. Then, you'll move the marquee onto the fabric, copy it, and deposit it on the mannequin to create a tie.

1. Choose the Lasso tool. In the Options bar set the feather radius to 2 px.

2. On Fred's shirt, draw the shape of the tie, as shown in Figure H1.15.

3. Choose the Rectangular Marquee tool. Place your cursor in the center of the marching ants. Click the mouse and drag it to one of the material swatches.

4. Choose the Move tool. Place the cursor inside the selection outlines and drag the tie back on to the shirt.

5. Deselect and save.

You can enhance the tie, as I have done in Figure H1.16, by painting portions of it with a low-opacity black to produce a shadow effect. See Chapter 12, "Using Channels and Quick Mask," to learn about painting.

## Cropping the Image

Now that you've finished Fred, let's throw away any unwanted parts of the image.

1. Choose the Crop tool ▣ . Place your cursor on the lower-left corner of the white background. Click and drag up and to the right to encompass about three-quarters of the white background, as shown in Figure H1.17. Release the mouse.

Figure H1.15

**The outline of the tie**

Figure H1.16

**The completed tie, with a shadow for depth**

Figure H1.17

**The Crop bounding box in place**

Figure H1.18

**The feathered selection border**

2. Adjust the Crop bounding box by dragging its corner handles.

3. Click the check mark to implement the crop.

4. Save the image.

## Adding a Background

To finish this portrait off, we'll add a soft-edged background.

1. Choose the Magic Wand tool. Set the tolerance to 32.

2. Click in the white background to select it.

3. Choose the Rectangular Marquee tool. In the Options bar, set the feather to 40 px.

4. Click the Subtract From Selection icon.

5. Click and drag about a half-inch or so from the upper-left edge down to the very bottom about an inch or so from the lower-right edge, as shown in Figure H1.18.

6. Click the Swatches tab in the Color/Swatches/Styles palette cluster. Choose a color by clicking a swatch (see Figure H1.19).

7. Press Option-Delete/Alt-Backspace to fill the area with color.

8. Deselect and save.

Figure H1.19

**Choosing a color in the Swatches palette**

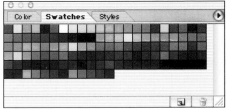

# CHAPTER 7

# Layering Your Image

*Photoshop images appear* on flat screens, but they are actually three-dimensional because of the power of layers. In the virtual world of the Photoshop workflow, layers are the third dimension. Beyond the height and width, they create depth.

Layers are critical to working dynamically in Photoshop. Fragments of an image saved on individual layers can be edited separately and moved independently of each other. The stacking order of layers can help determine the depth and position of visual elements within the picture plane. In short, working with layers gives you tremendous control over the image during the process of creating it.

This chapter will help you learn about:

- **Understanding the Layers palette**
- **Creating new layers**
- **Using layer styles**
- **Consolidating and blending layers**
- **Working with Type layers**

## Creating the Illusion of Depth

The illusion of depth on a flat surface is created by the use of techniques that mimic what we see in the world. Artists have used these techniques for centuries to create realistic images that resemble our visual reality. One technique, called *perspective*, achieves its affect by using converging lines that intersect at a horizon. An object whose contours align with the perspective lines appears to recede in space.

Another method involves modifying the relative scale of visual elements in an image. Larger objects appear closer to the viewer than smaller ones. Because this visual phenomenon is a naturally occurring characteristic of sight in the 3-D world, when we see it in a picture we subconsciously draw the conclusion that the objects exist in space when, in fact, the picture is two-dimensional.

The position of an object in an image also contributes to the illusion of depth. If one element blocks out part of another element, the obstructing element appears to be in front of the obstructed one. Another common device, atmospheric perspective, uses tonality to simulate distance. As objects recede in space, they appear lighter and less distinct due to the presence of dust and haze in the air.

The fact remains, however, that no matter how many devices are used to produce three-dimensionality, and no matter how deep the picture appears, unless its surface is textured, it is as flat as a pancake.

Photoshop images are somewhat of an exception to the flat-as-a-pancake rule. They appear on-screen as flat images of colored light, and they have a specific height and width. They can also have depth in the form of *layers*. A Photoshop layer is like a piece of clear glass (see Figure 7.1), and parts of the image can be pasted to the glass. If you have different parts of the image separated onto multiple layers, you can shuffle their position in the stack, allowing one part of the image to appear in front of another. Because the layers isolate each part of the image, you have the added advantage of being able to control the contents of each layer separately.

When a part of the image is isolated on an individual layer, it can be singled out and affected at any time. A layer can be moved horizontally or vertically, or repositioned anywhere in the stack, to help produce the illusion of depth. You can modify the color relations of pixels on superimposed layers and adjust their level of opacity. Special layer styles can be applied to produce realistic shadows, embosses, textures, patterns, and glowing effects.

## Looking at the Layers Palette

At the heart of all this power is the Layers palette (shown in Figure 7.2). It is the control center from which you perform most layer operations. By default, the Layers palette is clustered with the Channels and the Paths palettes. If the Layers palette is not displayed, you can access it by choosing Window → Layers or by pressing F7 on an extended keyboard.

Each layer in the palette is separated from the one directly below it or above it by a thin line. Each layer's row includes a thumbnail of the layer's contents, the layer's name, and any layer styles, masks, or locks applied to that layer. In the far left column is an eye icon which, when displayed, indicates that the contents of the layer are visible. Immediately to the right of this visibility indicator is another column that displays a brush icon if the layer is the target layer, a small chain icon if the layer is linked, or a mask icon if the layer is a Fill or Adjustment layer.

Figure 7.1

**Layers in a Photoshop document**

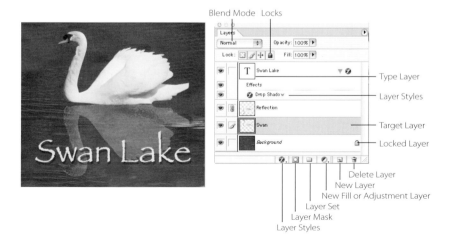

Figure 7.2

**The Layers palette**

Figure 7.3

**The Layers Palette pull-down menu**

Above the layer stack are Lock check boxes, which enable you to lock the transparency, editing, and movement of layer contents. At the top-left of the Layers palette is a list of blending modes that can alter the color relationships of layers in the stack. And to the right of the blending modes is the Opacity slider, which controls the level of transparency of a targeted layer's contents. In version 7, the Layer Style Advanced Blending Fill Opacity control has been moved from the Layer Styles window to the Layers palette.

You can access many layer operations from the palette pull-down menu (shown in Figure 7.3). Clicking the small triangular icon on the top-right of the palette reveals these options.

## Working with the Background

When you scan or import an image from another program and open it in Photoshop, the Layers palette displays one thumbnail, labeled *Background*. You can think of the Background as an image mounted to a board. If you were to cut away a portion of the image with an X-ACTO knife, you would see the board underneath—in this case, the background color behind the Background contents. The contents of all of the layers float on top of the Background. Unlike a layer, the Background is opaque and cannot support transparency. If the document contains more than one layer, the Background is always at the bottom of the stack and cannot be moved or placed in a higher position. When new layers are added to the document, their content always appears in front of the Background.

> If your image is composed entirely of layers, you can convert one of your layers into a Background. Target a layer and choose Layer → New → Background From Layer. The Background will automatically be deposited at the bottom of the stack.

By default, the Background is locked. If you want to move its contents, adjust its opacity, or reposition it in the Layers stack, you need to convert it to a layer. Like many of Photoshop's operations, there is more than one way to perform this task. To convert the Background into a layer from the menu, choose Layer → New → Layer From Background. To convert the Background from the Layers palette, double-click the Background's name or thumbnail to display the New Layer dialog box. If you click OK, Photoshop names the converted layer Layer 0 by default. You can use the default name, or you can enter a name for the new layer in the Name field and click OK.

Figure 7.4

**The New Layer dialog box showing the layer name Layer 0**

Alternatively, Option-double-click (Macintosh) or Alt-double-click (Windows) the Background's name or thumbnail to automatically change it into a layer named Layer 0 (see Figure 7.4).

The New Layer dialog box also lets you color-code your layer, adjust its opacity, and specify a blending mode. You can also group it with other layers if, for example, you're using it to make a clipping group. (Chapter 22, "Advanced Layer Techniques," describes clipping groups.)

## Naming Layers

Naming your layers is essential to establishing an efficient workflow. The default numbers that Photoshop assigns to new layers become quite anonymous when their content is too small to be recognized on the thumbnail or when there are 30 or 40 of them in the document. Instead of using the default name Layer 0, I recommend that you give the layer a name that readily identifies it. Naming each layer with a descriptive title is a fast way to organize the components of your image for easy identification.

To name a new layer, enter a name in the Name field of the New Layer dialog box and click OK. To rename a layer, double-click the layer's name. A box will appear around it. Type in the new name.

## Viewing Layers

You can conceal or reveal the content of a layer by clicking the eye icon in the first column of the Layers palette.

To reveal or conceal the contents of more than one layer at a time, click the eye next to each of the desired layers. To conceal all but one layer, press the Option/Alt key while clicking its eye icon. With the same key held down, click the icon again to reveal all layers.

### Choosing Your Thumbnail Size

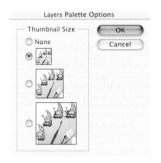

The thumbnails that represent each layer display its content in miniature. You can choose from three different sizes of thumbnails, or you can choose to display no thumbnail at all. To specify a thumbnail display, pull down the Palette menu and choose Palette Options. In the dialog box that opens (Figure 7.5), click the desired thumbnail size and then click OK.

Figure 7.5

**The Layer Palette Options menu determines the size of the thumbnails that are displayed.**

### Targeting a Layer

You can apply a Photoshop operation to affect the contents of a layer, but first you must target the layer you want. A *targeted* layer is active and ready to be edited. To target a layer, click its name, which appears to the right of the thumbnail. You will see a colored highlight in the text field and a brush symbol in the second column to the left of the layer's thumbnail (as in Figure 7.6). Only one layer can be targeted at a time; a targeted layer must be visible to be affected. Certain effects can be applied to multiple layers simultaneously by linking them (see the upcoming section titled "Linking Layers"), placing them in sets, or grouping them (see Chapter 22).

Figure 7.6

**The Swan layer is targeted.**

## Understanding Transparency and Opacity

Since transparency is by nature invisible, it is graphically displayed in Photoshop as a gray and white checkerboard. If you see an area on a layer that is displayed as a checkerboard,

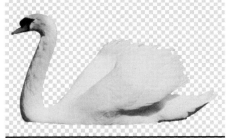

then the area is totally transparent. This means that either it is void of pixels or the pixels are completely transparent. If it's displayed as a combination of image and checkerboard, then it is semitransparent; and if it's displayed totally as image, then it's opaque. Figure 7.7 illustrates the difference between opaque and semitransparent images.

If only one layer is displayed and its contents are surrounded by areas of transparency, the image will appear against a gray and white checkerboard. If the color of the image is predominantly gray and the checkerboard becomes difficult to see, the color and size of the checkerboard can be changed in Transparency & Gamut Preferences to better reveal the image.

### Controlling Opacity

The Opacity slider enables you to adjust the level of transparency of all the pixels on a targeted layer, so that you can see through the image to the underlying layers in the stack. Click the arrow next to the Opacity field on the Layers palette; a slider pops up, which you can drag right to increase, or left to decrease, opacity. Or enter a value from 0 to 100 percent directly in the box.

If any tool other than the painting and editing tools is active, you can enter any number between 01 and 100 to change the Opacity value of the targeted layer.

Figure 7.7

**The swan at the top is displayed at 100% opacity; the swan at the bottom is displayed at 50% opacity.**

### Fill Opacity

In Photoshop 7, the Layer Style Advanced Blending Fill Opacity control has been moved from the Layer Styles window to the Layers palette. The slider enables you to add another opacity setting to a layer. This can be helpful when copying layers and making separate adjustments to the copied layer while maintaining the master opacity of the original layer.

## Changing Layer Order

The stacking order in the Layers palette determines the plane of depth where the visual elements appear. The content of the topmost layer in the Layers palette appears in the front of the image. The further down in the stack a layer is, the farther back its content appears, all the way back to the bottommost layer, or the Background.

You can change a layer's position in the stack and, consequently, its visual plane of depth in the image. In the Layers palette, click and drag the thumbnail or name of the layer you wish to move. As you drag up or down, you will see the division line between layers become bold (as in Figure 7.8). The bold line indicates the new location where the layer will appear when the mouse is released.

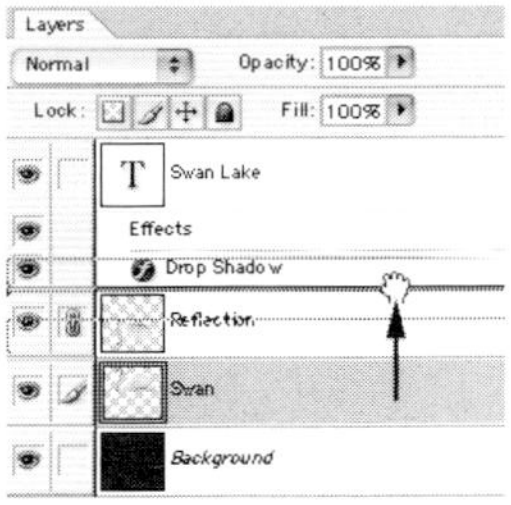

Another method of changing the position of the layer in the stack is to choose an option under Layer → Arrange, or use the equivalent key command. The Arrange submenu presents you with four options, as shown in Table 7.1.

Figure 7.8

**You can change a layer's position in the stacking order.**

| POSITION | MACINTOSH SHORTCUT | WINDOWS SHORTCUT | RESULT |
|---|---|---|---|
| Bring To Front | Shift-⌘-] | Shift-Ctrl-] | Moves the layer to the top of the stack |
| Bring Forward | ⌘-] | Ctrl-] | Moves the layer on top of the layer immediately above it |
| Send Backward | ⌘-[ | Ctrl-[ | Moves the layer under the layer immediately below it |
| Send To Back | Shift-⌘-[ | Shift-Ctrl-[ | Moves the layer to the bottom of the stack but in front of the Background |

Table 7.1

**Shortcuts for Positioning Layers**

## Linking Layers

Let's say you've positioned two elements of a logo on separate layers, and you are satisfied with their visual relationship to each other, except that they are a little too large and they need to be moved a half-inch to the left. You can transform or move two layers simultaneously by *linking* them.

To link one or more layers, target one of the layers. The target layer will display a paintbrush icon. Click in the column to the immediate left of the thumbnail on the layers that you want link to the target layer. A chain icon appears, like the one next to the Reflection layer in Figure 7.9. You can then choose the Move tool or any transformation function (Edit → Transform), and the layers will scale, rotate, distort, etc. as a group. (See Chapter 13, "Sizing and Transforming Images," for more on transformations.)

Linked layers are used primarily for transforming and moving multiple layers simultaneously. You can apply other effects to multiple layers by using specific layer-based operations. (These effects are described in more detail in later sections of this chapter and in later chapters of this book.)

Figure 7.9

**Linked layers are indicated by a chain icon.**

These operations include the following:

**Adjustment Layers** for color, brightness, and contrast adjustments and for color mapping functions (see Chapter 16, "Adjusting Tonality and Color").

**Layer Masking** to conceal and reveal portions of two sequential layers in the stack (see Chapter 22).

**Blending Modes** to apply a preprogrammed color formula to affect the relation between the pixels on a layer and the layer immediately below it in the stack (see Appendix C).

**Layer Sets** for grouping, opacity control, positioning of multiple layers in the stack, and transforming or moving layers (see the following section).

**Fill Layers** to apply a solid color, gradient, or pattern to an independent layer. When the opacity is adjusted, the Fill layer affects the underlying layer. A Fill layer also contains a layer mask, so that the color, gradient, or pattern can be superimposed onto a specific area of the image (see Chapter 10, "Creating and Applying Color").

**Clipping Groups** for using the content of one layer to clip portions of another (see Chapter 22).

## Grouping Layers in Layer Sets

Earlier versions of Photoshop supported a mere 99 layers; with its latest release, Photoshop now supports an unlimited number, with RAM being the only limiting factor. The potential to produce enormous quantities of layers makes a layer-management tool an absolute necessity.

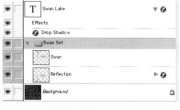

Figure 7.10

**The Swan and Reflection layers make up a layer set, which has been color-coded.**

*Layer sets* let you consolidate contiguous layers into a folder on the Layers palette. By highlighting the folder, you can apply certain operations to the layers as a group. The layers in a layer set, like Swan and Reflection in Figure 7.10, can be simultaneously revealed or concealed by clicking the eye icon for the set in the Layers palette. The whole set can be repositioned in the stack, moved, and—like linked layers—transformed using any of the transformation tools.

Although you can transform and reposition both layer sets and linked layers, layer sets differ from linked layers in that they contain contiguous layers—that is, layers that are sequenced immediately above or below each other in the stack. Layers that are linked can be anywhere in the stack.

There are a few different ways to create a new layer set:

- From the Layer menu, choose Layer → New → Layer Set.
- From the Layers Palette menu, choose New Layer Set.
- Click the Layer Set icon in the Layers palette. By default, the first layer set will be named Set 1.

With the first two commands, the Layer Set Properties dialog box appears (Figure 7.11). You can name the layer set, color-code it, and specify the color channels that comprise the image.

A fast way to create a layer set is to link the layers that you want in the set. Then choose Layer → New → Layer Set From Linked. All of the linked layers will be consolidated into one set. When you convert linked layers into a layer set, however, they become contiguous and their position in the stack may change.

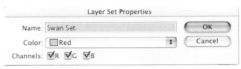

Figure 7.11

**The Layer Set Properties dialog box**

To add a layer to a set, click and drag it to the Layer Set folder. Then, release the mouse. To reveal the layers within the set, click the triangle to the left of the folder so that it points down. To conceal the contents of the layer set to eliminate clutter, click the triangle so that it points to the right.

## Locking Layers

Photoshop 7 offers four controls, or *locks*, in the Layers palette that prevent a layer from being modified (see Figure 7.12). Each lock is represented by an icon at the top of the palette; to lock a layer, target the layer and check the box for the lock type you want.

The lock types include the following:

**Lock Transparent Pixels**  This function is comparable to Preserve Transparency in earlier versions of the software. It protects the areas of the targeted layer that don't contain pixels from being edited. If you attempt to paint on a transparent area, for example, the tool will not respond, so in a sense, locking transparency works like a mask. The areas that do contain pixels will still respond to any Photoshop operation. Locking transparency does not protect transparent areas from the effect of transformations like scaling, rotating, or moving.

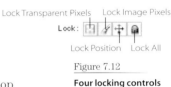

Figure 7.12

**Four locking controls**

**Lock Image Pixels**  The entire targeted layer is protected from editing functions like painting, color adjustments, or filters. You can, however, transform or move the content of a layer. Menu operations that you can't perform are grayed out. If you attempt to apply a tool function, you will be greeted by a circle with a line through it.

**Lock Position**  Checking this option prevents you from moving a targeted layer or applying Edit → Free Transform or any of the Edit → Transform operations such as Scale and Distort. When the Lock Position box is checked, these menu items are grayed out.

**Lock All**  You can protect a targeted layer from all editing functions by checking the Lock All box.

# Creating New Layers

It is often necessary to create a new layer, either to add new content to the image or to isolate an existing element. When a new layer is added, the file size of the document increases commensurate with the quantity of information on the new layer. Adding several new layers can significantly increase the amount of space the image consumes on your disk. This, however, is a small inconvenience for the power that layers deliver. As part of your workflow, though, you'll no doubt want to consolidate layers during the imaging process to decrease the file size (see "Consolidating Layers" later in this chapter).

## Creating a New Empty Layer

Here is an another example of redundant Photoshop operations. Two of these operations produce identical results, and one produces similar results with a slight twist. All three create a new layer. Let's try them:

- From the Layers menu, choose Layer → New → Layer to bring up the New Layer dialog box. Name the layer and specify its characteristics. Click OK.

- From the Layers palette pop-up menu, choose New Layer to bring up the New Layer dialog box (Figure 7.13). Name the layer and click OK.

- Click the New Layer icon 🔲 (next to the trash icon at the bottom of the Layers palette). A new layer, named Layer 1, appears in the stack immediately above the targeted layer. To rename the new layer, double-click its name and enter the new name in the Name field. You can also access the Layer Properties dialog box from the Layer menu or from the Layers Palette pull-down menu to rename the layer.

## Creating a New Layer with Content

There are two potential sources for the content of new layers: elements cut or copied from another layer or Background, and elements dragged and dropped from another document. Whatever its source, the end result isolates the content onto a separate layer so that it can be moved, edited, or rotated in the stack.

### Copying an Image to a New Layer

Figure 7.13

**The New Layer dialog box**

When you choose Layer → New → Layer Via Copy, the selected portion of the image is duplicated and moved to the same position on a new layer. By default, the first new layer you copy or cut is assigned a number that hasn't been used.

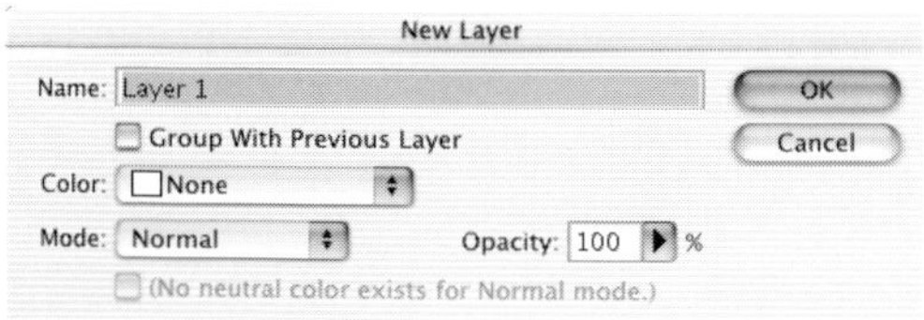

The name that Photoshop assigns to a new layer depends on the technique you choose to create the new layer and the existing content of the Layers palette. It will appear as Layer 0, Layer 1, or some other number. To avoid the confusion of inconsistent labels, rename your new layer immediately upon creating it.

To copy the contents of a layer to a new layer:

1. Target the layer or Background that you intend to copy.

2. Make an accurate selection of the area on the layer or Background using one of the selection tools or techniques.

3. Choose Layer → New → Layer Via Copy, or press ⌘/Ctrl-J. The content within the selection marquee is copied to a new layer and is placed immediately above the layer from which it was copied. The new layer automatically becomes the target layer.

   In Figure 7.14, I selected just the skull on the Background and copied it to a new layer.

4. Double-click the layer name's text to rename the layer.

5. Press Return/Enter to commit the name.

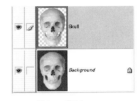

Figure 7.14

**Layer → New → Layer Via Copy**

When you copy or cut to a new layer, inspect the image edges against a contrasting solid fill background. Use one of Photoshop's matting techniques (Chapter 22) to remove any stray edge pixels.

### Cutting an Image to a New Layer

When you cut a selected portion of an image to a new layer, the content of the selection is either filled with the current background color (if it's on the Background) or replaced by transparency (if it's on a layer). It is transferred to the same position on a new layer.

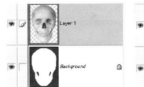 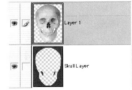

Figure 7.15

**When the selection is made on a background, the cut area fills with the background color (left), and when the selection is made on a layer the selected area creates a transparent hole (right).**

To cut a portion of an image to a new layer:

1. Target the layer or Background with the element(s) that you intend to cut.

2. Make an accurate selection of the area using one of the selection tools or techniques.

3. Choose Layer → New → Layer Via Cut, or press Shift-⌘/Ctrl-J. The content is cut to a new layer, leaving a transparent hole in the original layer or an area filled with the background color (if it was cut from the Background). The new layer is placed immediately above the targeted layer.

   In Figure 7.15 (left), I selected the skull on the Background, then I cut it to a new layer. In Figure 7.15 (right), I selected the skull on a layer and cut it to a new layer.

4. Double-click the layer's name to rename the layer, then press Return/Enter.

Figure 7.16

**You can drag a layer from the Layers palette and drop it on an image that is open on the desktop.**

## Dragging a Layer from Another Document

A layer from an open document (and all of that layer's contents) can be copied to another open document simply by dragging and dropping it. The layer will appear immediately above the targeted layer in the stack. The *source* document is the document from which you will get the layer. The *destination* document is where you will put the layer.

To drag a layer from a document:

1. Open the source document and the destination document so that they both appear on-screen.

2. Target the layer or Background on the Layers palette of the source document.

3. Click and drag the layer name or thumbnail from the source to the destination document until you see an outline of the layer. Release your mouse (see Figure 7.16).

4. Name the layer by double-clicking on its name.

The new layer will appear immediately above the targeted layer on the destination document.

## Dragging a Selection from Another Document

The contents of a selection can be copied from an open document and placed in another open document by dragging and dropping. When you drag and drop a selection, a new layer is automatically created in the destination document and will appear immediately above the targeted layer in the stack. Let's try it:

1. Open the source document and the destination document so that they both appear on-screen.

2. Target the layer or Background on the Layers palette of the source document.

3. Make an accurate selection of the area to be moved.

4. Choose the Move tool. Click and drag the selection from the source document's image window to the destination document's image window until you see a rectangular outline. Release your mouse when the outline appears where you want the selection to be placed (see Figure 7.17).

5. Name the new layer.

## Duplicating Layers

Two techniques produce identical results for creating an exact copy of a layer. The copy will be placed directly above the original layer; the name of the copy will be the name of the original plus the word *copy*. The new layer will have the same opacity, styles, and blending mode settings as the original. To duplicate a layer, do *one* of the following:

- Target the layer to be copied. Choose Duplicate Layer from the Layer menu or from the Layers palette pop-up menu.

- Drag the layer's name or thumbnail to the New Layer icon in the Layers palette. If you Option/Alt-drag, you'll be able to name the new layer from the Layer Properties dialog box that automatically appears. In the Destination field of the Layer Properties window, you can duplicate the layer to any open document or to a new document.

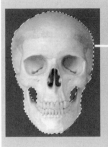

Figure 7.17

**You can drag an active selection from the image window and drop it on an image that is open on the desktop.**

## Removing Layers

You can eliminate layers using the Layers palette (deleting the contents of that layer in the process). To discard a layer, do *one* of the following:

- Target the layer to be deleted. Choose Delete Layer from the Layer menu or from the Layers palette pop-up menu.

- Drag the layer's thumbnail or name to the trash icon in the Layers palette.

- Target the layer and then click the trash icon, which brings up a dialog box to confirm the delete.

- Target the layer and then Opt/Alt-click the trash icon to directly delete the layer.

# Blending Layers

Imagine having two color slides on a light table. Let's say you sandwich a red transparent gel between the two slides. The image you see would be a combination of the bottom slide and the top slide affected by the tint of the gel. But suppose that, instead of just the tinted image, you had the ability to slide in more complex, specific effects, such as color saturation, color inversion, or color bleaching.

That's how *blending modes* perform. They are preprogrammed effects that determine the color relations between aligned pixels on two consecutive layers in the stack. Figure 7.18 demonstrates some of the many applications of blending.

Figure 7.18

**Examples of blending modes applied to an image**

A blending mode can be assigned to a layer a couple of different ways:

- Target the layer, then use the Mode pop-up list at the top of the Layers palette (directly under the Palette Title tab) to choose the desired blending option.

- Opt/Alt-double-click the layer name or double-click the thumbnail to display the Layer Style dialog box (see Figure 7.19). From the list on the left, choose Blending Options: Default. In the General Blending area, choose your blending mode and opacity level.

For a complete description of blending modes, see Appendix C.

The options in the General Blending area are identical to those at the top of the Layers palette: pop-up menus for choosing a blending mode and an opacity control. But by using the General Blending area of the Layer Style dialog, you have the additional ability to save the settings as a style and apply them to a different layer. (See "Using Layer Styles" later in this chapter.) When you adjust opacity and apply a blending mode from within the dialog box, the mode and opacity setting in the Layers palette change to reflect the adjustment.

## Advanced Blending

The Advanced Blending area of the Layer Style dialog box lets you control several different characteristics of the color relationships between the targeted and the underlying layer:

**Fill Opacity** This value controls the interior opacity of the pixels in the layer. If, however, the image has a style applied to it, such as Drop Shadow, Fill Opacity does not affect the style. To set, move the slider to select a percentage between 0 and 100 or enter a value in the field.

**Channels** You can choose which channel to blend. Choosing any one or two of the channels excludes the color information from the others; consequently, the pixels on the layer will change color depending on their color content.

**Knockout** You can use this option to cut a hole through the content of the layer. Knockout works hand in hand with the Fill Opacity and Blend Modes options. As you move the Fill Opacity sliders or change blending modes, Shallow knocks out the image just to the layer underneath it, and Deep punches a hole clear through all layers to the Background.

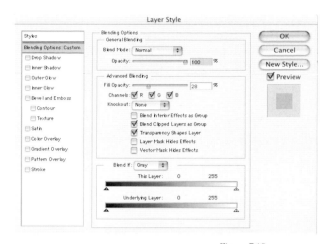

Figure 7.19

**The Layer Style dialog box with Blending Options displayed**

**Blend Interior Effects As a Group** If you check this box, the Fill Opacity and Blend If sliders affect any interior effects applied to the layer, like Inner Shadow or Inner Glow. If unchecked, the effects are excluded from blending.

**Blend Clipped Layers As a Group** If you check this box, the Fill Opacity and Blend If sliders affect layers that are included in a clipping group. This option, which is selected by default, causes the blending mode of the bottom layer in a clipping group to be applied to all layers within the group. Deselecting this option allows you to maintain the original blending mode and appearance of each layer individually. (Clipping groups are described in Chapter 22.)

**Layer Mask/Vector Mask Hides Effects** Check these options to use a layer or vector mask to hide a layer style effect rather than shape the effect at the edges of the mask.

**Blend If** You can choose the specific color components to be affected by the blend. Choose Blend If Gray to affect all of the colors, or pick a specific color channel (or channels) to affect. The Blend If color sliders let you accurately adjust the highlight, midtone, and shadow areas to be blended.

## Layer Styles

*Layer styles* jazz up your images with dazzling realistic enhancements like drop shadows, neon glowing edges, and deep embossing. They are really efficient canned effects that simplify operations that used to require tedious channel juggling and layer manipulation.

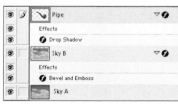

Figure 7.20

**Image with a Drop Shadow and a Bevel and Emboss effect**

When a layer has been affected by a style, an italic *f* icon appears to the right of its name in the Layers palette (like the one next to the Pipe layer or the Sky B layer in Figure 7.20). In Photoshop 7, the Layers palette can be expanded to reveal a list of the layer styles that have been applied, by clicking the small arrow to the left of the *f* icon. Clicking/double-clicking any one of these effects displays its controls so that you can modify it.

Layer styles apply their effects to the edges of the layer, so the content on the target layer should be surrounded by transparency.

## Using Layer Styles

If you want to create, define, or edit a layer style, access the Layer Style dialog box (Figure 7.21) by doing *one* of the following. If a layer is targeted when you open this dialog, the style you choose will be applied to the layer. You cannot apply a layer style to the Background.

- Choose Layer → Layer Style. Choose a style from the list.
- Choose Blending Options from the Layer Options pull-down menu. Click on a layer style from the list to display its controls.
- Double-click the layer's thumbnail.
- Click the Layer Style icon at the bottom-left of the Layers palette and drag to a layer style to display its controls.

From the Layer Style dialog box, you can also choose an effect. To display the extensive controls for each effect, click its name. Many of the controls have similarities, and experimentation with a live preview is the best way to see the result of your efforts. Under the Preview button is a swatch that demonstrates the effect on a square. This is very helpful in seeing the result of a combination of effects.

Figure 7.22 demonstrates several samples of the layer style effects. (A color version of this demonstration, Figure C5, is available in the color section.)

Figure 7.21

**The Layer Style dialog window displaying Drop Shadow controls**

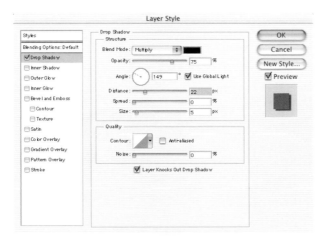

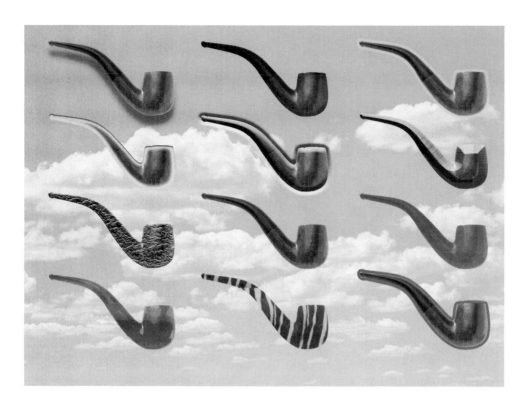

Figure 7.22

**Layer styles
demonstrated**

Each layer style provides a unique and potentially complex set of options. Experimentation with the controls and with combinations of styles is the key to producing the best possible effect for your particular image.

**Drop Shadow**  Every object (except vampires) casts a shadow if placed in the path of a light source. Drop shadows are a key element in creating credible, realistic images. The drop shadow follows the same shape as the pixels on the target layer. This is a fast way to give your image a realistic look. There are two sets of controls:

   **Structure**  determines the opacity, size, and position of the shadow.

   **Quality**  determines the contour of its edges and its texture.

**Inner Shadow**  As a drop shadow is cast outward, away from the layer content, an inner shadow is cast from the edge inward toward its center. Use this style to model your image or to create inner depth. The settings are similar to Drop Shadow for controlling the structure and quality of the effect, except that Choke, a term used in the printing industry to indicate an inward expansion, replaces Spread, a term for outward expansion.

**Outer Glow** This style is perfect for a neon look. It creates a halo of a light color around the outside edge of the layer's content that can be as soft- or hard-edged as you like, depending on the settings you choose.

**Inner Glow** The best way to describe this effect is a soft-edged, light-colored stroke. Use Inner Glow to create a halo from the edge of the layer's content inward.

**Bevel and Emboss** The Bevel and Emboss style applies a highlight and a shadow to the layer content to create the illusion of three-dimensional relief. You can choose from five styles of embossing, each of which applies a different kind of sculptured surface. The Structure and Shading options let you minutely control the appearance of the effect. You also have these options:

**Contour** Control the shape of the edge of your Bevel and Emboss effect by editing its contour. Double-click the name Contour on the Styles list. Choose a contour from the pop-up list. Adjust the range of the contour with the Range slider (see Figure 7.23). A smaller percentage decreases the range of the contour relative to the bevel; a larger percentage increases the range.

To create a new contour, click the icon to display the Contour Editor (Figure 7.24). Click the New button and name the contour. A dotted line on the graph displays the profile of the current contour. Edit the position of the anchor points by dragging them, or click the dotted line to place new anchor points. Check the Corner box if you want a corner point, or uncheck it if you want a smooth point. Drag the anchor points to modify the curve to the profile of the edge you want. The Input value represents the percentage of the horizontal position of an anchor point. Output represents the percentage of the vertical position of an anchor point. Click OK to save the new contour when you're satisfied with your settings.

As you create a contour, a live preview in the image window will display the results on your image.

Figure 7.23

**The Contour controls**

**Texture** The Bevel and Emboss Texture option lets you map a textural surface to your layer's content. Display the texture controls by clicking the word Texture in the Styles list. Choose a pattern from the pop-up list. The Texture controls use the Pattern presets as a source for textures (see Chapter 10 for more on patterns). Essentially, it applies the colorless texture of the pattern to the content of the layer. You can move the sliders to adjust the scale and depth of the texture. Checking the Invert box changes the appearance of the texture from emboss to relief.

You can reposition the texture while in the Texture dialog box by clicking the texture in the image window and dragging.

Link the textural style to the layer by checking the Link With Layer box. If you move the layer, the texture moves along with it. If the box is unchecked, the texture will remain in place while the layer moves.

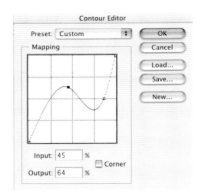

**Satin**  To produce the effect of light and shadow bouncing off a satiny surface, Photoshop applies a soft-edged shadow across the middle of the layer's content. Controls let you determine its size, position, opacity, and contour.

**Color Overlay**  This style is a no-brainer. It simply fills the layer's content with a color that you select by clicking the swatch. You can control its opacity.

Figure 7.24

**The Contour Editor**

**Gradient Overlay**  Similar to Color Overlay, Gradient Overlay applies a gradient to the pixels on the layer. You can choose a gradient from the current Gradient palette, or create one on-the-fly by clicking Gradient to display the Gradient Editor. (See Chapter 10 for more on gradients.) From the menu, you can control the opacity, style, angle, and scale of the gradient.

**Pattern Overlay**  If you have one or more patterns stored in the current Patterns presets, you can overlay a pattern on the layer content as an effect. This is similar to the Bevel and Emboss Texture option. The difference is that Pattern overlay applies the colors as well as the texture of the pattern. You can control the opacity and scale of the pattern, and you can link the pattern to the layer so that it will accompany the layer if the layer is moved horizontally or vertically.

**Stroke**  To apply an outline as an effect to the edge of the image, choose Stroke. You can determine the color and size of the stroke and whether it's placed on the inside, middle, or outside of the edge of the layer content. The best feature of this effect is Fill Type, which applies a gradient or pattern to the stroke; this is excellent incentive to use the Stroke layer style instead of the similar Edit → Stroke.

## Applying Layer Styles

There are several ways to apply a layer style. If you have a style defined and wish to simply apply it, target the layer, click the Layer Style icon at the bottom-left of the Layers palette, and choose the style from the list that pops up.

Use the Layer Style dialog box to apply a style by following one of these methods:

- Target the layer, choose Layer → Layer Style, select a style by checking its box from the Layer Style dialog box, and click OK.
- Double-click the layer's thumbnail or title; select a style and click OK.
- Target the layer, click the Layer Style icon at the bottom-left of the Layers palette, select a style, and click OK.

Checking the style's box in the Layer Style dialog box applies the style to the layer. To view the controls of a particular layer style, however, you must click the style's name.

### Saving Layer Styles

If you've applied one or more styles or blending options to a layer and you're satisfied with the result, you may want to save the style to later apply it to a separate layer. To save a style, click the New Style button in the Layer Style dialog window. You'll be prompted to name your new style.

## Working with Type Layers

When you enter type in Photoshop using the Type tool, a new layer is automatically created. The layer is conveniently named with the text. Type layers are pretty much like any other

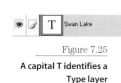

layer in that they can be edited, transformed, reordered in the stack, and modified by applying effects to them. The thumbnail of a Type layer is identified by a capital T. If you've entered type and want to edit it, double-click the thumbnail to automatically highlight it, as in Figure 7.25.

**Figure 7.25**

**A capital T identifies a Type layer**

Several Photoshop operations cannot be applied to Type layers, including color adjustments or filters that only affect pixels. Before a Type layer can be affected by these operations, it must first be *rasterized*. Rasterization converts the vector information of the type fonts into pixel-based information. Once you've rasterized the type, you can no longer edit it with the Type tool. To rasterize a Type layer, target the layer and choose Layer → Rasterize → Type.

For the big picture on generating and editing type, read Chapter 8, "Working with Type."

## Consolidating Layers

At some point during the process of creating a brilliant digital image, you will have accumulated more layers than you can shake a mouse at. This can present problems, because with the addition of each new layer, the size of your file will increase depending on how much information the layer contains. In the interest of streamlining your workflow, you should, from time to time, *merge* your layers. Merging layers combines the content of two or more layers into one. You can merge visible layers and linked layers, and you can merge down from a targeted layer. You can flatten the image so that all of the layers are consolidated into one Background.

A fast way to merge layers without losing them is to hold down the Option/Alt key and select a Merge function from the Palette menu. This merges the content of the layers into the targeted layer but doesn't delete the original layers. You can then check the merged layers before duplicating the image for flattening. To quickly flatten the duplicate image, conceal all layers from view except for the merged layer. Then choose Layer → Flatten Image → Discard Hidden Layers.

Before you flatten an image, be sure that you have finished editing the layer's content and no longer need the layer operations. It is wise to flatten a duplicate version of the image instead of the original, because once the image has been saved and closed, it cannot be unflattened.

## Merging Visible Layers

This operation merges the content of all the visible layers into one layer. You will probably use this method more than any of the others, because you can see in the image window exactly what the new merged layer will look like. Let's merge visible layers:

1. Only the layers you want to merge should be visible. In the Layers palette, click the eye icon next to any visible layer that you don't want to merge to conceal it from view.

2. Target one of the visible layers.

3. From either the Layer menu or the Layers Palette pop-up menu, choose Merge Visible.

   The contents of the visible layers will be merged into the targeted layer. That layer will retain its original name.

## Merging Linked Layers

This operation merges the content of all the linked layers into one layer.

1. In the Layers palette, click the second column to link the layers that you want to merge. Only the layers you want to merge should be linked.

2. Target one of the linked layers.

3. From either the Layer menu or the Layers Palette pop-up menu, choose Merge Linked.

   The images on the linked layers will be merged into the targeted layer, which keeps its original name.

## Merging Down

This operation merges the content of the targeted layer and the layer immediately below it into one layer.

1. In the Layer palette, target a layer.

2. From either the Layer menu or the Layers Palette pop-up menu, choose Merge Down. The layer retains the name of the bottommost layer.

## Flattening an Image

*Flattening* your image eliminates all layers and places all of the content onto one Background. Because many other programs aren't able to read Photoshop's native layers format, you will usually need to flatten the image when you are saving your image to a format such as EPS (for use in a desktop-publishing program), GIF, or JPEG (both for use on the Web).

The TIFF format supports Photoshop layers. Even so, when saving your file as a TIFF to be imported to another program, remember that layered documents have much larger file sizes and will consequently take longer to print. It's a good idea to flatten a duplicate version of the document before saving it as a TIFF that will be imported elsewhere.

To flatten your image,

1. Be sure all of your layers are visible. Photoshop will discard layers that are not visible.

2. Choose Flatten Image from either the Layer menu or the Layers palette pop-up menu.

# CHAPTER 8

# Working with Type

*Type is more than* just written words. It is an important part of the visual gestalt of any layout. How a word looks can communicate to a viewer as much as or more than how it reads. Photoshop's powerful set of tools and palettes can precisely control all the characteristics of typography. Combined with the application of layer styles, the typographical options are limitless.

Many of Photoshop's type functions resemble those of page-layout programs, and you may be tempted to use Photoshop to create text documents. But don't try to drive a nail with a screwdriver! Use the right tool for the job. When generating body copy, it's better to import your image into a page-layout program and then create or manipulate the text there. Where Photoshop really shines is in its ability to produce cool text effects and large display type for headlines, subheads, and graphic text. This chapter will introduce you to:

- **Typography 101**

- **Using the Type tools**

- **Applying character and paragraph specifications**

- **Working with Chinese, Japanese, and Korean type**

- **Warping text and rasterizing type**

- **New features in Photoshop 7**

## Type in Photoshop

Photoshop's type functions give you the ability to generate fully editable type directly on the image, without a cumbersome type window. You also have the ability to enter text in a bounding box, which empowers you to confine your text to a predefined area and to attribute paragraph characteristics such as indents and spaces to it. You can access many of these functions, including orientation, font, style, size, anti-aliasing, alignment, and color, on the Options bar when the Type tool is selected.

Additional type-specific characteristics, like leading, tracking, horizontal and vertical scale, and baseline shift, are accessed from the Character and Paragraph palettes. You can set type attributes before you enter text, or edit selected characters after you enter them. In addition, you have a complete set of tools to create and edit Chinese, Japanese, and Korean characters.

New to Photoshop 7 is a spell checker that insures accurate spelling—without having to thumb through your 3-volume (30-pound) paper copy of Webster's each time you're unsure of a word. Another new addition to the program is the Find and Replace command that enables you to search for and change words or characters.

The Warp Text palette gives you precise control over the bending and curving of type. You'll find that in most instances you won't have to import curved text from Illustrator, Free-Hand, or CorelDRAW.

Again, don't be so dazzled by Photoshop's sophisticated type features that you use it for page layout. You'll find it much easier to import your image into a page-layout program, like InDesign, QuarkXPress, or PageMaker, and generate the body copy there. For one thing, the file size of your page-layout documents will be much smaller than equivalent documents in Photoshop. For another, Photoshop's performance in managing large amounts of text is pretty clunky, even on the fastest computers. It's best to concentrate Photoshop's type features where they'll do the most good: on spot text, headlines, and other display copy—any text where graphic enhancements are needed.

## Typography 101

If you are going to create type on any software program, it's essential to understand the nature and terminology of type. Type has been around for a long time. Ever since humans decided to record their experiences as symbols, the conventions of typography have evolved. Type is more than just words. It is a powerful visual element, capable of expressing ideas. Your eye perceives the character forms, and your brain freely associates what it sees with what it knows—it translates the unique visual relationships of the text symbols into a voice.

That voice can have a gender; it can convey a particular time in history. It may have an accent from another language or culture. It can be humorous, serious, fluid, mechanical, or any other description. It can have a specific tempo and pitch. Type is a silent voice that delivers its message in words without sound.

Figure 8.1 identifies the traditional names for the key type features and dimensions that help define your type's voice. These characteristics, and many others, are explained in the following sections.

Figure 8.1

**Anatomy of type characters**

## Font

*Font* is the name for the style or appearance of a complete set of characters. Your choice of font can greatly influence the quality of the publication. The four categories of fonts include the following:

**Serif** fonts have a horizontal linear element on their extremities that guides the eye across the page.

**Sans Serif** fonts don't have the horizontal linear element.

**Cursive (or Script)** fonts are typographic versions of handwritten script.

**Display** characters are usually embellished with shapes or ornaments that endow them with a unique illustrative character.

## Size

In traditional typography, the *type size* of a character is determined by the distance from the top of a capital letter to the bottom of a descender. Size is traditionally measured in *points*, with 72 points in an inch.

## Style

By controlling the *style* of a character, you place a visual emphasis on its meaning. In Photoshop, style is chiefly a function of font *weight* (thickness or heaviness) and *obliqueness* (whether it leans). You can specify either of these two type characteristics by choosing a bold or italic typeface from a type family on your system or by applying faux styles from the Character palette. The weight or obliqueness of type creates emphasis or meaning when used in headlines, subheads, and character-based logos. A bold character headline, for example, may be used to indicate power or to simply ensure that it is the first thing seen by a viewer.

## Alignment

Aligning text is an important step in maintaining readability. The *alignment* choices in traditional page layout are flush left, flush right, centered, and justified. Photoshop lets you apply these alignment options to horizontally or vertically oriented type. Alignment of text within an image reacts directly with the composition. It is a way to stabilize the viewer's eye movement by creating visible margins around the text blocks that establish clean, fluid lines and spaces. Aligning text to other visual elements frames the contents of the page so that there is ample, consistent space between the edge of the page and the content.

## Leading

*Leading* is the typographic term that describes vertical spacing between lines; the word originates from the time when typesetters hand-set wooden or metal type. The space between lines was filled with lead slugs, which controlled the spacing. This term has been adopted throughout the industry as a way to describe the distance, in points from baseline to baseline, of rows of type characters. Type conventions apply autoleading for body copy to traditional type at 120% of the type's size.

## Tracking and Kerning

These terms refer to the space between characters. *Tracking* is the global space between selected groups of characters, and *kerning* is the space between two individual characters. Because each letterform has specific visual characteristics, characters are optically spaced. For example, in the top line of type in Figure 8.2, the capital *T* next to the lowercase *y* needs less space than the capital *H* next to the lowercase *i* to appear the same distance apart. Sometimes Photoshop-generated text needs manual kerning.

HighType

HighType

Figure 8.2

The characters in the top row, set using Photoshop's default tracking, seem to isolate the capital *T*. The text in the bottom row has been manually kerned to accommodate the optical spacing and to connect the capital *T* with the rest of the word.

## Horizontal and Vertical Scale

The horizontal and vertical *scale* of type can radically change its appearance, as seen in Figure 8.3. When you reduce the horizontal scale of a letterform (as in the second row of the example), you squeeze it from side to side. When you scale it "up" horizontally (to a percentage higher than 100), all of the vertical strokes appear fatter and the characters appear extended, as in the third row of type in the figure.

When you vertically scale a letterform (as in the fourth row of Figure 8.3), you stretch it from top to bottom. With scaling greater than 100%, the vertical strokes appear thinner and elongated relative to their size. The character appears condensed, even though it's at the normal horizontal width.

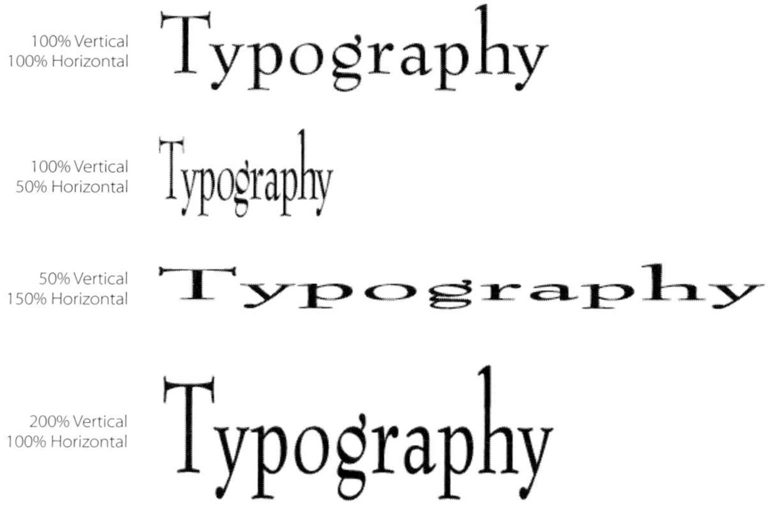

100% Vertical
100% Horizontal

Typography

100% Vertical
50% Horizontal

Typography

50% Vertical
150% Horizontal

Typography

200% Vertical
100% Horizontal

Typography

**Figure 8.3**

**Horizontal and vertical scale**

## Baseline Shift

Shifting the *baseline* of a character, as in Figure 8.4, moves it horizontally or vertically from its default starting position, or baseline. Unlike leading, which affects all of the characters in a paragraph, baseline shift can target individual or a group of selected characters and moves them up or down.

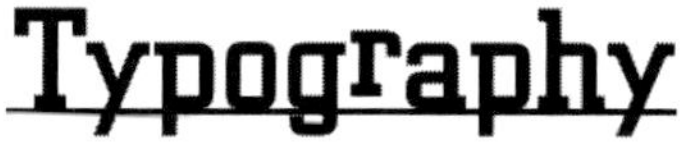

**Typography**

**Figure 8.4**

**The effect of baseline shift on a single character**

## Type Conventions

Typography is an art that has evolved over thousands of years and, like any art form, it has common-sense rules of thumb. Type conventions act as guides to help the artist or designer achieve readable, well-emphasized character combinations. The conventions emphasize certain visual elements so that the viewer's eye is gently guided through the text.

For the sake of continuity and clarity, I mention these conventions here, because when designing with type, they are a good place to begin. Remember, however, that you can ignore the conventions, break the rules, and get wild and crazy in the anything-goes world of graphic design, providing you don't lose sight of your goal: to visually communicate your ideas clearly and efficiently.

**Less Is More** Don't use more than two fonts, three sizes, or three styles in a design field. As a complicated example, a headline might be 36-point Gill Sans Bold, the subhead might be 20-point Gill Sans Demi, and the body text might be 12-point Garamond Medium.

**Stick with Standard Leading** Normal leading equals 120% of the type size, so if a character is 10 points, for example, its normal leading is 12 points. If your leading is too small—the lines

**A**
**R**
**T**

**S**
**A**
**V**
**E**
**S**

**L**
**I**
**V**
**E**
**S**

Figure 8.5

**Text generated with
the Vertical Type tool**

too tight together—you lose readability; if your leading is too loose, the reader's eye will wander instead of flowing smoothly from the end of one line to the beginning of the next.

**No Faux Styles** Whenever possible, avoid using faux styles—that is, styles applied by a software program to the text. If you want to use a boldface style, use the bold style from that font's family, because there are subtle differences in the characters.

**Kern and Track Your Text** Pay attention to the kerning and tracking of type. This is an area that is painfully neglected by many desktop publishers. Be sure the spacing looks natural. Although Photoshop auto-kerns its characters, it's wise to tweak the character spacing, *especially* when you apply warping or styles to the type. Look for consistent spacing of text by squinting your eyes. Correct gaps where the characters are too far apart or bunching where they are too close together.

**Use Ligatures** A *ligature* is a set of two characters that is designed to replace certain character combinations, such as fl and fi, to avoid spacing conflicts. Use ligatures whenever possible.

## Using the Type Tools

To generate text, choose the Type tool $\boxed{\text{T}}$ , click the point in the image where you want the text to appear, and enter the text from the keyboard. You can preprogram the Type tool prior to entering the text by entering values in the Options bar or in the Character or Paragraph palettes, or you can highlight the text after it has been entered and modify its specifications.

Use these functions to modify text:

- To highlight text so that it can be edited, click in front of it and drag over it.

- To select a word, double-click it.

- To select a line of text, triple-click it.

- To select all characters in a bounding box, quadruple-click anywhere in the box, or press ⌘/Ctrl-A (Select All).

When you select or format text on a Type layer, the Type tool shifts into edit mode. Before you can perform other operations, you must commit the changes by clicking the check mark or pressing Enter/Return, or cancel by clicking the Cancel symbol or pressing Escape.

There are four variations of the Type tool to choose from in the Type Tool cluster, as shown in Figure 8.6. At the top is the basic Type tool, or Horizontal Type tool, which you'll use most of the time; it generates a Type layer.

The variation immediately below it, the Vertical Type tool, generates a column of vertical characters, as seen in Figure 8.5. Next are the Horizontal and Vertical Type Mask tools, which generate a selection marquee in the shape of the specified character. They can be used for generating type on existing layers or for pasting visual elements into the type to produce interesting type/image combinations, as shown in Figure 8.7.

Figure 8.6

**The Type Tool cluster**

All of the type on a layer must be either vertical or horizontal.

The Type tool Options bar, shown in Figure 8.8, displays these type characteristics:

**Orientation** The icon to the right of the Type tool Preset picker toggles between a horizontal and a vertical orientation of type.

**Font** Choose a font and style from the menus.

**Size** Choose a size in points from the list, or enter a numeric value.

Figure 8.7

**An image pasted into a type mask**

**Anti-Alias** This setting will determine how the type blends into its background in varying degrees. None produces a jagged character, Strong makes a heavier character, Crisp a sharper character, and Smooth a smoother character.

**Alignment** You can align either flush left, centered, or flush right. The type aligns to the insertion point. When the type is vertically oriented, the top, center, or bottom of the text aligns to the insertion point.

**Color** Click the swatch and select a fill color for the type from the Color Picker.

**Warp Text** You can place your text on a path, twist it, or bend it using this function (see "Warping Text" later in this chapter).

**Character/Paragraph** This icon opens the Character and Paragraph palettes where you can enter global specifications for your text.

**Commit/Cancel** After you input your type specs, click one of these buttons to commit the edit or to cancel it.

Figure 8.8

**The Type tool Options bar**

## Entering Type in a Bounding Box

There are two ways of entering type in Photoshop: from a point or within a bounding box. The bounding box lets you control the flow of text (see Figure 8.9). As you enter text in the bounding box, it automatically returns at the end of each line. Once the bounding box has been drawn and entered, you can size the box to reflow the text.

To enter text in a bounding box, follow these steps:

1. Choose the Type tool.

2. Click in your image and drag to the size you want the bounding box to be. Release the mouse and the bounding box appears.

3. Set your type specifications in the toolbar and enter the text.

4. If needed, readjust the size of the bounding box by dragging any of the corner or side points.

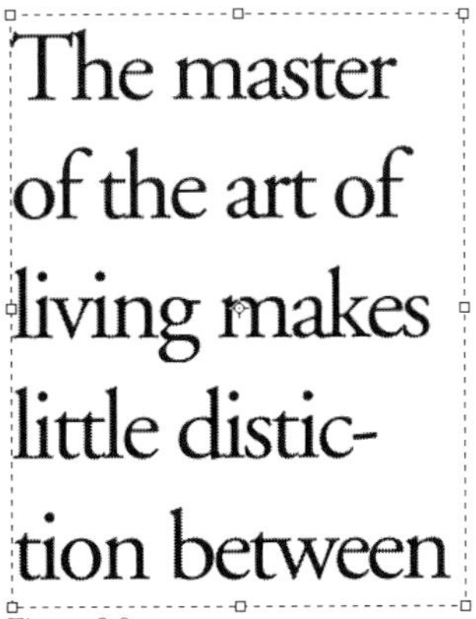

> The master of the art of living makes little distic-tion between

Figure 8.9

**A bounding box around paragraph text**

You can convert point text to paragraph text and vice versa. Target the Type layer and choose Layer → Type → Convert To Point Text or Convert To Paragraph Text.

# Applying Character and Paragraph Specifications

Photoshop gives you two palettes that expand your capabilities for generating text above and beyond those readily available in the Tool palette. To access the palettes, select the Type tool and click the Palettes button in the Options bar. The Character and Paragraph palettes appear.

## The Character Palette

This palette consolidates all of the character attributes into one floating palette. To access the Character palette (see Figure 8.10), you can either choose Window → Character or, with the Type tool selected, click the Palettes button in the Options bar.

You can designate the following characteristics on the Character palette. For most changes to these settings, you can click the Commit (check mark) button at the right end of the Options bar to apply your edits or the Cancel button if you change your mind. For most settings, pressing Return/Enter, choosing another tool, or targeting another layer will commit your changes.

**Size** To designate the size in points prior to typing, enter a value or choose a size from the list. If the text has already been entered, highlight the text and then enter or choose a value.

> If you need to work with other units when setting type, enter the number and then the unit abbreviation or name—inches (in), millimeters (mm), pixels (px), etc. Photoshop will automatically convert the value into the current type units specified in the preferences.

**Kerning** Is measured in thousandths of an em space. (An em space is a standard for type measurement. The width of an em space depends on the size of the text; it's usually about the width of the letter *m*.) The Metrics setting uses the font's default spacing. To kern manually, place your insertion point between the two characters and enter a value or choose a width from the list. Negative values decrease the spacing between characters; positive values increase the spacing.

**Tracking** Is akin to kerning and is also measured in thousandths of an em space. To change tracking, highlight the text, then enter a value or choose a width from the list. Like kerning, negative values decrease the space between characters, and positive values increase the space.

**Leading** Is measured in points from baseline to baseline. To change the leading, highlight the text, then enter a value or choose one from the list.

**Vertical/Horizontal Scale** Is measured as a percentage of normal scale. To change the horizontal or vertical scale, highlight the text and enter a value.

**Baseline Shift** Is measured in points. To change the baseline shift, highlight the text, then enter a value or choose one from the list.

**Color** To change the color, click the swatch and choose a color from the Color Picker.

**Style** These icons let you apply faux styles to your type. They include bold, italic, all caps, small caps, superscript, subscript, underline, and strikethrough.

**Language** You can choose a language for hyphenation and spelling conventions on selected characters.

**Anti-Alias** Redundant with the Options bar, this feature lets you choose an anti-alias method from the menu.

Figure 8.10

**The Character palette**

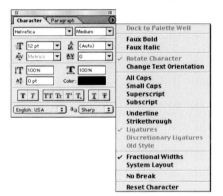

## The Character Palette Menu

Click the arrow in the upper-right corner of the Character palette to access more commands and options for your type characters:

**Faux Styles** If you don't have a bold or italic type font, you can apply a faux style by choosing Faux Bold or Faux Italic.

**Rotate Character** Select this option to rotate a vertical character 90 degrees to be horizontal. This option is available only for vertical text; otherwise, it will be grayed out in the pull-down menu.

**Change Text Orientation** This option changes all the text on a layer to a vertical orientation if the type is horizontal, or horizontal if the type is vertical.

**Case** Select a case option before typing: All Caps, Small Caps, Subscript, or Superscript. Or format text after it has been entered by highlighting all or part of the text on a Type layer. This option is also available on the palette interface by clicking one of the icons. (Selecting Small Caps will have no effect on text that was originally typed as capital letters.)

**Superscript, Subscript, Underline, and Strikethrough** These traditional type styles are repeated in the pull-down menu. Superscript and subscript characters are smaller and shifted above or below the text baseline, respectively. Underline places a line of corresponding weight beneath the character, and Strikethrough places a line in the horizontal center of the characters.

**Ligatures and Old-Style Numerals** If your font provides them, you can use ligatures and old-style typographic numerals by choosing Ligatures or Old Style from the Character Palette menu.

**Fractional Widths** The spacing between characters varies, with fractions of whole pixels between certain characters. Most of the time, fractional character widths provide the best spacing. Fractional widths, however, can cause small type to run together, making it difficult to read. To turn off this option so that the type is displayed in whole-pixel increments, choose Fractional Widths from the palette menu and clear the option.

**System Layout** This feature disables fractional width spacing and the anti-aliasing option that may be applied to the text.

**No Break** This feature prevents selected words from breaking at the end of lines to preserve the intended meaning of these words.

**Reset Character** Click this item to reset the Character palette to the defaults.

## The Paragraph Palette

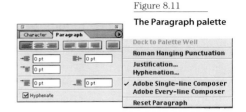

Figure 8.11

**The Paragraph palette**

The Paragraph palette (see Figure 8.11) specifies options for an entire paragraph, which is defined by Photoshop as one or more characters followed by a hard return. Each line of text entered at a point is a separate paragraph because it's separated by a return. Photoshop won't wrap multiple lines in one paragraph unless you resize it with a bounding box.

You can access the Paragraph palette by choosing Window → Paragraph. Or, with the Type tool selected, click the Palettes button on the Options bar, then click the Paragraph tab.

### Selecting Paragraphs

You can format a single paragraph, multiple paragraphs, or all paragraphs in a Type layer.

| **To Format This:** | **Do This:** |
| --- | --- |
| A single paragraph | Choose the Type tool and click between any two characters in a paragraph. |
| Multiple paragraphs | Select the Type tool and drag to highlight the text range of the paragraphs you want to select. |
| A Type layer | Target the Type layer that you want to affect in the Layers palette. |

### Aligning and Justifying Type

You can *align* text to one edge or *justify* text to both edges. You can align point text and paragraph text; you can justify paragraph text but not point text.

To specify alignment for horizontally oriented text, click the Left Align, Center, or Right Align icons at the top of the Paragraph palette. For vertically aligned type, these become Top Align, Center, and Bottom Align.

In order to justify type, it has to be paragraph text—that is, in a bounding box. When you choose a justification icon, the text is spread out so that both the left and right edges of the text align. The icons offer four options for aligning the last line of horizontally oriented type (Justify Last Left, Center, or Right, or Justify All) and, again, four options for vertically oriented type (Top, Center, Right, and Justify All).

### Indenting Paragraphs

An *indent* is the space between the text and the insertion point or the edge of the bounding box. You specify a paragraph indent by entering a value in the indention fields. You can specify a left, right, or first-line indent:

**Indent Left Margin**  indents the whole paragraph from the left edge of the bounding box.

**Indent Right Margin**  indents the whole paragraph from the right edge of the bounding box.

**Indent First Line**  indents the first line of text in the paragraph relative to the left indent.

### Adding Space Before and After

Enter a value in the Add Space Before Paragraph or Add Space After Paragraph fields in order to add space between paragraphs. The values entered will be the units specified in the Units & Rulers preferences (described in Chapter 4, "Navigation: Know Where to Go").

## The Paragraph Palette Menu

Click the arrow in the upper-right corner of the Paragraph palette to access commands that affect the punctuation, justification, hyphenation, and flow of the text.

### Hanging Punctuation

The Roman Hanging Punctuation option enhances the alignment of text by placing punctuation marks outside the margin. You can affect the following punctuation marks when this option is active: periods, commas, single and double quotation marks, apostrophes, hyphens, en and em dashes, colons, and semicolons.

To hang punctuation marks, choose Roman Hanging Punctuation from the Paragraph Palette pull-down menu.

### Justifying Text

Justification determines word- and letter-spacing defaults on justified text. To set justification options, choose Justification from the Paragraph Palette menu. The dialog box in Figure 8.12 appears.

> Justification options are applied to the entire paragraph. If you want to increase or decrease space for a few characters, use the Kerning or Tracking functions.

For the options in the Justification dialog box with three columns of settings, Photoshop will space text in order to stay between the Minimum and Maximum values, and will try to come as close to the Desired value as possible while balancing all the settings. The values you end up with are chosen not only by the spacing options, but also by things like the hyphenation settings and font size.

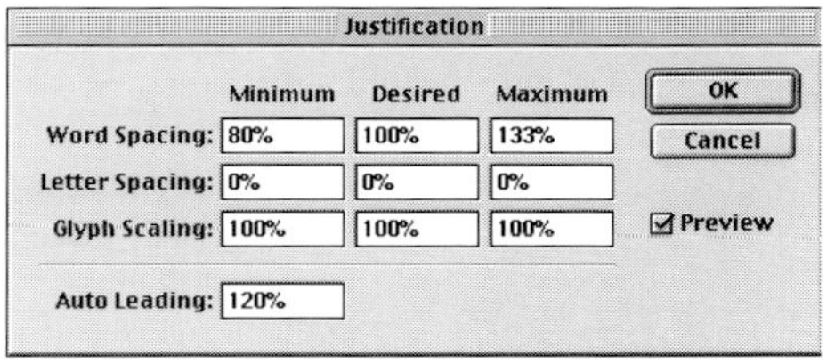

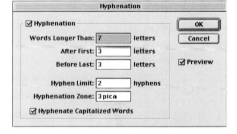

**Word Spacing** specifies the amount of space between words when the spacebar is pressed. Values range from 0 to 1000%; at 100% no additional space is added to the default spacing of the specified font.

**Letter Spacing** determines the normal distance between letters, which includes kerning and tracking values. Values range from 0 to 500%; at 100% no additional space is added to the default spacing of the specified font.

Figure 8.12

**Use this dialog box to set justification options**

**Glyph Scaling** scales the actual width of characters to justify them. Input a Minimum value (50%), a Desired value, and a Maximum value (200%) to fit characters into a justified line of text.

**Auto Leading** is the normal distance between baselines of text—120% of the font size by default; enter a different value if desired.

**Preview** lets you see the result of your specification in selected text before closing the window.

## Hyphenating Text

Hyphenation options determine where a word breaks to be hyphenated. To activate automatic hyphenation, click the Hyphenate box in the Paragraph palette. To set the following hyphenation options, choose Hyphenation from the palette pull-down menu to bring up the dialog box in Figure 8.13:

**Words Longer Than** specifies the minimum length, in letters, of a word to be hyphenated.

Figure 8.13

**The Hyphenation dialog box**

**After First** specifies the minimum number of letters at the beginning of a word before a hyphen.

**Before Last** specifies the minimum number of letters at the end of a word after a hyphen.

**Hyphen Limit** is the number of consecutive lines that can contain hyphens.

**Hyphenation Zone** is the distance at the end of a line of unjustified text that will cause a word break.

**Hyphenate Capitalized Words** does just that. Turn off this option to be sure headlines are not hyphenated. This only works with the Single-Line Composer.

**Preview** lets you see the result of your specifications on selected paragraphs before closing the window.

### Composing Text Lines

Composing methods determine possible line breaks, based on the hyphenation and justification settings. There are two composition methods and one option to choose from:

**The Every-Line Composer** looks ahead five lines to determine the line breaks. The result is more consistent spacing and less hyphenation. The Every-Line Composer is selected by default.

**The Single-Line Composer** composes text one line at a time. The result is more consistent spacing within a line but less consistent spacing and hyphenation among multiple lines. This option is preferable if you want to manually compose your type.

**Reset Paragraph** This option sets the paragraph to its previously formatted state before attributes from the Paragraph palette are applied.

## Working with Asian Characters

If you have the proper fonts installed, Photoshop can manage Chinese, Japanese, and Korean text. To access these options in the Character and Paragraph palettes, choose Edit ➔ Preferences ➔ General ➔ Show Asian Text Options.

### Tsume

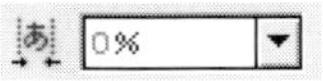

Figure 8.14

**Specify a character width in the Tsume field**

The majority of Asian characters are *monospaced*, meaning that all of the characters are the same width when using horizontal text and the same height when using vertical text. You can enter a percentage in the Tsume field in the Character palette (see Figure 8.14) to specify a character width for selected text. This decreases the size of each character but increase the proportional spacing between characters.

### Tate-chuu-yoko

The *tate-chuu-yoko* system (also called *kumimoji* and *renmoji*) "flips" certain nontextual items. You can improve the readability of vertical text by rotating numerals and acronyms so that they are horizontally oriented. To do this, highlight the characters that you want to rotate and choose Tate-chuu-yoko from the Character Palette pull-down menu.

### Japanese Composition

Spacing for Asian characters, numbers, and line breaks that can be applied to your Asian type fonts are determined by these options, which are based on Japanese text standards.

## MOJIKUMI

*Mojikumi* determines the composition of Japanese text, including character spacing between punctuation, symbols, and numbers, based on composition rules set forth in the Japanese Industrial Standards (JIS #4051).

Photoshop includes several mojikumi sets from which you can choose. They are accessible from the Paragraph palette's Mojikumi pop-up list.

## KINSOKU SHORI

You can choose different methods for processing line breaks. *Kinsoku shori* are characters that cannot begin or end a line, based on composition rules set forth in the Japanese Industrial Standards. Choose JIS Weak or JIS Maximum from the Kinsoku Shori pop-up list. Oidashi and oikomi are line-break rules as applied to kinsoku shori:

**Oidashi** is push-out line breaking, which increases the number of characters on a line by reducing the space between letters.

**Oikomi** is push-in line breaking, which decreases the number of characters on a line by increasing the space between letters.

You can choose either of these options from the Paragraph Palette pull-down menu. A check mark indicates which option is selected.

### Hanging Asian Punctuation

You can specify hanging punctuation in Asian text. Using hanging punctuation (called *burasagari*) forces punctuation marks to be placed outside the indent margins and evens the edges of the paragraph. Choose Burasagari from the Paragraph Palette menu. If the option is checked, it is active.

# Warping Text

You can bend type to conform to almost any type of curve. The Warp Text option 🔲 is accessible from the Type tool Options bar or from the Layer → Type menu. When you click the icon, the Warp Text dialog window appears (Figure 8.15). You can choose from 15 different styles (all demonstrated in Figure 8.16), each with its own set of precision controls.

There are so many combinations of styles and settings that it's impossible to list them all here. I'll show you how to warp a few lines of text in the Hands On project that follows this chapter, but play with these controls. Experiment with settings, sizes, and fonts so you'll be familiar with some of the wild, twisted type effects you can create.

Figure 8.15

**The Warp Text dialog box**

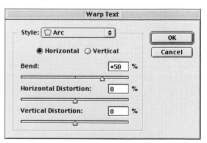

Figure 8.16

**The 15 Warp Text styles**

## Rasterizing Type

You generate Photoshop text using vector-based fonts, which preserve the ability to edit the text throughout the imaging process. Once you've generated the text, you can scale it and apply any layer style to it. You can also warp it or change its color. There are, however, Photoshop filters and color adjustment operations that do not work on vector-based type. If you want to apply those effects, you'll have to *rasterize* the type, or convert it into pixels.

Pixel-based type has its advantages and disadvantages. The main disadvantage is that once you render your type, it appears at the same resolution as the document. This is particularly problematic for small type on low-resolution documents, because there may not be enough pixels to do a decent job of smoothing the type's edges (as seen in the sample in Figure 8.17).

The advantage of pixel-based type is the ability to do pretty much anything to the image you please, such as pasting images into the type or applying artistic filters to it. To render your type into pixels, target the Type layer and choose Layer → Rasterize → Type.

Figure 8.17

**Crisp, vector-based type (top), and jagged, rasterized type (bottom)**

# Using the New Spell Checker

New to Photoshop 7, the spell checker will check the type-on-type layers, but will not check text that has been rasterized. To check your spelling, follow these steps:

1. Choose Edit ' Check Spelling to display the spell checker (see Figure 8.18).

2. If a Type layer is targeted, you can check the text exclusively on that layer or check the Check All Layers box.

**Figure 8.18**

**The spell checker**

3. The checker displays any words that are not in its dictionary and alternate spellings for the misspelled word. Click the correct spelling, or enter an alternate spelling in the Change To box. Then click the Change or the Change All button to respell all instances of the word.

   If the checker doesn't recognize additional words, it continues to display alternate spellings.

4. If the word is spelled correctly and is not in the dictionary—a person's name, for instance—you can click Ignore or Ignore All.

5. To add an unrecognized word to the dictionary, click Add.

6. When the spell checker finishes, it displays a prompt that the spell checking is complete (see Figure 8.19).

# Using the New Find and Replace Text Command

Find and Replace is a convenient method of locating and changing words in a document. It functions like the Find Change function in any word processor. The text needs to be on type layers and not rasterized for this operation to work:

1. Choose Edit → Find And Replace. The dialog box in Figure 8.20 appears.

2. Enter the word you want to locate in the Find What field and the word you want to replace it with in the Change To field.

**Figure 8.19**

**Spell checker prompt**

3. Check the following boxes as needed:

   **Search All Layers** searches additional layers, other than the targeted layer.

   **Forward** moves forward through the document as you click the Find Next button.

   **Case Sensitive** ignores words that are not in the same case, even if they are spelled similarly.

   **Whole Word Only** finds and changes an entire word rather than a fragment.

**Figure 8.20**

**The Find and Replace feature**

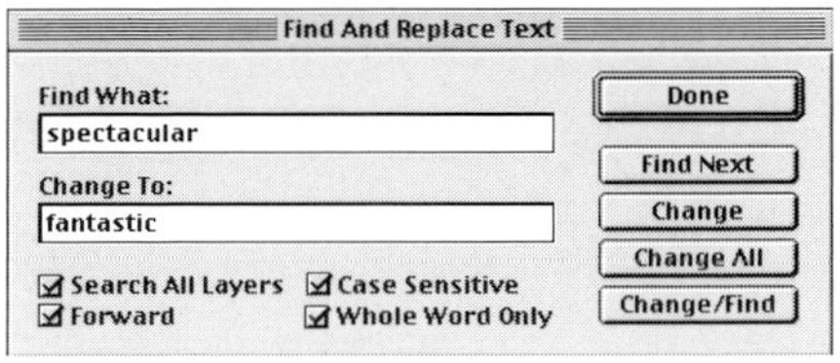

4. Click Find to locate the word and Change to change it.

5. Click Find Next to locate additional instances of the word.

6. Click Change All to change all instances of the word.

# Layers and Type

*Layers greatly increase your power* to manage your work. In this Hands On session, I'll put you through the moves of layers and type so that you can apply some of the powerful techniques from Chapters 7 and 8 to an actual project. You will see the advantage of organizing your layers into sets as you apply layer upon layer of digital images to produce a phantasmagoric poster. We will also take a crack at generating type, applying layer styles, and warping text.

Figure H2.1

**The beginning Flying Women file showing the content of the poster**

## Getting Started

Before beginning this Hands On exercise, delete or hide your preferences file. The section titled "Modifying Photoshop's Settings" in Chapter 5 details how to reset your preferences to Photoshop's defaults. Once you have launched Photoshop with default preferences, here's how to begin the Hands On project:

1. Insert the *Photoshop 7 Savvy* CD in your CD-ROM drive.

2. Choose File → Open; select and open `Flying_Women_start.psd` in the `HO2` folder on the CD.

3. Save the file to your disk as `Flying_Women.psd`. Figures H2.1 and H2.2 show the beginning and end images.

Figure H2.2

**The completed Flying Women poster**

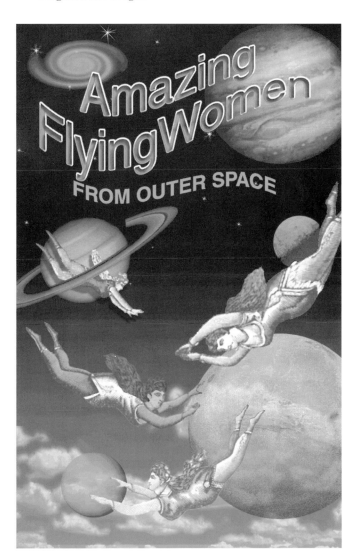

The color section in this book includes a color version of the first and last stages of the Amazing Flying Women poster (Figures C42 and C43).

# Arranging Layers

## Viewing Layers

Follow these steps to view your layers:

1. When you open the file `Flying_Women_start.psd`, you see only the transparency checkerboard, as shown in Figure H2.3. The Layers palette, however, reveals that the image contains two layer sets (containing two layers each), seven additional layers, and the Background. To reveal the contents of the Background, click the first column next to its thumbnail. An eye icon appears, and the Background image appears in the image window.

2. Reveal the contents of all layers: Option-click (Macintosh) or Alt-click (Windows) the eye icon of the Background. Figure H2.4 shows the image with all of the layers visible.

3. Then conceal the layers that we don't need right now. Click the eye icon next to the following layers or layer sets to conceal their content: Purple, Layer 1, Layer 2, and Blue. (Your image should look like Figure H2.4.)

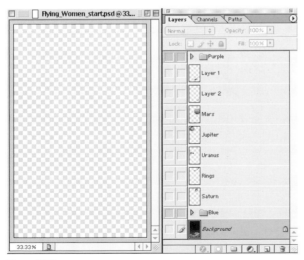

Figure H2.3

**The image window and the Layers palette of the Flying Women document**

Figure H2.4

**The image and Layers palette with the Purple and Blue layer sets, Layer 1, and Layer 2 no longer visible**

## Moving Layers

The contents of a layer can be repositioned horizontally or vertically within the image window. Follow these steps to move the planets into their vertical and horizontal positions on the image:

1. Choose View → Rulers to display the horizontal and vertical rulers.

2. Double-click the vertical or horizontal ruler to display the Units and Rulers preferences. Set the Units to Inches.

3. Target the Mars layer by clicking its thumbnail or its name, as shown in Figure H2.5.

4. Select the Move tool . In the Options bar, check Show Bounding Box. Place your cursor in the center of Mars, which is indicated by a little circle-cross. Click and drag until Mars aligns with the 12″ vertical and 8″ horizontal marks on the rulers (as in Figure H2.6). Release the mouse.

5. Target the Jupiter layer. Using the same technique as in step 2, place the center of Jupiter on the 2″ vertical and the 8″ horizontal ruler marks.

6. Save your work (press ⌘/Ctrl-S or use File → Save).

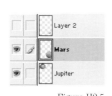

Figure H2.5

**Targeting the Mars layer**

## Moving Linked Layers

When items are linked, they can be moved or transformed simultaneously.

1. Conceal the Jupiter and the Uranus layers by clicking their eye icons in the Layers palette.

2. Target the Rings layer.

3. Click in the second column next to the Saturn layer. The link icon appears.

4. With the Move tool, drag and place the center of Saturn and its rings at the 7.25″ vertical and 3″ horizontal marks.

5. Reveal the Jupiter layer by clicking the eye icon in the Layers palette. The image should look like Figure H2.7.

## Naming Layers

To keep your document organized, name your layers:

1. Display Layer 1 and Layer 2 by clicking their eye icons. Double-click on the words *Layer 1*, and a box appears.

2. Type the words **Yellow Woman**.

3. Repeat the process for Layer 2, and rename it **Yellow Costume**.

Figure H2.6

**Aligning Mars on the ruler marks**

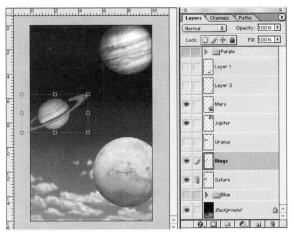

Figure H2.7

**The planets have been moved. Two layers (Saturn and Rings) are linked so that they can be moved as a unit.**

## Making a Layer Set

Layer sets organize your layers so that they can be easily managed:

1. Target the Yellow Woman layer. Click the Create A New Set icon on the Layers palette ⬜. A new Layer Set folder appears above the targeted layer.

2. Option/Alt-double-click the layer set. The Layer Set Properties dialog box appears. Rename the layer set **Yellow**. For Color, choose yellow.

3. Click the Yellow Costume layer and drag it on top of the Yellow Layer Set icon. The layer becomes part of the set, as shown in Figure H2.8.

4. Drag the Yellow Woman layer on top of the Yellow layer set. Notice that the layers inside the folder have been automatically color-coded in yellow.

5. Save your work.

Figure H2.8

**The two layers are part of the color-coded layer set.**

## Moving Items within a Layer Set

We've created our layer set, but the costume is not on the yellow woman yet. She might be getting cold, flying around in deep space in her underwear, so we need to dress her. You can reposition the contents of a layer and change its stacking order within the layer set:

1. Target the Yellow Costume layer, choose the Move tool, and drag the Yellow Costume onto the Yellow Woman.

2. Now the costume is behind the yellow woman. In the Layers palette, drag the Yellow Costume layer above the Yellow Woman layer within the layer set.

3. On the image window, use the Move tool to reposition the costume so that it aligns with the yellow woman.

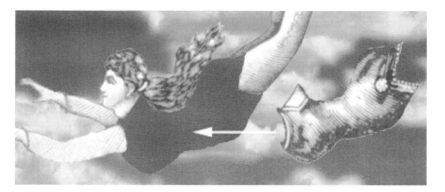

## Changing the Order of Layers

You can change the position in the stacking order of a layer or of a group of layers in a layer set. Use the order, from top to bottom in the Layers palette, to control which content is positioned in front of other image elements. Note that you can restack all of the layers within a set simultaneously—no other function does this.

1. Option/Alt-click the first column of the Layers palette to make the content of all layers visible. Notice that the Blue Woman is behind Mars.

2. To bring all of the layers in the layer set forward, they must be moved up in the stacking order. Place your cursor on the Blue Layer Set folder or name. Click and drag the layer set to the top of the stack. The woman and her costume now appear in front of Mars.

# Using Layers to Create and Edit

## Cutting and Copying Images to a New Layer

You can make new layers from the contents of existing layers, making it easier to apply effects to specific parts of your image.

1. Target the Uranus layer.

2. Option/Alt-click the eye icon of the Uranus layer to reveal only its contents against a transparent checkerboard, as in Figure H2.9.

3. Choose the Rectangular Marquee tool ⬚ . Draw a marquee around the blue planet.

4. Choose Layer → New → Layer Via Copy, or press ⌘/Ctrl-J. The selected planet is copied onto a new layer. Name the layer **Galaxy**.

Figure H2.9

**You can reveal a layer's contents against a transparent checkerboard, making it easier to apply effects.**

5. Target the Uranus layer again. Draw a rectangular marquee around the green planet.

6. Choose Layer → New → Layer Via Cut, or press Shift-⌘-J/Shift-Ctrl-J. The selected planet is cut to a new layer. Name the layer **Mercury** (see Figure H2.10).

Figure H2.10

**The new Mercury layer appears with the others.**

## Editing the Contents of a Layer

Follow these steps to edit the contents of your layers:

1. Target the Galaxy layer.

2. Option/Alt-click the eye icon of the Galaxy layer to reveal only its contents against a transparent checkerboard.

3. Choose the Move tool. In the Options bar, choose Show Bounding Box.

4. Click the upper right handle of the bounding box (see Figure H2.11) and drag downward to squash the circular planet into an oval. Press Return/Enter to implement the transformation.

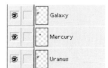

Figure H2.11

**The bounding box**

5. Choose Filter → Blur → Gaussian Blur → 4.4 pixels (as shown in Figure H2.12) to blur the edges of the oval.

6. Draw a rectangular marquee around the oval, as shown in Figure H2.13.

7. Choose Filter → Distort → Twirl, and set a value of 999 to twirl the oval into a galaxy (see Figure H2.14).

8. Press ⌘/Ctrl-D to deselect.

9. With the Galaxy layer still targeted, choose the Move tool and drag the Galaxy into the upper-left corner of the document so that its center aligns with the 1″ vertical and 2″ horizontal marks on the rulers.

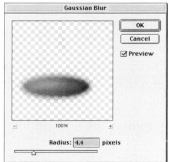

Figure H2.12

**The Gaussian Blur filter applied to the Galaxy layer**

10. View and target the Mercury layer. Press Shift as you drag Mercury to constrain its horizontal movement; reposition the planet so that its center aligns with the 6.5″ vertical and 8.75″ horizontal marks on the rulers.

11. View and target the Uranus layer. Move Uranus so that its center aligns with the 14″ vertical, 2.25″ horizontal marks on the rulers.

12. Save the document.

Figure H2.13

**The Galaxy selected with the Rectangular Marquee tool**

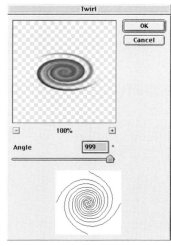

Figure H2.14

**The Twirl filter applied to the Galaxy**

## Moving Layers from Another Document

You can easily move layers from one document to another. Here we will move two linked layers.

1. In the Flying_Women.psd file, click the eye icon next to the Background and the Saturn and Ring layers to make them visible. Target the Saturn layer.

2. Open the file Red_Woman.psd from the HO2 folder on the CD, and target the Red Costume layer.

3. In Red_Woman.psd, click in the second column next to the Red Woman layer to link it with Red Costume.

4. Place your cursor on the Red_Woman.psd image. Press your mouse, drag the image, and place it on the Flying_Women.psd document. Release the mouse and two new layers appear between the Saturn layer and the Ring layer.

5. Choose the Move tool and position the Red Woman and the Red Costume between Saturn and its rings.

There are three different ways to drag layers and place them on another image. Make sure you use the right one:

- You can drag an individual layer from the Layers palette or from the image window to another image.

- To drag linked layers and maintain the linked relationship, you must target one of them and drag from the image window.

- To drag a layer set from an image, drag from the *name* or *folder* of the layer set in the Layers palette.

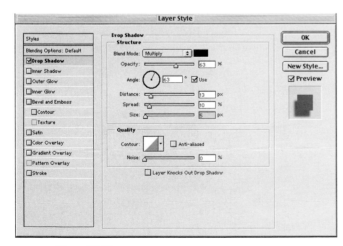

Figure H2.15

**Drop Shadow controls**

## Applying a Style to a Layer

A drop shadow adds realism and depth to an image. Creating the drop shadow as a layer style is easy:

1. With the Red Woman layer targeted, double-click the layer thumbnail to bring up the Layer Style dialog box.

2. Click the Drop Shadow option to display its controls (see Figure H2.15).

3. Set the following specifications, and then click OK. Your image should look like Figure H2.16.

| | |
|---|---|
| Opacity | 63% |
| Distance | 13 px |
| Spread | 10% |
| Size | 5 px |

# Entering Type

Photoshop 7's Type tool **T** is powerful for producing sophisticated text effects. Combined with Photoshop's layer styles, the graphic possibilities are endless.

1. Display all of the layers in the document by pressing the Option/Alt key and clicking the eye icon next to the Background.

2. Target the Purple layer set, which is topmost in the stack. This will ensure that the Type layer you are about to create will appear above all the other layers.

3. Choose the Type tool and enter the following specifications in the Options bar:

   | | |
   |---|---|
   | Font | Helvetica |
   | Size | 100 pt |
   | Anti-Alias | Smooth |
   | Alignment | Centered |
   | Color | Red |

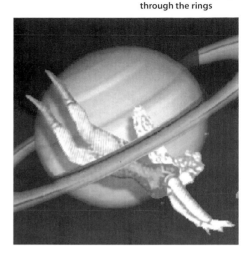

Figure H2.16

**The Red Woman flying through the rings**

4. Display the Character palette (Window → Character, or click the Palettes button on the Options bar); in the palette, set Leading at 100 pt.

5. Click the image, somewhere between the Galaxy and Saturn. (If necessary, you can reposition the type after you've entered it.) At the blinking insertion point, type this: **Amazing** <return> **Flying Women**. When you're finished typing, click the check mark on the Options bar. This will create a new Type layer named Amazing Flying Women.

6. Click the Text tool. Change the settings on the Options bar to Font: Helvetica Bold, Size: 45, and Color: Yellow. From the Character Palette pull-down menu, choose All Caps.

7. Type the words **From Outer Space**. Click the check mark in the Options bar to create a new Type layer. Your text should resemble Figure H2.17.

Figure H2.17

**The basic title for our poster**

## Warping Text

Photoshop 7 lets you bend and twist type to any shape:

1. Target the Amazing Flying Women layer and choose the Text tool.

2. Click the Create Warped Text button **T** in the Options bar.

3. Choose Style → Flag (see Figure H2.18).

4. Enter the following values and click OK:

| | |
|---|---|
| Bend | 50% |
| Horizontal Distortion | –34% |
| Vertical Distortion | 0% |

5. Target the From Outer Space layer.

6. From the Style list, again choose Flag.

7. Enter the following values and click OK:

| | |
|---|---|
| Bend | 66% |
| Horizontal Distortion | –24% |
| Vertical Distortion | 0% |

8. In the Layers palette, adjust the opacity of the From Outer Space layer to 55%. Your text should now look like Figure H2.19.

Figure H2.18

**Setting values for the Flag style**

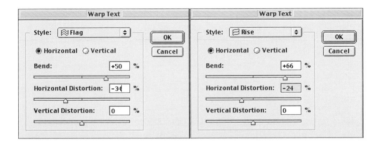

Figure H2.19

**Warped text**

## Applying Multiple Effects to Layer

We've seen how you can apply a drop shadow layer style to a layer. We'll now apply several different effects to a Type layer:

1.  Target the Amazing Flying Women layer.

2.  Opt/Alt-double-click the layer to display the Layer Style dialog box.

> When working in the Layer Style dialog, you must click the name of the style in order to display the individual layer style controls. Checking the box next to the name doesn't display the controls; it's an indicator that the effect has been applied to the current layer.

3.  From the Style list on the left, click the name Inner Shadow. The check box is automatically checked, and the Inner Shadow controls are displayed (see Figure H2.20).

4.  Set the following specifications (use the default values for settings that aren't listed here):

    | | |
    |---|---|
    | Angle | 63° |
    | Distance | 8 px |
    | Choke | 0% |
    | Size | 5 px |

5.  Click the Bevel and Emboss style. Set the following specifications (use the defaults for the remaining options):

    | | |
    |---|---|
    | Style | Outer Bevel |
    | Technique | Smooth |
    | Depth | 201% |
    | Direction | Up |
    | Size | 5 px |
    | Soften | 5 px |

6.  Click the Satin style.

7.  Click the Color Overlay style.

8.  Click the Stroke style. Set the Color to Yellow, and use the defaults for the other settings. Your text should now look something like Figure H2.2. Better, isn't it?

> It makes no difference in what order you apply the multiple layer styles.

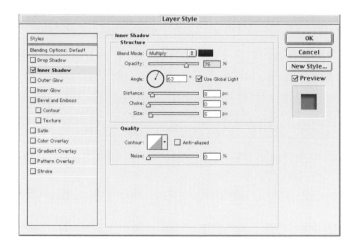

As I said earlier in the chapter, type is more than just words. By applying the type-twisting techniques and multiple effects that you learned in this chapter, you transform your type into a strong visual element that resonates with form, texture, and color. With such a multitude of controls, the choices are infinite.

## Adjusting the Opacity of a Layer Set

Now that all of the poster elements are in place, you can subdue the color of the planets so that the flying women stand out more:

1. Link all of the planet layers except Saturn and Rings. That includes Jupiter, Mars, Uranus, Mercury, and Galaxy.

2. Make a new layer set by choosing, from the Layers Palette pull-down menu, New Set From Linked.

3. Name the layer set **Planets**. In the Layers palette, adjust the opacity of the Planets layer set to 75%

## Merging Layers and Flattening the Image

In order to reduce the file size and to more efficiently manage your document, you can merge layers:

1. Click off the eye icons next to all the layers except for the Blue, Purple, and Yellow layer sets. Target the Purple layer set.

2.  Choose Merge Visible from the Layers Palette pull-down menu. The content of all three of the layers sets is merged into one layer (see Figure H2.21). Notice the reduction in the file size in the information field in the lower-left corner of the image window.

3.  Choose Image → Duplicate. Name the new image `Flying_Women_flat.psd`.

4.  Be sure all layers are visible, and make a note of the file size in the information field in the lower-left corner of the image window. From the Layers Palette pull-down menu, choose Flatten Image. Notice the dramatic reduction of the file size.

5.  Save the image.

Figure H2.21

**You can merge the contents of all three layers sets into one layer**

# CHAPTER 9

# Drawing Paths

*Photoshop provides several methods* for isolating areas of an image, as you saw in Chapter 6, "Making Selections." Still, making accurate selections can be difficult or time-consuming, because each image presents different problems. The Pen tool and the Paths palette add more capabilities to further enhance the accuracy and speed of making selections and defining the smooth edges. Once you've learned to draw with the Pen tool, you'll probably find it indispensable, because it can often be the easiest and fastest way to select areas that are defined by long, smooth curves.

This chapter covers topics that include:

■ **The Path tools and the Paths palette**

■ **Drawing and editing paths**

■ **Using paths to apply color**

■ **Paths and selections**

■ **Exporting paths**

■ **Vector masks and clipping paths**

■ **Paths and the Shape tools**

# What Is a Path?

If you have used any vector illustration software, then the Paths function in Photoshop should be familiar to you. Paths represent *vector objects* that mathematically define specific areas on an image by virtue of their shape and position. Vector objects are composed of anchor points and line segments, known as *Bézier curves*, like the ones shown in Figure 9.1 (see Chapter 3, "The Nature of the Beast," for more information on these terms).

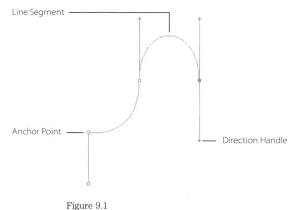

Figure 9.1

**Components of Bézier curves**

The Path tools enable you to create straight lines and curves with much greater clarity and precision than with the selection tools. If you create an open-ended path, you can then stroke it with a color to form a curved line (using the path as a drawing tool). If its two end points have joined, the path encloses a *shape*. You can then fill the shape with color, stroke it with an outline, or store it in the Paths palette (or the Shape library) for later use. It can also be converted into a selection, to which you can then apply some other Photoshop operation.

# The Path Tools

The primary Path tool is the Pen tool, located in the Tool palette. To choose the Pen tool, click

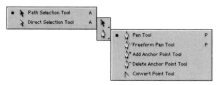

its icon or type **P**. If you hold down the mouse button, you can expand the Tool palette to display the other Path tools. Photoshop 7 has tools for drawing paths (Shift-P cycles through these) and tools for editing paths. There are also two tools designed specifically to select and move a path or a portion of a path. We'll explore these tools throughout the chapter, but here is a quick preview.

## Path-Drawing Tools

This set of tools includes the following:

**The Pen Tool**  Draws paths by clicking and dragging.

**The Freeform Pen Tool**  Draws a freeform line that converts itself into a path when the mouse is released.

**The Freeform Pen Tool with the Magnetic Option**  Sometimes simply called the Magnetic Pen, this tool intuitively defines edges based upon contrasting colors.

## Path-Editing Tools

This set of tools includes the following:

**The Add Anchor Point Tool**  Adds anchor points to existing paths.

**The Delete Anchor Point Tool**  Removes anchor points from existing paths.

**The Convert Point Tool**  Changes a corner point to a curve, or a curve to a corner point.

**The Path Selection Tool**  Selects and moves the path as a unit.

**The Direct Selection Tool**  Selects and moves individual anchor points and segments.

# Drawing Paths

Each path-drawing tool employs a slightly different method for creating a path outline. Learning to draw accurately with the Pen tools can be challenging at first, because drawing with Bézier curves is unlike any form of traditional drawing. With a little practice, however, as you become familiar with the process, your speed and accuracy will improve considerably.

## The Pen Tool

The Pen tool enables you to draw straight lines and smooth curves with a high degree of control and precision. The basic techniques and concepts used for drawing paths in Adobe Photoshop closely parallel those used in Adobe Illustrator. Usually, a path is drawn to follow the form of the area to be isolated, and then the path is edited and refined to a considerable degree of accuracy.

The Pen Tool Options bar displays options that enable you to modify its behavior. Before you draw the shape, specify in the Options bar (Figure 9.2) whether to make a new Shape layer or a new work path. This choice will affect how the shape can later be edited. If you choose the Shape Layer icon, Photoshop generates an independent Shape layer (see "Creating Lines and Shapes" near the end of this chapter). If you choose the Work Path icon, Photoshop draws an independent path and creates a work path in the Paths palette. For now we'll be working with Work Paths. Check the Auto Add/Delete feature to automatically add anchor points when one of the Pen tools is placed on a segment or to delete a point when a Pen tool is placed over an anchor point.

> Using the Zoom tool or the Navigator to view the image more closely greatly enhances your ability to draw with precision.

Creates a New Shape layer  Create Fill Pixels  Pen Tool  Shape Tools  Displays Geometry Options

☑ Auto Add/Delete

Creates a New Work Path  Freeform Pen Tool  Automatically Adds or Deletes Anchor Points

Figure 9.2

**The Pen tool Options bar**

## Straight Paths

The simplest of all paths consists of two anchor points joined by a straight line segment (anchor points that connect straight line segments are called *corner anchor points*). You add additional segments to the straight path by moving the cursor and clicking the mouse. The segments can abruptly change direction as the corners zigzag their way across the image.

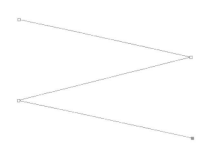

Take these steps to draw a straight path:

1. Select the Pen tool and click the image where you want to begin the path. An anchor point appears; release the mouse button.

2. Click (and release) your mouse at the next point on the image. A line segment with another anchor point appears between the two points.

3. Continue to move and click your mouse to produce a series of straight-line segments connected to each other by corner anchor points.

## Curved Paths

A curved path consists of two anchor points connected by a curved segment. *Direction handles* determine the position and shape of the line segment.

Take these steps to draw a curved path:

1. Select the Pen tool and place the cursor over the image where you want the path to begin.

2. Click your mouse *and drag*. An anchor point with a direction handle appears. Without releasing the mouse button, drag the handle in the general direction you want the curve to travel.

3. Release the mouse and move the cursor to the next point on the image.

4. Click your mouse *and drag*. A curved segment with another anchor point and direction handle appears. Drag in the opposite general direction of the curve.

5. With the mouse button still depressed, adjust the direction handle until the curved line segment is in the desired position, and then release the mouse.

### Tips for Drawing Curved Paths

Keep the following suggestions in mind as you practice drawing curved paths:

- Drag the first point in the direction of the peak of the curve and drag the second point in the opposite direction. Dragging the first and second point in the same direction produces an S curve, which is undesirable because its shape is difficult to control.

- Use as few anchor points as possible to assure a smooth path
- Place the anchor points on the sides of the curve, not on the peaks or valleys, to maintain better control and smooth transitions.
- A path is a continuous series of segments connected by anchor points. You can add anchor points to the middle of a segment, but you can only add segments to the end points of an open path.
- An anchor point can only connect two segments.
- If you stop drawing and want to add a new segment to a path, resume drawing by first clicking one of the end points with a Pen tool.
- If you are drawing an open path and want to begin a second path that is not connected to the first, press ⌘ (Macintosh) or Ctrl (Windows) to get the Direct Selection tool. Click off the path and release the keys. Resume drawing the new path.

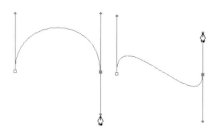

## Changing the Direction of a Curved Path

You can draw a scalloped path by changing the direction of the curve. When performing this operation, it helps to think of the Option/Alt key as a turn signal. In the following example, the segments will curve upward.

1. Select the Pen tool. Click the image where you want to begin the path and drag up. An anchor point with a direction handle appears. Without releasing the mouse button, drag to adjust the direction handle, then release.

2. Click where you want the next part of the curve. Click your mouse and drag down. A curved segment with another anchor point and direction line appears, as in Figure 9.3; release the mouse.

3. Place your cursor on the last anchor point and press Option or Alt (the turn signal!). See Figure 9.4.

4. Click and drag the direction handle up and release the mouse, as shown in Figure 9.5.

5. Move your cursor to the next location, click your mouse, and drag down. Adjust the segment so that the curve is the desired length and position (see Figure 9.6).

6. Repeat steps 3 and 4.

7. Repeat steps 2 through 5 until the desired number of curves are drawn, as in Figure 9.7.

Figure 9.3

**A curved segment with another anchor point and direction line**

Figure 9.4

**Placing the cursor on the last anchor point and pressing Option/Alt**

Figure 9.5

**Dragging the direction handle up**

Figure 9.6

**Drag and adjust to the desired position**

Figure 9.7

**Repeat to draw more curves**

### Adding a Curved Path to a Straight Path

Usually, paths you draw are combinations of straight and curved paths. These techniques combine the two into one continuous path.

1. Select the Pen tool and click the image where you want to path to begin. An anchor point appears; release the mouse button.

2. Click the next point on the image. A straight segment with another anchor point appears.

3. To add a curved segment, place your cursor on the last anchor point, and press Option or Alt while holding down the mouse button and dragging up.

4. Release your mouse button and move your cursor to the next location.

5. Click your mouse and drag down to finish the curve. Release the mouse when the size and position of the curve is achieved (see Figure 9.8).

Figure 9.8

**Adding a curved segment to a straight segment**

### Adding a Straight Path to a Curved Path

You can also begin with a curve and add a straight line to it:

1. Select the Pen tool, click the image where you want to begin the path, and drag up. An anchor point with a direction handle appears. Without releasing the mouse button, drag the direction handle in the direction of the curve.

2. Release the mouse and move the cursor to the next point.

3. Click your mouse and drag down. A curved segment with another anchor point and direction line appears. Release the mouse.

4. Place your cursor on the last anchor point, press Option or Alt, and click your mouse once.

5. Move your cursor to the next location and click your mouse to complete the segment.

### Closing a Path

By closing a path, you create a *shape*. To close a series of straight paths, draw at least two paths, and then place your cursor directly over the first anchor point. A little circle appears beside the pen cursor to indicate that the path is ready to be closed. Click the mouse. To close one or more curved paths, draw at least *one* path and click the first anchor point.

## The Freeform Pen Tool

Drawing with the Freeform Pen tool is very similar to drawing with the Lasso tool, introduced in Chapter 6. When you place your cursor on the image, click, and drag your mouse, the Freeform Pen will be followed by a trail that produces a path when the mouse is released (see Figure 9.9).

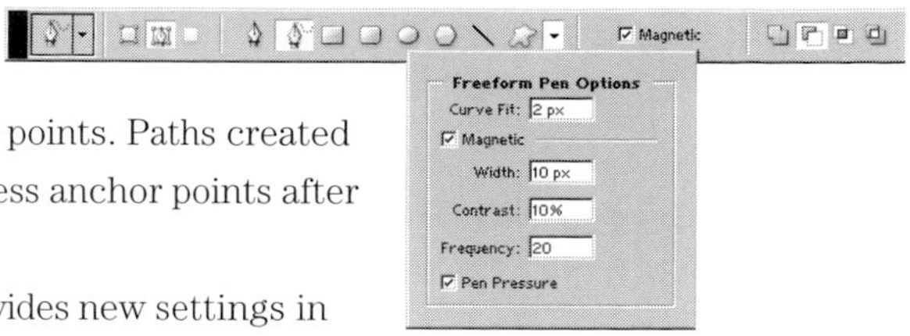

The Freeform Pen tool is a quick way to draw a curve, but it doesn't offer the same level of control and precision as the Pen tool. You can't control the number or placement of anchor points. Paths created by the Freeform Pen usually require editing or removal of excess anchor points after the path has been completed.

When you select the Freeform Pen tool, the Options bar provides new settings in the Geometry Options drop-down menu: *Curve Fit* and *Magnetic*. You can specify the Curve Fit between 0.5 and 10.0 pixels, to determine the sensitivity of the tool to the movement of your mouse. A lower tolerance produces a finer curve with more anchor points, whereas a higher tolerance produces a simpler path with fewer anchor points and fewer anchor points produce a smoother curve.

## The Magnetic Pen Option

The performance of the Freeform Pen tool with Magnetic checked (also called "the Magnetic Pen tool") is similar to the Magnetic Lasso (see Chapter 6). It automatically snaps to areas of high color contrast within an image as you drag. You define the area within which snapping will occur and the degree of contrast needed to trigger snapping. Where the Magnetic Lasso converts to a selection, the Magnetic Pen converts to a path. Thus, where the Magnetic Lasso is a good tool for cropping, say, a face out of a contrasting background, the Magnetic Pen is useful for defining its edges based on contrasting colors.

Figure 9.9

**The Freeform Pen tool draws an unrestricted path.**

To access the Magnetic Pen, select the Freeform Pen tool (click and hold the cursor on the Pen tool in the Tool palette, and choose the Freeform Pen from the fly-out; or type Shift-P once or twice to select the tool) and check the Magnetic box in the Options bar. Then use the Geometry Options menu to display the Magnetic options:

**Width**  Enter a distance in pixels from the edge that the tool will be active. Higher values mean the tool is "attracted" to the edge from a greater distance.

**Contrast**  Enter a value between 1% and 100% to determine the tool's sensitivity in detecting contrasting borders. Higher values detect edges of greater contrast, while lower values increase the tool's sensitivity to low-contrast edges.

> You can increase the detection width in one-pixel increments *while drawing* by pressing the ] key. You can decrease the width by pressing the [ key.

**Frequency**  Enter a value between 1 and 100 to establish the rate at which the Magnetic Pen places anchor points. Higher values place more anchor points over a shorter distance.

**Pen Pressure** If you are working with a stylus tablet, check Pen Pressure. As you drag, the pressure of the stylus will correspond to the Width setting. An increase of pressure on the stylus will thicken the pen width.

Take the following steps to draw with the Magnetic Pen:

1. Click the image to set the first point, near an edge of relatively high contrast.

2. Release the mouse button and drag slowly. A path will follow along the most distinct edge within the Pen width. Periodically, the Pen places anchor points along the specified border, while the most recent segment remains active (see Figure 9.10).

3. Press Return/Enter to end an open path. You can resume drawing the open path by clicking the last anchor point and dragging.

4. If you stop dragging and double-click, you create a segment that connects the last anchor point with the first one and closes the path. You can also close the path by hovering over the first anchor point until the little circle appears. Click once.

> You can temporarily turn off the Magnetic option by holding down the Option or Alt key with the mouse button depressed to draw a straight path, or with the mouse button released to draw a freeform path.

# Editing Paths

Once a path has been drawn, all or part of it can be moved or reshaped. Anchor points can be added or omitted, and corners can be converted into curves or curves into corners.

The path-editing tools include the Path Selection tool, the Direct Selection tool, the Add Anchor Point tool, the Delete Anchor Point tool, and the Convert Point tool.

## The Path Selection Tool

The black arrow, the Path Selection tool, selects all of the anchor points and segments of a path. You can then reposition the path anywhere on the image by dragging it with this tool.

> Another method of selecting a path is to use the Path Selection tool to click and drag a marquee that touches any part of the path. All the anchor points will appear solid, indicating that the entire path is selected.

Figure 9.10

**A path made with the Magnetic Pen "snaps" to a line of contrasting pixels.**

Figure 9.11

**Option/Alt-drag to duplicate a path.**

You can duplicate a path by dragging and dropping it with the Path Selection tool and the Option or Alt key depressed, as seen in Figure 9.11.

## Aligning Paths

Using the Path Selection tool, you can automatically align and distribute multiple paths and vector objects such as lines and shapes. You cannot, however, align or distribute shapes that are on separate layers. To align multiple paths, select two or more paths with the Path Selection tool by dragging a marquee that touches the objects, or by Shift-clicking the paths. From the Options bar, choose one of the alignment options shown in Figure 9.12.

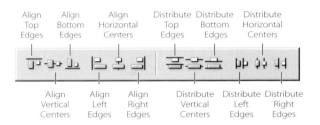

Figure 9.12

**Alignment features of the Path Selection tool**

The Align choices match up the edges or centers of paths and objects, as follows:

| | |
|---|---|
| Top Edges | Aligns the top edges of the path or vector object |
| Vertical Centers | Aligns the vertical midpoints |
| Bottom Edges | Aligns the bottom edges |
| Left Edges | Aligns the left edges |
| Horizontal Centers | Aligns the horizontal midpoints |
| Right Edges | Aligns the right edges |

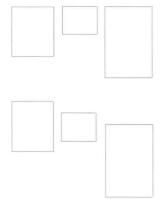

The Distribute choices position the edges or centers of paths and objects over equal distances, in these ways:

| | |
|---|---|
| Top | Distributes the top edges of the path or vector object |
| Vertical Centers | Distributes the vertical midpoints |
| Bottom Edges | Distributes the bottom edges |
| Left Edges | Distributes the left edges |
| Horizontal Centers | Distributes the horizontal midpoints |
| Right Edges | Distributes the right edges |

Figure 9.13 illustrates the difference between aligning and distributing.

Figure 9.13

**In the first row, the top edges are aligned. In the bottom row, the top edges are distributed.**

## The Direct Selection Tool

The Direct Selection tool selects or modifies a segment, or the position of an anchor point, on a path. It is an essential tool for revising and reshaping the path once it has already been drawn.

To select, move, or edit a segment or anchor point, choose the Direct Selection tool. Click on a segment or anchor point to select it. Click and drag an anchor point to reposition it or a segment to reshape it. To deselect a path, click anywhere on the image.

You can toggle from any of the Pen tools or path-editing tools to the Direct Selection tool by pressing the ⌘/Ctrl key.

### Reshaping Paths

To alter the shape of a path once it has been drawn, follow these steps:

1. Choose the Direct Selection tool.

2. Click an anchor point to select it.

3. Click and drag one of the anchor point's *direction handles* until the desired shape of the curve is achieved (as in Figure 9.14).

Figure 9.14

**Reshaping a path**

## Editing Anchor Points

After you have drawn a path around an area on the image, you may need to refine it by adding or deleting anchor points. When you do so, you increase your ability to edit the path.

It might be tempting to add dozens of anchor points, to facilitate the drawing of a path. That's not always a good idea, because too many extra points increase the path's complexity and compromise the smoothness of the shape.

### Adding and Deleting Anchor Points

To add an anchor point, choose the Add Anchor Point tool and click the path. A new anchor point will appear where you've clicked. To delete an anchor point, choose the Delete Anchor Point tool and click an anchor point. The two segments connected by the point will join into one.

### Converting Anchor Points

There are two types of anchor points. *Smooth points* connect curved or straight lines that "flow into" each other. *Corner points* connect lines that change direction abruptly. An anchor point can be converted from corner to smooth or smooth to corner (see Figure 9.15) by clicking the point with the Convert Point tool. Click a smooth point and it converts to a corner point; to convert a corner point, click it and drag out the direction handles until the desired curve is achieved, and release the mouse.

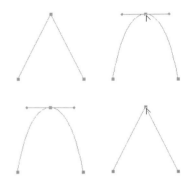

Figure 9.15

**Converting (top) a corner to a smooth point and (bottom) a smooth to a corner point**

## Transforming Paths

Like selection outlines and selection contents, paths can also be modified with the Transformation tools. Once a path has been drawn, you must select it with one of the arrow tools. If you select it with the Path Selection tool, you can employ any of the transformation operations in the Edit menu, including Free Transform, Scale, Rotate, Skew, Distort, Perspective, or Flip, to edit the entire path. If you select one or more points or segments with the Direct Selection tool, you can apply any of the transformation operations to the selected part of the path.

> To learn how to use Photoshop's transformation features, see Chapter 13, "Sizing and Transforming Images."

## Combining Paths

If you have drawn two or more paths that intersect, you can combine them into one path. Select both paths with the Path Selection tool by pressing your mouse button and dragging a marquee that touches both of them or by clicking them in sequence while pressing the Shift key. On the Options bar, click the Combine button. The elements of both paths combine into one continuous path.

## The Paths Palette

The Paths palette is the central control for all path operations. Like a layer or a channel, a path can be stored into a palette so it can later be edited or converted into a selection. You can access the Paths palette (Figure 9.16) by choosing Window → Paths. (If you still have the Paths palette in the default cluster—grouped with the Layers palette—pressing the F7 function key will also bring it up.)

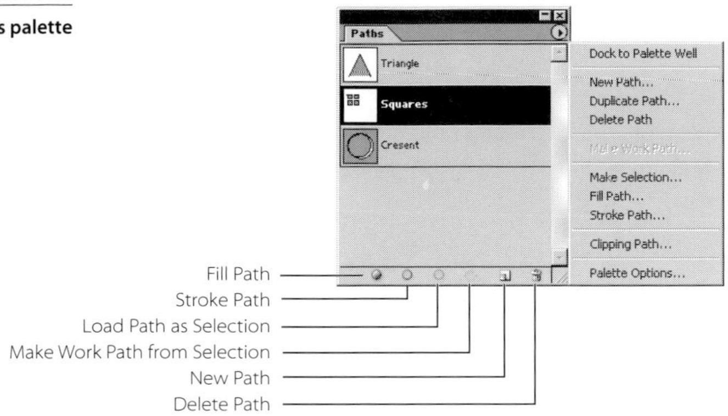

Figure 9.16

**The Paths palette**

Fill Path
Stroke Path
Load Path as Selection
Make Work Path from Selection
New Path
Delete Path

## Work Paths

When you begin drawing a path with the Pen tool, it appears as a thumbnail in the Paths palette, named Work Path. The work path is a temporary element that records changes as you draw new sections of the path. If you complete a path on an image, click the Pen tool, and draw another path, it will appear on the same Work Path thumbnail as the first path. To create separate additional paths, you must save the work path to the Paths palette.

You can increase or decrease the size of the Paths palette thumbnails, or turn them off, by choosing Palette Options from the palette pull-down menu and clicking the radio button next to the desired thumbnail size.

## Saving Paths

Saving a path to the Paths palette has a distinct advantage over saving selections as alpha channels (which are described in Chapter 12, "Using Alpha Channels and Quick Mask"): The file size of a document does not substantially increase with each saved path.

Once your path has been drawn and appears as a Work Path thumbnail, you can save it by choosing Save Path from the palette menu. A dialog box appears where you can name the path; if no name is entered, the path name defaults to Path 1. You can also save a path by dragging the Work Path to the New Path icon at the bottom of the palette.

The Paths palette lists saved paths from top to bottom in the order in which they were created. The paths can be reorganized within the list by clicking the path's name or thumbnail and dragging it to the desired location.

## Displaying Paths

To display a path, click the path's name or thumbnail image in the Paths palette. Photoshop allows only one path to be displayed at a time. When displayed, it will appear on the image. You can edit it, move it, add other paths to it, or delete portions of the path. To conceal a work path or saved path from view in the image window, click the empty portion of the Paths palette.

## Deleting Paths from the Image Window

To delete a path from the image, do one of the following:

- Select an entire path with the Path Selection tool. Press the Delete or Backspace key. If it's a work path, the path and its icon are deleted. If it's a saved path, the path is deleted from the image window, but its empty thumbnail remains in the Paths palette.

- Select a part of the path with the Direct Selection tool. Press the Delete or Backspace key once to delete the selected part of the path or twice to delete the entire path.

## Deleting Paths from the Palette

You may want to discard a path from the Paths palette once you are sure you will have no further use for it. To do so, target the path's name in the palette and perform one of the following operations:

- Drag the path thumbnail to the trash icon 🗑 at the bottom of the palette.
- Choose Delete Path from the Paths Palette pull-down menu.
- Click the trash icon in the Paths palette. In the dialog box that appears, click Yes.
- Target the path in the Paths palette. Press the Delete or Backspace key.

# Using Paths to Apply Color

You can apply color to an area of an image within a closed path or to the edge of a path.

## Filling a Path

To fill the area within a path, draw an open or closed path or display an existing path from the Paths palette by clicking its thumbnail. Choose a foreground color, and then choose Fill Path from the Paths Palette pull-down menu.

The Fill Path dialog box appears (Figure 9.17). Its top two fields are identical to the Fill dialog box in the Edit menu and are discussed in Chapter 10, "Creating and Applying Color." In the additional Rendering field, you can enter a feather radius for the edges of the path and check the Anti-Aliased option. Click OK when you have the settings you want.

You can fill a path with the current Fill Path dialog box settings by clicking the Fill Path icon ⬤ at the bottom of the Paths palette.

Figure 9.17

**The Fill Path dialog box**

## Stroking a Path

A path can be stroked with a line of a specific color and width. This is an important operation in Photoshop because it is really the only way to create smooth curved lines precisely. Try drawing one with the Paintbrush or Pencil; you'll see that it's quite difficult to achieve satisfactory results. Drawing an open path, editing it to your exact specifications, and then stroking it with a color produces perfect results every time.

Figure 9.18

**The Stroke Path dialog box**

To color the line of a path, draw a path or load one from the Paths palette. Choose a foreground color; then, from the Paths Palette pull-down menu, choose Stroke Path. The Stroke Path dialog box (Figure 9.18) appears; pick a tool from the pop-up list. When you click OK, the stroke will be painted with the current characteristics of the chosen tool as defined in the Options bar.

You can quickly stroke a path with the current tool characteristics set in the Stroke Path dialog box by clicking the Stroke Path icon at the bottom of the Paths palette.

# Converting Paths

The primary reason for using paths is the ease and facility with which you can precisely define regions of an image. While some of the selection tools offer unique selection techniques, there is nothing quite like the path operations to quickly and precisely surround an area.

Paths are easy to edit and require less real estate on your disk than selections saved as alpha channels. Eventually, though, you will need to convert your path into a selection before you can apply a Photoshop operation to the area it surrounds.

## Converting a Path into a Selection

When you convert a path to a selection using the Make Selection dialog box, you can specify the characteristics of your new selection and its relation to active selections on the image. To do this, target the path in the Paths palette and choose Make Selection from the Paths palette pull-down menu. The Make Selection dialog box is displayed (Figure 9.19), enabling you to choose the characteristics of the new selection:

Figure 9.19

**The Make Selection dialog box**

| | |
|---|---|
| Feather Radius | Sets a distance in pixels for feathering of the selection outline |
| Anti-Aliased | Determines whether the selection will possess an anti-aliased edge |
| New Selection | Makes a selection from the path |
| Add To Selection | Adds the area defined by the path to the active selection |
| Subtract From Selection | Omits the area defined by the path from the active selection |
| Intersect With Selection | Makes a selection from the overlap of the path and the active selection |

Click OK to convert the path into a selection.

Another way to convert a path into a new selection is by clicking the Load Path As Selection icon at the bottom of the Paths palette.

## Converting a Selection into a Path

To convert a selection into a path, draw a marquee with one of the selection tools. Choose Make Work Path from the Paths Palette menu. A dialog box is displayed that enables you to set the tolerance of the path in pixels. Tolerances with low values produce more complex paths with greater numbers of anchor points, while tolerances with higher values produce simpler paths. Click OK to convert the selection into a path.

You can also convert a selection into a path by clicking the Make Work Path From Selection icon ▨ at the bottom of the Paths palette.

# Importing and Exporting Paths

Photoshop paths can be used by other programs, where they can be modified. You can transfer a path directly from Photoshop to popular vector-based drawing programs like Illustrator or FreeHand, or vice versa, to take advantage of either program's unique path-editing features.

## Copy and Paste

If you're moving the path from Photoshop to a vector-based drawing program, you can select the entire path with the Path Selection tool and copy it to the Clipboard (by choosing Edit → Copy or pressing ⌘/Ctrl-C). Open a document in the other program and paste the path into it. The paths remain fully editable in either program.

When you paste a path from a drawing program into Photoshop, a dialog box appears that asks you to choose to place the path as a rasterized image (Pixels), a vector path, or a Shape layer, as seen in Figure 9.20.

Figure 9.20

**The Paste dialog box**

## Drag and Drop

You can drag and drop a path from Photoshop to Illustrator. With both programs running, select the path with the Path Selection tool. Drag the path onto the Illustrator pasteboard. The new Illustrator path is fully editable.

## Exporting Paths to Illustrator

If you can't run Photoshop and Illustrator simultaneously, you can export the file as a native Illustrator format (.ai) file using the File → Export → Paths To Illustrator command. In the dialog box that appears, for Write, choose Work Path. When you quit Photoshop, launch Illustrator, and open the document, the exported path will be fully editable in Illustrator.

Exported paths from Photoshop to Illustrator do not contain fill or stroke information.

## Using Vector Masks

When working with Photoshop graphical elements, it is sometimes necessary to "knock out" portions of an image—that is, make those areas invisible, so that elements in layers below can show through. This can be done using a *vector mask*. When you use a vector mask, the interior portion of the path will be displayed, and the area outside the path will be completely transparent (for more about layer masking, see Chapter 22, "Advanced Layer Techniques"). Vector masks are best used when you want a clean, crisp edge to your element—not always easy to create with regular selection methods!

To create a vector mask:

1. Draw a path around an area on the image that you want to isolate (see Figure 9.21). Use the Direct Selection tool to tweak it to your liking.

2. From the Paths Palette pull-down menu, choose Save Path, and give it a name.

3. With the path selected in the Paths palette, choose Layer → Add Vector Mask → Current Path from the main menu.

4. Now the path outline will clip out anything outside the path, making it invisible and letting any layer beneath show through. The vector mask is also represented in the Layers palette, to the right of your active layer. Notice also that you can use any layer styles you want (such as the drop shadow shown in Figure 9.22) with vector masks as well.

5. Deselecting the vector mask path in the Paths palette will hide the path outline, but you will still be able to edit it at any time by simply selecting it again. Of course, how you utilize this function is limited only by your imagination!

Figure 9.21

**Selecting the area with the Pen tool**

Figure 9.22

**Using a drop shadow**

# Using Clipping Paths

The Clipping Path option has essentially the same effect as the Vector Masks option, except that clipping paths are designed to be exported with your image into a vector illustration program (such as Adobe Illustrator) instead of embedded within a Photoshop layer.

To create a clipping path:

1. Create your path around an area of your image as before using the Path tools.

2. From the Paths Palette pull-down menu, choose Save Path, and give it a name.

3. Choose Clipping Path from the palette menu (see Figure 9.23).

4. Select the name of the path you want to convert to a clipping path from the pull-down submenu. Click OK.

5. For most paths, leave the Flatness setting blank. When you print the image, the printer's default flatness setting will be used to define the shape. However, if you experience printing problems, try saving the path with new settings (see the "Troubleshooting" sidebar).

Figure 9.23

**The Clipping Path dialog box**

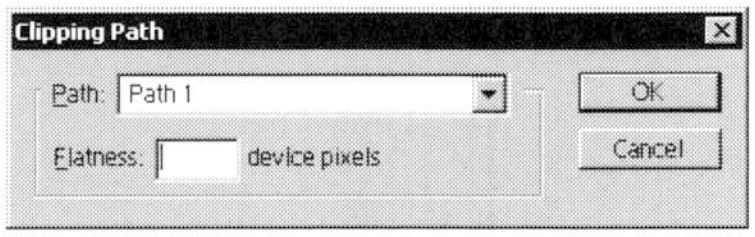

The path name is outlined (MacOS 9.0) or boldfaced (Win and MacOS X) in the Paths palette, indicating that it is a clipping path.

Images containing clipping paths must be saved in either EPS or TIFF format, depending on the program, and therefore can only be imported into programs that support these images. It's best to save a *copy* of the image so that the original image retains Photoshop's attributes.

To save an image with a clipping path as an EPS:

1. Choose File → Save As. Check the As A Copy option.

2. From the Format list, choose Photoshop EPS to display the EPS Options dialog box (Figure 9.24).

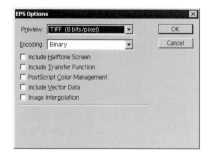

Figure 9.24

**EPS file options**

3. Choose a Preview option, depending on the type of computer and the platform you are using: Macintosh or Windows, 1 bit or 8 bit (see Appendix B, "File Formats," for a detailed explanation of the EPS Settings dialog box).

4. For the Encoding type, choose Binary.

5. Click OK.

6. Open a document in a desktop-publishing program or vector-drawing program, and place the EPS image. The clipping path should mask out everything outside the path, much as the vector mask does within Photoshop.

### TROUBLESHOOTING CLIPPING PATH POSTSCRIPT ERRORS

A raster image processor (RIP) is software on a computer or a device inside an imagesetter or PostScript printer that interprets a vector curve by connecting a series of straight line segments together. The *flatness* of a clipping path determines the fidelity of the lines to the curve. The lower the setting, the more lines are produced, and the more accurate the curve.

But if a clipping path is too complex for the printer's capabilities, it cannot print the path and will produce a limitcheck or PostScript error. Any printer can be jammed up with a complex clipping path, although you may find that a clipping path may print perfectly well on a low-resolution printer (300–600 dpi) because that device uses a higher flatness value to define the curve. The same clipping path may not print on a high-resolution imagesetter (1200–2400 dpi). If you run into printing problems on an image with a clipping path, troubleshoot them in the following ways:

- Increase the Flatness settings and resave the file. Flatness values range from 0.2 to 100. Enter a flatness setting from 1 to 3 for low-resolution printers and 8 to 10 for high-resolution printers.

- Reduce the number of anchor points in the curve by manually eliminating them with the Delete Anchor Point tool.

You can also re-create the path with lower Tolerance settings:

1. Target the path in the Paths palette.

2. Click the Load Path As Selection icon at the bottom of the palette.

3. Click the trash icon to delete the path but leave the selection.

4. Choose Make Work Path from the palette's pull-down menu. In the dialog box, decrease the Tolerance to 5 pixels (a good place to start).

5. Name and save the new work path.

6. Choose Clipping Path from the palette pull-down menu.

7. Save the file in EPS format.

# Creating Lines and Shapes

Photoshop 7 handles lines and shapes in a manner much like Illustrator. Like type, lines and shapes are vector objects (drawn and defined by paths). You draw a predefined shape using one of the Shape tools or a custom shape using the Pen tool. Once drawn, shapes can be edited by adjusting their anchor points with the path-editing tools. When you create a shape on a shape layer, it appears on an independent layer with a Vector Mask thumbnail next to a Color Fill Layer thumbnail.

The shape also appears as a separate path in the Paths palette. To apply any filter to a shape, it must first be *rasterized* or turned into pixels. If you flatten the image, shapes are automatically converted to pixels.

The Shape tool can instantly create precise shapes, such as rectangles, rounded rectangles, ellipses, polygons, lines, and custom shapes that are editable using the path-editing tools. When you click the Shape tool icon in the Tool palette, it expands to reveal all of the available tools. Once you've chosen a shape from this fly-out, click in the image and drag to size the shape.

## The Shape Tool Options Bar

As you choose a different shape from the Tool palette or from the Shape list in the Options bar, the Options bar changes to accommodate specific characteristics of the shape. Figure 9.25 illustrates the differences in the Options bar when the three different drawing options are selected.

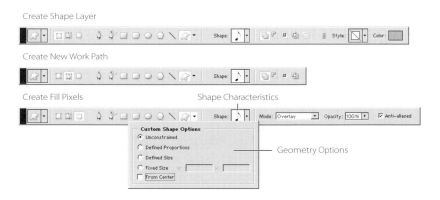

Figure 9.25

**The Options bar of the Shape tools**

| Options Bar Feature | Function |
| --- | --- |
| Create New Shape Layer | Makes a shape and a path on a new layer |
| Create New Work Path | Makes the path outline of the shape on an existing layer or Background |
| Create Fill Pixels | Fills an area with the foreground color in the form of the shape |
| Shape List | Lets you choose a shape |

| Options Bar Feature | Function |
|---|---|
| Geometry Options | Lets you enter specifications for the size and proportion of the shape |
| Style | Attaches a layer style to the Shape layer (available with New Shape Layer) |
| Shape Characteristics | Assigns values for the characteristics of a particular shape, or chooses a custom shape |
| Mode | Lets you select a blending mode for the shape (available only with Create Fill Pixels) |
| Opacity | Opacity slider for the shape (available only with Create Fill Pixels) |
| Anti-Alias | Applies an anti-alias to the shape (available only with Fill Pixels) |

## Drawing Shapes

To draw a shape, first choose a foreground color. Click the Shape tool in the Tool palette and choose a tool type from the expanded palette or from the Options bar. Click in the image and drag to form the shape.

Because shapes are vector objects, you can use the Path Selection tool, the Direct Selection tool, or the path-editing tools to move or edit a shape or to add and delete anchor points.

Each shape performs slightly differently. The Options bar of each shape lets you adjust its individual characteristics. For example, you can enter a value for the radius of the corners on the Rounded Rectangle tool, or for the number of sides on the Polygon tool.

### The Rectangles and Ellipse Tools

As with the selection Marquee tools, icons on the Shape tool Options bars let you add, subtract, intersect, or exclude areas from a shape as you draw. Clicking the arrow to the right of the Shape tool icons on the Options bar offers additional controls on a pop-up panel. When you choose the Rectangle, Rounded Rectangle, or Ellipse tool, the down-arrow button on the Options bar offers you these choices:

| | |
|---|---|
| Unconstrained | Checking this button sizes and proportions the shape as you draw. |
| Square (or Circle) | Checking this button constrains the shape. |
| Fixed Size | Input values for the shape's width and height. |
| Proportional | Enter values in the Width and Height fields to define the shape's proportion. |

| From Center | Check this box to radiate the shape from a center point. |
| Snap To Pixels | Aligns the shape to the on-screen pixels (Rectangle and Round-Cornered Rectangle only). |

To constrain the Rectangle or Round-Cornered Rectangle to a square or the Ellipse to a circle, hold down the Shift key as you drag.

## The Polygon Tool

When the Polygon tool is selected, a Size field in the Options bar allows you to set the number of the shape's sides. The Polygon Options panel choices differ from those of the other shapes. Figure 9.26 illustrates the wide variety of shapes you can create by adjusting these settings:

Figure 9.26

**Polygon examples**

| Radius | Enter a corner radius for a round-cornered polygon. |
| Smooth Corners | Rounds the corners of the polygon. |
| Indent Sides By | Enter a percentage value to curve the sides inward. |
| Smooth Indents | Rounds the indents. |

## The Line Tool

When the Line tool is selected, you can enter a value in the Options bar for the Weight of the line in pixels. Choices in the Line Options panel determine what type of arrow will appear at either end of the line. Check the Start or End boxes, or both, to produce an arrowhead at the beginning and/or end of the line (see Figure 9.27). Enter values in Width, Length, and Concavity for these characteristics of the arrowhead. Figure 9.28 demonstrates the wide variety of possibilities in these settings.

## The Custom Shape Tool

You can generate custom shapes with the Shape tool  . With the Custom Shape tool selected, the Options panel displays these options:

Figure 9.27

**Arrowhead characteristics**

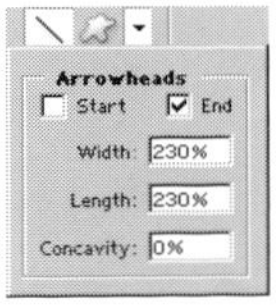

| Unconstrained | Manually determines the proportion of the shape as you draw. |
| Defined Proportions | Drag to constrain the proportion of the shape. |
| Defined Size | Draws the shape at the size it was created. |
| Fixed Size | Enter values for the shape in the height and width fields. |
| From Center | Radiates the shape from a center point. |

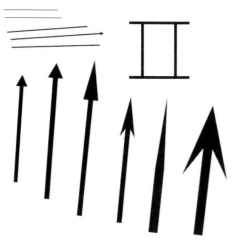

**Figure 9.28**

**Examples of lines, with and without arrowheads**

The Options bar Shape menu lets you choose from many predefined custom shapes. You can create additional shapes with the Pen tool and save them to this list (see Figure 9.29).

The pull-down submenu on the panel provides a list of commands that let you Save, Load, Reset, Delete, and Replace custom shapes, plus several palette-viewing options. The options at the bottom rung of the submenu replace the default list with additional shapes. With the All option, you can view a comprehensive list of all available shapes.

### PLACING CUSTOM SHAPES ON AN IMAGE

Applying predefined custom shapes is a snap. First, open an image or create one; then take the following steps:

1. Choose a foreground color.

2. Make a new empty layer by clicking the New Layer icon in the Layers palette.

3. Click the Shape tool in the Tool palette.

4. In the Options bar, click the Custom Shape icon to display the Shape Options panel. Click the Unconstrained radio button.

**Figure 9.29**

**The Shape list**

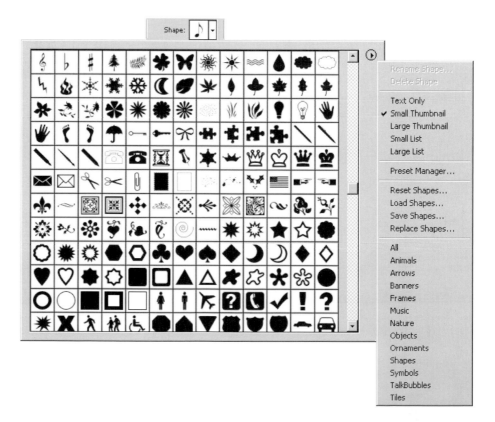

5. In the Options bar, click the Shape menu arrow to display the default custom shapes. Click the arrow on the panel to display the list of commands in the pull-down submenu; choose All to load all the additional shapes.

6. Click a shape in the Shape menu. Place your cursor on the image, click, and drag until the shape is the size and proportion you want. To reposition the shape, press the space-bar while dragging. Then release the mouse.

7. Optionally choose additional shapes from the Shape menu and repeat for all the shapes you want on your image layer. Your result might look like Figure 9.30.

Figure 9.30

**The dog poster adorned with custom shapes**

## DEFINING CUSTOM SHAPES

To create your own custom shape:

1. Use one of the Pen tools and draw a shape outline.

2. Choose Edit → Define Custom Shape.

3. Choose the Custom Shape tool. The new shape will appear in the Shape menu in the Shape tool Options bar.

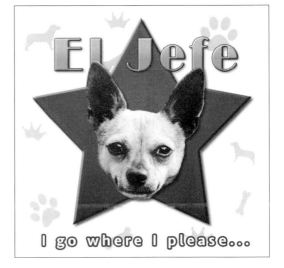

# CHAPTER 10

# Creating and Applying Color

*The methods used* by painters and computer artists differ in their physical application. Painters, of course, paint with pigment, where computer artists paint with light. The similarity, however, lies in the fact that Photoshop's painting functions are designed to simulate the real-life studio environment with a variety of virtual tools for applying color. Photoshop draws and paints with light, yet has the ability to simulate almost any effect that can be created on paper or canvas. These same capabilities can be greatly extended by applying artistic, textural, and brush stroke filters that can convert a photograph into anything—from a Rembrandt to a Picasso—instantaneously.

In this chapter, you'll learn about:

- **Understanding digital color**
- **Choosing colors, color modes, and color models**
- **Creating and modifying brushes**
- **Using the painting and editing tools**
- **Making and applying gradients and patterns**
- **Filling and stroking**

# Painting with Paint and Pixels

Applying color to a surface is one of the oldest and most common forms of self-expression. From the meticulous application of thinned glazes used to render exacting detail on photo-realistic paintings to pigment splashed by the gallon on Abstract Expressionist canvases, the application of color is the artist's way of whispering, speaking, or shouting.

Paint is indeed a versatile medium. Colors are made from minerals or organic substances, ground and then mixed with either an oil- or water-based vehicle that forms a liquid or paste to make them fluid enough to apply. It can be brushed, troweled, rolled, sprayed, poured, spattered, or thrown onto a surface. It can be mixed, blended, glazed, or smeared, thin or thick, to produce an infinite variety of colors and surface effects.

Photoshop's drawing and painting features allow you to use light instead of physical compounds on paper or canvas. Specifying digital color and applying it with one of the painting tools is fundamental to digital imaging. The painting tools go far beyond just the ability to apply color in an artistic capacity, however. They are essential for spot editing and photo retouching, creating textural surfaces, and image compositing.

# Understanding Digital Color

Every pixel in each color channel of your image is assigned a numeric value. These values can be translated into specific color systems that distribute the information depending on your needs. For example, the three-channel RGB system is used to display images on-screen, but the four-channel CMYK color system is designed to organize the information into color separations so that it can be printed on a printing press.

In Photoshop, you can choose a specific color system. Some of these systems are called color *modes*, like RGB, CMYK, Lab, and Grayscale, in which the information is organized into color *channels* with specific characteristics. Others, such as HSB, are called color *models* and are supported for your convenience, so that you can easily pick the exact color you want by determining its basic characteristics.

## Color Models and Modes

A color mode or model is a system of displaying or printing color. Photoshop supports the HSB color model and RGB, CMYK, Lab, Indexed, Duotone, Grayscale, Multichannel, and Bitmap color modes. To convert an image from one color mode to another, choose Image → Mode and select a color mode.

Because the *gamut*, or range of possible colors, of one color mode may be different from that of another, converting your image can sometimes present problems in the form of color shifts. See Chapter 15, "Color Management and Printing," for more on this issue and how to avoid it.

## DIGITAL IMAGING AND FINE ART

Since the introduction of computer painting and imaging software like Adobe Photoshop, there has been an ongoing debate in art circles about whether painting will be replaced by its digital counterpart. The controversy embraces many aspects of the meaning and purpose of art and especially its commercial value to collectors, museums, and galleries.

When it was first introduced, graphic designers and commercial illustrators immediately gravitated to photo manipulation and desktop-publishing software to replace traditional graphic arts techniques performed with paste-up, technical pens, and process cameras. It took almost a decade, however, for digital art to be taken seriously as a "real" art form by the art establishment of universities, galleries, and museums. This was due, in part, to reluctance by the institutions to accept a new medium, and to the limitations of hardware to produce archival-quality output. (*Archival* simply means that the ink won't fade and paper won't deteriorate over time.)

These days, however, many images we see hanging on the walls of museums and galleries are produced by computers. The recent introduction of direct, high-end printing to archival-quality paper with archival ink, as with Iris printers, or photographic output devices, like Light-Jet RGB printers, has made museum-quality computer art possible. Some of these direct-to-print digital images are photographic, and some are painterly. Because they can be systematically reproduced, they acquire the status of limited edition prints or photographs.

Owing to the unique differences of the processes of painting and computer art, one can hardly replace the other. Painting is a much more physical process than computer art. It requires broader movement of the body and direct contact with wet media, which intrinsically presents entirely different visual, tactile, and olfactory sensations. On a computer, most operations can be performed using the fingers, hand, and wrist in an environment that is free of the odors of solvents and the feel of the brush against a surface.

Just as the traditional visual arts have continued to thrive in our society as a means of self-expression, the computer has emerged as another dynamic art form. In addition, the computer has become an aid to the artist. With the capability of quickly creating multiple versions, it helps some artists visualize and refine the style, composition, and color relationships of their work.

## HSB Color Model

The HSB model uses the basic characteristics of color to define each color; HSB is the Color Picker's default model, as it is usually the easiest model by which to locate any given color quickly. Each possible color consists of the following characteristics:

**Hue**  is the *color* of light that is reflected from an opaque object or transmitted through a transparent one. Hue in Photoshop is measured by its position on a color wheel, from 0 to 360 degrees.

**Saturation**  or *chroma*, is the intensity of a color as determined by the percentage of the hue in proportion to gray from 0 to 100 percent. Zero percent saturation means that the color is entirely gray.

**Brightness**  or *value*, is the relative lightness or darkness of a color, measured from 0 to 100 percent.

### RGB Color Mode

The RGB mode represents the three colors—red, green, and blue—used by devices such as scanners or monitors to acquire or display color. Each range of color is separated into three separate entities called *color channels*. Each color channel can produce 256 different values, for a total of $256^3$, or 16,777,216, possible colors in the entire RGB gamut. Photoshop can display all of these colors, providing you have a monitor and video card capable of supporting 24-bit color.

Because RGB produces color with light, the more light that is added, the brighter the color becomes; hence, RGB is referred to as an *additive* color model (see Figure C10, left image, in the color section). Each pixel contains three brightness values—a red, a green, and a blue—ranging from 0 (black) to 255. When all three values are at their maximum, the color is pure white. Colors with low brightness values are dark, and colors with high brightness values are light.

### CMYK Color Mode

The CMYK (cyan, magenta, yellow, black) color mode produces a full range of color by printing tiny dots of cyan, magenta, yellow, and black ink. Because the colored dots are so small, the eye mixes them together. The relative densities of groups of colored dots produce variations in color and tonality. The more ink you add to a CMYK image, the darker it becomes; conversely, less ink produces lighter colors, and the absence of ink produces white. For this reason, CMYK is referred to as a *subtractive* color system (see Figure C10, right image, in the color section). You specify CMYK colors to ultimately segregate colors into color separations for use in the offset lithography printing process.

### Lab Color Mode

The CIE Lab color mode is an international color measurement system, developed in 1931 by the International Commission on Illumination (Commission Internacionale de l'Éclairage, or CIE). Lab color is *device independent*, meaning that the color model is based on the perception of the human eye rather than a mechanical ink or light system. Lab color consists of three channels: a luminance or lightness channel (L), a green–red component (a), and a blue–yellow component (b) (see Figure C8 in the color section). In the Color Picker, entering a value from 0 to 100 in the L channel controls the lightness or luminosity information, and values from +120 to –120 in the a and b channels control the color information.

Figure 10.1

**A grayscale and a bitmap image**

As a color model, Lab can be used to adjust the luminance and color of an image independently of each. Photoshop uses Lab as an interim color space when converting files from one color mode to another.

## Grayscale Mode

Grayscale is a mode that displays what we traditionally think of as a black-and-white image. A Grayscale image is composed of one channel with 256 possible shades of gray. Each pixel has a brightness value from 0 (black) to 255 (white). Sometimes Grayscale pixels are measured in percentages of black ink from 0 percent (white) to 100 percent (black). When color images are converted to Grayscale, their hue and saturation information is discarded, while their lightness, or *luminosity*, values remain intact.

## Bitmap Mode

Bitmap mode images (not to be confused with the Bitmap file format) are the simplest form of true black-and-white graphic image. They contain two types of pixels, literally black or white, and are used to create line art and digital halftones. Bitmap images contain only 1 bit of information per pixel, so their file sizes are much smaller than grayscale images, which contain 8 bits per pixel, or color images, which contain 24 bits per pixel. Figure 10.1 compares an 8-bit, 256-level grayscale image with a 1-bit, 2-color (black or white) bitmap image.

## Indexed Color Mode

Indexed color mode uses a maximum of 256 colors to display full-color images. When you convert an image color to the Indexed mode, Photoshop stores the color information as a color look-up table (CLUT). You can then use a specific palette to display the image to match the colors as closely as possible to the original. Because it contains fewer colors, Indexed color creates smaller file sizes, which is why it is often used when publishing files to the Web or to multimedia applications.

### Duotone Mode

Duotones are images that have been separated into two spot colors. Duotone modes support Monotone, Duotones, Tritones (images with three colors), and Quadtones (four colors). The Duotone color information is contained on one color channel. Photoshop displays a preview that is an RGB simulation of the ink combinations. Duotones and spot color are covered in more depth in Chapter 18, "Duotones and Spot Color."

### Multichannel Mode

The number of channels in a Multichannel document depends on the number of channels in the source image before it was converted. Each channel in a Multichannel document contains 256 levels of gray. This mode is useful for converting a Duotone image into separate color channels for the purpose of analyzing the color information. Multichannel will convert RGB to cyan, magenta, and yellow spot color channels and CMYK into CMYK spot color channels.

> Although RGB will convert to spot CMY, these are not true CMY separations that are press-ready; they are simply the theoretical subtractive opposites of the additive original.

You cannot print a color composite from Multichannel mode. Most export file formats do not support Multichannel. However you can save a Multichannel file in DCS 2.0 file format. See Appendix B, "File Formats."

## Choosing Colors

Picking a color in Photoshop 7 is as simple as squeezing paint from a tube. It is a matter of choosing a color from one of Photoshop's three color interfaces. In addition, you can sample colors directly from any open image.

There are two color swatches near the bottom of the Tool palette, representing the current *foreground* and *background* colors . The swatch on the left is the fore-ground color, which is applied directly by any of the painting tools. The default  foreground color is black. The background color on the right is applied with the Eraser tool or by cutting a selected portion of an image on the Background. The default background color is white.

You can reverse the foreground and background colors by clicking the curved arrow to the upper-right of the swatches. To restore the colors to the default black and white, click the icon at the lower left of the swatches.

> When you cut a portion from an image on a layer, the area becomes transparent.

## The Color Picker

To choose a foreground or background color, click its swatch; the Color Picker appears (see Figure 10.2; for a color version of this image, see Figure C7 in the color section). The Color Picker lets you choose from four methods of defining your colors: HSB, RGB, Lab, and CMYK. Your main tools in the Color Picker are a vertical slider and a large color field.

You can also set values for the following characteristics in the Color Picker:

**Hue**  This is the position of the color on a color wheel. When the H radio button is selected in the Color Picker, the vertical slider displays the spectrum of all of the available hues, and the color field presents that hue's saturation and brightness variations.

Notice that the top and bottom of the Spectrum slider are both red. If you drag the slider to the top or bottom of the color bar, the values in the Hue box are the same: 0 degrees. No, we are not taking the hue's temperature; we're determining its position on a color wheel. The vertical bar is actually a color wheel that has been cut and straightened at the 0 degree, or red, position. Drag the slider anywhere on the bar, and notice that the hue value changes to a number between 0 and 360 degrees. As you move the slider, the field to the left changes color.

**Saturation**  The color field on the left determines the saturation and brightness of the hue. Saturation is the intensity of a particular hue. There are two ways to determine the saturation of a color in the Color Picker: Enter a value in the Saturation box, or click or drag within the color field. If the value in the Saturation box is 100 percent, or if the circle on the color field is to the far right, the color will be as intense as it can possibly be. If a 0 is entered in the Saturation box, or if the circle is placed at the far left of the field, the color will be gray (saturation is therefore represented by the X-axis in the color field).

**Brightness**  The value of a color is controlled in a similar manner. Brightness is the lightness or darkness of a color. Lower values produce darker colors, with zero percent equaling black. Higher values produce lighter colors, with 100 percent equaling white when there is no color saturation or the lightest possible combination of hue and saturation. Click toward the bottom of the color field to darken the color or toward the top to lighten it (the Y-axis in the color field represents brightness).

## Active Parameters of Color

By default, the Color Picker opens in HSB mode with Hue as the active parameter. The slider represents the colors (hues) on the color wheel, and the field represents the saturation and brightness of the selected hue. The Color Picker can be changed to display several different configurations.

Figure 10.2

**The Color Picker**

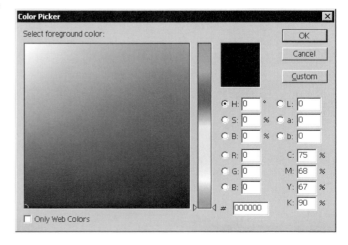

The Color Picker can be configured for HSB, RGB, Lab, and CMYK active parameters by clicking a radio button next to the desired model. The vertical bar then represents the selected characteristic in the selected model. When the S radio button is active, for instance, the active parameter of the Color Picker shifts to Saturation mode and the vertical bar becomes a Saturation slider. The color field now displays hue and brightness variations. If you click or drag in the field, to the left or right, you affect the hue; if you click or drag up or down, you affect the brightness.

When the B radio button is checked, the active parameter of the Color Picker shifts to Brightness, and the vertical bar becomes a Brightness slider. The color field now displays hue and saturation variations; clicking in the field or dragging the circle to the left or right affects the hue, and dragging it up or down affects the saturation.

In the case of RGB and Lab, when a color channel's radio button is selected, the vertical slider displays the variations of color within that channel, and the color field becomes the other two color channels, one represented horizontally and the other represented vertically.

The color swatch at the top of the Color Picker has two parts. The bottom of the swatch shows the current color setting; the top shows the color you've selected in the Color Picker.

## Specifying CMYK Colors

Let's say a client walks into your office and wants you to add a logo to an image with specific CMYK color values to correspond to the official corporate colors of the business. Once you've scanned the logo, you can define the colors in the Color Picker and fill the logo with the exact tint values of cyan, magenta, yellow, and black needed to produce the corporate color.

To define and apply CMYK colors:

1. Click the foreground swatch to display the Color Picker.
2. Enter the CMYK percentage values in their boxes.
3. Click OK. The color appears as the foreground color.
4. Select the area to be filled.
5. Press Option-Delete (Mac) or Alt-Backspace (Win) to fill the selected area.

## The CMYK Gamut Warning

You would think that, because CMYK is represented by four color channels instead of three, there would be more colors available in this color mode. But in fact, a high percentage of black plus any combination of cyan, yellow, and magenta usually yields black, and this greatly limits the possibilities of CMYK. The CMYK gamut is so small that some colors, especially highly saturated ones, cannot be produced at all. The color section includes a schematic comparison of the gamut of visible, RGB, and CMYK colors (see Figure C9).

If you choose a color in HSB, Lab, or RGB that is outside the printable range or gamut of
CMYK, you will see the percentage values in the CMYK boxes. You will also see a CMYK
Gamut Warning next to the color swatch in the Color Picker. The small swatch below
the warning represents how the color will print. Some CMYK colors, especially highly saturated colors, can vary significantly from their RGB counterparts. If you get a warning, you
may want to specify a different color for a closer match, or be prepared to accept considerable
variation of the color on the printed piece.

## Specifying Web Colors

In HTML, colors are coded with a combination of six hexadecimal characters so that World
Wide Web browsers can read and display them. Not all browsers can display all colors. You
can use the Color Picker to assure that the colors you use are browser-safe.

To specify a Web color, check the Only Web Color box at the bottom of the Color Picker. The
color bar and color field then limit themselves to 216 Web-compatible colors; note the banding
in Figure 10.3, indicating that the color field no longer has a continuous, nearly infinite color set.
When you click any variation, the color's six-character hexadecimal number appears in the # box
(each character pair represents the channels R, G, and B, respectively). If you know the Web
color's number, you can select that color simply by entering the number in the # box.

Like CMYK colors, Web colors have a very limited gamut compared to RGB. When the
Only Web Colors box is cleared, the Color Picker displays a Web Color Gamut Warning
next to the large swatch in the Color Picker. The small swatch below the warning shows how
the color will be seen on Web browsers.

It is very hard to control exactly how even Web-safe colors are seen on browsers. A lot
depends on the quality and age of the viewer's monitor, what system palette they are using,
and how the brightness and contrast controls are set. The Web-safe colors feature lets you
choose colors that will not radically change when viewed on other monitors of the same
quality and calibration as the one you are working on. They also produce dither-free solids.

It is not absolutely necessary to use the Web-safe
palette when creating graphics for the Web since the
limited gamut can reduce color options and overall
image quality. The option is there in the event that
some viewers may not be able to view more than 8-
bit color with older video cards/monitors. However,
though the image may look slightly better to these
users, overall it would appear less than marvelous to
the majority of users capable of viewing 24-bit color.
As the curve of technology improves with time, and
older equipment declines in use, this becomes less
and less of an issue. Use your own judgment.

Figure 10.3

**When Only Web
Colors is checked, the
Color Picker restricts
itself to browser-safe
possibilities.**

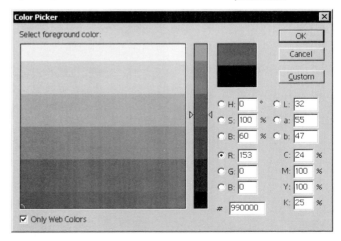

## Specifying Custom Colors

Photoshop supports the PANTONE Matching System, which is a group of inks used to print spot colors. Where CMYK mixes only four colors to produce a full-color spectrum, PANTONE inks are solid colors used to print rich solid or tinted areas. The PANTONE system is recognized all over the world; a PANTONE ink can be specified in the U.S. and printed in Japan, for example, simply by telling the printer its number. Photoshop also supports other matching systems, such as ANPA, DIC, Toyo, Focoltone, HKS, and TRUMATCH (a CMYK computer color-matching system).

To specify a custom color:

1. Click a color swatch to display the Color Picker.

2. Click the Custom button to display the Custom Colors dialog box (see Figure 10.4).

3. From the Book pop-up list, choose the desired matching system.

4. Enter the color's number using the keypad. You can, instead, scroll through the color list using the slider; when you find the color you want, click it.

5. Click OK.

In Photoshop 7, the PANTONE library specifications have changed to match the new 2000 guide. This change could cause some confusion if some software uses the older PANTONE library definitions while new applications use the updated definitions.

Unlike past versions of Photoshop, these color library files are no longer built into the application, but are now contained in preset files known as Color Books. It is now possible to remove unwanted library color choices to streamline the menu.

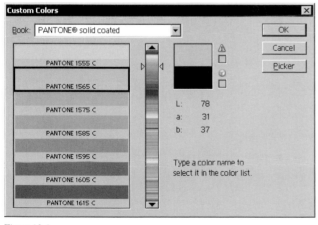

Figure 10.4

**Choosing custom colors**

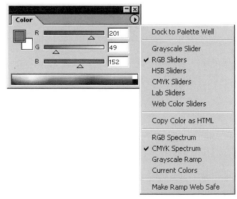

Figure 10.5

**The Color palette**

## Using Color Palettes

While the Color Picker displays all of the color characteristics and models in one integrated field, it is sometimes cumbersome to use because it is not *context sensitive*. A context-sensitive palette will respond immediately to your commands without having to click an OK button. On the other hand, you must display the Color Picker by clicking the foreground or background swatch, then choose a color model and a color, and, finally, you must click OK. This process can be time-consuming because of the many steps involved. Instead, you may want to use the context-sensitive Color and Swatches palettes that conveniently float on the desktop.

Figure 10.6

**The Swatches palette**

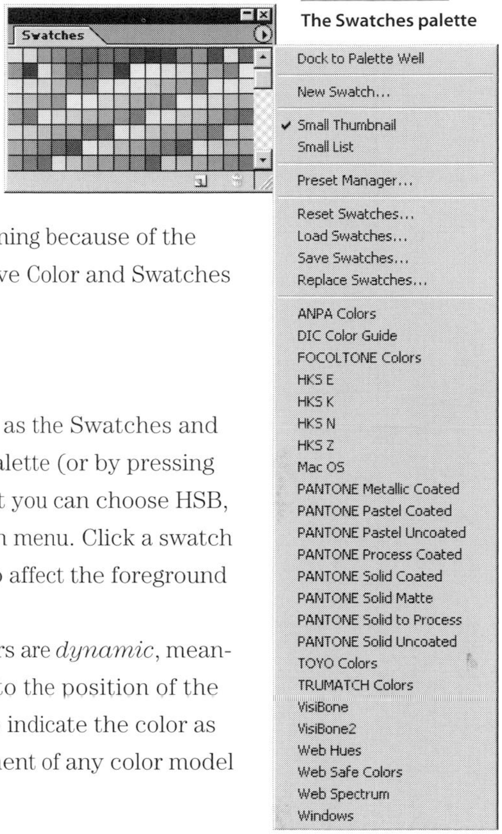

### The Color Palette

The Color palette (Figure 10.5) is in the same default palette cluster as the Swatches and Styles palettes. You can access it by choosing Window → Show Color Palette (or by pressing the F6 function key). By default, the RGB color model is displayed, but you can choose HSB, Grayscale, CMYK, Lab, or Web Color sliders from the Palette pull-down menu. Click a swatch in the upper-left corner of the palette to designate whether you want to affect the foreground or background color.

The position of the sliders determines the color. By default, the sliders are *dynamic*, meaning that a gradient bar displays the selected color that corresponds to the position of the sliders. The Tool and Color palette swatches simultaneously change to indicate the color as you drag the slider. You can also enter specific values for each component of any color model in boxes to the right of the sliders.

> The fastest way to select a color is to click or drag in the spectrum bar at the bottom of the
> Color palette to designate an approximate color. Release the mouse, and the color will
> appear as the foreground color. Then move the sliders to tweak the color until you get
> exactly the color you want.

### The Swatches Palette

To display individual swatches of color, choose the Swatches palette (Figure 10.6) from the palette cluster. You can choose from predefined colors, or add and save new colors. See Table 10.1 for tips on doing swatch techniques.

Table 10.1

**Swatch Techniques**

| SWATCH TECHNIQUE | HOW TO DO IT |
|---|---|
| Selecting a foreground color | Click the desired color; it will appear as the foreground swatch on the Tool palette. |
| Selecting a background color | Press the ⌘/Ctrl key while clicking the color. |
| Adding a color | Place your cursor in the blank space below the color swatches. The cursor changes to a paint can. Click your mouse, name the color, and the foreground color will appear in the palette as a new swatch. |
| Deleting a color | Press Option/Alt and click the swatch. Or, Control-click/right-click and select Delete Swatch from the shortcut menu. |
| Saving a Swatch palette | Once you've added colors to the swatches, you may want to save the palette for use in other documents. From the Swatches Palette menu, choose Save Swatches. Designate a folder in which to store your palette. |
| Loading swatches | To access a saved palette, choose Load Swatches from the Swatches Palette menu. (New Swatches palettes can also be loaded from the Preset Manager found in the Edit menu.) You can then access the swatch from the folder in which you saved it, or choose a specific palette like PANTONE, Focoltone, ANPA, or Web-Safe Colors from the list. |
| Resetting swatches | The Reset Swatches command on the Palette menu restores the swatches to the Photoshop default palette. |
| Naming a swatch | Color swatches can be named for identification. To name a swatch, double-click it and enter the name in the Swatch Name dialog box. Or Control-click/right-click and select Rename Swatch. |

# Introduction to Brushes

Figure 10.7

**The Options bar Brush Preset Picker and menu**

Photoshop provides you with an abundant supply of built-in brushes that can be used to apply color to your image in a variety of ways with the painting and editing tools. In addition, you can create new brushes and control such characteristics as size, hardness, spacing,

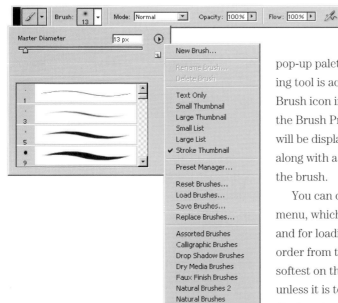

roundness, and angle. You can also make custom brushes in virtually any shape.

The preset brushes are displayed by means of a pop-up palette from the Options bar whenever a painting or editing tool is activated. Click the small arrow to the right of the Brush icon in the Options bar to open the pop-up palette called the Brush Preset Picker (Figure 10.7). By default, the brushes will be displayed with a thumbnail view of each loaded brush tip, along with a brush stroke view. Clicking on the view will select the brush.

You can change the display characteristics in the Palette menu, which also has options for renaming and deleting brushes and for loading additional brush sets. The default brushes go in order from the smallest and hardest on top to the largest and softest on the bottom. Each brush is displayed at actual size unless it is too big to fit in the thumbnail view, in which case it is displayed with a number that indicates its diameter in pixels.

When a brush tip is selected by clicking on it in the Brushes palette, the brush stroke view will display in the larger view window at the bottom of the palette. If you hold your mouse cursor over any brush tip in the Brushes palette long enough for the brush name to appear as a tool tip, you will then be able to merely hover the cursor over the other brush tips to quickly view the brush stroke displays in the view window.

In Photoshop 7, you can also view, select, and load the brushes via the Brushes palette (Window→ Brushes), which, by default, is located in the Palette Docking Well, but can be moved out of the well or clustered with other palettes. The Brushes palette (See Figure 10.8) is also used to design customized brushes and to control various brush dynamics. The palette can be toggled on and off with the Brushes Palette icon in the Options bar, or by using the shortcut key F5.

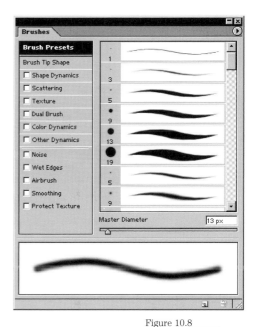

## Creating a New Brush

A brush tip is a specific shape with several options pertaining to it that will affect the way it appears when applied with brush strokes. You can easily create new brush tip shapes from selected areas of an image and use the editing options to achieve the desired look.

To create a custom brush, follow these steps:

1. Select an area of an image with a selection tool.

2. Choose Edit → Define Brush. The Brush Name dialog box appears, as seen in Figure 10.9.

3. Name the brush and click OK.

4. Choose a painting tool. The custom brush is now available as a choice in the Brushes palette.

Figure 10.8

**The Brushes palette**

## Modifying Brushes

Brush tips have several basic characteristics that can be adjusted with options located in the Brush Tip Shape portion of the Brushes palette when a painting or editing tool is activated.

Open the Brushes palette. To the left of the brush display window, you'll see a list of choices. At the top of the list is Brush Presets, which has the same function as the Brush Preset Picker in the Options bar pop-up palette noted earlier. The second option is Brush Tip Shape—select it and notice the assortment of settings that appears in the right portion of the palette (see Figure 10.10).

Figure 10.9

**Naming your custom brush**

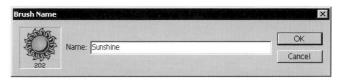

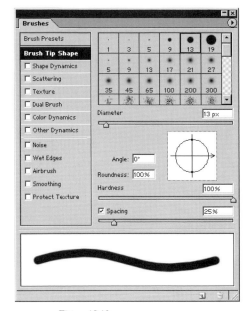

Figure 10.10

**The Brush Tip Shape settings**

Select a brush tip to experiment with the different settings while viewing the changes in the brush stroke display window at the bottom of the palette:

**Diameter** determines the size of the brush, from 1 to 2500 pixels. Use the Diameter slider, or enter a numerical value, to change the size. The Use Sample Size button can be used to reset to the original diameter.

**Angle** rotates the angle of the brush tip by degrees from the horizontal axis. You can drag the horizontal axis (the line with an arrow at the end running through the circle) in the interactive display window, or type in a numerical value.

**Roundness** adjusts the roundness of the brush shape. Drag the dots along the vertical line running through the circle in the display window, or type in a numerical percentage value. 100% gives the full roundness of the brush, while 0% gives a linear shape.

**Hardness** adjusts the hardness of the edges of a brush by using a percentage of the brush diameter as a basis; for instance, if a brush is set to 50% hardness, the 50% consisting of the central core will be hard, and the remaining 50%, consisting of the outer edges, is gradually softened through a gradient transition.

**Spacing** affects how frequently color is deposited by the brush tip as you create a brush stroke, determined by percentages of the brush diameter, from 0% to 1000%.

> Higher-resolution documents need larger brushes; for example, a 72-pixel brush on a 72 ppi document will paint a stroke 1 inch in diameter. The same brush will paint a half-inch stroke on a 144 ppi document.

### Saving Modified Brushes

When you modify a preset brush tip using the Brush Tip Shape options in the Brushes palette, the modifications will apply only as long as you have the brush activated, but will revert to the default original settings when you change brush tips or brush tools. To save a modified version of a brush tip, first make the desired modifications, and then click the Create New Brush icon located at the bottom of the Brushes palette. This will bring up the Brush Naming dialog box—name the modified brush, click OK, and it will be added to the currently open set of brushes. It will then be available for use with all the painting and editing tools.

A word of caution, however: If the brush set containing the new brush is later reset to the defaults, the new brush will be lost. Adding the modified brush permanently to a brush set requires saving the entire set through the Palette menu's Save Brushes option. Saving the set using the original set name will replace the default set with the modified set, or if the set is renamed during the saving operation, the modified set will then be saved as a new set.

## More Brush Dynamics

Photoshop 7 includes many new options for adding variable elements to the brushes. Two of the key variables you'll work with when manipulating these options are Jitter and Control, found under the Shape Dynamics tab:

**Jitter**  determines the randomness of the given effect, measured by percentage. 0% equals no change, while 100% brings about the maximum amount of change.

**Control**  contains a drop-down menu of choices pertaining to the way in which you wish to control the variation of the jitter; the Off setting chooses no control, while Fade will allow you to input a specified number of steps with which to fade the effect. Pen Pressure, Tilt, and Airbrush Wheel allow you to vary the effect based on those properties of a pressure-sensitive pen/tablet if you use one instead of a mouse.

### Setting Brush Dynamics

As with the Brush Tip Shape options, you access the new options in the Brushes palette. Clicking on the name of the option (rather than clicking in the check box) will bring up its settings (for those that have extra settings) as well as select it. The new options include the following:

**Shape Dynamics**  establish the variation of shape in the brush marks along a brush stroke, according to size, minimum diameter, angle, roundness, and minimum roundness (see Figure 10.11).

**Scattering**  regulates the numerical amount of brush tip marks contained in a stroke, as well as how they are distributed (or *scattered*, if you will), according to randomness, direction, count, and count jitter (see Figure 10.12).

**Texture**  incorporates a chosen pattern into the brush tip, resulting in the appearance of painting with a texture, as shown in Figure 10.13.

  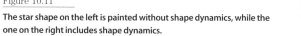 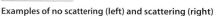

Figure 10.11

**The star shape on the left is painted without shape dynamics, while the one on the right includes shape dynamics.**

Figure 10.12

**Examples of no scattering (left) and scattering (right)**

**Dual Brush** combines properties of two brush tips: the primary brush tip being the tip selected using the brush presets, and the secondary (dual) tip then selected in the Dual Tip options, with extra settings of diameter, spacing, scatter, and count to be applied to the secondary tip (see Figure 10.14).

**Color Dynamics** adjust how paint varies over the course of a stroke, according to foreground and background color, hue, saturation, brightness, and purity (see Figure 10.15).

**Other Dynamics** adjust how paint varies over the course of a stroke, in regards to opacity and flow (see Figure 10.16).

**Noise** adds a noise effect to the outer edges of brush tips, resulting in a sort of frayed-edge appearance (see Figure 10.17), especially noticeable when used with soft brushes.

**Wet Edges** permits color to build up along the edges of the brush strokes, simulating a watercolor style, as in Figure 10.18.

**Airbrush** allows you to apply color similarly to the way a real airbrush operates, by spraying to build up the color gradually.

**Smoothing** generates smoother curves in brush strokes.

**Protect Texture** locks the texture pattern and scale so that it will remain the same for all brushes.

Figure 10.13

**Examples of a non-textured (left) and a textured (right) brush stroke**

Figure 10.14

**Examples of a single tip and a dual tip brush stroke**

 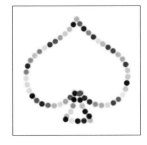  

Figure 10.15

**Examples of a brush stroke with (right) and without (left) color dynamics**

Figure 10.16

**Examples of a brush stroke with (right) and without (left) other dynamics**

Figure 10.17

**Brush stroke with (right) and without (left) noise**

Figure 10.18

**Brush stroke with (right) and without (left) the Wet Edges option**

# Using the Painting and Editing Tools

You use the painting and editing tools to manually apply color or to modify an area of the image. With the exception of the Gradient and Paint Bucket tools, the painting tools rely on the motion of your hand and choice of brush tip to distribute the color or apply an effect. Each tool has its own unique set of characteristics. You can access the painting and editing tools by clicking them in the Tool palette or by pressing the appropriate shortcut key on the keyboard. (The letter in parentheses after some of the tool names in the following sections indicates its keyboard shortcut.) The behavior of the painting and editing tools can be adjusted by setting certain characteristics in the Options bar.

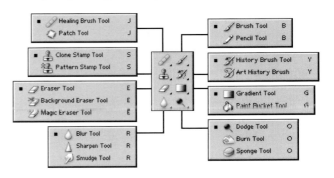

You can usually toggle between tools in an expandable tool cluster in the Tool palette by simultaneously pressing the Shift key and the tool's keyboard shortcut.

## The Painting Tools

The painting tools include the Brush tool and the Pencil; these tools are designed to simulate real studio painting techniques by emulating their real-life counterparts.

### Brush Tool (B)

You apply color to the image with the Brush tool 🖌 by clicking your mouse and dragging. By default, the stroke is a solid color. You can adjust the characteristics of the tool to alter the quality of the paint stroke with the following options:

**Color Blending Modes** Blending modes control the relation of the color that is being applied to the existing colors on the image, and are available for most of the painting and editing tools. The Normal blending mode, at 100% opacity, applies the color as if it were painted straight out of a tube (subject to the settings of the particular brush being used, of course). Other blending modes produce less predictable results and require a bit of experimentation. For a complete list of blending mode characteristics, see Appendix C, "Blending Modes."

**Opacity** The transparency of the stroke is controlled with the Opacity slider, going from 0% to 100%. When painted on a colored surface, the transparent or translucent stroke will reveal the pixels underneath it.

**Flow** The Flow control adjusts how quickly the paint flows by percentage; 100% results in complete coverage, while a lower flow percentage reduces the amount of virtual paint in the brush.

**Airbrush** Use the Airbrush option to spray color as if using an actual airbrush—i.e., building up the color by dragging the cursor slowly or stopping while still spraying.

If the Airbrush option is activated in the Options bar, it will be checked in the Brushes palette as well, and vice versa.

> In previous versions of Photoshop, the Airbrush option was a separate tool. While there is no longer an Airbrush tool, the airbrush capability is now incorporated as an option in many of the painting and editing tools.

### Pencil (B)

The Pencil ![pencil icon] is the only tool that produces an aliased, or hard-edged, stroke. Use the Pencil to draw crisp horizontal or vertical lines or stair-stepped diagonals. Like the Brush tool, you can adjust the opacity or assign a color mode to the stroke.

You can use the Pencil as an eraser by checking the Auto Erase box. If you start painting on an area containing the foreground color, the Auto Erase function replaces it with background color. If you start painting on an area containing any color other than the foreground color, the Pencil paints with the foreground color.

## The Editing Tools

The editing tools include the Clone Stamp, Pattern Stamp, Healing Brush, Patch, History Brush, Art History Brush, Eraser, Background Eraser, Magic Eraser, Blur, Sharpen, Smudge, Dodge, Burn, and Sponge tools. While the editing tools don't apply color directly to the image, they are essential for manipulating small regions within the image and modifying existing colors. Many of the editing tools have filter counterparts that produce the effect over larger areas, but the tools offer the dexterity and control of a smaller hands-on operation.

## Clone Stamp (S)

Use the Clone Stamp 🖫 to copy an area of the image and paint it elsewhere with a brush. The Clone Stamp is perfect for cloning textures from one small area of the image to another.

To clone an area, you must first sample it:

1. Choose the Clone Stamp from the Tool palette.

2. Choose an appropriate brush from the Brush Preset Picker on the Options bar.

3. Press the Option/Alt key and click your mouse on the point that you want to copy.

4. Release your mouse and reposition the cursor where you want the sample to be painted.

5. Click your mouse and begin painting. As you paint, the tool will begin copying the point of the image that was sampled. A small cross will indicate the area that is being copied as you drag the brush across the image.

Check the Aligned option to maintain the alignment of the Clone Stamp brush with the original sampled area. Each time you release the mouse, move the brush, and resume cloning, the alignment will persist depending on where the brush is in relationship to the original sampled point (as seen in the middle image in Figure 10.19). If Aligned is not checked, each time you click, you restart cloning from the original sample point as the source of the image.

If the Use All Layers option is checked, the Clone Stamp image is sampled from all of the visible layers. If it is cleared, the image is sampled from only the targeted layer.

## Pattern Stamp (S)

Use the Pattern Stamp 🖫 to paint an area with a repeating pattern that you choose from the Pattern pull-down menu on the Options bar. Photoshop provides you with several default patterns in the list, or you can define your own (see "Creating Patterns" later in this chapter.)

The Aligned option works in the same manner with the Pattern Stamp as it does with the Clone Stamp. By checking the Impressionist option, the pattern will be applied with an Impressionist-style painting effect.

Figure 10.19

**An original image (top), with aligned (middle) and non-aligned (bottom) clones**

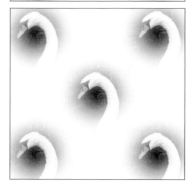

### Healing Brush (J)

New to version 7 of Photoshop, the Healing Brush  functions in a manner very similar to the Clone Stamp, in that it enables you to sample a chosen area of an image by pressing Option/Alt as you click the desired area, and then paint the sample into another area. The difference with the Healing Brush is that when the sampled area is painted into the new area, it seemingly absorbs the texture, lighting, and shading of the surrounding pixels, creating a virtually seamless blend. This capability makes it an invaluable tool for tasks such as photo retouching, as shown in Figure 10.20.

> Due to the healing algorithm that combines the source and target pixels, you can't heal to a transparent layer.

### Patch Tool (J)

The Patch tool , which is also a new addition to version 7, works in much the same way as the Healing Brush, except that it gives you the ability to heal a selected area with a sampled area, rather than using a brush. This can come in handy when you have a large area that needs to be repaired. You can either make the initial selection with the Patch tool activated, or you can use any of the other selection tools to make the selection first, and then switch to the Patch tool. The Patch tool can then be used in either of the following two ways:

- Select the area that you wish to repair, choose Source in the Options bar, and then drag the selection marquee over the area from which you want to sample.

- Select the area from which you want to sample, choose Destination in the Options bar, and then drag the selection marquee over the area you wish to patch.

You can also make a repair using a pattern, by first choosing a pattern from the Pattern Picker in the Options bar and then clicking Use Pattern.

> For more about the Healing Brush and the Patch tool, refer to Chapter 19, "Image Retouching," and Hands On 7, "Restoring a Color Photo."

### History Brush (Y)

The History Brush restores a portion of the image to a former state, or a previous point in the image's history. Choose the History Brush, target a state in the History palette, choose a brush size, press the mouse, and drag across the image. For more information about the History Brush, see Chapter 11, "Altered States: History."

## Art History Brush (Y)

This tool is quite handy for creating instant Impressionist effects, as illustrated in Figure 10.21. Its behavior is really wild—like an industrial-strength Smudge tool, Paintbrush, and Blur tool all in one. It paints with stroke clusters that vary in color depending on the color of the area you are painting on. When you paint with the Art History Brush 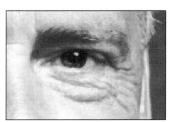, color is deposited rapidly in several directions.

Choose from a list of characteristics in the Options bar that affect the style of the stroke and the rapidity in which it is deposited:

**Style** determines the size and shape of the strokes that are deposited. Choose from a list that includes Tight, Loose, Short, Long, Dabs, and Curls options.

**Area** determines the width of the region in which the strokes will be deposited, from 0 to 500 pixels. Higher-resolution files need higher values.

**Tolerance** restricts the areas that can be painted; a low tolerance allows you to paint all image areas, while a higher tolerance limits painting capabilities to areas that differ considerably in color from the source state or snapshot.

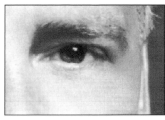

Figure 10.20

**After initially sampling a portion of smooth skin texture, it takes only a few dabs with the Healing Brush to miraculously eliminate the wrinkles from around the eye in this photo.**

## Eraser (E)

The Eraser  performs differently depending on whether you're working on the Background or a layer. When working on the Background, the Eraser replaces the area with the background color in the Tool palette. When erasing on a layer, it replaces the layer content with transparency. If the transparency option on the layer is locked, then the pixels are replaced with the background color.

The Eraser offers three modes in which to work: Brush, Pencil, or Block. The characteristics of each tool are inherent in the erasure.

Figure 10.21

**The version on the right has been altered with the Art History Brush, giving it an Impressionist look.**

You can erase the image back to a History state by clicking the first column in the History palette to set a source and choosing the Erase To History option from the Options bar.

### Background Eraser (E)

The Background Eraser tool functions like a combination of the Magic Wand tool and the Delete key command, in that it lets you sample and set a tolerance to determine what range of color will be erased. You can also determine the sharpness of the remaining edges. The Background Eraser erases to transparency on a layer, or automatically converts the Background into a layer when applied there.

Use these options to control this tool:

**Erasing Modes** control what pixels will be erased. Choose:

> **Discontiguous** to erase all of the pixels within the Tolerance range on the entire layer
>
> **Contiguous** to erase pixels of the sampled color that are adjacent to each other
>
> **Find Edges** to erase pixels of the sampled color that are adjacent to each other but better preserve the sharpness of the edge pixels of the remaining image

**Tolerance** controls the range of colors to be erased. Low Tolerance erases colors that are similar to the sampled colors; High Tolerance erases to colors that are more diverse in range.

**Sampling Option** determines the method in which the colors will be chosen:

> **Continuous** samples colors continuously as you drag, erasing areas of different colors.
>
> **Once** samples a color when you first click and then continues to erase only that color. Use this option to erase areas of solid color.
>
> **Background Swatch** erases areas that are the current background color.

Check the Protect Foreground Color box to ensure that areas of the foreground color are not erased.

### Magic Eraser (E)

The Magic Eraser erases all pixels of similar color within the tolerance range when you click the color you want to erase. It allows you to isolate the erasure to specific colors.

These settings control the tool:

**Tolerance** in the Options bar controls the range of colors to be erased. Low Tolerance erases colors that are similar to the sampled colors; high Tolerance erases to colors that are more diverse in range.

**Anti-aliased** creates a smoother appearance along the edges of the erased areas.

**Contiguous** determines what pixels will be erased. When checked, you erase only *adjacent* pixels of the color. With Contiguous unchecked, the Magic Eraser erases all pixels of the color on the layer.

**Use All Layers** determines where the information will be erased. With this option checked, the Magic Eraser erases through all of the visible layers; without this option, it erases only the pixels on the target layer.

**Opacity** determines the strength of the erasure.

## Blur (R)

The Blur tool softens the region it is applied to by decreasing the relative contrast of adjacent pixels. Use it to blend colors and soften edges, or to reduce the focus of a background. Increase the Strength setting in the Options bar to strengthen the effect.

## Sharpen (R)

The Sharpen tool increases the relative contrast values of adjacent pixels. As you drag over an area, the pixels randomly change color. The more you drag, the more diverse the colors of the adjacent pixels become. Increase the Pressure setting in the Options bar to increase the intensity of the effect.

Sharpening fools your eye into thinking an image is in focus. This tool can be used to enhance portions of an image that you want to emphasize or as a quick fix for photographs that are slightly out of focus.

> The Luminosity blend mode for the Sharpen tool reduces the randomness of the sharpened effect by replacing pixels with colors closer to the original image.

## Smudge (R)

Use the Smudge tool to simulate charcoal or pastel effects. As you drag with the Smudge tool, you move one area of color into another while blending and mixing the colors as you move them.

Checking the Use All Layers option smudges areas of colors on different layers (otherwise, the Smudge tool blends areas only on the targeted layer). If you check the Finger Painting box, you mix the current foreground color into the smudged area.

## Dodge (O)

Dodging is a technique used by photographers in the darkroom to overexpose or lighten specific areas of an image. In Photoshop, the Dodge tool performs a similar function by increasing the brightness values of pixels as you paint with it. The Dodge tool's Options bar lets you concentrate the effect on a specific range of tonality by choosing Highlights, Midtones, or Shadows from the Range pull-down menu. Adjusting the exposure will weaken or strengthen the effect.

### Burn (O)

Photographers burn an image in the darkroom to underexpose or darken areas of an image. Photoshop's Burn tool ◐ darkens by lowering the brightness values of pixels as you move it over the image. As with the Dodge tool, the Options bar lets you pick a range of pixels to affect by choosing Highlights, Midtones, or Shadows from the menu. Again, adjusting the exposure will weaken or strengthen the effect.

### Sponge (O)

The Sponge tool ◐ changes the intensity of a color as it touches pixels. From the Options bar, choose either Saturate to enhance a color or Desaturate to diminish the color and push it toward gray.

> Using the Dodge, Burn, or Sponge tool at full strength can often be overpowering. When you use these tools, try lowering the Exposure or Pressure setting to between 5% and 20% and making multiple passes to gradually build up the effect.

## Painting Tool Shortcuts

Here are a couple of shortcuts that will increase your dexterity in handling the painting tools and performing tasks that could be otherwise difficult:

- For horizontal and vertical lines, press Shift as you drag up or down, left or right.
- For a straight line in any other direction, click and release your mouse, then move the cursor to a new location and Shift-click.

# Making and Applying Gradients

In nature, we see countless variations of color that subtly blend into one another as light and shadow intermingle into dimensional forms. The ability to gradually blend colors is essential to the credibility of any realistic image. Photoshop gradients blend multiple colors into each other, or into transparency, over a specified distance.

## Choosing Gradients

Choose the Gradient tool ▦ from the Tool palette and notice how the Options bar configures itself. At the far left is a preview bar, or *gradient swatch*, with a down arrow; clicking in this swatch calls up the Gradient Editor, while clicking the arrow pops up a simpler Gradient Picker panel. Both display all saved gradients, beginning with the several preinstalled gradients. The default gradient creates a fill that blends from the foreground color to the background color. Another gradient, called Foreground To Transparent, fills from the current foreground color to transparency. Use it to gradually fade a single color or multiple colors. You can choose from the gradients on the default list that comes with Photoshop, and you can create new ones.

If you click the arrow at the upper-right of the Gradient Picker pop-up panel, you will display the Gradient Options pull-down menu. The first group of commands on this menu lets you reset, load, save, or replace gradients. The second group displays different ways of viewing the gradients in the menu, either by thumbnail or by name. At the bottom of the menu is a list of additional premade Photoshop gradients.

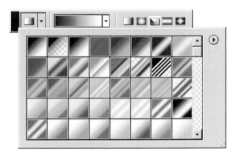

On the Options bar, to the right of the gradient swatch, are icons for the five gradient types, which blend the color in unique ways (as demonstrated in Figure 10.22). Choose one to indicate in what direction you want your gradient built.

| Gradient Type | Effect |
|---|---|
| Linear | Applies a continual gradient over a specified distance from beginning point to end point. |
| Radial | Radiates around a center point to its end point. |
| Angle | Radiates clockwise around a center point. |
| Reflected | Creates two linear gradients on each side of a center point. |
| Diamond | Radiates from a center point into a diamond blend. |

## Making Custom Gradients

Gradient Editor is used to edit existing gradients, or to make new custom gradients and add them to the list. You can also save and load entire gradient palettes from the Gradient Editor or from the Preset Manager.

You can call up the Gradient Editor (Figure 10.23) by clicking the gradient swatch in the Options bar. Click a gradient in the Presets list to select it. The gradient preview bar shows the gradient's colors, their proportional distribution, and the position of any transparency. These characteristics can be edited.

Figure 10.22

**The gradient types**

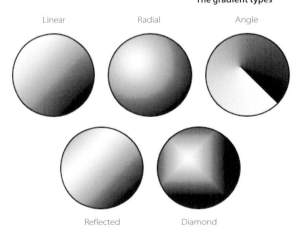

Linear  Radial  Angle

Reflected  Diamond

Figure 10.23

**The Gradient Editor**

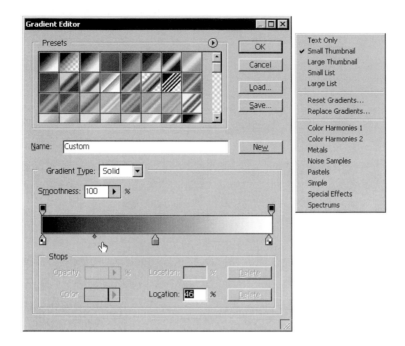

## Editing Gradient Color

The house-shaped markers along the *bottom* of the color bar are *color stops*, and determine where a solid color ends and where a gradient begins. You can assign a color to a color stop by clicking it to highlight it. Move the cursor off the Gradient Editor and onto the image, the Color palette, or the Swatches palette to sample a color. Another method of choosing a color is to double-click the color swatch in the Stops area to display the Color Picker. To redefine a stop's location, drag it left or right, or set a value in the Location field as a percentage of the gradient's length.

The small diamond under the preview bar marks the *midpoint* of the transition between the two colors that are being blended. Move it to redistribute the relative color proportions of the gradient.

To add a color to a gradient, click underneath the preview bar and a new color stop will appear. Determine a color for the color stop, drag the stop into position, and adjust the color's midpoint. To delete a color, drag its color stop off the Gradient Editor.

## Editing Gradient Transparency

The house-shaped markers along the *top* of the gradient preview bar determine where transparency ends and where it begins. To blend transparency into the gradient, click a transparency stop and enter a percentage value in the Opacity field. Drag a stop to determine its location, or enter a number in the Stops area.

If transparency is set anywhere along the gradient, a diamond on top of the preview bar marks the center point of the transparency range. Move the midpoint to redistribute the proportion of transparency in the gradient.

To add a transparent area to a gradient, click above the color bar. Determine an opacity value in the Opacity field, move the stop into position, and adjust its midpoint. To delete a transparency, drag the transparency stop off the Gradient Editor.

## Editing an Existing Gradient

You can edit existing gradients by adding, subtracting or redistributing their colors:

1. Choose the Gradient tool and click the gradient swatch on the Options bar to display the Gradient Editor.

2. At the top of the Editor is a list of presets—the gradients that have already been saved. Double-click the gradient you want to edit. The Gradient Name dialog box appears. If desired, enter a new name and click OK.

3. On the preview bar in the Gradient Editor, you see the configuration of color and transparency of the selected gradient as determined by the number and position of the color and transparency stops and the midpoint diamonds. Slide the stops to the left or right to adjust the color or transparency proportions. Slide the midpoint diamonds to adjust the centers of the blend.

4. Add a color by clicking under the preview bar to create a new stop.

5. Double-click the stop to display the Color Picker. Choose a color for the stop and click OK.

6. When satisfied with the edited gradient, click OK to leave the Gradient Editor. The edited gradient now appears in the Options bar.

7. Choose a Gradient tool, click in the image, and drag. Release the mouse to apply the gradient.

## Making a Noise Gradient

The Noise option under Gradient Type in the Gradient Editor adds random colors to a gradient depending on the predefined colors you choose. The results can be somewhat unpredictable, so experiment to achieve the best results.

To create a noise gradient:

1. In the Gradient Editor, under Gradient Type, choose Noise, as shown in Figure 10.24.

2. For Roughness, choose or enter a percentage. This will determine the strength of the noise.

Figure 10.24

**Choosing the Noise type in the Gradient Editor dialog**

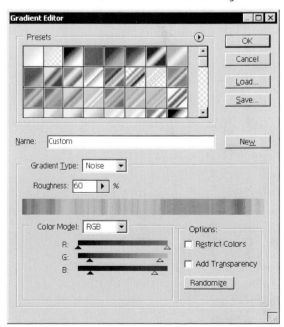

3. Choose a color mode or model—RGB, HSB, or Lab. The effect will vary significantly with each system.

4. Check Restrict Colors to prevent oversaturation.

5. Check Add Transparency to create a transparent gradient.

6. Click Randomize to preview variations of the effect.

### Creating a New Gradient

Follow these steps to make your own gradient:

1. Click the gradient swatch on the Options bar to display the Gradient Editor.

2. Click the New button. The Name field displays the name of the currently selected gradient, and the preview bar displays its properties.

3. Enter a name for the new gradient. It's easy to be thrown by the fact that the name and properties of the new gradient are the same as the current gradient. It's important to change the name immediately to avoid confusion.

4. Target each of the color or transparency stops and change their colors and locations as described under "Editing an Existing Gradient," earlier in this chapter.

5. Add color or transparency stops if desired by clicking under or over the preview bar.

6. Click OK to finalize the gradient and to select it into the gradient swatch.

## Applying Gradients

All gradients are applied over a specified distance (see Figure 10.25). You choose the Gradient tool, click the image where you want the gradient to start, and drag in the desired direction. Release the mouse where you want the gradient to end. You will fill a selection if one is active, or the entire Background or layer if no selection is active. The distribution of the gradient depends on its color content and the positions of the stops, but just as important are the placement of the cursor and the length and direction you drag on the image.

Press Shift while dragging to constrain the gradient to a vertical, horizontal, or 45-degree angle.

## Creating Patterns

You can fill a selection with a repeating pattern. A pattern can be any image contained within a rectangle, or *tile*, that defines its top, bottom, left, and right edges.

To create a pattern in Photoshop:

1. Select an area on an image using the rectangular marquee.

2. Choose Edit → Define Pattern.

   The rectangular marquee must have a feather radius of zero pixels. In other words, it cannot have a feathered edge. It can, however, have an anti-aliased edge. If you select an area on the image and you find that the Define Pattern command is grayed out in the Edit menu, check the rectangular marquee's Options bar to be sure that the Feather Radius reads 0 px.

3. If you look in Edit → Preset Manager → Preset Type → Patterns, you'll see that the pattern has been added to the list.

   You apply patterns to the image with the Pattern Stamp, the Fill command, the Paint Bucket, the Healing Brush, and the Patch tool or as a Pattern Fill layer (see the sections on these features elsewhere in this chapter).

# Filling and Outlining

You may find it difficult or time-consuming to paint large areas of the image and impossible to paint the outline of a shape. Photoshop provides several alternatives that automatically perform these tasks.

### The Fill Command

Filling an area changes its pixels to a designated color:

1. Before an area can be filled, it must first be selected. Make an accurate selection with any of the selection tools to define the area. If the selection is feathered, the area that is filled will have a soft edge.

2. Choose Edit → Fill. The Fill dialog box is displayed (Figure 10.26).

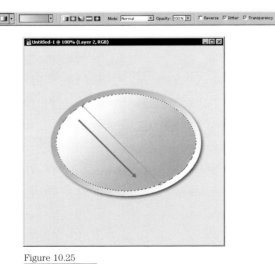

Figure 10.25

**Applying a gradient includes choosing its direction.**

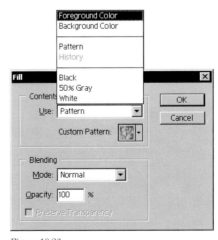

Figure 10.26

**The Fill dialog box**

3. From the Use pop-up list, choose a color or method to fill your selection:

| Color or Method | Effect |
| --- | --- |
| Foreground Color | Fills the selected area with 100% of the current foreground color |
| Background Color | Fills the selected area with 100% of the current background color |
| Pattern | Fills the selected area with a pattern chosen from the Pattern menu |
| History | Fills the selected area with a selected state in the History palette (see Chapter 11) |
| Black | Fills the selected area with 100% black or an RGB value of 0 red, 0 green, 0 blue |
| 50% Gray | Fills the selected area with 50% black; an RGB value of 128 red, 128 green, 128 blue; or HSB values of 0 h, 0 s, 50 b |
| White | Fills the selected area with 0% black or an RGB value of 255 red, 255 green, 255 blue |

4. Choose a blending mode and opacity. (See Appendix C for details on blending modes.)

5. If you are filling a layer, you can choose to preserve the transparent areas and fill only the areas that contain pixels by checking the Preserve Transparency box.

6. Click OK.

A fast method of filling an area with 100% of the foreground color is to press Option-Delete/Alt-Backspace. To fill an area selected on the Background with 100% of the background color, press Delete or Backspace.

### The Paint Bucket (G)

The Paint Bucket tool works like a combination of the Magic Wand tool and the Fill command, in that it will fill an area with color based on the tolerance, or range of color, of the target pixels.

To fill with the Paint Bucket:

1. Expand the Gradient tool in the Tool palette and choose the Paint Bucket.

2. In the Options bar, choose the type of fill—either the foreground color or a pattern. If filling with a color, choose a foreground color from the Color palette, Swatches palette, or Color Picker.

3. Set the blending mode and opacity for the fill.

4. Set the tolerance to determine the range of adjacent pixels to be colored. Higher tolerances color a wider range of pixels.

5. If you want only adjacent pixels to be colored, check the Contiguous box. If the box is not checked, all of the pixels within the tolerance on a targeted layer will be affected.

6. Check the Anti-Aliased box if you want the fill to extend into the edge pixels of the selection or image.

7. Check the All Layers box if you want the tolerance measured and the fill applied through multiple layers.

8. Place your cursor on the area you want to affect, and click your mouse.

## Using Fill Layers

Another unique method for filling an area is using a Fill layer. Fill layers are more dynamic than the traditional methods of filling large areas of color, because they combine the potential of the Fill command with the flexibility of layers. You can create Fill layers with solid colors, gradients, or patterns (Figure 10.27).

> See Chapter 7, "Layering Your Image," and Chapter 22, "Advanced Layer Techniques," for more on how to manipulate Fill layers.

### Creating a Solid Color Fill Layer

Follow these steps to create a Solid Color Fill layer:

1. Choose Layer → New Fill Layer → Solid Color.

2. The New Layer dialog box appears, with the layer named Color Fill 1 by default. Enter a name for the layer to better identify it and click OK.

   As with any layer, you can group the Fill layer with the one immediately above it, forming a clipping group. Choose a color from the list if you want to color-code it, then choose an opacity setting and a blending mode.

3. The Color Picker is displayed. Choose a color and click OK.

4. The new layer that appears in the Layers palette has a layer mask linked to it and is represented by the thumbnail to the left of the layer name. A layer mask enables you to conceal portions of the image by painting on it.

> If you make a selection prior to creating a Fill layer, the new Fill layer will fill only the selected area and create a layer mask that conceals the unselected areas. The layer mask thumbnail that appears in the Layers palette displays the revealed area as a white shape and the masked area as a black border.

Figure 10.27

Solid Color, Gradient, and Pattern Fill layers (top to bottom)

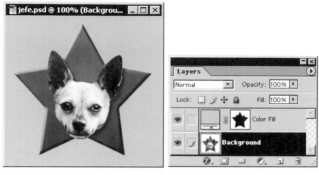

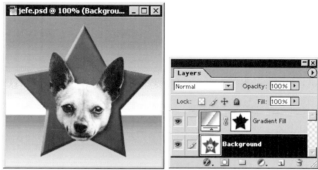

## Creating a Gradient Fill Layer

To create a Gradient Fill layer:

1. Choose Layer → New Fill Layer → Gradient.

2. The New Layer dialog box appears. The name of the new layer defaults to Gradient Fill 1. Enter a name for the layer to better identify it. Click OK; the Gradient Fill dialog box appears (see Figure 10.28).

3. The colors of the gradient default to the last gradient chosen. If you want a gradient other than the one presented, click the down arrow to the right of the gradient swatch to choose a saved gradient, or click the swatch itself to display the Gradient Editor and create a new one. In the Gradient Fill dialog, set the following specifications:

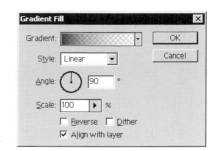

Figure 10.28

**The Gradient Fill dialog**

**Style** Choose a gradient type from the Style pop-up list.

**Angle** Enter a number, or click the diagram, to choose an angle to control the direction of the gradient.

**Scale** Choose a scale, by clicking on the arrow and moving the slider or by entering a value, to control the gradient's relative distribution over an area.

**Reverse** Check Reverse to flip the gradient's direction over the entire layer.

**Dither** Check Dither to soften the blending of the gradient. Dithering may help prevent banding that sometimes occurs when the Gradient is printed.

**Align With Layer** If the gradient is contained within a selection, check Align With Layer to distribute the gradient within the selection; not checking this box distributes it over the entire layer but reveals only the selected portion.

4. Click OK to fill the layer.

## Creating a Pattern Fill Layer

A pattern chosen from the Pattern presets can be applied to a layer in the same way a Solid Fill or a Gradient Fill can:

1. Choose Layer → New Fill Layer → Pattern.

2. The New Layer dialog box appears, with the layer named Pattern Fill 1 by default. Enter a name for the layer to better identify it and click OK; the Pattern Fill dialog box appears (see Figure 10.29).

3. Click the down arrow to choose a pattern, and set the following options:

**Scale** Choose a percentage to determine the size of the pattern.

**Snap To Origin** You can move the pattern by placing your cursor on it on the image window, or you can snap it back to its origin by clicking the Snap To Origin button.

Figure 10.29

**The Pattern Fill dialog**

**Link With Layer** Checking this box aligns the pattern's layer mask to the layer.

**Create A New Preset From This Pattern** Click the small document icon to save the pattern to the Presets.

Once they have been created, Color Fill, Gradient Fill, and Pattern Fill layers can be edited by double-clicking their thumbnails in the Layers palette to reveal the Color Picker, the Gradient Fill dialog, or the Pattern Fill dialog, respectively. Unlike regular layers filled with pixels, these dynamic effects will resize if the canvas is resized.

## Outlining with the Stroke Command

The Stroke command in Photoshop outlines a selection border with a color. Strokes can vary in width and relative position on the selection border, as you can see in Figure 10.30. A feathered selection will soften the edge of the stroke.

To apply a stroke to a selection:

1. Make a selection with any of the selection tools.

2. Choose a foreground color.

3. Choose Edit → Stroke. The Stroke dialog box appears (Figure 10.31).

4. Set the following attributes:

    **Width** Enter a value in pixels, between 1 and 250, for the stroke width.

    **Color** Click the swatch to reveal the Color Picker. Choose a stroke color and click OK.

    **Location** The Inside option places the stroke on the inside of the selection outline; Center centers the stroke between the inside and the outside of the selection outline; and Outside places the stroke on the outside of the selection outline.

    **Blending Mode** Choose a blending mode from the pop-up list to affect the relationship of the color that is being applied to the existing colors on the image. (See Appendix C.)

Figure 10.30

**You can position your stroke in different places relative to the selection.**

Stroke Inside

Stroke Center

Stroke Outside

Feathered

**Opacity**  Set the opacity from 1% to 100%.

**Preserve Transparency**  If the image is on a layer surrounded by transparency, checking the Preserve Transparency option will prevent the transparent area from being stroked. Depending on selection and stroke location, if you place the stroke on the outside of a selection on a transparent layer, and you choose this option, you may not see any results.

5. Click OK to apply the stroke.

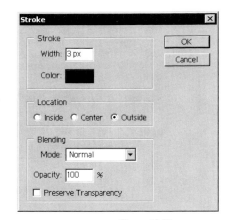

Figure 10.31

**The Stroke dialog box**

# CHAPTER 11

# Altered States: History

*As we've seen* in previous chapters, the application of such fundamental procedures as using layers during the editing process helps to keep an image dynamic. As you work, you can make changes to the image, or even just a portion of the image, one step at a time, until the results are satisfactory. In this chapter, we'll examine Photoshop's capability to take a step backward as well as forward. In this respect, I like to think of Photoshop as the "bachelor's software": you *never have to make a commitment*—that is, until you finally settle down and publish your work.

Photoshop takes the concept of bachelor's software to the max with the extreme flexibility of its History palette. The History palette is Photoshop's answer to the concept of multiple undos. Where some programs provide a system of undoing operations backwards in sequence, Photoshop's interactive History palette features both sequential and nonlinear editing.

This chapter explores Photoshop's undo and history features. In addition, Hands On 3, "Painting, Paths, and History," immediately following this chapter, will put you through the moves using the information covered in Chapters 9, 10, and 11 on history, paths, and painting.

In this chapter, you'll learn about:

- **Undoing what you've done**

- **Photoshop's Time Machine**

- **Working with snapshots**

- **Editing history**

# Undoing What You've Done

Even the most accident-prone among us will find that it's almost impossible to do any *permanent* damage while working in Photoshop, because Photoshop can instantly undo errors. You never have to compromise, because you can reverse any operation. With this in mind, you can feel secure while experimenting freely with your images.

## The Undo Commands

There are several techniques that reverse unwanted edits. Let's say you are carefully cloning out the blemishes on Uncle Herman's portrait. You've had one too many double espressos, and your hand is a bit jittery. You slip, you drag a little too far, and you place a rather unsightly blotch on the tip of his nose.

An easily corrected mistake? Yes! The first course of action is to head straight to the top of the Edit menu and select Undo, which will instantly revert the image to the moment before you made the ill-fated clone stroke. When you order Undo, you get a new command on the Edit menu—Redo—which restores the undone action. You can toggle back and forth between the previous artwork (Undo) and the later look (Redo) by selecting the command again, or better yet, use the key commands in the list below.

There are two additional commands in the Edit menu that apply to the Undo operations:

**Step Backward**  This undoes the last command and then continues backward through the operations you've performed, undoing them one at a time. As the operations are undone, you see them disappear one by one in the image window.

**Step Forward**  If you've applied the Step Backward command more than once, you can restore the undone operations by choosing Edit → Step Forward. As the operations are redone, you see them appear one by one in the image window.

As you apply them, the Step Backward and Step Forward commands move one by one through the state list in the History palette. See "The History Palette" later in this chapter.

You'll use these operations so frequently that it's worth remembering their corresponding key commands:

| Command | Windows | Macintosh |
|---|---|---|
| Undo | Ctrl-Z | ⌘-Z |
| Step Backward | Ctrl-Alt-Z | ⌘-Option-Z |
| Step Forward | Shift-Ctrl-Z | Shift-⌘-Z |

By default, Ctrl/⌘-Z will toggle between Undo and Redo in Photoshop, although in ImageReady (see Chapter 25, "Web Design with Photoshop and ImageReady"), the default command for Redo is Ctrl/⌘-Shift-Z. Recall from Chapter 5, "Setting Up the Program," that you can change the key command preference for Redo in both programs via Edit → Preferences → General.

## Begin Again

Another lifesaving operation reverts the image to the last time you saved it. Suppose you've been working on an image for ten minutes since your last save, and you decide that somewhere along the line you went astray and the image is not going in the direction you want it to. You have gone too far to make corrections, so you decide you want to begin again. Choose File → Revert, and the image will be reopened to the last saved version.

If you are working on a newly formed image that has not yet been saved, the Revert command will be grayed out in the File menu.

# Photoshop's Time Machine

The *history* of a Photoshop image is simply a record of work that has been performed on it. Photoshop automatically records every edit, operation, or technique that you apply to an image. As you work, each event, called a *state*—whether it's a paint stroke, filter, color correction, or any other operation—is listed in the History palette (Figure 11.1). You can target a specific state on the list and display its contents in the image window. Like riding in an H.G. Wells time machine, you can freely move through the history of the document, alter states, and in so doing affect the outcome of the final image.

The History states are not layers. They do not contain isolated parts of the image per se. Rather, each state is a record of how the image looked after a specific tool or operation was applied to it. The history is exclusively a record of the changes to the image during the current work session. Once the image is closed, the history is wiped clean, and when you reopen the document, the history begins again. The history cannot be saved or transferred to another image. Program changes to preferences, palettes, color settings, and Actions are not recorded.

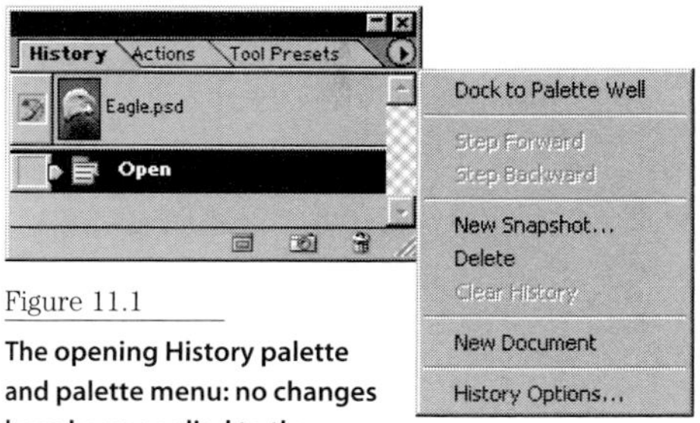

**Figure 11.1**

The opening History palette and palette menu: no changes have been applied to the image yet.

## The History Palette

The recorder for all of the states is the History palette, which you access by choosing Window → History. By default, when the image is opened, the History palette displays a snapshot of the image as it appeared when it was last saved. It is from this point on where you will make changes to the image. Each time you perform an operation, the History palette

Figure 11.2

**The History palette after a few operations**

produces a state with the name of the operation or tool that was used—for example, Brush Tool, Levels, Smudge Tool, etc. The most recent state is at the bottom of the History stack; note that in Figure 11.2, the act of opening the document appears at the top. The higher the state appears in the stack, the earlier in the process the state was created.

## Changing History

They say you can't change history, but in fact, you can. If you want to move backward in time and see a previous state, click it in the History palette. The image window will display the image as it was during the targeted state. All states below it in the History palette are grayed out.

> Be careful! If you work on the image with a state targeted earlier than the most recent, all states below it will be deleted. You can still use the Undo and Step Backward features to get back to where you were, but you would lose all your new work.

For example, if you paint a brush stroke with the Brush tool while an earlier state is targeted, all states below it will be replaced by the state called Brush Tool. Later I'll show you how to avoid this by using the Non-Linear History option.

## Increasing History States

What allows Photoshop to remember all of the History states is, of course, memory. Each state is stored in your computer's RAM or on the scratch disk. When you exceed the current limit on states, the oldest state is deleted to make room for the most recent state. The number of History states is limited to 20 by default. You can increase or decrease the default number of History states by selecting Edit → Preferences → General → History States and entering a number from 1 to 1000.

Specifying an excessive number of History states earmarks memory for the History cache and takes the allocation away from Photoshop's other operations. This could compromise Photoshop's performance. Whenever possible, keep the number of states at the default.

## Looking at History Options

You can change the behavior of the history by checking options in the History Options window. In the History Palette pull-down menu, choose History Options to view or change these settings (see Figure 11.3):

**Automatically Create First Snapshot**  Produces a snapshot of the original image upon opening it and places its thumbnail at the top of the History palette (see the next section, "Working with Snapshots").

**Automatically Create New Snapshot When Saving**  Generates a snapshot of the current state when saving and adds its thumbnail to the top of the History palette.

**Allow Non-Linear History** Allows you to discard or edit a previous History state without deleting more recent states.

**Show New Snapshot Dialog By Default** Automatically displays the Snapshot dialog box when a new snapshot is created, prompting you to name the snapshots as they are made.

Figure 11.3

**Use this window to change the behavior of the history**

# Working with Snapshots

At any point in time, you can save the current image to a snapshot (see Figure 11.4). By saving a snapshot, you can explicitly preserve various states of the image. Snapshots don't count toward the History state limit; they're saved—period—and you don't have to worry about that state being discarded when the limit is exceeded. But of course, they use up memory and, like the rest of the history, are discarded when the file is closed.

Figure 11.4

**The History palette with a snapshot**

## Saving Snapshots

Click the History Palette pull-down menu and choose New Snapshot. The dialog box that appears allows you to name the snapshot and determine which combination of layers the snapshot will be made from.

**Full Document** Makes a snapshot of all the visible layers and the Background.

**Merged Layers** Makes a snapshot of all the layers and merges them into one layer.

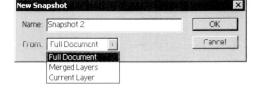

**Current Layer** Makes a snapshot of the currently targeted layer.

A fast way to make a snapshot is to target a History state and click the Create New Snapshot icon 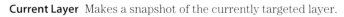 at the bottom of the History palette. By default, it will be given a name based on the snapshot number (Snapshot 1, Snapshot 2, etc.). To rename it, simply double-click the name in the palette and type in a new one.

## Saving a Snapshot As a New Document

If you want to work on multiple versions of an image or preserve it in a particular state, you can save a snapshot as a new document.

1. Save the History state as a snapshot.

2. Target the snapshot in the History palette and choose New Document from the pull-down menu.

3. Choose File → Save As and save the document to a location on your disk.

You can quickly make a new document from a snapshot by dragging the state to the Create New Document From Current State icon ▣ .

### Deleting Snapshots

When you no longer need your snapshots, you can discard them. Here are several ways to do it.

- Drag the snapshot to the trash icon in the lower-right corner of the History palette.

- Click the snapshot and choose Delete from the History Palette pull-down menu.

- Click the snapshot and then click the trash icon.

## Editing History States

The primary purpose of Photoshop's history is to keep the editing process dynamic. There are several ways to use the History palette to keep the workflow flexible so that you can experiment freely and confidently.

For all history operations, to target a state, click it in the History palette.

### Deleting History States

Sometimes you'll want to delete a state. Try any of these commands:

- Drag the state to the trash icon at the bottom of the History palette.

- Target the state, and then choose Delete from the palette's pull-down menu or click the trash icon.

- Target a state. All states beneath it will be grayed out. Perform an edit to the state and the grayed-out states will be purged.

- Choose Clear History from the palette's menu to clear all of the states except the last state. Clearing the history retains the snapshots.

- Choose Edit → Purge → Histories. All the states but the one at the bottom of the list will be deleted. This option cannot be undone. The snapshots are retained.

### Non-Linear History

If you delete a state, then by default, you'll also eliminate all of the more recent states (those underneath it in the palette). You can, however, change this default. From the History Palette pull-down menu, choose History Options and check Allow Non-Linear History.

The Allow Non-Linear History option gives you the ability to eliminate or edit a state in the History palette and still preserve all of the states below it in the stack. For example, you can target a state, make changes to it, save the altered state as a snapshot, target the most recent state, and continue working on the image. Experiment carefully with this option, because you can produce strange and unexpected results.

## The History Brush

The History Brush tool ![icon] enables you to paint with a chosen state. You can use the History Brush to re-establish portions of a state even if you've edited them later on. The Source column at the far left of the History palette tells Photoshop which state you want to paint with.

For example, suppose you paint a brush stroke on an image. As you continue to work, each time you perform an operation, a new state is added. If you later decide that you only want to retain half of that original brush stroke, here's how to do it:

1. Open the History palette.

2. Look through the states from bottom to top in sequence, until you find the state where you made the brush stroke.

3. Click the Source column to the left of the previous state, just above the state with the brush stroke. A History Brush icon appears in that column.

   By choosing the state previous to the brush stroke as the Source, you are telling the History palette that this is what you are going to want the corrected portions of the image to look like. You are actually painting with the previous state in order to eliminate a portion of the brush stroke.

4. Choose the History Brush from the Tool palette and retarget the most recent state.

   If the Allow Non-Linear History option is not selected, you must target the last state in the history if you want to avoid losing the intervening states.

5. Paint over the portion of the brush stroke you want to cover up with the chosen previous state.

## Painting with a Snapshot

You can use a snapshot in a similar manner when using the History Brush. Suppose you take a snapshot of an edit you made with a filter. After undoing the filter or eliminating its state, you can selectively apply the snapshot to specific portions of the image. If you save the snapshot as the full document or a single layer, the History Brush will paint from one layer to the corresponding layer on the targeted state. (The color section of the book includes a demonstration of painting with the History Brush. See Figures C11a–c.)

To paint with a snapshot:

1. Apply a filter, brush stroke, color adjustment, or any other effect to an image.

2. Choose Make Snapshot from the History Palette pull-down menu.

3. Choose Edit → Undo to undo the effect.

4. Click the Source column next to the new snapshot.

5. Choose the History Brush from the Tool palette. Choose a brush size and specify opacity and other brush characteristics in the Options bar.

6. Paint on the areas of the image that you want to affect.

## Other History-Editing Features

There are a couple of history-editing features scattered throughout the program that you should be aware of:

**The Eraser Tool**  With the Erase to History option selected, the Eraser tool erases to a designated History state. You must designate the History state by clicking the Source column in the History palette next to the state you wish to erase to.

**Fill from History**  Choose Edit → Fill → Use History to fill a selected area with a designated state. You must designate the History state by clicking the Source column in the History palette next to the state you wish to fill with.

## The Art History Brush

This tool is called the Art History Brush ![icon], because it's quite handy for creating instant Impressionist effects (Impressionism being an important movement in the history of art). And I mention it here only because it is in the History Brush fly-out on the Tool palette. But it does not use the history to alter the image as the History Brush does, except, like any other tool or operation, its effects are recorded as a state each time you apply it. (See Chapter 10, "Creating and Applying Color," for a complete description of the Art History Brush tool and a demonstration of what it can do.)

# Painting, Paths, and History

*When working on an image* in Photoshop, we almost never use just one particular tool or technique exclusively. In nearly every real-world project, we draw upon the array of tools available. In this lesson, you'll combine many of the basic tools and techniques introduced in Chapters 9, 10, and 11—painting colors, working with paths, and using the History palette—to create a virtual *painting* from a basic line-art image.

## Getting Started

To ensure that your settings match the settings shown in this Hands On exercise, you may wish to hide your preferences file before beginning, and then restart Photoshop to create a clean version. The section titled "Modifying Photoshop's Settings" in Chapter 5 details how to temporarily reset your preferences to Photoshop's defaults. You can restore your customized, personal settings when you're done.

Once you've launched Photoshop with default preferences, you are ready to begin the Hands On project. Figure H3.1 shows the drawing you'll start with, and Figure H3.2 shows the finished version. (You can get a better preview of it by opening the `Seahorse_end.tif` file in the H03 folder on the CD.) See also Figures C44 and C45 in the color section for the beginning and completed seahorse images.

Take these steps to begin:

1. Insert the *Photoshop 7 Savvy* CD into your CD-ROM drive.

2. From the H03 folder on the CD, open the file `Seahorse_begin.psd` (see Figure H3.1).

3. Choose File → Save and save the file to your disk.

You'll notice by looking in the Layers palette of the `Seahorse_begin.psd` file that there is a Background with four layers above it. The layers labeled Plantlife, Painting, and Extras are empty, while the Outline layer contains the basic seahorse shape.

You will work on each of the different layers during the exercise, but it is important to keep them in their original stacking order throughout the editing process.

## Painting the Main Character

We'll start the first portion of the lesson by selecting our central character—the seahorse—and then make use of several of the painting tools to color, shade, highlight, and texturize the skin within the selected area. Once this process is completed, the Path tools will be used to create an eye.

### Selecting the Painting Area

To begin the project, you'll use a selection tool to select the outer areas, and then invert it to select the seahorse.

1. Target the Outline layer.

2. Click the Magic Wand tool ![icon] to activate it. In the Options bar, check to make sure the tolerance is set to 32, with the Anti-aliased and Contiguous boxes both checked.

3. In the image window, click once in the white area outside the seahorse outline.

4. Hold down the Shift key to add to the selection (or click the Add To Selection button in the Options bar), and click inside the small circular area created by the curl of the seahorse's tail. All image areas outside the outline are now selected, as evidenced by the "marching ants" of the selection marquee.

Figure H3.1

**The project begins with a simple line-art image.**

Figure H3.2

**Our line-art character will develop a bit more personality after a Photoshop paint job.**

5. Invert the selection via Select → Inverse (use Shift-⌘-I for Macintosh and Shift-Ctrl-I for Windows) so that the seahorse, rather than the outer area, is now selected.

6. The marching ants could prove to be a bit distracting in this project, but you can hide them from view by choosing View → Show → Selection Edges, and clicking to clear the option.

## Painting the Base Color

Now that the area is selected, the next course of action includes choosing a base color and using the Paint Bucket tool to apply it.

1. Target the Painting layer.

2. Choose Window → Swatches, and click the Pastel Green Cyan color in the Swatches palette to set it as the foreground color. (This was my color choice, but feel free to make your seahorse any color you like.)

3. Activate the Paint Bucket tool ; make sure the Fill choice in the Options bar is set to Foreground, and click inside the seahorse to fill it with color (see Figure H3.3). Even though the marching ants are hidden from view, the selection is still active, so you don't have to worry about staying within the lines.

Figure H3.3

**The coloring process begins by filling the selected area in the Painting layer with a base color.**

## Shading and Highlighting

To add shading and highlights, we could use darker and lighter shades of the same color, but we'll take a shortcut and simply utilize some of Photoshop's specialty painting tools to achieve the desired look.

1. Activate the Burn tool and choose a medium soft brush, such as Soft Round with a size of 17 pixels. While still on the Painting layer, paint along the seahorse outline, and then along and just below each body ridgeline to give those ridges a bit of depth by shading. Switch to a smaller soft brush to shade the smaller areas, such as the ridges along the tip of the tail. See the first part of Figure H3.4 for an example of the shading process.

2. Activate the Dodge tool  now, and once again choosing the 17-pixel Soft Round brush, paint just above the body ridges and inside the larger areas to add highlighting (see the second part of Figure H3.4). Paint inside the inner part of the eye area until it becomes very light, almost white. Just as before, switch to a smaller soft brush to perform the more detailed work in the smaller areas.

3. Activate the Sponge tool. In the Options bar, set the mode to Saturate and the flow rate to 15%; then click the Airbrush icon to enable the airbrush capabilities. As you learned in Chapter 10, "Creating and Applying Color," the Airbrush option provides the ability to build up an effect just as a real airbrush would do. Choose a 27-pixel Soft Round brush, and then sweep the Sponge tool over any of the lighter areas that you wish to brighten up with more saturated color, holding it in place longer in areas you wish to make more colorful, such as the fins and "mane" of the seahorse.

4. To blend the shaded and highlighted areas, activate the Blur tool, and choose a medium soft brush. Make a quick pass over the entire seahorse. The Blur tool's effect can be very subtle, but you'll notice that it does help to achieve a smoother transition between the different shades.

Reminder: Any time you make a mistake or simply don't like the result of an operation, click a step back in the History palette to restore the image to a previous state.

Figure FH3.4

**The Burn (left) and Dodge (right) tools make easy work of shading and highlighting.**

## Adding a Texture with the History Brush

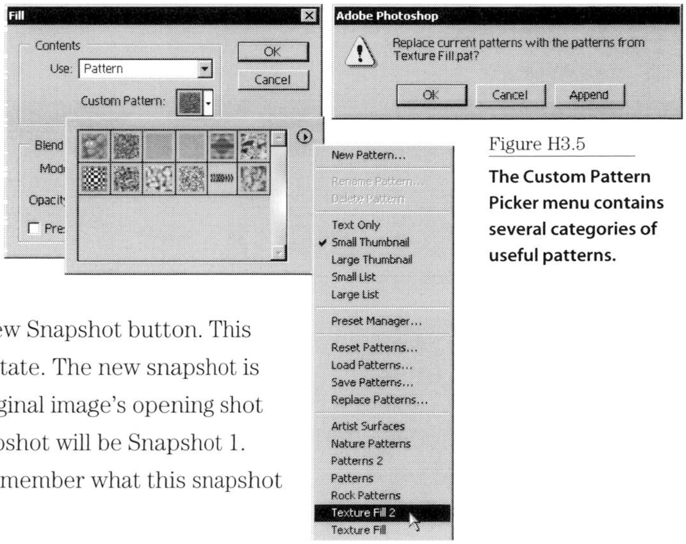

Your seahorse now has the basic coloring in place, along with flawlessly smooth skin. But since smooth skin is generally not characteristic of seahorses, you'll remedy the situation by using a combination of snapshots, a pattern fill, and the History Brush tool to give the skin a textured appearance.

1. In the History palette ⬚ , click the Create New Snapshot button. This creates a snapshot of the image in the current state. The new snapshot is located in the History palette just below the original image's opening shot (`Seahorse_begin.psd`). By default, the new snapshot will be Snapshot 1. Change this name to Smooth Skin so you will remember what this snapshot contains and can find it later.

2. Go to Edit → Fill and, in the drop-down menu under Contents To Use, choose Pattern. Click the Custom Pattern Picker to open the pattern window, and use the button to bring up the menu list (see Figure H3.5). Click Texture Fill 2 to load the texture patterns. This brings up a pop-up window asking if you want to replace the current patterns with the Texture Fill 2 patterns; click OK.

3. Once the Texture Fill 2 patterns are loaded, they will appear in the Pattern Picker window. Choose the pattern called Shingles (which happens to be the first one), and click OK. Your seahorse will be entirely filled with the texture, as in Figure H3.6.

4. In the History palette, click the Create New Snapshot button to create a snapshot of the image now filled with texture, and name it Skin Texture.

5. Click in the Source column next to the Skin Texture snapshot to set it as the source for the History Brush tool. The History Brush icon will appear in the column.

6. Target the Smooth Skin snapshot (see Figure H3.7). Once you do, you will no longer be able to see the texture in the actual image.

**Figure H3.5**

The Custom Pattern Picker menu contains several categories of useful patterns.

**Figure H3.6**

The skin-texturing procedure begins by filling with a texture pattern.

Figure H3.7

**Targeting the Smooth
Skin snapshot**

7. Activate the History Brush  . Choose a medium-size soft brush. Set the mode to Overlay so that when the texture is applied with the brush, it will overlay the color of the seahorse, blending it rather than just painting in the grayscale texture. Set the opacity to 50%.

8. Paint the texture into the body of the seahorse, as in Figure H3.8. Switch to a smaller brush size to paint the more detailed areas, such as the face, tail, and fin.

> Even when you're painting from a snapshot with the History Brush, you can still use the History palette as usual to go back a step if you make a mistake.

## Softening the Outline

Now that you've completed the skin coloring and texturing, you'll move on to the finer details, such as giving the black outline a somewhat less harsh appearance.

1. Target the Outline layer.

2. Activate the Smudge tool  , and choose the 9-pixel Soft Round brush, Normal Mode, and Strength at 50%.

3. You may wish to use your Zoom tool  to zero in on specific areas for the smudging process. Begin by going along the perimeter of the seahorse outline with the Smudge tool. This will smudge the harshness of the drawn lines into a softer, more painted appearance, so that the lines become more like shading. Remember, you still have the selection around the seahorse (although you have the marching ants hidden from view), so you will stay within the lines while working on the Outline layer, just as you did on the Painting layer.

4. After you've made your way around the perimeter, begin smudging the lines inside the body area. If you feel the lines are a bit too smudgy, take a few steps back by way of the History palette, and then turn down the Strength in the Options bar, or switch to a smaller brush before continuing. Don't worry about keeping the lines perfect, though— this is the fun part where you can reshape, smear, and blend them to your heart's desire. See Figure H3.9.

5. Once you've completed the outline softening process, you will no longer want to keep the area selected, so use Select → Deselect (⌘/Ctrl-D) to remove the selection.

> If you've had to close and reopen your image at any time during the lesson, your selection will have been disabled, and you'll need to reselect the seahorse just as you did in the first part of the project. In Chapter 12, "Using Alpha Channels and Quick Mask," you'll learn to save selections in your image as alpha channels.

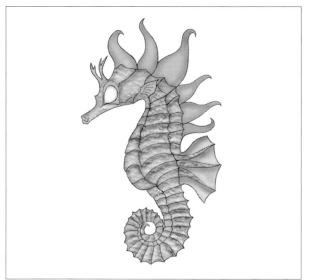

Figure H3.8

**By using the History Brush to apply the texture from a snapshot, you can be choosy about which areas to texturize.**

Figure H3.9

**The seahorse outline takes on a softer blended appearance after a session with the Smudge tool.**

## Using a Path to Shape the Eye

To complete the seahorse portion of your image, you'll employ the Path tools to create an unusually shaped, cartoon-style eye. (See Figure H3.10 for a visual step-by-step of the eye creation.)

1. Target the layer labeled Extras.

2. Zoom in on the eye area.

3. Activate the Ellipse tool ![icon], and set it to Paths in the Options bar (see Figure H3.11).

4. Place an ellipse in your image, approximately as large as the white of the eye area (Figure H3.10, square A).

5. Go to Edit → Transform Path → Rotate, type **125** into the Set Rotation area in the Options bar (see Figure H3.12), and click the Commit Transform button (Figure H3.10, square B).

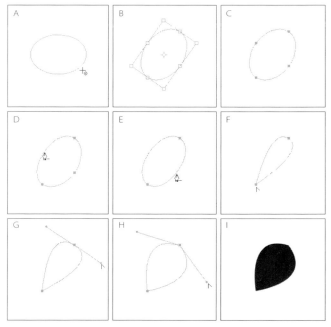

Figure H3.10

**The eye is formed with the Ellipse tool in Path mode, and then manipulated to the desired shape before filling with color.**

6. Activate the Path Selection tool ▶ . Click inside the path to select it (Figure H3.10, square C), and then drag the path to the eye area, placing it directly over the white of the eye.

7. Activate the Delete Anchor Point tool ✍ , click on the point in the upper-left side of the path to delete it (Figure H3.10, square D), and then click on the lower-right point to delete it as well, leaving a sort of egg shape (Figure H3.10, square E).

8. Activate the Convert Point tool ⌐ , and click the lower-left point to convert it to a corner point (Figure H3.10, square F).

9. For the upper-right point, click and drag the handle toward the lower right to bring the shape into something like an upside-down teardrop (Figure H3.10, square G). After that, use the handles one at a time to shape the path similarly to the line around the white of the eye (Figure H3.10, square H).

10. If necessary, use the Path Selection tool again and drag the path to the proper positioning. You'll want the path to be just a tad smaller than the white part. If it is too large or small, go to Edit ➔ Transform ➔ Scale, and use the resulting bounding box to scale to the correct size.

11. Set the foreground and background colors to default black and white by either clicking the tiny black and white swatch in the toolbox or using the keyboard shortcut D.

12. Go to Window ➔ Paths to bring the Paths palette into view. There you will see the work path you just created. Click the menu button in the upper-right corner and choose Fill Path. Under Contents, choose Foreground Color, and click OK to fill the path with the black foreground color (Figure H3.10, square I).

13. Click the palette's menu button again and choose Delete Path.

Figure H3.11

**Setting the Ellipse tool to Paths**

Figure H3.12

**Setting the rotation area**

## Adding Highlights to the Eye Shape

Now that you have the basic black eye shape in place, you'll add highlights to liven it up so that it won't have such a flat appearance (see Figure H3.13).

1. Activate the Pen tool ✍ . Set the option to Paths in the Options bar.

2. Zoom in very closely on the eye shape. With the next few steps, you will create a wedge-shaped path in the upper right portion of the eye.

3. Click to place your first point approximately in the center of the shape.

4. Move the Pen straight up and then slightly off to the right to place the second point at the upper-right outer edge of the eye.

5. Moving down, place two more points along the edge of the eye, each falling just a bit below the last one.

6. Finally, close the path by clicking the point you first placed in the center of the eye.

7. If you feel the wedge is too large or small, go to Edit → Transform → Scale, and use the resulting bounding box to scale to the correct size. If necessary, use the Path Selection tool to drag the path to reposition it.

8. Go to Window → Paths to bring the Paths palette into view. Click the palette menu button and choose Fill Path. Choose White for the fill color and click OK.

9. Click the palette menu button again and choose Delete Path.

10. Activate the Brush tool 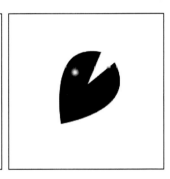 ; set the Foreground color to white in the toolbox, and choose the Soft Round 5-pixel brush. Click once just to the left of the wedge highlight to create a specular highlight.

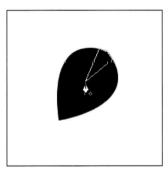  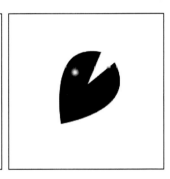

Figure H3.13

**Highlighting the eye shape with the Pen and Brush tools**

# Creating the Background

Now that you have the basic character finished, you'll move on to adding a background environment.

## Applying Color as a Diagonal Gradient

To begin creating the background setting, you'll use the Gradient tool to place the initial colors for the water.

1. Target the Background.

2. Click the foreground color swatch in the toolbox to bring up the Color Picker, and choose a shade of light blue. Choose a medium blue, perhaps with a bit of purple tint, for the background color.

3. Activate the Gradient tool  and choose Linear Gradient in the Options bar. Then open the Gradient Picker in the Options bar and choose Foreground To Background, as in Figure H3.14.

4. Place your cursor in the upper-left corner of the image, click, and drag to the lower-right corner, thereby placing your Linear Gradient at an angle.

Figure H3.14

**Choosing the Foreground To Background option**

## Using a Pattern Fill for the Water

A pattern fill will now be added to give the background a watery quality while still retaining the gradient effect.

1. From the H03 folder on the CD, open the file water.psd.

2. Go to Edit → Define Pattern. The Pattern Name dialog box will pop up for you to name the pattern—keep the default water.psd name, and click OK.

3. Go back to the Seahorse image, and with the Background still targeted, go to Edit → Fill. Choose Pattern as the fill content, and then click the water.psd pattern in the drop-down menu. Fill in 25% for the Opacity value, and click OK.

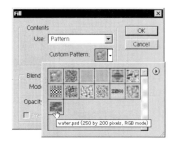

By choosing a reduced opacity for the pattern fill, you permit the gradient background color to partially show through the pattern, as seen in Figure H3.16.

## Forming the Plant Life with Custom Shapes

With the Custom Shape tool, you'll add more details to the image by creating plant life using built in custom shapes.

1. Target the Plantlife layer.

2. Use the Swatches palette to choose dark green as the foreground color.

3. Activate the Custom Shape tool , and choose Fill Pixels from the Options bar.

4. Open the Custom Shapes Picker in the Options bar, click on the menu button, and choose Nature from the menu list to replace the current default shapes with the nature shapes.

5. Scroll to the last row of shapes now showing in the Shapes Picker, and choose Grass 3 (see Figure H3.15).

6. Click and drag a few of the grass shapes into your image, making them different heights and widths for variety.

7. Go back to the Custom Shapes Picker and choose Grass 2 this time. Click and drag a few of these grass shapes into your image, making them different heights and widths, as in Figure H3.17. To add variety, you can choose different green colors for the different grasses.

8. To give the grass some shading quickly and easily, go to Layer → Layer Style → Satin. Leave the default settings in the dialog box, and click OK.

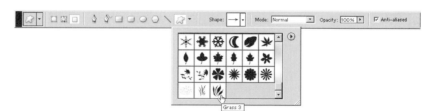

Figure H3.15

**Choosing from the nature shapes**

Figure H3.16

**The water pattern fill over the gradient**

Figure H3.17

**By using Photoshop's built-in custom shapes, we add plant life to the waterscape instantly.**

## Using a Pattern Fill Layer to Build Up the Water

To add more of a motion effect to the water, let's utilize the Scale option in a Pattern Fill layer:

1. With the Plantlife layer still targeted, choose Layer → New Fill Layer → Pattern.

2. In the resulting dialog box, name the pattern **Water**, set the blending mode to Soft Light and the Opacity to 75, and click OK (see Figure H3.18).

3. In the Pattern Fill dialog box, choose the water pattern you used previously (water.psd). By using a Pattern Fill layer, you can scale the pattern to a different size—use the slider to scale it up to around 155% (see Figure H3.19).

The Pattern Fill layer enables the water pattern to not only blend with the water below it, but to give the impression of water flowing over the plants (See Figure H3.20).

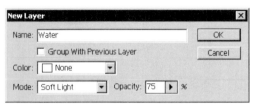

Figure H3.18

Use the New Layer dialog box to set the water's blending mode and opacity.

Figure H3.19

Use the Pattern Fill dialog box to scale the pattern to a different size

Figure H3.20

**A Pattern Fill layer intensifies the water effect.**

## Creating and Cloning the Bubbles

To complete the background environment, you'll use the Gradient tool in a selected area to form a few bubbles in the water.

1. Target the Extras layer.

2. Activate the Elliptical Marquee tool and create a circular selection in the upper-left portion of your image. Don't worry if it's not exactly a perfect circle, but make it fairly close to circular.

3. Set the foreground color to black.

4. Activate the Gradient tool . In the Options bar, use the Gradient Picker to choose Foreground To Transparent. Set the Gradient as Radial, and place a check mark in the Reverse box, as shown in Figure H3.21.

Figure H3.21

**Choosing the Foreground To Transparent option**

5. Click in the lower-right portion of the selection just a short way from the edge, and move up toward the upper left until you've gone a bit past the outer edge of the selection marquee (see Figure H3.22) and release. This will create a radial gradient centering from your starting point. Deselect (⌘/Ctrl-D).

6. Activate the Brush tool. Set the foreground color to white; choose a soft brush and paint in a specular highlight in the upper-left portion, similar to the highlight you painted in the eye earlier.

7. Repeat steps 2 through 6 to create another bubble of a different size than the first.

8. Activate the Clone Stamp tool .

9. Option/Alt-click on a bubble you wish to reproduce.

10. Choose another location and simply brush in the new bubble.

11. Repeat steps 9 and 10 until you have as many bubbles as you wish.

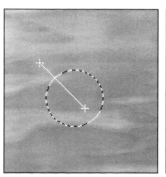  

Figure H3.22

**The bubble creation procedure adds the finishing touches to the project.**

# CHAPTER 12

# Using Channels and Quick Mask

*It's raining outside.* You're quite comfy in front of your computer working on an assignment to colorize a black-and-white group photograph of 34 mariachis. You've spent the last half-hour carefully outlining each one of their pants, tunics, and sombreros with the selection tools. You're about to apply the Hue and Saturation command to simultaneously color all of their costumes a brilliant turquoise. You hear thunder in the distance! The lights flicker! Your screen goes dead.

Fortunately, you've been regularly saving your work. You restart your computer, launch Photoshop, and open the image. The 34 mariachis are there, but without the precious selection marquee over which you labored for so long.

If you haven't saved the selection, more than an hour of work has just gone down the tubes. Before you utter a stream of unprintable obscenities, however, remember that you've learned a valuable lesson: Save your selections as alpha channels.

This chapter will explore:

- **What are channels?**

- **Looking at the Channels palette**

- **Editing alpha channels**

- **Using Quick Mask**

- **Performing channel operations**

# Photoshop Channels

You can use two types of channels in a Photoshop document. *Color channels* are graphic representations of color information. They are an integral part of the image. Having access to this information enables you to perform powerful modifications and corrections to the image's appearance and color relationships. *Alpha channels* are selections that have been made with the selection tools and stored for later use.

Color channels are composed of information segregated by color. Each color channel is actually a separate grayscale image. When you view the color channels superimposed on each other in an image, you see the full-color composite image. For a detailed description of color channels, see Chapter 3, "The Nature of the Beast."

An alpha channel is also a grayscale image. Like a color channel, it can support 256 shades of gray. Unlike a color channel, however, an alpha channel does not contain information that contributes to the image's appearance. And instead of the values of gray representing tonality or color, they represent the areas of opacity, semitransparency, or transparency of a mask.

Photoshop provides many features that help you isolate parts of the image so that you can perform edits and adjustments to them. It's helpful to think of an alpha channel as a tool that you create, store, and later use to isolate a region so that a tool or command can ultimately be applied to it.

## Alpha Channels and File Size

Bear in mind that although alpha channels are stored selections and do not affect the way the image appears, they are perceived by Photoshop as part of the image, and therefore increase the file size of the image proportionally each time you save a selection. Photoshop supports a maximum of 24 channels (except in bitmap images and 16-bit images, which don't support alpha channels) in a document. Images with alpha channels can become quite large and consume a great deal of disk space, so it is best to delete your alpha channels when you are sure you are done with them.

# Looking at the Channels Palette

Channels are displayed in the Channels palette (Figure 12.1). To access the Channels palette, choose Window → Show Channels, or you can press F7 to display the Layers/Channels/Paths cluster.

The composite channel appears at the top of the palette. The individual color channels appear underneath, each labeled with the name of the color that they represent and a key command that displays them in the image window. As in the Layers and History palettes, the first column, to the left of the thumbnail, displays or conceals an eye icon that tells you what you can see—in this case, it indicates what channels are displayed. Clicking to turn off the

Figure 12.1

**The Channels palette with the alpha channel loaded on the image**

eye next to the red channel, for example, reveals the content of the green and the blue channels. Clicking the composite channel eye reveals the full-color image.

If you save a selection to an alpha channel, it is placed underneath the color channels in the stack in the order in which it was created.

## Saving Selections as Alpha Channels

Because making an intricate selection can sometimes be difficult or time-consuming, Photoshop enables you to store selections to the Channels palette so that they can be used when you need them. It is wise to save a selection as an alpha channel if the selection is complex, if you need to refine it, or if you are going to use it more than once.

To save a selection:

1. Make a selection with one of the selection tools.

2. Choose Select → Save Selection.

3. In the dialog that appears (Figure 12.2), designate the document where the selection will be saved, and determine the following settings:

   **Document** You can save a selection as an alpha channel to the document where the selection was made or to any open document that is the exact same height, width, and resolution. The names will appear in the Document pop-up list. Choosing New creates a new document with no color channels and one alpha channel in the Channels palette.

Figure 12.2

**The Save Selection dialog box**

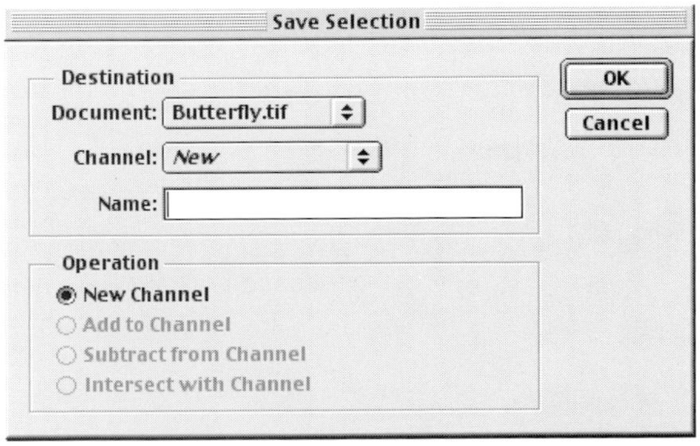

**Channel** Choosing New here makes a new channel. You can name the new channel in the Name field. If you don't name it, the saved selection will appear on the Channels palette titled as Alpha 1, 2, etc. Selecting a channel name in the Channel pop-up list writes over an existing channel.

**Saving the Selection As a Layer Mask** You can save a selection to a layer mask from the Channels dialog box if you created a layer mask on the image. The name of the layer mask defaults to Layer Mask 1 (see Figure 12.3). It appears in both the Layers palette and the Channels palette. (See Chapter 22, "Advanced Layer Techniques.")

4. If you have an active selection on the image and you choose a channel name to write over, the Operation area presents you with the following four options. To choose, click the radio button next to the operation.

**New Channel** discards the original mask channel and replaces it with an entirely new alpha channel.

**Add To Channel** adds the new selected area to the alpha channel.

**Subtract From Channel** removes the new selected area from the alpha channel.

**Intersect With Channel** creates an alpha channel of the area where the original channel and the new selection overlap.

5. Click OK to save the selection.

You can quickly save a selection as a new alpha channel by clicking the Save Selection As Channel icon at the bottom of the Channels palette.

Figure 12.3

Saving a selection as a layer mask

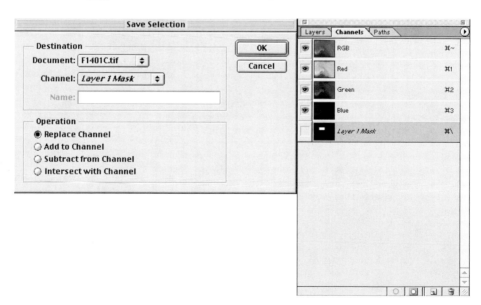

## Viewing Color Channels

It is often necessary to examine a color channel in black and white to better observe the brightness relationships of its pixels. By default, color channels are displayed in the Channels palette as black-and-white thumbnails and in the image window as grayscale images. You can display color channels in their native color by choosing Edit → Preferences → Display & Cursors → Color Channels In Color.

To display or conceal a color channel, click the first column to the left of its thumbnail, or press one of the keys displayed in Table 12.1.

| MODE | RGB | CMYK | LAB | GRAYSCALE & INDEXED | MULTICHANNEL |
|------|-----|------|-----|---------------------|--------------|
| ⌘/Ctrl-~ | Composite RGB Channel | Composite CMYK Channel | Composite Lab Channel | Gray Channel | Cyan |
| ⌘/Ctrl-1 | Red | Cyan | Lightness | Gray Channel | Cyan |
| ⌘/Ctrl-2 | Green | Magenta | a | Alpha 1 | Magenta |
| ⌘/Ctrl-3 | Blue | Yellow | b | Alpha 2 | Yellow |
| ⌘/Ctrl-4 | Alpha 1 | Black | Alpha 1 | Alpha 3 | Black |
| ⌘/Ctrl-5 | Alpha 2 | Alpha 1 | Alpha2 | Alpha 4 | Alpha 1 |

Table 12.1

**Color Channel Modes**

## Viewing Alpha Channels

Once an alpha channel has been saved, you can display it or conceal it in the Channels palette. As with viewing color channels, you view or conceal alpha channels by clicking the eye icon to the left of the channel's thumbnail.

Once a selection has been saved as an alpha channel, it can be viewed independently in the image window (see Figure 12.4). To view a channel:

1. Click in the box to the right of the channel's thumbnail to make it visible.

2. Click the eye next to the composite channel at the top of the palette to conceal it.

   Or, press Option (Macintosh) or Alt (Windows) and click its thumbnail or name.

   Or, press ⌘/Ctrl and the appropriate number key (see Table 12.1).

By default, black represents masked areas, white represents selected areas, and gray represents semitransparent areas.

When both color channels and alpha channels are visible, you see the alpha channels as superimposed translucent color overlays. By default, the overlays are 50% red, which is designed to resemble Rubylith, a traditional masking film used in the graphic arts industry (see Figure C12 in the color section).

Figure 12.4

**An alpha channel displayed in the image window**

## Using the Channel Options

You may need to change the color of an alpha channel overlay if you are looking at more than one channel at a time or if the content of the image closely resembles the color of the overlay.

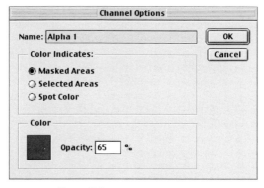

If you double-click the thumbnail of the alpha channel, the Channel Options dialog box appears (Figure 12.5). You can then set display options for that channel. The radio buttons in the Color Indicates area let you choose masked areas or selected areas to be displayed as color overlays, or if you are working with spot colors, you can designate a spot color channel (described in Chapter 18, "Duotones and Spot Color").

Always check the Channel Options dialog to see if masked areas or selected areas are represented by color. Look at the alpha channel in the image window by its thumbnail. When color represents masked areas, the masked area will appear black and the selected area will appear white. The reverse is true when color represents selected areas.

Figure 12.5

**The Channel Options dialog box**

To change the color of a mask:

1. Double-click the channel thumbnail to display the Channel Options dialog.

2. Click the swatch to bring up the Color Picker.

3. Choose a color and click OK.

You can specify the opacity of the mask from 0% to 100%, which affects only the way you see the mask and not its masking characteristics. Reducing the opacity helps you see the image more clearly through the mask.

## Loading Selections

Once saved to the Channels palette, the alpha channel can be loaded as a selection. Loading a selection surrounds the area with a selection marquee just as if you outlined it with a selection tool.

To load a selection:

1. Choose Select → Load Selection.

2. In the Load Selection dialog box, the options are similar to the Save Selection dialog. From the Document pop-up list, choose the name of the document where the channel was made. This list will display all alpha channels from all open documents that are the same height, width, and resolution.

3. From the Channel pop-up list, choose the source channel to be loaded. This list displays all alpha channels and layer masks from the current document. The Invert box loads an inverse selection of the mask.

4. If you have an active selection on the image, the Operation area presents four options:

**New Selection** loads a new selection on the image, replacing any currently selected area if there is one.

**Add To Selection** adds the loaded selection area to an active selection marquee.

**Subtract From Selection** omits the loaded selection area from an active selection marquee.

**Intersect With Selection** loads the area where the loaded selection and an active selection marquee intersect.

5. Click OK to load the selection.

A faster method is to load a selection by dragging its icon to the Load Channel As Selection icon  at the bottom of the Channels palette. You can rename the channel by double-clicking on its name and then typing the new name.

# Editing Channels

It is sometimes desirable to change portions of the channel using the painting or editing functions. If, for example, you missed a small part of the selection while using the Lasso tool, you can alter the contents of the mask channel with the Brush tool to include the areas that were excluded from the original selection. Any painting or editing function that can be applied to a grayscale image can be applied to an alpha channel.

## Fine-Tuning Alpha Channels by Painting

Suppose that after having saved a selection, there are inaccuracies visible on the mask that weren't visible on the selection marquee. You can fine-tune these and other flaws by painting directly on the alpha channel.

Here's a practice exercise on how to save and alter the contents of an alpha channel:

1. Open the file titled `Alpha_Head.psd` from the `Ch12` folder on the *Photoshop 7 Savvy* CD.

2. Choose the Magic Wand tool and select the blue background. Click the Add To Selection icon and three or four times to select all of the Background.

3. Choose Select → Inverse to select the head.

4. Click the Save Selection As Alpha Channel icon in the Channels palette. The channel will be named Alpha 1. Double-click the name and enter the word **Head**.

5. View the alpha channel in the image window by pressing Opt/Alt and clicking its name or thumbnail. The black-and-white channel will appear in the image window.

6. The foreground and background color swatches in the Tool palette have changed to black and white. This is because a channel is a grayscale image and does not support color. Choose the Brush tool, Airbrush, Pencil, or any tool that deposits foreground color.

Figure 12.6

**Painting on the alpha channel (left) alters the selection when the channel is loaded (right).**

7.  Display the composite channel but be sure that the Alpha 1 channel is targeted. You'll see a red color where the channel masks the Background. Paint out the eyes with red, as shown in Figure C13 in the color section (see also Figure 12.6). The resulting painting will, by default, alter the selection to mask the newly painted areas when the selection is loaded.

8.  To see the result, use Select → Load Selection, and choose Alpha 1 from the Channel pop-up list.

Painting with a shade of gray creates a partially masked area; the degree of masking depends on how light or dark the gray is. The darker the shade of gray, the more an area will be masked; applying black will produce areas that are entirely protected, while painting with white will entirely erase the painted area.

## Performing Channel Operations

You can perform several operations within the Channels palette that change the structure of the document. Some of these operations produce shifts in the color mode, and some disperse the channels into several documents.

Because of the radical changes to the color information, it is always a good idea to make a copy of the document before implementing most of these channel operations. To duplicate the document, choose Image → Duplicate.

## Duplicating Channels

When you duplicate a targeted channel, you get an exact copy of it in the Channels palette. You should duplicate the channel if you want to experiment with modifying it by painting, applying a filter effect, or any other editing function. Also duplicate the channel if you want to inverse and save it for alterations, as seen in Hands On 3, "Painting, Paths, and History." Click the arrow in upper-right corner of the Channels palette and scroll down to the Duplicate Channel command.

| Dock to Palette Well |
| --- |
| New Channel... |
| Duplicate Channel... |
| Delete Channel |
| New Spot Channel... |
| Merge Spot Channel |
| Channel Options... |
| Split Channels |
| Merge Channels... |
| Palette Options... |

> The Duplicate Channel option will be dimmed if the composite channel is targeted, because you can duplicate only one channel at a time.

A fast way to duplicate a channel is to drag it to the New Channel icon 🗐 at the bottom of the Channels palette.

## Deleting Channels

You can delete a targeted channel from the document by choosing Delete Channel from the Palette pull-down menu. You can delete alpha channels and maintain the integrity of the image, but when you delete color channels, the color mode of the image will change to Multichannel (see the section titled "Using Multichannel" later in this chapter). If you delete the red channel of an RGB image, for example, the remaining color channels will convert to magenta and yellow. (Multichannel documents always default to CMYK descriptions.) You cannot delete the composite channel.

A fast way to delete a channel is to drag it to the Delete Current Channel icon (the trash icon) 🗑 at the bottom of the Channels palette.

## Splitting Channels

Photoshop can split a document's channels into independent Grayscale documents. The title of each window is automatically appended to the channel's color name as a suffix in the image title bar at the top of the window. For example, a CMYK document named Box will be divided into 4 channels: Box_C, Box_M, Box_Y, and Box_K. Alpha channels will be converted to separate Grayscale documents. This option is useful as a first step in redistributing channels or for making a single document out of the channels information. This is not a process you'll use every day, unless you're a printer who needs to isolate the color information to a single document or if you have very specialized needs to analyze the channel information. The new documents are not automatically saved, so you should save them to your hard disk.

To split a channel, first flatten the image. Choose Split Channels from the Channels palette pull-down menu. When you perform this operation, the original document is automatically closed.

## Merging Channels

Separate channels can be merged into a single Multichannel document by choosing Merge Channels from the Channels Palette pull-down menu. The images must be open, grayscale, and the exact same height, width, and resolution. A dialog box appears that allows you to assign a color mode to the image, based on the number of images open. Three open images will produce an RGB, Lab, or Multichannel image; four open images will produce a CMYK or Multichannel image. Click OK and another dialog enables you to determine the distribution of the color channels. You can create some rather surprising color distortions by switching color information between channels.

One of the most common uses for this command is when prepress users have to recombine an EPS DCS 1 or 2 file that has lost the composite preview file, which links the separations together. A new EPS DCS file can be created that includes the composite preview file and the high-resolution separations.

## Using Multichannel

You can divide an image's channels into an individual series of channels. When you choose Image → Mode → Multichannel, the new channels lose their color relation to each other and appear as individual Grayscale channels within a single document, so there is no composite channel. This is useful if you want to separate the color information of a composite channel like a Duotone, Tritone, or Quadtone and view the color information of each ink color separately. (Chapter 18 goes into more detail on image features like Duotones and spot colors.) The Multichannel operation converts the red, green, and blue channels on RGB images into separate cyan, magenta, and yellow channels within the same the same document.

## Mixing Channels

Channel Mixer is a Photoshop feature that enables you to adjust the color information of each channel from one control window. You can establish color values on a specific channel as a mixture of any or all of the color channels' brightness values. The Channel Mixer can be used for a variety of purposes, including:

- Creating an optimal grayscale image from an RGB or CMYK file
- Making a high-quality sepia tone from a CMYK or RGB file
- Converting images into alternative color spaces
- Swapping color information from one channel to another
- Making creative color adjustments to images by altering the color information in a specific channel

To learn how to use the Channel Mixer, see Chapter 16, "Adjusting Tonality and Color."

## Using Spot Color Channels

The spot channel features in the Channels Palette pull-down menu are used to create images that are output to film for printing on printing presses. They are most frequently applied to grayscale images for two- and three-color print jobs. They are also used on four-color process (CMYK) images when additional areas of solid rich color, varnishes, and special inks are specified. Spot colors are usually printed with PANTONE or other custom color inks. See Chapter 18 to learn how to work with spot colors.

# Using Quick Mask Mode

As you become more proficient in Photoshop, the speed of performing tasks will become more crucial to your particular style of work. As you understand the relations of tool functions and begin to recognize the logic and similarity of the various windows, palettes, and toolbars, you'll want to explore shortcuts that accelerate your work. Selecting areas on a Photoshop image can be the most time-consuming part of the image-editing process; Quick Mask mode can accelerate the selection making and enhance the precision.

Quick Mask mode is an efficient method of making a temporary mask using the paint tools. Quick Masks can quickly be converted into selections or stored as mask channels in the Channels palette for later use. By default, the Quick Mask interface is similar to the channels interface in that Photoshop displays a colored overlay to represent the masked areas. You can toggle directly into Quick Mask mode on the Tool palette by pressing the letter Q or clicking the Quick Mask icon ▣▣ .

> Quick Mask is versatile way of making or editing selections using many of Photoshop's painting and editing tools. You can even use the selection tools to define areas of the Quick Mask to edit.

When you choose Quick Mask mode from the Tool palette, a temporary thumbnail labeled Quick Mask, in italics, appears in the Channels palette. The thumbnail will change appearance as you apply color to the Quick Mask (see Figure 12.7).

## Quick Mask Options Window

The Quick Mask Options dialog (see Figure 12.8) is almost identical to the Channels Options dialog, and can be accessed by double-clicking the Quick Mask icon.

To practice creating a mask in Quick Mask mode, follow these steps:

1. Open the file `Guitar.psd` from the `Ch12` folder on the CD.

2. Click the Quick Mask icon in the Tool palette. Notice that the foreground and background swatch colors in the Tool palette become black and white.

3. Choose the Brush tool from the Tool palette. Set brush options in the Options bar.

4. Choose a brush from the Brush menu and paint over the guitar. Painting on a Quick Mask is similar to painting on an alpha channel with the composite channel visible. By default, as you paint, if the foreground color is black, the paint tool will deposit a red color. If the foreground color is white, the paint tool will erase the mask color.

5. When you have completed painting the guitar, click the Edit In Standard Mode icon from the Tool palette. The masked area is outlined by a selection outline. By default, the areas that were painted are now excluded from the selection. You've selected the Background. If you want to select the guitar, choose Select → Invert to invert the selection.

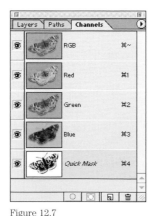

Figure 12.7

**A Quick Mask thumbnail in the Channels palette**

Figure 12.8

**Quick Mask Options dialog box**

6. After all that work, you should save the selection to an alpha channel. Click the Save Selection As Alpha Channel icon at the bottom of the Channels palette.

> If you want to be sure that the area is completely masked, set the Opacity slider in the Brush Options bar to 100%. Setting the opacity to 50%, for example, will paint with translucent color; the result will be that the painted area will be only partially masked.

Once a Quick Mask has been made, I recommend that you carefully examine it for missed areas and pinholes. It is quite easy to make mistakes because it can be difficult to see omissions and errors on the image. The best way to examine the Quick Mask is to view it as a grayscale image. You can see the Quick Mask as a grayscale by turning off the eye icon on all the other channels in the Channels palette except for the one to the left of the Quick Mask. Examine it carefully to assure that the masked areas are solid and opaque. If necessary, apply more paint to deficient areas. (See the Hands On section that follows this chapter for a demonstration.)

Quick Mask is ideal for cleaning up selections that you have made with one of the selection or marquee tools. You can paint a few pixels at a time with a small brush or with the Pencil tool, greatly enhancing the precision of making selections.

# Channels

*The goal of this project* is to make a selection of part of an image—some chickens—using the Quick Mask technique. You will save the selection as an alpha channel, duplicate it, and make it into a Gradient Mask. A filter will then be applied to the background through the Gradient Mask to give the chickens movement and life.

## Getting Started

Hide or discard your preferences file before beginning this Hands On exercise. The "Modifying Photoshop's Settings" section in Chapter 5 details how to temporarily reset your preferences to Photoshop's defaults. Once you have launched Photoshop with default preferences, open the file `Chickens_in_Motion_start.psd` (Figure H4.1) in the `HO4` folder on the *Photoshop 7 Savvy* CD. To see a color preview of the before and after (Figure H4.2) versions of the image, check Figures C46 and C48 in the color section. Save the file to your disk.

Figure H4.1

**The original chickens, standing around**

Figure H4.2

**The chickens in motion**

# Selecting the Chickens

You'll start by selecting the white portion of the chickens. Follow these steps to begin:

1. With the Magic Wand tool ![magic wand], try to select the chickens. Click them once; press the Shift key and click again. You'll see that, because the colors of the chickens are close to the background, it is impossible to isolate them.

2. Click the lightest area of a chicken with the Magic Wand tool. Click the Add To Selection icon in the toolbar ![add to selection] and continue to select the lightest areas. Select as much as you can, but not too much (see Figure H4.3).

3. Click the Quick Mask icon ![quick mask] in the Tool palette, or type **Q**. What you've selected so far becomes your Quick Mask.

4. Choose the Paintbrush. Click the Reverse Colors icon ↰ in the Tool palette, or type **X**, so that white is the foreground color. Choose a brush and begin to erase the red transparent color on the chickens. Carefully paint to the edges. If you make a mistake and paint outside the edge, reverse the colors so that black is the foreground color, and paint out the mistake.

5. When you get to the chickens' red combs, it becomes difficult to see where to erase the red color. Change the color of the mask by double-clicking the Quick Mask thumbnail in the Channels palette. In the Quick Mask Options dialog, click the swatch, choose a green color from the Color Picker, and click OK. (See Figure C47 in the color section for a comparison of a red and a green mask.)

6. Reduce the opacity of the Quick Mask to 30% for a better view of the background.

7. Erase the mask from the chickens and their legs with the Paintbrush tool, using white as a foreground color.

8. Once you've completed that selection, choose the Lasso tool and select the wall they are standing on (as in Figure H4.4) and the parts of their feet that extend upward slightly from the wall.

Figure H4.3

**Select the chicken parts by selecting the lightest areas of the chickens first.**

Figure H4.4

**Selecting the wall**

9. Be sure that white is the foreground color. Press Option-Delete (Mac) or Alt-Backspace (Win) to delete the green mask from the wall area. Press ⌘-D/Ctrl-D to deselect.

10. When the Quick Mask of the chickens is complete, click the Normal Mode icon, or type **Q**, to convert the mask into a selection.

11. Save the document.

## Saving and Cleaning Up the Alpha Channel

Follow these steps to repair and save your selection as an alpha channel:

1. Click the Save Selection As Channel icon ▣ in the Channels palette to quickly save the selection. A thumbnail labeled Alpha 1 appears in the palette. Deselect.

2. Click the thumbnail to display the alpha channel in the image window. Notice that there are some flaws—areas that you missed or edges that are not sharp (see Figure H4.5). Choose the Paint-brush, choose white as a foreground color, and paint out the flaws in the white area of the alpha channel.

3. While making repairs to the edges, you may want to see the image. Click the eye next to the RGB composite channel to reveal the image and the alpha channel at the same time.

4. When the alpha channel is complete, save the document (File → Save or ⌘/Ctrl-S).

Figure H4.5

**The flaws in the alpha channel**

## Duplicating and Modifying the Channel

Follow these steps to copy and edit the alpha channel:

1. Drag the Alpha 1 channel 🔲 to the New Channel icon at the bottom of the Channels palette to duplicate it. The new channel is named Alpha 1 Copy.

2. Choose Image → Adjust → Invert to reverse the colors of the channel, making the black areas of the channel white and the white areas black (Figure H4.6).

3. Double-click the channel thumbnail. Name it **Gradient Mask**.

4. The Gradient Mask channel ◌ should be targeted. Click and drag the Gradient Mask channel to the Load Selection icon at the bottom of the Channels palette to select the

white area of the Alpha channel. You can also select the white area with the Magic Wand tool.

5. Press the D and then the X key to make the foreground color black and the background color white 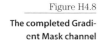 (or click the Switch Colors double-arrow icon on the Tool palette swatches). Choose the Gradient tool and click the Radial option in the Options bar. Click and drag from the center out toward the edge of the document to modify the areas surrounding the chickens with a gradient, as in Figure H4.7. Your alpha channel should then look like Figure H4.8.

Figure H4.6

**The inverted alpha channel**

Figure H4.7

**Drag the gradient on the inverted alpha channel.**

Figure H4.8

**The completed Gradient Mask channel**

## Filtering and Adjusting the Selection

Now we'll apply a filter and an adjustment through the selection to affect the image. To filter and adjust your selection:

1. Click the RGB composite channel to target it.

2. Load the Gradient Mask channel by dragging it to the Load Selection icon at the bottom of the Channels palette. Your image should look something like Figure H4.9.

3. Choose Filter → Blur → Radial Blur, and set these options:

   Amount: 100

   Blur Method: Zoom

   Quality: Best

4. Click OK.

5. You'll want to further enhance the image by adjusting its brightness through the Gradient Mask channel. Target the RGB composite channel. With the Gradient Mask channel still loaded, choose Image → Adjustments → Auto Levels. Choose Edit → Fade Levels to modify the effect.

6. Deselect (⌘/Ctrl-D) and save (⌘/Ctrl-S).

Figure H4.9

**The loaded selection**

# CHAPTER 13

# Sizing and Transforming Images

*Photoshop documents can be* resized and transformed in several ways. Resizing usually (though not always, as you'll see in this chapter) involves resampling, which changes the pixel information of an image. When you reduce the size of an image in this way, you inevitably discard pixels. When you resample to enlarge an image, you add new ones. These operations can significantly affect the look of the final published work. This chapter will clarify issues related to image size and help you best determine the methods to choose when scanning, sizing, and transforming an image to achieve optimal results at the printer.

This chapter will help you understand:

- **Resolution and image size**
- **The Crop tool**
- **Canvas size**
- **The Resize Image Assistant/Wizard**
- **Transformation operations**

# What Is Resolution?

Resolution determines the quality of an image and how much detail can be displayed or printed. There are several important terms relating to resolution you should be aware of:

**Image resolution**  The number of pixels that occupy a linear inch of a digital image, usually measured in pixels per inch (ppi).

**Monitor resolution**  The number of pixels that occupy a linear inch of a monitor screen (72 ppi for most Macintosh RGB monitors, 96 ppi for Windows VGA monitors). This resolution never changes, as it represents the physical matrix of the monitor.

**Image size**  The physical size and resolution of an image.

**Printer resolution**  The number of dots that can be printed per linear inch, measured in dots per inch (dpi). These dots compose larger halftone dots on a halftone screen or stochastic (random pattern) dots on an ink-jet printer.

**Halftone screen**  The dot density of a halftone printed image, measured in lines per inch (lpi) or, in rare instances, lines per centimeter (lpc). A halftone screen is a grid of dots. The tonality of a printed image is determined by the size of the dot within the specific matrix. Table 13.1, later in the chapter, lists some standard values.

Optical systems allow us to collect and organize visible light. Each type of optical system breaks up light in its own unique system of units. Though each system determines resolution differently, the more information that can be collected or printed, the better the quality of the image. Let's take a look at reality through several optical systems that allow us to collect and organize visible light.

## The Human Eye

Probably the most perfect optical device is the human eye. Our eyes collect light through a lens called the *cornea* and focus it on a light-sensitive field called a *retina*. Color and tonal information are transmitted through the optic nerve and interpreted by the brain into a completely continuous-tone reality. When an image is *continuous-tone*, there are no visible divisions between colors and shades. Our eyes enable us to see reality as a seamless fabric of color and form. The closer we look at something, the more detail we perceive.

### DPI VS. PPI VS. LPI

Dots per inch (dpi) and pixels per inch (ppi): The two terms are often confused. Manufacturers often refer to the resolution capabilities of their scanners in dpi, but a scanner creates pixels and a printer prints dots. In this book, I use *ppi* when referring to pixel resolution from a scanned image or on a monitor. I use *dpi* when I refer to the output of a printer and *lpi* for the screen frequency of a halftone screen.

## The Traditional Camera

The traditional camera is a mechanical replica of the human eye. It, too, collects light through a lens and focuses it on a light-sensitive field—but this field is made of film or paper coated with chemicals called *emulsions* that, when developed, respond to light. The grain of the emulsion determines the maximum visual depth of the image. Photographic grains are microscopic, which allows photographic images to be produced at exceptionally high quality. Even though photographs are termed as "continuous-tone" in the industry, when a photograph is enlarged too much, its grains become visible, which can diminish its quality.

## Scanners and Digital Cameras

The scanner and digital camera are two other optical devices that "see" tonality and color. In Chapter 14, "Capturing Images," I discuss how these devices work in more detail. Suffice it to say that scanners and digital cameras collect red, green, and blue color information and interpret it into units called *pixels*. Like all digital information, these pixels are assigned numbers that identify their color content. A computer is needed to decipher these values. A video card and monitor are necessary to display them. Since the image is constructed of individual units of color, it is a mosaic of colored squares. Each pixel is like an individual building block. The more pixels contained within the image, the more information there is, and hence, the more detail can be displayed (see Figure 13.1).

Should a pixel-based digital image be considered continuous-tone or not? That's a matter of ongoing debate in the industry. One of the best discussions of the issues involved can be found at www.deluxacademy.com/articles/digitalphoto/contone.html.

Figure 13.1

**Identical images at different resolutions: The image at 30 ppi (left) and the image at 300 ppi (right)**

## Halftone Screens

Printing an image with ink on paper presents a unique set of problems. How does a mechanical device like a printer communicate tonality to a flat piece of paper? Because it must distribute ink, it needs a method that will portray the tonal range without smearing the ink. To accomplish this task, printing technologies divide the ink into individual dots on a grid called a *halftone screen*. On traditional halftone screens used for black-and-white images, the size of the dots determines the darkness or lightness of an area (see Figure 13.2). Areas on

Figure 13.2

**A halftone screen, enlarged to show tonal density**

the screen that contain larger dots are darker than areas with smaller dots (which allow more of the paper to show through, providing a lighter perceived tone). With full-color images, four different colored halftone screens—one each of cyan, magenta, yellow and black—called *color separations*, are used. These colors combined in varying densities on the screens can produce a full range of color. The finer the halftone screen, the more detail can be displayed. The line frequency of the halftone screen is determined by the type of printing that is being performed. Table 13.1 is a list of common line frequencies used in various types of printing.

Table 13.1

**Typical Halftone Screen Values**

| VALUE | DEFINITION |
| --- | --- |
| 65 lpi | This value produces a coarse halftone screen, suggested for screen printing. |
| 85 lpi | This value works well for newsprint and porous paper stock. |
| 133 lpi | This value produces finer detail. It's used on web presses for printing medium-quality weekly magazines, books, and other jobs on uncoated paper. |
| 150–175 lpi | These frequencies are suitable for brochures, pamphlets, and commercial printing on coated stock. |
| 200–300 lpi | These values produce the finest images with lots of detail and color depth. You might use this option when creating annual reports or fine art prints. |

Screen frequencies higher than 200 lpi are not as common as 175 lpi or less. The physical demands of printing finer screen rulings often prohibit their successful use. To avoid difficulties, ask your print shop early in the process about stock requirements and other details related to the choice of screen frequency.

## Ink-Jet Printers

Some ink-jet printers produce colored dots similar to a halftone screen when viewed from a distance. These ink-jet printers, however, use a *stochastic* or *frequency modulated* screen to produce tonality. Whereas a halftone screen is a grid with a fixed number of lines where the size of the dots will vary, a stochastic screen produces dots of a uniform size. Instead of the size of the dot, it is the number and distribution of dots that determine tonal value and color density (see Figure 13.3).

## Image Resolution Vs. Monitor Resolution

*Image resolution* refers to the number of pixels per linear inch collected at the scanner or digital camera. The monitor resolution is a fixed matrix of pixels. When an image with the same resolution as the monitor is displayed at actual size, it appears at its actual physical size, because at 100%, one image pixel equals one monitor pixel. If the image has a higher resolution, it will appear larger than its physical size. For example, a 4" × 5" image that is 300 ppi will appear three times larger at 100% than an image that is 4" × 5" at 100 ppi. If you copy and paste (or drag and drop) an image that is the same physical size but a lower resolution to a document of higher resolution, the pasted image will reduce in physical size (see Figure 13.4).

To get a preview of the printed size of an image, choose Print Size from Photoshop's View menu. The image displays at the size at which it will print, no matter what its resolution.

## Determining Resolution

The physical size of an image is its height and width when printed. Its resolution is the number of pixels that occupy a linear inch of a digital image, measured in pixels per inch (ppi). You determine this resolution when you scan an image or shoot a digital photo at a given setting. To acquire sufficient information to produce good quality images from your high-resolution imagesetter or laser printer, scan your images at 1.5 to 2 times the screen frequency of the halftone screen you will use for printing (again, see Table 13.1 for common halftone screen frequencies). That means if your image is going to be printed in a newspaper or in a newsletter, scan it anywhere from 128 to 170 pixels per inch (1.5 or 2×85 lines per inch).If your image will be printed in a glossy magazine, scan your image at 225 to 300 ppi (1.5 or 2×150 lpi). The image size should be scanned at 100% of the size it will be printed.

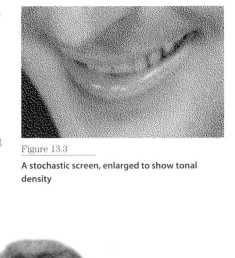

Figure 13.3

**A stochastic screen, enlarged to show tonal density**

Figure 13.4

**The small monkey was dragged and dropped from a 72 ppi file that was 6" wide by 7.2" deep onto a file that was the same physical size but with a resolution four times greater, or 288 ppi.**

Should you use 1.5 or 2? Whether to use the higher or lower setting depends on the content of the image. If you are scanning images of big puffy clouds, for example, where the content is intrinsically soft, use the lower setting to decrease file size. If sharpness is critical to your image, then scan at the higher setting.

If you're going to print only to desktop ink-jet printers or wide format printers, I recommend that you scan your images at a minimum of 1/3 the desired print resolution. For example, for a print resolution of 720 dpi, you will need to set the scan resolution to 240 dpi or higher. If you are going to increase the size of the printed image, then you should scan at a higher resolution. This equates to common scan resolutions of 120 ppi, 240 ppi, and 480 ppi—although anything over 360 ppi is probably overkill. If you scan a picture at 600 dpi and print it at 300 dpi, you can increase its physical size by a factor of two without compromising its quality.

Line art or bitmap content is different. Ideally, scan at the same resolution as the printer's dpi resolution or in evenly divisible units of the printer's resolution. For example, you would scan at 360 ppi for a 1440 dpi print. See `http://support.epson.com/webadvice/wa0216.html` for more information.

## Resampling Image Resolution

Resampling the resolution of your image lets you determine the number of pixels in the image. When you resample down, you discard pixels. When you resample up, you create new pixels. Usually the results are okay when you decrease the size of an image, but I don't recommend that you increase the size or resolution of an image by a large amount. Photoshop creates new pixels using predefined interpolation algorithms that produce a loss of sharpness and dulling of color (see Figure 13.5). If you need a larger image, rescan it properly, taking into account its output size.

Exceeding the optical resolution of a scanner is essentially the same as resampling up in Photoshop. It will produce less than desirable results. For best results, don't exceed the scanner's optical resolution.

A third-party plug-in called Genuine Fractals does a fairly decent job of resampling images up with a minimum loss of quality. Developed by Altamira and now available through LizardTech, `www.lizardtech.com/products`, it comes in several versions for different purposes.

Figure 13.5

**A close-up of an image scanned at 288 ppi (left) and one scanned at 72 ppi and resampled up to 288 ppi (right)**

The image resolution and the physical size of an image are interchangeable values. For example, an image that is 4"×5" at 72 ppi has the same amount of information an image that is 2"×2.5" at 144 ppi has. Therefore, you can enlarge an image to a larger physical size with no loss of quality if you reduce its resolution without resampling. To perform this operation, follow these steps:

1. Open the file lemon_machine.psd.

2. Choose Image → Image Size. The Image Size dialog box appears. The image has a width of 2.267", a height of 2", and a resolution of 300 ppi.

3. Clear the Resample Image box, which also clears the Constrain Proportions box and grays out the option.

4. Enter a new value into the Resolution field. In this example, change the resolution from 300 ppi to 150 ppi, decreasing the resolution of the image by half but doubling its physical size to 4.533"×4" (see Figure 13.6).

5. Click OK to apply the changes.

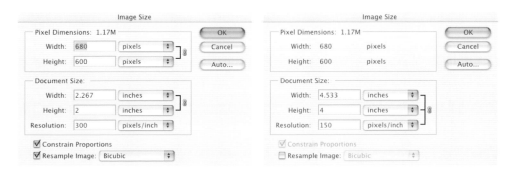

Figure 13.6

**The Image Size dialog box before (left) and after (right) resizing without resampling**

When you clear Resample Image, as in the above example, your image retains its original pixels while changing only its print size. In contrast, resampling changes the image resolution and/or physical size. This occurs by adding pixels to increase an image's physical size or resolution, or removing pixels for a smaller size or lower resolution.

To use this feature, check the Resample Image box in the Image → Image Size dialog box and pick from one of the three algorithms listed: Nearest Neighbor, Bilinear, or Bicubic. Each of these choices determines how Photoshop adds or removes pixels from your image:

**Nearest Neighbor** evaluates an adjacent pixel. Use this option for line art desktop icons, software interface screen captures, or anytime that anti-aliasing creates artifacts.

**Bilinear** averages the four pixels above, below, and on either side for smoother transitions.

**Bicubic** produces the best results on photographic images by averaging the eight closest neighbors and adding a sharpening effect to increase the contrast. As a rule of thumb, I suggest you select Bicubic for photographs.

The default interpolation settings are found under Edit → Preferences → General. The default interpolation is also active when using transformation commands such as Edit → Free Transform or Edit → Transform → Distort And Perspective and on several of the distortion filters like Spherize or Pinch. This default preference can be altered on an image by image case using the Image Size command, as necessary.

## Constraining and Unconstraining Proportions

When you enable the Resample Image feature, you have the option to constrain the image's proportions. When selected, the Constrain Proportions check box ensures that image height will vary proportionately with the width. Change one dimension, and the other will automatically update to preserve proportionality. When you deselect this option, the link between height and width disappears, and you will increase the height or width independently. Your image, in this case, will stretch disproportionately vertically or horizontally.

You can turn off Constrain Proportions only when you allow image resampling. Without resampling, proportions remain automatically constrained, as shown by the link icon.

## The Crop Tool

Sometimes the best way to resize your image is to eliminate part of it. The Crop tool enables you to trim down your images precisely. (You can also select an area with the Rectangular Marquee or Elliptical Marquee tool and then choose Image → Crop, but with these tools you sacrifice the flexibility and control of the Crop tool's features.) In Photoshop 7, the Crop tool is found in the default Tool palette on the left column in the third row.

To perform a basic crop with the Crop tool, open the `mandrill.psd` file from the `Ch13` folder on the CD and follow these steps:

1. Choose Image Duplicate to make a copy of the image so that you can preserve your original.

2. Choose the Crop tool from the Tool palette.

3. We want to crop the black border out of the picture. Drag the mouse to define the bounding box. As you can see in Figure 13.7, the area outside your crop will darken, highlighting your selection.

4. Fine-tune your crop interactively. Use the handles to encompass more or less of the image, and move the bounding box by placing the cursor inside its boundaries and dragging.

5. To crop, click the Commit (check mark) button ⊘ ✓ in the Options bar or press Return (Mac) or Enter (Win). You can also double-click inside the cropping area to commit your crop. Figure 13.8 shows the result of applying the crop. If you decide to cancel the crop, press the Esc key or click the Cancel (X) button.

Figure 13.7

**After you make the initial cropping selection, areas outside the Crop bounding box will darken. Use the handles to fine-tune your selection.**

Figure 13.8

**Applying a crop removes all areas outside your selection from the image.**

You can turn the crop shield on and off by checking or clearing the Shield Color box in the Crop tool Options bar. Choose a color for the shielded area by clicking the swatch or the opacity by choosing or entering a value.

## Rotating a Crop

One of the Crop tool's most useful features allows you to crop down to a *rotated* area. To practice simultaneously cropping and rotating an image, start, as above, by opening the `mandrill.psd` file from your CD.

1. Choose Image Duplicate to make a copy of the image.

2. Choose the Crop tool from the Tool palette, and highlight your initial crop area, just as in Figure 13.7 in the previous procedure.

3. Move your mouse just outside any of the corner selection handles until the cursor ↻ changes to the curved rotation icon.

The Crop Rotation option becomes active when the cursor is anywhere outside the crop selection; when the cursor is too close to the selection, a Crop Selection Resize icon will be active.

4. Drag the mouse to rotate the selection, as in Figure 13.9. Further adjust your selection using any of the handles until you're satisfied with the new, rotated crop.

5. As before, click the Commit (check mark) icon in the Options bar. Photoshop crops the image, rotating it as needed, as you can see in Figure 13.10.

The Crop tool can be used to increase the size of a cropped area if the height and width values entered are greater than the original size.

Figure 13.9

**With the Crop tool, you can rotate the bounding box to encompass a diagonal area.**

Figure 13.10

**The resulting crop, after rotation and cropping.**

## Cropping to Size

With the Crop tool, you can trim your image to a fixed size and new interpolated resolution by entering values for the height, width, and resolution. The Crop bounding box automatically constrains to your specified image size.

1. Duplicate the mandrill.psd again. Choose the Crop tool from the Tool palette.

2. Locate the Width and Height fields in the Options bar. Enter **4** inches for the width, **6** inches for height, and **72** (ppi) for the resolution (see Figure 13.11).

3. Drag the bounding box. It will automatically be constrained within the proportions you enter in the Width and Height fields. No matter what part of the mandrill the bounding box encompasses, its contents will be 4" wide by 6" high and 72 ppi when the Crop is applied. You can still rotate the bounding box as described above.

4. Commit your change (click the check mark icon in the Options bar or press Return/Enter) to finish cropping your image.

Figure 13.11

**The Crop Options bar**

Most cropping is usually performed with the width, height, and resolution fields left blank. The Clear button on the Options bar will clear the number fields so that no resampling takes place. The Front Image button on the Options bar fills the current active document's width/height/resolution into the number fields.

## Perspective Cropping

Once you've drawn a Crop marquee, the Options bar presents several additional options. The Perspective option allows you to adjust the corner anchor points of the bounding box independently. This feature is useful if you want to distort an image as you crop it or to fit an image's content into a rectangular document of a specific size. When you implement the crop, the image area will distort to conform to the new document's height and with (see the example in Figures 13.12 and 13.13).

Figure 13.12

**The Perspective crop option lets you crop an irregular shape into a rectangle.**

Figure 13.13

**The image after perspective cropping**

# Trimming an Image

The Trim command automatically eliminates edge pixels of a specific color to quickly refine the edges of an image. Let's trim the mandrill image:

1. Duplicate the mandrill.psd again.

2. Choose Image → Trim. The Trim dialog box appears (see Figure 13.14).

3. Check the color you want trimmed, or if the image is on a layer, you can remove a transparent edge. In this case, we want to remove the black rectangular border from all four sides.

4. Click OK. The entire border is removed and the image is cropped to a new size.

Figure 13.14

**The Trim dialog box**

## Sizing the Canvas

The *canvas* is the surface on which the image resides. The Canvas Size command produces more space around the image and more pixels to work with. When you apply this operation, the new canvas is filled with the background color if the image has a background. If there is no background, the new canvas is transparent, so you should first choose a background color from the Color Picker, Color palette, or Swatches palette.

Choose Image → Canvas Size to access the dialog box that allows you to expand or shrink your canvas. Enter a new value for the width and/or the height, select an anchor, and click OK.

The Current Size field indicates your file size for the current canvas size, and the New Size field indicates the file size of the image with the new height and width values. Photoshop 7 enables you to enter a relative size for the canvas. Check the Relative box and enter the amount you want to add to the existing canvas.

The anchor buttons control where the new canvas will be added. Click the center button, and the canvas will grow equally on all sides. Click the bottom-right button to adjust the left and top sides only.

When using the Canvas Size dialog box, you can work in any of eight units: percent, pixels, inches, centimeters, millimeters (a new option in Photoshop 7), points, picas, and columns. For example, you may want to increase your canvas width to 150 percent.

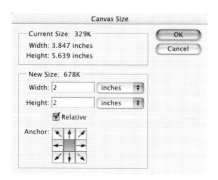

Figure 13.15

**Canvas Size dialog**

In the following example, you will expand your canvas a couple of different ways. Open `sonny_and_cher.psd` from the `Ch13` folder on the CD. First, let's add some canvas to the image, which will produce an even, white border around the image and more space on which to work.

1. Choose White as a background color. Choose the Image → Canvas Size menu option (see dialog box in Figure 13.15).

2. Expand the canvas size by 2" on each side. Check the Relative box and enter **2** in the Height and Width fields. Click on the center box to anchor the image to the center. Click OK.

3. As an alternative, anchor the image to the bottom-left corner. Enter the same Relative values and click the lower-left box. The results are shown in Figure 13.16.

**Figure 13.16**

Expanding the canvas produces new areas around the image. On the left is the original image. The middle image was anchored in the center and canvas added evenly around it. On the right, the image was anchored at the bottom-left corner.

## Rotating the Canvas

To rotate the entire image rather than a single layer or selection, use the Rotate Canvas commands. These menu options, which are found under Image → Rotate Canvas, will reorient your entire document:

**180°** Rotates the image so that it appears upside-down. The image retains its left-to-right orientation.

**90° CW** Rotates the canvas by 90 degrees in a clockwise direction.

**90° CCW** Rotates the canvas by 90 degrees in a counterclockwise direction.

**Arbitrary** Displays the Rotate Canvas dialog box (see Figure 13.17). Specify a precise angle by entering a number in the Angle field, choose CW or CCW (clockwise or counterclockwise), and click OK.

**Flip Canvas Horizontal** Mirrors the image across the vertical axis. Each picture element will mirror horizontally, so items from the right will appear on the left and vice versa. Writing and other features will appear reversed.

**Flip Canvas Vertical** Mirrors your image across the horizontal axis with vertical mirroring. Do not confuse this menu option with 180-degree rotation. This command will alter picture elements through mirroring, whereas the standard rotation will not.

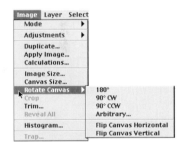

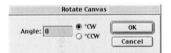

**Figure 13.17**

The Rotate Canvas dialog box

# Getting Help with Resizing Images

Photoshop provides the Resize Image Assistant (Macintosh) or Wizard (Windows) to help you determine the best possible options for size and resolution. When you use the Resize Image Assistant/Wizard, Photoshop duplicates your document. The operation has no effect on the original.

This interactive tool, seen in Figure 13.18, guides you through the entire process of changing your image size:

1. Choose Help → Resize Image and wait for the Resize Image Assistant /Wizard window to appear. Follow the directions and make the appropriate choices.

Figure 13.18

**Resize Image Assistant**

2. Choose Print or Online, depending on how you will use the image. Then click Next. In this exercise, let's assume we're preparing an image for print, which is slightly more complicated than preparing one for the Web.

   When preparing an image for online use rather than for print, you need only enter a new pixel count (the unit pull-down list does not appear in this case) and allow Photoshop to resize the image for you. The Web resize process ends after this step.

3. Set the new image height and width. These values are linked and vary proportionately; if you choose a new, larger height, the width will automatically update to a proportionately larger value. You can choose from any of five units on the pull-down lists to the right of each text field: inches, centimeters, points, picas, and columns. Pick the unit that works best for your project, and enter a value into either the Height or Width fields. After you've entered the new value or values, click Next.

4. Choose a halftone screen frequency and click Next. This value refers to the lines per inch (lpi) at which the image will be printed.

5. Next, set the image quality level for your picture. Do this by moving the slider between 1× and 2×. The higher the number, the better the image quality and the larger the file size. In the Results area below the slide bar, you can see the size of the original image, the new image, and the pixels per inch that will be produced. After selecting an image quality, click Next.

*Image quality level* refers to the proportion between the final image resolution and the screen frequency you picked in the previous step. When you pick a value between 1.5 and 2 times the screen frequency, you're assured of creating images at the highest quality the printer can produce. Because you include more information, the printer can create smoother and more realistic transitions.

6. Wait for Photoshop to complete your transformation. When the confirmation box appears, click Finish.

# Transforming Your Image

Photoshop allows you to stretch, squeeze, rotate, and otherwise alter your image selections. Each of these operations can be found in the Edit → Transform submenu (see Figure 13.19). You can apply any of them to a selection or to an independent layer. Many of these transformations act very much like the canvas operations discussed earlier in this chapter. However, they differ in some ways: They affect only your current selection or the active layer (and any layers linked to it), and they simultaneously affect all of the layers in a layer set.

You'll save time and effort if you isolate the item to be transformed to its own layer before performing a transformation. The advantage is that Photoshop lets you apply the transformation to the contents of a layer without having to make a selection.

Figure 13.19

**The Transform submenu**

### Scaling a Selection

*Scaling* refers to how you change the size of a portion of the image by stretching or squeezing it along one or both dimensions. For example, you might stretch the contents of a layer or selection along the vertical axis to create an excessively tall, fun-house-mirror look. Similarly, you might shrink your selection symmetrically along both axes to reduce its size proportionally. To use this feature, choose Edit → Transform → Scale. This menu command turns your selection marquee into an interactive bounding box (like the one in Figure 13.20) that allows you to apply a variety of scaling operations to your selection:

**Resize along Both Axes** Drag one of the bounding box corners. The new bounding box will follow your mouse movement. Release the mouse, and the selection will resize to the box you've chosen.

Figure 13.20

**You can apply a variety of scaling operations in an interactive bounding box.**

**Resize Proportionately along Both Axes**  Hold down Shift while dragging a bounding box corner. The new bounding box will increase or decrease in size as you move the mouse, but it will retain the proportions of the original selection. Release the mouse to finish the resize task. The example that follows demonstrates this operation.

> Shift-drag a bounding box to change the size without changing the proportions.

**Resize along One Axis**  Drag one of the four midpoint handles on the bounding box. This stretches your selection along one axis while retaining the dimension of the other axis. The bounding box will stretch or shrink as you move the mouse. Release the mouse, and the selection resizes to the new dimension.

To practice resizing, follow these steps:

1. Open the `ge_radio.psd` file, found in the `Ch13` folder on your CD.

2. The image is separated into two layers and the Background. The radio is covering some of the ad text, and we need to fix that. Target the Radio layer and choose Edit → Transform → Scale.

3. Hold down the Shift key while dragging a corner handle to reduce the size of the radio proportionally, as shown in Figure 13.21.

4. After scaling, position the image by placing the cursor inside the bounding box and dragging.

Figure 13.21

**The result of dragging the Scaling bounding box inward while pressing the Shift key to constrain proportions**

5. Click the check mark in the Options bar to implement the rotation and the move.

## Rotating a Selection

You can *rotate* a selection or the content of a layer by turning it around a point. Rotation allows you to change a selection's diagonal orientation. To rotate an image, choose Edit → Transform → Rotate.

In rotation, it's important to understand the concept of the *point of origin*. You find it whenever you create an interactive bounding box. It looks like a tiny compass rose and appears initially in the exact center of your bounding box.

The center point defines the fulcrum around which the rotation turns. In the left image in Figure 13.22, the center point remains in the middle as I manually rotate the image counterclockwise. In the right image, I moved the center point to the lower left, outside the box, and rotated the image around it.

Figure 13.22

**The image rotated manually around a center point within the box (left), and the point of origin moved to the lower left outside the box and the image rotated (right).**

To move your center point, simply drag it to its new location. Here are several tips that will help you place your center point:

- Your center point's location need not lie within the selection's bounding box. Select any spot on your image to place your point. You can use this feature to rotate around your picture's corners or around an important design feature.

- If you drag the center point back near the original central location of your selection, the point will automatically snap back to this default. This allows you to return the center point to its initial position after you experimented with moving it.

- Hold down the Shift key when moving the center point to constrain the point to several key axes: horizontal, vertical, and 45-degree diagonals.

- The center point location is shown in the first fields of the Options bar, $x$ and $y$.

## Performing the Rotation

Once you set your center point, you're ready to rotate your selection. To perform your rotation, move your mouse to just outside of the bounding box. The cursor will change, becoming a small arc with arrows at each end. When you see this cursor, you're ready to rotate. Simply drag the mouse and the selection's bounding box will rotate along with your mouse movements. Release the mouse and the image will update, the selection rotating to match the new border.

The following tips might help you while rotating:

- Hold down Shift while rotating to limit your rotation to increments of 15 degrees. This allows you easy access to such important and common angles as 30, 45, and 60 degrees.

- Sometimes your hand slips when making an important rotation. Choose Edit → Undo (or ⌘/Ctrl-Z) to reverse any rotation by one manipulation. This option leaves you within the rotation but undoes your last movement.

- Press the Esc key to cancel all rotation operations.

- To commit your rotation, press Return/Enter, double-click inside the boundary, or use the Options bar.

• The Options bar will show you the exact degree of rotation you selected in the fifth field, the one marked by an angle symbol. To specify an exact angle of rotation, type the value into this field. Remember to use negative numbers for counterclockwise rotation and positive numbers for clockwise rotation.

### Other Rotations and Flipping

The Edit → Transform submenu offers five standardized transformations. These options work the same as their Image → Rotate Canvas counterparts, but they affect only the active selection or layer, and offer you one-click access to some of the most common image modifications:

| Command | Action |
| --- | --- |
| Rotate 180° | Rotates your selection by 180 degrees, turning it upside down. |
| Rotate 90° CW | Rotates your selection clockwise by 90 degrees. |
| Rotate 90° CCW | Rotates your selection counterclockwise by 90 degrees. |
| Flip Horizontal | Mirrors your selection across the vertical axis, creating a horizontal reflection. |
| Flip Vertical | Mirrors your selection across the horizontal axis, creating a vertical reflection. |

## Skewing, Distorting, and Applying Perspective

These three functions—skewing, distorting, and applying perspective—all share a common basis: Each allows you to alter your selection by slanting image elements. Open the ge_radio.psd image on the CD and try them out. They work as follows:

**Skew** This function slants your selection along one axis, either vertical or horizontal. The degree of slant affects how pitched your final image will become. To skew, drag one of the handles of the bounding box. The border will update after each drag. When skewing, you can move each corner independently (affecting only one border side), as shown in Figure 13.23, or you can drag the handle at the center of an edge to skew parallel borders symmetrically.

**Distort** When you distort a selection, you can stretch either of its axes. Unlike skewing, slanting is not restricted to a single border at a time. Drag a corner and both adjacent edges will stretch along that corner (as in Figure 13.24). If you drag a border midpoint, you will stretch or shrink your selection along that edge. You can also drag the selection from any point in the middle to relocate it.

Figure 13.23

**Slant an image with the Skew command**

Figure 13.24

**Distort the image by adjusting the handles on the bounding box**

**Perspective** The Perspective transformation will squeeze or stretch one edge of a selection, slanting the two adjacent sides either in or out, as shown in Figure 13.25. This produces an image that mimics the way you perceive a picture slanted at a distance. To create a perspective, you drag a corner in only one direction, either horizontally or vertically. As you drag, you either pinch together one end of the picture or pull it out.

> To create skewed perspectives as easily as simple perspectives, drag any border midpoint to slant your results.

These three transformations share some common traits. Here are some tips that apply to all three operations:

- You can enter an angle into the Angle field in the Options bar to rotate your selection at the same time that you skew, distort, or change perspective.

- Choose Edit → Undo to reverse your last manipulation without leaving the interactive mode that allows you to skew, distort, or change perspective.

- To finish your transformations, click the check mark in the Options bar or press Return/Enter. You can also double-click inside the boundary to implement the transformation.

- To cancel your transformation, press Esc, or click the Cancel button in the Options bar.

- Since image transformations resample the image data, multiple transformations should be applied to the image before implementation.

Figure 13.25

**Applying perspective to the image creates diagonal lines that intersect at a horizon point.**

## Using the Free Transform Tool

Photoshop provides an interactive bounding box you can use to scale, rotate, or move the selection or layer contents. This combines the features of several of the tools described in the last sections in a handy, Swiss-Army-knife sort of transformation. You can access this command in several ways:

- Choose Edit → Free Transform.
- Press ⌘/Ctrl-T.
- When using the Move tool, click Show Bounding Box in the Options bar.

Once you've activated free transformation, you can directly access its features from the bounding box:

- Drag the center point as needed. It works exactly as described in "Rotating a Selection" earlier.

You cannot move the Move tool's center point.

- Move your mouse just outside any of the eight squares on the bounding box, and your cursor will change to a quarter-circle with arrows on each end. You are now in Rotate mode, and can use all of the rotation techniques described earlier.
- Move the mouse over any of the borders, and you can scale them horizontally or vertically.
- Move the mouse over any of the corners to scale them by dragging. You can use all of the scaling techniques described previously.
- Hold the ⌘/Ctrl key while dragging a corner and enter Distort mode. The corner will drag independently of the rest of the selection.
- To duplicate the selection you wish to transform, hold down Option/Alt while you transform it.
- If the cursor is inside the selection but not on the center point, you can move the selection.

# Transforming with the Move Tool

The Move tool ⊕ has become the transformation shortcut in Photoshop that transforms images on-the-fly. No more fishing around in the Edit menu for transformation features—you simply choose it and use it. When you choose the Move tool, the Options bar displays the Show Bounding Box check box. When you check the box, a bounding box surrounds the selection or the content areas of a layer. You can move, rotate, or scale the bounding box as you would with the Free Transform feature, or use the input fields to alter the layer contents numerically. The Options bar displays alignment options for the bounding box, as in Figure 13.26.

Align Top Edges       Align Left Edges
Align Vertical Centers   Align Horizontal Centers
Align Bottom Edges     Align Right Edges

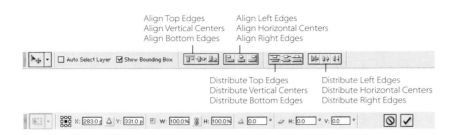

Distribute Top Edges       Distribute Left Edges
Distribute Vertical Centers   Distribute Horizontal Centers
Distribute Bottom Edges     Distribute Right Edges

Figure 13.26

**The Move tool
Options bar**

To use the Move tool, follow these steps:

1. Open a file.

2. Make a selection or target a layer.

3. Choose the Move tool. If a selection is active, you can align the contents of a layer with the top, bottom, middle, or sides of the marquee by clicking an icon in the Options bar.

4. Check the Show Bounding Box option.

5. Move, rotate or scale the image manually as you would the Free Transform command.

6. If you rotate or scale the image, the Options bar changes to display numerical values. Enter values for the $x$ and $y$ coordinates of the center of the bounding box. You can also enter values for the width, height, angle, and horizontal and vertical skew of the bounding box.

7. Click the check mark in the Options bar to commit the transformation or the cancel icon to cancel it.

# CHAPTER 14

# Capturing Images

*The process of digital imaging* begins when the image is captured. Two types of devices may be used to convert light into pixel information. The scanner or the digital camera acts as the eyes of the computer. These devices "see" color and interpret it into numerical data. Learning to use a digital camera or a scanner properly are important skills, and there are many variables that enter into producing a quality image capture. In addition to image size and resolution, contrast adjustments and hardware limitations must be taken into consideration. This chapter will introduce you to the best methods for inputting your image so that you can be assured of producing the best possible results in Photoshop.

You'll learn about:

- **Scanners and digital cameras**
- **Digitizing issues**
- **Scanning images**
- **Attributes of digital photographs**

# Scanners and Digital Cameras

A variety of hardware is available that captures image data in a form that your computer and, particularly, Photoshop 7 can understand. These technologies transform visual information into digital data. They work by translating analog values from light into digital levels that you can store and manipulate on your computer. As a preview of the issues this chapter will explore, Table 14.1 summarizes the factors that determine the quality of a scanner or digital camera.

<table>
<tr><td rowspan="11">Table 14.1<br><br>**Factors That Determine the Quality of an Image Capture Device**</td><td>**FACTOR**</td><td>**MEANING**</td></tr>
<tr><td>Optical Resolution</td><td>The maximum number of pixels per linear inch the device can create from information it gathers from a reflective or transmissive image.</td></tr>
<tr><td>Scanning Elements</td><td>Charge-Coupled Device (CCD) (better quality) or Complementary Metal-Oxide Semiconductor (CMOS) (less expensive).</td></tr>
<tr><td>Interface</td><td>The computer program that controls the device's behavior.</td></tr>
<tr><td>Scanning Modes</td><td>RGB, CMYK, Grayscale, Lab.</td></tr>
<tr><td>Document Dimensions</td><td>The maximum physical size of the image to be captured. In the case of a flatbed scanner, that would be limited to the size of the bed.</td></tr>
<tr><td>Dynamic Range</td><td>How extensively the device can retain detail, especially in the highlight and shadow areas of an image. The higher the Dynamic Range the more information the scanner can collect.</td></tr>
<tr><td>Speed</td><td>The length of time it takes the device to capture an image.</td></tr>
<tr><td>Bit Depth</td><td>How much information the device attributes to each pixel.</td></tr>
<tr><td>Passes</td><td>Some older scanners require three passes to collect the data—one each for red, green, and blue. Single-pass scanners are usually faster.</td></tr>
</table>

## Scanners

Scanners convert opaque images, or positive or negative transparencies, into digital data. A scanner measures the color content and tonal variations and converts the data it collects into pixels. Each pixel is assigned a value for its red, green, and blue components or, if the image is black-and-white, a grayscale value.

### Flatbed Scanners

A flatbed scanner bounces light off opaque art and directs the bounced light to a series of detectors that convert color and tonal variations into digital values. Flatbed scanners produce images composed of pixels. Compare flatbed scanners by evaluating the number of pixels produced per inch—the more pixels the scanner can produce, more detail the image will have. When choosing a scanner, be aware of the difference between its optical and interpolated resolution. *Optical* resolution is the amount of data that the scanner can collect optically. *Interpolated* resolution uses software to increase the resolution by manufacturing pixels. This can produce the undesirable softening of an image. Dynamic range is also a critical factor. A good consumer-grade flatbed scanner can currently be purchased for less than $100 to more than $3000 for "prosumer" models.

### Transparency Scanners

Instead of bouncing light off a piece of opaque art, a transparency scanner passes light through the emulsions on a piece of negative film or a color slide. In general, the quality of this light is better and less distorted because it is stronger than reflected light. A transparency scanner's *dynamic range* determines its ability to distinguish color variations and highlight and shadow detail. If you're going to purchase a transparency scanner, look for one with a high dynamic range (3.0–4.0) and a high optical resolution (2700–8000 dpi). Good transparency scanners for 35mm slides range in price from $400 to $2000. Transparency scanners are also available for 2.25"×2.25" and 4"×5" film, but these are significantly more expensive.

Transparency adapters are available for flatbed scanners, but these devices don't usually produce the quality scan that a dedicated transparency scanner can produce.

### Drum Scanners

Drum scanners are analog devices and have been used in the graphics industry for years. The opaque art or transparency is taped to a drum that spins very rapidly while the scanner's sensors record a small tightly focused area of color and tonal information. Older drum scanners output to process color film separations, converting the information directly into halftone dots. Newer drum scanners convert the information to pixels first. The advantages of using a drum scanner are the precise control it offers over color balance and contrast, the fine detail it allows, and its ability to scan large flexible reflective art. Drum scanners can produce outstanding quality color separations; however, they are gradually being replaced by high-end flatbed and transparency scanners.

## Digital Cameras and Video

Every digital camera (still or video) contains a two-dimensional array of detectors that convert the light from an entire image into pixels, or digital values. Light enters the camera through an optical lens and is focused onto the detectors. Two types of detectors dominate the digital camera market: the higher-quality charge-coupled devices (CCDs) and the less expensive complementary metal-oxide semiconductor (CMOS) chips. CMOS detectors are much more prone to noise and distortion.

The size and quality of the detector determine the amount of data a digital camera can collect. Inexpensive digital cameras produce ever larger and more detailed images, but most cameras cannot produce the level of picture information provided by the most common, inexpensive scanners. The appeal of digital cameras, however, is immediately apparent—their portability and the streamlining of workflow they allow by eliminating the need for the film processing.

Fair-quality digital cameras now cost somewhere around $500. Semiprofessional ("prosumer") digital cameras are high-resolution, self-contained units that don't have a single fix-mounted high-quality zoom lens. These cameras can cost between $1000 and $2000. Professional single-lens reflex (SLR) 35mm digital cameras with interchangeable lens systems are available that can produce digital images at high speeds comparable to any 35mm slide. These are significantly more expensive, ranging from $3000 to $30,000. Digital backs that attach to 120mm and 4"×5" film cameras are also available and quite pricey.

Professional SLR digital cameras, like the Canon EOS D30 or the Fuji S1 Pro, which has a Nikon body, use interchangeable lens systems. The lenses are compatible with their analog counterparts but have a different focal length when used on a digital camera. Normally, the conversion factor is 1.3. For example, a 35mm lens on an optical camera will produce a 50mm image on a digital camera, and a 105mm telephoto portrait lens will produce the equivalent of about a 135mm image.

> Many photo processors will digitize your traditional photographs. For a few dollars per roll, they will digitize your film and either ship the resulting files to you on a CD, upload them to a Web site, or both.

## Digitizer Boards

These special-purpose computer cards transform analog video signals into digital image data. Image sources for this technology include television signals and the output from VCRs and traditional (non-digital) video cameras. Such sources produce a picture screen (or *frame*) by sending out a stream of image information. Digitizer video boards, sometimes called "frame grabbers," wait until an entire screen has been received and then display it. Select the Capture function for your board, and you can grab one screen at a time.

This method of image capture produces the noisiest and poorest-quality pictures. Most video systems depend on motion to allow your brain to interpret between successive frames, providing the illusion of greater image quality. As I'm sure you've seen, when you hit the Pause button on your VCR, the actual images are quite raw and low-grade.

## Digitizing Issues

No matter which technology you use to capture your images, you should bear in mind the kinds of problems you may encounter capturing digital images. Some of these problems are unavoidable. With others, preemptive measures can ensure that you create the highest-quality image possible.

> Some scanning software, like Nikon's Digital ICE for its line of transparency scanners, can automatically repair many scanning flaws.

**Noise** Random values—*noise*—may inadvertently be added to and distributed across a digital picture. Noise is primarily a result of digitizing technology Video capture boards create the most noise, scanners the least. To help limit noise, shoot your pictures or video with as much ambient light as possible. Image noise appears most pronounced in the blue channel. (See Figures C14a, C14b, and C14c in the color section.) You can correct noise to a certain extent by applying the Despeckle or Gaussian Blur filters to the blue channel (see the accompanying sidebar).

### REMOVING IMAGE NOISE AND ARTIFACTS

An image's blue channel usually contains the most noise and artifacts. The blue channel is the least critical to the human visual system—but it is still necessary for producing full-color images. Instead of blurring the blue channel directly, a better technique is to duplicate the background of a flattened image. On the new layer that is created, change the blending mode to Color so that detail is not affected and then apply the Despeckle or Blur filter conservatively on this layer. Merge or flatten the two layers into one. Indirect filtering in this case leads to superior results, while remaining artifacts can be removed directly in their respective channels with the Blur tool, instead of being globally filtered.

**Artifacts** Unintentional image elements are sometimes produced by an imaging device or a compression scheme like a low-quality JPEG (again, see Figures C14a, C14b, and C14c in the color section). Artifacts can also result from dirty optics. Make sure to clean your lenses and dust both your scanner bed and lid to help avoid artifacts in your pictures. Also be sure originals are clean of dust, fingerprints, and other surface marks.

**Resolution** The *resolution* of a digitizing device is measured by the pixel count per unit of measure it produces: the higher the pixel count, the better the potential image quality. Keep this in mind when purchasing a scanner or digital camera. In general, when capturing an image, use a higher resolution than you will ultimately need. You can always use Photoshop's Image Size command to reduce the resolution to a more manageable picture size. Be cautious about increasing resolution or resampling "up." When Photoshop adds pixels by interpolation, the image may lose its contrast and sharpness.

Chapter 13, "Sizing and Transforming Images," shows how to determine scan resolution.

**Bit Depth** *Bit depth* refers to the capability of your scanner or digital camera to capture pixel information. The more bits a capture device allocates to each pixel, the more colors can be produced. The most common color depth, 8 bits per channel (or 24-bit RGB color), can produce 256 shades of red, green, or blue for a total of 16,777,216 digital values or colors.

"High bit" images consisting of 36-bit color (three channels with 12 bits per pixel) and 48-bit color (three 16-bit channels) can produce billions or even trillions of color combinations at the expense of much greater file sizes and a limit to the operations that Photoshop can perform.

> "High bit" files need to be duplicated and reduced to regular bit depth for output to print. This process will average out the larger amount of possible channel values in higher bit data into regular 8-bit data, which will theoretically be superior to a file that has been scanned in 24-bit image mode. Some photographers swear by this process. Chapter 3, "The Nature of the Beast," discusses bit depth in more detail.

**Moiré Patterns** These are optical anomalies produced when one pattern is imposed over another. In Photoshop they are usually created by scanning preprinted halftones or optical repeating patterns that produce interference with the screen's matrix of image pixels, as in Figure 14.1. Editing moiré patterns can be problematic because they can vary significantly from image to image, depending on the scan and halftone resolutions and the screen angles. You can avoid them by scanning only continuous-tone images or by using the scanner's descreening function, described below. You can sometimes reduce moiré patterns by changing the angle of the art on the scanner bed. After the image has been scanned, rotate it back with the Crop tool. This technique requires some experimentation. Also note that eliminating the moiré noise from the most pronounced channel (usually the blue) can reduce or eliminate moiré patterns.

Figure 14.1

**Scanned directly from a magazine, this image contains heavy moiré patterns caused by the interference of the original halftone screens, the image pixels.**

# Scanning Images

Photoshop provides direct integration with most scanner control software. And, although you can open a previously scanned image, you can also scan images directly into Photoshop. The File → Import submenu offers direct access to any installed scanners, as you can see in Figure 14.2, where my VistaScan TWAIN device appears as a file type. Of course, this menu will vary with the scanning software currently installed.

Figure 14.2

The Import menu offers direct control of installed scanners.

After you select a scanner from the submenu, its controlling dialog box will appear, as seen in Figure 14.3. The illustration represents the software that drives a UMAX Astra e5420 scanner. The software for your scanner may look different, but most scanner control software allows you to work with the attributes shown here:

**Type** Most interfaces offer you the opportunity to choose between multiple scanners.

**Beginner/Advanced** Typically you can choose between a Beginner mode that offers limited control using everyday terminology and an Advanced mode, like the one shown here, that offers precision scanning options.

**Resolution** Enter a value to determine the pixel count. Be aware that some scanner software refers to resolution in DPI (dots per inch) instead of the PPI (pixels per inch) used by Photoshop.

**B&W or Color** Most scanners allow you to select between a grayscale or color scan. Grayscale images typically use about a third of the memory of color images.

**Descreen/No Descreen** The function will diffuse dots produced by scanning preprinted images from newspapers or magazines, for example. Use it to eliminate moiré patterns produced by the interference of the image's halftone screen with the resolution pixels of the scanner. The scan can take considerably more time.

Figure 14.3

A typical scanning software dialog box, offering Beginner and Advanced modes

**Preview** The Preview feature performs a quick, low-quality scan you can use to crop the image to eliminate unwanted areas.

**Filter** This option applies a sharpening operation to the image after the data has been collected. In most cases, it's better to use Photoshop's Unsharp Mask filter after the image has been scanned, because it affords more control.

**Auto Adjustment** Check this box in order to perform automatic contrast adjustments to the image. In most cases it's better to scan the image and perform a Levels or Curves adjustment in Photoshop.

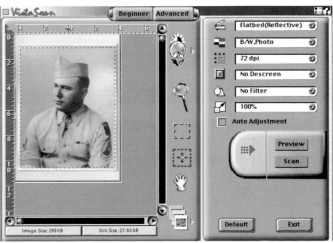

**Scan** Every scanner provides a Scan button to initiate the scanning process. As the scan proceeds, you will usually see a progress bar indicating what percentage of the document has been scanned.

## Other Uses for Scanners

Flatbed scanners are designed to scan images that are drawn, painted, or printed on flat sheets of film or paper. They can also be used to scan text if Optical Character Reading (OCR) software is installed on the computer. OCR software can convert a scanned image of text, usually saved as a TIFF, to an editable text document. OCR software does this by recognizing the shapes of characters and applying conversion algorithms to produce an editable text document of significantly smaller file size.

There are also non-traditional uses for scanners that you may want to try for fun. A scanner can be used to scan three-dimensional objects. Place the object on the bed of the scanner and position the cover over the object. Cover the entire scanner with a piece of black cloth to prevent light leaks. You can scan any object that fits on the bed.

Just for fun, you might also try scanning your hand or even your head. Remain very still during the process of the scan. Or try moving a little to produce some really weird results. Don't stare directly into the light, of course; and make sure you clean the glass after this twisted little adventure.

## Digital Photographs

Digital photographs share many traits with scanned images but also have some unique attributes of their own. Here are some of the ways in which they differ:

**Size** Low- and medium-quality digital cameras produce, in general, smaller images than scanners do. Their image size is limited to the capacity of their CMOS or CCD chip. Their resolutions and file sizes also depend on the amount of data their detectors can collect and process. Advertising materials often describe the resolution of a digital camera measured in *megapixels*, an abbreviation of the total number of pixels in the entire image. For example, a 5.5-megapixel camera will employ a CCD that can convert the image into approximately 5,500,000 pixels.

**Functionality** Digital cameras work best when used in the same way you'd use a traditional camera. Many do not capture pages or printed photographs particularly well, although they can be used in a pinch to create relatively low-resolution copies of printed material.

**Blue Channel** The blue channel accumulates more noise than the red or green channels. This can be quite pronounced in a digital photograph. To correct this problem the blue channel can be blurred slightly with the Gaussian Blur or Despeckle filter.

**Noise** Noise in digital photographs tends to be the product of low lighting conditions. One of the best ways to avoid noise in digital snapshots is to increase ambient light. Of course, an even better method is to purchase better-quality equipment with high-end sensors.

# PART II

# Photoshop Color

Photoshop is about color! *When you encircle an area on an image with a selection tool and make any modification to it, you are really only changing the color values of designated pixels. It comes as no surprise then, that there are numerous methods to perform this operation, and therein lies Photoshop's ultimate power.*

*Color can present itself on your monitor in a variety of ways. These "color working spaces" affect how you see color. Much of your editing depends on your perceptions of the on-screen image. Color management and color correction are critical factors in the quality of the image. This section of Photoshop 7 Savvy looks at managing, correcting, and mapping color and preparing files for their ultimate destination.*

# CHAPTER 15

# Color Management and Printing

*You've labored long and hard* to get the color exactly right. You've used all the tricks—Levels, Curves, Selective Color, Color Balance, Adjustment Layers, the Unsharp Mask filter (covered in Chapter 16, "Adjusting Tonality and Color")—and the image looks perfect on the monitor. Unfortunately, what your printer just spit out looks quite different. Those beautiful sky blues and brilliant magentas have turned to gloomy grays and muddy maroons. Furthermore, the image looks quite different from monitor to monitor.

If you're a digital artist or graphic designer using Photoshop to print color images, you probably frequently ask yourself two very important questions: How can I be confident that the color on my monitor will be matched by the color of the printer? And how can I trust that the color on *my* monitor will look like the color on *your* monitor? These questions are about how you *manage* color from one device to another, and that's what this chapter is about.

In this chapter, you'll read about:

- Why we need to manage color

- Managing color between monitors

- Converting colors

- Printing images

## Color Management—A Brief History

In the years before the desktop publishing revolution, professional color systems were used in the creation and modification of high-quality printing and publishing. These methods of color management relied on what is called "closed-loop" color, the idea being that nothing ever escaped the system. No outside files were accepted, and no files were ever allowed to leave the system except in the form of separated film, ready for printing. Looking back, those were the "good ol' days" when the reliability of color was—mostly—under control. The systems were expensive, and compared to today's computers, very slow. But they worked.

Desktop technologies created a *distributed* model for color production. Some of the work was done on a computer that wasn't connected to a prepress color system. It was the differences between systems—different monitors, different viewing conditions, and different software applications—that created the need for color management.

Scientists went to work on the problem in the late 1980s, developing a model for color management that would eventually provide software tools to ensure that color would match, location-to-location and device-to-device. The first practical color management system, Apple ColorSync, arrived in 1991 and has undergone improvements since. Over the years, the idea of color management has migrated to most professional software applications—including Adobe Photoshop. Today most computers and operating systems have a facility for color management, and most applications have built-in support for color management. The challenge is getting it to work.

In the fall of 1998, the Adobe Photoshop development team rocked the design and printing community with a completely new outlook on color. The release of Photoshop 5 got the attention of all color practitioners in the digital imaging world. Prior to Photoshop 5, the color that was displayed depended entirely on the monitor, and there are so many different types of monitors that the colors in an image on one monitor may very well appear dissimilar to the same image viewed on another monitor.

## The Color Working Space

What revolutionized digital color was the introduction of the concept of a specific environment for handling color. This environment, called a *color working space* (CWS), is independent of the monitor and can be chosen by the user. Under this model, it is possible to scan, save, edit, and store an image with a CWS attached to it. When the image is saved and then opened, its appearance will display the characteristics of the CWS. The image is embedded with an ICC (International Color Consortium) profile, information that describes the color characteristics or *gamut* of the CWS. The image can then move from one computer to another with its profile and will appear the same on different monitors.

The CWS concept created the opportunity for Photoshop to accommodate images from scanners and other sources whose color gamuts exceed the available colors on a monitor. The CWS allows for color to be captured, modified, stored, and output without affecting the color gamut of the original.

# A Window into a Window

To grasp the concept of color working space, imagine that the image you see on your monitor exists on a separate, parallel plane, just behind your monitor, and that your monitor acts like a window into the image. The image you see may be the entire image, but it might not be. It might be distorted by the window's characteristics or size. Perhaps the window is not perfectly transparent, perhaps it is slightly tinted, or perhaps light is reflecting off its surface, causing the colors to appear muted.

In fact, computer monitors really behave like windows into our images, modifying the "reality" of the actual image and displaying something that is appropriate to the monitor's abilities, but not always to the qualities of the image itself.

For professional graphic artists, the monitor is an excellent window into the image. This is true because we spend considerable sums of money on quality monitors that have good color gamuts and a range of brightness that will allow us to see *almost* all the qualities of the image in Photoshop. But lesser monitors don't provide such an undistorted view.

## Monitor Quality

To better understand this, consider the monitor. Monitors are light emitters: they create light from electrical energy. A cathode ray tube (CRT) monitor like the one on your computer is a television-like picture tube. As illustrated in Figure 15.1, it uses electrons beamed at the monitor's face from the back of the picture tube to stimulate mineral phosphors that are coated on the inside of the face of the tube, creating light of a single color on the face.

Figure 15.1

**A cross-section of a cathode ray tube showing the separate high-voltage amplifiers for the red, green, and blue signals**

The electrons are invisible to the human eye, but when they strike the coating, the phosphors react, emitting visible light in a spectrum that is within the color gamut of human vision. Activating those phosphors in combination with others causes "color" to be created on the face of the picture tube.

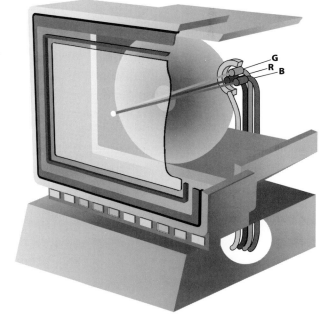

As with many electromechanical devices, there is considerable variability in the manufacture of picture tubes and in the quality of minerals used to coat the inside of the tube. Some computer monitors sell for less than $100, while others sell for more than $3500. In addition to the size of the monitor, there are quality issues to take into account when evaluating a monitor's color. Is the color quality of a sub-$100 monitor likely to be very good? How will it compare to the color quality of a graphic-arts–quality monitor designed for critical color decisions? Cost-cutting measures taken by the makers of low-cost monitors include coating the monitor with phosphors of inconsistent quality or low purity. It might be possible to reduce manufacturing costs by reducing the quality control checks that are made in manufacture to ensure that each monitor meets the company's standards. By contrast, a graphic-arts–quality monitor will be made from components that cost more to make, more to test, and more to deliver to the end user.

## Monitor Profiles

A monitor's characteristics are described by its ability to display pure red, green, and blue colors as bright, clear components of an image. In the visual arts we use such colors, and the millions of color permutations possible when mixing them together, to make our photos and illustrations. In order for Photoshop to display an image correctly, it must know the characteristics of the monitor you are using. To do this, we provide Photoshop with a piece of software called a *monitor profile*.

There are several ways to create a monitor profile. The easiest method is to make a visual calibration of your monitor using version 5 or later of Adobe Gamma to test and adjust the appearance of the monitor, and then save the resulting information as a *color profile* (see Chapter 5, "Setting Up the Program").

Installed on your system along with Photoshop, Adobe Gamma is a software monitor calibrator that builds a monitor profile. To use it, follow the on-screen instructions. Windows 2000 and XP and MacOS 8.5 through X also offer calibration software packages bundled with their operating systems and accessible from their monitor display settings. These programs are very similar to Adobe Gamma.

### CRT VS. LCD

Liquid crystal display (LCD) monitors contain a gooey liquid compound sandwiched between two thin grids of transparent electrodes and two polarizing filters. The electrodes can selectively turn the cells (or pixels) in the grid on to create the image you see on screen.

You can see an LCD display in room light, but were it not for the back and edge lighting of the monitor, the image would appear at low contrast except when viewed head on. Even though LCD monitors have been greatly improved over the past few years, the colors you see on screen are, to a degree, dependent on the angle at which you view the image. Because a certain degree of distortion can be expected from most LCD monitors, graphic arts professionals prefer CRT displays.

LCD monitors are no longer used exclusively on laptops. Apple stopped making CRT monitors and now makes only LCD monitors, which are integrated into its latest iMacs or purchased separately as "flat panel displays." If you are interested in precision color accuracy, it's wise to invest in a CRT monitor. You'll also need an additional video card.

Some monitors are "self calibrating." That is, the software that drives them automatically readjusts their characteristics based on a preprogrammed profile as they vary over time from wear. These monitors, however, should be periodically calibrated manually to ensure that the designated white point and gamma are consistent with your preferred working environment.

Adobe Gamma and its Windows and Macintosh counterparts are visual calibration systems. In other words, the settings are based on the perceptions of the viewer, and are to some degree subjective. A visual calibration system can only create a very generalized profile.

Precision calibration of a monitor can be achieved by employing a device called a *colorimeter*. A colorimeter is a worthwhile investment if accurate color is critical to your task. For example, if you are doing a significant amount of color correction for output to color separations or high-end RGB or inkjet prints, it's essential to work in a predictable color environment from session to session.

Monitor characteristics change over time. You should calibrate your monitor a minimum of once per month.

### ACCURATE CALIBRATION WITH A COLORIMETER

A colorimeter attaches to the screen with suction cups. It measures the color temperature, gamma, and white point of the monitor (see "The Yin/Yang of Color" later in this chapter if you aren't already familiar with those basic characteristics of any monitor). For this demo, I've chosen to use a ColorVision Spyder, which currently costs about $300. The device is bundled with software (either ColorCal or its professional version, OptiCal) that analyses the data and writes an ICC profile based on the measured output of the monitor. The software provides instructions to take you through the calibration process.

Here's a step-by-step overview of monitor calibration with the ColorVision Spyder.

1. Be sure that the monitor has been on for at least one half hour before calibrating. Plug the Spyder into a USB port on the computer.

2. Next, launch the software. After the initial splash screen you'll see the OptiCal interface. Choose a monitor to be calibrated (if you have more than one monitor connected to your computer).

3. Choose the type of monitor, either CRT or LCD. The window also displays the date of your last calibration.

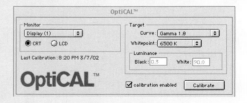

*Continued on next page*

## ACCURATE CALIBRATION WITH A COLORIMETER

4.  In the Target field choose a target Curve. This will depend on the type of system you are working on, either Gamma 1.8 for Mac or Gamma 2.2 for Windows.

5.  Choose a white point. For most printing applications, 6500K (Kelvin) is the white point of choice.

6.  Click the Calibrate button. You are told to set your monitor's contrast controls to the maximum 100% and the brightness controls to the minimum. Then adjust the brightness control so that the logo shown here is just barely visible. Click the Next button.

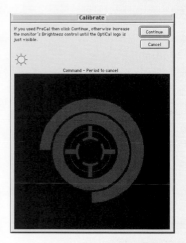  

7.  Attach the Spyder to the screen on the graphic. Click the Next button.

8.  The software displays a series of color fields—pure red, green and blue, and a variety of grays. The Spyder measures the temperature and feeds the information to the software.

9.  When the calibration is complete, OptiCal asks you to save your profile.

Colorimeters like the Spyder have the advantage of producing a consistent monitor environment from session to session, ensuring the accuracy of the color you see on screen during the editing process.

## The Viewing Environment

Professionals in the printing and publishing industries have known for years that to achieve good color on a computer monitor you need (among other things) to put the monitor into a "proper" viewing environment. The International Organization for Standardization (ISO) and its partner national organizations recently adopted a new color standard for viewing color for the photographic and graphic arts industries worldwide. Called ISO 3664, the standard dictates, among other things, that a proper viewing environment is a workspace without windows or skylights—no natural light at all. They also specify that the color of the walls should be neutral gray (the ISO committee specifies the color Munsell N5 through N7). The walls should be absent of colorful artwork, and the artist in front of the computer should be wearing neutral clothing, preferably gray or black. Room lighting recommendations in the ISO standard are for very low, preferably diffuse lighting of the proper 5000 K temperature.

Is this a happy place to work? It's pretty dull, but it's a workplace where color can be viewed most accurately. Some design studios and professional prepress operations have such a workplace but reserve it for "soft proofing" visits, which provide an opportunity for workers to go into the "cave" only long enough to approve color on-screen.

## Determining a Monitor Profile

Just having a calibrated monitor and a proper viewing environment are not enough. You must tell your operating system about the profile, setting it as the system profile. Then, when you launch Photoshop, it will use your monitor profile for some of its color display calculations.

There are two ways to tell your system about the monitor profile you have created on a Macintosh. In MacOS 9.2 and earlier, under the Apple menu, choose Control Panels → Monitors and click the Color icon; from the ColorSync menu, choose a profile. Or choose Control Panels → ColorSync directly from the Apple menu to display the dialog box. Click the Set Profile button and choose a profile from the list. In OS X, from the Apple menu choose system Preferences → Hardware → Display → Color. Then, from the resulting menu, choose a profile.

In Windows 98, 2000, and XP, choose Start → Settings → Control Panel → Display → Color Management. (Windows 95 and NT do not support color management.)

> The Windows path will depend on the video board you have installed. For some boards, you may have to choose Control Panel → Display → Settings → Advanced → Color Management.

Choose the system profile or the profile you created with Adobe Gamma or the colorimeter. The computer will know how to correct the color displayed on your monitor through the profile, making adjustments on the fly to all images displayed on screen.

Photoshop automatically looks to the operating system to get the name of the current monitor profile, and you cannot change that setting from within the latest version of Photoshop. But it is possible to "turn color management off" in the Color Settings control panel. This has the effect of returning Photoshop 7 to the functionality of Photoshop 4, limiting the color gamut to that of the monitor and disabling all color-space conversions.

## The Yin/Yang of Color

When we discuss the *gamuts* of color working spaces, we must understand that the gamut of a monitor is a triangular space with its corners in the red, green, and blue areas of an industry-standard color chart. The gamut chart in Figure C15 in the color section plots the available colors of a device (a monitor, for example) compared to the gamut of colors humans can see—and the differences are extreme.

All of the color spaces of the world of graphic arts and photography converge inside a large triangle that falls well within the colors of human vision. With Photoshop's support for the color working space, we want to choose a space that is adequate to accommodate most if not all the colors of our output device, while providing a reasonable view of that color on our monitor.

Unfortunately, the color system used for printing color on paper is the physical opposite of the color system used to emit light on the face of a monitor. With light-emitting devices, the unit creates, and mixes, colors from the three additive color primaries—red, green, and blue. When you add equal parts of full intensity red, green, and blue light on a monitor, you get white.

The vibrancy and brightness of these primary colors on a picture tube are usually far greater than they can ever be on the printed page, because the printing process begins with the available white light in the viewing environment, and then filters out components of that light to simulate color. The processes are called *additive* (for light-emitting devices) and *subtractive* (for printed or reflected light products).

When you put pigment on a sheet of paper, superimposing the primary colors of ink (cyan, yellow, magenta) on top of each other, in an ideal world you would get pure black, but in reality, because of impurities in the ink, you get something that approximates deep, yucky brown. (Technical term!) Because pigments subtract light components from the white light in the environment, they reduce its intensity, making it less bright than unfiltered light. Subtractive colorants always reduce the amount of light reflected back at the viewer, and thus it's very hard for the printed page to compete with the bright color on good computer monitor. And there we have the classic yin/yang of color—the conflict between the two scientific principles of color reproduction—and another reason we need color management in our lives. The strengths of emitted light on a monitor are the weaknesses of colors on the printed page.

If we want to reproduce the best color possible on the printed page, while still displaying the color in the same images, we must acknowledge and accept the weakness of the monitor relative to the printed page, and vice versa. The compromise we must learn to accept is that there are colors at the blue, magenta, and vibrant green points of the triangle that we can display on a monitor, but cannot print with the standard four-color ink sets used on ink-jet printers and four-color process printers.

## Making a Colorful Match

Choosing a color working space that is appropriate to the printed page is critically important so that we don't force Photoshop to remap the colors in an image. We want to pick a working space that is not too big (so we don't add colors that are out of the printable range) and not too small (so we don't omit colors needed to accurately represent the image).

The gamut chart in the color section (Figure C15) shows the comparative gamuts of several of Photoshop's color working spaces. Superimposed in yellow is the gamut of standard printing inks on gloss paper (called the SWOP Coated gamut).

## Gamma

*Gamma* is a measurement of the monitor's contrast and saturation. It is expressed as a number, from 1.0 to about 2.5, that describes the curvature of a mathematical contrast curve. The Macintosh has traditionally used a gamma of 1.8, which is relatively flat compared to television. Windows PCs use a 2.2 gamma value, which provides more contrast and saturation. The gamma of Windows is closer to the "natural" appearance of the world, while the 1.8 gamma adopted by the Macintosh is more like the contrast achieved by printing on good paper. If you are working on images destined for television, the World Wide Web, or multimedia, it's better to use a gamma of 2.2. If your destination is the printed page, a gamma of 1.8 to 2.0 may be more appropriate.

## Getting to Know RGB Color Working Space

The color working space is, as already mentioned, a plane for holding and handling images in Photoshop that is independent of the monitor. The RGB color working spaces of Adobe Photoshop 7 include five standard color spaces. Photoshop also has the ability to choose others that that are designed for other working environments or offer special qualities. Each has a combination of characteristics, including its color temperature, gamma, and white point (the phosphor settings for "white"). White is a variable thing in the world of computer-generated color, because the effective "whiteness" of the non-image areas is a key component in getting the color on the screen to match the color that is produced by a printer or a commercial printing press.

### sRGB IEC61966-2.1

Of the color spaces available, sRGB (the *s* stands for *standardized*) is the smallest. This means that it puts serious limitations on the colors available in your color palette in Photoshop. The sRGB space, designed by Microsoft and Hewlett-Packard, is well suited to corporate computer monitors and images destined for viewing on the World Wide Web. It is also suitable for output to low-end desktop inkjet printers. sRGB has taken a lot of flack for being destructive to images with large color gamuts, and indeed it is. But, if you look at the purpose of sRGB—making images look good on corporate computers—the color space makes more sense and is useful for its intended purpose.

It is set as the default color working space in Photoshop 7 (as it was in 5 and 6), and that is the root of the controversy surrounding it. Adobe allows you to change this setting—but most people don't realize that it is important to do so. Use sRGB as your color working space, or convert images to this space, when developing images for display on the Web or output to desktop inkjet printers. Otherwise, use one of the following.

### Adobe RGB (1998)

The Adobe RGB (1998) color working space is large enough to accommodate graphic arts images and most scanned images, and allows for good representation on most high-quality monitors. Adobe RGB (1998) has a white point of 6500 K, which is in line with the latest ISO standard (ISO 3664) for color viewing in critical color conditions. Its gamma is 2.2. Adobe RGB (1998) is also able to accommodate conversions to CMYK for printing with good results; very little of the CMYK color is clipped or remapped in the process.

> Don't confuse the *K* that crops up in color discussions about white point with *K* for kilobytes or black (as in CMYK). Here it stands for degrees Kelvin; 6500 K is approximately the "temperature" of outdoor ambient light in the middle of a clear day.

### Apple RGB

The original "graphic arts" monitor was the Apple 13-inch RGB monitor. It created an industry, providing color previews to millions of users from 1988 to about 1995, when it was replaced by better and larger monitors. Based on a Sony picture tube, the Apple monitor had good color saturation and a small but reasonable color gamut. The Apple RGB color working space is a good choice for converting images from unknown sources. Almost all the stock photos made between 1988 and 1995 were made with computers and scanners connected to an Apple 13-inch monitor; and although the quality of monitors has improved substantially since then, that monitor still represents the colors of the era. This Apple RGB working space uses 6500 K color temperature for white and a 1.8 gamma, which is relatively flat in appearance.

## ColorMatch RGB

The Radius PressView monitor was, for years, the viewing standard of the graphic and visual arts. Almost all professional color work was created on monitors in this class. Now discontinued, the PressView will live on in the form of a color working space that matches its characteristics.

ColorMatch RGB represents a good gamut of colors, a 1.8 gamma, and a 5000 K white point, which causes some monitors to turn a sickly yellow color. Use this one if it causes the colors on your screen to look good while maintaining a pleasant white. If your monitor turns yellowish, switch to Apple RGB, which has similar characteristics, as that will deliver a bluer white and a more attractive appearance on many monitors. If you have a PressView, this is an excellent working space for you.

## Color Sync RGB—Generic RGB Profile

This matches the color profile currently set in the Apple ColorSync control panel (Figure 15.2). From this control panel you can choose from a list of ICC monitor profiles that are found in the ColorSync profiles list in the System Folder.

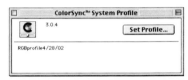

## Monitor RGB

This profile sets the color working space to the current monitor profile. Use this working space if other programs you will use to view the image do not support color management.

Figure 15.2

**The ColorSync System Profile window**

## Other Color Working Spaces

We are able to choose or load other RGB color working spaces that were the primary spaces in Photoshop 5.0 and 5.5. These appear, along with several dozen others, in the Edit → Color Settings (Windows and MacOS 9) and Photoshop → Color Settings (MacOS X) dialog box under Working Spaces RGB. They include:

**CIE RGB** The International Commission on Illumination (CIE) is an organization of scientists who work with color. CIE standards determine how we measure and describe color in every field of human endeavor. This working space is based on the CIE standard RGB color space, a 2.2 gamma, and Standard Illuminant E white point. Its gamut of colors is slightly larger than that of the Apple monitor, and it works almost identically when opening or converting images from older files, those that were created and saved from early versions of Photoshop.

**NTSC (1953)** The North American Television Standards Committee established a color gamut and a white point for television in the U.S. that is maintained to this day. Use this color space if you are working on images that will be displayed on television. The gamma is 2.2, and the white point is a very cool-blue Standard Illuminant C.

**PAL/SECAM** PAL and SECAM are European and Asian standards for television color and contrast. As with the NTSC setting above, if your work is destined for television outside North America, this setting is appropriate. The gamma is 2.2, and the white point is 6500 K.

**SMPTE-C** A movie industry standard, SMPTE-C is compliant with the Society of Motion Picture and Television Engineers standards for motion picture illuminants. It has the same white point as the two television standards, above, and its color temperature is 6500 K.

**Wide Gamut RGB** Adobe created this color working space to accommodate images created on the computer, where vibrant greens, bright reds, and cobalt blues are created and must be maintained. This color space is particularly well suited to work that is destined for an RGB film recorder. The gamma is 2.2, and the white point is a yellowish 5000 K, especially useful to those recording onto "electronic" color transparency films. Wide Gamut may sound attractive to those who believe that more is better, but in fact, too large a color gamut can be damaging to many images. Wide Gamut color remapping will result in strange color shifts in images. Know what you are doing before using this space.

There are numerous RGB spaces available for profiles of specific monitors, laptop computers, printers, or working conditions. You can save and load specific profiles from other sources, or you can make your own using Adobe Gamma or a colorimeter.

## Color Settings

Photoshop 6 made significant changes to the color settings, which remain intact in this latest version. Photoshop uses ICC color management at all times (even when color management is technically "off"). The settings you select for color handling can make a huge difference in the appearance and reproduction of color.

Figure 15.3

**The Color Settings controls**

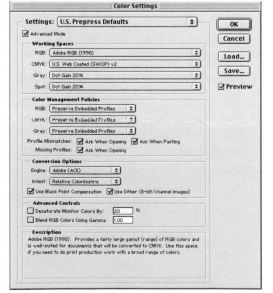

Choose Edit → Color Settings (Windows and MacOS 9 and earlier) and Photoshop → Color Settings (MacOS X) to access the primary color control window (Figure 15.3). It has two modes: Standard and Advanced. (The Conversion Options and Advanced Controls areas shown in the figure are hidden if you clear the Advanced box.)

You should configure color settings prior to opening a document or creating a new document. The Color Settings dialog box controls your color working spaces, your color management policies, and your settings for what should happen when Photoshop opens an image that either has no embedded profile or has one that is different from the current color working space.

First, set your Color Settings defaults according to the kind of work you do. Choose a setting from the Settings pull-down menu at the top of the window. If you are unsure, a good place to start is with U.S. Prepress Defaults, which includes the Adobe RGB (1998) color space and typical North American standards for printing color, U.S. Web Coated (SWOP) v2. This is a good space for both RGB and CMYK colors, and will cause little, if any, harm to images handled by the program.

> Any change to the defaults will create a custom setting.

## CMYK Working Space

If you plan to convert your image from RGB mode to CMYK, you can choose a color working space for CMYK. If you have a four-color (CMYK) profile for a printer, for example, or a printing press that you normally use, you can set it if it's on the list. If you don't have a custom profile to use, there are several "generic" CMYK profiles you can load. For North America, you can use the SWOP (Specifications for Web Offset Publications) standard profiles. There should be at least two in your system, one for gloss papers and another for uncoated papers. If you are outside North America, choose either Eurostandard (coated or uncoated) or the Japan Standard profiles as appropriate to your location. These CMYK profiles will be used when you convert to CMYK with the Mode → CMYK or Mode → Convert To Profile functions, and the results will be acceptable.

## Creating a Custom Profile

You can configure a custom profile in Photoshop if you know the specifications of your output device. Check the Advanced box in the Color Settings dialog box and click the CMYK Workspace menu. Choose Custom CMYK to display the dialog box shown in Figure 15.4, which resembles the Photoshop Printing Ink and Separation Setup from Photoshop 4 and earlier or the built-in CMYK settings of Photoshop 5. Enter the specifications for your printing environment, including the following:

**Name** Reflects the specifications found under Ink Options.

**Ink Colors** Choose a profile based on the printing environment and paper stock.

> If you choose Custom from the Ink Colors menu, you can enter *Yxy* or Lab values derived from a specific hardware device (as shown in Figure 15.4) or click on a swatch and choose a color from the Color Picker.

**Dot Gain** Enter a percentage for the amount the dot will shrink or expand (from −10% to +40%) when ink is applied to a substrate on a printing press. The Curves option lets you apply dot gain values to each of the CMYK channels individually instead of a global setting for all four channels.

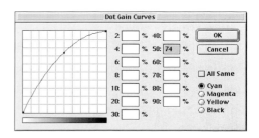

**Separation Type**  Choose a separation type:

> **GCR**  (Gray Component Replacement) Black ink replaces cyan, magenta, and yellow to create neutrals and colors. CGR separations tend to be darker and more saturated, and they produce better gray balance.
>
> **UCR**  (Under Color Removal) Black replaces cyan, magenta, and yellow in only the neutral areas to use less ink and produce more detail in the shadows. Because UCR uses less ink, it is used on more porous paper like newsprint or uncoated stock.

**Black Generation**  Available with GCR, this determines how dark the cyan, magenta, and yellow must be before it adds black to the mix. Select Light to use black sparingly or Heavy to really lay it on. None prints no black, and Maximum prints black over everything.

**Black Ink Limit**  Enter the percentage of the maximum amount of black that can be printed on the page.

**Total Ink Limit**  Designates the total amount of cyan, magenta, yellow, and black that can be applied to the page, ranging from 200% to 400% (with 300% being common for printing on coated stock).

**UCA**  (Under Color Addition) Available with GCR, adds cyan, magenta, and yellow where the black ink is sparsely distributed.

**Gray Ramp**  Reflects the distribution of color in graph form. You cannot edit the graph but you can observe the lines to check the results of your settings.

> It is essential to consult your printer to determine what specifications best suit the printing environment before applying your custom profile to the image.

## Loading a Custom Profile

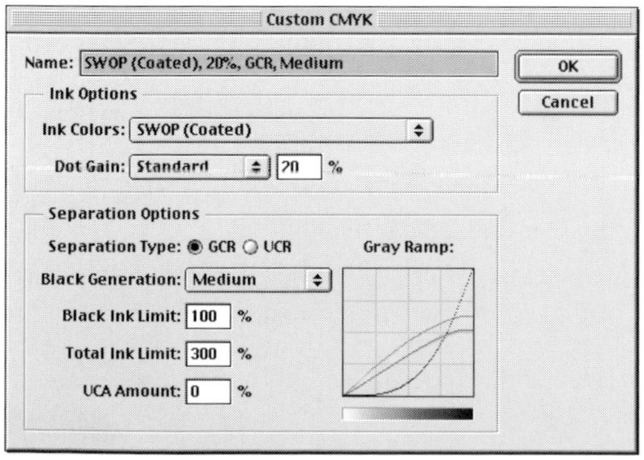

Figure 15.4

**The Custom CMYK dialog box**

If you are printing to a CMYK device that provides a custom profile, or if you've created a custom profile using a spectrophotometer or a profile-writing program like ColorVision's Pro-filer Plus, you can load it as your CMYK workspace. Check the Advanced box and click on the CMYK Workspace menu. Choose Load CMYK and locate the profile in the directory.

## Color Management Policies

*Color management policies* determine how Photoshop deals with color profiles when opening a document. You can specify how Photoshop will deal with documents that have no embedded profile, or whose profile differs from that specified in the Color Settings dialog box.

If we simply reopen a file on the same machine, using the same color working space speci-fied in the Color Settings dialog box, the file will open without interruption. But if we move the file to another machine running Photoshop, or we open an image that came from another machine, Photoshop puts on the brakes, asking, in effect, "Wait. This file is not from around these parts. What should I do with it?"

Putting the responsibility for controlling how files are opened on the user, Photoshop asks you to set one of the policies for each type of file we might be opening, RGB, CMYK, and Grayscale. Our choices for these policies are:

**Off**  When a file type's Color Management Policies option is set to Off, files with unknown profiles will be opened with color management turned off. This causes Photoshop to behave more like Photoshop 4 (Adobe calls it "pre–color management"), where the Color Working Space color gamut limits the color available in any image.

**Preserve Embedded Profiles**  Opening images that already have a color working space profile embedded will retain that space. Any new documents will be created within the current color working space. This is a safe approach to opening files with embedded profiles, as it will allow these images to be opened without making any modification to the color working space of the image. After working on the file, it's possible to save the document and retain the embedded profile. When importing color to an RGB or grayscale document—cutting and pasting an image from another with a different profile document, for example—appearance takes prior-ity over numeric values. When importing color to a CMYK document, numeric values takes priority over appearance.

**Convert To Working RGB/CMYK/Grayscale**  (This option changes according to the image type.) This will cause mathematic conversion, remapping all the color values in the image to the current color working space. This conversion can cause drastic changes in the color of an image from a color space much smaller or much larger than the current space; however, it is the preferred method for converting from other color spaces to the CWS and does not usu-ally cause problems.

> Whenever Photoshop opens an image into a working space other than the default, it will mark the title bar with an asterisk to indicate that it is not using the default working space.

## The Embedded Profile Mismatch Dialog Box

In the Color Settings dialog, there are three Ask When Opening or Pasting check boxes. These determine the behavior of Photoshop when opening an image with no profile or a mis-matched profile, or when pasting an image into a Photoshop document. It is a very good idea to check each of these boxes so that you can decide, on a case-by-case basis, how to deal with these variables as they arrive. When you open or paste from a mismatched image, the Embedded Profile Mismatch dialog box (Figure 15.5) will appear, displaying the name of the embedded profile. (If the file has no profile at all, the Missing Profile dialog comes up instead; that feature is described in its own section later in this chapter.)

Although it takes a few seconds to make these choices as they occur, the result is a conscious decision, and a skill that can be learned over time.

Of course, there may be circumstances under which you would want all CMYK images with mismatched profiles to be mapped to your current CMYK working space. If this is the case, you can set that CMYK working space in the menu in the Color Settings dialog box, and then clear the Profile Mismatches check box to cause this to occur every time an image is opened. (However, doing that will also cause RGB images to open into your RGB working space without notice.)

## Opening Images with Missing Profiles

When you open an image with no profile, Photoshop displays the Missing Profile dialog box (Figure 15.6), where you can choose from several options.

| | |
|---|---|
| Leave As Is | The image will not be color-managed and will display in the CWS. |
| Assign Working RGB | The current RGB working space is assigned to the image. |
| Assign Profile | The image will be assigned a profile selected from the pop-up menu. |

The Assign Profile setting has a secondary check box that will subsequently convert the document to the current working space. This will result in the image taking on the embedded profile of the current working space when it is saved. The net effect of this is to assign the colors to a working space that you think is the correct one for the original image, then convert it to the current working space so its embedded profile will be adequate for the reproduction plans you have.

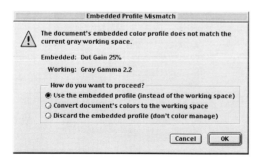

Figure 15.5

**Photoshop can alert you that the image you're opening or pasting from doesn't use your current color profile.**

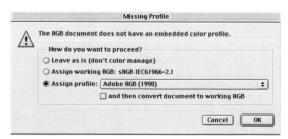

Figure 15.6

**The Missing Profile dialog box**

Passing images through this dialog requires some thought. If you know (or can guess) the source of the image, it is best to assign a profile appropriate to that source. For example, if the image comes from a source for which you have a profile, assign that profile. Converting to the working space after the assignment will cause the current working space profile to be embedded when the image is saved. It does not otherwise change the color in the image.

For example, say you open an image from a Digital Stock disc that was created prior to the common use of ICC profiles. Though Digital Stock scanned everything with a calibrated monitor, the images themselves were not embedded with a scanner profile. Later, when ICC profiles became more common, Digital Stock (later acquired by Corbis) made the profile available; applying that profile to the image results in the image being adjusted correctly for display.

But what if you don't have the right source profile? It's easy enough to try a few to find a workable solution to your problem. If you assume that the image was scanned and saved on a Macintosh computer using an Apple 13-inch RGB monitor, you can assign the Apple RGB working space to the image.

If you think that the image comes from a Windows PC with a "standard" monitor, try sRGB and the result will probably be good enough. There is not much difference between the Apple 13 and sRGB color spaces, and images processed into those spaces will look almost identical (apart from overall brightness differences between the 1.8 Macintosh gamma and the 2.2 Windows gamma).

But if the processed image seems flat and lacking in color, it is likely that it came from a larger color space like Adobe RGB (1998); Choose Image → Mode → Assign Profile. Assign the Adobe RGB 1998 profile. It will probably look much better. Remember that for this technique to work, your monitor must be calibrated. If not, the image you see on screen may not be the image you'll see in print.

# Advanced Color Settings

Checking the Advanced Mode check box at the top of the Color Settings dialog displays two sets of additional settings, Conversion Options and Advanced Controls. The Conversion Options area, the Engine setting (Figure 15.7), allows us to set or change the color management "engine" that is used for color conversions. Depending on the options available on your computer, those options range from a selection of two to six or more.

## Engine

Adobe has its own color management engine (in the parlance of the industry this is called a CMM, or color management module): Adobe Color Engine (ACE). Other CMMs you might encounter include Apple ColorSync, Heidelberg, Kodak, Imation, Agfa, X-Rite, and Microsoft.

Figure 15.7

**The Engine conversion options**

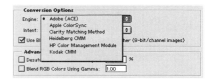

Which engine should you choose? Each company suggests that its CMM uses a superior method of polynomial voodoo to convert color. Adobe similarly claims that theirs is superior. A good suggestion is to use a CMM that is available in all of the applications you use to manage color. This will ensure that color is not being converted differently between applications. For example, if you use Adobe Photoshop to make some conversions and QuarkXPress (through Apple ColorSync) to make others, then it would be a good idea to set Photoshop to use Apple ColorSync, so that all your conversions are done with the same mathematical "engine."

In reality (and with apologies to the various authors of these CMMs), the net effect of a color management engine is essentially the same. Even experts can discern only very subtle differences, so it's not worth a lot of worry. You are certainly welcome to try various combinations of engines and rendering intents, and decide for yourself.

## Conversions through Rendering Intent

The next item under Conversion Options is cryptically named Intent (see Figure 15.8). The ICC has established a set of four "rendering intent" settings under which color conversions can be made. Each has a purpose, and each can be used to maximize the quality of your images for a particular task. Rendering intents cause the color of an image to be modified while it is being moved into a new color space. These modifications can appear as subtle changes or glow-in-the-dark shifts that make color images look very odd. Here we will examine them and identify their purposes.

**Figure 15.8**

**The Intent conversion options**

### Perceptual

Perceptual is a rendering intent designed to make photos of generalized subjects look "good" when converted to a new color space. The Perceptual rendering intent uses a method of remapping colors that preserves the relationships between colors to maintain a "pleasant" appearance. Though color accuracy will often suffer, the appearance of the image will generally follow the appearance of the original scene. Most photo applications default to Perceptual rendering, and Photoshop does this also. Most people find it pleasing, but read on before making a decision about your imaging policies.

### Saturation

Saturation is for business graphics and illustrations made with solid colors. Of the four intents, it is the easiest to understand and the easiest to use. Saturation rendering will result in bright, fully saturated colors in solid areas, and fairly strong contrast applied to differences in color. Saturation rendering sacrifices color accuracy for sharp contrast and saturation. It simply lives up to its name.

If you convert images from EPS illustration programs like Adobe Illustrator, the Saturation rendering intent will result in a better-looking image after conversion than the other intents. Saturation is best used when converting graphs or financial presentations.

## Relative Colorimetric

Relative Colorimetric rendering is a method where color precision is preferred over saturation, resulting in a more accurate conversion of colors into a new color space. Adobe recommends that Relative Colorimetric rendering be used for most color conversions. One of the key components of this rendering intent is its handling of white. Relative Colorimetric rendering moves the white of the image to the white point of the working space, which usually means (as they say in the ad biz), "whiter whites and brighter brights" than in the original.

> Relative Colorimetric should always be used with Black Point Compensation; otherwise, shadow detail will plug up, because the black points in the conversion are not mapped correctly.

## Absolute Colorimetric

This rendering intent is very much like the Relative intent, except that it renders the whites differently. Whites in the source will remain the same in the resulting file. While this sounds obscure, it produces an image that can be used effectively for proofing files that will print on nonwhite or off-white papers (like newsprint). Absolute Colorimetric is a rendering intent that is designed for those who have a very specific reason for using it; otherwise, avoid it.

## Black Point Compensation/Dither

There are two additional settings in the Color Settings dialog under Conversion Options: Use Black Point Compensation and Use Dither (8-Bit/Channel Images). Black Point Compensation is generally left checked, as it is used to maintain saturation of solid black in conversions where the normal behavior of a conversion would desaturate blacks.

An example of this can be seen when converting RGB images to CMYK for print. If we leave this box unchecked and make a conversion (Image → Mode → CMYK), the darkest blacks will often be remapped to the closest color that is within the gamut of the destination profile, which might include an adjustment for dot-gain error or what is called *total ink coverage*. This adjustment will desaturate the solids in order to keep their value below the total ink coverage number, but will result in some washed-out colors where a solid would be better. Black Point Compensation corrects this problem.

The Use Dither checkbox causes 8-bit images to be *dithered* when converted to 8-bit images of another color mode. Dithering is a method of alternating tonal value steps in tiny steps to smooth out tonal shifts. Checking this setting will result in smoother gradations in the converted file. Though the resulting files will likely be larger, the result is usually worth the price.

## Advanced Controls

Two controls in the Color Settings window were added in Photoshop 6: Desaturate Monitor Colors By and Blend RGB Colors Using Gamma. Though recommended for "advanced users only," these settings can have a positive impact on the accuracy of the preview of images on our monitors.

### Desaturating Monitor Colors

This option instructs Photoshop to desaturate colors by a specified amount when displayed on the monitor. This option can be helpful when attempting to view the full range of colors in images with color gamuts larger than that of your monitor. An example of this might be viewing on any monitor an image whose color working space is Wide Gamut RGB. Since the gamut in Wide Gamut is larger than any production monitor, this function will simulate the tonality of the image—even though the monitor can't display the actual color beyond the range of its phosphors. Be careful, though—using this feature can cause errors between the displayed color and final output color.

### Blending RGB Colors

The Blend RGB Colors Using Gamma setting controls the blending of RGB colors on screen. When the option is selected, RGB colors are blended using a selected curve. The range of values available here is between 1.0, which is linear (it has no effect), and 2.2, which creates slightly higher-contrast edge transitions.

When the option is not selected, RGB colors are blended in the document's color space, matching the color display behavior of other applications.

## Previewing in CMYK

The world of graphic arts reproduction is changing, and many printing firms are now using a fully color-managed workflow in preparation for printing. Those who do so want you to provide your images to them in RGB color, with embedded working space profiles.

Printers request these files because there is no "generic" CMYK separation that is correct for all different types of paper and ink sets. The separation made for sheet-fed offset on uncoated paper is drastically different than the separation made for web-fed glossy paper. Printers want control over this conversion.

When an image is destined for the printed page, it is necessary to preview the image before sending the file to the printer. You also need the ability to preview an image in CMYK without making the *conversion* to CMYK. Photoshop provides the Proof Colors control, which allows the on-screen preview to simulate a variety of reproduction processes without converting the file to the final color space.

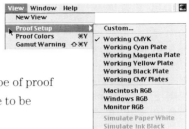

Figure 15.9

**The Proof Setup menu allows you to assign any profile and rendering intent as the proof destination.**

To prepare for and carry out an on-screen proof, first tell Photoshop what kind of proof you want to see. Choose View → Proof Setup (Figure 15.9) to select the type of proof to preview. The top option is for Custom setups, which allow essentially any profile to be applied for the proof.

Once the setup has been completed, you can view a "soft proof" the image on screen by choosing View → Proof Colors or pressing ⌘-Y (Mac)/Ctrl-Y (Win). The image will change temporarily to preview in the color space you've chosen in the Setup window. Options include proofing CMYK, each channel individually, or the CMY colors without black. Three RGB monitor profiles are also available, one for a generic Macintosh monitor, one for a generic Windows monitor, and one for the monitor set as Monitor RGB. Where possible, Photoshop will look to the operating system to get the assigned profile for the monitor for this proofing simulation.

### Simulate Paper White and Ink Black

One of Photoshop's proofing capabilities is its ability to show the white point of the converted image as either a *bright white*, using the monitor's white as the target, or the *paper white*, as measured and calculated in the ICC profile. When working with papers like newsprint and other nonwhite substrates, you can get a better simulation of the actual product if you check the option for Paper White at the bottom of the View → Proof Setup menu. The image will darken significantly and show a proof that more accurately represents the appearance of the image on the nonwhite substrate.

Simulating Ink Black in the proof setup will cause the proof to represent the actual measured black of the profile rather than a solid black as dark as the monitor might make it. When this happens, you will see the darkest black from the measured profile, and the image will usually shift away from deep, solid black to a slightly lighter charcoal image. On most images, the differences are very hard to see. Some profiles are able to represent the dark blacks and the paper white with tremendous range, and these will cause less of a shift on the screen during a proof event.

### Show Out-of-Gamut Colors

Almost always, there are colors in an image that exceed the color gamut of the reproducing device. These colors are not going to print correctly when converted to CMYK and put on a press. To preview the colors that will not print accurately, you can ask Photoshop to highlight the out-of-gamut areas on screen with a special color by choosing View → Gamut Warning. Usually these colors are very small amounts of relatively unimportant information in an image, but checking is a good idea because the out-of-gamut color might be *the most important* color in the image.

In the Ch15 folder of the *Photoshop Savvy 7* CD, I've included a photo of Venice's gondolas from Photo Disk (gamwarn1.tif) that shows color and tonality very nicely on screen. But when Gamut Warning is turned on (gamwarn2.tif), the colors that exceed the currently selected CMYK profile are shown in medium gray. These areas, some of them crucial to this particular image, indicate that the colors on the printed sheet will not look as vibrant as the colors in the original. For more on viewing and selecting out-of-gamut colors, see Chapter 21, "Making Difficult Selections."

> If the image contains a great deal of gray so as to make the gamut warning less distinct, you can change the warning color in the Transparency & Gamut preferences (see Chapter 5).

## Converting Files

In spite of the color-managed workflow options, many Photoshop practitioners prefer to make their own CMYK conversions. Some printers insist that all files arriving for output be CMYK. To make such conversions, we must set the proper ICC color profile in the Color Settings window, and then make a change of Mode to CMYK. Remember that the quality of a color separation made in Photoshop depends on the quality of the CMYK profile.

### Converting Profiles

It's possible to convert your color mode and profile by using Image → Mode → Convert To Profile. This dialog box (Figure 15.10) allows you to select from RGB, CMYK, and other profile types, and also select the rendering intent for the image you're making. If you choose a profile that requires a change in color mode, Photoshop makes the switch; for example, if you're in an RGB file and select a CMYK profile, your file ends up in CMYK mode.

### Assigning Profiles

*Figure 15.10*

**The Convert To Profile dialog box**

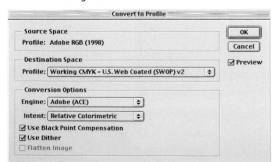

To reassign an image from one profile to another *without changing color mode*, use Image → Mode → Assign Profile to display the dialog box shown in Figure 15.11. This is helpful if an image was opened with color management turned off, and you want to assign a profile to the image so it can be processed in an ICC-compliant workflow. When working in RGB, only RGB profiles are available in this menu, and only CMYK are available profiles for those images.

## Grayscale Profiles

Converting from color to black-and-white (also called monochrome or grayscale) in early versions of Photoshop was less than ideal. Photoshop's luminance-only conversion was seldom optimal. Converting with the Channel Mixer made it better, but the ability to use proper grayscale ICC profiles for grayscale conversions makes it even better.

The image in Figure 15.12 was converted with the 25% Dot Gain Grayscale. Notice how nicely the image appears in one color. In early versions of Photoshop, conversions using Image → Mode → Grayscale were often "too mechanical" to have much artistic value, and the methods using the Color Mixer and calculations were too tedious to be effective in production. Using a profile, the conversion not only is correct for the reproduction process, but results in a more pleasing image than in past versions.

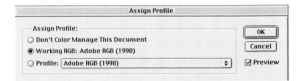

Figure 15.11

**The Assign Profile dialog box**

## Spot Color Profiles

Photoshop treats spot color profiles like grayscale profiles and applies them in the same way. There are standard profiles loaded by the program, which are based on various dot gain values. If you are inclined to make your own profiles, it's a process of printing a gray ramp scale (it is printed automatically by Photoshop if we choose Calibration Bars when printing) and then measuring the resulting target patches with a reflective densitometer.

Figure 15.12

**An image converted from color to grayscale using the Mode → Grayscale command**

## DOT GAIN

When a liquid comes in contact with a piece of paper, the capillary action of the paper's fibers spreads the liquid as it's absorbed. You can easily see this by placing a droplet of water on a piece of tissue.

Ink applied to paper on a printing press produces the same result. The size of the ink dot increases, spread by capillary action. This phenomenon is known as *dot gain*. Porous papers like newsprint absorb ink at a faster rate than coated stocks, producing greater dot gain. Some lower-grade papers will spread an ink dot as much as 40%, while glossy coated stocks will barely gain 10%. The profiles for CMYK, grayscale, and spot color in Photoshop attempt to predict the dot gain based on the qualities of specific paper types. With these profiles the halftone dots on film output will be smaller to compensate for the spreading ink when it is applied to paper.

What you are measuring is *dot area*, the ratio of ink to paper for a selected spot on the printed page. If you read the 50% patch, for example, you will get a value of 73 in typical gloss offset environments. To build a profile, you enter the actual measured values of dot area into a custom dot gain table (Figure 15.13), accessible from the Color Settings dialog box by choosing Custom Dot Gain from either the Gray or Spot pop-up lists in the Working Spaces area. Saving the resulting curve creates an ICC profile.

A custom dot gain table allows you to enter actual grayscale performance curves, which are then used to compensate for the gain you experience. These curves are translated into grayscale and spot color profiles by Photoshop.

Figure 15.13

**A custom dot gain table**

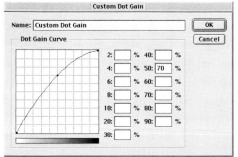

Once you create these profiles in Photoshop, they are available to any application that supports ICC profiles. To save a custom profile, use the Gray or Spot pop-up list in the Working Spaces area of Color Settings and choose Save Gray or Save Spot. The effect of using ICC grayscale profiles on images to be converted for monochrome printing is to create a file that is optimized for reproduction on the measured paper and ink which was used to make the dot area measurements. It is, in essence, a method for matching the image to the printing capabilities of the chosen process.

## Printing from Ink-Jet Printers

Once you've completed your image, assigned RGB profiles to it, and converted it (or not converted it, depending on the circumstances), you can print it. The majority of desktop ink-jet printers use the RGB information to convert the image to CMYK on the fly, so with those printers you should not convert to CMYK because the printer.

Ink-jet printing results can vary dramatically from model to model because of their different gamuts. If you have the printer's profile, the results will be more predictable. If you don't have the profile of a specific printer, you can improve the results on ink-jet printers by printing the image in RGB and letting the printer software do the conversion on the fly. You can then use the print as a proof to recalibrate your monitor (using Adobe Gamma) to display the image as close to the proof as possible. Save the Adobe Gamma settings to be used specifically for editing images printed on the target printer. Make your adjustments to the image based on the on-screen display and save the image as a separate file, identifying it for the specific printer. This is a funky, trial-and-error way to match the printed image to the monitor, but it works if you're willing to pull a number of prints and tweak adjustments to get as close a match as possible.

A more accurate and reliable method is to invest in a spectrophotometer and take a reading from the print, and then plug the information into the spectrophotometer's software and load the resulting profile into the Color Settings dialog box. Unfortunately a system like this can be quite costly.

A cheaper option is to use the profile creation services of a consultant. You print and mail the print target; they read it and e-mail you the profile. This way, no hardware investment is needed by the end user.

## The Printing Dialogs

Several dialog boxes offer similar functions for ultimately printing your image. They are Page Setup, Print With Preview, Print, and Print One Copy.

### Page Setup

Choose File → Page Setup to determine the paper size, orientation, and scale of the image. The dialog box will include different options depending on your installed printer, sometimes including some of the same options found in the Print with Preview dialog box.

### Print With Preview

Choose File → Print With Preview to display a printing dialog box with a preview on the left side of the screen. Set up your printing specifications (Figure 15.14). The preview image on the left side of the screen displays the image's size in relation to the paper.

Position specifies the location of the printed image on the current paper size. Scaled Print Size lets you increase or decrease the image size while maintaining the image's constrained proportions. Check the Scale To Fit Media box to size the image to fit the paper. Check Show Bounding Box to manually scale and reposition the image by dragging. If you have an active selection, you can then choose to print only that part of the image with the Print Selected Area option.

Figure 15.14

**The Print With Preview
dialog box**

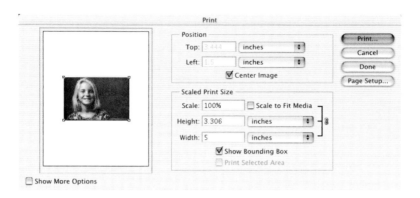

Check the Show More Options box to expand the dialog box. In the expanded area, a pop-up list offers two sets of settings, Output and Color Management.

## Output Options

Some of these options are demonstrated in Figure 15.15.

**Background**  Choose a color from the Color Picker for the area surrounding the image.

**Border**  Enter a value from 0.00 to 10.00 points in points, inches, or millimeters to produce a black border around the image.

**Bleed**  Enter a value from 0.00 to 0.125 inches to specify the width of the bleed. When printed, crop marks will appear inside rather than outside the image.

**Screen**  Enter values for screen frequency, angle, and shape for the halftone screens or individual color separations.

**Transfer**  This function is designed to compensate for poorly calibrated printers. If a printer is printing too dark, for example, adjust the curve to lighten the image to achieve better results.

**Interpolation**  Check this box to automatically reduce the jagged edges that would be created when a low-resolution image is resampled up for printing.

**Calibration Bars**  Selecting this option produces an 11-step grayscale wedge for measuring dot densities with a densitometer. On CMYK images, a gradient tint bar is printed on each separation.

**Registration Marks**  These marks, including bull's-eyes and star targets, are used to register color separations.

**Crop Marks**  These marks show where the page is to be trimmed.

**Captions**  Prints text entered in the File Info box.

**Labels** Prints the file name on images.

**Emulsion Down** Prints the emulsion side of the image down so the type is readable when it is on the back of the film. Most plate burners in the United States use emulsion-down negatives.

**Negative** Prints a negative image. Most printers in the United States use negative film to burn plates.

### Color Management Options

You can color-manage the image while printing. Let's say that your image is set up with profiles for prepress output to an imagesetter to make color separations, but you're going to print to an ink-jet printer to proof the image. You can temporarily convert the document to a more appropriate profile, like sRGB1e61966-2.1, just before you print. If you're printing to a PostScript printer like a laser printer or imagesetter, you can designate PostScript color management.

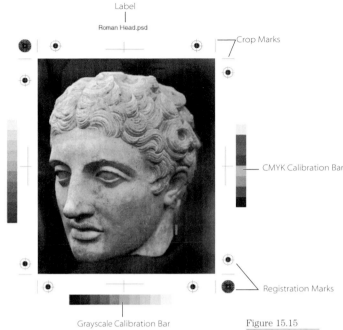

Figure 15.15

**A printed image with various Output Options selected**

Choose a source space: Document uses the current *color* settings as a profile for the printed image, Proof uses the current *proof* settings. Under Print Space, choose a working space from the Profile list. You can also choose a rendering intent.

And of course, click the Print button to print the image.

## Print

You can also choose File → Print to display the Print dialog box (Figure 15.16). The options here will depend on the printer you have selected. Some of the functions found in the Print dialog box may be redundant or irrelevant, like specifying multiple pages and collation. (Photoshop does not support multiple-page documents.)

## Print One Copy

This quick print option (File → Print One Copy) prints the image with the current defaults. No dialog box appears.

Figure 15.16

**The Print dialog box**

## Preflight Checklist

As a final note, I've provided a very general checklist of operations you should perform to ensure accuracy at the printer. These operations are covered in this chapter and throughout *Photoshop 7 Savvy*.

1. Calibrate your monitor.

2. Scan the image at the proper resolution.

3. In the Color Settings dialog box, choose the appropriate color profiles for display and printing.

4. Open the image. Duplicate it, crop it, and adjust its color.

5. Edit the image using Photoshop's tools and commands.

6. Duplicate the image again and flatten it.

7. Apply the Unsharp Mask filter.

8. Under File → Page Setup, choose an orientation (portrait or landscape).

9. In the Print with Preview dialog box, set up the image for printing, choosing print size and position on the page, and, if necessary, attach crop marks, labels, etc.

10. Print the image. This will be a proof.

11. If necessary, recalibrate your monitor and print the image again.

# CHAPTER 16

# Adjusting Tonality and Color

*Almost every photograph* that finds its way onto your computer—whether it is scanned, copied from a Photo CD, transferred from a digital camera, or downloaded from the Web—will need some color adjustment, from minor tweaking to major surgery. Inferior photographic techniques, like bad lighting, poor focus, or under- and over-exposure, are a major cause of color problems in images; however, other variables can significantly degrade color and tonality. The type and quality of the equipment that is used to digitize the image is a factor—an expensive film scanner with a high dynamic range can "see" many more variations of tone than an inexpensive digital camera.

In the process of capturing an image, software interprets the information collected by the scanner or digital camera. The algorithms used to describe the subtle variations of color and to assign values to the pixels can vary. Consequently, the color range, or *gamut*, of each device often differs considerably.

Inevitably, you will use Photoshop's color adjustment features to enhance contrast and remove color casts—two basic operations that compensate for the multitude of variables that can occur during input.

In this chapter, you will learn about:

- **Measuring tonality and color**
- **Making quick adjustments**
- **Working with levels**
- **Adjusting curves**
- **Balancing color**
- **Mixing channels**
- **Using Adjustment layers**
- **Applying the Unsharp Mask filter**

## Measuring Tonality and Color

When you first open an image, you should scrutinize it carefully to determine what the colors on your monitor represent. Be aware that sometimes the on-screen image doesn't accurately represent the image's actual colors. First, be sure to calibrate your monitor using Adobe Gamma or a hardware device to create an accurate on screen image before performing any color adjustments (see Chapter 5, "Setting Up the Program," and Chapter 15, "Color Management and Printing").

Next, look at the image's *histogram* to determine the distribution of tonal values within the image and whether the image has sufficient detail. To view the histogram, choose Image → Histogram.

To more accurately display the actual tonal values within an image, you should avoid using the Image Cache to generate the histogram. Choose Edit → Preferences → Image Cache (Mac) or Memory & Image Cache (Win). Clear the Use Cache For Histograms box, quit the program, and then relaunch it. (See Chapter 5 for more on setting memory preferences.)

### Histograms

A histogram is a graph composed of lines that show the relative distribution of tonal values within an image. The more lines the graph has, the more tonal values are present within the image. The height of a line represents the relative quantity of pixels of a particular brightness. The taller the line, the more pixels of a particular brightness the image contains (see the example in Figure 16.1). The histogram looks like a mountain range on some images, because there can be a total of 256 tonal values represented at one time, and the lines are so close together that they create a shape. The dark pixels, or shadows, are represented on the left side of the graph; the light pixels, or highlights, are on the right. The midtonal ranges are therefore shown in the central portion of the graph.

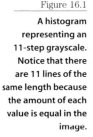

Figure 16.1

**A histogram representing an 11-step grayscale. Notice that there are 11 lines of the same length because the amount of each value is equal in the image.**

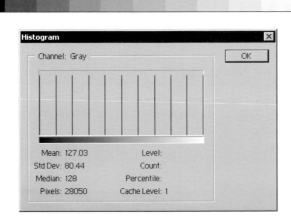

When you choose Image → Histogram, the numbers below the graph to the left represent statistical data about the image's tonality. The numbers in the right column indicate values about a specific level or range. To view data about a specific level, place your cursor on the graph and click your mouse. To display data about a range of pixels, click the graph and drag to the left or right to define the range (see Figure 16.2). The data is organized in the following way:

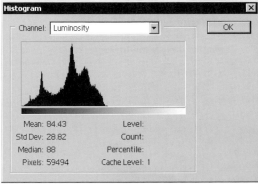

Figure 16.2

**Selecting a range of tonal values within the Histogram window. Note the data now listed in the right column.**

| Value | Definition |
|---|---|
| Mean | Average brightness value of all the pixels in the image (0–255.00) |
| Std Dev | The standard deviation, or how widely brightness values vary |
| Median | The middle value in the range of brightness values |
| Pixels | Total number of pixels in the image or in a selected portion of the image |
| Level | The specific pixel value, between 0 and 255, of the position of the cursor if you place it on the graph |
| Count | Total number of pixels in the level |
| Percentile | Percentage of pixels equal to and darker than the level |
| Cache Level | The current image cache setting |

A histogram can tell us about tonal characteristics of an image. For example, a histogram where tall lines are clustered on the left side of the graph and short lines are on the right side indicates that the image is dark, or *low key*. A histogram where the tall lines cluster on the right side of the graph indicates that the image is light, or *high key*. Compare Figures 16.3 and 16.4.

Figure 16.3

**A histogram representing a dark, or *low key*, image**

Figure 16.4

A histogram represent-
ing a light, or *high key*,
image

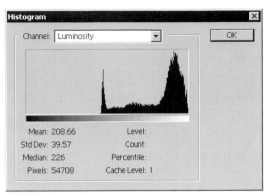

Histograms can also indicate deficiencies in the image. For example, a histogram devoid of lines on both the left and right ends of the graph indicates that most of the pixels are in the midtone range; therefore, the image lacks highlights and shadows and is of poor contrast (a "muddy" image). A histogram that has gaps in the graph could indicate that there is insufficient color detail in the image (see Figure16.5).

Figure 16.5

Histograms represent-
ing an image with poor
contrast (left) and an
image with insufficient
detail (right)

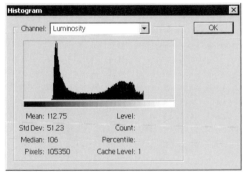
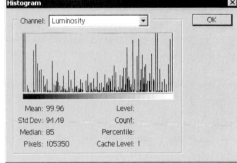

## The Info Palette

The Info palette enables you to accurately measure the color of a single pixel and to determine the average color of a group of pixels. You can use these areas as markers when you make adjustments to the image. To access the Info palette, choose Window → Show Info. By default, the Info palette displays Actual Color (current color model) and CMYK fields, the $x$ and $y$ coordinates of the position of the cursor, and the height and width of the selection (see Figure 16.6). Place your cursor on the image. As you drag over the image, the numeric values for the exact pixel under the cursor are displayed.

Click one of the eyedroppers in the palette to display an options menu. You can configure the options to display CMYK, RGB, HSB, Grayscale, Lab, Total Ink, or Opacity information. The two options at the top of the menu display the values for the actual color or for the potential proof colors when previewing an image prior to CMYK conversion. The proof color numbers are displayed in italics to distinguish them from actual color numbers.

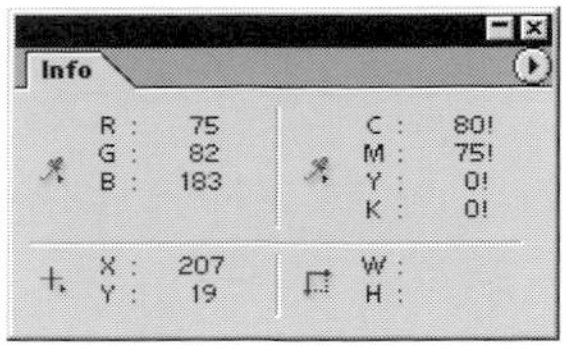

Choosing Palette Options from the Info Palette pull-down menu lets you pick from other color spaces for each of the information fields (Figure 16.7).

The modes in the Info Options pop-up lists are the following:

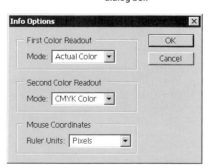

Figure 16.6

**The Info palette displaying the pixel values**

| Setting | Explanation |
| --- | --- |
| Actual Color | Color values of the current mode of the image |
| Grayscale | Density of black ink that would be deposited if the image were printed in black and white |
| RGB | Color of the numeric brightness values, from 0 (black) to 255 (white) of each of the red, green, and blue channels |
| Web Color | RGB hexadecimal equivalents of the sampled color |
| HSB | Hue, saturation, and brightness values of the sampled color |
| CMYK | Percentages of cyan, magenta, yellow, and black that would be output to process color separations |
| Lab | Lightness (L), green–red (a), and blue–yellow (b) values of a CIE Lab color image |
| Total Ink | Cumulative percentage of ink densities of the combined CMYK separations in a four-color process print |
| Opacity | Cumulative level of opacity on all of the visible layers of an image |

## The Eyedropper Tool

When using the Info palette, it is often more accurate to measure a group of pixels than just one, in order to get a better idea of the general tonality of a specific area. When you configure the Eyedropper tool to sample an average, the readings in the Info palette, or in any other operation that uses the Eyedropper to sample color, will reflect the new configuration.

In the Eyedropper Options bar, choose Point Sample to sample a single pixel. Choose 3 By 3 Average to sample the average color of a 9-pixel square, or 5 By 5 Average to sample the average color of a 25-pixel square. You will usually get the best results by averaging a 3×3 square; however, on high-resolution images greater than 400 pixels per inch, you may want to try the 5×5 option. See both options in Figure 16.8.

Figure 16.7

**The Info Options dialog box**

In Photoshop 7, you now have the ability to select colors from outside your image window—even outside of the Photoshop application itself! If you need to select a certain hue from another application, a Web browser window, or your desktop wallpaper, you can do so by simply clicking *and holding* the Eyedropper tool inside the image window, and then *dragging* the tool to any point outside the active image window (see Figure 16.9). The color of any on-screen pixel your cursor hovers over will be reflected within the current foreground color swatch—releasing the mouse will select that particular color.

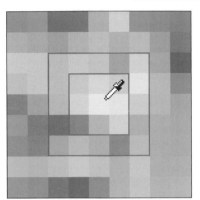

Figure 16.8

**The Eyedropper tool can sample the average color value of a 3×3- or a 5×5-pixel area.**

## The Color Sampler Tool

The Color Sampler tool ![icon] is a way to mark areas of the image for before-and-after comparisons of color adjustments. Prepress professionals, for example, often find this tool useful to adjust areas to target CMYK values.

To place a color marker, expand the Eyedropper tool in the Tool palette and choose the Color Sampler. Place the cursor on the image and click your mouse. The cursor leaves a marker, and the Info palette expands to display the data for that particular marker, as in Figure 16.10.

Using the Shift key with the regular Eyedropper tool also invokes the Color Sampler.

Figure 16.9

**Selecting a hue with the Eyedropper tool**

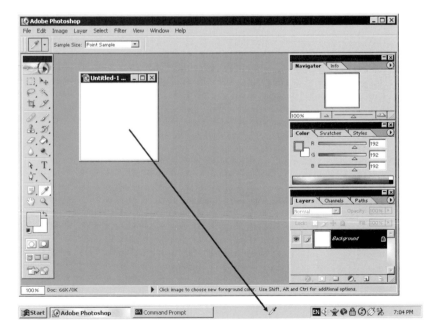

You can sample up to four colors and record the information in the Info palette. To change the color space of a marker, click the arrow next to the Eyedropper icon in the Info palette and drag to the desired color space in the pull-down list shown previously in Figure 16.7.

To move a marker you've already placed, choose the Color Sampler tool and drag the marker to a new location. To delete it, choose the Color Sampler tool and drag the marker off the image window, or choose the Color Sampler tool, press Option/Alt, and click the marker. The Options bar can also delete all placed Color Samplers with one click.

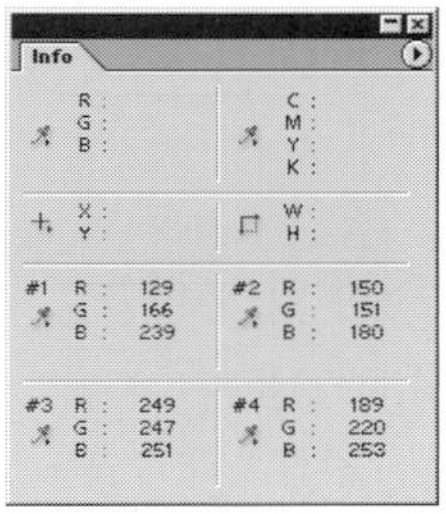

**Figure 16.10**

An image with Color Sampler markers and the expanded Info palette

While a color adjustment is being made to the image, the Info palette displays two numbers for each value, divided by a slash, as seen in Figure 16.11. The number on the left is the numeric value of the sampled color prior to the adjustment, and the number on the right represents the new values of the color after the adjustment. You can compare these values and, with a bit of experience reading these numeric color relations, determine the effect the adjustment will have on the targeted area.

**Figure 16.11**

The number to the left of the slash is the value before the adjustment, and number to the right is the value after.

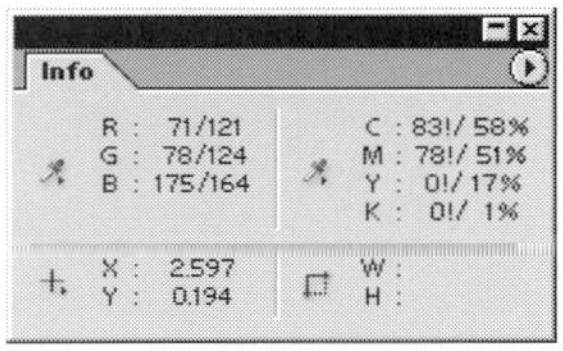

## Making Quick Adjustments

They say "never sacrifice accuracy for speed." Sometimes, however, expedience is a virtue, and you can therefore use one of Photoshop's semiautomatic operations to perform fast adjustments and correct simple, common problems. These commands can change tonal values in an image quickly, but they also lack the precision and control of the high-end adjustment features.

Using the semiautomatic adjustment features hands over the control of how your image looks to the software. Photoshop is not always the best judge of the aesthetic qualities of your image, so use common sense when applying these commands. Occasionally, you will luck out and they'll work just fine. But more often than not, they likely won't achieve the same quality of results one could achieve with a more hands-on approach.

### Brightness/Contrast

**Figure 16.12**

The Brightness/Contrast dialog box

Choose Image → Adjustments → Brightness/Contrast to perform a global adjustment of brightness or contrast to a selected area or to the entire image. The top slider (see Figure 16.12) controls how dark or light the image appears, by pushing the pixel values lower when you move the slider to the left or higher when you move the slider to the right. The slider on the bottom increases or decreases the contrast by changing the pixel

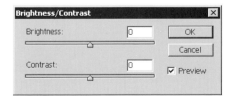

values toward the midtone range when you move the slider to the left, or toward the highlight and shadow ranges when you move the slider to the right. Check the Preview box to see the results.

> It's a good idea to make sure the Preview check box, found in all of the adjustment operations, is always checked in order to see the changes to the image before OK'ing them.

## Auto Levels

If you choose Image → Adjustments → Auto Levels, Photoshop makes the lightest pixel in each color channel white and the darkest pixel black. It then distributes all of the other pixels in between proportionately. By default, the Auto Levels command ignores the lightest and darkest 0.5% extremes when choosing the lightest and darkest colors so as to choose more representative colors. If you use Auto Levels, watch the image carefully, because it can potentially introduce or remove color casts.

You can change the default 0.5% white-point and black-point percentage by choosing Image → Adjustments → Levels or Curves. Click the Options button and enter a value from 0% to 9.99% in the Black Clip or White Clip box. Adobe recommends a number between 0.5% and 1% for the least color distortion.

## Auto Contrast

Choose Image → Adjustments → Auto Contrast to adjust the overall contrast relationships in an image. Like Auto Levels, Auto Contrast maps the lightest highlight to white and the darkest shadow pixel to black. Unlike Auto Levels, Auto Contrast maintains the color balance. By default, the Auto Contrast command clips the lightest and darkest 0.5% of the light and dark extremes so as to choose more representative colors.

## Auto Color

New to Photoshop 7, Auto Color attempts to correct the image's contrast by first mapping the brightest highlight to white and the darkest shadow to black, and then neutralizing the midtones. (It attempts to map any grays in the image to the most neutral shade of gray, thereby removing any aberrant color casts in the image.) Auto Color, for an automated tool, is actually pretty effective much of the time. Your mileage may vary, of course.

> Often I find that the semiautomatic tools do actually perform alterations needed within the image, but may perform them *too well*, creating an overadjustment. You can correct this by using Edit → Fade to fade the last applied color adjustment and to tone it down to a level between the original and the auto-adjusted result. This will often result in a more subtle, natural finish.

## Variations

If you need a little help visualizing what a color adjustment might look like, choose Image →
Adjustments → Variations. The Variations command displays thumbnails of potential adjustments (like the ones in Figure 16.13) in the color saturation and value of the image, enabling
you to visually choose the most appropriate alternative. The two thumbnails at the top of the
window display the original image, labeled Original, and the current image with adjustments,
labeled Current Pick. The circle of thumbnails below shows what the image will look like if
you add more of a specific color. The Current Pick thumbnail, which is in the center of the
circle, changes as you click any one of the color thumbnails. To undo the addition of a color,
click the thumbnail opposite it to introduce its complementary color and neutralize the effect.

You can increase and decrease the amount of color to be added, by moving the Fine/
Coarse slider: Fine produces small adjustments, and Coarse produces large ones. You can
choose to focus the adjustments on specific areas of tonality by clicking the Highlights,
Midtones, or Shadows radio buttons.

Clicking the Saturation radio button transforms the color circle into three thumbnails. Click
the left thumbnail to desaturate, or the right thumbnail to saturate, the image.

The field at the right controls the brightness of the image. Click the top thumbnail to
lighten the image and the bottom to darken the image.

As you use the Variations command, you may notice the proliferation of highly saturated
color in the thumbnails. These are gamut warnings, and they're there to alert you that some
of the colors may be outside of the range of the current color space, which could result in
areas of flat or dithered color. To turn off the gamut warning, clear the Show Clipping box.

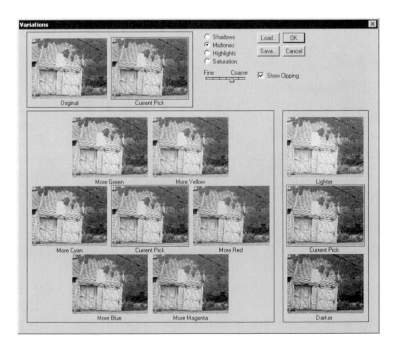

Figure 16.13

**The Variations
dialog box**

## Working with Levels

The Levels command displays an image histogram, which you can use as a visual guide to adjust the image's tonal range. Levels initially gives you three points of adjustment. The black slider on the left of the graph determines the darkest pixel in the shadow areas, which is called the *black point*. The white slider on the right determines the lightest pixel in the highlight area, called the *white point*. Move the black and white sliders to adjust the shadow and highlight extremes, respectively, of the image. The middle or gamma slider determines the median value between the black and white points. Move the slider to the right to decrease the median value, thereby making all values lower than the median darker, or to the left to increase it, making all values higher than the median lighter.

Where Input Levels increase contrast, Output Levels decrease contrast. Move the white slider to the left and the black slider to the right to reduce the range of contrast in an image. You can eliminate the extremes of the highlight and shadow in an image. Printers frequently do this to control ink coverage in preparing files for the press. For example, if the black arrow is moved from 0 to 12, values below 5% (equivalent to a 95% dot value) won't print.

When you perform a Levels adjustment, you are actually reassigning pixel values. For an example, suppose you have a low-contrast image like the photograph in Figure 16.14 (a mountaintop view, from Pu'u Kalena on Oahu, hastily taken with a lightweight, inexpensive camera).

Figure 16.14

**This landscape shot definitely needs more contrast.**

Follow these basic steps to increase the contrast in this picture:

1. Open the image in the `Ch16` folder on the *Photoshop 7 Savvy* CD titled `mountaintop.psd`.

2. Choose Image → Adjustments → Levels. The histogram displays the deficiency in the highlight and shadow areas, where the absence or shortness of lines indicates there are few pixels.

3. Move the white slider toward the center until it is aligned with the lines on the right of the graph, or until the Input Level box on the right reads about 189.

4. Move the black slider toward the center until it is aligned with the lines on the left of the graph, or until the Input Level value on the left reads around 26.

5 Click OK.

6. Choose Image → Adjustments → Levels again. The range of pixel values in the histogram has been redistributed to encompass the length of the entire graph. The lines that had a value of 26 now have a value of 0 (black), and the lines that had a value of 189 now have a value of 255 (white).

Figure 16.15 shows the histogram before and after the correction. Look at the before (Figure 16.14) and after (Figure 16.16) versions of the landscape here and in the color section (Figures C16 and C17) to see the difference this can make in your image.

## Adjusting Channels

If you perform a Levels adjustment on the composite channel, you have only 3 points of adjustment. If you adjust the levels of each channel individually, you have 9 points of adjustment in an RGB or Lab color image and 12 points of adjustment on a CMYK image. This triples or quadruples the power of the Levels command; it can also produce weird color combinations. To choose a specific channel in which to work, scroll down the Channel pop-up list in the Levels dialog box. (See Hands On 5, "Image Size, Transformation, and Color Adjustment," to try this operation out.)

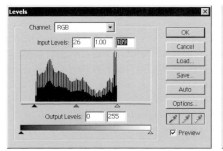
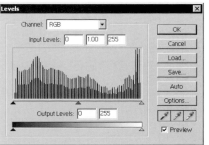

Figure 16.15

**Sample Levels dialogs, before and after adjustment**

Figure 16.16

**This photo, though still no Ansel Adams shot, does look quite a bit richer and cleaner than it did before!**

When adjusting the levels of individual channels, you may need to reset the Levels adjustment several times before producing the right combination of values. To do so, press the Option/Alt key. The Cancel button becomes the Reset button. Click it to begin again. Note that this cancels all of the operations that you have performed in the dialog box, not just the individual channels. To cancel only the last operation, press ⌘/Ctrl-Z.

## Determining White and Black Points

You can use the Levels command in Threshold mode to locate the highlight and shadow areas of an image. You can then assign specific values to those points to redistribute all of the other pixel values between those values.

### Finding the Highlight and Shadow Points

Use this technique to determine the lightest and darkest areas of the image:

1. Be sure that the composite RGB channel is selected from the Channels palette.

2. Open the Levels dialog box (Image → Adjustments → Levels) and check the Preview box.

3. Press Option/Alt and slowly drag the white Input Level slider to the left. A high-contrast preview appears. The visible areas of the image are the lightest part of the image.

4. Repeat the process with the black shadow slider, dragging it to the right to identify the darkest areas of the image.

You can assign specific values to the darkest shadow areas and the lightest highlight areas of an image and then redistribute the brightness information based on the light and dark extremes of the image. Prepress professionals frequently determine CMYK values for highlight and shadow areas based on the characteristics of their printing presses. When you determine the white point, it is often best to use the lightest printable area of the image that *contains detail*, not a specular white that when printed will contain no ink. The shadow area will be the darkest area that contains detail, not an absolute black.

## Setting the White Point

You can determine a specific RGB value for the white point of the lightest highlight areas:

1. To set the target RGB values, open the image `rockycliffs.psd` from the `Ch16` folder on the CD (see Figure 16.17). Before (Figure C18) and after (Figure C19) versions of this image are included in the color section.

2. In the Eyedropper Options bar, set the Eyedropper tool to 3 By 3 Average.

3. Choose Image → Adjustments → Levels.

4. *Double-click* the white eyedropper. The Color Picker appears.

5. Enter values for the highlight to prepare the image for print. Enter these recommended RGB values if you are printing on white paper: –240R, 240G, 240B. The grayscale density is a 6% dot (you can determine the highlight density by subtracting the Brightness value, B, in the Color Picker from 100').

   The RGB values will vary depending on the RGB color space you are working in. I'm working in Adobe RGB (1998) as a color setting (see Chapter 15). The point is, you're going to shoot for about a 4% to 6% neutral gray mix.

6. Locate the lightest area on the image. Do not choose a specular highlight, which will be pure white; instead, choose the lightest area that will contain detail. In the case of the landscape shot, it's along the brightest edge of the clouds. Click the area to set the highlight.

## Setting the Black Point

Determine a specific RGB value for the black point of darker shadows:

1. Double-click the black eyedropper. The Color Picker appears.

2. Enter RGB values for the shadow. Use these recommended values if you are printing on white paper and working in the Adobe RGB (1998) color space: 13R, 13G, 13B. The Grayscale density is a 95% dot. (As with the highlight value, you can determine the shadow density by the subtracting the Brightness value, B, in the Color Picker from 100.)

**Figure 16.17**

**The landscape, before the Levels adjustment**

When the values are converted to CMYK, the total ink coverage should not exceed 300%. You can input other values of ink in the CMYK fields—depending on the paper, printer, and press you are using—but it is important to maintain three equal RGB values to assure neutrality.

3. Locate the darkest area on the image that still contains detail. In this case, it's the bottom of the foremost hillside. Click your mouse there to set the shadow. The landscape should now look like Figure 16.18.

The process for determining the white point and the black point is the same for both the Levels and the Curves operations. I'll discuss curves just a couple of pages on.

## Saving and Loading Levels Settings

Once you've made a correction to the image, you may want to apply it to another image with the same color problems. Let's say you shot a roll of film at the wrong ASA and consequently underexposed all of the images. You can adjust one image and apply those settings to the entire group by first saving and then loading the settings.

To save and load a setting:

1. Choose Save from the options on the right side of the Levels dialog.

2. Choose a folder in which to save the settings, name them, and click OK. Click OK again to close the Levels dialog box. Now that you've saved them, you can reload them at any time.

3. To load the settings, choose Load from the options on the right side of the Levels dialog.

4. Locate the folder where the settings were saved, and click Open to open the settings.

# Adjusting Curves

Figure 16.18

**The landscape after adjusting the levels**

Curves are Photoshop's most powerful color adjustment tool. Where levels give you the ability to change three to nine points of adjustment, curves enable you to map many more. You

can adjust an image's brightness curve to lighten or darken an image, improve its contrast, or even create wild solarization affects.

When you open Image → Adjustments → Curves, Photoshop displays the Curves dialog box (Figure 16.19).

## Refining the Graph

By default, the graph is divided into 16 squares, each representing 16 brightness levels. Press your Option/Alt key and click the graph to refine the grid into 100 squares, representing the total 256 brightness levels for finer adjustment. The horizontal axis of the graph represents the *input* levels, or the colors of the image before the adjustment. The vertical axis represents the *output* levels, or the color of the image after it has been adjusted. By default, for RGB images, dark colors are represented by the lower-left corner, and light colors are represented by the upper-right corner of the graph. The diagonal line from bottom-left to top-right represents the brightness levels of the image. Adjustments are made to the image by changing the shape of this line.

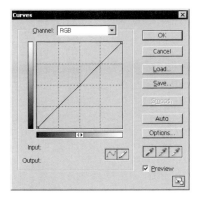

Figure 16.20 provides an illustration of the power of curves. The basic photograph (a) is perhaps slightly underexposed in the shadows. If you click the center of the diagonal line in the Curves dialog and drag it toward the upper-left, you will lighten the image, as in (b). If you bend it toward the lower-right, you will darken it (c). If you perform either of these operations, you alter the position of the midtones.

A classic S curve, as shown in (d), will increase the contrast of the image by darkening the shadows and lightening the highlights. A roller-coaster curve (e) pushes the pixel values all over the graph and creates wild solarization effects.

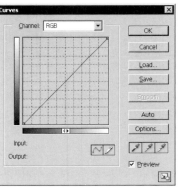

Figure 16.19

**The default Curves dialog box shows a 16-cell graph (top); Option/Alt-clicking the grid changes it to a 100-cell graph (bottom).**

## Using the Brightness Bar

The horizontal brightness bar below the graph represents the direction of the values of the graph. By default, for RGB images, the light values are on the right and the dark values are on the left, but they can be switched easily by clicking the center arrows. If you reverse the graph, the light values will switch to the bottom and left, and the dark values to the top and right. If you are working on an RGB or Lab image and you switch the direction of the brightness bar, the numeric input and output values change from a measurement of channel information to ink coverage. This can be useful if you are planning to convert your image to CMYK.

The default Curves dialog box for a CMYK image is reversed from the RGB or Lab image. The brightness bars display dark values on the top and light values on the bottom. The input and output values are the percentage of ink coverage.

## Choosing Graph Tools

Choose a graph tool ⟨image⟩ from the Curves dialog to edit the brightness curve. The Point tool is selected by default. Click the curve to establish anchor points, which can then be moved by dragging them with your mouse. As you drag, you can see the changes to your image if the Preview box is checked.

Figure 16.20

**Examples of curve adjustments**

(a) The Unadjusted Image

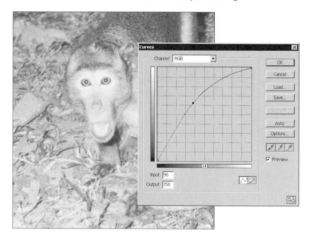

(b) Lighten

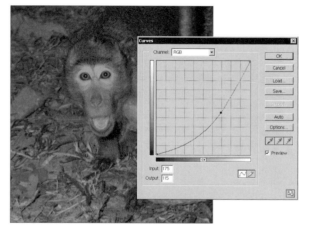

(c) Darken

(d) Contrast

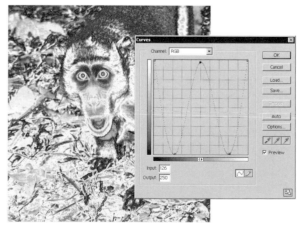

(e) Solarize

The Pencil tool  lets you draw freeform on the curve by clicking and dragging on it. It performs very much like Photoshop's Pencil tool. If you want to draw a straight line, click once, press Shift, and click elsewhere.

In Photoshop 7, you can click the Expand button in the lower-right corner of the Curves dialog box to enlarge the dialog, making it easier to work with.

## Changing Input and Output Values

When you move the cursor over the curve, the input and output values change to reflect its position relative to the horizontal and vertical axes of the graph. You can click a point on the curve and enter new values for that point in these boxes, which will result in bending the curve.

## Adjusting Channels

If you perform a Curves adjustment on the composite channel, you affect all of its channels simultaneously. As with levels, you can work with more precision by adjusting the channels individually. To choose a specific channel in which to work, scroll through the Channel pop-up list in the Curves dialog box. You can also select a combination of channels by Shift-selecting them in the Channels palette before opening the Curves dialog box.

## Making a Lock-Down Curve

It often helps to work with a *lock-down curve* so that other colors in the image are unaffected when you make an adjustment. A lock-down curve stabilizes the curve and prevents it from bending. The brightness values that are affected when manipulating the curve can then be better controlled. To make a lock-down curve, follow these steps:

1. Choose Image → Adjustments → Curves to open the Curves dialog box.

2. Press Option/Alt and click the grid to display the 100-cell grid.

3. Place your cursor on the diagonal line at the exact point where the horizontal and vertical grid lines intersect. Click your mouse.

4. Click each intersection point along the diagonal line, as in Figure 16.21.

5. Choose Red from the Channel pop-up list. Repeat the process.

6. Repeat the process for the Green and Blue curves. This way, if you need to lock down a specific channel, the curve will be contained within the file.

Figure 16.21

**A lock-down curve**

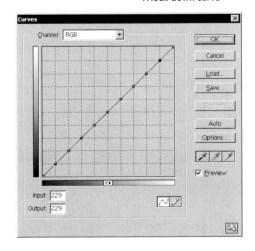

7. Choose Save, and designate a location for your curve. Name the curve **lockdown_curve.acv** and save the file. You can now load the curve on any RGB document in any channel at any time. A file of the same name is provided in the **Ch16** folder on your CD.

## Determining the Position of a Color

You can pinpoint a color and determine its exact location on the curve. You can then place an anchor point and make a precise spot adjustment to that color only.

To determine the location of a color:

1. Open the file **flower.psd** in the **Ch16** folder on the CD.

2. Choose Image → Adjustments → Curves to display the Curves dialog box.

3. Choose Channel → Red.

4. Choose Load from the options on the right side of the dialog. Load the lock-down curve you made in the previous section.

5. Place your cursor on the reddish portion of the flower petal. Press Option/Alt, and click the mouse. Observe the circle on the graph as you move your cursor (Figure 16.22). Press your ⌘/Ctrl key and click the mouse to place an anchor point.

6. Place your cursor on the anchor point, click your mouse, and drag straight upward until the Output reads around 217, as in Figure 16.23. The targeted red in the flower intensifies because you've increased its brightness value. All the other colors in the image, such as the greens in the leaves and stems, are left at their original values because you locked them down.

Figure 16.22

**Determining the anchor point**

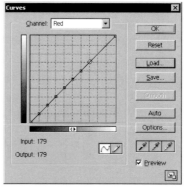

## Saving and Loading Curve Settings

As with levels, once you've made a Curves adjustment to the image, you can save the settings and load them to another image:

1. Choose Save from the options on the right side of the Curves dialog box.

2. Choose a folder in which to save the setting, name it, and click OK.

3. To load the settings, choose Load from the options on the right side of the Curves dialog.

4. Locate the folder where the settings were saved and click Load to load the settings.

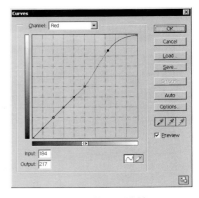

Figure 16.23

**Adjusting the curve**

# Balancing Color

After the tonal values have been corrected, you may want to make further adjustments to eliminate color casts, oversaturation, or undersaturation. Color in the image can be balanced using several different methods:

**Color Balance**  is used to change the overall color mix in an image.

**Selective Color**  adjusts the quantities of cyan, magenta, yellow, or black in specific color components.

**Levels and Curves**  adjust the brightness values of individual channels (see the previous sections in this chapter).

**Hue/Saturation**  changes the basic color characteristics of the image (see Chapter 17, "Modifying and Mapping Color").

**Replace Color**  replaces the hue, saturation, and brightness of specified areas (see Chapter 17).

**Channel Mixer**  blends colors from individual channels (see the section titled "The Channel Mixer" later in this chapter).

## Color Balance

Color balance is used to adjust the overall mixture of colors in the image and especially to eliminate color casts. To use the Color Balance command, be sure that the composite channel is targeted in the Channels palette. Then follow these steps:

1. Choose Image → Adjustments → Color Balance to display the Color Balance dialog box seen in Figure 16.24. (You can also bring this up with the keyboard shortcut ⌘/Ctrl-B.)

2. Click the Shadows, Midtones, or Highlights radio button to select the tonal range in which you would like to focus your adjustment.

3. Check Preserve Luminosity to maintain the tonal balance of the image and affect only the colors.

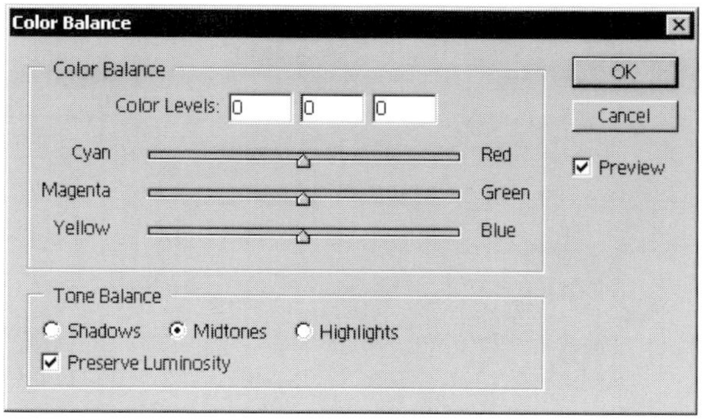

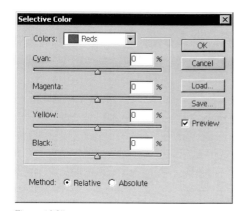

Figure 16.24

**The Color Balance dialog box**

Figure 16.25

**The Selective Color dialog box**

4.  To increase the amount of a color in an image, drag a slider toward it. To decrease the amount of a color, drag the slider away from it.

    Each color slider represents two color opposites. By increasing the amount of a specific color (by moving the slider toward its name), you, in effect, decrease its opposite.

## Selective Color

The Selective Color command is designed to adjust CMYK images; however, you can use it on RGB images, too. Selective color lets you determine the amount of cyan, magenta, yellow, and black that will be added to predefined color ranges. This is especially good for prepress professionals who need to control ink densities.

Follow these steps to use this command:

1.  Target the composite channel in the Channels palette.

2.  Choose Image → Adjustments → Selective Color; the Selective Color dialog box (see Figure 16.25) appears.

3.  From the Colors pop-up list, choose the color range you want to affect. The list shows reds, yellows, greens, cyans, blues, magentas, whites, neutrals, and blacks. Adjust the CMYK sliders to determine how much of each process color the target color will contain. (Some colors may not contain any of the process color, so they will not be affected.)

4.  Choose a method:

    **Relative** changes the existing quantity of process color by a percentage of the total. For example, if you start with a pixel that is 80% cyan and add 10%, 8% is added to the pixel (10% of 80 = 8), for a total of 88% cyan. You cannot adjust specular white with this option, because it contains no color.

**Absolute** adds color in absolute values. If, for example, you start with 30% cyan in the pixel and add 10%, you end up with a pixel that is 40% cyan.

5. Drag the sliders to the right to increase the amount of the process color component in the selected color or to the left to decrease it.

## The Channel Mixer

The Channel Mixer enables you to adjust the color information of each channel from one control window. You can establish color values on a specific channel as a mixture of any or all of the color channels' brightness values.

The Channel Mixer can be used for a variety of purposes, including:

- Creating an optimal grayscale image from an RGB or CMYK file
- Making a high-quality sepia tone from a CMYK or RGB file
- Converting images into alternative color spaces
- Swapping color information from one channel to another
- Making color adjustments to images by altering the color information in a specific channel
- Creating weird-looking stuff

The Channel Mixer does not add or subtract colors per se; it combines values from each channel with those of the target channel. The effect is similar to copying the Red channel, for example, and pasting it on the Blue channel. The Channel Mixer, however, offers much greater control by allowing you to vary the degree of the effect.

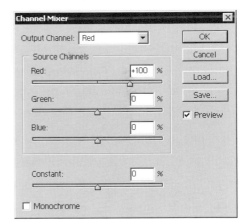

To use the Channel Mixer:

1. Target the composite channel in the Channels palette.
2. Access the window by choosing Image → Adjustments → Channel Mixer.
3. Target the channel to be affected by choosing the Output Channel from the pop-up list.
4. Adjust the color sliders to modify the color relations between channels.

### Swapping Colors within Channels

You can adjust color information globally on a particular channel or within a selection marquee, so that portions of the image can be quickly altered, corrected, or converted independently while previewing the results.

When you choose a channel by name from the Output Channel pop-up list, the value next to the corresponding Source Channel's color slider reads 100%, which represents the total amount of that color in the image. The values can be increased to 200% or decreased to –200%.

The performance of the Channel Mixer depends on the color mode of the image. When working in CMYK, increasing the numeric value of the color cyan or dragging its slider to the right increases the amount of cyan in the Cyan channel. Decreasing the numeric value or dragging to the left subtracts cyan from the channel. Adjusting the color slider of any other color, such as magenta, while the Cyan channel is targeted changes the amount of the cyan in the Cyan channel based on the relation between the brightness values of magenta and cyan.

When working in RGB mode, the Channel Mixer performs differently. Increasing the numeric value shifts the selected color toward the color of the selected channel, while decreasing the value shifts the color toward its complement. (As with CMYK, the limits of these changes are 200% and –200%.) You can therefore decrease the value of red if you target the Red channel and move the Red slider to the left, which shifts the color toward cyan—the complement of red on the color wheel. Targeting the Green channel and moving the Green slider to the left shifts the color toward magenta. Targeting the Blue channel and moving the Blue slider to the left shifts the color toward yellow.

The Constant slider is like having an independent black or white channel, with an Opacity slider added to the targeted color channel to increase or decrease the channel's overall brightness values. Negative values act as a black channel, decreasing the brightness of the target channel. Positive values act as a white channel, increasing the overall brightness of a channel.

Increasing the brightness of a color channel does not necessarily mean that the image will become lighter. It actually adds more of the channel's color to the image. You can demonstrate this by targeting the Blue channel, for example, and moving the Constant slider to the right. Any image becomes bluer. Drag it to the left, and it becomes more yellow (the complement of blue on the color wheel).

## Making Optimal Grayscales

Converting a color image directly to a perfect grayscale was once a hit-or-miss process. With the Channel Mixer, you can easily make a perfect grayscale from an RGB or CMYK image by manual correction and previewing.

When you convert an RGB image to a grayscale, Photoshop uses an algorithm to convert the brightness values from the 16 million colors in its three color channels into 256 shades of gray in the gray channel. By applying the Channel Mixer to the unconverted RGB file, you can control how the image looks prior to the conversion. By moving the sliders, you can emphasize brightness and contrast within the image.

To convert an RGB image to grayscale:

1. Check the Monochrome box in the Channel Mixer.

2. Adjust each of the color sliders until optimal contrast is achieved.

3. Move the Constant slider to darken or lighten the image.

4. When you're satisfied with the results, click OK.

5. Choose Image → Mode → Grayscale to convert the image.

# Using Adjustment Layers

When you apply an adjustment operation like Levels, Curves, Hue/Saturation, or the Channel Mixer to an image, you directly affect the information on a layer or on the Background. The only way to change these operations is to return to them in the History palette, which can have complicated and unexpected results if you've done a lot to the image since. Photoshop's Adjustment layers segregate the mathematical data of the adjustment to a separate layer that can be re-edited at any time during the imaging process. Adjustment layers are very handy indeed, and another element in Photoshop's arsenal that keeps the process dynamic.

## Creating an Adjustment Layer

Follow these steps to create an Adjustment layer:

1. Choose Layer → New Adjustment Layer and select the type of Adjustment layer you want from the submenu.

2. The New Layer dialog box appears. Name, color-code, and set the opacity and blending mode of the layer, if desired.

3. The Adjustment dialog appears. Make the adjustment and click OK. The new Adjustment layer appears on the Layers palette.

4. The Adjustment layer has an attached layer mask (as in Figure 16.26), which lets you selectively conceal portions of the adjustment. (See Chapter 22, "Advanced Layer Techniques," for more on layer masks.)

By default, an Adjustment layer affects all of the layers below it in the layer stack. You can, however, designate an Adjustment layer to affect *only* the layer immediately below it in the stack. Option/Alt-click the line that separates the Adjustment layer and the layer just below it. The grouped layer becomes indented and displays a clipping group icon, indicating that the two layers are now grouped. You ungroup an Adjustment layer in the same way.

You can also group a layer by clicking the Group With Previous Layer check box in the New Layer dialog box.

Figure 16.26

**An Adjustment layer,
with thumbnails for the
adjustment and for a
layer mask**

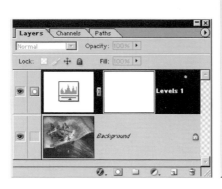
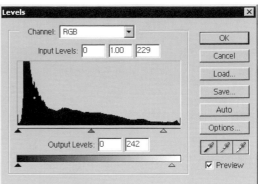

## Masking Portions of an Adjustment Layer

The ultimate power of Adjustment layers is the ability to selectively apply an adjustment to
the image and to interactively apply blending modes. An Adjustment layer can act as a mask
so that you can conceal portions of the effect. To try out this process, display the Layers
palette and follow these simple steps:

1. Open an image.

2. Choose Layer → New Adjustment Layer → Hue/Saturation.

3. In the Hue/Saturation dialog box, drag the Hue slider to radically alter the color scheme
   of the image. Click OK.

4. In the Layers palette, target the Adjustment layer.

5. Choose black as a foreground color and white as a background color in the Tool palette
   by pressing D, then press X to reverse colors.

6. Choose the Paintbrush. Paint any area of the image until the colors are restored to their
   original color. If you make a mistake, you can paint out the mistake with white.

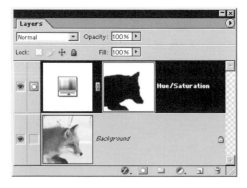

Using this masking method with Adjustment layers is an effective
way to isolate a portion of an image and to apply color manipulations
to it without affecting the rest of the composition. It works well, for
example, when you want to alter the color depth/contrast of the background portion of an image without affecting the subject of the photo,
or vice versa.

Also note that most filters work with the Adjustment layer masks.
This can come in handy sometimes—for example, when you want to

separate color adjustments between subject and background, but don't want an abrupt change, you can apply Filter → Blur → Gaussian Blur to soften the edges of your color adjustment (an extreme blurring can create an interesting "halo effect" sometimes). Using a Black-to-White gradient, instead of the Paintbrush tool, is also a good way to soften color variations within an Adjustment layer mask.

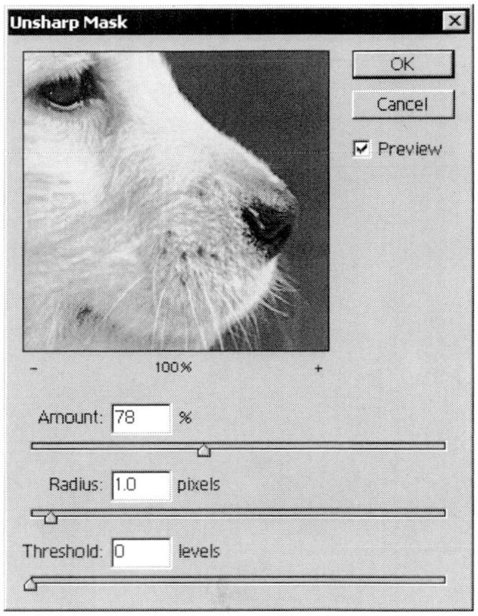

## Applying the Unsharp Mask Filter

You might ask, "What is a filter description doing here in the color adjustment chapter?" The answer is that the Unsharp Mask (USM) filter is a contrast-adjustment tool that goes hand-in-hand with color correction, and if used properly, it can further enhance the color relations and contrast of the image and make it really "pop."

USM exaggerates the transition between areas of most contrast while leaving areas of minimum contrast unaffected. It can help increase the contrast of an image and fool the eye into thinking fuzzy areas of the image are in focus.

To apply the USM, choose Filter → Sharpen → Unsharp Mask (see Figure 16.27). The USM filter has a preview in which you see a thumbnail version of the image. You can reduce or enlarge the preview by clicking the – or + signs. This is helpful if you want to compare the affected preview to the original 100%-sized, unsharpened image. Check the Preview box to see the effect on the image itself.

You'll have a chance to practice unsharp-masking the image at the end of Hands On 5.

Figure 16.27

**The Unsharp Mask interface**

### IF IT'S A SHARPEN FILTER, WHY IS IT CALLED "UNSHARP" MASK?

Many of the operations performed in Photoshop today were derived from traditional optical techniques performed in a process camera. Back in the old days before computers, a special mask was cut to protect parts of images when they were being "bumped," or exposed to increase their contrast. This mask would leave important flesh tones and other critical areas unaffected while enhancing the contrast of the most prominent edges to produce the illusion of sharp focus. Since the area within the mask was being protected and the area outside the mask was being sharpened, the term for the process came to be known as an *unsharp mask*. Photoshop essentially performs the same operation, only digitally and with more control and less labor.

To apply the USM, move one of its three sliders:

**Amount**  By moving this slider or entering a value from 1% to 500%, you determine how much sharpening will be applied. The higher the value, the more the image will be sharpened. Applying only an amount, however, will not sharpen the image. In order to see the effect, you must also specify a radius.

**Radius**  By moving the Radius slider or entering a value, you control the thickness of the sharpened edge. Lower values produce thinner, sharper edges; higher values produce wider edges with more overall sharpening of the entire image.

**Threshold**  To control the numeric value of adjacent, contrasting pixels, move the Threshold slider. This slider determines how different the pixels must be from the surrounding area before they are considered edge pixels and sharpened. It also restores smooth areas that acquire texture when the amount and radius are applied—the higher the value, the greater the restoration. Too much threshold will reverse the effect of the USM.

The goal in sharpening an image is to apply as much USM as possible without blowing out areas, shifting colors, creating dark or light halos, or amplifying noise and unwanted detail. These flaws can make the image appear garish or artificial. You can avoid most problems by applying one or more of the following methods.

## Small-Dose Technique

USM works better in smaller doses. Apply USM several times with smaller settings, keeping the amount and radius lower and the threshold higher. Sharpen gently several times with the same low settings. Press ⌘/Ctrl-F to reapply the filter with the same values, or reduce the values slightly each time.

Keep a close watch on the image as you sharpen it. Sharpen the image until it appears a little too sharp. To see an overall comparison, toggle between the original thumbnail in the History palette (Window → Show History) and the last line of the History list where sharpening was applied.

## Flesh-Tone Technique

This technique works particularly well on flesh tones. The problem presented by flesh tones when applying any sharpening filter is the tendency to increase the texture of the skin so that it appears rough or porous. To avoid this problem, apply a larger amount and a smaller radius. Keeping the radius low affects only the edge pixels while reducing the sharpening of noise and unwanted detail. Adjust the threshold to eliminate excess texture in the flesh tones and other areas of low contrast.

## Lab-Mode Technique

This method is specially designed to avoid color shifts. In essence, you will be applying your sharpening to the brightness information only. Like RGB mode, Lab mode segregates the image data into three channels. In RGB, however, red, green, and blue channels each contain 256 brightness levels. In Lab mode, the information is divided into an *a* channel (red and green hues), a *b* channel (blue and yellow hues), and an *L*, or lightness, channel (the brightness information). The L channel is where the USM will be applied.

1. Choose Image → Duplicate to make a copy of your image.

2. Choose Layer → Flatten Image.

3. Use Image → Mode → Lab Color to convert to Lab mode. Don't worry, there is no appreciable loss of color information in this conversion as there is when you convert from RGB to CMYK.

4. Choose Window → Channels. Target the Lightness channel by clicking its thumbnail.

5. Click the eye next to the composite Lab channel in the Channels palette so that the full-color image is visible in the image window.

6. Choose Filter → Sharpen → Unsharp Mask.

7. Move the Amount, Radius, and Threshold sliders to produce the desired effect.

# CHAPTER 17

# Modifying and Mapping Color

*Color is* one of the most significant factors in our visual experience of the world around us. Humans react to color emotionally. Cool, subdued colors can calm our senses, and hot, saturated colors can excite and motivate us. Color affects the decisions of our daily lives, like whether we purchase a certain product or cross the street. It affects our physical and mental space and contributes to our sense of well being.

Since color plays such an important role in our lives, how we use it to communicate ideas is essential to the success of our images. As we have seen, Adobe Photoshop provides numerous ways to apply and adjust color. In this chapter, we explore features that can radically alter existing colors in an image—*color-mapping* operations that go beyond brightness and contrast adjustments and simple color fills. These operations provide the means to alter the basic characteristics of color while maintaining the image's detail. You can use these commands to change the entire color scheme of your image or create eye-popping graphic effects, like vibrant posterizations, high-contrast art, and textured halftones.

In this chapter, you will learn about:

- **Altering the hue and saturation**
- **Replacing the colors in an image**
- **Limiting the number of colors in an image**
- **Producing graphic effects using halftones**

# Altering Hue and Saturation

You find most of the color-mapping operations under the Image → Adjustments submenu. You use this same menu to access the brightness and contrast operations, like Levels and Curves, and color-correction features, like Color Balance and Selective Color (see Chapter 16, "Adjusting Tonality and Color"). The Hue/Saturation command lets you alter the basic color characteristics of your image. When you choose Image → Adjustments → Hue/Saturation, you are presented with a dialog box with three sliders (Figure 17.1). Each slider *remaps* a different color characteristic.

## Changing Hue

If you drag the Hue slider to change relative color relationships of the image or selection, you can produce some really beautiful and unexpected color combinations. I encourage you to experiment with color images to get a feel for the Hue/Saturation command and to experience its potential. You'll find that changing the reality of an everyday landscape into a brilliant fauvist work of art is fun and easy. With these tools in hand, after all, who can resist the temptation to transform, with the click of a mouse, a humdrum blue sky to an electric fuchsia and the ordinary green leaves on the trees to bubble-gum pink?

The numeric values you see in the Hue/Saturation dialog box are based on the affected color's position on the color wheel, and expressed in degrees. Values in the box reflect the amount of rotation from the original color. Moving the slider to the right, or a positive value, indicates a clockwise rotation of the color wheel. Moving it to the left, to a negative value, indicates a counterclockwise rotation.

Figure 17.1

**The Hue/Saturation dialog box**

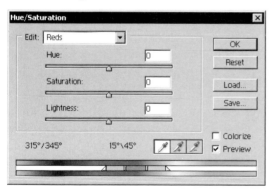

The color bars at the bottom of the palette are a graphic indicator of how the colors change as you move the Hue slider. By default, the color bars are aligned. The top color bar represents a color wheel that has been cut at the 180-degree point, or blue. As you move the Hue slider, the top color bar remains in place and represents the entire range of colors prior to the change. The bottom color bar is dynamic. It moves as you drag the Hue slider and realigns with the colors on the top bar to reflect the relative change of colors.

## Adjusting Hue

The Edit pop-up list at the top of the dialog box enables you to target a specific range of colors to adjust. The colors are divided into basic color ranges of 90 degrees each, including the *overlap* (the amount that the colors adjacent to the target color on the color wheel are affected). The Master option (the default range) permits the entire spectrum of color to be affected when you move the Hue, Saturation, or Lightness sliders. The other options perform as follows:

| Edit Option | Targets (on the Color Wheel) |
|---|---|
| Reds | Colors to be affected from 0 to 45 degrees clockwise and 360 to 315 degrees counterclockwise |
| Yellows | Colors to be affected from 15 to 105 degrees clockwise |
| Greens | Colors to be affected from 75 to 165 degrees clockwise |
| Cyans | Colors to be affected from 135 to 225 degrees clockwise |
| Blues | Colors to be affected from 195 to 285 degrees clockwise |
| Magentas | Colors to be affected from 255 to 345 degrees clockwise |

When you choose a color from the Edit list, you can limit the changes to a specific range of hues. An adjustment slider appears between the two color bars, telling you which colors are being affected and letting you increase or decrease the range of hues to be affected, by dragging left or right in these ways:

- To change the range of color to be affected, drag the dark gray horizontal bar to move the entire adjustment slider.
- To extend the range of color and the amount of overlap, drag the light gray horizontal bars.
- To change the range while leaving the overlap unaffected, drag the white vertical bars.
- To adjust the overlap while leaving the range fixed, drag the white triangles.

## Sampling with the Eyedroppers

The familiar eyedroppers that we saw in the Levels and Curves dialog boxes perform a slightly different function here. Once again, their performance is controlled by the presets made to the Eyedropper tool in the Options bar: Point Sample, 3 By 3 Average, or 5 By 5 Average. In the Hue/Saturation dialog box, they are used to pick specific colors to be adjusted. Choose the eyedropper that best suits your purposes:

**The Eyedropper** samples a pixel or set of pixels, depending on the options selected for the Eyedropper tool in the Options bar.

**The Plus Eyedropper** lets you add to the sample range by dragging over pixels in the image window.

**The Minus Eyedropper** lets you subtract from the range by dragging over pixels in the image window.

When you sample a color from an image with an eyedropper, the Edit pop-up list will at times produce an additional category, titled Reds 2 or Blues 2, for example. The new category includes the 90-degree range of default color categories with the specific, sampled hue at its center.

Once you sample the color on the image with an eyedropper, drag the Hue, Saturation, or Lightness sliders to affect that color.

## Adjusting Saturation

In a similar fashion, you can adjust the intensity of the colors in an image by dragging the Saturation slider. The default saturation value on the center of the slider is 0, which represents the relative saturation of the color. You can move the slider to the right—up to as much as +100%, where the affected colors will be fully saturated, producing intense neon colors— or to the left, to –100%, where the colors will be completely desaturated, or gray.

Most of the time your values will fall somewhere between the two extremes. You can enhance a color and make it "pop" by pushing the Saturation slider between +20% and +40%. On the other hand, if you're interested in muted pastel colors, drag the slider –20% to –40% to the left to diminish the saturation.

> You can perform a quick, total desaturation of an image or a selection by choosing Image → Adjustments → Desaturate. This operation accomplishes the same thing as moving the Saturation slider to –100 in the Hue/Saturation dialog box.

## Adjusting Lightness

You can edit the brightness values of an image by moving the Lightness slider. Drag it toward the left to darken the image or selection, or to the right to lighten it. The 0 point marks the input lightness value of the image. The extremes are +100% lightness, which produces white, and –100% lightness, or black.

If an area of your image is very light and you find that adjusting the Hue and Saturation sliders has no effect on it, darken it a little by dragging the Lightness slider to the left. Then drag the Hue and Saturation sliders. The light areas will begin to change to a color.

> Don't like the results of your first try? At any time, you can reset the Hue/Saturation and other dialog boxes to the default by pressing Alt/Option and clicking the Reset button, or press ⌘/Ctrl-Z to undo just the last operation.

## Colorizing

With this function, you can create those cool effects that you see in movies like *Schindler's List* or in magazine ads, where the entire image is black-and-white except for one area that displays a brilliant spot of color. Before a black-and-white image can be colorized, you must change its mode from Grayscale to one that supports color, like RGB, CMYK, or Lab. The appearance of the grayscale image will be unaffected by this conversion.

When you colorize an image or selected area, you convert gray pixels to colored pixels. Gray pixels have RGB values that are equal. For example, the RGB values for black are red = 0, green = 0, and blue = 0. The RGB values for white are red = 255, green = 255, and blue = 255, and the RGB values for medium gray are red = 127, green = 127, and blue = 127. When you colorize a group of pixels, you shift the red, green, and blue components to disparate values.

When you check the Colorize box, the Hue and Saturation sliders change to represent absolute values instead of relative ones. The default hue that is produced when you check the Colorize box is the current foreground hue. The Hue slider now reads from 0 degrees on the left to 360 degrees on the right, and the current foreground color's position on the color wheel is displayed.

To change the hue, move the slider until you see the color you want, or, more precisely, enter its position on the color wheel (in degrees) in the Hue Value field. The Saturation slider reads from 0% to 100% and defaults at 25%. Move the slider to the right to increase intensity or to the left to decrease intensity. The default lightness of the pixels remains unchanged, as does the Lightness slider. It continues to display relative values between –100 (black) and +100 (white). By colorizing, you apply color to the image without affecting the lightness relations of the individual pixels, thereby maintaining the image's detail.

Let's go through colorization step-by-step so you get the hang of how it operates. For this exercise and the one that follows, I've already selected pieces to be colorized onto separate layers. In later projects, you'll combine selecting or sampling with color adjustments.

1. Open the file `Roses.psd` (Figure 17.2) in the `Ch17` folder on the *Photoshop 7 Savvy* CD.

2. Notice that the file is in Grayscale mode. Choose Image → Mode → RGB. You'll be presented with a dialog box asking if you want to merge the layers before the mode change—choose Don't Merge.

3. When you initially apply colorization, the selection is colored with the foreground color. Click the Default Color icon, or press the D key, to restore the foreground color to black and the background color to white.

   Note that the default foreground color, black, is actually pure red hue, 0 degrees on the color wheel, with 0% saturation and 0% brightness.

4. Choose Window → Layers and target the layer named Red Rose.

5. Choose Image → Adjustments → Hue/Saturation.

6. Click the Colorize box. The rose turns red (the foreground color), along with the dab of paint falling from the paintbrush in the image.

7. Move the Saturation slider to 90% to increase its intensity. Click OK.

Figure 17.2

**The Hue/Saturation adjustment will add a much needed splash of color to the grayscale roses image.**

8. Target the Stem layer, and choose Image → Adjustments → Hue/Saturation again.

9. Click the Colorize box. The stem turns red.

10. Set the Hue to 90; the stem turns green. Set the Saturation to 20 to decrease its intensity. Set the Lightness to –30. Click OK. (See the result in the color section, Figure C20.)

The Hue/Saturation command can be assigned to an Adjustment layer. You can then make changes to the colors of the image throughout the imaging process. For more about Adjustment layers, see Chapter 16.

## Matching Colors

You can use the Hue/Saturation feature to sample a color from one image or selection and apply it to another image or selection, thereby perfectly matching the colors. Here's how:

1. Open the file from your CD, in the Ch17 folder, named Fish.psd.

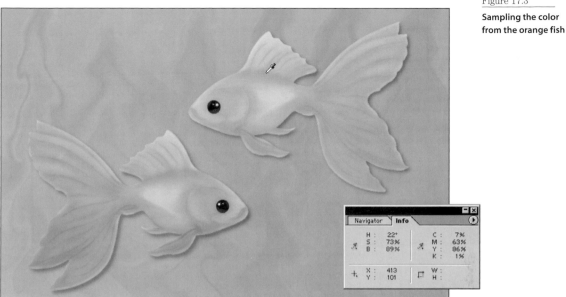

Figure 17.3

**Sampling the color from the orange fish**

2. To make it easier to target specific areas of the image, I have separated it into three layers. Target the Orange Fish layer.

3. Choose the Eyedropper tool . In the Options bar, set the Sample Size to 3 By 3 Average.

4. Choose Window → Info. In the Info Palette pull-down menu, choose Palette Options. For First Color Readout, select HSB Color in the Mode submenu. Click OK.

5. Place the cursor on a midtone region of the orange fish (I chose the area along the top of the fish, just below the fin). Click your mouse to sample the color as a foreground color. Note the Hue and Saturation reading in the Info palette; in this case, it's 22 for the Hue and 73 for the Saturation (see Figure 17.3).

6. Target the Pink Fish layer. Choose Image → Adjustments → Hue/Saturation. Be sure the Preview box is checked; check the Colorize box (see Figure 17.4).

7. If you sampled hue 22 as specified in step 5, then it is now the current foreground color. The Hue slider will read 22 when you click the Colorize box. If you did not sample the color, enter 22 in the Hue box and 73 in the Saturation box. (If necessary, you can also adjust the Lightness slider up or down a bit to best match the orange fish.) Click OK, and the two fish look as though they come from the same school.

Figure 17.3 also appears in the color section, as Figure C21.

Figure 17.4

**The Hue/Saturation dialog box**

# Replacing Color

With Photoshop, you can do more than just alter the hue, saturation, and lightness of an image. You can sample a specific range of colors and automatically replace it with a different range of colors, without affecting the rest of the image. This is particularly useful if you need to change a similar color that is scattered throughout an image.

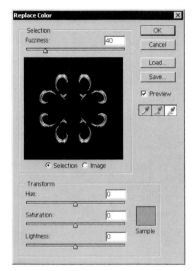

Figure 17.5

**The Replace Color dialog box**

When you choose Image → Adjustments → Replace Color (see Figure 17.5), you get a dialog box that is a combination of two powerful Photoshop operations: the Hue/Saturation command and the Color Range command. This dynamic duo can quickly perform miraculous color swapping. The Color Range command makes selections based on colors you sample in the image. (See Chapter 21, "Making Difficult Selections," for details on how to use Color Range.) The Replace Color dialog box combines this powerful feature with hue, saturation, and lightness controls so that you can precisely sample colors and then instantly replace them. Once again, before you enter the Replace Color dialog box, I recommend that you change the settings on the Eyedropper tool to 3 By 3 Average.

The default Replace Color dialog box displays a black mask of the image. Be sure the Preview box is checked. Choose an Eyedropper from the Replace Color dialog box, and click the color in the image window that you want to change. The mask reveals white portions that designate where the changes will be made. If you choose the Plus Eyedropper, you click and drag over areas to add colors. If you choose the Minus Eyedropper, you drag over colors and delete them from the replacement. The mask reflects the changes you make.

Once you select the colors to replace, the next step is to move the Hue, Saturation, and Lightness sliders to produce a new range of color. As you drag, the affected colors change in the image window. If you don't nail all the areas that you want to change when you sample with the Eyedropper, sample again with the Plus Eyedropper to extend the range. For a little more control, drag the Fuzziness slider to the right. If you click the Image radio button under the mask, you see the image before the change. You can then compare the "before" version in the Replace Color dialog box to the "after" version in the image window prior to committing to the alteration.

Let's take a crack at replacing colors:

1.  From the Ch17 folder on the CD, open the image Recolor.psd (see Figure 17.6).

2.  Choose the Eyedropper tool. (In the Options bar, be sure you set the sample size to 3 By 3 Average.)

3.  Choose Image → Adjustments → Replace Color. Make sure the Selection radio button under the preview window in the dialog box is checked.

4.  Click on one of the gold areas in the image to sample the color. Notice how the mask in the preview window changes to include the sampled gold areas.

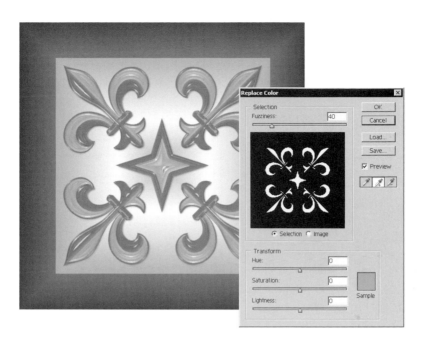

Figure 17.6

**You can recolor all the gold areas in this image with a couple waves of your mouse.**

5. Now choose the Plus Eyedropper. Drag over any gold portions of the image that did not get included in the first sampling. Be careful not to touch the surrounding colors.

6. Move the Hue/Saturation sliders to change the colors. I've specified Hue = –120, Saturation = +20, and Lightness = +10 to make the gold areas a light shade of purple.

7. If there are significant portions of the image that are still gold, drag over the areas with the Plus Eyedropper. If you include too much in the selection, use the Minus Eyedropper to remove some. If you need to extend the color just a little bit, move the Fuzziness slider to the right. Or, if you want to decrease it, move the slider to the left.

8. Click the Image radio button to compare before and after versions. When satisfied with the replacement, click OK. Check the color section, Figure C33, to see the color change in this image.

## Rearranging Colors

Photoshop's color-mapping features enable you to limit the number and range of colors in your image. You can automatically produce higher levels of contrast, convert your images into line art, produce images that resemble serigraphs (silk-screen prints), and change your image from a positive to a negative. With so many choices for transforming your image, no doubt you'll never again be satisfied with just an ordinary photograph. Let's go through them one by one and determine what they do and how they work. You can find all of these features on the bottom rung of the Image → Adjustments submenu.

## Equalizing the Contrast

You can use this command to alter the contrast of an image. It analyzes the color information in each channel, and maps the darkest pixel it can find to black and the lightest pixel to white. It then evenly distributes the color information between the two extremes. This doesn't mean that the image will contain black or white—only that, in at least one channel, there will be a pixel with a value of 0 and a pixel with a value of 255. Also, it doesn't mean that the image will be a higher contrast, only that the contrast values will be distributed over a larger range. The results can vary depending on the image. See Figure 17.7 for an example of the effect. You can also see a color version of this image, Figure C23, in the color section.

## Inverting Color Values

You can use the Invert feature to create negatives, because it expertly converts every color in the image to its exact opposite. If you're working on a 256-level grayscale image, black (0) will become white and white (255) will become black. All other values will also switch; a light gray will become its dark gray counterpart if inverted. For example, if a pixel has a brightness value of 230 (that is, 255 – 25), it will have a value of 25 when converted (0 + 25), as in the example in Figure 17.8. You can also see a color version of this image, Figure C22, in the color section.

Figure 17.7

**Before and after applying the Equalize command**

Figure 17.8

**Before and after applying the Invert command**

Invert works the same way on RGB color images; they are converted channel-by-channel. Invert doesn't produce color film negatives very well, however, because it omits the colored tint, called an *orange mask*, that is found in such negatives. You can use the Invert command and later make a color adjustment with the Color Balance or Variations commands to add an orange tint, but this will require some experimentation.

Because the operation converts the color values of each color channel, the results can vary substantially depending on the image's color mode.

If you invert an alpha channel, the selection it produces will be equal to an inverted selection. You can check the Invert feature in the Levels and Curves command to create negative effects as well; there is also an Invert Adjustment layer.

## Adjusting the Threshold

When you choose Image → Adjustments → Threshold, you map all of your colors to either black or white. The Threshold dialog box displays a histogram of all the brightness values of your image. You drag the slider to the left or right to determine its midpoint. Values on the right side of the slider are white. As you drag to the left, more pixel values are included on the white side and the image gets increasingly lighter. As you drag to the right, more pixel values are included on the black side and the image gets increasingly darker. Figure 17.9 demonstrates several threshold midpoints. See the color section for a color version of this image, Figure C24.

Threshold is useful for turning photographs into high-contrast line art, an effect formerly achieved by copying generations of images on a photocopier or by shooting extremely high-contrast film. Threshold has the advantage of being able to determine exactly how much of the image will be black and how much will be white and, therefore, offers far more control than traditional techniques. Threshold is also quite handy for making alpha channels from color channels for use on those seemingly impossible selections, as you will see in Chapter 21.

Figure 17.9

**The original image (top) remapped to threshold levels of 85, 128, and 200**

## Using the Posterize Feature

Where Threshold divides an image into two colors, Posterize lets you choose the number of colors in which to divide the image. The problem is you have no direct way of controlling how the colors are mapped. Choose Image → Adjustments → Posterize to bring up the Posterize dialog box (see Figure 17.10), and input a Levels value from 2 to 255. Posterize applies the value to each channel of the image, so if you enter 2 while working in an RGB image, for example, you actually produce 8 colors ($2^3$).

Figure 17.10

**The Posterize dialog box**

These effects can be interesting depending on how many colors you input into the Levels field. By breaking up the image into flat areas of color, with occasional dithering where the edges are ambiguous, you can achieve a much more graphic appearance to your image. Unfortunately, the results are also unpredictable.

You can, however, use Posterize to determine the number of colors and how they are distributed in your image. The following workaround will give you the ability to create flat areas of color with more precision and control. The results can vary, depending on your image and color choices. With this method, you can achieve an effect resembling a serigraph used on silk-screen posters with bright, vibrant colors, or tone down an image with pastel colors:

1. Open the RGB image `player.psd` in the `Ch17` folder on the CD (Figure 17.11).

2. Choose Image → Mode → Grayscale to convert the image to a black-and-white version.

3. Choose Image → Adjustments → Posterize. Enter a Levels value of 4 (you can enter any amount from 2 to 255, but we'll use 4 for this demo). Click OK. Notice that the image is now divided into four shades of gray: white, light gray, dark gray, and black, as in Figure 17.12.

4. Choose Image → Mode → RGB to convert the image back to RGB so it can support the color we are about to apply to it.

5. From the Tool palette, choose the Magic Wand tool  . Set the Tolerance to 1 and clear the Anti-Aliased and Contiguous options. Click an area of white to select all of the white in the image.

6. Choose Window → Show Swatches. Pick a light color from the Swatches palette.

7. Use the Paint Bucket tool or Press Option-Delete (Mac) or Alt-Backspace (Win) to fill the selected areas with color.

8. Repeat steps 5, 6, 7, and 8 on the areas of light gray, dark gray, and black, choosing a darker color each time to replace the gray shades.

To see different color versions of this image created using the effect described here, see Figures C25 and C26 in the color section.

Figure 17.11

**The original image**

Figure 17.12

**The posterization workaround lets you control the number of colors in your posterized image.**

## Applying Gradient Maps

You can apply a Gradient Map to an image to adjust the equivalent grayscale range of an image to the colors of a specified gradient fill. An image mapped to a three-color gradient, for example, will change the highlights into gradations on the left end of the gradient, midtones to gradations in the middle of the gradient, and shadows to the gradation of the right endpoint.

To apply a Gradient Map, follow these steps:

1. Open an image. Choose Image → Adjustments → Gradient Map to bring up the dialog box in Figure 17.13.

2. To choose a gradient fill, click the triangle to the right of the gradient fill displayed in the Gradient Map dialog box and then click a swatch.

   If you click the gradient fill, you can edit it or create a new gradient fill.

3. If desired, select one or both of the gradient options:

   **Dither** applies random noise to smooth the gradient and reduce banding effects.

   **Reverse** switches the direction of the gradient fill, reversing the gradient map.

See the color section for a color version of the original image, Figure C27a, and the image with the Gradient Map applied, Figure C27b.

# Creating Digital Halftones

A *halftone* is an image in which ink or toner is transferred to paper, and consists of dots on a grid. The resolution, or number of lines per inch (lpi), of a halftone depends on the printer's capabilities. The number of dots on a traditional halftone is finite and depends on the grid's lpi. The tonal densities of an image are determined by the size of the dots—the larger the dot, the more ink is deposited, and the darker the area appears.

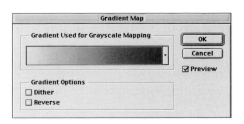

Figure 17.13

**Gradient Map dialog box**

Most ink-jet printers, however, produce a *stochastic*, or frequency modulated, dot pattern, in which the tonal density is expressed not by the size, but by the number of dots deposited. That's why the resolution claimed by desktop ink-jets (commonly 720×1440) is usually higher, though not necessarily better, because the dots are smaller and distributed in a random pattern. When you send an image to a printer, Photoshop, in tandem with the printer driver software, automatically and transparently converts the tonal information contained in pixels into dot density information that the printer's "marking engine" uses to construct your image. Fortunately, you don't have to do any of the math!

Before you begin to create an image for print, you should be aware of the necessary ratio of pixels per inch (ppi) to line screen (lpi) to produce quality halftones. For more on this, see Chapter 13, "Sizing and Transforming Images."

Photoshop also has built-in tools that let you convert your images to bitmaps and take over the halftoning process before you send your image to the printer. The term *bitmap* describes images that are composed of pixels, each containing one bit of information. That means the pixels are either black or white. When you turn an image into a bitmap, Photoshop simply converts all of the tonal information into a series of black or white elements composed of— you guessed it—pixels. You can then print the bitmap on your laser printer as black-and-white line art or as a fully composited halftone. Even better, you can choose from a variety of bitmap types and patterns to produce specialized graphic effects.

You can't directly convert an RGB, CMYK, or Lab image into a halftone. You must first convert your image into Grayscale. Bitmapped images do not support layers, alpha channels, filters, or any operations involving color—in fact, about the only things you can do with them are invert them or paint on them with black or white. Because they contain only one bit of information per pixel, the file sizes of bitmaps are relatively small.

Choose Image → Mode → Bitmap to convert your Grayscale. In the Bitmap dialog box (see Figure 17.14), choose a resolution for the bitmap. The higher the resolution, the smoother the elements that define it will be. If you want a one-to-one ratio with your laser printer, set it to the printer's output resolution (commonly 300, 600, 800, or 1200 dpi).

Next, choose a method from the Use pull-down menu:

**50% Threshold** converts the image to a black-and-white, line art bitmap with the midpoint at 128. The difference between this function and the Threshold command discussed earlier in this chapter is that the Threshold command works on color and grayscale images. It converts the image to black and white but retains the bit depth and, hence, the editability of the image. Plus, you can control the midpoint level, which lets you determine what pixels will be converted to white and what pixels will be converted to black. Bitmap images, on the other hand, are extremely limited as far as how they can be edited and what Photoshop operations they support. Another drawback is that 50% Threshold simply converts the image to black and white using the midtone pixels of 127 and 128 as the dividing line. In the bigger scheme of things, you may be better off using the Threshold command.

**Pattern Dither** applies a preprogrammed, geometric pattern to define the image's tonality. Unfortunately, it produces rather undesirable results, which have a tendency to close up when output to a laser printer.

**Diffusion Dither** applies a mezzotint pattern to the bitmap. The image is defined by a multitude of stray pixels peppered throughout the image. The effect can pleasantly soften the image but can also darken it. You may want to expose the image to a Levels adjustment to lighten it before you convert it to a bitmap using the Diffusion Dither option.

**Halftone Screen** is by far the most useful option of the lot. When you choose Halftone Screen, the dialog box in Figure 17.15 appears. Enter a value for the frequency (lpi), angle of the screen, and dot shape.

**Custom Pattern** uses a pattern that you select from the Pattern pull-down menu to define the tonality. The results can run from really interesting to incredibly ugly. Smaller patterns usually create effects that are more desirable.

To see variations of the potential results, open an image and apply each option in turn. See Figure 17.16 to get a quick idea of the possibilities. It may be difficult to see some differences at low monitor resolution or when printed to some printers.

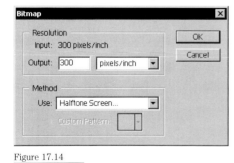

Figure 17.14

**The Bitmap dialog box**

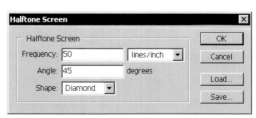

Figure 17.15

**The Halftone Screen dialog box**

When you view many of these bitmap effects on your monitor at certain sizes, you may see a strangely textured on-screen picture. This phenomenon is called a *moiré pattern* and is a result of the dot patterns of the image clashing with the matrix of the pixels on your monitor. Don't worry, the image will not print with these moiré patterns. There is not much you can do about this visual noise except to find a different size in which to view the image.

Original

Halftone Screen

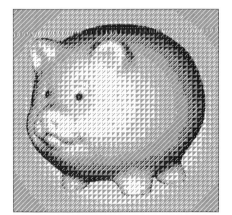

Pattern Dither

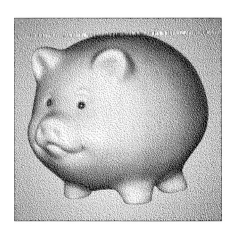

Diffusion Dither

Figure 17.16

**The results of converting an image to Bitmap mode using different methods**

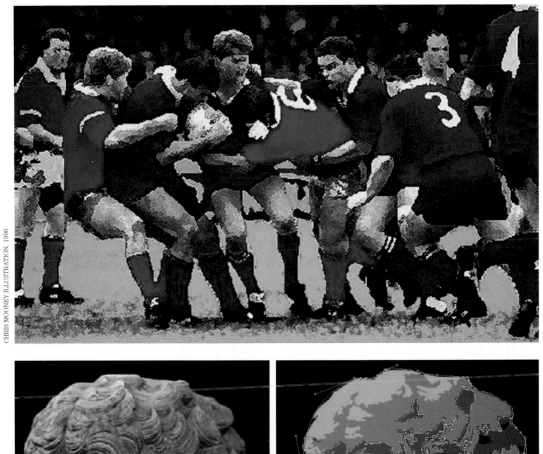

▲**Figure C1** A photograph altered to look like a painting using Photoshop's brushes and filters [Chapter 1]
▼**Figure C2** A raster image composed of pixels (left) and a vector version of the same image (right), composed of shapes constructed from Bezier curves [Chapter 3]

▲**Figure C3**  Paul Signac, *The Port at Sunset* [Chapter 1]
▶**Figure C4**  Detail of a four-color process image. The Pointillist movement influenced the development of the four-color process. [Chapter 1]

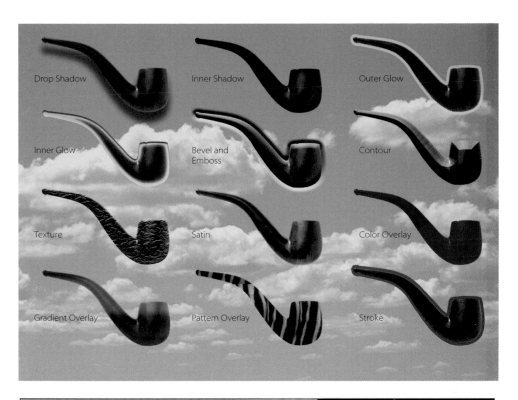

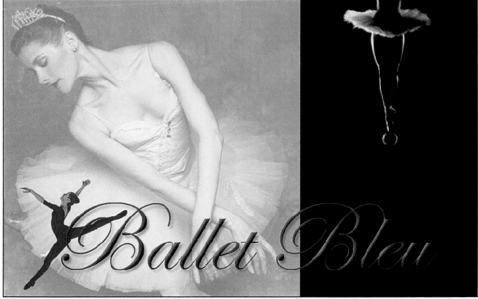

▲**Figure C5**  Layer Styles applied to the pipe [Chapter 7]
▼**Figure C6**  The finished Ballet Bleu homepage [Hands On 9]

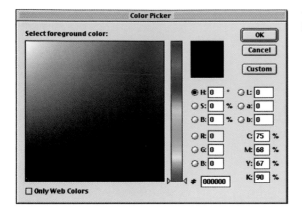

◀**Figure C7** The Color Picker [Chapter 10]

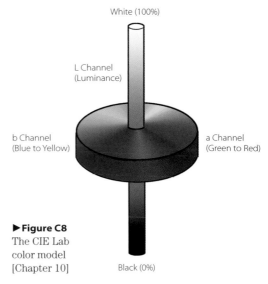

White (100%)

L Channel
(Luminance)

b Channel
(Blue to Yellow)

a Channel
(Green to Red)

▶**Figure C8**
The CIE Lab
color model
[Chapter 10]

Black (0%)

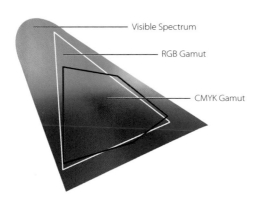

Visible Spectrum

RGB Gamut

CMYK Gamut

▲**Figure C9** A schematic comparison
of the gamut of visible, RGB, and CMYK
colors [Chapter 10]

▶**Figure C10** The RGB
(left) and CMYK (right)
color models [Chapter 10]

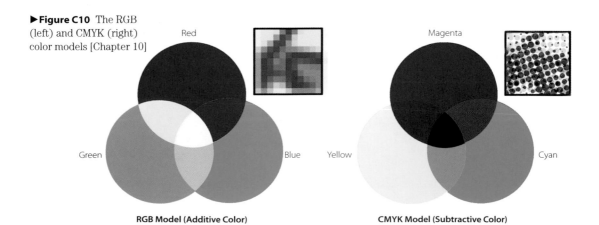

Red

Green

Blue

**RGB Model (Additive Color)**

Magenta

Yellow

Cyan

**CMYK Model (Subtractive Color)**

▲**Figure C11a** The original image from which a
snapshot has been taken. [Chapter 11]

◄**Figure C11b** The image after a Hue/Saturation adjustment
►**Figure C11c** Portions of the image have been painted back to the original with the snapshot

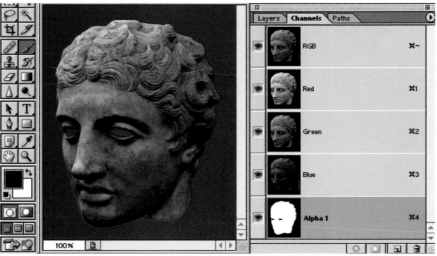

▲**Figure C12**  An alpha channel overlaid on an image [Chapter 12]

▼**Figure C13**  Painting on the alpha channel (left) alters the selection when the channel is loaded [Chapter 12]

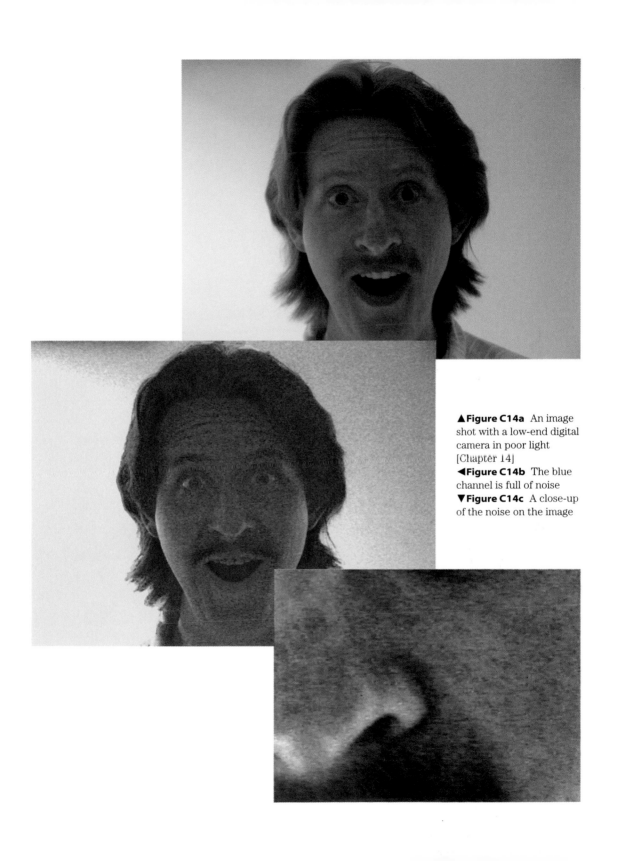

**▲Figure C14a** An image shot with a low-end digital camera in poor light [Chapter 14]
**◄Figure C14b** The blue channel is full of noise
**▼Figure C14c** A close-up of the noise on the image

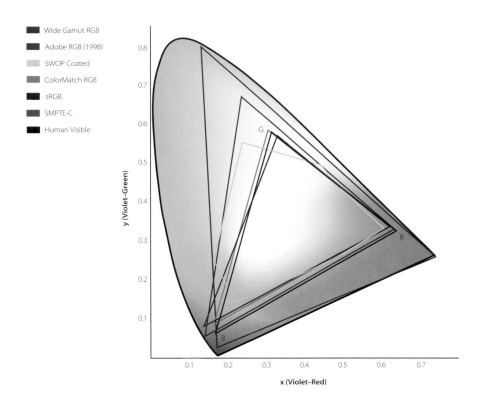

y (Violet–Green)

0.8
0.7
0.6
0.5
0.4
0.3
0.2
0.1

G

R

B

0.1  0.2  0.3  0.4  0.5  0.6  0.7

x (Violet–Red)

▲**Figure C15** The color gamuts of various working spaces [Chapter 15]
◀**Figure C16** This landscape needs more contrast. [Chapter 16]
▼**Figure C17** The landscape after adjusting the contrast [Chapter 16]

▲**Figure C18**  The landscape before the Levels adjustment [Chapter 16]
▼**Figure C19**  The landscape after adjusting the levels [Chapter 16]

▶**Figure C20** The Hue/Saturation adjustment will add a much needed splash of color to the Grayscale roses image. [Chapter 17]

▼**Figure C21** Sampling color from the orange fish [Chapter 17]

▲**Figure C22** Before and after applying the Invert command [Chapter 17]
◄**Figure C23** Before and after applying the Equalize command [Chapter 17]

▲ **Figure C24** The original image (top) remapped to threshold levels of 85, 128, and 200 (bottom, left to right) [Chapter 17]

▲**Figure C25** The original image [Chapter 17]
◄**Figure C26** The posterization workaround lets you control the number of colors in your posterized image. [Chapter 17]

▲**Figure C27a**  The original image [Chapter 17]
▼**Figure C27b**  The image with the gradient map applied [Chapter 17]

**Figure C28** These four images illustrate how Duotones can affect the mood of a photograph. [Chapter 18]

▲**Figure C29a**  The spot color applied over a knockout [Chapter 18]
▶**Figure C29b**  The spot color has been applied directly over the image.
▼**Figure C29c**  The spot color with tonal variations applied over a knockout

▲**Figure C30a** The original
image [Chapter 20]

▲**Figure C30b** Mezzotint,
Grainy Dots

▲**Figure C30c** Pointillize

▲**Figure C30d** Crystallize

▲**Figure C30e** Color Halftone

▲**Figure C31a**  The effect of the
Trace Contour [Chapter 20]
▶**Figure C31b**  Glowing Edges
▼**Figure C31c**  Find Edges filters

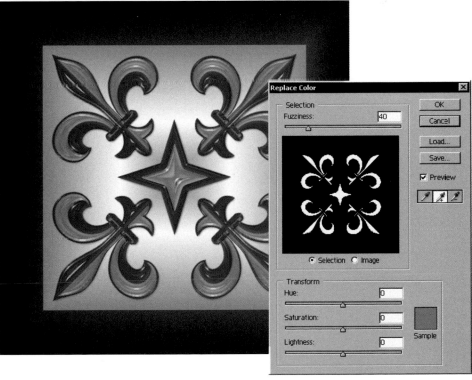

▲**Figure C32** The final Electric Telephone image with the lightning clipped and modeled with the layer mask [Chapter 22]

▼**Figure C33** The result of recoloring all the gold areas in this image [Chapter 17]

◀**Figure C34a** The original image [Chapter 20]

▲**Figure C34b** The Artistic → Watercolor effect

▲**Figure C34c** The Artistic → Palette Knife effect

▲**Figure C34d** The Sketch → Crosshatch effect

▲**Figure C34e** The Sketch → Ink outlines effect

◀**Figure C35** The cat with the cast shadow set to 40% opacity [Chapter 22]

▶**Figure C36** The shadowless cat [Chapter 22]

◀**Figure C37** The completed Uninvited Guest image [Chapter 22]

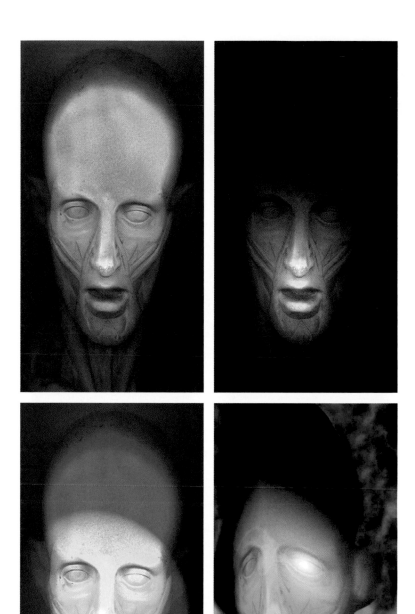

◀**Figure C38a** The original image [Chapter 20]
▶**Figure C38b** Light source from below

◀**Figure C38c** RGB lights
▶**Figure C38d** A combination of filter effects

◀**Figure C39a** The original Apples image [Chapter 24]

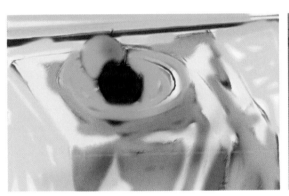

▲**Figure C39b** The broadly painted source

▲**Figure C39c** Subtract mode at 50% opacity

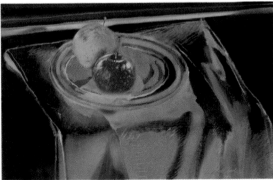

▲**Figure C39d** Multiply mode at 50% opacity

▲**Figure C39e** Exclusion mode at 100% opacity

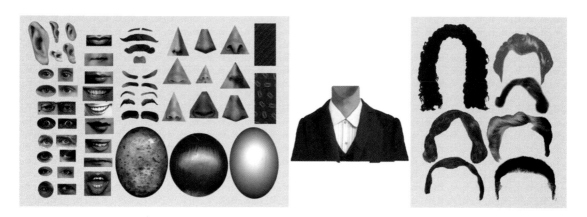

▲**Figure C40** The beginning pieces for the Fred Photato Head project [Hands On 1]
▶**Figure C41** The completed Fred Photato Head [Hands On 1]

▲**Figure C42** The beginning Flying Women file showing the content of the poster [Hands On 2]
◀**Figure C43** The completed Flying Women poster [Hands On 2]

▲**Figure C44** The original seahorse starts with a piece of line art. [Hands On 3]

▲**Figure C45** Our line-art character will develop a bit more personality after a Photoshop paint job. [Hands On 3]

▶**Figure C46** The original chickens, standing around [Hands On 4]

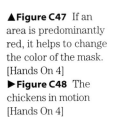

▲**Figure C47** If an area is predominantly red, it helps to change the color of the mask. [Hands On 4]

▶**Figure C48** The chickens in motion [Hands On 4]

▲**Figure C49**  The beginning Sonoran
Desert image [Hands On 5]
▶**Figure C50**  The finished Sonoran Desert
image [Hands On 5]

▲**Figure C51**  The beginning image [Hands On 6]
▼**Figure C52**  The finished Duotone with the spot color graphic and type [Hands On 6]

▲**Figure C53** The original image lacks rich colors and appears flat. [Chapter 24]

▲**Figure C54** Stacking layers with similar content and applying a blending mode and opacity and fill adjustments can greatly enhance an image's contrast and color. [Chapter 24]

▲**Figure C55**  The beginning image needs
restoration. [Hands On 7]
▶**Figure C56**  The completed image after
restoration [Hands On 7]

▲**Figure C57** The beginning Flamingo Hotel image with its Layers palette [Hands On 8]

▲**Figure C58** The finished Flamingo Hotel showing all of its guests [Hands On 8]

# Image Size, Transformation, and Color Adjustment

*Often, an image* needs more than minor color correction. This project covers a variety of techniques to correct color and tonality, including Levels, Auto Levels, Curves, Color Balance, Adjustment Layers, and Unsharp Masking.

Figure H5.1

**The start of the Sonoran Desert image**

## Getting Started

Hide or discard your preferences file before beginning this exercise. The "Modifying Photoshop's Settings" section in Chapter 5 details how to temporarily reset your preferences to Photoshop defaults. You can restore your customized personal settings when you're done.

1. Open the file named sonoran_desert.psd (Figure H5.1) in the H05 folder on the *Photoshop 7 Savvy* CD. (See Figure H5.2 for the completed image.) To see a color preview of the before and after versions of the image, look at Figures C49 and C50 in the color section.

2. Save the file to your disk. Close the file.

Figure H5.2

**The finished Sonoran Desert image**

## Choosing a Color Space

Calibrate your monitor using the Adobe Gamma software as described in Chapter 5 or a colorimeter as described in Chapter 15. The image for this exercise is going to be printed in a tourist brochure using four-color process. Before opening the document, choose an appropriate color space:

1. In Windows and MacOS 9.2 and earlier, choose Edit → Color Settings. In MacOS X, choose Photoshop → Color Settings. The Color Settings dialog box is displayed.

2. From the Settings pull-down menu, choose U.S. Prepress Defaults, as shown in Figure H5.3. Note that the RGB working space for this setting is Adobe RGB.

3. Open the Sonoran Desert image file you previously saved to your disk. Since you've changed the working color space to U.S. Prepress Defaults, and the image does not contain an embedded profile, you will be now be presented with the Missing Profile dialog box. Choose to assign working RGB (which is now Adobe RGB) to the image, and click OK.

Figure H5.3

**U.S. Prepress Defaults color setting**

## Cropping the Image

The image has a black border around it and is at a slight angle. You'll need to crop it to eliminate the unwanted areas and adjust its angle relative to the page.

1. Choose the Crop tool ⌞ᴛ⌟ . Place your cursor in the upper left of the image. Click and drag down and to the right to encompass all four corners of the inner image area.

2. Since the border around the image is black, we'll change the color of the crop shield so that we can distinguish the crop area from the border. In the Options bar, double-click the shield swatch and choose a color other than black.

3. Hover your cursor close to the outside of a corner point of the marquee until the rotation icon appears. Click and drag to rotate the marquee so that it aligns with the angled edges of the inner image area.

4. Click and drag the corner and side points as needed to adjust the size of the crop marquee so that it encompasses only the image areas, but none of the black border, as in Figure H5.4.

5. Click the check mark in the Options bar to commit the crop.

Figure H5.4

**The Crop marquee in place**

## Sizing the Image

The final physical size of the image has to be 5″ wide to fit in the brochure. Resize the image using the Image Size command:

1. Choose Image → Image Size. Change the width to 5″. The height automatically changes to 7.41″. (The height may vary, depending on how you cropped the image.) The resolution remains at 300 ppi, which is the required resolution for printing to a high-quality printed publication.

2. Click OK.

3. Press ⌘/Ctrl-S to save.

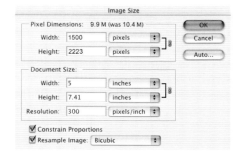

## Adjusting Levels

Next you'll adjust the image's levels:

1. From the Layers menu, choose New Adjustment Layer → Levels. The layer should name itself Levels 1; click OK.

   In the Levels dialog box (Figure H5.5), notice the histogram: Most of the pixels are clumped into the center, which indicates that the image needs a contrast adjustment. The graph is also devoid of lines in the highlights and shadows. (The spike on the right represents the pixels in the sky.) You can increase the overall contrast by spreading the highlights, midtones, and shadows over a broader range of values by moving the sliders.

2. Move the White slider toward the center until the output level reads 226. Move the Black slider until it reads 30. The contrast is improved, but we can be more precise. Undo the adjustment by pressing the Option (Mac) or Alt (Win) key and clicking Reset.

3. Choose Red from the Channel pop-up list. Drag the Highlight Input slider on the right toward the center until it just touches the beginning of the "mountain range" on the histogram. The value should read 218, as in Figure H5.6.

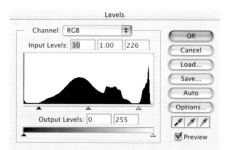

Figure H5.5

**RGB levels**

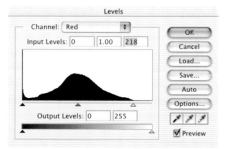

Figure H5.6

**Red channel adjustments**

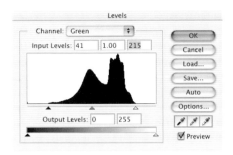

Figure H5.7

**Green channel adjustment**

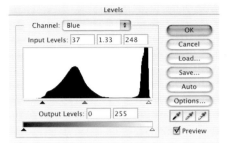

Figure H5.8

**Blue channel adjustment**

4. Choose Green from the Channel pop-up list. Adjust the Input values to 41 for the shadow, 1.00 for the midtone, and 215 for highlight, as in Figure H5.7.

5. Choose Blue from the Channel pop-up list. Move the sliders toward the center. Adjust the Input values to 37, 1.33, and 248, as in Figure H5.8.

6. Click OK.

7. Save.

## Balancing Color

Now the image looks a lot brighter but has a slightly yellow color cast. Use the Color Balance feature to correct the color cast:

1. Make a new Adjustment layer. This time, choose Layer → New Adjustment Layer → Color Balance. Click OK in the naming dialog box.

2. In the Color Balance dialog box, be sure the Preview box is checked to see the results as you work.

3. Click the Midtone radio button. Move the Yellow–Blue slider toward +15, as in Figure H5.9. This reduces the amount of yellow in the image and produces more natural-looking color in the midtones.

4. Click the Highlight radio button. Move the Yellow–Blue slider to +8, as in Figure H5.10. This produces more neutral colors in the lighter regions of the image.

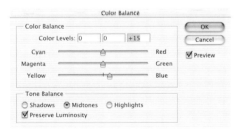

Figure H5.9

**Adjusting the midtone color balance**

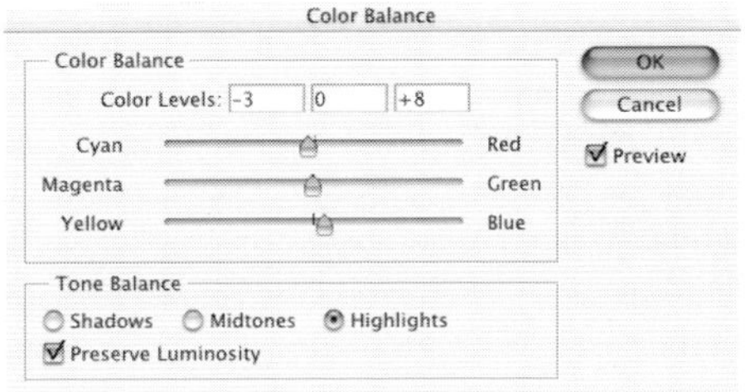

Figure H5.10

**Adjusting the highlight color balance**

5. Move the Cyan–Red slider toward Cyan to –3 to produce a slightly cooler image.

6. Click OK. The image has lost its yellow cast and the color looks more natural.

7. Press ⌘/Ctrl-S to save the document.

## Adjusting Curves

The image is now looking good, having adjusted its contrast and eliminated the color cast, but it would be nice to bring out a little more of the red in the mountains. The Curves feature is by far the most powerful of the color adjustment tools; it enables you to be quite specific about the range of color to adjust.

1. Choose Layer → New Adjustment Layer → Curves. In the resulting New Layer dialog box, keep the default name for the new adjustment layer and click OK to bring up the Curves dialog box.

2. Click the enlarge icon  to expand the dialog box. This will give you more control over the adjustment.

3. Press Option/Alt and click the graph to see the finer grid.

4. Because you want to enhance the reds in the mountains, choose the Red channel.

5. Choose Load, and open red_lockdown_curve.acv in the H05 folder on the CD.

6. Click and drag over the red rocks; notice that the cursor turns into an eyedropper and a little circle appears that moves up and down the curve, which indicates the range of the red pixels on the curve that we want to affect. Press ⌘/Ctrl, and click and drag the mouse to deposit an anchor point on the highest spot on the curve where the circle moves.

Figure H5.11

**The Curves adjustment**

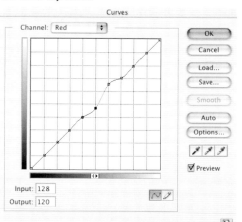

7. Click the new anchor point on the curve and drag it straight upward about half a cell. The mountains become redder.

8. Click the adjacent anchor point down and to the left of the point you just adjusted and drag it straight down just a small amount (see Figure H5.11). The area around the rock becomes greener, producing more contrast.

9. Click OK.

10. Save.

Be prudent in the amount you adjust the curve. Too great an adjustment will produce posterization and dithering. It's always a good idea to zoom in on a portion of the affected area and scrutinize it carefully after you've made the adjustment—but before you close the dialog box. Press ⌘/Ctrl-spacebar to zoom in and Option/Alt-spacebar to zoom out.

## Adding Canvas

The photographer who took the picture lopped off the top of the cactus. You'll need to add a new top, but first you'll have to expand the canvas:

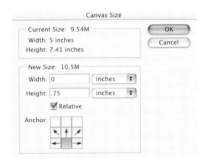

Figure H5.12

**The Canvas Size dialog**

1. Set white as the background color.

2. Target the Background.

3. Choose Image → Canvas Size.

4. In the Canvas Size dialog box, check the Relative box and enter **.75** inches for the height (see Figure H5.12).

5. Anchor the image at the bottom middle.

6. Click OK. The image should look like Figure H5.13.

## Adding Sky

We can make the sky more interesting with a few clouds:

1. Target the Background. Choose the Magic Wand tool . Set the tolerance to 100. Clear the Contiguous box in the Options bar. Click the blue area of the image to select it. Click the Add To Selection icon in the Options bar, and keep clicking on the blue until you select all of it.

2. Check the Contiguous box in the Options bar. Drop the tolerance down to 32. Click the white area to add it to the selection.

3. Open the document in the H05 folder on the CD titled big_sky.psd.

4. Choose Edit → Select All (⌘/Ctrl-A) and then Edit → Copy (⌘/Ctrl-C).

Figure H5.13

**The desert with the new canvas**

Figure H5.14

**The Move tool's
Options bar**

Figure H5.15

**The desert with the
new canvas**

5. Make the Sonoran Desert document active. Choose Edit → Paste Into to create a new layer. Double-click the layer's default name and rename it **Big Sky**. Notice that the layer has a layer mask.

6. Choose the Move tool ![move tool]. In the Options bar, choose Show Bounding Box (see Figure H5.14). Move and size the sky to fit the image by adjusting the corner and side points. Click the check mark in the Options bar to commit the transformation. The image should look like Figure H5.15.

7. Save the document.

## Topping Off the Cactus

Next, use the right arm of the large cactus to create a top. Since the union has to be seamless, you'll use a layer mask to blend the two elements together.

1. Target the Background. Zoom in on the right arm. In the Options bar, set the feather radius to 1 pixel. With the Magnetic Lasso tool ![lasso tool], select a portion as in Figure H5.16. To better conceal the union of the cactus and the arm, make the bottom line irregular.

2. Choose Layer → New → Layer Via Copy. Name the new layer **Cactus Top**.

3. In the Layers palette, drag the Cactus Top layer to the top of the stack.

4. Choose the Move tool and check Show Bounding Box in the Options bar. Drag the arm to the top of the cactus. Size and rotate it into position. Click the check mark in the Options bar to implement the transformation.

5. Choose Layer → New Adjustment Layer → Hue/Saturation. In the New Layer dialog box (Figure H5.17), choose Group With Previous Layer to confine the adjustments to the Cactus Top layer only.

6. Move the Hue and Saturation sliders until you match the color of the bottom part of the cactus. I set the hue to –35 and the lightness to +5 (see Figure H5.18).

7. Link the Hue/Saturation layer, the Cactus Top layer, the Big Sky layer, and the Background. Choose Layer → Merged Linked.

8. Press ⌘/Ctrl-S to save the document.

Figure H5.16

**The selected cactus arm**

## Enhancing the Saturation

The image is taking shape, but we need to create more depth and richness in the foreground foliage and the cacti while maintaining less saturation in the mountains to allow them to recede in the distance.

**New Layer dialog**

1. Target the Background. Choose Layer → New Adjustment Layer → Hue Saturation.

2. Move the Saturation slider to +15 and the lightness slider to –4, as in Figure H5.19. Click OK.

3. Target the Hue/Saturation Layer mask in the Layers palette. Choose a Soft 200-pixel brush. With black as the foreground color, paint out the sky and the mountains to diminish the effect in those areas.

Figure H5.18

**Hue/Saturation dialog**

4. In the Options bar, set the brush opacity to 50%, and paint out the grass at the bottom of the image. Your layer mask should look something like Figure H5.20.

5. Double-click the Layer thumbnail icon on the Hue/Saturation Adjustment layer. In the resulting dialog box, move the Hue slider to +10 to add green to the cacti (see Figure H5.21).

6. Save the image.

## Using Auto Levels

Next, let's drag and drop an image of a cactus wren onto the new image, and then apply a quick adjustment to it:

Figure H5.19

**Adjusting the saturation and lightness in the Hue/Saturation dialog box**

1. Open the file `wren.psd` in the `H05` folder on the CD.

2. Choose the Magic Wand tool and set the tolerance to 32.

3. Click the blue background of the image.

4. Choose Select → Inverse to select the cactus and the bird.

5. Choose the Lasso tool, and click the Subtract From Selection icon ⬜ in the Options bar. Omit the cactus from the selection by dragging around it with the Lasso tool while holding down Option/Alt. Carefully outline the bottom of the bird's feet, as shown in Figure H5.22.

Figure H5.20

**The Hue/Saturation layer mask**

6. Choose the Move tool. Click and drag the selected Wren layer to the Sonoran Desert image and release the mouse. A new layer will be created in the Layers palette. Name the layer **Wren** and click OK.

7. Choose Layer → Matting → Defringe. Enter **2** pixels to remove the edge pixels around the wren (see Figure H5.23).

8. With the Wren layer targeted, choose Image → Adjustments → Auto Color. The color of the wren will shift from muddy brown to more pleasing desert hues. In addition, the contrast will be improved.

9. In the Options bar, check Show Bounding Box. Press Shift to constrain the proportion of the bird as you drag a corner handle. Drag inward until the bird is a reasonable size for the Sonoran Desert scene, then release the mouse. Double-click inside the bounding box to initiate the transformation.

10. Place your cursor inside the marquee. Drag the wren and place it on the top of the large saguaro cactus, as in Figure H5.24. Adjust size and rotation if needed.

11. Choose File → Save and save the document.

## Applying USM

Figure H5.21

**Use the Hue slider to adjust the image's hue**

The image is practically complete, but let's see if we can get a little more punch out of it. Because we are going to flatten the image, we should make a copy of it first:

1. To duplicate the image, choose Image → Duplicate. Name the image **sonoran_desert_flattened**.

2. From the Layers Palette pull-down menu, choose Flatten Image.

3. Choose Image → Mode → Lab Color to convert the image so as to avoid color shifts when sharpening.

Figure H5.22

**The wren, selected**

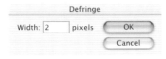

Figure H5.23

**The Defringe dialog box**

**The wren, sized and positioned**

Figure H5.25

**The Channels palette with the Lightness channel targeted and the composite channel displayed**

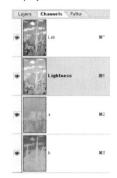

4. Display the Channels palette. Target the Lightness channel. You should be viewing the composite channel in the image window, but only the Lightness channel should be highlighted, as in Figure H5.25.

5. Choose Filter → Sharpen → Unsharp Mask. Set the amount to 75%, the radius to 3 pixels, and the threshold to 6 levels (see Figure H5.26).

6. Click OK.

7. Press ⌘/Ctrl-S to save the document.

## Converting the Image to CMYK

If you are outputting the image to four-color process color separations, it's wise to convert it to CMYK first so that you can make any necessary adjustments and accurately predict how the image will print. First, preview the document, then follow these steps:

1. Duplicate the flattened sharpened image. Name it **sonoran_desert_cmyk.psd** and place it next to the original RGB image on-screen, making sure it's active.

2. In the View menu, make sure that Proof Colors is checked, and then choose View → Proof Setup → Working CMYK to display the image in the CMYK setup that you selected in the color settings. In this case, it's U.S. Web Coated (SWOP) v2, which is part of the U.S. Prepress Defaults selected earlier in this project. By comparing it to the RGB image, you'll notice there are minor color shifts in the sky of the CMYK preview file, but let's convert the file as is.

3. Choose Image → Mode → CMYK to convert the file.

4. Save the image.

If there are radical color shifts, use the adjustment commands in the Image menu to restore the color.

Figure H5.26

**Applying the Unsharp Mask filter to the image is the final step in enhancing the contrast.**

# CHAPTER 18

# Duotones and Spot Color

*Most images printed* from Photoshop are printed in process colors. Printing presses use cyan, magenta, yellow, and black ink spread on individual metal or plastic plates and impressed onto paper to print color images. Similarly, ink-jet printers deposit ink from cartridges containing the CMYK colors. From time to time, however, the occasion arises when you need to create images using custom color ink systems, either for a specific look or for reasons of economy. Photoshop has two functions that are designed to prepare images for printing using custom colors: Duotones and spot colors. These systems depend on color information found in the Channels palette.

In this chapter, you'll discover:

- **The nature of Duotones**
- **How to make Duotones, Tritones, and Quadtones work**
- **How to create spot color channels**
- **Printing Duotones and spot color**

## Why Use Duotones?

Duotones are a source of disagreement in the printing industry. Some press professionals call them a waste of two-color press time. Others claim they can turn otherwise lackluster halftones into subtle works of art. Duotones, and their siblings Tritones and Quadtones, print grayscale images using two (or three or four) separate inks. Usually the inks are colored, but occasionally you'll see a Duotone created using two black plates. Proponents claim that two blacks can attain a richness and depth out of reach of the simple halftone; critics say it's just one black plate too many. They may never reach an agreement.

No such controversy exists over the use of spot colors. Pressroom shelves are lined with tubs of premixed and mixable inks, and now with six-and eight-color presses becoming more and more common, combinations of four-color process, spot colors, and/or varnishes are being used with greater frequency. Photoshop's spot color channels provide a tool for creating and separating spot colors for printing.

Duotones and spot color differ from process color. Process color produces a complete color and tonal range by mixing cyan, magenta, yellow, and black ink in varying densities. On the other hand, Duotones and spot color involve printing specific premixed ink colors on a substrate. Even though Photoshop deals with them in different ways, they appear together in this chapter. You'll have a chance to try them out for yourself, and then you can decide where you come down on the Duotone question.

## What Are Duotones?

When a grayscale digital image is converted to a halftone and printed with black ink on paper, the shades of gray that you created on your computer are represented by the size and concentration of dots. The black ink is still black, no matter what size you make the dot. It just can't quite represent all 256 levels of gray found in the grayscale image.

Duotones can help you achieve a wider tonal range in a grayscale image by using more than one shade of ink to fill in the gaps. You can enhance the detail and texture in an image. If you're printing a two-color book with halftones, adding the second color to the halftones can add an elegant touch. Duotones using a dark and a metallic ink can impart an opaque, antique quality, while lighter pastel shades might approximate a hand-tinted look or other variations, as you can see in Figures C28 in the color section.

Duotones do present one potential problem. Because two (or several) inks are being superimposed on one another, it is possible to generate too much ink. If the distribution of ink is not dealt with properly, it could saturate the paper and fill in the spaces between the fine halftone dots. That's why Photoshop's Duotone mode features a Curves palette in its dialog box, so that you can adjust each ink level individually…but we'll get to that in a minute.

# Working with Duotone Mode

Suppose you start with a color photo you've scanned. Open your RGB image, and then look in the Image → Mode submenu. You'll see that the Duotone mode is grayed out, unavailable as an option. In order to convert an image to Duotone mode, you have to first convert it to Grayscale mode. Wait! Before you do that, it's best to correct tonal and color values first, using Levels, Curves, or the other adjustment features discussed in Chapter 16, "Adjusting Tonality and Color." Get the image exactly where you want it before you reduce it to a single channel. In fact, take a look at your color channels individually. You may find something there you like (the Green channel in an RGB image may contain a convincing microcosm of the whole, for example). Even better, use the Channel Mixer to get the perfect grayscale image. Once you're happy with it, choose Image → Mode → Grayscale. If you want to do any further tweaking, do it while you're in Grayscale mode. *Then* choose Image → Mode → Duotone (Figure 18.1). Now you're in Duotone country.

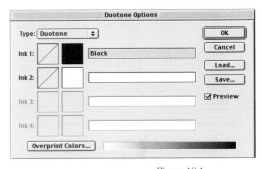

Figure 18.1

**The Duotone Options dialog box**

The Duotone Options dialog box lets you choose a type–that is, the number of inks you want to use, up to four. Monotones are just colored halftones, Duotones use two inks, Tritones three, and Quadtones…you guessed it. You can set curves and choose colors individually for each ink. Click an ink's color box to bring up the Color Picker. If you want to use printing ink colors, click Custom. There you can view a wide variety of swatch books to choose your ink colors. (See the section in Chapter 10, "Creating and Applying Color," on custom colors.) Check with your printer for the availability of inks.

If you plan to import the Duotone into a page layout document, keep an eye on the names of your inks. Make sure the Duotone ink has exactly the same name as in the other application's color dialog. You can always come back to the Duotone Options dialog box and change the name of the ink if you have to.

Figure 18.2

**Choosing the color of Duotone ink**

By default, the Ink 1 color is designated Black. If you choose any type other than Monotone, the new ink color(s) are empty (white) by default.

To choose an ink, click the swatch and the Custom Colors dialog box is displayed. The default book (a term derived from the fact that ink manufacturers produce color swatch books to display their inks) is PANTONE solid coated (as in Figure 18.2). Choose an ink color from the list, and click OK. Define additional inks in the same way. The color bar at the bottom of the dialog box displays the range, from light to dark, of the

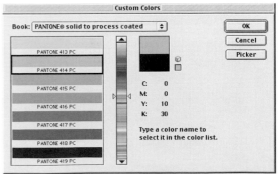

color mix you've specified. The image window also has a live preview. When you specify colors, the image displays the changes on-screen.

When you define ink colors for Duotones, Tritones, and Quadtones, make sure the darkest ink is at the top and the lightest at the bottom. When Duotone images print, the inks are applied in the order in which they appear in the dialog box. Allowing the darker inks to print first provides for a uniform color range from shadows to highlights.

## Duotone Curves

Duotone curves let you control the density of each ink in the highlights, midtones, and shadows. Click the curve thumbnail for any ink to display the corresponding Duotone Curve dialog box (Figure 18.3). Here you can adjust the curve to define ink coverage for each color. Or enter values in one of the 13 percentage fields.

When you first convert a file to Duotone mode, the curves are straight by default. If you leave the curve straight, Photoshop will distribute the ink evenly across the entire tonal range of the image. If all of the curves on a Duotone are straight, you'll end up with a dark, muddy mess. It's best to apply colors to suit the needs of the image in question; generally, you'll want dark inks densest in the shadows, somewhat lighter inks in the midtones, and light colors enhancing the highlights.

You have two ways of adjusting the curves in the Duotone Curves dialog. Either type numeric settings for ink percentages in the boxes provided, or drag inside the curve's grid to adjust the curve directly. Like the Curves dialog box we encountered in Chapter 16, the grid's horizontal axis expresses the gradations in the image from white (highlights) on the left to black (shadows) on the right. The vertical axis maps ink density, increasing as you go up. Click anywhere on the line and drag up or down to add or subtract ink in that part of the curve. As you adjust the curve, the numbers change accordingly in the percentage boxes to reflect the changes you make. Likewise, when you type numbers in the percentage boxes,

Figure 18.3

**The Duotone Curve dialog box**

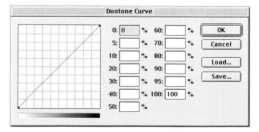

the curve adjusts itself to match. The first curve shown in Figure 18.4 retains the selected color in the shadow areas, while reducing the amount of ink to be printed in the highlights. The second curve concentrates its ink in the midtones and highlights, while the third enhances the highlights only. The final illustration is the Duotone Options box showing the curves for all three inks.

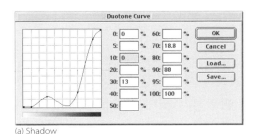

(a) Shadow

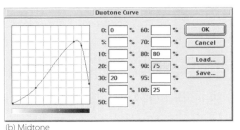

(b) Midtone

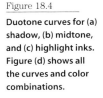

Figure 18.4

**Duotone curves for (a) shadow, (b) midtone, and (c) highlight inks. Figure (d) shows all the curves and color combinations.**

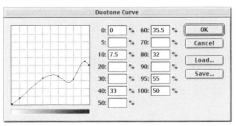

(c) Highlight

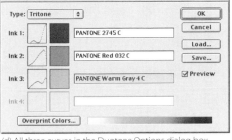

(d) All three curves in the Duotone Options dialog box

Save the curves you create in the Duotone Curves dialog by clicking the Save button; the program prompts you to choose where to save the curve file. Likewise, you can load curves you've already created by clicking Load and opening an earlier adjustment. The "master" Save and Load buttons in the Duotone Options dialog box will allow you to save or load a *complete set* of curves, inks, and overprint colors.

Photoshop provides several sample settings for Duotones, Tritones, and Quadtones that you can use to see how these options work. Use them as a starting point for experimentation and adventure.

Let's load some Duotone curves.

1. Open the file in the Ch18 folder on the CD, Rancho_Linda_Vista.psd (Figure 18.5).

2. Choose Image → Mode → Duotone. For the Type, choose Duotone. The Duotone Options dialog box is displayed.

3. Click Load to browse for the preset curves. These curves are located in the Photoshop 7.0\ Presets\Duotones\Duotones\PANTONE Duotones folder; choose one of the Duotone presets in that folder. Click Load to load the Duotone set and OK to apply the settings.

4. To make changes to your settings, try different inks, or to tweak the curves, just go back to Image → Mode → Duotone, and your previous settings reappear with the Duotone Options dialog. Make the changes you desire and click OK. See Figures C11 and C28 in the color section for examples of the images with some of the Duotone curves applied.

Figure 18.5

**The Rancho Linda
Vista image**

## Multichannel Mode

If you look in the Channels palette of a Duotone image, you will see only one channel, labeled
Duotone (or Tritone or Quadtone). Where are the channels representing the inks you've chosen? Photoshop creates Duotones by applying the various curves you've defined to a single-
channel image. To view the channels independently, you must convert the image to
Multichannel mode (Image → Mode → Multichannel).

In Figure 18.6, you see the Channels palette with the Tritone channel. Next to it, the
*same image's* palette has been split into three independent channels, listed separately,
and ordered according to the ink color names. If you make any changes or adjustments in
this mode, you will not be able to return to Duotone mode. You can print directly from Multichannel, and you will get two, three, or four separated prints called color separations, one for
each color. The advantage of using Multichannel is that the three channels can be edited
independently.

Figure 18.6

**The Channels palette
of the same Tritone
image, in Duotone
mode (left) and Multi-
channel mode (right)**

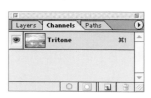

## Overprint Colors

*Overprint colors* are two or more unscreened inks that are printed one on top of the other. The order of how the inks are laid down can affect the final outcome. The Overprint Colors dialog box displays a chart that shows how different pairs of colors (or groups of three or four) will blend when printing. If you click any of the color swatches, the Color Picker comes up and allows you to replace the color. The new overprint colors will be applied to the image but only affect how the image appears on-screen. These settings do not affect how the image prints; use Overprint Colors to help you *predict* how colors will look when printed. Thus, you should only use this function on a calibrated monitor.

You can superimpose one ink over another in Duotone mode by using the same curve for each color. This is not a recommended practice because the results can look muddy from excessive ink. Where the Overprint Colors feature helps predict a color shift is on two or more solid, transparent areas of spot color that are super-imposed over each other.

## Using Spot Color Channels

Spot colors are additional inks used in a print job other than black or process colors. The inks can be overprinted on top of the grayscale or CMYK image or independently. Each spot color requires a plate of its own. Spot colors are printed in the order in which they appear in the Channels palette, from top to bottom. Spot color channels are totally independent of the color mode of the image; that is, the spot colors are not blended with the other channels in a grayscale, RGB, or CMYK image. Spot color channels are also independent of layers—you cannot apply spot colors to individual layers.

Here are some of the likes and unlikes of spot color:

- Spot color channels are like layers in that they are independent of and separate from the Background image.
- Spot colors are unlike layers in that they cannot be merged with the rest of the image and still remain as spot colors.
- Spot color channels are like color channels in that they exist only in the Channels palette.
- Spot color channels are unlike color channels because, by default, they print separately from the rest of the image.

Figure 18.7

**The frying pan image**

## Creating Spot Colors

Let's try creating a spot color:

1. Open the grayscale image `frying_pan.psd` (Figure 18.7) in the `Ch18` folder on the CD. Save it to your disk.

2. Choose Window → Channels to display the Channels palette (Figure 18.8.). Load Alpha 1, which is a selection of the egg yolks, by dragging it to the Load Channel icon ⬡ .

3. From the Channels palette pull-down menu, choose New Spot Channel. Your selection fills with red (the default spot color) and becomes the new spot color channel. The New Spot Channel dialog appears.

4. By default, the spot color is red. Click the color swatch to bring up the Color Picker. Choose Custom Colors and choose a premixed ink, such as PANTONE 1225 C. The spot color channel will be named automatically with the name of the selected ink, as shown in Figure 18.9.

### SOLIDITY VS. OPACITY

Entering a value in the Solidity box lets you control the viewing density of the spot color channel. The Solidity control is for visual reference only. It's there to help you visualize what an ink may look like when printed in a tint value from 0% to 100%.

Solidity is not to be confused with Opacity. Opacity affects the amount of color applied to an image with the paint tools, or the transparency of an image on a layer. Solidity is a visual reference, and does not affect the image unless you merge the spot colors with the other color channels. It then applies the tint value of the color to the image and is no longer a spot color.

If you want the spot color ink to print as a tint, you have to create a gray (instead of black) selection in the spot color channel. Spot color inks always print full intensity unless your selection mask in the spot color channel itself contains a gradation or tint. Printing inks are usually transparent. When printed over the image, the spot color will mix with colors underneath it.

5. Choose your solidity (see the sidebar on the difference between solidity and opacity) and click OK.

When your new spot color channel has been created, it resides in the Channels palette just below the separate channels of the color mode you're working in. In a grayscale image, Spot Color 1 follows Black; in an RGB image, Spot follows Blue. You cannot move spot color channels up above the regular color mode channels, unless you convert your image to the Multichannel mode. Likewise, alpha channels follow spot color channels in the pecking order. As with Duotone mode, spot color channels print in the order in which they're listed in the Channels palette.

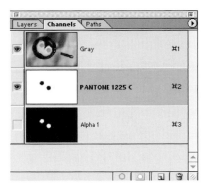

Figure 18.8

The frying pan with the spot color channel in the Channels palette

## Viewing Spot Colors

If you're viewing the image in the composite view, and your spot channel is active, the foreground color becomes the channel's spot color, with white as the background color. The foreground color swatch, however, will appear black, white, or a shade of gray depending on the brightness of the selected color. If you're viewing the spot color channel independently of the composite, the foreground color is white and the background color black. You can edit a spot color channel exactly as you would an alpha channel: use painting tools, selection tools, filters, type, placed artwork, etc. to impose the image you want to print.

Figure 18.9

The Spot Channel Options dialog box showing the name of the selected ink

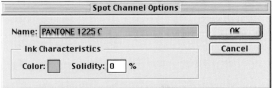

Special rules apply to type in spot color channels. In fact, in Photoshop 7, type behaves in spot channels the way that type used to, before Adobe made it editable. In other words, when you apply type to a spot color channel, the text shows up as a selection outline on the channel; then you fill it. Once you deselect it, it's no longer editable—except in the ways you would normally edit a selection.

## Knocking Out Spot Colors

If you don't want your spot color to overprint another spot color or a part of the underlying image, you can create a *knockout.* A knockout prevents ink from printing on part of the image so the spot color can print directly on the paper. Thus, no blending of ink occurs in the desired area. Activate the channel that you want to knock out. Choose Select → Load Selection,

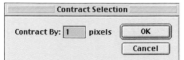

Figure 18.10

**Contract Selection
dialog**

and load the spot color channel in question. Choose Select → Modify → Contract (or Expand) to adjust the fit of the knockout. (See Hands On 6, "Duotones and Spot Color" following this chapter to try this.)

You can create a trap at this point by slightly reducing or enlarging the selection outline to allow a small outline of both inks to overprint. This way, no white space appears between two colors when the job is printed. Once you have your selection adjusted to fit, press Delete (Mac) or Backspace (Win) to eliminate the underlying image. Now the spot color can imprint unimpeded.

> Lighter-colored inks are usually *spread*, meaning that the knockout hole stays the same size, while the original spot color shape that prints over the hole is expanded slightly. Darker inks *choke*, meaning that the spot color shape stays the same size, while the knockout hole is contracted slightly to form the trap.

You can also select a portion of the image, copy it, and then attribute a spot color to it using its tonal qualities. We will use this technique on the Froggy image to create a different spot color effect.

To create a spot color from a tonal area on the image with a knockout:

1. Open the image `froggy.psd` in the `Ch18` folder on the CD. Save it to your disk as `froggy_knockout.psd`.

2. Choose Window → Channels to display the Channels palette. Load Alpha 1 by dragging it to the Load Channel icon, to select the spots on the frog's back.

3. Choose Edit → Copy to copy the image to the Clipboard.

4. Choose Select → Modify Contract to create a 1-pixel choked trap, as seen in Figure 18.10.

5. Press D to set the default black and white foreground and background colors. Press your Delete key to create the knockout, as in Figure 18.11. Deselect.

6. Load Alpha 1 again. From the Channel Options pull-down menu, choose New Spot Channel. Choose a PANTONE color for the channel.

7. Press ⌘/Ctrl and click on the spot color channel to select it. When viewed close-up, the selection should slightly overlap the knockout, as in Figure 18.12.

8. With the spot color channel targeted, choose Edit → Paste Into to paste the tonal image of the frog's skin into the selection. The image should look like Figure C29c in the color section.

> Figures C29a ,C29b, and C29c in the color section show examples of the Froggy image with various applications of spot color.

## Other Uses for Spot Color

Spot color can be used to create varnish plates and dies as well as color plates. Varnishes are simply unpigmented inks. Apply them to highlight areas of an image or to coat the image with a glossy surface. Dies are shaped forms used to cut paper. Remember those birthday cards that have an oval hole cut to reveal George Washington's face on the dollar concealed within? That's die-cutting. Precise shapes can be created by using spot color channels; those shapes can then be printed as negatives, which are then used to create the die.

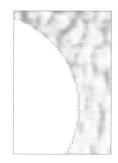

Figure 18.11

**The frog with the knockout**

# Printing Duotones and Spot Color

Printing Duotones and spot colors presents its own set of challenges. For one thing, in this book, the Duotones and Tritones were created using two or three custom color inks. But the color section of the book is printed using four-color process. So the Duotones and Tritones had to be converted to CMYK before printing, which can result in darker, less distinct colors than premixed inks provide.

If you want to import your Duotone into another application, you'll have to save it in EPS format. Only EPS preserves Duotone mode's color information properly. If you save it in another format, the additional curves simply won't be recognized; only Ink 1 will end up printing. Spot color channels, however, are supported by PSD, TIF, EPS, PDF, and DCS2 formats.

A special problem common to Duotone and spot color jobs is the difficulty in proofing. Most color proofers convert everything to CMYK when printing; custom ink colors simply aren't recognized. If you have Duotones composed of, say, black and magenta, things will work out fine. But a proofing device can't recognize those painstakingly chosen PANTONE colors unless it can read the color's CMYK equivalents. You have to fake it out by either renaming the colors (in which case you don't get a true color proof) or by converting it to CMYK (same result). This is part of the reason some printers are loath to work with Duotones; they feel as though they're working blind, since no real accurate proof is available to guide them.

The problem is similar but not quite as worrisome with spot colors. When you print a job with spot colors on your printer, a composite is printed, and the spot color channels print out

Figure 18.12

**The selection showing the trap**

separately only when you image film or plates. Once again, proofs can be created, but only by compromising the integrity of the color channels. When you choose Merge Spot Color Channels from the Channels palette menu, the spot color is converted to your image's color mode and blended in with the other channels. The spot color channels are eliminated at this point. You end up with a composite image incorporating your spot colors (now defined as RGB or CMYK colors). It's important to have the spot colors in the right order before taking this step. Different Solidity settings can produce different results when merging. Layered images flatten during this procedure. And once again, you run the risk of altering the color matching, since the CMYK inks reproduce colors differently than premixed inks. If you want a composite CMYK proof of the spot color image, always duplicate the file first. Print the duplicate image to your ink-jet or other proofing device and print the separations to an imagesetter or laser printer from the spot color original.

If you plan on importing an image with spot color channels into another application, you must save it in Photoshop's DCS 2.0 format. This is the only format that will allow other applications to recognize the individual spot color channels.

Hands On 6, which follows this chapter, will give you further practice applying these features.

# Duotones and Spot Color

*Here is a chance* for you to work in Duotone mode and with spot color channels. In this exercise, you'll convert a grayscale image into a Tritone to enhance its tonal depth, create more drama in the image, and bring out its details. Then you'll place a graphic element and some type on the image using a spot color. Finally, you'll convert it to an entirely different mode to be able to observe the channels as separations.

## Getting Started

Discard or hide your preferences file before beginning this Hands On exercise. The "Modifying Photoshop's Settings" section in Chapter 5 shows how to reset your preferences to Photoshop's defaults. You can restore your customized, personal settings when you're done.

Once you've launched Photoshop with default preferences, here's how to begin the Hands On project:

1. Insert the *Photoshop 7 Savvy* CD in the CD-ROM drive.

2. Choose File → Open; select and open the image in the HO6 folder on the CD named cow_tri_start.psd (Figure H6.1).

   Full-color versions of the beginning and final stages of this project are included in the color section (see Figures C51 and C52). To follow along on-screen, you can preview the finished image by opening cow_tri_fin.psd from the HO6 folder on the CD.

3. Save the file to your disk as cow_tri_now.psd.

4. Choose Image → Mode → Duotone.

5. From Type, choose Tritone.

6. Click the top color swatch. The Color Picker appears. Choose Custom Color. In the Book field, choose PANTONE Coated. Type **4625** on the keypad, or scroll down the list and find PANTONE 4625 C (it's a dark brown).

7. Click the second color swatch. On your keypad, enter **375** to designate PANTONE 375 C, a medium-bright green for the midtones. Click OK.

8. Click the third color swatch. Click in the middle of the slider. Move the slider until you find PANTONE Yellow 012 C. Click OK.

## Adjusting Curves

Now we'll adjust the curves of each color for precise control over the distribution of ink in the highlights, midtones, and shadows.

1. Start with the shadows: In the Custom Colors dialog box, click the PANTONE 2765 swatch to display the Duotone Curves dialog box. The values you'll enter in the next few steps are shown in Figure H6.2; clear any presets from fields that aren't listed here.

2. In the Percentage fields, enter the following values: For 0%, enter **0**. For 50%, enter **30** to reduce the amount of darker ink in the lower midtones. For 80%, Enter **100** to boost the coverage in the shadows; this will help increase contrast. For 90%, enter **95**. For 100%, enter **100**; we'll keep the darkest ink at full intensity in the deepest shadows.

3. For PANTONE 375, enter the following values to distribute the color in the midtone range: For the 0% field, enter **0**. For 40%, also enter **0**; we want to keep coverage of the middle ink very light in the lighter midtones. For 50%, enter **40** to keep coverage lighter in the midtone range. For 70%, enter **70**; now we're evening out the curve. For 100%, enter **70**. Continue to pull this lighter color out of the deepest shadows.

4. For PANTONE Yellow 012, enter the following values. For the
   0% field, enter **30** to load this ink into the brightest highlights.
   For 30%, enter **15**. For 100%, enter **10**. All but the brightest
   highlight areas will contain almost none of the lightest ink.
   This helps prevent muddying the image. When you're finished,
   your Duotone Options dialog box should look like Figure H6.3.

## Adding the Beef Graphic

The Beef graphic is on an independent layer. We want to add a little
spot of color to give the image that extra twist.

1. Choose Window → Layers.

2. Make the Beef layer visible by clicking the visibility column
   next to its thumbnail in the Layers palette. Target it. It shows
   up in contrast against the white area of the cow's flank.

3. Choose the Magic Wand tool. Clear the Contiguous box in the
   Options bar. Click on any black portion of the beef symbol.

4. Conceal the Beef layer.

5. While the selection is active, reveal the Channels palette. The
   Tritone channel is at the top of the palette. Two other saved
   selections appear below.

6. From the palette's pull-down menu, choose New Spot Channel.
   Set the Solidity to 0 so you can see how the spot color will
   print.

7. Click the color swatch to reveal the custom color list. Choose a PANTONE color to apply
   to the Beef symbol. I chose PANTONE Warm Red (its shortcut is W in the custom Color
   Picker). We'll allow the red on the eye and the tag to overprint on the very light coverage of mainly PANTONE Yellow 012 on the light area of the cow's flank.

8. Click OK in both dialog boxes.

## Adding Type

Finally, we'll add some type as a new spot color channel, using
PANTONE Yellow 012, which as you'll notice, is one of the colors
used in the Tritone.

1. Click the Channels palette to activate it.

2. Create a new spot color channel, choosing PANTONE Yellow
   012 as your color.

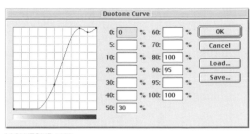

(a) PANTONE 4625

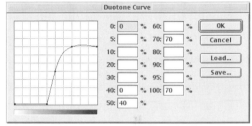

(b) PANTONE 375

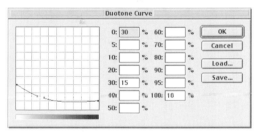

(c) PANTONE Yellow 012

Figure H6.2

**Duotone curves for
(a) PANTONE 4625,
(b) PANTONE 375, and
(c) PANTONE Yellow 012**

Figure H6.3

**After setting the
Duotone curves**

3. Using a nice fat font, with good large letters, type in the words **All Cows Eat Grass**.

4. Now, target the Tritone channel. Select Modify → Contract. Enter 1 pixel in the box and click OK. Now, making sure the background color is white, press Delete to fill the type selection with white. This knocks out the other colors from behind the yellow type. Figure H6.4 shows the text knocked out of the background, and Figure H6.5 (which also appears in the color section as Figure C52) shows the final version of the Duotone with the spot color and knocked-out type.

> The spot color channel can be directly output only from Photoshop, as it will not be recognized from the Duotone Mode EPS file when imported into layout or illustration software. The Duotone mode file can be duped, split into Multichannel, then saved as EPS DCS 2, so that the imported image will contain the Tritone separations and the spot color.

## Converting to Multichannel

In order to see the content of the separated channels, it's a good idea to convert the image to Multichannel mode. You can look at the channels to get a better understanding of how Duotones and spot colors distribute ink when they are printed.

1. Choose Image → Mode → Multichannel. In the Channels palette, the three Tritone channels are separated and named for their PANTONE colors, and the one spot color channel is at the bottom of the list.

2. Go to Edit → Preferences → Display And Cursors → Color Channels → In Color.

3. Click the eye icon of each channel, one at a time, to observe the densities of each color as it will be printed on paper.

4. If you have a printer, print the document and see how the colors are separated.

Figure H6.5

**The finished Duotone with the spot color graphic and type**

# PART III

# Photoshop Savvy

Now that you've covered *all the basics, you're ready to start combining techniques. The chapters in Part III cover advanced Photoshop techniques that will help you up the amperage of your images. In the following pages you will learn about the art and science of image restoration and how Photoshop techniques can revive those old images. We'll also look at the world of Photoshop filters and how they can produce everything from a minor correction to a complete transformation of your images.*

*Also covered are advanced selection, layer, and overlay techniques that help you better manage the image during the editing process. You'll also learn how to automate operations in order to streamline your workflow.*

*Chapters in Part III include:*

# CHAPTER 19

# Photo Retouching

*Since the introduction* of the box camera by Kodak in the early part of last century, photography has become a popular pastime, practiced by countless people. If your attic is anything like mine, there are no doubt hundreds of photographs sitting in envelopes or boxes that haven't been looked at for years. We don't throw these images away, because they are valuable to us and are part of our legacy. Many of these images are of relatives who have passed on and are the only living reminder we have of their lives.

Unfortunately, few of us have the time or money to create an environmentally safe archive for the original images, and so, with the passing of time, many of these photographs remain neglected and begin to fade or collect dust, scratches, and abrasions. This chapter is about restoring those long-neglected pictures.

You'll learn about:

- Scanning old photographs

- Removing dust and scratches

- Restoring contrast

- Adding missing pieces to a photograph

- Revitalizing color

- Browsing an archive

# Problems with Old Photographs

Several common problems can occur in old photographs, and the particular problems in a photograph will determine the best strategy for its reconstruction. Here is a list of problems you are likely to encounter:

**All or part of the photo is faded.** This problem results from the deterioration of the emulsion on an image, caused by exposure to ultraviolet light, air, or fluctuating temperatures. (It could also result from an image that was overexposed to begin with.) Sometimes the photograph may be perfect on one side and fade gradually to the other.

**The photo has a color cast.** A color photograph may have washed-out colors or a yellow or red cast over its entire surface. This may be the result of the emulsion's chemical reaction with air or paper.

Figure 19.1

This photograph is not worth the effort that it would take to restore it. Critical parts of the image are missing. There is hardly any detail in the highlight areas, and it is blurred, faded, stained, and covered with scratches and dust.

**The image is wrinkled, torn, scratched, or covered with spots.** Wrinkles and scratches are often a result of mistreatment of the photograph. Spots will develop from exposure to dust. Images stored in a damp environment can collect mold that appears as large or small splotches.

**The surface is textured.** Many old photographs were printed on textured paper. The removal of this surface can present problems during the retouching process.

**Part of the photograph is missing.** A vital portion of the image like a hand or a face may have a severe scratch on it or may be missing entirely. A corner may be missing or an area of the photograph may have peeled or faded away.

**Bad photography** The image may have superfluous elements like phone lines or portions that are out of focus. The image may have been shot at the wrong moment, the composition may be unbalanced, or the image may be underexposed or overexposed.

Photo restoration can be extremely labor-intensive. Some images are simply beyond repair. Experience will show you which images are worth restoring and which ones, like the photo in Figure 19.1, would be a waste of a lot of time and effort.

# Scanning Old Photographs

If you've read Chapter 14, "Capturing Images," you are aware of the many types of input devices available to scan images. Before scanning an old photograph, you'll want to examine the image closely. Observe the darkest and lightest areas of the image and see if there is detail within these areas that needs to be preserved. If so, you may want to adjust the contrast using the scanner software's brightness and contrast features. Don't expect to correct the entire image. Adjust the image just enough to capture the details. You can later make more refined adjustments in Photoshop. Observe the digital image carefully. If you haven't captured the detail you want, rescan it at different settings. You can also make multiple scans of the same photo at different settings and composite the best parts of each image into a master image. This technique, though labor-intensive, will enable you to combine the enhanced detail of the highlights, midtones, and shadow areas into one optimal image.

Scanning at higher resolutions helps preserve detail. Scan the image at 300 pixels per inch or higher on a flatbed scanner. If the image is especially small, you may want to increase the scale and the resolution. Avoid exceeding the scanner's optical resolution if possible. For example, if the scanner's optical resolution is 600 dpi, you can scan it at 300 dpi and 200% size.

There is no advantage to scanning a black-and-white photograph in RGB mode; that will only produce an image with a larger file size. In most cases it will require desaturation to eliminate discoloration. If there are stains on the image, scanning it in RGB will exaggerate them. For best results, scan the photo as an 8-bit grayscale. If you later decide to add color or a sepia tint to the image, you can convert it to RGB mode (Image → Mode → RGB Color), and adjust it using the Image → Adjustments → Hue/Saturation command. (See Chapter 17, "Modifying and Mapping Color," and Hands On 7, "Restoring a Color Photograph," which follows this chapter.)

# Removing Dust and Scratches

The Dust & Scratches filter (choose Filter → Noise → Dust & Scratches) was created for the purpose of removing those ugly artifacts that are unavoidable when scanning old photos. With its Radius and Threshold sliders to help define edges, the Dust & Scratches filter is a powerful tool for eliminating a good deal of the unwanted debris from an image. If you're scanning a batch of old pictures from your grandmother's scrapbook, or that old team shot from your high school yearbook, Dust & Scratches works wonders. It can also help a great deal in getting rid of moiré patterns that may appear when scanning printed halftones.

When using the Dust & Scratches filter, select small areas of similar texture in which to work. Each area of the image may require different settings. Applying it to the entire image all at once can result in a loss of detail. Use the minimum Radius and Threshold you need to achieve the best results (as in Figure 19.2).

The Dust & Scratches filter has two controls, Radius and Threshold. Radius blurs, and Threshold restores. When you move the Radius slider to the right you effectively blur the areas of most contrast. Move the Radius slider until the specks or scratch lines disappear, but do not overblur the image. Next move the Threshold slider just enough to restore the surrounding texture but not enough to restore the specks.

Figure 19.2

**The area selected (left), and the filter applied (right)**

Be cautious when using the Dust & Scratches filter. If you go too far with it, you could end up losing detail along with the unwanted specks. Sometimes a little elbow grease and the Rubber Stamp tool will be necessary to finish the job. When used in tandem with the Unsharp Mask filter, Dust & Scratches can work wonders. (See Chapters 16, "Adjusting Color and Tonality," and 20, "Using Filters.")

For practice with the Dust & Scratches filter using the publicity photo that is partially shown in Figure 19.2, open `dust_and_scratches.psd` in the `Ch19` folder on the *Photoshop 7 Savvy* CD.

## Adding Missing Elements

Often with old photographs, large areas have been scratched beyond recognition or are missing completely. Based on the severity of the problem, you'll have to decide the best approach to restoration. In many cases, Photoshop's tools and commands can be combined to remedy these problems, but some parts of photographs may be too damaged to restore. If, for example, the face of a person is missing from an image, I recommend that you avoid trying to paint it back in, as this will prove to be a virtually impossible task to accomplish with any credibility. A better approach might be to composite the face from another photograph or, if that's not possible, fill the area with neutral gray.

## Cloning

Small areas that are missing can be repaired with the Clone Stamp tool . I recommend that you first make a rough selection around the area so as to avoid applying the clone to unwanted areas. To practice using the Clone Stamp tool, follow these steps:

1. Open the file `clone_practice.psd` from the `Ch19` folder.

2. With the Lasso tool, select the torn area on the left side of the image, as shown in Figure 19.3.

3. Choose the Clone Stamp tool from the Tool palette. Place the cursor on the area of texture below and outside the selection. Choose a soft brush from the Brushes palette. Place the cursor inside the selection, click the mouse, and drag. You'll probably need to sample more than once to achieve good results.

4. Press the Option (Mac) or Alt (Win) key and click the mouse to sample the area. (Notice that the cursor turns into a target.) Release the mouse and the key.

5. After you're finished cloning within the selection marquee, deselect the area and clone any disparate edges that might have resulted. Carefully blend the edges of the region with the areas surrounding it.

6. Repeat the process for the other torn areas. Be sure to sample from areas of similar texture and value.

Figure 19.3

**Cloning a selected area**

You can perform this process on an empty layer with the Use All Layers option checked. This technique offers the advantage of sampling from the entire image and cloning to a new layer.

The Clone Stamp tool provides two options in the Options bar:

**Aligned Checked:** The clone is aligned with the original sample. When you clone and release the mouse and clone again, the alignment on the original sample is maintained.

**Aligned Unchecked:** Each time the mouse is released and the cloning is resumed, the original sample is repeated.

The Clone Stamp tool can also be used to remove unwanted elements or to add texture to the image. Careful observation of variations in color and texture of the image are crucial in determining the best place to sample for cloning.

## Applying the Healing Brush

In many ways, the Healing Brush tool  performs like the Clone Stamp. The process of sampling is similar, but the application of the sampled areas to the image differs. When the sampled area is painted onto the target area, it takes on the characteristics of the surrounding pixels, thus creating a seamless blend.

To try out the Healing Brush, follow these steps:

1. Open the `heal_me_patch_me.psd` file from the `Ch19` folder on the CD.

2. Zoom in on the scratch above the baby's head.

3. Choose the Healing brush and a 19-pixel brush from the Brush menu. Press the Option/Alt key and click in the area about a half-inch above the scratch to sample it, as in Figure 19.4.

4. Release the Opt/Alt key. Move the cursor onto the scratch. Drag the mouse to the left. As you drag, the scratch is replaced by the sample. When you release the mouse, the sample blends seamlessly into the surrounding pixels, as seen in Figure 19.5.

Figure 19.4

**Sample the image first.**

Figure 19.5

**The healed image**

## Using the Patch Tool

The Patch tool , which is also a new addition to version 7, is similar to the Healing Brush, except that it gives you the ability to patch a selected area. This works well on large areas in need of repair. You can either make the initial selection with the Patch tool activated, or you can use any of the other selection tools to make the selection first, and then switch to the Patch tool.

The Patch tool can be used in either of the following ways, depending on the specifications in the Options bar:

**Source**  Drag the selection marquee over the area from which you want to sample. It will sample the area and automatically copy it over to the area to be patched.

**Destination**  Select the area from which you want to sample. Drag the selection marquee over the area you wish to patch.

To see how the Patch tool works follow these steps:

1. Open the file `heal_me_patch_me.psd` on the CD.

2. Choose the Patch tool. Check Source in the Options bar.

3. Drag a marquee around the scratch on the man's face (Figure 19.6).

4. Place your cursor within the marquee. Drag the marquee slightly to the left and up, as in Figure 19.7. Release the mouse, and it automatically creates a patch, as seen in Figure 19.8.

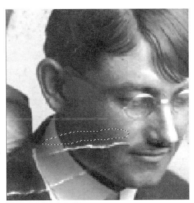

Figure 19.6

**Select the image first.**

Figure 19.7

**Move the selection to the area that you want to sample.**

Figure 19.8

**The sampled area is patched.**

## Duplicating and Manipulating Larger Areas

Sometimes the area you need to fix on the image is too big or too inconsistent to clone. Or you may find that it needs more precision than the Clone Stamp tool can offer. If there is a similar area on the image that can be duplicated, try this technique, using the image shown in Figure 19.9.

1. Open the file `duplicate.psd` in the `Ch19` folder.

Figure 19.9

**Areas of an image that are missing or damaged can be replaced.**

2. Choose the Lasso tool. In the Options bar, set the feather radius to 10. With the Lasso tool, encircle the missing right eye. The selection should be a little bit larger than the scratch, as shown in Figure 19.10.

3. Place the cursor inside the selection. Press the mouse button and drag the selection marquee without its contents to the "good" eye.

4. Choose Layer → New → Layer Via Copy to copy the contents of the selection to a new layer.

5. Choose Edit → Transform → Flip Horizontal to flip the eye.

6. Choose the Move tool. In the Options bar, check Show Bounding Box. Drag the eye and place it on the missing area. To rotate it into position, place the cursor outside the bounding box near any corner until you see the Rotate icon. Then click and drag (see Figure 19.11).

7. When the eye is in position, merge the background layer with the new layer. Choose Merge Visible from the Layer Options pull-down menu.

8. Clean up any unrepaired areas with the Clone Stamp tool or the Healing Brush tool.

9. Choose the Rectangular Marquee. Drag a rectangular selection around the baby's head. Choose Filter → Liquify. Warp the image slightly so that it not quite symmetrical with the left eye.

10. Choose the Dodge tool 🔍 . Dodge the areas under the eye to better match the surrounding tones.

Figure 19.10

**The selected area**

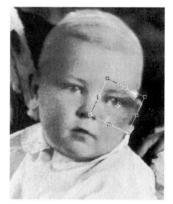

Figure 19.11

**The eye, flipped and in position**

11. Using the Clone Stamp tool, eliminate the scratch on the woman's head.

12. You can eliminate additional debris with the Dust & Scratches filter. Figure 19.12 shows the final result.

## Adjusting Contrast

The contrast of many old photographs diminishes over time because of the instability of the emulsion used to create the print. This emulsion may react chemically with nonarchival photo paper or it may have been exposed to sunlight; both of these may cause discoloring or fading. These problems can usually be remedied by adjusting levels or curves, as long as there is enough detail on the photograph to begin with. Highlight areas that have washed out will be more difficult to restore, often requiring careful cloning, compositing, or passes with the Burn tool.

Figure 19.12

**The completed image**

Frequently, however, contrast problems are more complex. When a photo has developed a gradual fade from one side to the other, as in Figure 19.13, the problem can be more difficult to fix. You may need to use special masks to apply precision contrast adjustments to the image.

Figure 19.13

**An image whose contrast fades from right to left**

To get an idea of how these problems might be corrected, try this technique:

1. Open the file gradual_fade.psd from the Ch19 folder.

2. Choose Layer → New Adjustment Layer → Levels. In the New Layer dialog box that appears, click OK. The Levels dialog box appears. Click OK again.

3. Target the Adjustment layer's layer mask by clicking on its thumbnail.

4. Press the D key. Click the Foreground and Background icon ◼ in the Tools palette to choose black as a foreground color and white as a background color.

5. Choose the Gradient tool. In the Options bar, choose the Linear Gradient icon ▭ . Make sure that the Foreground to Background gradient is selected from the Gradient Picker.

6. Click and drag the gradient from right to left. Press the Shift key while dragging to constrain the gradient horizontally.

7. Double-click the Levels 1 Adjustment Layer thumbnail. The Levels dialog box appears.

8. Move the Black Shadow slider to the right until the input level reads 69. Move the Gray Input slider to the right until the midtone input level reads .97, which will optimize the contrast on the left side of the image (see Figure 19.14). Click OK.

9. Repeat steps 2 through 5.

10. Target the layer mask of the Levels 2 layer. Click and drag the gradient from left to right.

11. Click on the Levels Adjustment layer thumbnail. The Levels dialog appears.

12. Move the Black Shadow slider to the right until the input level reads 45. Move the White Input slider to the right until the highlight input level reads 190, which will optimize the contrast on the right side of the image (see Figure 19.15). Click OK.

Figure 19.14

**The same image with a levels adjustment applied through the gradient layer mask**

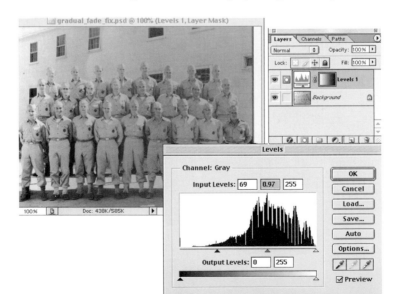

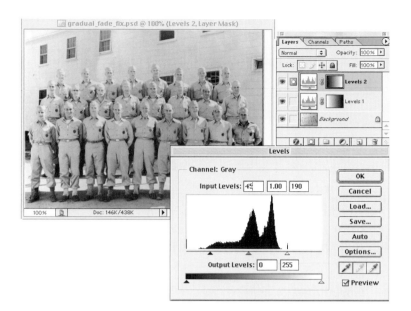

Figure 19.15

**The same image with a levels adjustment applied through the reversed gradient layer mask**

13. Now we'll perform a global contrast adjustment to optimize the contrast of the entire image. Once again, choose Layer → New Adjustment Layer → Levels. Click OK in the New Layer dialog box. The Layer will be named Layer 3 and will appear above Layer 2 in the stack. This time, move the Black slider to the right until the input level reads 16 and the White slider to the left until the input level reads 238. Click OK.

14. Save the image. Figure 19.16 shows the final result.

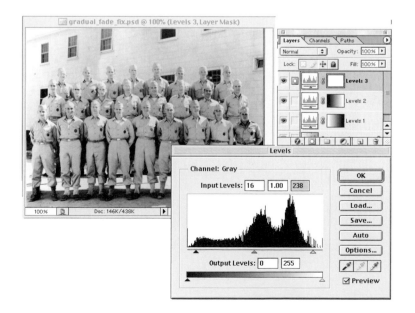

Figure 19.16

**The completed image with a global levels adjustment applied**

## Making a Digital Archive

Having performed miracles on that old photograph, you should store your work in an archive, where it is readily accessible. Most commonly, images are stored in JPEG format to reduce file sizes, using the highest settings to avoid data loss. The disadvantage of saving to JPEG format—if you expect to do any further work with the image—is that you will end up discarding all of your layers and alpha channels in the process. You may want to save a version of the image in Photoshop format and another version in JPEG.

Archives are usually burned to a CD or a DVD; either provides an inexpensive storage medium with room for plenty of images. To review the content of the archive, you can use Photoshop 7's new File Browser. Using this tool, you can quickly scan the contents of your archive in thumbnail form and open the desired image.

For efficient review of an archive's contents, you should place all the images in the same folder. Once you've done that, choose File → Browse. The File Browser window appears, displaying the contents of the folder you last browsed (see Figure 19.17). Choose the desired folder from the topmost field. Click on an image in the image list to see a version of it in the preview field. The preview area can be expanded or contracted by dragging its top and bottom borders. The Field below the preview presents information about the image. Double-click or Control/right-click an image to open it.

If you want further practice in photo restoration, try Hands On 7, immediately following this chapter. There, you'll use some techniques introduced in earlier chapters, as well as what you've learned here.

Figure 19.17

**The new File Browser window**

# Restoring a Color Photograph

*The restoration of color* photographs presents a unique set of problems. In addition to the usual dust and scratch repairs and contrast adjustments, the color emulsions can change with time, producing severe color casts. The best way to remove these color casts and restore natural color varies with each situation, but in general some specific tools are commonly used to make these adjustments. Usually, Levels, Curves, Color Balance, and the arsenal of color correction features covered in Chapter 16, "Adjusting Tonality and Color," work in combination with Adjustment layers and layer masks. In addition, you can use the Hue/Saturation and Replace Color features to make modifications to specific areas of color.

In this Hands On exercise, you will restore a color photograph by employing some of these techniques. The before and after versions of the image can be seen in the color section (see Figures C55 and C56).

## Cropping the Image

The scanned photograph we're going to work on is shown in Figure H7.1. As you can see, it has several problem areas.

1. Open the file `color_photo.psd` in the H07 folder on the CD.

2. Choose the Crop tool  . Click and drag from the top-left corner inside the yellow border to the bottom right. Click the check in the Options bar to commit the crop or the cancel icon to cancel it .

Figure H7.1

**The scanned photograph before restoration**

Figure H7.2

The scratch before and
after repair with the
Healing Brush tool

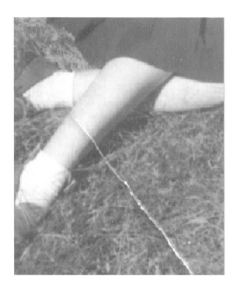 

## Removing the Scratch

The first problem we're going to fix is the scratch across the lower left. This scratch goes across both the grass and the woman's ankle, so we will need to sample both areas separately to fix it.

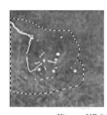

Figure H7.3

The area selected with
the Patch tool

1. Choose Photoshop 7's new Healing Brush tool [icon].

2. Select a soft brush from the Brushes palette. Place the cursor on the grass. Press Option (Mac) or Alt (Win), and click the mouse to sample an area.

3. Heal the scratch with your sample. You may want to sample more than once.

4. Sample the ankle and repair the scratch. (The result should look like Figure H7.2.)

5. Save the image.

## Restoring a Scratched Area

Next we'll work on the scratched area in the upper-left corner, using the new Patch tool.

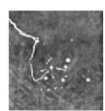

Figure H7.4

The scratched area
before and after the
repair made with the
Patch tool

1. [icon] Choose the Patch tool. Drag a selection encircling the scratched area of the image in the upper-left corner, as in Figure H7.3.

2. Place your cursor in the center of the marching ants. Click and drag the selection to an area of similar texture on the right side of the photo, near the woman's head.

3. Release the mouse. The area is completely restored. See how it looked with the scratch and now without in Figure H7.4.

# Adjusting Contrast and Color

Adjusting levels by individual channels offers more control than a global adjustment to the RGB channel. We will use this technique on an Adjustment layer to improve the contrast and balance the color.

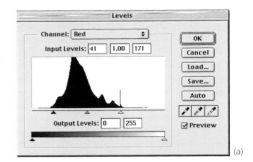

1. Choose Layer → New Adjustment Layer → Levels. Click OK in the New Layer dialog box.

2. At the top of the dialog box, choose the Red channel from the pull-down menu. Move the Black slider to the right until the input field reads 41. Move the White slider to the right until the input reads 171 (see Figure H7.5a).

3. Choose the Green channel from the pull-down menu. Move the Black slider to the right until the input field reads 10. Move the White slider to the left until the input reads 145 (see Figure H7.5b).

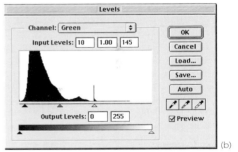

4. Choose the Blue channel from the pull-down menu. Move the Black slider to the right until the input field reads 11. Move the White slider to the left until the input reads 92 (see Figure H7.5c).

5. You'll see a dramatic improvement in the color balance and contrast. Click OK.

## Color Balancing

There is still a slight red cast on the image. We can eliminate that with the Color Balance feature, which was introduced in Chapter 16.

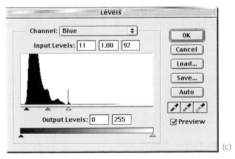

Figure H7.5

**The Levels dialog boxes, showing red levels (a), green levels (b), and blue levels (c)**

1. Choose Layer → New Adjustment Layer → Color Balance.

2. In the Color Balance dialog box, click the Highlight radio button (see Figure H7.6a).

3. Move the Cyan–Red slider toward Cyan until it reads –6. Move the Yellow–Blue slider toward Yellow until it reads –6.

4. Click the Midtone radio button (see Figure H7.6b).

5. Move the Cyan–Red slider toward Cyan until it reads –6. Move the Magenta–Green slider toward Green until it reads +4.

6. Click the Shadow radio button (see Figure H7.6c).

7. Move the Cyan–Red slider toward Cyan until it reads –7.

8. Click the Preview box twice to see the before-and-after changes, and click OK.

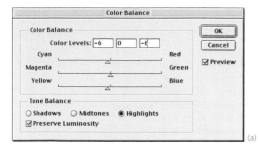

(a)

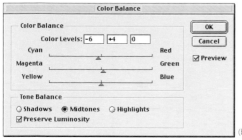

(b)

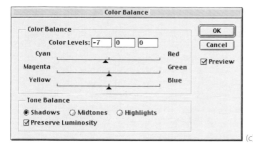

(c)

Figure H7.6

The Color Balance dialog boxes, showing highlights (a), midtones (b), and shadows (c)

## Replacing the Shoulder

A severely torn area like the right shoulder can be replaced and modified using other parts of the image. To replace the shoulder, follow these steps:

1. ✳ Choose the Magic Wand tool. In the Options bar, enter a Tolerance value of 80. Click inside the white tear to select it.

2. Choose Select → Modify → Expand → 6 pixels.

3. Choose Select → Feather → 4 Pixels.

4. Choose Select → Transform Selection. Then choose Edit Transform → Flip Horizontal. Click the check mark to implement the transformation.

5. Drag the selection and place it on the opposite shoulder, as shown in Figure H7.7.

6. Choose Layer → New → Via Copy. Double-click the layer name, name the layer **Shoulder**, and hit Return/Enter.

7. Choose the Move tool. Click and drag the shoulder and position it on the left shoulder, as shown in Figure H7.8.

8. Target the Background. Choose the Clone Stamp tool. Clone the uncovered areas of the tear.

9. Click on the eye columns next to the two Adjustment layers to conceal them.

10. Check the Use All Layers box in the Options bar. Place the cursor on the forearm, press the Option/Alt key, and click the mouse to sample it. Clone out some of the folds near the shoulder to alter its appearance, as in Figure H7.9.

11. Link the Shoulder layer and the Background. From the Layer Options palette, choose Merge Linked.

12. Click on all of the eyes in the Layer palette to reveal the adjustment.

Figure H7.7

Using the selection on the opposite shoulder

Figure H7.8

**The replacement shoulder in place**

Figure H7.9

**The finished shoulder**

## Coloring the Grass

The grass in our photo is quite brown, so next we'll color it. The best way to color the grass is to select the woman first.

1. Target the Background. Choose the Magnetic Lasso tool 🪧 . Encircle the woman as accurately as possible. You may need to use the Quick Mask (see Chapter 12, "Using Alpha Channels and Quick Mask") or another selection technique to tweak the results of the selection.

2. Choose Layer → Via Copy. Name the new layer **Woman**.

3. Target the Background. Choose Layer → New Adjustment Layer → Hue and Saturation. In the Hue/Saturation dialog box, move the Hue and Saturation sliders until an adequate shade of green is achieved (see Figure H7.10).

## Coloring the Ribbon

At this point, we've finished the restoration; but making one more change to the image will allow us to practice using the Replace Color feature from Chapter 17, "Modifying and Mapping Color." We're going to change the color of the ribbon:

1. Choose the Rectangular Marquee tool. Drag a selection around the ribbon.

Figure H7.10

**The Hue/Saturation dialog box**

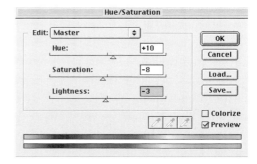

2. Choose Image → Adjustments → Replace Color. Choose the Plus Eyedropper tool and drag it over the ribbon. You will see a selection mask in the window, as shown in Figure H7.11.

3. Drag the Hue, Saturation, and Lightness sliders until you have the desired color.

4. When the image is completed it should look like Figure CXX in the color section.

5. If desired, flatten the image, or better yet, save both a flattened version and the layered version to your disk.

Figure H7.11

**The selection mask in the Replace Color dialog box**

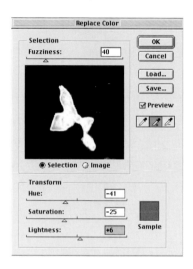

# CHAPTER 20

# Using Filters

*When images created* in Photoshop really make your eyes pop out, chances are good that *filters* were involved. Like many of Photoshop's other techniques, filters have their origin in the analog world of photography. A photographer uses a filter to correct or enhance lighting, and to create or adjust anomalies of perspective. Photoshop's filters take on these tasks and expand them far beyond the traditional tools.

You've applied filters in previous chapters to retouch images and enhance contrast. Here, you'll see further that with filters, you can adjust focus, eliminate unwanted artifacts, alter or create complex selection masks, breathe life into less-than-perfect scans, and apply a range of effects previously unavailable to the traditional photographer. Filters also have the capability to completely destroy anything recognizable in an image and turn it into a swirling mass of pixels gone wild.

In this chapter, you'll look at the wonders filters can achieve. You'll learn about:

- **Filter basics**
- **Constructive and destructive filters**
- **Effects filters**
- **Filters that render**
- **The Amazing Liquify filter**
- **New in Photoshop 7: Pattern Maker**

# Filter Basics

Filters are nothing more than mathematical formulas that alter the features of pixels or groups of pixels in specified ways. What can be changed for any individual pixel are its brightness value, saturation, and hue, and its position in relation to other pixels. These changes are limited. What allows for the great variation among filter effects is the way they can alter groups of pixels over a specified range, following specific constraints. Some work subtly; others can be brash and flamboyant. Some effects gain strength when used gently and reapplied; sometimes a filter can be mitigated or softened by fading the effect. The Fade command extends the range and usefulness of filters by allowing you to use layer-like blending modes to blend the filter effect back into the original image.

It's beyond the limits of our space here to delineate every possible effect offered by Photoshop's filters. Rather, some of the most useful ones will be discussed in detail. I encourage you to play and experiment with filters to discover for yourself their vast potential. Keep in mind that when you're working with standard, automated special effects, they are available to every person who uses the software. Some of those effects, if applied generically, are immediately recognizable by anyone who's ever used them and can compromise the "magic" of the image. It's a good idea to be aware of what's available, but practice will indicate which techniques have more range of possibility and staying power; creativity will guide you to apply them in unusual or not-so-obvious ways. Sometimes the most effective special effect is the one that remains invisible.

## Activating and Deactivating Filters

By choosing commands from the Filter menu, you can apply your filter of choice to the entire image, or confine it to a selected area. The Filter menu provides a long list of submenus, some of them long in turn. You can add or remove filters from these lists by placing items inside, or deleting them from, the Photoshop application's `Plug-Ins` folder. If you find there are large groups of filters you rarely use, you can save Photoshop valuable memory space by removing those from the `Plug-Ins` folder. If a day comes when you can't get away without applying one, just slip it back into the `Plug-Ins` folder and it's available once again. Plenty of third-party plug-ins are available for special occasions; they can be treated the same way.

> If you hold down ⌘-Option (Macintosh) or Ctrl-Alt (Windows) when you launch Photoshop, you can specify which plug-ins folder you want to use for that session.

## Filter Previews

When you're applying an effect as powerful and image-altering as some filters can be—and certain filters are among Photoshop's most memory-intensive functions—it's good to have some idea of what to expect. Most filters provide a preview inside the dialog box. In fact, the previews in version 7 have been greatly improved. You can zoom in or out by clicking the + and – buttons, and drag inside the preview box to scroll to the part of the image you wish to preview. Other filters, such as the majority of corrective filters, allow you to preview the effect in the image window itself; just click the Preview box or button. When the blinking bar below the Preview box disappears, the program has finished building the preview. Still other filters, such as most in the Distort and Stylize submenus, provide no preview whatsoever. These non-previewable filters are generally among those that consume massive amounts of memory to apply.

## Fading Filters

Don't like how strong that filter effect comes on? You can mitigate the effect by using the Edit → Fade command. Fade allows you to blend the filter effect in with the original image, just as you would with a separate layer. Fade offers a dialog box containing the same options you see in the Layers palette—that is, you can control Opacity from 1% to 100% and use any of the blending modes (with the exception of Behind and Clear). The Fade command is available immediately after a filter is applied. If you take any other action affecting the image, Fade becomes grayed out in the Edit menu.

> To reapply a filter with the same parameters a second time, simply press ⌘/Ctrl-F. If you want to apply that same filter again but change the options, press ⌘-Opt-F or Ctrl-Alt-F. The last-used filter's dialog box appears, allowing you to make changes before reapplying.

## Filter Types

Rather than go through the list filter by filter, let's divide them up by what they can do. First, we'll look at the *constructive* filters—those that are used to modify and enhance images for printing or screen display. *Destructive* filters are an entirely different animal. These equations can take your image and turn it inside out. Their entire purpose is to displace pixels, more or less radically redistributing image elements. Other filters provide *fine-art effects*, mainly textures and painterly techniques. In addition to these types, there are filters for preparing images for video, for creating a digital watermark, and custom filters that allow you to create your own effects.

# Constructive Filters

Four groups of filters provide tools to help improve image quality by changing the focus, or by smoothing transitions within an image. These filters belong to the Filter → Blur, Noise, Sharpen, and Other submenus. These groups are the bread and butter of Photoshop filtering, the workhorses that are put to frequent, day-to-day use.

The constructive filters complement one another. For instance, Blur's effect is the opposite of Sharpen; Median acts on an image in exactly the opposite way from Add Noise. These complementary effects will be delineated in greater detail below.

## Blur Filters

The Blur group contains six individual filters: Blur, Blur More, Gaussian Blur, Motion Blur, Radial Blur, and Smart Blur. Like their Sharpen counterparts, Blur and Blur More are fully

Figure 20.1

**The Gaussian Blur dialog box**

automated. You click, the filter does its job, and that's that—no dialog box, no user input, no control. They diminish contrast, resulting in softer, smoother edges and transitions. Much more powerful than either of these is Gaussian Blur, named for 18th-century German mathematician Carl Friedrich Gauss. Gauss's work with number theory and distribution patterns made him a pioneer of modern mathematics. He is ultimately responsible for the distribution curves employed in the filter that bears his name (he'll crop up again in Photoshop when we get to the Add Noise filter), and he was one heck of a dancer.

But seriously, if you learn to manipulate the niceties of the Gaussian Blur, you'll never need the Blur and Blur More filters. Even with only one variable in its dialog box (Figure 20.1), Gaussian Blur offers much more control. By entering a number from 0.1 to 250 or by sliding along the Radius slider, you tell Gaussian Blur to apply its softening curve to a range of adjacent pixels. Lower values produce a slight, subtle blur effect, which can be used to smooth out rough transitions or blotchy areas; higher values can blur the image beyond recognition. You can create shadow effects by applying this filter to underlying layers. Figure 20.2 shows some of the Gaussian Blur filter's range.

With the Blur filters (as well as other filter types), the degree to which a given setting affects a particular image depends on the resolution of the image. The higher the resolution, the greater the settings have to be in order to achieve the effect.

Figure 20.2

**The original image (left); the image with the Gaussian Blur filter applied (right)**

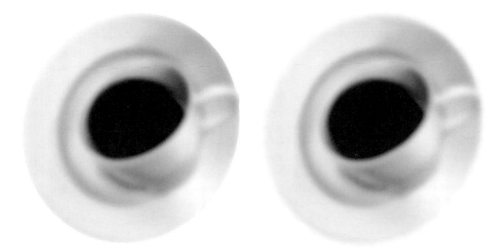

Figure 20.3

**Gaussian Blur applied (left) within a selection and (right) to the unselected image.**

Radically different effects can be achieved with Gaussian Blur, depending on whether you're applying it to a selection or freely to an image or layer as a whole. If Gaussian Blur is applied within a selection outline, its effect remains more or less constrained within the selected area. If you apply it to a layer or an entire image, the curve is allowed to carry its effect across the full range of the image. Compare the left image in Figure 20.3, where Gaussian Blur is applied within the confines of a selection, to the right image, where the same parameters were used on the entire layer.

Figure 20.4

**The Mode option in the Smart Blur dialog box protects edges while blurring.**

The Smart Blur filter (Figure 20.4) is a kind of counterpart to Unsharp Mask in that it applies its blur to the open or continuous areas of an image while retaining edge definition. Like Unsharp Mask, Smart Blur offers the option of defining what it sees as an edge and how far the effect should extend. It's often used for creative effects on line drawings. The Radius and Threshold settings work the same as in Unsharp Mask.

The options in the Quality pop-up list control the smoothness of the effect, with the High setting, logically enough, providing the smoothest transitions. The Mode control offers various methods of applying the blur. Normal mode applies the effect, well, normally, as seen in Figure 20.5. The Edge Only and Overlay Edge options trace the edges with white lines. Edge Only shows the edges as white lines against a black background, while Overlay Edge superimposes white edge lines over the visible image. The Normal mode is most likely the one you'll end up using 99% of the time with Smart Blur. Other edge-finding filters like Filter → Stylize → Find Edges and Filter → Stylize → Trace Contour allow more control over your image and more interesting visual effects.

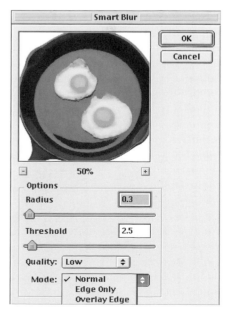

Figure 20.5

**The original image
(left); the effect of the
Smart Blur filter (right)**

The Blur submenu contains two more filters that apply a blur along motion lines. Motion Blur (Figure 20.6) allows you to specify a direction of movement, expressed as an angle in degrees and a distance in pixels. Your image spreads out along a path in a linear distribution in the direction and distance indicated.

Radial Blur offers a different kind of directional movement in its dialog box. Two Blur Method options are available in this filter: Spin and Zoom. Spin distributes pixels by rotating them around a chosen center point, while Zoom's blur radiates pixels out from the center. The Radial Blur dialog box (Figure 20.7) shows a Blur Center field containing a grid pattern. Click or drag the center point to reposition the starting point of the Spin or Zoom anywhere in your image. Enter an Amount to define how far the blur extends. (Why this slider is named Amount here but named Distance in the Motion Blur filter is a mystery. They both accomplish the same thing.)

Draft, Good, and Best are offered as options under the Quality button. If Draft is chosen, the effect takes less time to accomplish, but the blur is applied more roughly; Best provides a smoother blur but requires more time and memory capacity. Figure 20.8 compares the effects of the Motion Blur and Radial Blur filters.

Figure 20.6

**The Motion Blur
dialog box**

Try combining filters using the Fade command. Filter → Stylize → Wind used in tandem with the Motion Blur filter can produce an enhanced blast of directional movement. The Radial Blur Spin filter can create interesting concentric patterns when used together with Filter → Distort → Zig Zag. Or try the Radial Blur Zoom option and blend with Filter → Stylize → Extrude.

## Noise Filters

You'll find the next group of filters in the constructive category in Filter →
Noise. Add Noise, Dust & Scratches, and Median all allow user control; the
Despeckle filter is an automated effect that does its work without benefit of a
dialog box. Like its "hands-off" counterparts in the Blur and Sharpen submenus, Despeckle's effects are easily surpassed by its more powerful siblings
Dust & Scratches and Median. These three filters work in various ways to eliminate noise; Filter → Noise → Add Noise, believe it or not, adds noise to an image.

### Add Noise

When you Add Noise to an image, the result is a grittier, grainier look—a bit of texture. Noise
can work wonders in helping to smooth tonal transitions; it can help prevent banding in gradations and stair-stepping in your tonal range. In a grayscale image, noise is added in black,
white, and gray grains; in color images, noise is added individually to each color channel, producing natural-looking hues of noise that blend together at random. Figure 20.9 shows the
Add Noise dialog box with its three option areas.

**Amount**  Enter a number from 0.1% to 400% to set a color range for your noise. This controls how far the noise can differ from the existing pixel colors—the higher the number, the
greater variation in color of the added noise.

**Distribution**  Two options are available to define the way noise is distributed across an
image. If you click the Uniform button, colors are applied at random throughout the image.
Otherwise, Photoshop applies the noise in a Gaussian curve (you were warned that Carl

Figure 20.7

**Click in the Blur Center box to position the Spin or Zoom starting point.**

Figure 20.8

**The hanging bulb: The original image (left); with Motion Blur applied to a 300ppi image (center) (Angle –9, Distance 50); with Radial Blur applied (right) (Amount: 18, Method: Spin centered at top-left corner, Quality: Good)**

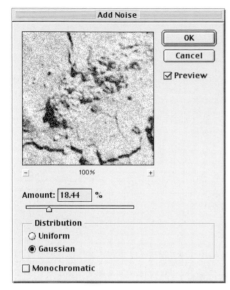

Friedrich would turn up again). Gaussian generally results in a more pronounced effect than Uniform delivers.

**Monochromatic** Check this box if you wish to distribute noise uniformly across all color channels. Otherwise, Add Noise applies its effect randomly to each channel separately, resulting in more color variation. Monochromatic ends up producing grayscale noise; if you're working on a grayscale image, the effect is the same whether or not you check this option. Take a look at Figure 20.10 for some samples of noise in action.

### Dust & Scratches

The Dust & Scratches filter was created for the purpose of removing those spots and splotches that many old photos have acquired from years of neglect or abuse. Because it's used for photo restoration, the Dust & Scratches filter is covered at length in Chapter 19, "Photo Retouching," and further demonstrated in Hands On 7, "Restoring a Color Photograph."

### Median

The Median filter is similar to Dust & Scratches, but its dialog box lacks the Threshold slider. Median is used to average the numerical values of adjacent pixels that are based on the Radius setting (with a range of 1 through 100). Median ignores pixels that are radically different so that the effect reflects a center-weighted average. The result is a softened, molded quality almost like a mild posterization. Higher values can destroy image detail, though, so take it easy on this one. Figure 20.11 provides one example of the Median filter at work.

## Sharpen Filters

The Sharpen group contains four filters: Sharpen, Sharpen Edges, Sharpen More, and Unsharp Mask. The first three of these are fully automated—that is, the user has no control over their effect. When you click one of these, no dialog box appears. Photoshop simply

Figure 20.10

**The original image (left); Add Noise, Gaussian (right), Amount: 64 has been applied.**

applies the predefined effect of increasing contrast. Sharpen increases contrast overall; Sharpen More has a stronger effect; and Sharpen Edges focuses on the areas of highest contrast in an image.

Much more powerful than any of these is Unsharp Mask, which we visited in Chapters 16 ("Adjusting Tonality and Color") and 19. Unsharp Mask gets its unusual name from an old photographic technique of shooting through a blurred negative as a mask to increase the edge contrast in a film positive. Photoshop's engineers have transformed that arcane bit of low technology into an incredibly useful enhancement tool. Its three-variable dialog box allows for minute adjustments and a very fine level of control. If the other three Sharpen filters were discarded, Photoshop users would still have all the sharpening capability they'd ever need with this one tool.

The Unsharp Mask dialog box (Figure 20.12) appears when you choose Filter → Sharpen → Unsharp Mask. These options appear for your input:

**Amount**  Values from 1% to 500% can be entered to define the degree of sharpening—the higher the value, the greater the effect.

**Radius**  Defines the thickness (from 0.1 to 250 pixels) of an edge. As illustrated in Figure 20.13, lower values produce crisp, sharp edges, while higher values define edges as thicker and generate greater overall contrast throughout an image.

**Threshold**  Entering a value from 0 to 255 allows Unsharp Mask to determine what's considered an edge. The number indicates the difference in brightness values necessary to recognize an edge. Lower numbers include lots of pixels in the effect; the higher the number, the more exclusive the value.

These three variables work together to do the job of heightening focus and contrast. A little experimentation and practice may be in order to find the right combination of settings to achieve the desired effect. Subtle effects can be produced by keeping the Amount setting under 100%; raising it over 300% can create results that some may consider undesirable.

Sometimes repeated applications of a lower Amount setting can produce better results than a single application at a higher setting.

When identifying edges, Unsharp Mask uses the Radius setting as its criteria. The effectiveness of this setting depends entirely upon the resolution of the image. Screen images and Web graphics will require a much lower setting (say, in the 0.5 range) than high-resolution images intended for fine printing (usually nicely sharpened in the 2.0 range.)

Figure 20.11

**The Median filter with a Radius of 17**

Figure 20.12

**The Unsharp Mask dialog box includes options that are common to many filters.**

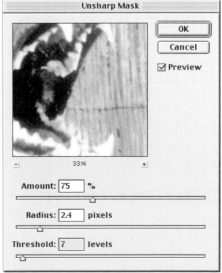

Figure 20.13

Unsharp Masking with various Radius settings. The original image (upper left); Radius of 2 (upper right);
Radius of 100 (lower left); Radius of 250 (lower right).

Radius values can be set all the way up to 250, but the higher values produce results more suitable for special effects than for day-to-day image correcting.

Raising the Threshold value has the effect of increasing the definition of an edge. In other words, higher values require more contrast between pixels to be recognized as an edge; lower values recognize edges between pixels with closer brightness values.

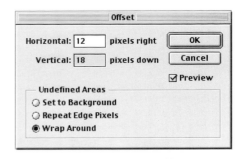

Figure 20.14

**The Offset dialog box**

## Other Constructive Filters

Some other useful constructive filters reside in the Filter → Other submenu. Filter → Other → Offset (Figure 20.14) is effectively a "Move tool in a (dialog) box." You enter numbers in the Horizontal and Vertical fields to tell Photoshop how far to move a selection. Positive numbers move the image to the right or down; negative numbers move it to the left or up. You can make the same precise moves by using the arrow keys in conjunction with the Move tool. The difference is that Offset allows you to determine what happens to the unselected areas by clicking one of its three radio buttons. Set To Background fills the emptied area with the current background color. If the image to be moved is on a layer, then the Set To Background option changes to Set To Transparent and the emptied area will become transparent. Repeat Edge Pixels fills the area with duplicates of the pixels at the edge of the selection, while Wrap Around takes pixels from the opposite side of the selection and duplicates them. These settings reappear frequently in some of the destructive filters we'll see shortly, particularly those in the Filter → Distort and Filter → Stylize submenus.

### Minimum and Maximum

The effect of the Minimum and Maximum filters will be familiar to anyone who has spent time in a lithography darkroom. In order to make colors in a printed image overlap, or *trap*, printers would change the colors' borders to allow one of the colors (generally the lighter of the two) to spread into the other. When applied to a masking channel, the Minimum filter shrinks the selection. The number you specify using the Radius slider is the amount your selection contracts. Maximum does the exact opposite: Input a Radius amount, and the filter expands your selection precisely by that number of pixels. This way you can create precise traps mathematically. Masks created using Maximum and Minimum can be used to overlap different colored areas so that just the right amount of trap is created. This prevents dreaded white space from showing where two colors meet during printing.

### High Pass

The High Pass filter offers a tool for finding and isolating areas of high contrast. On its own, it seems at first glance an awkward and unlikely filter. But when applied to individual color channels or to selection masks, it can help create interesting line effects or imbue

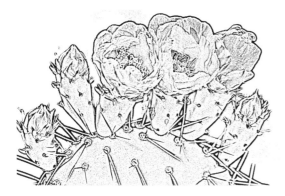

Figure 20.15

**The High Pass filter is applied to a 300ppi image. Step 1: High Pass, Radius 7 (top). Step 2: Threshold, Level 120 (center). Step 3: The Opacity slider in the Layers palette adjusted to 50% (bottom).**

unremarkable images with added color. High Pass's Radius slider allows a range from 0.01 to 250 pixels. Lower numbers leave your image a flat, midrange gray. Higher values let the higher-contrast areas show through in lighter gray. This isn't so great when applied to an image as a whole, but try applying this filter to individual color channels and you have a completely different animal. If you increase contrast by applying High Pass to individual color channels, you end up adding color at either end of the scale.

You can achieve a line-drawing effect by using High Pass in combination with the Threshold command and then reapplying the modified image to the original. Figure 20.15 shows how this can be achieved. First, make a duplicate layer of your image, and apply High Pass to the duplicate, using the Radius to find a desirable effect. Choose Image → Adjust → Threshold at the desirable value. Then use the Opacity slider in your Layers palette to blend the line image with your original. Voilà! a line-drawing effect.

## Destructive Filters

Now that the constructive filters have displayed their image-correcting prowess, it's time for a little fun. The special effects in the Filter → Distort, Pixelate, and Stylize submenus take your precious pixels and shove them about with wild impunity. With these filters, you can turn images inside out, explode and reassemble them, or boil the life out of them, leaving you with an indigestible goo. Used with care, they can be useful friends; used unwisely, they'll turn on you viciously. These filters are undoubtedly the cool members of the gang; they look good and offer a fun night out, but ultimately they're not quite as responsible as the constructive filters. And some are just plain dumb.

### Distort Filters

The common purpose of the filters in the Distort submenu is to transport pixels in your image across specifically defined patterns. For instance, Spherize gives the impression that your image has been wrapped around a ball. Twirl fixes the center point of your image and spirals the pixels around it, clockwise or counterclockwise. Shear provides an axis along which you can curve or lean your image.

The Distort filters are among the most memory-intensive of any of Photoshop's operations. To save yourself a lot of time watching the progress bar, do your experimenting with these filters on a lower-resolution version of your image. When you arrive at the effect you desire, make notes about the settings that produce the effect, and scale up those settings to apply the filter to your high-res version.

Filter values need to be greater for high-resolution images.

## Diffuse Glow

Diffuse Glow seems to be misplaced in the Distort submenu, rather than among its kin, the Stylize filters. It gives the effect of viewing the image through a diffusion filter. You can set the level of Graininess, and define Glow and Clear parameters.

## Glass

Glass, too, seems to belong elsewhere than with the Distort effects, perhaps among the Texture filters. Glass uses a hardwired variable displacement map effect similar to Distort → Displace (see the "Displace" section later in this chapter). Its effect approximates viewing your image through a glass lens (defined in the Texture pop-up menu). You also have the option of applying a texture of your own, using the Load Texture dialog box. You'll find this option in some of the Effects filters as well. Look for it in Artistic → Rough Pastels and Underpainting, Sketch → Conté Crayon, and especially Texture → Texturizer. These art effects offer a set of textures, but you can apply a pattern of your own making by saving it as a grayscale file in Photoshop format.

## Ocean Ripple

Ocean Ripple, Ripple, Wave, and Zig Zag all offer methods of introducing degrees of wiggliness into your image. (Some might also include Glass in this group; it applies a rippling effect with the added element of texture.) Of these, Wave is by far the most powerful and the most mysterious. Compare Zig Zag's user-friendly dialog with Wave's scientific control panel (Figure 20.16).

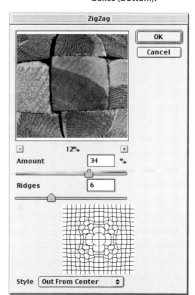

Figure 20.16

**Compare the Zig Zag (top) and Wave dialog boxes (bottom).**

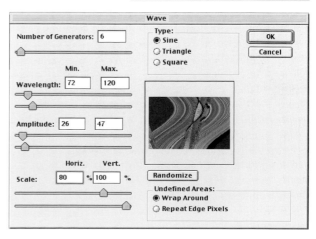

## Wave

The Wave dialog is where some of Photoshop's mathematical underpinnings become most transparent. Too bad they couldn't provide a box with knobs you could twiddle like an old-fashioned synthesizer. You can input the number of wave Generators, define minimum and maximum Wavelength and Amplitude levels, Scale the wave effect horizontally and vertically, and choose between three Types of waves. And when in doubt, just click Randomize; Photoshop will make up its own wave parameters. Figure 20.17 shows some of the effects these filters can accomplish.

## Pinch and Spherize

Pinch and Spherize are opposite sides of the same coin. If you apply a negative Amount in the Pinch dialog box, you get a Spherize-like effect; if you go negative in Spherize (Figure 20.18), the result is a lot like a Pinch. The difference is that Pinch maps your pixels onto a rounded cone, while Spherize maps the image onto—you guessed it—a sphere. Spherize offers the added option of allowing you to constrain the effect to the horizontal or vertical axis, or both. These two filters don't cancel each other out, though. Compare the effects of each in Figure 20.19.

## Polar Coordinates

The Polar Coordinates filter (illustrated in Figure 20.20) takes the corners of your image and brings them together to form a circle. Or the reverse: it takes the center and maps it out to the corners. Back in the old days, applying Polar Coordinates Rectangular to Polar was one of the few ways you could get type in a circle in Photoshop. Now that the Type tool offers that capability much more flexibly, Polar Coordinates can go back to what it does best: changing squares into circles.

Figure 20.17

**Comparison of filter applications: Ripple (a); Ocean Ripple (b); Zig Zag, Around Center (c); and Wave (d)**

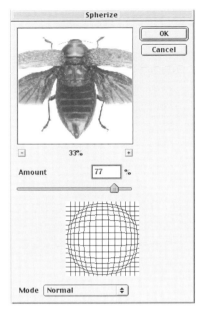

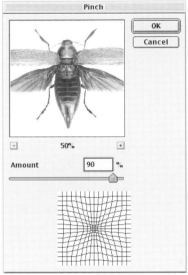

Figure 20.18

The Spherize dialog box is similar to Pinch, except for the extra Mode (axis) option at the bottom.

Figure 20.19

Pinched and Spherized images. (top left) Spherize, +100%; (top right) Spherize, –100%; (center) the original image; (bottom left) Pinch, +100%; and (bottom right) Pinch, –100%

Figure 20.20

**The Polar Coordinates filter applied to the prickly pear**

### Shear

Shear, as mentioned above, places your pixels along a curve. When you first open the Shear dialog box, you see a grid with a vertical line down the middle. You can take this vertical and angle it so it leans either way. This is akin to the Skew effect you get in the Transform functions. But if you click anywhere along the line, you can add points that turn the line to a curve. Now your image can distort along that curve in ways that Transform → Skew and Distort can't achieve, as I've done with the light bulb in Figure 20.21. Radio buttons help you designate how the undefined areas will be treated: you can either wrap the image around or have the edge pixels repeat. If you don't like your curve, click the Defaults button and start over.

### Twirl

The Twirl filter takes your image pixels and rotates them along a spiral. The center of the selection rotates while the edges remain in place. The Twirl dialog (Figure 20.22) offers two directions, expressed in minus and plus degrees, from 1 to 999. Since a circle is 360°, the full application of 999° gives you a spiral with almost three rotations. A positive value maps the spiral in a clockwise direction, while applying a negative number twirls your image counterclockwise.

## Displace

The Displace filter is a bit different than others in the Distort submenu. It relies on the use of displacement maps to reconfigure your image pixels. Like Distort → Wave, Displace retains quite a bit of its hard-science background, making it harder to predict without a lot of experimentation or mathematical know-how.

The Displace filter uses the brightness values in another image, called a *displacement map*, to relocate pixels. If the displacement map is a grayscale image with a single channel, pixels in the image that align with the black areas of the map are moved to the right and down, depending on your specifications in the dialog box. Pixels that align with the white areas of the map are moved to the left and up.

If the image has two or more channels, as in a grayscale image with an additional alpha channel or an RGB image, the first channel (Gray for grayscale and Red for RGB) determines horizontal movement and the second channel (an alpha channel for a grayscale image or the Green channel for an RGB image) determines vertical movement. The other channels in the image are not used. Areas of the image that align with the black pixels on the first channel are moved to the right, and areas that align with the white pixels are moved to the left. Areas of the image that align with the black pixels on the second channel are displaced down, and the areas that align with white pixels are moved up. Of course, the amount of displacement depends on the specifications you enter in the dialog box.

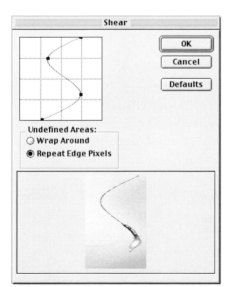

Figure 20.21

**The Shear dialog box**

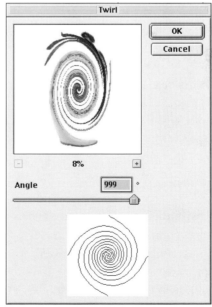

Figure 20.22

**You can Twirl from –999˚ *to 999˚*.**

You can access Photoshop's displacement maps (find them in the `Plug-Ins` folder in the Photoshop application folder) or create your own. Displace lets you define horizontal and vertical scale, and you get to say how you want undefined areas to be handled. You can also tell Photoshop whether to tile the displacement map or scale it to fit your image.

## Pixelate Filters

In general, the Pixelate filters break up and rearrange your image into variously shaped groups of pixels. As I mentioned previously, it would be impossible to fully describe every effect, let alone demonstrate them all visually. I'll just hit the high points here.

### Facet, Fragment, and Color Halftone

Neither Facet nor Fragment offers a dialog box; they simply apply their effects without so much as a by-your-leave. Of the two, Facet has a more pleasing, irregular, sort of hand-colored effect. Color Halftone's controls include a Radius input, and four screen angles boxes. It takes an awfully long time to apply this clunky effect, which can be achieved with more finesse using Filter → Sketch → Halftone Pattern.

### Crystallize, Mosaic, and Pointillize

Crystallize, Mosaic, and Pointillize all offer a Cell Size slider in their dialog boxes, which allows you to designate how many pixels will be used to create a cell or clump of grouped color. Larger values result in great big groupings of pixels that rob your image of detail. Smaller values can create more interesting artistic effects, mainly by increasing color contrast from cell to cell.

### Mezzotint

The Mezzotint filter offers several ways of adding largely uncontrollable noise to your image, in the form of dots, lines, or strokes. It's like the bullyish big brother of Add Noise without the slider. Mezzotint turns grayscale images black and white; RGB images are reduced to six colors (red, green, and blue and their complements cyan, magenta, and yellow) plus black and white.

Figure C30 in this book's color section shows the effects of some of the Pixelate filters.

## Stylize Filters

Some filters in the Stylize submenu deal with the edges of your image in one way or another; others map image pixels into geometric shapes.

### Solarize

Solarize is unique in dealing solely with color shifts. Its effect is similar to combining a photographic negative with a positive. All blacks and white become black, grays remain gray, and other colors become their negative equivalent. You have no control over this filter.

## Tiles and Extrude

Tiles and Extrude are the two Stylize filters that map to shape.
Tiles breaks your image up into squares. You can define how
many tiles fill a row across your image, how far the tiles can
offset from each other, and how the areas between tiles will
be filled. But the effect is rather flat; the Texture → Mosaic
Tiles filter creates a textured effect (with grouting options)
that is much more realistic.

## Extrude

The Extrude filter is similar to Tiles, except that the mapping
doesn't stay in two dimensions. The tiles or blocks extend into
space. You can make your extruded elements block- or pyra-
mid-shaped, and options are offered for the size and depth of
the extruded shapes. In addition, you can decide whether you
want incomplete blocks left out, and whether the fronts of
square blocks should remain solid or contain image detail.
Finally, you can arrange your extruded shapes randomly or
arrange them by level. Figure 20.23 presents two sample
Extrusions.

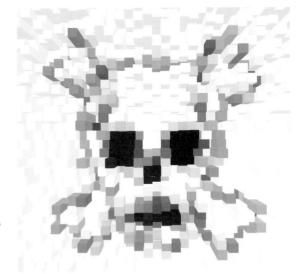

## Find Edges, Glowing Edges, and Trace Contour

Find Edges, Glowing Edges, and Trace Contour all provide
ways of getting a color outline of your image. (Remember the
technique of using High Pass and Threshold to create line art,
and include that method in this repertoire of edge-building
tricks.) Find Edges is a no-options effect that draws colored
lines around the edges of your image. Glowing Edges does the
same, except that you can determine the width, brightness,
and smoothness of your edges. Look at the examples in the
Color Section, and notice that Glowing Edges, if left to its defaults, is nothing more than an
inverted-color version of Find Edges. Or vice versa: If you want control over Find Edges, just
use Glowing Edges instead and then invert the results.

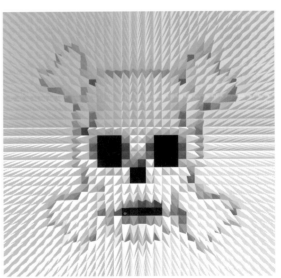

Figure 20.23

**The Extrude filter, set
to Blocks, Random,
Solid Front Faces (top)
and Pyramids, Level-
based (bottom)**

Trace Contour (Figure C31a in the color section) creates colored contours but leaves all non-
edge areas white. You can define a threshold above or below which Trace Contour will determine
what constitutes an edge. This one seems to require a bit of fading and blending to make it interesting, while Find Edges and Glowing Edge produce a more visually appealing effect.

To practice using Stylize filters, you can use the file `Stylize.psd` in the Ch20 folder on the CD.

### Diffuse

Diffuse works in a manner similar to the Dissolve brush or blending mode, in that it diffuses the edges of your selection. Because of this similarity, this filter's usefulness is rather limited; you can accomplish more by applying the brush or blending mode to an image. It does have a nice effect on type selections, though.

### Wind

The Wind filter offers three "strengths" of wind effect: plain old Wind, a Blast of wind, or a Staggeringly strong wind, coming either from left or right. This filter is notoriously time-consuming, so try it on a grayscale or low-res image for a preview of the effect.

### Emboss

And so we arrive at Emboss, perhaps Stylize's most interesting and entertaining offering. Figure 20.24 shows the Emboss dialog box with its Angle, Height and Amount options. You

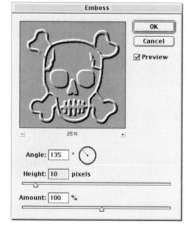

Figure 20.24

**The Emboss filter is arguably one of the most overused.**

can input your angle numerically, or slide the circle icon around to find the direction of light Emboss applies. Height is the distance of apparent bas relief you get, and Amount specifies the black-and-white value of edge pixels. Higher values create more contrast, while lowering the value gives the image an overall gray cast.

Emboss is one of those filters people really like to overuse on its own. Look at magazine ads and you'll recognize this frequently used effect. Its true power comes when applied to layers and blended, when faded back into the original image, or when applied individually to color channels. For an effect of color relief, use the Fade command and apply it using the Hue or Luminosity mode. This allows you to retain the colors in your image, while allowing the Emboss effect to reveal itself.

# Effects Filters

This group of filters for the most part produce a variety of studio techniques traditionally achieved in drawing, painting, and photography.

## Artistic, Brush Strokes, Sketch, and Texture

Artistic, Brush Strokes, Sketch, and Texture are the four groups of filters once called Gallery Effects. These all approximate different kinds of fine art, painterly techniques. With some of them, the results resemble effects that it would take several passes with standard Photoshop filters to achieve. The Artistic effects attempt to reproduce the effects of traditional art media, such as Watercolor, Dry Brush, and Fresco. Brush Strokes turns your image into various styles of color strokes, like Crosshatch and Sprayed Stroke. Sketch filters use your foreground and background colors to replace your image colors while creating textures. If you want to get some of the original color back, just use your Fade command. Its usefulness is not to be underestimated. Finally, Texture applies depth and, well, texture to your image. The Texturizer filter gives you the most play, allowing you to supply and apply your own textures. You can also scale your texture, define Height and Relief values, and determine the direction of light playing across the image. Take a look at Figure 20.25, and the color version of these images as Figure C34 in the color section, for a variety of artistic effects.

**Figure 20.25**

**Examples of the Artistic filters.**

(a) Original image

(b) Artistic ➤ Watercolor

(c) Artistic ➤ Palette Knife

(d) Sketch ➤ Crosshatch

(e) Sketch ➤ Ink Outlines

Artistic, Brush Strokes, Sketch, and Texture filters are not available in Lab, Indexed, or CMYK modes. If you're working in any of those modes, you must convert to RGB or grayscale mode before you can apply these effects.

# Render Filters

The Filter → Render submenu contains an interesting mix of lighting and texture effects, plus the 3D Transform filter. Clouds and Difference Clouds both reside here; to apply either of these filters to your image, simply choose the command. A hazy mixture of foreground and background colors fills your selection. Choose the filter again, and the cloud pattern changes. Every time you choose this filter, the cloud patterns shift. If you hold down the Option or Alt key while choosing, the colors create a more pronounced effect. Difference Clouds works in the same way as Clouds, but you end up with inverted colors (if you started with blue sky and white clouds, you now get orange sky with black clouds). Apply the filter again and your colors reinvert, back to blue and white.

Lens Flare produces a simple lighting effect. A preview box shows a replica of your image where you can move the pointer to find your flare center. The Brightness slider allows you to adjust brightness from 10% to 300%. Three lens shapes are offered: 50–300mm Zoom, 55mm Prime, and 105mm Prime. The result is a refraction, like light glinted back off a distant object.

Lens Flare and Lighting Effects, a much more powerful lighting tool, operate only on RGB images.

Some of these effects require a long time to compute and render.

## Lighting Effects Filter

The Lighting Effects dialog box (Figure 20.26) offers a wide range of options for simulating the play of spotlights or floodlights over your image. Imagine you're hanging lights in a gallery, shining a flashlight into a dark cave, or driving down a wooded road at night. Any of these lighting situations can be duplicated with these versatile options.

At the top of the dialog box, the Style menu provides a wide array of lighting styles. These preconfigured effects can serve as a starting point to add your own touches. In addition, the Light Type area allows you to create your own effects, which you can then save to the Style list. You're given options for Intensity and Focus, and you can choose a color for your light effect. You can define properties such as Gloss (Matte or Shiny finish), Material (ranges from Plastic to Metallic), Exposure, and Ambience. A color swatch lets you define the tint of the Ambience, which refers to ambient or overall lighting, separate from the spot or special lighting.

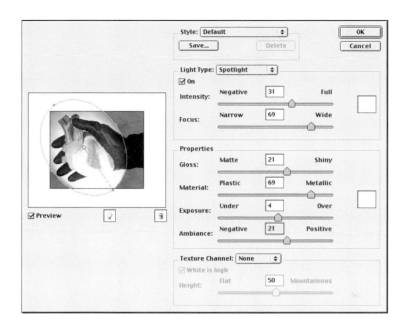

Figure 20.26

**The Lighting Effects
dialog box**

In the Texture Channel section, you can designate one of the channels (red, green, blue, or alpha) as a texture map—that is, a grayscale image where the light areas become peaks and dark areas become valleys. If you uncheck the White Is High box, the effect is reversed and the white areas become the valleys. Pick a Height somewhere between Flat and Mountainous, and you're set.

Inside the Preview area, you'll see a lighting footprint that shows you how the light source you've chosen will be applied. If you're working with a Spotlight or Omni, you can grab the handles and change the shape of the light. Clicking the Focus Spot (the end of the preview radius) allows you to change the angle of lighting. You can change the angle but not the shape of a Directional style of light. Keep in mind that the smaller the light footprint, the brighter or more intense the light. As you increase the size of the footprint, the light spreads out and dims accordingly. When you get an effect you like, click the Save button. Photoshop invites you to name your new lighting style, which will then appear in your Style menu.

Figure 20.27 (also shown as Figure C38 in the color section) demonstrates a few Lighting Effects. LFX_Dummy.psd is included in the Ch20 folder on the CD for you to experiment with lighting effects.

Figure 20.27

Examples of the Lighting Effects filter. The original image (upper left); Default light expanded and rotated so that the source is from below (upper right); RGB lights moved to various locations (lower left); A combination of filter effects (lower right). Filter → Render → Clouds was applied to the background. A blue omni was shined on the face from below. The 50–300mm lens flare was added. Finally, the image was 3D transformed.

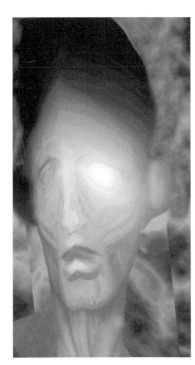

## Texture and 3D Filters

Texture Fill, also found in the Filter → Render submenu, is a tool for filling your selection with a previously created texture. Some textures are provided in Photoshop's \Presets\Textures folder directory in Windows. You can also create your own Texture Fill files, by saving any grayscale image in Photoshop format. When you choose Filter → Render → Texture Fill, you are prompted to find a texture file to apply. Just pick one and go. These fills work just like the ones in Filter → Texture → Texturizer.

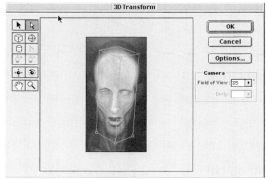

Figure 20.28

**The 3D Transform dialog box**

3D Transform allows you to map images to three-dimensional shapes: cubes, spheres, and cylinders. Figure 20.28 shows its dialog box, and Figure 20.29 illustrates some examples. In the preview window, you can position and size the shape of your choice. The shape you choose appears as a green wire frame over your image, which you can then manipulate using the tools from the left panel of the dialog box.

Figure 20.29

**Various effects of the 3D Transform filter**

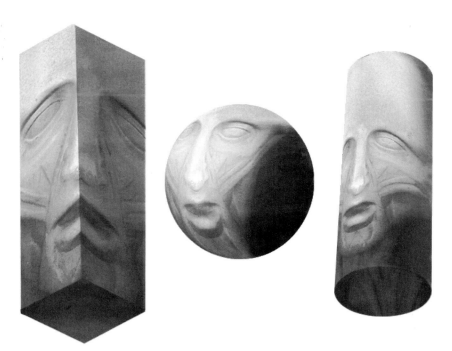

The Selection and Direct Selection tools enable you to move the wire frame and alter its size and shape. The Rotate tool lets you apply a rotation; the Pen tools allow you to add, subtract, or convert points along the path of the wire frame to more exactly fit the shape you desire; and a Scaling tool lets you increase or decrease its size. If you arrive at a shape that's impossible for Photoshop to render, the wire frame turns red. The filter's Dolly Camera option magnifies or shrinks the object, as if you were rolling a camera toward or away from it. Once you're satisfied with what you've set up, click OK and let the filter apply itself. This toolbox-within-a-filter is also one of the hallmarks of the Liquify and new Pattern Maker features.

# Other Filters

Two filters exist in a category by themselves, being neither constructive nor destructive.

## Video

The Video → NTSC Colors filter has one purpose: to convert the colors of an image for transfer to videotape. This filter is not a color space. It converts your RGB images to NTSC (North American Television Standards Committee)-compatible colors.

If you continue to work on an image after using this filter, you may introduce incompatible colors. A better solution is to close the file, head to the Color Settings, and choose the NTSC RGB color space as your working RGB space. Then reopen the file and OK the profile conversion in the dialog box that appears.

The Video → De-Interlace filter regenerates missing interlacing rows from video grabs. When you capture an image from a video device, the results may be less than satisfactory due to the interlacing used by the video program to compress file sizes. The De-Interlace filter restores the image by replacing pixel data. The result is that the image appears smoother. You can choose to replace interlaced fields by duplication or interpolation.

## Digimarc

The Digimarc filter lets you embed a digital watermark on your image to protect your copyright. It's particularly useful to professionals who license their work. Code is added to the document as noise and is usually imperceptible to the human eye. The watermark can endure most editing, even filters and file conversion.

To embed a digital watermark:

1. Choose Filter → Digimarc → Embed Watermark.

2. You must first register with Digimarc Corporation to get a creator ID. Click Personalize to launch your browser and access the Digimarc Web site at `www.digimarc.com`, or call the phone number in the dialog box.

3. Enter the PIN and ID number in the creator ID box. Click OK.

4. In each field, enter information about the image, including the copyright date and usage information.

5.  Select a Visibility and Durability value. The more visible the watermark is, the more durable it is.

6.  Click OK.

After you've embedded the watermark in an image, test its durability with the Signal Strength meter. Choose Filter → Digimarc → Read Watermark. The meter will tell you under what conditions the watermark will survive a specific intended use.

## The Liquify Filter

The Liquify filter, introduced in Photoshop 6, has regained its rightful place in the Filters menu. (They had originally placed it in the Image menu, but we all knew it was really a filter.) Liquify is, at its heart, a set of painting tools that distort pixels and transform areas of an image. Imagine using Distort filters on the fly with brushes. You can also mask off areas to protect them from change, or reconstruct unwanted distortions. In Photoshop 7, Liquify has gained a few features—nothing earthshaking, but enough to give it a little extra heft.

Filter → Liquify presents a set of transformation tools that you can work with in great detail before actually applying. Get everything exactly the way you want (Liquify has fully functional previewing capabilities), and when you click OK, your whole session of warping/ transforming takes effect. Figure 20.30 shows the Liquify dialog box.

Liquify makes pixels warp and flow within an image. It contains its own complete set of painting and masking tools, along with a Reconstruct tool that allows you to reverse the distortion. There are several Reconstruct modes, so you can apply a partial or complete reconstruction at will. You can have a mesh grid overlay your image area to show the amount of

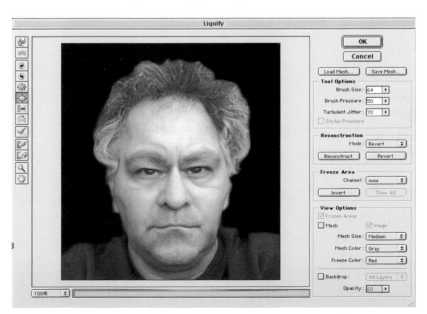

Figure 20.29

**You can Liquify extensively within this "subinterface."**

warping or reconstruction that's taking place, then you can save the mesh and apply it to an entirely new image regardless of the image's size or resolution.

Let's first look at the Liquify painting tools (the top eight icons in Figure 20.31), which work somewhat like a set of distortion filters. Instead of individual brushes, you're provided with a Brush Size slider and a Pressure slider. In Photoshop 7, they've added a new setting here called Turbulence Jitter. These sliders control the size and opacity of the various tools:

**Warp**  This pushes pixels along as you drag. If you hold the mouse down and drag longer, the effect is enhanced. Short, gentle drags of the mouse can move changes along slowly and precisely. Generally applies the effect like a smudge tool.

**Turbulence**  This new tool is another Liquify "brush" that applies the pixel-pushing effect more radically. If you hold the mouse down the pixels merge and melt like a piece of film burning in the projector. It's as if a randomizing Wave filter is at work inside the confines of the brush size. Changing the numbers on the Turbulence Jitter slider slows down or speeds up this effect.

**Twirl Clockwise and Twirl Counterclockwise**  These tools rotate pixels. Don't confuse them with the Twirl filter discussed earlier in this chapter. Unlike that tool, they cause pixels to rotate faster at the edges of the brush than at the center.

**Pucker and Bloat**  These tools squeeze your pixels in or out. Pucker pinches pixels under its drag, and Bloat moves them away from the center of the brush.

**Shift Pixels**  This tool moves pixels at a 90-degree angle to the way you're moving the brush. Dragging moves pixels to the left of your mouse path; Option/Alt-drag moves pixels to the right.

**Reflect**  This tool drags along a mirror image of the pixels perpendicular to your brush.

Once you've made some distortions, you can use the Reconstruct tool to completely or partially restore your image to its initial state. Masking brushes (the Freeze tool creates a mask, Thaw erases it) allow you to freeze or thaw selected areas of your image—that is, protect them from the transformations underway, or release the protection. You're also able to select an alpha channel to freeze areas.

Also notice in the toolbar that the familiar Zoom and Hand tools have been added to Liquify in Photoshop 7. You can now zoom in on a specific area of the image you are distorting and navigate anywhere you need to go inside the zoom.

Now that you've had your way with your image and it's warped all over creation, you're having second thoughts. Can you get it back without canceling the Liquify effect and starting all over again? Sure—that's what the Reconstruct tool is for. But Reconstruct is much more

Figure 20.31

**The Liquify tool palette**

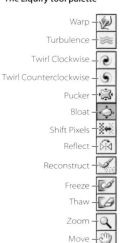

Warp
Turbulence
Twirl Clockwise
Twirl Counterclockwise
Pucker
Bloat
Shift Pixels
Reflect
Reconstruct
Freeze
Thaw
Zoom
Move

than a History Eraser. The reconstructions you apply can be fodder for further distortions. Look back at Figure 20.30 to see Liquify's Options area, on the right side of the dialog box. In the Mode pop-up list of the Reconstruction area, you have several options for regulating the degree and type of reconstruction, ranging from Rigid to Loose. Each one offers a slightly different degree of reconstructing capability. In fact, by the time you get to Loose, you're continuing to distort the image, but at least you're going back the way you came. If you want to reconstruct back to before a certain set of distortions, just click the Revert button in the Reconstruction area; then use the brush to enact your reconstruct.

> If you undo an action while transforming in the Liquify display, any mask designating a frozen area will be eliminated. You must re-create or rechoose a mask to keep the area frozen as you proceed.

Among the Reconstruction modes, Displace moves pixels in unfrozen areas to match the displacement of a reference point. This mode can be used to reconstruct the image to a specific point. Amplitwist is used to duplicate the displacement, rotation, or scaling of a reference point. Affine matches displacement, rotation, scaling, and skew of a reference point.

The Freeze Area options give you various ways of protecting segments of your image from distortion. Click to select an alpha channel to apply, or create your own. The View Options area provides options for the way you look at Liquify. Most important of these is the Mesh option. What is at first a regular square grid takes on the shape of the transformations you apply. This can be useful when applying reconstructions, by letting you see how close to square you're able to return.

A new section at the bottom of the Liquify dialog box in Photoshop 7 allows you to blend in your current Liquify experiments with the existing image. When you click the Backdrop button, you can adjust the opacity of the original image to allow it to merge with the Liquify effect.

When you're done making selections, click OK and watch Image → Liquify perform its magic. See Figure 20.32 to see some truly horrifying Liquify transformations. For practice, you can go to the Ch20 folder on the CD to obliterate and abuse sample files in the Things-to-Liquify folder.

## New in 7.0: Pattern Maker

Right up there under Extract and Liquify at the top of the Filters menu is a new feature called Pattern Maker. With this tool (Figure 20.33 shows its window), you can take any selection from any part of your image and generate repeating tiles based on your selection, the entire image, or the contents of the Clipboard.

Figure 20.32

**These three images show the application of the Liquify Filter and how it can be used to distort facial characteristics to produce wild caricatures.**

Like the Liquify tool, Pattern Maker offers you considerable control over its application. At the top-left corner of the window are the familiar Marquee, Zoom, and Hand tools. With Pattern Maker, the Marquee allows you to select an area of the image from which to generate patterns. However, the dialog box also gives you the options of using the Clipboard contents, the entire image (via the Use Image Size button), or an area you define with the handy Width and Height inputs.

In addition, you can Offset the spacing of your tiles horizontally or vertically and specify an offset Amount percentage. Changing the Smoothness settings to 1, 2, or 3 can enhance blending of the edges of your tiles; while increasing the Sample Detail allows greater precision in the formation of your sample. Keep in mind, though, that the farther you push the sample detail up, the more time Photoshop will take to generate the tiles. If you go all the way up to the maximum of 21, you could be in for a long wait while your sample generation grinds away.

Once you've chosen a sample, click the Generate button to see elements of your sample repeated in place of your original image, tiled to fill the image area. Keep pressing Generate Again, and new patterns replace one another in the image window. You can view the entire series of patterns you've generated in the Tile History area. The Tile History window shows the current generated sample as an individual unit. Up to 20 of these tiles can be stored (after that, the earliest ones are discarded as you produce more). By clicking the arrow buttons at the bottom of the dialog box, you can view each set of tiles sequentially. To delete one, click the trash can icon to the right; to save one, click the disk icon to the left. A dialog appears that shows you the pattern you've chosen and allows you to name it. Your new pattern will be saved at the end of Photoshop's list of default patterns, available for use with the rest, just as if you've made a selection and then chosen Edit → Define Pattern. You can use this option to save generated patterns without ever altering your image. If you press Cancel at this point, your saved patterns will remain, but your image will return to its original state.

Use the Preview area to see what you're doing. Choose either Original or Generated to let Pattern Maker show you your original image, or the current generated pattern. You can opt to view the tile boundaries as a line in the color (default green) you define. You can change this color just as you would the mask color in the Channels palette. Clicking the color swatch takes you to the Picker, where... well, you know what to do by now. If Tile Boundaries is checked, colored lines will show you the area covered by each individual tile.

> Using any of the methods in the Tile Generation section will override any Marquee selection you might have made.

If you get lost in all this pattern generation, just look down at the bottom of the dialog, where all is displayed in an orderly fashion. You can check up on your zoom magnification, Image Size in pixels, and Tile Grid (how many tiles fit across and down in your image size). You can also see the size in pixels of anything you've stored in the Clipboard; under Preview, you can be informed of which of the generated tile patterns you're looking at. Figure 20.34 (next page) shows some sample patterns generated from the desert image.

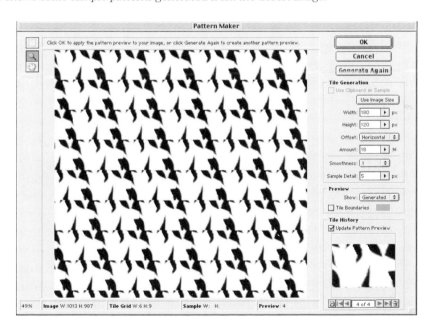

Figure 20.33

**The Pattern Maker interface**

Figure 20.34

The original image (left)
and two of the many
possible patterns
generated from
it (center; right)

# CHAPTER 21

# Making Difficult Selections

*In Chapter 6,* we covered the basics of selection making. You saw that the selection tools provide several manual techniques, like the Marquee and Lasso tools, to isolate areas of an image. Photoshop also has a few semiautomatic selection tools, like the Magic Wand and the Magnetic Lasso that select pixels based on their brightness or contrast values. The Quick Mask extends selection-making abilities to the painting tools for even more control, and the Pen tool lets you make accurate selections with Bezier curves.

Sometimes, however, areas of an image seem impossible to select because they have ambiguous surroundings or complex content. What do you do with these problem images, short of canceling all appointments, turning off the phone, and sitting in front of the computer for the next week, one by one encircling each pixel?

In this chapter, you will learn how to select those really tough areas with a few tools and techniques that, if they don't make these selections easy, at least get the job done with a minimum of effort. You will learn about:

- **Making selections with color channels**
- **Working with color range**
- **Selecting out-of-gamut colors**
- **Modifying selections**
- **Extracting images**

# Making Selections with Color Channels

You can use an image's color information to make really difficult selections. The differences in the contrast levels of the red, green, and blue channels can often provide a method of isolating portions of the image that would seem impossible to select. You'll use this technique and a combination of Photoshop's painting tools and filters to select from images like Figure 21.1, where the background and foreground are complex and almost indistinct, so that isolating the model and her hair from the background would otherwise be virtually impossible. Be warned that this process can be quite labor-intensive, so roll up your sleeves and make it happen.

Figure 21.1

**It's close to impossible to select this model's hair with traditional selection tools, but you can use color channels to do it.**

1. Open the image `Hair_Select.psd` in the `Ch21` folder on the CD.

2. Open the Channels palette (Window → Channels, or F7 on the keyboard if you still have it clustered with the Layers palette). Click the Red, Green, and Blue channel thumbnails to display each channel in grayscale in the image window. Determine which channel has the most contrast between the hair on the model and the background. In this case, it's the Red channel.

3. Target the Red channel, and duplicate it by choosing Duplicate Channel from the Channels palette pull-down menu, or by dragging it to the New Channel icon at the bottom of the palette. The channel will be named Red Copy.

4. Choose Image → Adjustments → Levels and increase the contrast of the Red Copy channel by dragging the sliders inward. Click OK. I set the input levels in this image to 71, 1.00, and 216.

5. Choose Filter → Other → High Pass. Set the radius to 9.9. The High Pass filter will flatten the colors of the image and make the division between the hair and background even more distinct (see Figure 21.2).

6. Choose Image → Adjustments → Threshold. This operation will turn all of the pixels either black or white. I set the Threshold value to 123 (Figure 21.3) to maintain the distinction between the hair and the background.

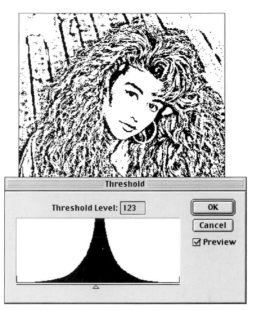

Figure 21.2

**Apply the High Pass filter to enhance the distinction between the hair and background.**

Figure 21.3

**Apply a Threshold adjustment to the duplicate Red channel, to map the pixels to either black or white.**

7. Choose the Paintbrush and block in, with black, the larger areas on the Red Copy channel that you want masked.

8. With a smaller brush, block out the additional areas close to the hair so that the channel resembles Figure 21.4. You may want to view both the Red Copy channel and the RGB image to paint as close as possible to the edge of the hair.

9. When you've finished painting, view the RGB and Red Copy channels by clicking their eye icons in the Channels palette. With the Lasso tool , select the interior of the model as close to the solid part of her hair as possible, as in Figure 21.5.

10. Choose Select → Feather and give the selection a 2-pixel feather radius. Choose white as the foreground color and press Option-Delete or Alt-Backspace to fill the interior of the selection with white. The selection should look like Figure 21.6.

11. Now that we've isolated the model, we're going to place her on a different background. Open the file `Desert.psd` from the `Ch21` folder on the CD.

Figure 21.4

**The Red Copy alpha channel with the areas around the model painted black**

Figure 21.5

**Select the solid area of the hair with the Lasso tool while viewing the RGB and Red Copy channel.**

12. Click the Hair image. Target the RGB channel. Load the Red Copy by dragging it to the Load Selection icon ⊙ in the Layers palette to select the model.

13. Choose the Move tool ▶₊ ; drag the image from the Hair image window and drop it onto the Desert image.

14. Some of the colors in the extremities of the model's hair have washed out a little in the process of moving her. To restore those areas, choose the Sponge tool 🧽 . In the Options bar, choose Saturate.

15. Choose a soft brush and make a few passes on the frizzy areas of the hair to intensify those colors.

16. You can make a few light passes on the very edge of her hair with the Eraser tool 🩹 and a small brush set at 40% or 50% opacity to further enhance the effect, as in Figure 21.7.

17. Choose Layer → Matting → Defringe → Radius 1px to eliminate any unwanted edge pixels.

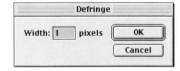

Figure 21.6

**The finished selection**

Figure 21.7

**The finished image**

# Working with Color Range

The Select → Color Range command is ideal for selecting areas of similar color within the image or within a selection outline. In Chapter 17, "Modifying and Mapping Color," we used a similar technique, Image → Adjustments → Replace Color, to substitute colors. Color Range operates in very much the same way, but instead of altering color it produces an accurate selection marquee around the specified areas of similar color.

This tool really helps you in situations where you have a lot of small areas of similar color situated throughout the image. With so many scattered areas of color, a tedious task can be simplified, as we shall see.

Figure 21.8

**The Color Range dialog box**

When you choose Select → Color Range, the dialog box (Figure 21.8) presents you with a mask of the image. The Select pull-down menu lets you choose a specific color range to sample, and it will automatically select all of the pixels within the range. You can choose to select Reds, Yellows, Blues, Magentas, Greens, Cyans, Highlights, Midtones, Shadows, or Out-of-Gamut colors.

If you want more control, however, the best approach to making a selection is to choose the default, Sampled Colors. You use the familiar eyedropper tools to sample the colors you want to select from the image. I recommend that you change the setting in the Eyedropper tool Options bar to 3 by 3 Average. Click in or drag over the image with the Eyedropper to select colors. Drag over the image with the Plus Eyedropper to increase the range of colors selected or with the Minus Eyedropper to decrease the range. The Fuzziness slider also extends the range of selection into adjacent pixels. Check the Invert box to invert the selection.

The radio buttons under the mask let you view the selection mask on the image as you drag the eyedropper, or adjust the Fuzziness slider to accurately determine the range of the selection. The Selection Preview pull-down menu lets you choose from Grayscale, White Matte, Black Matte, Quick Mask, or None modes in which to view the mask in the image window. These preview modes help you better determine what areas of the image will be selected and what areas will be masked. Choose the one most appropriate to the tonal or color content of your image. For example, you'll probably choose White Matte if the image is particularly dark, because the mask will be more visible.

### Selecting a Sampled Color Range

Let's try selecting part of an image using Color Range.

1. Open the file `sparks.psd` in the `Ch21` folder of the CD.

2. In the Tool palette, choose the Eyedropper tool. Change the setting in the Options bar to 3 by 3 Average.

3. Select the left portion of the image with the Rectangular Marquee (see Figure 21.9).

4. Choose Select → Color Range. With the Plus Eyedropper tool, drag over a portion of the shower of sparks. Watch the mask in the Color Range dialog box (Figure 21.10).

Figure 21.9

**Select a portion of the image first, and then choose Color Range to refine the selection.**

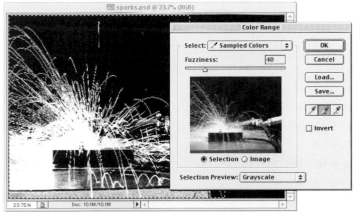

Figure 21.10

**The Color Range dialog box with a mask of the shower of sparks**

5. From the Selection preview, run through the masking options one by one to determine what part of the image will be selected.

6. Move the Fuzziness slider to extend the selection to include as much of the sparks as possible.

7. Click OK to select the sparks.

Depending on the fuzziness and the range of color that was selected, portions of the welder may be included, in which case you'll need to deselect those areas by choosing the Lasso tool, choosing the Subtract From Selection icon in the Options bar, and encircling them. Think about how much time you saved by using this technique. It certainly would have been labor-intensive to select these areas with the Magic Wand tool, even with the Contiguous option turned off. Color Range lets you collectively select those colors that are dispersed throughout the image simply by dragging over them. The finished selection is shown in Figure 21.11.

Figure 21.11

**The final selection**

## Selecting Out-of-Gamut Colors

Another unique function of the Color Range command is its ability to isolate unprintable colors. Chapter 15, "Color Management and Printing," describes Photoshop's color management features and shows how you can compensate for out-of-gamut colors. In the Edit → Color Settings dialog box, you can specify a CMYK profile for a device or printing environment that has its own unique CMYK gamut. When you prepare an image for process color printing, the profile affects how the image is converted into CMYK from its working mode (usually RGB). If you choose View → Gamut Warning, Photoshop will display a gray mask that shows you which colors are out of gamut. If you choose View → Proof Setup → Working CMYK (Photoshop's default) and then View → Proof Colors, you can preview on-screen how the image will look when printed, before you convert it.

> Toggle in and out of Proof Colors by pressing ⌘/Ctrl-Y to compare the CMYK preview to the RGB display. You can also use Window → Documents → New Window for soft-proofing CMYK.

You'll want to pull the out-of-gamut colors back into the CMYK range before you convert the image, so that you can perform final edits with the knowledge that what you see on screen is as close as possible to what you'll get when you print. But first you'll have to select the out-of-gamut colors, and the method you'll use is buried deep within the Color Range dialog box.

To select and adjust out-of-gamut colors, for an image that will be printed on a sheet-fed printing press, follow these steps:

1. Choose Edit → Color Settings. From the Working Spaces, RGB menu choose Adobe RGB 1998. From the CMYK pull-down menu, choose U.S. Sheetfed Coated v2. Click OK.

2. Open the file `chiles.psd` from the `Ch21` folder on the CD.

3. Make a duplicate of the document (Image → Duplicate). Name the copy `chiles_CMYK.psd`.

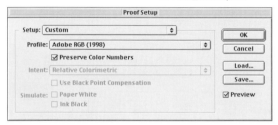

4. Place both images on the screen side by side.

5. Click `chiles.psd` to activate it. Choose View → Proof Setup → Custom. From the Profile menu (Figure 21.12), choose Adobe RGB 1998 to display the original image in RGB mode. You'll keep this image on screen for reference.

Figure 21.12

**Use the Proof Setup dialog box to choose the current CMYK working Space.**

6. Activate `chiles.psd`. Choose View → Proof Setup → Working CMYK and then View → Proof Colors. You'll notice that the colors in the CMYK proof are less saturated than in the RGB image.

7. Choose View Gamut → Warning to view the out-of-gamut colors, as in Figure 21.13. They appear as gray shapes on the chilies. Press Shift-⌘-Y (Mac) or Shift-Ctrl-Y (Win) to turn the Gamut warning off.

8. Choose Select → Color Range. Choose Out Of Gamut from the bottom of the Select pull-down menu (Figure 21.14). The dialog box displays a mask of the out-of-gamut colors.

9. Click OK. As shown in Figure 21.15, the marquee on the image displays a selection outline.

Figure 21.13

**The Gamut warning displays the out-of-gamut colors as gray shapes**

Figure 21.14

**Selecting out-of-gamut colors with the Color Range dialog**

Figure 21.15

**The out-of-gamut colors selected**

10. Choose Select → Feather → Radius; 3px to create smooth transitions between colors when you increase their intensity.

11. Press ⌘/Ctrl-H to hide the edges of the selection.

12. Choose Layer → New Adjustment Layer → Hue/Saturation. In the Hue/Saturation dialog box (Figure 21.16), move the Hue slider to +8 and the Saturation slider to +61, to more closely match the RGB image.

> You can also experiment with other adjustments, including Levels, Curves, Color Balance, Selective Color, the Channel Mixer, or Variations to produce optimum results.

13. You can compensate for diminished intensity by experimenting with variations of hue, saturation, and lightness to produce better results while maintaining the colors within the CMYK gamut. However, on most images you will never achieve the full intensity of the RGB image.

## Extracting Images

Earlier we used RGB channels to isolate images with fuzzy, complex, or indefinable edges from their background. Another option is to use the Filter → Extract command for this purpose. The results might not be as precise as the channels method, but you can, by trial and error, isolate problem edges with much less effort. The Extract command is actually a mini-program, complete with a subinterface (Figure 21.17), that measures subtle differences of the edge of an image by its color and brightness content and then determines how best to isolate the region.

Figure 21.16

Make adjustments in the Hue/Saturation dialog box so that the CMYK image matches the RGB original as closely as possible.

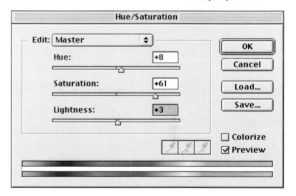

> In Photoshop 7, the Extract command has been moved out of the Image menu and put into the Filter menu, along with Liquify and the new Pattern Maker command.

The general technique is to use the Edge Highlighter to define the image's edges; you then fill its interior and preview it. You can refine and preview as many times as you like until you have all of the image and none of the background. You then extract it, which deletes undefined areas and places the image on a transparent layer.

> Because of the radical transformation that Extract produces, you should first duplicate the image or make a snapshot of it.

Figure 21.17

**The Extract dialog box**

Edge Highlighter —
Fill —
Eraser —
Eyedropper —
Cleanup —
Edge Touchup —
Zoom —
Hand —

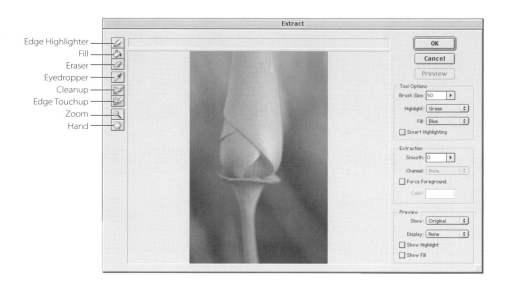

Specify the following tool options in the dialog panel:

**Brush Size** Enter a value or drag the slider to specify the width of the Edge Highlighter tool, which defines the boundary of the image.

**Highlight** Choose a color to display the edge boundary that you draw with the Edge tool.

**Fill** Choose a color to display the interior fill inside the boundary.

**Smart Highlighting** This option helps you keep the highlight on the edge, especially when the edge between the foreground and background is sharp with similar color or texture. To toggle Smart Highlighting on or off while you drag, press the ⌘/Ctrl key.

To practice extracting an image, choose Filter → Extract and open the file iris.psd in the Ch21 folder on the CD.

1. Set the Highlight color to red and the Fill color to blue.

2. Choose a 24px Brush Size. Select the Edge Highlighter tool ![icon] and drag along the edge of the flower to highlight the edge of the object you want to extract. Draw the highlight so that it slightly overlaps both the foreground and background regions around the edge, to cover areas where the foreground blends into the background.

3. Use a smaller brush to precisely highlight edges that are more defined, like the area around the flower's base. Use a larger brush to highlight the fuzzy edges around the petals, loosely covering the soft transitions. Don't highlight the bottom or top of the flower, only the sides.

4. If you make a mistake, erase the highlight. Select the Eraser tool ![icon] from the dialog box, and drag over the highlight. This tool is available when a highlight exists. You can completely erase the highlight by pressing Alt-Backspace or Option-Delete.

> To toggle between the Highlighter and the Eraser while drawing an edge, press the Option or Alt key.

5.  To fill the flower, select the Fill tool . Click inside the outline to fill its interior (see Figure 21.18).

> If the image is especially intricate or lacks a clear interior, make sure that the highlight covers the entire edge. To highlight the entire object, press Ctrl-Backspace (Win) or ⌘-Delete (Mac), and then select Force Foreground. Use this technique with areas that contain tones of a single color.

## Viewing the Extraction

Click Preview to view the extracted image. The edges of the flower will be soft, and the area around it will be transparent, like the one in Figure 21.19. You can better see the result of the extraction if you view it using the following techniques:

*   In the Show menu, switch between previews of the original and extracted images.

*   Use the Display menu to preview the extracted object as a grayscale mask or against a white matte or a black matte. To choose a colored background, choose Other and a color from the Color Picker. To display a transparent background, choose None.

*   Select the Show Highlight or Show Fill option to display the object's extraction boundaries or interior.

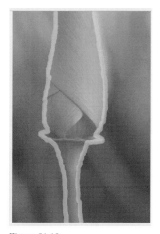

Figure 21.18

**The highlighted and filled flower**

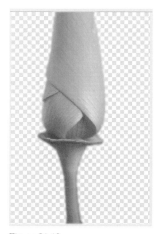

Figure 21.19

**Previewing the completed flower**

## Refining the Extraction

Several tools let you alter the edges and interior of the extraction, adding areas to the extraction or eliminating unwanted pixels.

### The Cleanup Tool

You can edit and refine the extraction with the Cleanup tool ⬜, which is only available when you preview the extracted image. The Cleanup tool subtracts opacity. If you make multiple passes, it will have a cumulative effect. Drag over an area to erase it to transparency. Press the Option/Alt key while painting with the Cleanup tool to restore opacity.

> The Eraser and Fill tools can also be used to edit the previewed image. The Eraser restores the edge to transparency. Clicking a filled area with the Fill paint bucket removes the fill.

### The Edge Touchup Tool

Use the Edge Touchup tool ⬜ to edit the extraction boundaries. The tool, which is available when you show the extracted image, sharpens the edges of the extracted image. It has a cumulative effect as you make multiple passes over the edge. If there is no clear edge, the Edge Touchup tool adds opacity to the image or makes the background more transparent.

### The Smooth Control

To help remove stray artifacts in the extraction, click on the right arrow next to the Smooth field in the Extract dialog box. Enter a value in the field or drag the Smooth Slider. The higher the number, the greater the radius of pixels that will be affected. When you are finished editing, click Preview again to view the edited extraction. You can edit and preview the extraction as many times as you like until you achieve the results you want.

To apply the final extraction, click OK. All pixels on the layer outside the extracted image are eliminated. If necessary, use the History brush ⬜ or the Background Eraser ⬜ to touch up stray edge pixels and flawed areas.

# CHAPTER 22

# Advanced Layer Techniques

*Chapter 7, "Layering Your Image,"* introduced the
importance of layers to Photoshop images, and compared a layer to a piece of clear acetate.
You learned that you can separate parts of your image onto independent layers in order to
maintain a dynamic workflow. You also learned how to reshuffle layers in the stack so as to
reposition their plane of depth in the picture, and how to link layers or create layer sets in
order to organize your work. We changed a layer's opacity to be able to "see through" it,
experimented with blending modes to dramatically alter the color relationships of layers,
and applied cool special effects like drop shadows and bevels.

In this chapter, we explore more of Photoshop's layer capabilities and look at techniques
that empower you to combine visual elements in unique and rather surprising ways.

You'll learn about:

- **Creating and controlling layer masks**
- **Seamless compositing**
- **Grouping layers**
- **Casting shadows**

## Working with Layer Masks

When you work in Photoshop, you rely on masks to perform many of its editing tasks. Masking, as discussed in Chapter 6, "Making Selections," is a way to isolate a part of an image, which you do when you make a selection. In Chapter 12, "Using Alpha Channels and Quick Mask," we worked with Quick Masks to extend the power of selecting to the painting tools. In the same chapter, we looked at ways to store selections as alpha channels so that they could be used at any time during the editing process. Selections, alpha channels, and Quick Masks all work to the same ends: to protect an isolated region from the application of a tool or operation. Layer masks are a little different. Instead of protecting an area of the image from an operation, they reveal or conceal it from view.

When you adjust the Opacity controls on the Layers palette, you change the transparency of the entire layer so that the content of layers beneath it in the stack will be visible. But when you apply a layer mask to an image, you can control the transparency of a particular part of the layer. Layer masks use the same visual vocabulary as alpha channels to perform their tasks with a slightly different twist. On an alpha channel, by default, black fully protects an area, white fully exposes an area, and gray partially exposes an area. On a layer mask, black completely conceals an area, white fully reveals an area, and gray partially reveals an area.

Make a layer mask by choosing Layer → Add Layer Mask → Reveal All or Hide All. If you choose Reveal All, the mask thumbnail appears white and begins by *revealing* the entire layer. As you paint with black, you conceal portions of the targeted layer. If you choose Hide All, the mask thumbnail appears black and begins by *hiding* the entire layer. As you paint with white, you reveal portions of the layer. A thumbnail appears in the Layers palette to the right of the targeted layer's thumbnail. When you click the layer mask thumbnail, it displays a double border to indicate that it is ready for editing. By default, the layer mask is targeted after it is created and is indicated in the title bar of the document. By default, the layer mask is also linked to the layer, indicated by the chain symbol.

> Not having the correct layer or layer mask targeted is perhaps the most common mistake made by users.

## Controlling Layer Masks

Once you've created a layer mask, you can control it in the following ways:

**Activating and Deactivating a Layer Mask**  Press Shift and click the layer mask to turn it on or off, or choose Layer → Enable or Disable Layer Mask.

**Viewing a Layer Mask**  Press Option (Macintosh) or Alt (Windows), and click the mask thumbnail to view the layer mask in the image window.

**Making a Selection from a Layer Mask** Press ⌘ (Mac)/Ctrl (Win) and click the layer mask to generate a selection outline.

**Moving a Layer's Mask and Contents** Click between the two thumbnails to reveal or conceal the link icon. When the two thumbnails are linked and you drag on the image with the Move tool, both the image on the layer and layer mask move as a unit. When the link is not visible, only the content of the targeted thumbnail will move.

**Removing a Layer Mask** Choose Layer → Remove Layer Mask → Discard or Apply. Discard removes the layer mask and does not apply the effect. Apply removes the layer mask and applies the effect directly to the pixels of the layer. You can also drag the Layer Mask icon (not the Layer icon) to the trash can on the Layers palette.

## Making Layer Masks

To understand how layer masks work, let's use one to conceal parts of an image. To practice creating a layer mask, follow these steps:

1. Open the file `coffee_time.psd` in the `Ch22` folder on the CD (see Figure 22.1).

2. The image is composed of two layers: the cup and the pattern layer behind it.

3. Open the file `uninvited-guest.psd`.

4.  Choose the Magic Wand tool. In the Options bar, set the tolerance to the default and select the white area around the beetle. (You may have to click more than once.)

5. Choose Select → Inverse or Shift-Cmd/Ctrl-I to select the beetle.

6.  Choose the Move tool. Place your cursor on the beetle, press the mouse button, and drag the selection onto the cup. Place it on top of the coffee. Name the new layer **Guest**.

Figure 22.1

The `coffee_time` image and its Layers palette

7. Notice that there is a white fringe around the beetle resulting from the anti-alias of white background that was selected. To remove it, choose Layer → Matting → Defringe. In the Defringe dialog box (see Figure 22.2), enter **1** pixel. (To learn more about removing edge pixels, see the section titled "Seamless Compositing" later in this chapter.) See Figure 22.3.

8. Choose Layer → Add Layer Mask → Reveal All. A Layer Mask icon appears in the Layers palette that is, by default, targeted for editing.

9. Choose black as the foreground color and white as a background color. Choose the Brush tool. Choose a 21-pixel Soft brush from the Brushes palette. In the Options bar, set the opacity to 100%. Pass over the topmost portion of the beetle's body. Set the opacity to 50% and make several passes as you work your way down the beetle's body. Reduce the opacity to 35% as you near the middle part of the beetle's body. The result should be a gradual fade on the layer mask, producing the illusion that the beetle is emerging from the depth of the coffee.

10. Apply the same technique to the legs. You can produce realistic transparency with this technique, as shown in Figure 22.4. Press Option/Alt and click the layer mask thumbnail to view the layer mask, seen in Figure 22.5.

11. To enhance the effect, choose the Magic Wand tool. Set the feather radius in the Options bar to 1 pixel. Target the Cup layer and click on the coffee to select it. Choose Filter → Distort → Zig Zag → Pond Ripples → Amount → 35 Ridges→ 5.

If you make a mistake, choose white as a foreground color and erase it.

Figure 22.2

**Defringe dialog box**

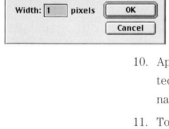

Figure 22.3

**The two images combined with the white fringe removed**

Figure 22.4

**The transparency effect created by the layer mask**

Figure 22.5

**The layer mask**

12. Double-click the cup icon to display the Layer Styles dialog box. Click on the name Drop Shadow to reveal the Drop Shadow controls. Set the opacity to 35%, the angle to 39 degrees, the distance to 22 pixels, and the size to 7 pixels.

13. As a final touch, paint a shadow of the front leg on the cup in 30% gray, then blur it slightly with the Blur tool. The image should look like Figure 22.6, which can be seen here and in Figure C37 of the color section.

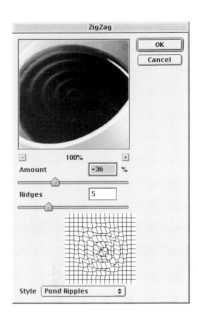

## Seamless Compositing

You often see advertisements in glossy magazines that you know have been "Photoshopped." The non sequitur and the neosurreal images are dead give-aways, and sometimes they are amazingly clever. The image may have a brilliant concept, dazzling colors, and a truly dynamic composition and be perfect in every way—except for a few out-of-place edge pixels. It is unfortunate when a great work of commercial art is just short of perfection, especially when Photoshop has built-in bandages to cover every possible boo-boo.

*Matting* is the key to clean composites. When you select an image, the anti-alias programmed into the selection tool selects edge pixels. When you drag the selection onto another image, the stowaway edge pixels can't be seen until they reach their destination. When you see them, it's usually a row of one or two pixels that are significantly darker or lighter than the color behind them, as in Figure 22.7.

Figure 22.6

**The completed image**

You can easily eliminate unwanted edge pixels by using Photoshop's matting functions. The matting functions eliminate those nasty little fellows and blend your image into the layers beneath it. There are three ways to matte an image, and if your edge pixels are particularly stubborn, there's also a workaround that does the job every time.

In order to matte an image, it must be on an independent layer surrounded by transparency. The three options include:

**Defringe** Choose Layer → Matting → Defringe, and enter a value in the dialog box that is displayed (see Figure 22.2 earlier in this chapter). Defringe is a very effective method of eliminating the off-color edge pixels selected by the anti-alias because it replaces the color of the edge pixels with the colors of the nearby pixels on the layer.

**Remove White or Black Matte** Choose Layer → Matting → Remove White Matte or Remove Black Matte to darken the white edge pixels or lighten the black pixels. This is helpful if you are moving a selection from a white or black background to another background.

**Workaround for Stubborn Edge Pixels** If none of these operations works to your satisfaction—and sometimes you just can't eliminate enough of that edge—here's a neat workaround:

1. Select the image pixels on the layer by pressing ⌘/Ctrl and clicking the thumbnail.

2. Choose Select → Modify → Contract. Enter the amount (in pixels) to contract the selection. View the edge close-up to see how far into the image the marquee has contracted. Undo and enter different values if necessary.

3. Choose Select → Inverse.

4. Choose Select → Feather, and feather the selection 1 pixel.

5. Press Delete/Backspace to delete the edge.

   Or, choose Layer → Add Layer Mask → Reveal All to convert the selection into a layer mask that will conceal the edge pixels.

Figure 22.7

The hand grenade on the top is surrounded by light-colored edge pixels. On the bottom, the edge pixels were removed by defringing.

## Clipping Groups

When you group layers together, you can perform some very interesting graphic tricks. You can literally "tattoo" one image onto the other. With the help of layer masks, layer opacity, and blending modes, you can mold and model the image into superbly realistic forms.

In order to join two layers into a clipping group, the image on the bottom layer must be surrounded by transparency. The layer to be clipped will appear one step higher in the stack. When a layer is clipped, it fills the shape of the image on the layer below it; in other words, the bottom layer acts as a mask to clip the layer immediately above it.

To try out clipping groups, let's clip two layers together to create an "electric" telephone, and then use blending modes and a layer mask to enhance the effect:

1. Open the file in the Ch22 folder on the CD named electric_telephone.psd. The image is separated into three layers: the topmost is the Lightning layer, the middle is the Telephone, and the bottom is the black background (see Figure 22.8).

2. To create a clipping group, press Option/Alt and click between the Lightning and Telephone layers (see Figure 22.9).

3. Experiment with blending modes to enhance effect. Target the Lightning layer and choose Hard Light from the pop-up menu at the top of the Layers palette. The lightning becomes more saturated. Try Pin Light and Linear Light, too. Adjust the Opacity slider to modify the effect.

Figure 22.8

**The beginning electric telephone image is composed of three layers.**

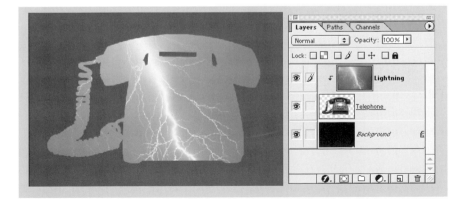

Figure 22.9

**After Option/Alt-clicking between layers, the Lightning layer is shown as a clipping group to the Telephone layer.**

Figure 22.10

**The final image altered
with a layer mask**

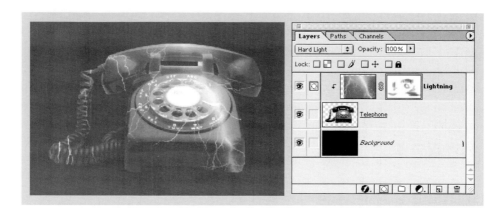

4. You can also add a layer mask to subtly model the telephone. With the Lightning layer targeted, choose Layer → Add Layer Mask → Reveal All.

5. Be sure that the layer mask is targeted. Choose black as a foreground color. Choose the Paintbrush and set its opacity in the Options bar to 20%. Choose a Soft brush from the Brush panel. Paint on the telephone in various places to diminish the effect of the lightning and to enhance the phone's three-dimensionality. If necessary, paint multiple passes to achieve the effect shown in Figure 22.10. Look at the telephone in the color section (Figure C32) to see what happens to your telephone when a bolt of lightning hits a power line!

## Casting Shadows

In Chapter 7, we looked at how to create realistic drop shadows using Photoshop's built-in layer styles. *Cast shadows* are a little different. A drop shadow is quite simply a gray, semi-transparent, soft-edged duplicate of the image from which it is dropped. A cast shadow has all the qualities of a drop shadow, except that it is distorted by the direction of light and the terrain on which it rests. Using layers, you can create a very convincing cast shadow and blend it perfectly into its surroundings.

You can see the beginning and end images from the following steps in the color section (Figures C35 and C36):

1. Open the black_cat.psd file in the Ch22 folder on the CD. The image is composed of two layers named Cat and Background (Figure 22.11).

2. Duplicate the Cat layer by dragging it to the New Layer icon. Name the layer **Shadow**.

3. Lock: ☐ ✐ ✛ 🔒  Check the Transparency lock. Choose black as a foreground color and press Option-Delete/Alt-Backspace to fill the contents of the layer with black. Uncheck the Transparency lock.

4. Drag the Shadow layer between the Cat layer and the Background layer (Figure 22.12).

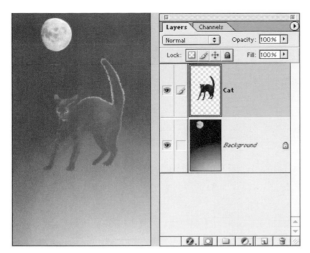

Figure 22.11

**The shadowless cat**

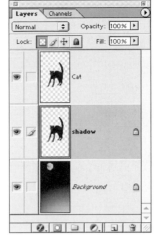

Figure 22.12

**The stacking order of the layers in the Layers palette**

5.  Choose Edit → Transform → Flip Vertical to flip the shadow. Then choose Edit → Transform Distort (see Figure 22.13). Distort the marquee so that the contents of the shadow layer appear to lie on the ground, as in Figure 22.14. You may have to play with this a little to get it to look convincing. When you're satisfied, commit your transformation by pressing Return/Enter.

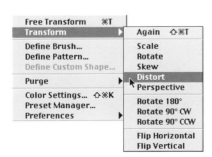

Figure 22.13

**The Edit → Transform → Distort option**

Figure 22.14

**Distort the cast shadow so that it appears to lie on the ground.**

6. Choose Filter → Blur → Gaussian Blur (see Figure 22.15). Drag the slider to 2.3 to soften the edges of the shadow. Click OK.

7. Move the Opacity slider on the Shadow layer to 40% to make it transparent, as you can see in Figure 22.16.

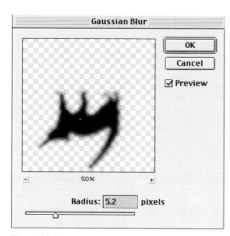

Figure 22.15

**The Gaussian Blur dialog box**

Figure 22.16

**The cat with the cast shadow set to 40% opacity**

Advanced layer techniques extend your capabilities. These methods empower you to manipulate the image content and keep the editing process dynamic. Learn them and practice them—you'll find them indispensable.

# Advanced Layers

*In this project,* you'll try out some of the advanced layer techniques by making layer masks, clipping groups, and a drop shadow and applying matting to clean up edge pixels.

 In the HO8 folder on the CD, open the file `hotel_flamingo_start.psd`. Save the image to your disk. To view the beginning and completed versions of the Flamingo Hotel image, see Figure H8.1 (which is also presented as Figure C57 in the color section) and Figure H8.2 (Figure C58 in the color section).

Hide or discard your preferences file before beginning this Hands On exercise. The "Modifying Photoshop's Settings" section in Chapter 5 details how to temporarily reset your preferences to Photoshop defaults. You can restore your customized personal settings when you're done.

Figure H8.1

**The beginning image (left) with its Layers palette (right)**

## Placing the Parrot in a Window

The image has been divided into two layers and a background. You'll start by dropping in an image from another document, and creating a layer mask to place the parrot in a window of the hotel.

1. Open the file `mr_parrot.psd`.

2. Target the Parrot layer.

3. Choose the Move tool . Drag the Parrot layer to the hotel image. Align it on the fourth large window from the left, as seen in Figure H8.3.

4. Reduce the opacity of the Parrot layer to 60% so that you can see the window behind it.

5. Choose Layer → Add Layer Mask → Reveal All.

6. Choose the Brush tool and a 19-point Hard-Edged brush from the Brush menu in the Options bar. Choose black as a foreground color. With the layer mask targeted, carefully paint out the background and portions of the parrot to give the appearance that the parrot is partially inside the window. Restore the opacity to see the result, as in Figure H8.4.

7. Save your work.

Figure H8.3

**The parrot aligned on the window**

Figure H8.4

**With the layer mask targeted, paint out the background to give the appearance that the parrot is partially inside the building.**

Use the Burn tool to darken areas of the parrot closest to the window to heighten the effect.

## Placing the Crane in the Window

Next you'll place the crane in the window using a layer mask, but with a different twist for concealing the background.

1. Open the File `dr_crane.psd`. Choose the Move tool. Drag the Background onto the hotel image. Align it on the second window from the right. Name the layer **Crane**.

2. Choose the Magic Wand tool. Set the tolerance to 50. Click the blue areas around Dr. Crane to select them.

3. Choose Select → Inverse.

4. Choose Layer → Add Layer Mask → Hide All. The bird disappears, but you can see the selection marquee.

5. In the Tool palette, choose white as the foreground color.

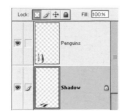

Figure H8.5

**The crane in the window and the Layers palette displaying the layer mask**

6. Press Option-Delete (Mac) or Alt-Backspace (Win) to fill the selected area on the mask and reveal the bird. Check carefully to be sure that all of the blue field has been removed. If there are any edge pixels showing, erase them with the Eraser tool.

7. Deselect. Reduce the layer's opacity to 60%. Choose the Brush tool and select black as a foreground color; on the layer mask, paint out the lower-right portion of the crane so it appears to be partially in the window, as shown in Figure H8.5. Restore the layer to 100% opacity.

8. To enhance the effect, target the Crane layer thumbnail 🖼 and pass over it with the Burn tool to darken the bottom edge of the crane.

9. Save your work.

# Casting the Penguins' Shadow

In these next steps, you'll make an additional layer and distort its contents to cast a shadow.

1. Target the Penguins layer and make it visible. From the Layers Palette pull-down menu, choose Duplicate Layer; name the layer **Shadow**.

2. Drag the Shadow layer beneath the Penguin layer.

3. Check the Transparency lock (see Figure H8.6). Choose black as the foreground color and press Option-Delete or Alt-Backspace to fill the contents of the layer with black. Uncheck the Transparency lock.

4. Choose Edit → Transform → Distort. Distort the marquee so that the contents of the Shadow layer appear to lie on the ground, as in Figure H8.7. You may have to play with this a little to get it to look convincing. When you're satisfied, press the Return/Enter key.

5. Choose Filter → Blur → Gaussian Blur (see Figure H8.8). Drag the slider to 2.3 to soften the edges of the shadow. Click OK.

6. Change the layer to Multiply Blend mode. Move the Opacity slider on the Shadow layer to 40% to make it semitransparent, so that it rests on the ground texture.

7. Save your work.

Figure H8.6

**Layers palette with Transparency lock**

You can use this same shadow technique to create shadows for the flamingo, the parrot, and the crane.

Figure H8.7

**Distorting the penguins' shadow**

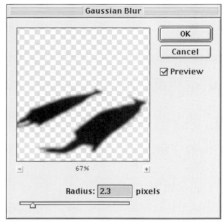

Figure H8.8

**Gaussian Blur dialog box**

# Matting and Placing the Flamingo

Matting removes unwanted pixels that result from selecting and cutting or copying an image from another document or layer.

1. Open the file `Flamingo.psd`.

2. Choose the Magnetic Lasso tool . Drag around the edge of the flamingo, as in Figure H8.9, until you've selected it.

3. Choose the Move tool and drag the flamingo onto the hotel image. Name the new layer **Flamingo**.

4. The flamingo is too large, so let's reduce its size by 50%. Still using the Move tool, check Show Bounding Box in the Options bar. Place your cursor on the upper-left corner of the bounding box, click and drag inward a little bit, and release the mouse. The Options bar now changes to allow you to input numeric values for the transformation (see Figure H8.10).

5. Click the link icon between the Width and Height fields to constrain the proportion of the flamingo. Enter 50% in the Width field. Click the check mark on the Options bar to confirm the transformation.

6. Move the flamingo so that its neck aligns with the center window in the second row of windows from the top (the eighth from the left side).

Figure H8.9

**Selecting the flamingo with the Magnetic Lasso**

Figure H8.10

**Width and Height fields**

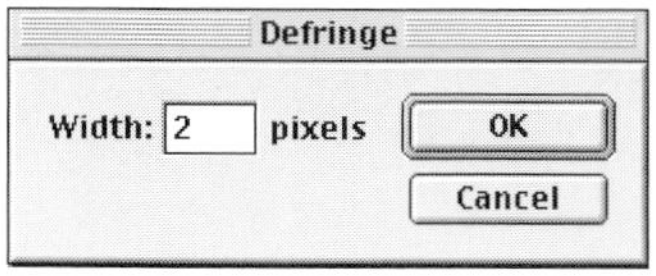

Figure H8.11

**Defringe dialog box**

7.  Choose Layer → Matting → Defringe to eliminate the edge pixels. Enter **2** pixels in the dialog box and click OK (see Figure H8.11).

8.  Choose the Eraser tool and erase the bottom part of the flamingo so that it looks as though its neck is sticking out of the window (see Figure H8.12).

9.  To enhance the effect, use the Burn tool to darken the bottom part of the flamingo's neck.

10.  To further enhance the image, use the cast shadow technique to create a shadow for the flamingo.

11.  Save your work.

## Using Vector Masks

Vector masks are similar to layer masks in that they are designed to conceal parts of an image. (Read about vector masks in Chapter 9, "Drawing Paths.") Follow these steps to use one to conceal part of a seagull:

1.  Open the file `Gulls.psd`.

2.  Select the frontmost gull with the Magnetic Lasso tool.

3.  With the Move tool, drag the selected gull and drop it on the top corner of the hotel. Name the new layer **VectorGull**. Defringe if necessary.

Figure H8.12

**The flamingo and the cast shadow**

4. From the Layers menu, choose Add Vector Mask → Reveal
   All. A vector mask appears next to the VectorGull layer.

5. Choose the Pen tool 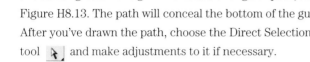. Ensure that the paths and not
   shape layer option is selected. Click along the top edge of
   the building below the gull to create a triangular path, as in
   Figure H8.13. The path will conceal the bottom of the gull.
   After you've drawn the path, choose the Direct Selection
   tool 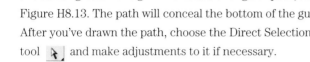 and make adjustments to it if necessary.

6. Save the image.

Figure H8.13

**Creating the
vector mask**

## Creating a Clipping Group

The easiest and most flexible method of placing the gulls in the sky is to create a clipping
group with a Sky layer.

1. Drag the Gulls layer immediately above the Background.

2. Target the Background. Choose the Magic Wand tool and set the tolerance to 50. Click
   on the white area above the hotel.

3. Choose Layer → New → Layer Via Copy. Name the new layer **Sky**.

4. Place your cursor on the line between the Sky layer and the Gulls layer above it. Press
   Option/Alt and click your mouse. The Gulls layer is now clipped to the Sky layer, taking its shape.

5. Target the Gulls layer. Choose the Move tool; drag the Gulls layer inside the clip until
   you are satisfied with its position.

6. Target the Gulls layer. Drop the layers and the fill to 67% to subdue the gulls a
   little. The image should look like Figure H8.2 (see the image's Layers palette in
   Figure H8.14).

7. Save the image.

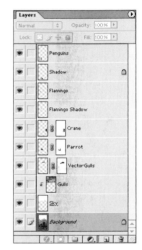

Figure H8.14

**The Layers palette of the
Flamingo Hotel image**

On the CD in the H08 → More Birds folder, there are additional images to add to the
Flamingo Hotel to practice layer mask techniques.

# CHAPTER 23

# Automating the Process

*When working in Photoshop,* you often repeat tasks. For example, if you publish a lot of work on the Web, you may regularly convert files from RGB to Indexed color mode before you save them as GIFs. Here's another: Let's say you want to place all of the images in a folder into a single document to make a contact sheet for comparison. Opening, sizing, and pasting the images can be tedious, time-consuming work.

Building a Web site is a lot of work too. Wouldn't it be nice if there was some way to accomplish this by simply pressing a button? This chapter is about Photoshop's magic buttons called Actions and Automation. These operations can greatly accelerate your workflow by automatically performing tedious and repetitious tasks. You can perform most Actions and automations on either single or multiple documents, and you can save them and store them for later use.

You'll learn how to:

- Set up an Action
- Apply Actions to a batch of images
- Create contact sheets, picture packages, and a Web photo gallery
- Create Droplets

# Creating and Applying Actions

When a multimillion-dollar Hollywood movie is produced, everybody involved in the production, including the director, actors, and cinematographer, follows a script. A script is simply written dialog with accompanying directions. Just like the movies, computers also use scripts. Unlike actors, however, computers never ad-lib; they follow the script to the letter! When you record an Action, you are actually writing a script that tells the software what sequence of operations to perform. Fortunately, recording a script for Photoshop is a lot easier than writing a script for a movie.

Almost any single operation or sequence of operations can be recorded into an Action, except for some of the manual tools like the Airbrush and Paintbrush. You can program an Action to select the Paintbrush, but you can't create an Action to paint with that brush. Likewise, the zoom tools, window commands, and view commands cannot be recorded. The tools from which you can record an Action are the Marquees, Polygon, Lasso, Magic Wand, Crop, Slice, Magic Eraser, Gradient, Paint Bucket, Type, Shape, Line, Note, Eyedropper, and Color Sampler. You can record many of the menu commands, but you can't make an Action out of program preference changes.

Before you record an Action, envision the end product first. Try to imagine what you want the image to look like. Then ask yourself what processes need to be applied in order to accomplish that end. It's also a good idea to "walk through" and test the steps before recording them.

As you will see, Actions are flexible. You can create a sequence of Actions and then apply a single Action from the sequence to your image. Or you can apply the same Action with different settings to the image.

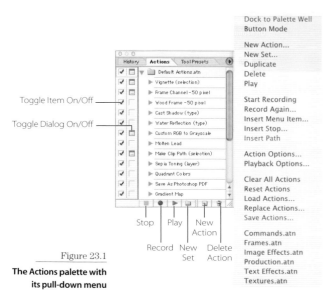

Figure 23.1

**The Actions palette with its pull-down menu**

## The Actions Palette

Actions are recorded and played in the Actions palette, shown with its pull-down menu in Figure 23.1. Choose Window → Actions to access the palette. When you first open the palette, you see a "set" called Default Actions.atn. A *set* is simply a folder where groups of Actions are stored. Every Action must be contained within a set.

Expand the Default Actions set by clicking its down arrow. You'll see a list of Actions that Adobe includes with Photoshop. Actions are applied to the image in sequence from top to bottom. When a check mark appears in the Item On/Off box (in the far-left column of the palette) next to an Action or set's name,

it will be applied to the image when played. If
the item isn't checked, the Action will be
skipped. By checking or clearing the Item
On/Off boxes, you can determine which
Actions will be applied in a sequence. When
the Dialog On/Off box (in the second column of
the Actions palette) is checked, the Action will
pause to display a dialog box so that you can
change the settings.

Figure 23.2

**The toddler, selected**

The pull-down menu provides commands to
save, load, duplicate, and create new Actions
and sets. Button mode displays a button interface on the Actions palette; in this mode, you
simply click an Action's name to run it with the
default or existing settings. The bottom section
of the Actions pull-down menu provides many
additional default Actions. Just click one of these Actions to load it in the Actions palette.
Experiment with the default Actions and get to know their capabilities.

> Actions can be nested within other Action Sets; you'll notice that the Actions inside the
> Default Actions set have, in turn, substeps. These are also Actions, but for clarity, I'll refer to
> these "sub-Actions" as *operations within an Action*.

## Applying an Action Step by Step

To see how the Actions palette applies commands to an image, let's try running one of the
Default Actions. In this exercise, we'll create a vignette of an image.

1. Open the `Toddler.psd` file in the `Ch23` folder on the CD. Duplicate the file (Image →
   Duplicate) and save the copy to your disk.

2. Choose the Elliptical Marquee ⬚ . Place your cursor
   on the center of the image.
   Click Option/Alt and drag to generate an elliptical selection from a center point (see
   Figure 23.2).

3. Expand the Default Actions set. Target the Vignette
   Action and expand it to display the sequence of operations contained within the Action (see Figure 23.3).

Figure 23.3

**The Vignette Action
and its operations**

4. We will use the default settings, so click each of the Dialog On/Off icons ▣ in the second column on the left, to turn off each one.

5. Target the Vignette Action and click the triangular Play button ▶ at the bottom of the Actions palette. When the Action has finished running, the image should look like Figure 23.4.

## Recording an Action

Of course, you can create your own Actions and apply them to images. You can name, color-code, and specify a function key for an Action so that all you have to do is press the key to apply it. We'll go through making an Action step by step as we perform a tonal adjustment, eliminate moiré patterns, convert, and colorize an image. We'll work on two images cut from an old yearbook.

Figure 23.4

**The Vignette operations applied to the toddler image**

1. Open the file Becky_1964.psd from the Ch23 folder on the CD.

2. Choose Window → Actions. From the pull-down menu, choose New Set. Name the set **Yearbook Photos**, as in Figure 23.5.

Figure 23.5

**New Set dialog**

New Set

Name: Yearbook Photos        OK
                             Cancel

3. From the pull-down menu, choose New Action. In the dialog box, name the Action **Becky** (see Figure 23.6). From the Function Key menu, choose Shift F2. Click the Record button ● on the Actions palette. The button turns red to remind you that your next steps will be recorded.

Figure 23.6

**New Action dialog**

New Action

Name: Becky                          Record
Set: Yearbook Photos        ↕        Cancel
Function Key: F2   ↕   ☑ Shift  ☐ Command
Color: ☐None   ↕

4. Choose Image → Adjustments → Levels. Drag the Black Shadow slider until the value in the box reads 10. Drag the White Highlight slider to 189 and the Gray Midtone slider to 1.34. Click OK.

5. Choose Filter → Blur → Gaussian Blur, and set the Radius to 1.0 to eliminate the moiré pattern.

6. Choose Filter → Sharpen → Unsharp Mask and set the following values: Amount: 66%, Radius: 3.4 pixels, Threshold: 2 levels.

7. Choose Image → Mode → RGB Color to convert the image so that you can colorize it.

8. Choose Image → Adjustments → Hue/Saturation and check Colorize. Enter 239 for the Hue, 12 for the Saturation, and 0 for the Lightness. Click OK.

9. Click the Stop Recording ■ button. The Actions palette should look like Figure 23.7, and the image should look like the "after" version in Figure 23.8. We'll use this recorded set throughout this chapter.

Figure 23.7

**The Actions palette with the Year-book Photos Actions Set and the Becky Actions**

Watch out—you need to exercise caution when recording. Remember that almost anything you do is being recorded. If the image does not appear the way you want it to or if you if you make a mistake, stop recording, drag the Action or Action Set step to the trash, and rerecord it.

Figure 23.8

**The Becky 1964 year-book image before (left) and after (right) the Yearbook Photos set was applied**

## Applying Actions to Another Image

Obviously, the main purpose of using Actions is to repeat a command or series of commands. But because the settings often need to be readjusted to achieve good results on a different image, you can stop the Action during the process of applying it. In this exercise, you'll apply the Actions recorded in the preceding section to a second image, which will require that you change some of the settings as the action is playing.

1. Open `Becky_1965.psd` from the `Ch23` folder on the CD.

2. In the Actions palette, click the Dialog On/Off icons (in the second column) next to Levels, Gaussian Blur, and Unsharp Mask to turn them on, so that the Action will pause and present the operation's dialog box. You can make the necessary changes to accommodate the different image and then continue to run the action.

3. Target the Becky Action and press Shift-F2. The Play button turns red.

4. As the action runs, enter new values in the dialog boxes as they appear. Levels: 15 for the shadow and 220 for the highlight; Gaussian Blur 0.8; Unsharp Mask Amount 47%, Radius 2.9 pixels, and Threshold 4 levels. Click OK in each box. The new settings are applied, and the Action continues to run. The Convert Mode and Hue/Saturation operations are applied without interruption. The image will look like Figure 23.9.

Figure 23.9

**The Becky 1965 image, before (left) and after (right) the Becky Actions have been applied**

## Inserting a Stop

You can pause any Action in order to perform a task that is not recordable, such as painting a stroke with the Paintbrush. To insert a stop:

1. Select the Action or operation at the end of which you want to insert the stop.

2. Choose Insert Stop from the Actions Palette pull-down menu.

3. In the dialog box that appears, type a message that reminds you what to do manually (see Figure 23.10). Check the Allow Continue box if you want to display a dialog box that lets you choose to stop or continue. Click OK.

Figure 23.10

**Record Stop dialog box**

## Undoing an Action

Because an Action is a sequence of operations, choosing Edit → Undo or pressing ⌘-Z (Mac) or Ctrl-Z (Win) will undo only the last operation in the sequence, not the entire Action. Instead, press ⌘-Option-Z or Ctrl-Alt-Z as many times as necessary to step backwards through the operations. You can also undo a sequence of Actions by clicking the state in the History palette just above the first applied state of the Action.

## Saving and Loading an Action

Once you've compiled a series of operations into an Action, you'll want to save the Action to your disk. From the Actions pull-down palette, choose Save Actions with the Action Set targeted. Then choose a destination on the disk. Add the extension `.atn` to the Action's name. (Even Mac users should do this, both to anticipate platform problems and to identify the file as an Action.) To load an Action, choose Load Action from the pull-down menu and locate the file where you saved it.

Actions must be saved and loaded in sets.

## Controlling the Speed of an Action

The Playback Options dialog box (from the Actions palette pull-down menu) lets you control how fast an Action is played. Choosing Accelerated plays the Action as quickly as possible (see Figure 23.11). Step By Step waits until the Action is finished and the image redrawn before playing the next Action. Pause lets you enter a number in seconds between operations within an action.

Figure 23.11

**Playback Options dialog box**

### Editing, Moving, and Discarding an Action

You can edit the settings of an operation within an Action when it's not running by double-clicking its name in the Actions palette. A document must be open in order to do this (although you can insert a stop with no document open). The operation's dialog box appears so you can change the settings. The next time you run the Action, the new settings will be applied.

Actions can be repositioned in the stack. An Action's position in the stack can greatly affect the final outcome of the image. To reposition an Action, click and drag it within the Actions palette; release the mouse when it's positioned in the desired location.

To discard an Action, drag it to the trash icon in the Actions palette.

### Inserting Unrecordable Commands

Some menu items that cannot be recorded as Actions can be inserted at the end of an Action. To insert a menu item:

1. Target an Action in the Actions palette by clicking it.

2. Choose Insert Menu Item from the Actions palette pull-down menu.

3. With the Insert Menu Item dialog box displayed, choose a command from the menu at the top of the screen.

## Automation Operations

So far we've applied Actions to images manually. Hmmmm… manual automation? Sounds like an oxymoron, doesn't it? Wouldn't it be really cool if we could apply Actions automatically while we were away from the computer, maybe strolling in the park or dining out? "Why would he mention it if it couldn't be done?" you might be asking yourself right now. Yes, it can be done. And there are several ways to do it….

### Batch Processing

You can apply actions to multiple files within a folder by choosing File → Automate → Batch; the Batch dialog box is shown in Figure 23.12. This formidable-looking interface lets you apply a set, a group of Actions, or a single Action. You can batch-process a group of images within a folder, or from an external source such as a digital camera or scanner with a document feeder. (But note that your scanner or digital camera may need an Acquire plug-in to support batch processing.) You can then automatically save the images within the folder, or save them to new folders leaving the originals unchanged.

For better performance when batch-processing images, go to the History palette. Decrease the number of saved History states and turn off Automatically Create First Snapshot.

To batch-process a group of images, choose File →
Automate → Batch. Under Play, choose the Set and
Action that you want to run from the pop-up lists.
Then choose your input method from the Source list:

**Figure 23.12**

**The Batch dialog box**

**Import**  Applies the images on a scanner or digital
camera.

**Opened Files**  Plays the Action on open files.

**Folder**  Runs the Action on all of the images within a
selected folder. Click Choose to locate and select the
folder, and then select the following check-box
options as desired. (You can also apply the Action
within the File Browser.)

> **Override Action "Open" Commands**  Ignores any
> Open commands that are part of the Action, to
> ensure that the images are opened from specified
> folder. Select this option when you want Open commands in the Action to refer to the
> batched files, rather than to the filenames specified in the Action. If you enable this
> option, the Action must contain an Open command because the Batch command will not
> automatically open the source files.

> **Include All Subfolders**  Affects the contents of any folders within the selected folder.

> **Suppress Color Profile Warnings**  Turns off the color policy and profile mismatch
> messages.

For the Destination, choose from these options for the batch-processed files from the
Destination pop-up list:

**None**  Leaves the files open without saving changes (unless the Action included a Save
command).

**Save And Close**  Saves the files in the source folder.

**Folder**  Lets you specify a new location for the batch-processed files. Click Choose to locate
and select the folder, and enable the following check-box option if desired.

> **Override Action "Save In" Commands**  Ignores any Save As commands that are part of
> the Action, to ensure that the specified files are saved to the destination folder. Select
> this option when you want the Save As commands in the Action to refer to the batched
> files, rather than to the filenames and locations specified in the Action. If you enable this
> option, the Action must contain a Save As command because the Batch command will
> not automatically save to the destination file.

The Batch command always saves the files in the same format as the original. To create a batch-processing operation that saves files in a new format, record the Save As or Save A Copy command. Designate a location within the Action, followed by the Close command. In the Batch dialog box, choose None for the Destination.

### File Naming

File naming is available if you selected a folder as the destination. You can determine how batch-processed files will be named, as well as their platform compatibility.

Choose from pop-up menus or type into the fields to create file-naming conventions. Determine the naming convention for the document name, identification number or letter, date, and filename extension. The fields let you change the order and formatting of the filenames. For File Name Compatibility, choose Windows, MacOS, and/or Unix.

### Error Processing

You can choose an option for error processing from the Errors pop-up menu. Stop For Errors pauses the operation until you OK the error message. Log Errors To File records any errors in a separate log file. The error message appears after the process is complete. Click Save As and name the error file.

### Creating and Using Droplets

A Droplet is a mini application that can play an Action. You can apply a single Action or series of Actions by dragging a file or folder onto the Droplet's icon. This way you don't even have to open the program in order to apply the Action—the Droplet will automatically do that for you. The Create Droplet dialog box is quite similar to the Batch dialog box. To create a Droplet from an Action, choose File → Automate → Create Droplet (Figure 23.13).

Under Save Droplet In, click Choose. Determine a location for the Droplet. Choose a Set and an Action from pop-up menus. Set the Play and Destination options for the Droplet as described for the Source and Destination options in the earlier section "Batch Processing").

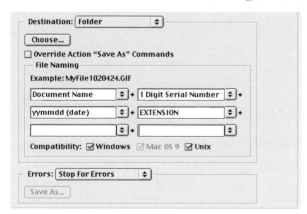

Figure 23.13

**The Create Droplet dialog box**

## Using a Droplet to Apply an Action

Let's make a Droplet from the Becky Action we recorded in the previous section, "Recording an Action," and apply it to an image.

1. Choose File → Automate → Create Droplet.

2. In the Create Droplet dialog box, do the following: For the Save Droplet In option, click Choose and choose the Desktop of your computer. For Set, choose Yearbook Photos; for Action, choose Becky.

3. In the Play section, clear the check boxes for Override Action "Open" Commands, Include All Subfolders, and Suppress Color Profile Warnings.

4. For Destination, choose Folder. Click Choose and determine a location for the Droplet's icon.

5. Leave the default filenames, and the Stop for Errors default.

6. Click OK and the Droplet will appear  in the specified location.

7. On your desktop, open the Ch23 folder on the CD. Drag the icon of the Vicky.psd image onto the Droplet icon.

8. The adjustments for this photograph will be different from the ones recorded in the Action. As the Levels, Gaussian Blur, and Unsharp Mask dialog boxes appear, make adjustments to improve the image.

9. Open the image in the destination folder to observe the changes to the image. Your image should look better, perhaps something like Figure 23.14.

Figure 23.14

**Vicky before (left) and after (right) after being dragged to the Droplet**

# Other Automation Commands

The File → Automate commands are a group of commonly used Actions consolidated into a dialog box. You can configure options that vary the outcome of the image. Some of the Automate commands convert files to other formats or construct files into contact sheets.

## Conditional Mode Change

You can change the color mode of a document while in an Action by recording File → Automate → Conditional Mode Change. Choose the modes that you need changed, or click

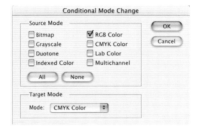

All to choose any mode. If your Action encounters a file in an unchecked mode, it will leave that file unchanged. Then choose a target mode. Click OK and the document's mode will be converted to the target mode. The advantage of Conditional Mode Change (over, say, the Image → Mode submenu) is that this command allows your Action to avoid any error messages that occur when an image is required to be in a specific color mode, or is already in the desired mode.

## Contact Sheet II

This command produces a new document of thumbnail previews on a single sheet from the files in a folder. Choose File → Automate → Contact Sheet II to display the Contact Sheet dialog box (Figure 23.15). Choose a source folder from which to make the document, and specify a width, height, resolution, and mode for the document. In the Thumbnails field, Place determines whether the sequence of files will be placed horizontally or vertically. Choose the number of columns and rows. Check the box if you want to add the file's name as a caption, but be aware that this will make the images somewhat smaller. You can also choose a font and a size for the caption. The preview on the right side of the dialog box displays the layout of the contact sheet.

I've provided a folder of images on the CD so you can try out making a contact sheet.

1. Choose File → Automate → Contact Sheet II.

2. Click Choose. On the CD in the Ch23 folder, click the Contact_Sheet folder, then click Choose.

3. In the Contact Sheet II dialog box, use these settings:

| | |
|---|---|
| Width | 8 |
| Height | 10 |
| Resolution | 72 |
| Mode | Grayscale |
| Place | Across first |
| Columns | 3 |
| Rows | 3 |

4. Check the Use Filename As Caption box. For Font, choose Arial; for Font Size, enter **10**.

5. Click OK… and wait! This process can take a while. But eventually, an image that looks like Figure 23.16 will appear on-screen.

## Fit Image

This command will fit an image to a specified width or height without changing its aspect ratio. Keep in mind that this operation resamples the image, changing the amount of data in the image. When entering the Width and Height in pixels, the command chooses the smaller of the two numbers in which to configure the image.

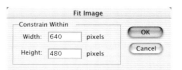

## Multi-Page PDF To PSD

Use this command to convert the pages of an Adobe Acrobat PDF document into separate Photoshop files. Choose the source folder and page range of the PDF file, specify the resolution and color mode of the new Photoshop documents, and choose a destination folder.

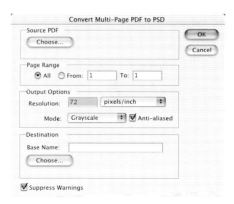

## Picture Package

The Picture Package command creates a document with multiple copies of an active image on a single page. This feature is used to assemble a sheet of multiple copies of one image, the kind you might receive from a portrait studio, for example. The Picture Package dialog box (Figure 23.17) lets you choose an image from a file, folder, or the frontmost document open in Photoshop. Choose from a list of layout options and a resolution and mode for the new document. The display on the right of the dialog box shows a preview of the picture package layout.

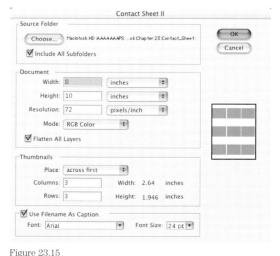

Figure 23.15

**The Contact Sheet II dialog box**

Figure 23.16

**The contact sheet**

Figure 23.17

**The Picture Package dialog box**

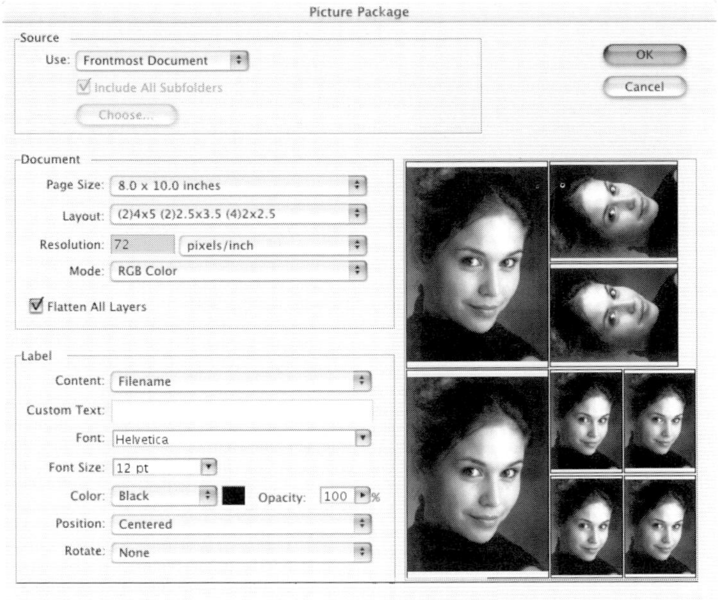

## Web Photo Gallery

The Web Photo Gallery feature is a quick way to put your images online and offers a number of sophisticated navigational features that simplify Web publication. It automatically creates an HTML document, an index page, individual JPEG image pages, and hyperlinks to your specifications. Photoshop generates the code and the source files and places them in folders that can be uploaded to your FTP site. To create a Web site, choose File → Automate → Web Photo Gallery. A dialog box (Figure 23.18) is displayed.

**Styles** Choose from Simple, Table, Vertical Frame, or Horizontal Frame styles with several variations of backgrounds and automated slide shows. The graphic on the right of the dialog box displays the layout.

**Email** This feature generates a mail link in the Web site with the e-mail address you specify.

**Extension** Choose from three characters (.htm) or four characters (.html) as a filename extension on your HTML-coded documents. Three-character extensions are a better bet for displaying your site on older browsers.

**Folders** Choose a source folder from which the JPEG images will be generated. Select a destination folder for the HTML documents and image folders that are created.

**Options** When you choose an option from this pull-down menu, the field changes to display its specifications. Enter the desired configuration for the site's elements:

**Banners** Specify a site name, photo credit, contact info, and copyright information. Date the site and choose type specifications for the HTML text that is generated.

**Large Images** Choose the size and quality of the large JPEG images. You can also specify a border size and title content.

**Thumbnails** Choose the size, layout, titles, and font usage for the site's thumbnail images.

**Custom Colors** Select the gallery's background, banner, and link colors. Click a swatch and choose a color from the color picker.

**Security** Enter labels and copyright information for the gallery images.

Figure 23.18

**The Web Photo Gallery dialog box**

# CHAPTER 24

# Overlay Techniques

*One of Adobe Photoshop's* greatest strengths is its ability to combine images. In Chapters 7 and 22 you mastered the power of compositing with layers. Image parts separated into layers can effectively be superimposed on each other. Furthermore, images from multiple sources can be collaged together and precisely tuned with layer masks and clipping groups. We saw in Chapters 6 and 21 that, like layers, alpha channels can also be combined. The process of combining images from multiple sources takes many forms and is one of Photoshop's most useful features. In this chapter, we're going to look at industrial-strength image compositing.

You will learn how to:

- **Superimpose images to enhance their quality**
- **Create artistic effects by applying images**
- **Use calculations to combine complex selections**

# Layer-Based Compositing

Imagine that you have two different transparencies on a light table, one on top of another. When you look at them through a magnifying loupe, you see the effect of combined colors on the two superimposed images. Opposite colors like reds and greens may cancel each other and produce areas of dark gray, while colors that are closer to each other on the color wheel, like reds and yellows, may produce richer, more saturated oranges.

Now imagine that you have duplicates of the *same* transparency on the light table, and you are able to "sandwich in" filters that produce a variety of color relations between the two superimposed images. In Photoshop, these are the *blending modes,* and you apply them to an image in the Layers palette. The blending modes, which are described in Appendix C and illustrated in the Color Section, can be used to enhance color on an image. When you super-impose one layer on another, you can apply a layer effect to alter the color relationships and then precisely control the result by adjusting the opacity of the layer.

To demonstrate this effect, open the file `Rinocerose.psd` from the `Ch24` folder on the CD. Figure 24.1 shows before and after versions of the image. (See color versions, C53 and C54, in the color section.) The original image on the left is divided into two layers. It lacks rich colors and appears flat.

1. Hide the Rose layer by clicking the eye symbol  next to it in the first column of the Layers palette. Target the Rose layer.

Figure 24.1

**The original image (left) lacks rich colors and appears flat. Stacking layers with similar content and applying a blending mode and opacity and fill adjustments can greatly enhance an image's contrast and color (right).**

2. Choose the Magnetic Lasso  and drag it around the rhinoceros. The Magnetic Lasso will most likely not make a perfect selection, so you'll need to add to and subtract from the selection with the Lasso tool ⌇ or the Quick Mask ▣ .

3. Choose Layer → New → Layer Via Copy to copy the rhino to a new layer. Name the new layer **Rhino**.

4. Target the new layer and choose Vivid Light from the Mode pull-down menu. It looks more saturated but a little too "contrasty."

5. Drag the Fill slider to 88% to diminish the contrast. Drag the Opacity slider to 76% to bring out a little more detail in the shadow areas.

6. We'll now enhance the rose. Click the Rose layer's eye icon again.

7. Drag the Rose layer to the New Layer icon to duplicate it. Name the layer **Vivid Rose**.

8. Choose Linear Light from the Mode menu, and reduce the fill to 55% to enhance the detail.

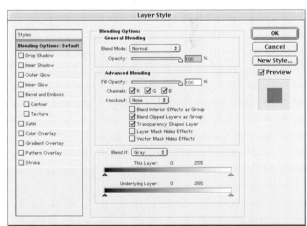

The image now appears much richer. The colors in the targeted areas are more saturated and have better contrast. Experiment with creating additional layers and applying different blend modes at varying degrees of opacity to vary the effect.

## Excluding Colors

Use Photoshop's Layer Style dialog box (Figure 24.2) to exclude colors in the image. Advanced Blending excludes targeted information in a specific channel. With the exclusion sliders, you can omit colors of a specific brightness value. To demonstrate how these sliders work, open the file `Heavenly_Roses.psd` (Figure 24.3) from the `Ch24` folder on the CD.

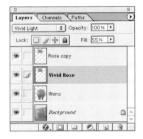

1. The image is divided into a layer and a Background. Double-click the Rose Layer icon, to display the Layer Style dialog box.

2. First, clear all of the Channels boxes. The image of the roses disappears. Now check the red (R) box only. The channel information from the Red channel appears and affects the underlying layer. The Red channel appears to contain most of the detail of the red rose.

Figure 24.2

**The Advanced Blending controls in the Layer Style dialog box**

Figure 24.3

**The Heavenly Roses image**

If you were to look at the information for the Rose layer in the Channels palette, you would see that the Red channel contains most of the detail of the red rose and more pixels with higher brightness values.

3. Check the green box and uncheck the red and blue boxes. Notice that there is more detail on the green rose when the green box is checked. The same is true for the blue rose.

4. Check all of the boxes to display the roses in full color.

   You will now use the exclusion sliders to omit pixels of a specific brightness value within each channel.

1. Make sure Blend If is set to Gray.

2. Move the black This Layer slider to the right until the shadow value reads 90, as in Figure 24.4. The darker pixels in the roses disappear.

3. Press Option (Mac) or Alt (Win) and click Reset. In the Blend If pull-down menu, choose Red. Move the black This Layer slider to the right until it reads 90. The dark pixels on the green and blue roses disappear, but almost all of the pixels on the red layer remain.

4. Press the Option/Alt key and click Reset. Now move the white slider to the left, until the highlight value reads 96. The red rose almost completely disappears.

If you use exclusion sliders to omit pixels of a specific brightness range from the layer, you force colors to disappear. This can produce harsh color transitions and jagged edges. You can diminish the effect by adjusting the Fuzziness setting, which softens the transition. Here's how: Press Option/Alt and click Reset. This time, press the Option/Alt key as you drag the *left half* of the white slider to the left. The effect on the red rose produces a softer edge, as in Figure 24.5.

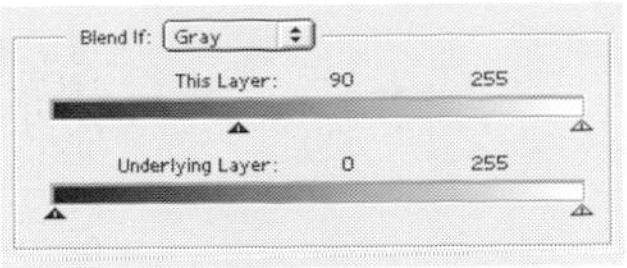

Figure 24.4

**Setting the channel options to Gray and the black exclusion slider to 90**

## Channel-Based Compositing

Adobe once counted channel-based compositing among Photoshop's most powerful features. The extensive layer compositing techniques introduced in recent versions of Photoshop have, to a certain extent, made this capability redundant. It still, however, allows you to apply additional modes that, even in Photoshop 7, have not been added to the Layers palette. Photoshop's two channel-based compositing techniques are the Apply Image command and the Calculations command.

## Apply Image

The Apply Image command applies a source image to the target image. To use Apply Image, both images have to be open on the desktop. The images must be exactly the same physical size and resolution.

First, let's look at the Apply Image dialog box (Figure 24.6) to understand what its commands do. To access it, choose Image → Apply Image.

**Source** This is the image that is applied, or overlaid. Choose the desired image from the pop-up list.

**Layer** The pop-up lists all of the layers and the Background in the source image. You can overlay all the layers if you choose Merged.

**Channel** Select the channels you apply to the image from this list. If you choose the composite channel (RGB, CMYK, etc.), the entire channel will be mixed.

**Invert** Check the box to invert the contents of the selected channel. Pixels that are black will be applied as if they are white and vice versa.

**Target** This is the image that is active. The target lists the channel(s) and layers that the image will be applied to.

**Blending** The pop-up list displays the blending modes in which the color will be applied (see Appendix C, "Blending Modes," for a description of each mode).

**Opacity** Enter the opacity of the mode.

Figure 24.5

**You can achieve softer transitions by pressing the Option or Alt key while dragging half of a slider.**

Figure 24.6

**You can use the Apply Image dialog box for channel-based compositing.**

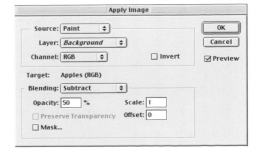

**Preserve Transparency**  This check box leaves transparent areas on a layer unaffected.

**Mask**  Checking this option masks off a part of the source image. When you choose Mask, the Apply Image dialog box expands. From the menus, choose an image and a layer. Choose a

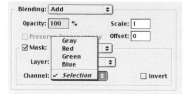

color channel, an alpha channel, or an active selection on the source image to isolate the application of the affect.

**Scale and Offset**  If you choose either the Add or Subtract modes, you can enter values for scale and offset. These values are used in the calculation to determine the brightness values of the superimposed pixels. (See Appendix C.)

The Apply Image command can produce some beautiful artistic effects. You can vary the results by choosing different settings. We'll start with a sepia watercolor, then apply a broadly painted version of the image and mitigate the effect by adjusting the blending modes and the opacity.

1. Open the `Apples.psd` file in the `Ch24` folder on the CD (Figure 24.7). For this exercise, refer to the full-color versions of this image included in the color section (Figures C39a–e).

2. Choose Image → Duplicate to make a copy of the image. Name the new image **Paint**.

3. With the painting tools, color the image with broad strokes as in Figure C39b.

4. Click the `Apples.psd` image to make it active.

> The image that is active will become the target image.

5. Choose Image → Apply Image. Enter the following, then click OK:

| | |
|---|---|
| Source | Paint image |
| Layer | Background |
| Channel | RGB |
| Blending | Subtract |
| Opacity | 50% |

6. Try different combinations of modes, channels, and opacities to produce vastly different results.

## Overlaying Graphics

Apply Image can also be used to produce interesting overlay graphic effects. In Chapter 17, "Modifying and Mapping Color," we created a posterization and a halftone from the same image. You can combine these two types of images to produce a strong posterized halftone effect. You can vary the effect by applying different values, modes, and opacities.

1. Open the images `Listerine_poster.psd` and `Listerine_halftone.psd` from the `Ch24` folder on the CD.

Figure 24.7

**Use this sepia-toned watercolor to experiment with the Apply Image command.**

2. Click on `Listerine_halftone.psd` to activate it. Choose Image → Mode → Grayscale to convert the bitmapped image to a grayscale.

Channel-based compositing techniques do not work on Bitmap images. It is therefore necessary to convert their mode.

3. Click `Listerine_poster.psd` to activate it. It will be the target document.

4. Choose Image → Apply Image. Enter the following specifications and click OK:

| | |
|---|---|
| Source | `Listerine_halftone.psd` |
| Layer | Background |
| Channel | Gray |
| Blending | Add |
| Opacity | 40% |

The halftone image is applied to the target. (Figure 24.8 shows the before and after results.)

5. Try different combinations of modes, channels, and opacities to produce different results.

Figure 24.8

The posterized
image (a), the
halftone (b),
and the halftone
superimposed on
the posterized image
using the Apply
Image feature (c).

(a)  (b)  (c)

Figure 24.8

The posterized image (a), the halftone (b), and the halftone superimposed on the posterized image using the Apply Image feature (c).

## Calculations

Despite the complexity of its dialog box, the Calculations command actually performs a rather simple operation—it creates only one channel. Image → Calculations works exclusively to combine two source channels into a new channel. Like the Apply Image command, it calculates the numerical values of pixels and applies a mode or mathematical formula to produce results. The difference is that it uses the information on individual channels to produce a new selection, a new alpha channel, or a new document. The Calculations command has three purposes: to create a new grayscale image, or to combine two masks into either a single alpha channel or an active selection.

Like Apply Image, this command requires the images to be exactly the same height, width, and resolution. When you go to Image → Calculations, you see the Calculations dialog box (Figure 24.9). It's quite similar to the Apply Image dialog box; the only difference is the additional source. The two source areas let you choose two channels to combine.

Let's combine a couple of alpha channels to see how the Calculations command works.

1.  From the Ch24 folder on the CD, open the document Cowpoke.psd (Figure 24.10).

2.  Look at the Channels palette. Alpha 1 is a channel of the circle surrounding the cowboy; Alpha 2 is the outline of the cowboy. You are going to combine the two channels into a third.

3. Choose Image → Calculations. Enter the following:

| | |
|---|---|
| Source 1 | Cowpoke.psd |
| Channel | Alpha 1 |
| Source 2 | Cowpoke.psd |
| Channel | Alpha 2 |
| Blending | Difference |
| Result | New Channel |

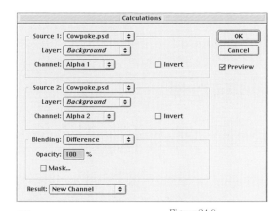

Figure 24.9

**The Calculations dialog box**

4. Click OK, and Photoshop creates the Alpha 3 channel, which combines Alpha 1 and Alpha 2 (see Figure 24.11).

5. You can also use the Calculations command to blend channels from two source documents and create a new grayscale document. Open the file Cowboy_Sky.psd from the Ch24 folder on the CD. Then click Cowpoke.psd to reactivate it.

6. Choose Image → Calculations. Enter the following:

| | |
|---|---|
| Source 1 | Cowpoke.psd |
| Channel | Gray |
| Source 2 | Cowboy_Sky.psd |
| Channel | Blue |
| Blending | Darken |
| Result | New Document |

Figure 24.10

**The cowpoke image and its Channels palette**

7. Click OK. A new document is created, combining the composite Gray channel of the Cowpoke.psd document and the Blue channel from the Cowboy_Sky.psd document (see Figure 24.12 on the next page).

The Calculations feature is complex, to say the least, and as always there are several workarounds that perform the same operations. Mastering it, however, gives you the skills you need to quickly combine channels, and that can extend your selection-making capabilities.

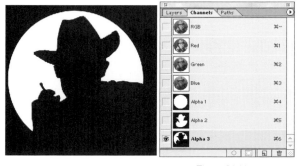

Figure 24.11

**The new combined alpha channel**

Figure 24.12

This image was created by using Calculations to combine the Gray channel of the cowpoke with the Blue channel of the cowboy sky.

# PART IV

# Photoshop, WWW, and DV

As you've seen, *Photoshop is versatile at producing images for print media. It is the tool of choice for preparing files for CMYK conversion and for output to any printing device. Photoshop's versatility extends further into the world of electronic publications like Web sites. With Photoshop in combination with its Web-authoring sibling, ImageReady, you can produce killer interactive Web sites with animations and rollovers. Furthermore, Photoshop is a great program for preparing files for output to digital video nonlinear editing systems like Adobe Premier. The two chapters in Part IV cover how you can use Photoshop for publishing images to the Web and with digital video.*

# CHAPTER 25

# Web Design with Photoshop and ImageReady

*The Web* is the world's most recent and dynamic publishing phenomenon. It gives you instant access to an enormous amount of information and entertainment. The Web is like having at your fingertips a several-million-volume encyclopedia that is revised hourly with the latest information. In addition to being able to access information, you can also publish your ideas and images instantaneously on the Web. Photoshop has many features that enable you to efficiently publish images to the Web.

Adobe, recognizing the need for streamlined, Web-specific software, bundles ImageReady with Photoshop to provide powerful tools to the Web designer. ImageReady can help you create images and generate HTML code for browser-ready Web sites. ImageReady is fairly easy to learn because, in many respects, it closely resembles Photoshop. In fact, the two programs share many of the same capabilities.

This chapter covers the cool Web-related stuff that Photoshop and ImageReady can do. It will take you through several step-by-step processes so that you can begin creating, optimizing, and adding interactivity to images and animations for the Web.

This chapter includes these topics:

- **Creating Web page elements**
- **Optimizing images**
- **Slicing graphics**
- **Working with transparency**
- **Creating an animation**
- **Creating image maps and rollovers**

## Web Features in Photoshop

Photoshop supports numerous image formats, which makes it ideal for importing scans and graphics from sources such as Photo CDs, digital cameras, and video captures. Once you edit an image, you can easily save it or export it to a Web-compatible image format such as JPEG, GIF, or PNG. You can take advantage of the unique characteristics of each format including file size, progressive rendering, transparency, and compression.

Photoshop's user-friendly Layers palette is ideal for separating portions of an image so that they can remain editable throughout the creative process. This empowers designers to lay out entire Web sites within Photoshop and then use the elements created on the layers. The original files remain intact and can be modified as necessary. The Layers palette is also quite useful for creating and organizing simple animation sequences. These layer stacks are saved and re-opened in Adobe ImageReady and have the capability of generating animated images.

## ImageReady and Photoshop

When you open ImageReady, your first observation may very well be that it looks a lot like Photoshop, and indeed it performs in very much the same way. It contains many of the same tools, filters, commands, and palettes of its bigger, older sibling. ImageReady's strength is its ability to prepare files for the Web, an ability it shares, in part, with Photoshop's Save For Web option. However, it also provides the additional capability of creating rollovers, image maps, and animations.

The primary difference is that in place of the extensive printing features of Photoshop, ImageReady has numerous powerful operations for Web file preparation. Instead of print-specific adjustments, color settings, and gamut tools, there are (among others) the Image Map tool, default browser preview, and the Slice, Rollover, Image Map, Animation, and Optimize palettes. Another major difference is Photoshop's ability to save a document to many different formats, including those that support printing and desktop publishing, video, and the Web. ImageReady, on the other hand, is designed to save optimized files exclusively to Web formats—GIF, JPEG, PNG—and the Photoshop format, PSD.

> If you use the Export Original command, you can save in BMP, PCX, TGA, TIF, PICT, and PXR formats, and you can save an animation as a QuickTime movie.

## Designing Page Elements in Photoshop

Photoshop's unique interface makes it perfect for developing Web elements. Follow the exercises in this chapter to become accustomed to designing for the Web using Photoshop. I'll demonstrate by building a few types of Web graphics.

## Creating a Margin-Style Background

A margin-style background is a common visual element that helps unify the design of a Web page. It serves as a visual compass because it fills the entire vertical depth of the document no matter how tall it may be. Furthermore, a margin can help establish the ordered division of information by separating the background into vertical blocks. It is also a perfect way to infuse the page with interest and character by adding a splash of color or texture.

A margin background is simply a pattern that is configured so that the image repeats vertically but not horizontally. Because all Web backgrounds tile from the left topmost corner into the available space, we have to ensure that we create a strip long enough so that the tile doesn't appear to repeat along the horizontal axis.

Figure 25.1

**Choosing margin-style background settings in the New dialog box**

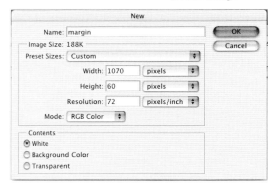

To create a margin-style background:

1. Choose File → New.

2. Name the file **Margin**.

   Don't worry about the `gif`, `jpg`, or `png` extension at this point. Because the default Saving Files preferences is Append File Extension, Photoshop will automatically add the extension when the document is saved.

3. Enter a width of **1070** pixels and a height of **60** pixels (Figure 25.1).

   The width of 1070 pixels in this image ensures that the image will not repeat at monitor resolutions of 1024×768 or lower. However, at higher resolutions, you run the risk of the image repeating. For this reason, some Web designers prefer to set their margin background widths to 1280.

4. Set the resolution to 72 pixels per inch.

5. Choose RGB Color for the Mode.

6. Under Contents, choose White.

Figure 25.2

**Choosing an image size**

7. Click OK.

   Now, fill a portion of the file with color.

1.  Click the Rectangular Marquee tool to display its settings in the Options bar.

2. Choose Fixed Size from the Style pull-down menu; enter **108 px** for the width and **60 px** for the height, as shown in Figure 25.2.

3. Click the image in the top-left corner of the document.

4. Open the document `margin_texture.psd` on the `Ch25` folder on the *Photoshop 7 Savvy* CD.

5. Choose Select → Select All. Choose Edit → Copy.

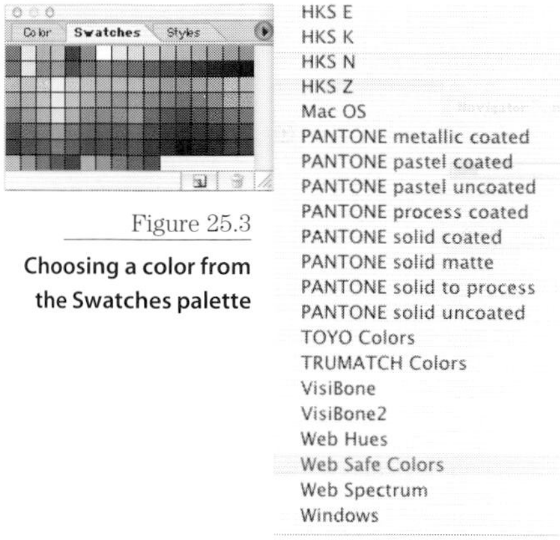

Figure 25.3

**Choosing a color from the Swatches palette**

HKS E
HKS K
HKS N
HKS Z
Mac OS
PANTONE metallic coated
PANTONE pastel coated
PANTONE pastel uncoated
PANTONE process coated
PANTONE solid coated
PANTONE solid matte
PANTONE solid to process
PANTONE solid uncoated
TOYO Colors
TRUMATCH Colors
VisiBone
VisiBone2
Web Hues
Web Safe Colors
Web Spectrum
Windows

6. Click on the margin document. With the Rectangular Marquee still active, choose Edit → Paste Into.

7. From the Swatches Palette pull-down menu, choose Web Safe Colors (see Figure 25.3). Click a light color to choose it.

8. In the Layers Palette, target the Background.

9. Press Option-Delete (Mac) or Alt-Backspace (Win) to fill the marquee with the foreground color.

You can now choose what to do with the file:

- Save the file in native Photoshop format, layers intact, for future use or modification in Photoshop (always recommended).

- Duplicate the image and save it for the Web in GIF, JPEG, or PNG format (see "Saving for the Web" later in this chapter).

- Import the file into ImageReady for processing.

- Once the file is optimized, load it into your HTML editor as part of your Web page. When the image is loaded as a background, it will repeat vertically as a pattern and appear to be a continuous design down the depth of the page (see Figure 25.4).

Figure 25.4

**The margin-style background as a Photoshop document**

- When you open the Web page in the browser, it appears as a seamless margin, as in Figure 25.5.

## CHOOSING A WEB-COMPATIBLE COLOR

There are three ways to choose colors that are Web-compatible:

- Choose Window → Swatches. From the pull-down menu in the upper-right corner of the palette, choose Web Hues, Web Safe Colors, Visibone, or Web Spectrum. Any of these color palettes displays the 216 Web-safe colors; the palettes consist of the same colors organized differently. If you hover your cursor over any color in the palette, its hexadecimal name will be displayed.

- You can click the foreground color in the Tool palette to reveal the Color Picker and check the Only Web Colors box. Move the slider on the color bar to scroll through the hexadecimal hues and then pick a color from the color field.

- Choose Window → Swatches. From the pull-down menu in the upper-right corner of the Color palette, choose Web Color Sliders. Drag the sliders to pick a color.

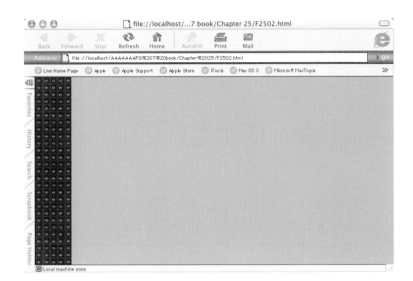

Figure 25.5

**The margin-style background as it repeats vertically in the browser**

## Creating a Seamless Background in Photoshop

An alternative to the margin-style background is a background-repeating tile, also referred to as *wallpaper*. In most cases, you will want the pattern to be subtle so as not to compete with the information that floats on top of it.

Wallpaper patterns were the first wave of background graphics. You've probably seen lots of them, in all kinds of styles. They can be problematic for a number of reasons: if they're too dark or busy, for example, they interfere with the readability of images and hypertext. They're also demanding on the designer—making them completely by hand takes a bit of skill.

If you design them properly, however, seamless backgrounds can create an extremely attractive look for your site. The following are some general guidelines to use when creating tiles:

- Individual tiles should be at least 50 pixels by 50 pixels.
- Do *not* interlace background graphics.
- Use light colors so that images and text will float on the background.

Follow along as I create a tile using Photoshop 7:

1. Open the CD file `Web Clouds.psd`.
2. Display the Layers palette. Choose Layer → New → Layer From Background.
3. Name the new layer **Clouds 1**.

4. 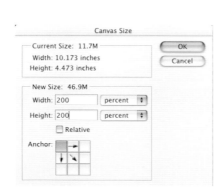 Drag the Clouds 1 layer to the New Layer icon to create a new duplicate layer. Name the layer **Clouds 2**. Repeat the process two more times, naming the additional layers **Clouds 3** and **Clouds 4**.

5. Choose Image → Canvas Size, and increase the width and height of the canvas to 200 percent (see Figure 25.6). Anchor the image in the upper-left corner of the canvas. Click OK.

6. Target the Clouds 2 layer. Choose the Move tool and drag the layer to the upper right of the document.

7. Choose Edit → Transform → Flip Horizontal.

8. Target the Clouds 3 layer. Choose the Move tool and drag the layer to the lower left of the document.

9. Choose Edit → Transform → Flip Vertical.

10. Target the Clouds 4 layer. Choose the Move tool and drag the layer to the lower right of the document.

11. Choose Edit → Transform → Flip Vertical, and then Edit → Transform → Flip Horizontal.

12. Zoom in close to the document to assure that the layers butt up against each other and that there is no space between them. If there is, choose the Move tool and nudge them into place with the arrow keys. The image should look like Figure 25.7.

13. From the Layer Options pull-down menu, choose Merge Visible.

14. Move the Opacity slider to 50%.

15. Save the document as a JPEG using the Save For Web feature. (See the section titled "Saving for the Web" later in this chapter.) When displayed on the browser, the background should look like Figure 25.8.

Figure 25.6

**Canvas Size dialog box**

Figure 25.7

**The seamless background tile**

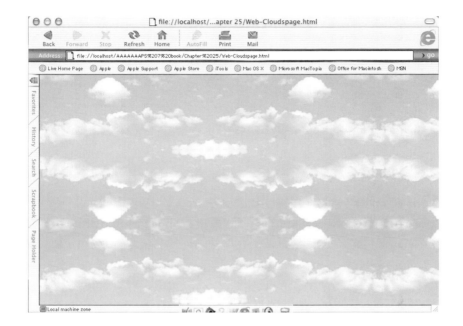

Figure 25.8

**The seamless back-ground on a browser**

## ImageReady's Tile Maker

ImageReady has a built-in tile maker that can help smooth out some problems that you may encounter when creating continuous, or seamless, background images. One such problem is that if each tile's edge is slightly different, those edges will show where the tile repeats. The effect is somewhat disturbing!

To correct or avoid this problem:

1.  If Photoshop is running, click the Jump To icon  in the Tool palette. Open the file `Tile.psd`.

2.  Select Filter → Other → Tile Maker. The Tile Maker dialog will appear (see Figure 25.9).

3.  Click the Blend Edges radio button. You can select the amount of pixels for blending; I've left it at the default of 10. I've also left the Resize Tile To Fill Image option checked. This expands the file where necessary to make the blending as seamless as possible.

4.  Click OK.

5.  Optimize and save your file.

You can now view your file within an HTML page or import it into GoLive to begin designing your page. The result is a smoother, more attractive background (see Figure 25.10).

Figure 25.9

**The Tile Maker dialog box**

## ImageReady's Kaleidoscopic Tiles

While working to make your background tile seamless, you might have noticed the Kaleidoscope Tile option in the Tile Maker dialog. This is a neat background effect with endless design possibilities!

To create a kaleidoscope background:

1. Open or create an image. You can start with the textured tile developed in the previous section.

2. Select Filter → Other → Tile Maker. When the Tile Maker dialog appears, click the Kaleidoscope Tile option.

3. Click OK. You now have a kaleidoscope tile (see Figure 25.11).

4. Once done with the kaleidoscopic effect, you can blend the edges of the tile. Select the Tile Maker filter again and blend the edges of the image for smooth results (see Figure 25.12).

## Web File Formats

Images need to be saved in one of several formats in order to be read by browsers. JPEG, PNG, GIF formats, and their variations are briefly described here. Look in Appendix B, "File Formats," for more detailed descriptions.

Figure 25.10

**The original image (top), and the image after the Tile Maker filter has been applied (bottom).**

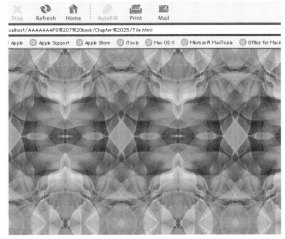

Figure 25.11

**A kaleidoscope tile**

Figure 25.12

**The kaleidoscopic background tile on a browser**

You can use a wide range of effects and source images before applying the kaleidoscope effect.

## OPTIMIZING YOUR IMAGES IN PHOTOSHOP

When it comes to optimizing Web graphics with Photoshop, you have several options. First, you can use the built-in Save For Web feature, which many Web designers opt to do. Or you can choose to optimize in ImageReady, which has many features similar to those in the Save For Web dialog. Another choice is to optimize by hand and save as JPEG, or use Indexed color mode. You can save as CompuServe GIF (GIF86a) and PNG, but ultimately Save For Web gives you the most choices, the best previews, and the best information.

Using the Save For Web feature or employing ImageReady puts some excellent power tools into your hands. Without them, you have to rely on testing and experience in order to make the best decisions.

## JPEG (Joint Photographic Experts Group)

JPEG is a lossy compression format. It supports 24-bit color and is used to preserve the tonal variations in photographs. JPEG compresses file size by selectively discarding data. A higher-quality setting results in less data being discarded. Low JPEG settings result in blocky areas within the image and a profusion of artifacts, or blotchy spots. JPEG compression can degrade sharp detail in images and is not recommended for images with type or solid areas of color. See Figure 25.13 for a comparison of JPEG settings.

Each time you save the file as a JPEG, you discard more data. To avoid progressive deterioration, you should save JPEG files from the original image, not from a previously saved JPEG.

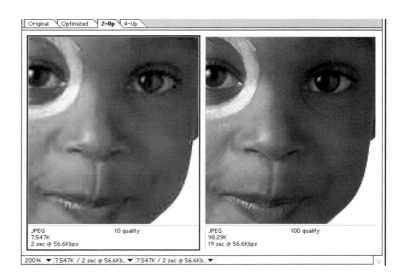

Figure 25.13

**JPEG compression-quality comparisons: (left) Low and (right) Maximum**

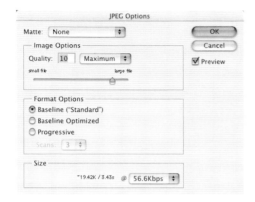

Figure 25.14

**JPEG dialog**

If you use the JPEG Options dialog box (File → Save As → JPEG) to save an image, you can specify characteristics of the JPEG (see Figure 25.14).

The JPEG format does not support transparency. When you save an image as a JPEG, transparency is replaced by the *matte* color. Use the background color of the Web page as the matte color to simulate transparency. Choose Matte to select a color for the background of an image that is on a transparent layer. The color will fill the areas where there are transparent pixels when the image is seen on the browser. If your image is going to be displayed over a pattern or multiple colors, save it as a transparent GIF.

In the Image Options field, enter a quality value from 0 to 10, or choose Low, Medium, High, or Maximum from the pull-down menu.

Choose a format option by clicking the radio buttons:

**Baseline ("Standard")** displays the image after it has downloaded.

**Baseline Optimized** displays the image from top to bottom as it downloads.

**Progressive** allows you to specify 3, 4, or 5 scans. These have the effect of progressively displaying low-resolution versions of the image as it is downloading. Use this option to hold your viewer's attention while the image loads.

In the Size field, the number on the left of the slash is the file size. The number on the right is the download rate, which you can determine by choosing a modem baud rate from the pull-down menu.

## PNG-8 and PNG-24 (Portable Network Graphic)

The PNG-8 format is similar to GIF 8-bit color. It uses 256 colors, supports transparency, and is lossless, but is not supported by older browsers. PNG-24 is an excellent format because it combines the attributes of JPEG and GIF in lossless compression. It supports 24-bit color and is fine for saving photographs to the Web because it preserves tonality. Like GIF, PNG-24 preserves the sharp detail found in line art, logos, and type. It also supports transparency and matting.

Another great feature of the PNG-24 format is that it supports *multilevel* transparency, in which you can preserve up to 256 levels of transparency to blend the edges of an image smoothly into a background color. This seems like the dream format, doesn't it? The only (minor) drawback is that versions of the major browsers from 1999 and earlier don't support it, and it takes awhile before the latest browsers are used by the majority of Web users. Take this into consideration when deciding to use the PNG formats.

### GIF (Graphics Interchange Format)

The GIF format is used primarily for saving images with solid areas of color and sharp edges, like line art, logos, or illustrations with type. It is also the format for saving animations produced in ImageReady.

Unlike JPEG, the GIF format uses lossless compression. Yet because GIF files are 256 colors or fewer, optimizing an original 24-bit image as an 8-bit GIF can degrade the image. You can create lossy GIFs, which produce much smaller files but sometimes produce artifacts similar to those found in JPEG images. You can control the number of colors in a GIF image and adjust the dithering options to simulate the effect of blending.

You can save a file as a GIF in two ways. Choose File → Save As → CompuServe GIF to bring up the Indexed Color dialog box, where you can optimize the image. (See "Exporting to GIF" later in the chapter.) The second method is by using the Save For Web option.

## Saving for the Web

The Save For Web feature is a "subinterface." It contains numerous options for saving files to Web formats, and can compare the effects of different settings on up to four images at once. Figure 25.15 shows the Save For Web dialog box. It behaves very much like a plug-in application, with full features contained within the dialog box itself.

The Save For Web dialog contains the following tab options:

**Original**  shows the image in its original state.

**Optimized**  shows the image with whatever Web optimization features you select.

**2-Up**  displays the original image next to the optimized image.

**4-Up**  provides a look at the original image with three possible optimization results.

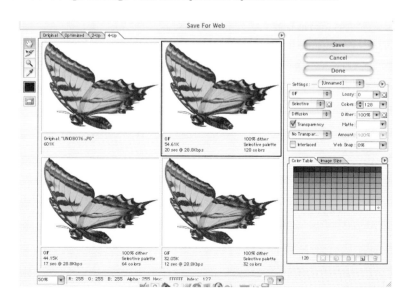

Figure 25.15

**The Save For Web dialog "subinterface"**

The Preview menu is accessible from the small arrow on the right of the image window. It has several options, including the ability to simulate what a graphic looks like on different computers. This feature allows you to make cross-platform decisions about your Web graphics. It also displays several different baud rates (see Figure 25.16). Choose one to determine the amount of time your image will take to download. The value is displayed below the image window.

The right side of the Save For Web dialog box offers numerous file format and color controls:

**Settings** This option provides a pop-up menu of preconfigured settings for saving images as GIFs, JPEGs, and PNGs.

**Optimized File Format** This option provides a pop-up menu of possible file formats, including GIF, JPEG, PNG, and WBMP (for wireless Web surfers on mobile phones).

**Color Reduction Algorithm** This option is available for GIFs. In most cases, you'll want to select Web.

**Dithering Algorithm** Standard dithering options are provided for the GIF format. Work with these to see which gives you the best results.

**Lossy** This option allows you to create lossy GIFs. You'll sacrifice quality, but you will reduce the file size.

**Colors** This pop-up menu allows you to specify the exact number of colors you'd like to include in your image.

**Transparency** This option produces transparency if you are saving the image as a GIF or PNG image and the image is on a transparent layer.

Figure 25.16

**Baud rates**

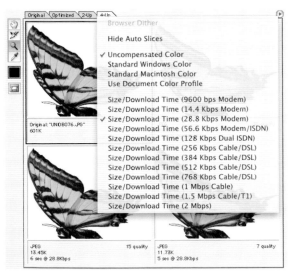

**Dither** If you select a dithering algorithm, this slider allows you to precisely control the amount of dithering that occurs in the image.

**Web Snap** If you are using a color palette other than the 216 Web-safe colors, this slider allows you to adjust the number of colors that snap to the Web palette.

**Interlaced** Select this option if you want your image to be rendered progressively.

**Color Table** The color table allows you to see the exact colors being used in the optimized image when using PNG-8 and GIF images. Colors with dots in the center are Web-safe colors. The arrow to the right above the color table displays a menu that allows you to select, sort, lock, shift, save, and load colors.

**Image Size** This palette (see Figure 25.17) allows you to change the physical dimensions of the image you are saving.

The annotations under the image(s) denote the format type, file size, the download time on a selected modem, plus the various characteristics of a selected group of settings. Click the arrow at the top of the tabbed display to choose additional options for the display and annotations.

When working with the Save For Web dialog, remember that the variations you apply to an image do not influence your original image. Instead, the image is saved as a new file. You can save your choices by using the Save Settings feature if you like the way that a particular combination of options worked for you.

**Figure 25.17**

**Image Size palette**

I like to use the 4-Up option to display at once as many options as possible, so I can compare settings and results. The goal is to get the perfect balance of good-looking graphics and a low file weight.

Now let's go through the by-hand optimization process so you can effectively optimize your graphics to retain their good looks yet weigh little for fast load times. I'll use the same graphic, once with a solid background and once preserving transparency, but you can use the general process defined here to optimize any of your GIF and JPEG images.

## Using Indexed Color

Before you save an image, you can reduce the number of colors, and thus its file size, by changing its color mode from RGB to Indexed. Converting the file to Indexed color substantially reduces the number of colors in the document. By reducing the number of colors, you reduce the image's file size. See the practice steps in the next section to learn how to convert your image to Indexed.

> If the image you're working with naturally lends itself to transparency, you can save the image as a transparent GIF in the Save For Web dialog box. Images containing transparency need to be on layers surrounded by a transparent area. Since Indexed color does not support layers, check the Transparency box in order to maintain the transparency when the image is finally saved as a GIF.

## Exporting to GIF

GIF (Graphics Interchange Format, or CompuServe GIF) is a common format used to optimize and export graphic files to the Web. We'll save the same image to GIF format using Save For Web, first with an opaque and then with a transparent background:

1. Open the `mallard.psd` file in the `Ch25` folder on the CD.

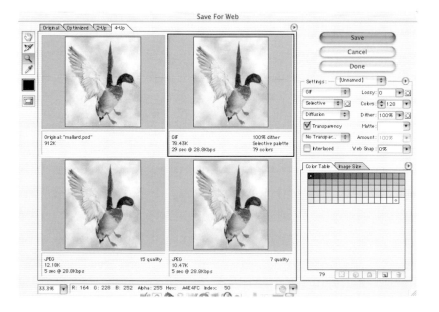

**Figure 25.18**

**The Indexed Color dialog box**

2. Choose Image → Mode → Indexed Color. A prompt will appear asking if you want to flatten layers. Click OK. The Indexed Color dialog box appears (Figure 25.18). For Palette, choose Local (Adaptive).

3. You can change the number in the Color field to reduce the number of colors in the document and its file size. Enter 80 in this field, and observe the preview of the image, whose quality does not change significantly.

4. Dithering blends the areas of color together and helps the image look less posterized. In this instance, choose Diffusion in the Dither field and an amount of 75% to see the result.

5. Choose File → Save For Web (see Figure 25.19). Click the 4-Up tab. The dialog box displays the original image in the upper-left and three additional images.

6. Choose GIF from the pop-up menu. Notice that the color table displays the 80 colors that were designated in the Indexed Color dialog box.

7. Click the top-right image. You will configure this image first.

8. Under Settings you can choose a preset format; under the Optimized File Format menu, choose GIF. For Color Reduction Algorithm, choose Adaptive. For Color, scroll down the list trying different options to achieve the best possible image with the fewest number of colors.

9. Click the other images and try different settings to compare the results.

10. Click the best image and click OK. Name the image and choose a location in the Save File dialog box.

**Figure 25.19**

**Save For Web with the GIF option selected, displaying the color table**

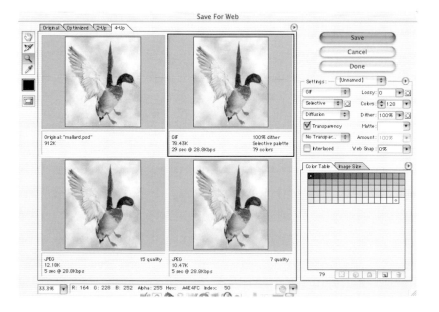

## Saving the Image As an HTML File

When you click the Save button, the Save Optimized As dialog box appears (Figure 25.20), giving you four options. Select an option from the preference setting in the Settings menu:

| Setting | Description |
|---|---|
| Default Settings | Photoshop's default settings. |
| Background Image | Settings for background tiles. |
| Custom | Any variations to the above settings will be saved as custom settings. |
| Other | Configures new settings. |

Figure 25.20

**The Save Optimized As dialog box**

### Setting File-Saving Preferences

If you choose the Other option, the Output Settings dialog box is displayed (see Figure 25.21). You can set four categories of options in the Output Settings dialog box. These options configure the preferences for files saved for publication to the Web. Choose a category from the pop-up list (HTML, Slice Name, Background, or Saving Files).

#### HTML

Choose from these HTML formatting options:

**Tags Case**   Selects the case for HTML tags: uppercase, initial cap, or all lowercase.

**Attributes Case**   Selects the tag attribute case: uppercase, initial cap, second initial cap, or all lowercase.

**Indent**   Determines a means for code indention: use the authoring software's default tab settings, a specific number of spaces, or no indention.

**Line Endings**   Selects a platform for line-ending compatibility: Mac, Windows, or Unix.

Use one of these options to embed comments into the HTML code:

**Include Comments**   Imbeds ImageReady comments in the HTML code.

**Always Quote Attributes**   Places quotation marks around all tag attributes. This option is necessary for compatibility with some early browsers. It is not recommended to always quote attributes. Quotation marks are used when necessary to comply with most browsers, even if this option is deselected.

Figure 25.21

**The Output Settings dialog box**

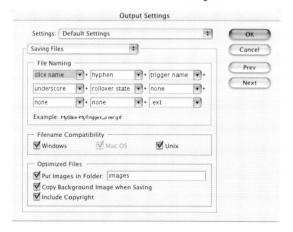

**Always Add Alt Attributes**  Generates HTML with blank attributes when attributes are not specified.

**Close All Tags**  Generates close tags for all elements.

**Include Zero Margins on Body Tag**  The body tag code includes attributes to produce zero margins.

### SLICES

You can set HTML naming conventions for slices by entering text or choosing from the menu items. This will configure the code to specific or universal browser compatibility. Choose from the following slice output options:

**Generate Table**  Aligns sliced images in an HTML table.

**Empty Cells**  Indicates how to fill empty table data cells (slices without content):

- Select GIF, IMG W&H to use a one-pixel spacer GIF with width and height in the IMG tag.
- Select GIF, TD W&H to use a one-pixel spacer GIF with width and height in the TD tag.
- Select NoWrap, TD W&H to code a non-standard NoWrap attribute on the table data and place width and height in the TD tags.

**TD W&H**  Determines when to place width and height attributes for table data: Always, Never, or Auto (recommended).

**Spacer Cells**  Says when to place a row and a column of empty spacers around the table: Always, Never, or Auto (recommended). Spacer cells align slice boundaries in tables where slice borders do not line up to prevent the table from breaking apart in some browsers.

**Generate CSS**  Creates cascading style sheets for slices.

**Referenced**  Refers to how the cascading style sheet will be referenced in the HTML code: by ID, inline, or by class.

**Default Slice Naming**  Determines naming conventions for slices.

### BACKGROUND

To designate the characteristics of a background, choose the Background preference category. You can specify the following configurations:

**View Document As**  To designate the current image as a background, choose Background. To designate a background to be used with the current image, click Image. Specify the location path in the path field.

**BG Image**  To specify a solid color that will be displayed while the image is downloading or through areas of transparency, choose a color option.

**SAVING FILES**

Choose from these file-saving options:

**File Naming** Choose items from menus, enter values, or test for saving Web images. Items include preferences for saving the document's name, slice name if the image has been cut into slices, rollover state if the image contains a rollover created in ImageReady, file creation date, slice number, punctuation, and file extension. You can reconfigure the filenames, for example, using a different abbreviation to name the file.

**Filename Compatibility** Select one or more options to make the filename compatible with Windows, Macintosh, and Unix platforms.

For optimized files, choose from these options:

**Put Images in Folder** Consolidates sliced images into a separate folder when saving (not the folder with the HTML document). This folder is called Images by default, or you can rename it.

**Copy Background Image When Saving** Check this box to preserve the background settings of an image that is being used a background.

**Include Copyright** Check to include copyright information with the image. You add copyright information for an image in the Image Info dialog box.

Figure 25.22

ImageReady's live preview allows you to see changes in a file as you make them. The Optimize palette enables you to format the image to your chosen specifications.

> These options can be set in ImageReady by choosing File → Save Optimized or File → Save As Optimized → Settings → Other.

## Optimizing Images in ImageReady

The Save As Optimized feature in ImageReady is very similar to the Save For Web feature in Photoshop. ImageReady's optimization capabilities include the following:

**Live Preview** Whenever you are working on a file in ImageReady, you can automatically see changes based on file type and optimization choices (Figure 25.22).

**Choice of File Types** ImageReady supports GIF, JPEG, PNG, and PSD. Depending upon the file and your needs, you can adjust accordingly.

**User-Level Control** While ImageReady gives you immediate optimization choices, advanced users can use options to customize their graphic output.

While you don't really need a working knowledge of optimization to use ImageReady, you will no doubt be empowered by understanding the basic rules of thumb when it comes to optimization:

- Use GIFs when working with line art, flat color, and few colors.

- Use JPEGs for photographs and for art with many colors, shadows, and light gradations.

- PNGs are useful for broad application, but they are not supported by older browsers.

## Working with GIFs in ImageReady

The Optimize palette displays options for saving images as GIFs, JPEGs or PNGs.

1. Open the file `mallard.psd` in the `Ch25` folder on the CD.

2. Click the 4-Up tab to display four versions of the image. Click the second image. Choose Window → Optimized to display the Optimize palette.

3. In the Settings pop-up list, choose GIF 128 Dithered. Compare the optimized version to the original. The original's size is approximately 209 KB compared to the optimized version of about 50 KB (see Figure 25.23). In this particular image, there is not a great variation in quality, but the file size has been substantially reduced.

4. Click the third image. In the Optimize palette, reduce the number of colors to 2. Typically, this will be too few colors for most images, but it's a good idea to get a feel for how the image would look at the lowest possible compression of only 3 KB.

### GETTING INFORMATION ABOUT FILE SIZES

Information about the file size of your images is available in the Save For Web option in Photoshop or the image window in ImageReady. You can display different information in each of these windows:

- Select one of the tabs in the image window. Choose one of the options: Original, Optimized, 2-Up, and 4-Up. I like to set this option to 2-Up, which gives a comparison between the original file size and current file specifications.

- In Photoshop, the information is at the bottom of each image. By clicking on the arrow at the top-right of the window, you can choose a baud rate at which to recalculate the information.

- In ImageReady, choose information from the arrows at the bottom of the menu. The first arrow indicates the size in which you are viewing the image. The second two arrows offer additional information, including the image's type, file size, and the possible speeds at which it will be downloaded.

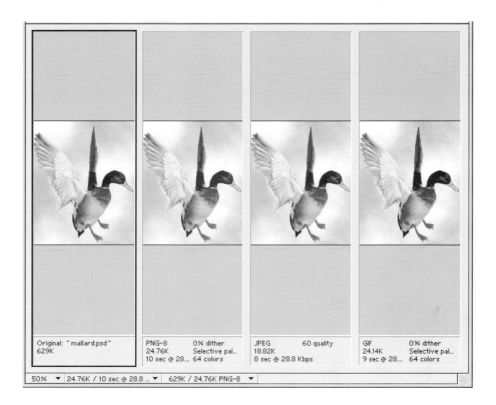

Figure 25.23

The original Mallard is on the left at 629K. The second image displays the PNG-8 128 at 24.76K. The third image is a high quality JPEG and is only 18.82K, and at the bottom right is a 64 color GIF with a file size of 24.14K.

5.  On the fourth image, bring the color number to 32, which gives you a great look but even better compression at about 30 KB than you had at the auto setting.

6.  Choose File Save Optimized As to save the GIF.

You can now make additional selections for your GIF, such as interlacing or transparency using the Optimize palette settings. Interlacing allows the GIF image to appear progressively on the page, and transparency is discussed later in the "Matting" section.

## Preparing JPEGs in ImageReady

For photographs and any image with significant amounts of gradations in light or shadow, JPEG is the file format of choice for the best look and compression. You can optimize an image as a JPEG to produce the best results for your photographs.

1.  In ImageReady, open the file `Liberty.psd` in the Ch25 folder on the CD.

2.  When the file is open, go to the Optimize palette and choose JPEG from the File Format pull-down menu.

3.  Click the 2-Up tab on the image.

4. View the image using Maximum, High, Medium, and Low JPEG settings in the Optimize palette. Try to find the setting that gives you the best quality and compression without causing artifacts on the image (Figure 25.24).

You can make further, custom adjustments by using the Quality slider bar. For example, if the quality at the Medium setting (30) is fine, but the Low setting (10) is showing artifacts, try moving the slider to a setting of 20 and seeing how the image's look and size add up.

5. Select File → Save Optimized. Name your file. The Format pop-up list provides the following options:

**HTML Only** saves an HTML file with the images written into the code.

**HTML And Images** saves an HTML file with the images written into the code and a separate folder of the image or slices.

**Images Only** saves only the image or slices.

Figure 25.24

The extremes of JPEG settings. Notice the deterioration and artifacts in the image on the left, which is set to JPEG Low to produce a file size of only 7.5 KB, but at the expense of image quality. The image on the right maintains quality, at 98 KB, set to JPEG High 100.

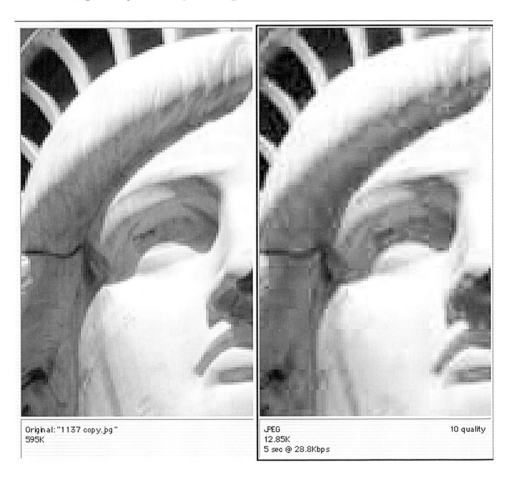

Original: "1137 copy.jpg"
595K

JPEG                                    10 quality
12.85K
5 sec @ 28.8Kbps

6. Choose HTML And Images to create a document and files that are Web-ready. ImageReady will generate the image in a separate folder as well as the HTML file. You can now view your HTML file in the browser of your choice.

These kinds of decisions are the heart and soul of image optimization for the Web. It's always a balance of good looks and quick load times, and always based within the context of the page with which you are working.

> To progressively render a JPEG, check the Progressive box. This enables supporting browsers to display the image incrementally.

## Creating a Transparency Mask in Photoshop

If you'd like an image to appear seamless against a patterned or solid background, you need to either make an image transparent or matte the image on the background color. This technique is especially important to use whenever your image isn't a rectangle.

The streamlined features in File → Save For Web have replaced the GIF89a Export of former versions as the method of creating transparent GIF images. In order to create transparency on an optimized Web image, the image must be on a layer surrounded by transparency. Let's knock out the background of an image:

1. Open the file in the Ch25 folder on the CD titled Liberty.psd.

2. Choose the Magic Wand tool  . In the Options bar, set the tolerance to 32 and clear the Contiguous box. Click on the blue area surrounding the Statue of Liberty.

3. Choose Select → Inverse to select the statue.

4. Choose Layer → New → Layer Via Copy to isolate a copy of the statue on a separate layer.

5. Target the new layer. Click off the eye icon on the Background.

6. Choose File → Save For Web (see Figure 25.25). Choose GIF from the pop-up list and enter **16** for the number of colors. Notice that the Transparency option is active and the image is displayed on a checkerboard, indicating transparency.

7. Choose 2-Up.

8. Optimize the image as you did the opaque GIF. Try different settings and compare the results.

9. Click the best image and click OK. Name the image and choose a location in the Save File dialog box. The image should look like Figure 25.26 on the browser.

Figure 25.25

**Choosing Save For Web and GIF with transparency**

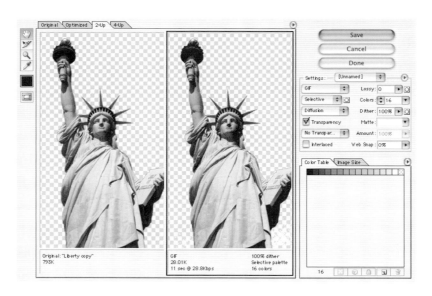

Figure 25.26

**The transparent GIF displayed on the browser with the clouds background tile**

## Matting

Browsers support either opacity or transparency. Unlike Photoshop, they do not display semitransparent layers. The idea of matting is to blend the edges of a shape with the background design of a page to simulate semitransparency and smooth out some of the rough edges. Transparency in Photoshop is layer-based—in other words, the transparent areas that surround an area of a layer will be transparent in the browser. If you want an image to float on a patterned background, matting can help soften those edges. To apply matting to an image, follow these steps:

1. Open the file titled `Tile.psd` in the `Ch25` folder on the CD. Choose the Eyedropper tool and sample a midtone green from the image. Click the foreground color swatch in the Tool palette to display the Color Picker. Check Only Web Colors. Write down the hexadecimal number of the color.

Figure 25.27

**The New dialog box**

2. Choose File → New (see the dialog box in Figure 25.27). Name the file **emerald_forest**. From Preset Sizes, choose 468×60 Web Banner. Set the mode to RGB and the contents to Transparent. Save the file in Photoshop format.

3. Choose the Type tool. Type the words **Emerald Forest**. I used Herculanum Bold, 64 point, but you can use any typeface you please.

4. Color the type yellow and add a Bevel and Emboss style to the text (see Figure 25.28).

5. Choose File → Save For Web. From the Settings pop-up menu, choose GIF 32 Dithered, as in Figure 25.29.

Figure 25.28

**The Emerald Forest text with the Bevel and Emboss layer style applied**

6. Click on the matting swatch. Choose Other to bring up the Color Picker. Check Web Colors Only. Enter the hexadecimal value you recorded. This will place a green mat around the type to blend it into the pattern tile on the Web page.

7. Click Save. You can now display the image in the browser (as in Figure 25.30) against the patterned background.

Figure 25.29

**The Save For Web settings**

Figure 25.30

**The Emerald Forest text displayed without matting (above). The Emerald Forest text displayed with matting on a patterned background (below).**

## Slicing Images in Photoshop and ImageReady

A group of small images downloads more efficiently in a browser than one large image. In Photoshop or ImageReady, you *slice* a Web image in order to divide it into smaller files to accelerate download time or to assign different compression or file formats to various parts of an image, particularly animations. Slicing is the process of cutting an image into pieces, saving the individual parts as image files, and writing an HTML document that reassembles the slices on-screen. This increases the efficiency of displaying the images on the browser by decreasing the download time.

You can slice the image with the Slice tool 🖊 in either program. To slice an image, choose the Slice tool from the Tool palette, click the mouse, and drag the cursor where you want the slice.

> Slices can only butt up against each other or butt up against the top, bottom, or sides of the image. You cannot cut a slice out of the center of the image unless it is adjacent to other slices.

The individual slices are saved as separate files, and an HTML document with table code is written that reassembles them on the browser. You can select a slice with the Select Slice tool either from the Tool palette in Photoshop and ImageReady or within the Save For Web dialog box in Photoshop. The slice can be repositioned, or different options can be designated for the slice.

By default, when you choose the Slice tool, you see that the image is really one slice. The number 1 appears in the upper-left corner of the slice. Each time you create a slice, a new sequential number is assigned to it (see Figure 25.31).

When you're satisfied with your slice arrangement, save the image using the Save For Web option. You can select an individual slice by choosing the Slice Select tool. If desired, you can optimize the slices individually or, if no slices are selected, as a group.

Figure 25.31

**The image before slicing, with the guides in place**

Figure 25.32

**After slicing, Photoshop and ImageReady number the slices.**

Another method of creating slices is to set guides and convert them:

1. Open the image `Bio_Web_Site.psd`, in the `Ch25` folder on the CD, in ImageReady.

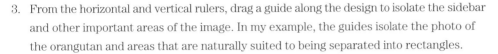

2. Choose View → Rulers.

3. From the horizontal and vertical rulers, drag a guide along the design to isolate the sidebar and other important areas of the image. In my example, the guides isolate the photo of the orangutan and areas that are naturally suited to being separated into rectangles.

4. Under Slices, choose Create Slices From Guides.

5. Select File → Save Optimized. When the Save As dialog appears, select HTML And Images from the Save As Type drop-down menu, and All Slices from the Slice menu. Click Save. Your image should now look like Figure 25.32.

You can make a slice into a link to connect it to another Web page or URL. Click the slice you want to make into a link. Activate the Slice palette (choose Window → Slice or, if the palette is visible, click the Slice tab). Enter the Name of the slice and the URL.

ImageReady saves the separate images, as well as the HTML, that are necessary to lay them out properly.

To view the results, open the HTML file in your browser, and you'll see that ImageReady maintains the integrity of your design while optimizing the sliced images in the best possible fashion.

## Creating Image Maps in ImageReady

An *image map* is an area of an image that links the site visitor to another Web page or URL. You can set up multiple areas in the image called hotspots. Where slices let you define only rectangular areas as links, image maps let you define circular, polygonal, or rectangular regions.

To define an image map as a region of the entire image, use the Image Map tools:

1. Choose one of the Image Map tools from the Tool palette. The choices are rectangle, circle, or polygon, as shown in Figure 25.33.

2. Drag over the area you want to make into an image map.

3. Click the Image Map tab to display the Image Map palette.

4. Name the image map and assign a URL to it. Now when visitors click that area of the image (like the beetle in Figure 25.34), their browser will transport them to that URL.

Figure 25.33

**Image Map tools**

Figure 25.34

**An image map defined by the Polygon Image Map tool and the Image Map palette**

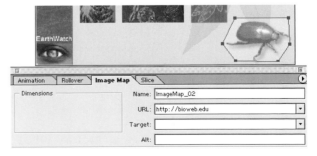

Figure 25.35

**The Heart image separated from the Background**

You can also make a layer-based image map:

1. In the Layers palette, target the layer you want to make into an image map.

2. Click the Layer menu and choose New Layer-Based Image Map Area.

3. Click the Image Map tab to display the Image Map palette.

4. Name the image map and enter a URL.

## Using Photoshop to Prepare Animations

Because Photoshop's Layers palette allows you to successively stack one transparent layer on top of another in sequence, it serves as a very effective cell animation program.

You can target an image on one layer, copy the layer, and apply a small increment of a filter, movement, or other operation. Copy the layer again and apply the operation one more time. Continue this process until the animation is complete. Incidentally, you can record the duplicate layer function and the operation into an action, and quickly automate your task.

Here is a step-by-step example of preparing a Photoshop animation:

1. Open the `Beating_Heart.psd` image in the `Ch25` folder on the CD. In my document, the Heart image has been separated from its background and named Layer 1 (see Figure 25.35).

2. Go to Window → Actions.

3. From the Actions Palette pull-down menu, choose New Set. Name the set **Animation**.

4. From the Actions Palette pull-down menu, choose New Action. I named mine **Heart Beat**. Assign the F2 key as a key command. Click Record and OK.

5. Drag Layer 1 to the New Layer icon to duplicate it.

6. Choose Filter → Distort → Spherize. Set the amount to 25% and the mode to Normal, as seen in Figure 25.36.

7. Stop recording.

Figure 25.36

**Settings on the Action palette**

8. Target Layer 1. Run the action by pressing the F2 key. A new layer is created called Layer 1 Copy. On the new layer, the heart appears to have grown a little.

9. Each time you target the new layer, repeat the action. Repeat the process four more times by pressing the F2 key. The heart will grow a little bit each time as each new layer is created. Name each layer with a sequential numeric value from 1 to 5 (as in Figure 25.37), so that when you do the animation in ImageReady, you'll have no problem keeping them organized.

The animation file is complete. Save it as a Photoshop file named `beating_heart_layers.psd`, layers intact. In order to create the beating heart animation and convert the file to animated GIF format, you'll import it into ImageReady.

# Creating a GIF Animation in ImageReady

Another very attractive aspect of ImageReady is that you can create layer-based animations. In Photoshop, we created the Beating Heart document; now, in ImageReady, we'll give it life.

1. With Photoshop running and the layered Beating Heart document open, launch ImageReady by clicking the Jump To icon. The Layers palette shows five layers and the Background, displaying an eye icon next to only the Background and Layer 1.

2. Choose Window → Animation. The frame in the Animation palette displays the visible portions of the image (see Figure 25.38).

> Each frame in ImageReady's Animation palette displays the current visible layers. You create an animated sequence by making a new frame and then making visible only those layers that you want to appear in that frame.

3. Click the Duplicate Current Frame icon [icon] to insert a frame in the Animation palette, or choose New Frame from the palette pull-down menu. Click off the eye icon for Layer 1, and click it on next to Layer 2. Leave on the eye next to the Background.

4. Repeat the process, adding new frames for Layer 3, 4, and 5. Your Animation palette should look like Figure 25.39.

5. At this point, you may want to see the result. Click Play to see the first half of the beating heart animation: The heart expands and suddenly contracts. So for the second part of the animation, we'll create a smooth contraction. We create the second half of the animation by using the same layers but in reverse order.

6. Click the Duplicate Current Frame button and make the contents of Layer 4 and the Background visible.

7. Repeat the process for Layers 3 and 2; the Animation palette should look like Figure 25.40.

8. In order to create a smoothly animated sequence, we want each frame to appear for the same amount of time. To set the speed between each frame, select all the frames by choosing Select All Frames from the Animation Palette pull-down menu. Choose the arrow on the lower right of each frame, and set a uniform delay time for each frame (or choose a duration for each frame individually).

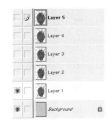

**Figure 25.37**

**The Layers palette after the animation action has been applied**

**Figure 25.38**

**The image, the Layers, and the Animation palette displaying the visible portion of the image**

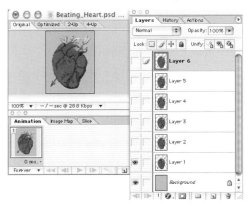

Figure 25.39

**The Animation palette with the first half of the animation**

Figure 25.39

**The Animation palette with the first half of the animation**

9. Next, you'll want to set up the iterations of the animation, or how many times it loops. Forever is only appropriate when the animation keeps looping in a constant motion, which is best for slower, subtler animations. Setting the animation to Once may be appropriate if the animation is particularly large and detailed. You can also set the animation to loop a custom number of turns.

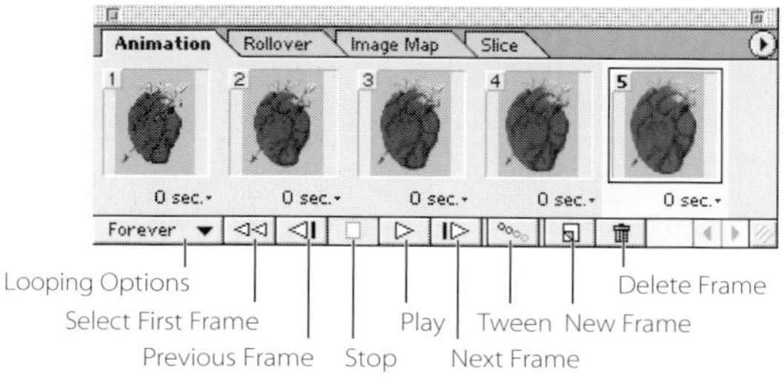

10. To add a smooth transition between points on an animation, use the Tween option from the Animation Palette drop-down menu. Tweening, or "in betweening," will automatically add a blur so that a smooth transition occurs between frames.

11. To view your animation, click the Play button at the bottom of the Animation palette. The animation will cycle in the originating file. At this point, you can stop the animation and make any adjustments that you feel are necessary.

12. Once you're happy with your animation, save it as a GIF by choosing File → Save Optimized, then name the file and click Save.

## Creating Rollovers in ImageReady

A *rollover* is a mini animation that is implemented by the behavior of your mouse. It's intended to add interactivity to your Web page. Like animations, rollovers depend on layers for their behavior. You designate a rollover on an image by changing the visibility of a layer's content.

To create a rollover, you should slice your image or create an image map so that the portion that contains the rollover is independent from the rest of the image.

1. In ImageReady, open the file `Bio_rollover.psd` from the `Ch25` folder on the CD. To simplify the process I have merged all of the layers in the document except for the ones needed for the rollover. The Background and the Legs 1 layer are visible, as shown in Figure 25.41.

2. Choose the Slice tool and drag a rectangle over the lower-right corner of the image to slice the beetle. Other slices will also be displayed. The beetle is the slice we want, so click it with the Slice Select tool 🔪, accessible by expanding the Slice tool in the Tool palette. It will be numbered Slice 03, as you see in Figure 25.42.

Figure 25.40

**The Animation palette with the completed animation**

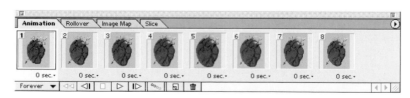

3. Choose Window → Rollovers to display the Rollovers palette, which contains a thumbnail of the entire image, named Normal, and a thumbnail of the slice, named Bio_ Rollover_03.

4. Target Bio_ Rollover_03. Click the New Rollover State icon. A thumbnail appears in the Rollovers palette, named Over State. Click *off* the eye next to the Legs layer, and click *on* the eye next to the Legs 2 layer, as in Figure 25.43.

5. To see the rollover, choose File → Preview In and choose a browser. Place your mouse on the beetle and the legs move. Remove the mouse and the legs are restored to the Normal state.

6. When the rollover is complete, you can optimize the image slice by slice. Choose the Select Slice tool from the Tool palette, click the individual slices one by one, and optimize them individually with the Options palette.

7. Save the entire page as an HTML document. Choose File → Save Optimized → HTML And Images.

## Changing Rollover States

You can program other states into a rollover and create additional rollover frames. Click the Options menu in the Rollovers palette and choose Rollover Options.

The Rollover State Options dialog box (Figure 25.44) gives the following State options:

**Normal** The image doesn't change; this is the default, or nonanimated, state.

**Over** The state changes when the mouse is hovered over the image or slice. Over is the default setting for the second rollover state.

**Down** The state changes when the mouse is clicked and held down in the area.

**Click** The state changes when the mouse is clicked and released over the area.

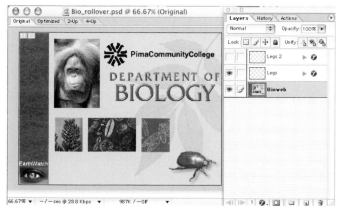

Figure 25.41

**The Background and the Legs 1 layer are visible.**

Figure 25.42

**The document showing the beetle slice**

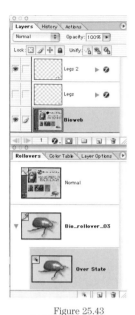

Figure 25.43

**The document, the Layers palette, and the Rollovers palette**

Figure 25.44

**Rollover State Options dialog box**

Web browsers, or different versions of a browser, may process clicks and double-clicks differently. Some browsers leave the slice in the Click state after a click and in the Up state after a double-click; other browsers use the Up state only as a transition into the Click state, regardless of single- or double-clicking. Be sure to preview rollovers in various Web browsers.

**Out**  The state changes when the mouse is moved off the area.

**Up**  The state changes when the mouse is released within the area.

**Custom**  This option lets you enter a custom behavior. You must write JavaScript code and add it to the HTML file in order for this to work.

**Selected**  Implements a rollover state when the user clicks the mouse on the slice or image map area. The state is maintained until you activate another selected rollover state, and other rollover effects can occur while the selected state is active. Note that if a layer is used by both states, the layer attributes of the Selected state override those of the Over state.

Check Select Use as Default Selected State to activate the state initially when the document is previewed in ImageReady or loaded into a Web browser.

**None**  The state does not change.

# Web Design and ImageReady

In this Hands On project, you'll lay out a Web site in Photoshop and use ImageReady to prepare the files for publication. The project is intended to take you through some of the Web features of Photoshop and ImageReady, but you will also use image-editing commands covered in previous chapters. The goal of this project is to assemble a home page for Ballet Bleu, an international ballet company (Figure H9.1)

To see the finished version from this exercise, see Figure C6 in the color section.

Figure H9.1

**The finished home page**

Figure H9.2

**Settings for the new document**

# Getting Started

Quit Photoshop and discard or hide your preferences file before beginning this exercise. The "Modifying Photoshop Settings" section in Chapter 5 details how to reset your preferences to Photoshop defaults temporarily.

Launch Photoshop and choose File → New. Name it **Ballet_ Bleu.psd** in preparation for saving to disk. Enter **768** for the width and **480** for the height. The resolution should be 72 ppi and the contents should be white, as in Figure H9.2.

These pixel dimensions work for displaying a browser on a 17" monitor. If you want to prepare the image for display on a 13" monitor, then make the image 585 pixels wide by 300 pixels deep. You will then need to resize the images to fit.

## Opening the Ballerina Image

The beautiful ballerina is a large part of the background image on the Web site. In these first steps, you'll drag it from its window onto the Web page:

1. Open the file `ballerina.psd` in the H09 folder on the CD. Choose the Move tool ⊕ and drag and drop the image to the left side of a new document. A new layer is created. Name it **Ballerina**.

2. Choose Edit → Preferences → Transparency And Gamut → Grid Size: None to display the Ballerina against a white background.

3. Adjust the opacity of the Ballerina layer to 40%.

## Creating a Background

Since we're going to slice the image in ImageReady, we don't have to worry about creating a seamless background. But we will fill the empty portion of the background:

1. Choose the Magic Wand tool ⊠ . Click the transparent area of the Ballerina layer to select it.

2. Choose Window → Swatches. From the Swatches Palette pull-down menu, choose Web Safe Colors, as seen in Figure H9.3. The Web Safe Colors swatches let you choose from the 216 colors that are displayed uniformly on the World Wide Web.

3. Choose black (#000000) from the Swatches palette.

If you hover your mouse over a swatch, the color's hexadecimal name will be displayed.

4. Target the Background. Press Option-Delete (Mac) or Alt-Backspace (Win) to fill the selection with black.

5. Deselect by pressing ⌘/Ctrl-D.

6. The image should look like Figure H9.4

## Entering the Type

Another way to choose Web color is with the Color Picker. Next, you'll color the type with a hexadecimal that you choose from the Only Web Colors feature:

1. Choose the Type tool. Click the color swatch in the Options bar. In the Color Picker, check Only Web Colors. Choose a bright red, or enter a value in the Hexadecimal box. As you can see in Figure H9.5, I entered #FF0033. Click OK.

2. I used 160-point Edwardian Script ITC for the font, but you can use another typeface. Type the words **Ballet Bleu** in the lower part of the image.

3. Click the Commit button (the check mark icon) in the Options bar to initiate the type.

4. Double-click the Type layer to display the Layer Style dialog box.

5. Check Drop Shadow and set the opacity to 50%; use all of the other defaults.

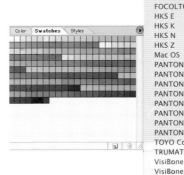

Figure H9.3

**Choosing Web Safe Colors**

Figure H9.4

**The image with the ballerina and black area filled**

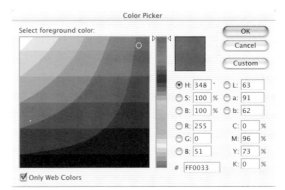

Figure H9.5

**The Color Picker**

Figure H9.6

**The styled text**

Figure H9.7

**The Logo in position**

6. Click the name, then choose Bevel & Emboss → Inner Bevel from the pull-down menu. I used the Smooth technique with a depth of 201%. The type should look like Figure H9.6.

## Adding the Logo

The logo is a graphic element that will later be used as a rollover on an image map in ImageReady. Follow these steps to create two layers, one for each state of the rollover:

1. Open the CD file titled `Logo.psd`. Choose the Move tool and drag the Logo layer from the Layers palette onto the Ballet_Bleu image so that it appears to the left of the B.

2. Drag the Logo layer and place it under the Type layer, as in Figure H9.7. Name it **Logo Black**.

3. Duplicate the layer by dragging it to the New Layer icon. Name the new layer **Logo Blue**.

4. Choose Layer → New Adjustment Layer → Hue Saturation.

5. In the New Layer dialog box, click Group With Previous Layer (see Figure H9.8) to apply the adjustment to the Logo layer exclusively.

6. In the Hue Saturation dialog box, check Colorize.

7. Move the Hue slider to 215, the Saturation slider to 100, and the Lightness slider to +21, as in Figure H9.9.

8. Press ⌘/Ctrl-S to save the document.

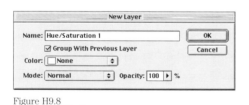

Figure H9.8

**The New Layer dialog box**

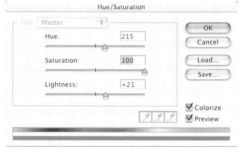

Figure H9.9

**The Hue/Saturation dialog box**

## Adding the Animation Images

Next, we'll prepare our images for an animation sequence. First, we drag and drop them into Photoshop's Layers palette, and then animate them in ImageReady.

1. Target the Ballerina layer.

2. Open the file `animation_images.psd` in the `H09` folder on the CD.

3. Target the topmost layer (1) in the stack. Click the second column in the Layers menu of each layer to link all eight images together.

4. Choose the Move tool. From the image window, drag the layers and drop them on the Ballet Bleu image. Place them in the upper middle of the black rectangle, as in Figure H9.10.

5. Press ⌘/Ctrl-S to save the document.

## Jumping to ImageReady

Now we can open the document in ImageReady and slice it into smaller, more manageable pieces. We'll then create an animation, a rollover, and an image map. Finally, we'll save all the elements as an HTML document for publication to the Web.

1. Click the Jump To icon  in the Tool palette. ImageReady launches, and the Ballet Bleu Photoshop image darkens. An ImageReady version appears in a new window.

2. Choose the Slice tool and use it to divide the image into six rectangles (slices), as shown in Figure H9.11. One slice should contain the images you will use for the animation. Your goal is to cut up the image into six parts.

Another method of creating slices is to drag guides into the position where you want the image to be sliced. Then choose Slices → Create Slices From Guides.

> If need be, you can readjust or reposition the slices by dragging their edges with the Slice Select tool.

**Figure H9.10**

**The Web page with the ballet images**

**Figure H9.11**

**The sliced image**

## Animating the Images

ImageReady can create layer-based animations. Follow these steps to animate the numbered layers and fade them into each other:

1. In the Layers palette, display the eye icons next to all layers *except* for the eight numbered layers.

2. Choose Window → Animation. The frame in the Animation palette displays the visible portions of the image. For the first frame, click the eye icon next to Layer 1 to make it visible.

Remember that each frame in the Animation palette in ImageReady displays the current visible layers. You create an animated sequence by making a new frame and then making visible only those layers that you want to appear in the frame.

3. Click the Duplicate Frame icon  to insert a frame in the Animation palette. In the Layers palette, click the eye icon next to Layer 1 to conceal it, and the icon next to Layer 2 to reveal it.

4. Repeat the process, adding new frames for layers 3, 4, 5, 6, 7, and 8 and changing the layer visibility for each. When completed, your Animation palette should look like Figure H9.12.

5. At this point, you may want to see the animation. Click the Play button ▶ to display it in the image window.

6. Currently, the animation runs too fast. To slow it down, go to the Animation Options pull-down menu and choose Select All Frames. Click the small arrow next to one of the frames and set the delay to 2 seconds.

7. Target Frame 1. Set the delay to 20 seconds. This means that the animation will stop for 20 seconds on the Frame 1 image and then repeat.

8. You may want to set the *iterations* of the animation, or how many times it loops. Forever is only appropriate when the animation keeps looping in a constant motion. Setting the animation to Specific may be appropriate for certain animations like this one. From the Looping Options menu, enter **5**, which means that the animation will display 5 times on the browser and then stop.

Figure H9.12

**The Animation palette displaying the eight frames**

## Creating an Image Map

An image map defines an area on the image that will be interactive. Follow these steps to make the logo a link to another Web page:

1. Choose the Polygon Image Map tool . Draw a shape around the logo, as in Figure H9.13.

2. Choose Window → Image Map. In the URL field, enter **http://cyberdance.org** (see Figure H9.14). This links the image map to another Web site. (Note that the URL must include the entire address, as in `http://cyberdance.org`.)

   If you want to link the logo to another Web page on this site, you will have to create a place for it in the same folder as the Ballet Bleu Web page for this to work. The title of the page should include the HTML extension, as in `aboutballetbleu.html`.

Figure H9.13

**Identifying the image map**

## Creating a Rollover

Like animations, rollovers depend on layers for their behavior. You designate a rollover on an image by changing the visibility of a layer's content. Follow these steps to create a rollover and change the color of the logo:

1. In the Layers palette, be sure that the Logo Black layer is displayed and the Logo Blue layer is concealed.

2. Choose Window → Rollovers to display the Rollovers palette, seen in Figure H9.15.

3. Click the ImageMap_01 thumbnail. In the Rollover Options menu, choose New Rollover State. An Over state appears in the palette, as shown in Figure H9.16.

4. In the Layers palette, conceal the eye next to the Logo Black layer and reveal the Logo Blue layer.

Figure H9.14

**Image Map dialog box**

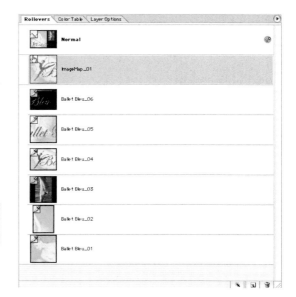

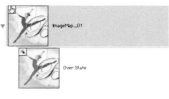

Figure H9.16

**Rollover states**

Figure H9.15

**The Rollovers palette**

## Previewing the Page

Before saving the optimized file, it's a good idea to look at it in your browser, and test the animation, the rollover, and the image map. Choose File → Preview In and choose a preferred browser from the submenu. The preview displays the Web page and the source code for the document, as shown in Figure H9.17. When the image opens, the animation will run. Place your mouse on the logo; the dancer will change color. Click your mouse, and you will be transported to the cyberdance.org Web site.

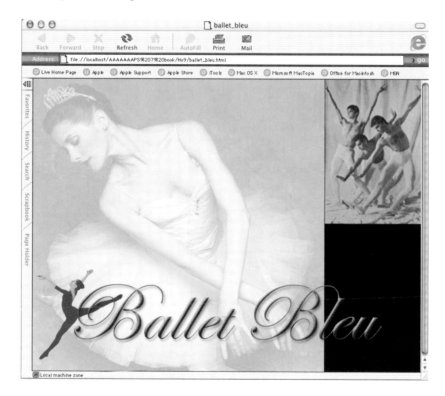

## Optimizing the Images

When the image is complete, you can optimize it slice by slice. To do this, choose the Select Slice tool from the Tool palette. Then click the slices one by one and optimize them individually with the Options palette, or select them as a group and apply the same settings.

Follow these steps to reduce the file sizes of our slices:

1. Choose the Slice Select tool ![icon].

2. Press Shift while selecting slices 1, 2, 4, and 6.

3. In the Optimize palette, choose JPEG Medium for the settings, as in Figure H9.18.

4. With the Slice Select tool, click on Slice 3. In the Optimize palette, choose the setting GIF 64 Dithered (see Figure H9.19) to decrease the file size of the animation and preserve its appearance.

5. Choose File → Save Optimized As → HTML And Images. The slices and animation will be divided into separate images and inserted into an image folder. It's important not to remove the images from the folder, as the HTML code refers to these images within the folder hierarchy.

Figure H9.18

**Optimize palette showing a JPEG setting**

Animations need to be saved as GIFs.

## Publishing Your Page

Having brought your page to life, you are ready to publish it to the Web. Photoshop and ImageReady are good tools for creating simple Web pages with slices, as well as straightforward cell animations and rollovers. For more complex animations, you may want to try Macromedia Flash or Adobe LiveMotion. To create and manage larger, more sophisticated Web sites, you'll find what you need in programs such as Adobe GoLive, Macromedia Dreamweaver, or Microsoft FrontPage.

Figure H9.19

**Optimize palette showing a GIF setting**

Many professional Web designers still prefer to assemble their Web pages in HTML code. They claim the code is cleaner than that generated by WYSIWYG (What-You-See-Is-What-You-Get) editors. I recommend that you at least learn basic HTML code, so that you can understand the structure of Web pages and troubleshoot any problems that may result from code that is too complex or that is not universally compatible with all current browsers.

# CHAPTER 26

# Photoshop and Digital Video

*Photoshop as a graphic tool* is not confined to the world of print and Web images. Professional video editors incorporate the creative power of Photoshop into video post-production. They make titles "pop" out of the background with beveling and embossing. They strip images and add filters, color, and textures with mattes and transparency, sculpting their vision and ultimately incorporating those images into a medium that has both motion and sound. Editors are not limited to using what a camera records; a creative editor can make the television or computer screen defy its two-dimensional environment.

Remember the last time your Aunt Marge dragged out the videotapes of last year's family reunion? You watched hours of bouncing and zooming video images—at the end of the session, you needed motion-sickness pills.

Before, the only way to get these videos cleaned up and trimmed down to a more palatable viewing experience was to pay an expert with sophisticated editing equipment. Now, the world of digital video has placed professional tools in the hands of anyone with a computer.

This chapter helps you prepare Photoshop still images and titles for video. Later, you can combine these images with digitized video in an NLE program like Adobe Premiere. This chapter covers:

- **Nonlinear editing**

- **Video formats**

- **Preparing Photoshop images and titles for digital video**

- **Floating and layered images**

## What is Nonlinear Editing?

The costs of professional digital video tools have come down to such an extent that almost anyone can move into the world of digital video nonlinear editing. *Nonlinear editing (NLE)* is the random access of video storage. With NLE, you can access images through bins set up during the capture, or digitizing, of the video media (digital or analog) and place them along a *timeline* (Figure 26.1) on your computer screen. You no longer have to wait for the tape to shuttle from one end of a videotape to another just to access a shot during the edit. Once the images are stored on a drive, they can be accessed in whatever order you desire, and the order of the edited timeline can be moved around easily.

Figure 26.1

**Example of an Adobe Premiere timeline**

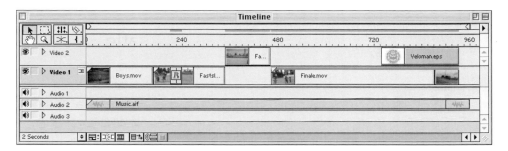

NLE systems like Adobe Premiere allow you to apply effects, titling, image layering, multiple audio tracks, and audio mixing. These elements can be accomplished in real time if you have a professional system, or, if you don't mind waiting for your video to render, you can get the same results on an inexpensive system.

## Exploring Video Formats

Another advantage of NLE is that you can save your project to various formats. You can record back to digital or analog video formats, or you can use various software CODECs (compression-decompression schemes) that compress or decompress the video images and sound. This process reduces storage requirements and data rates, enabling you to save the project for distribution via the Web, CDs, or DVDs. You can create QuickTime movies and capture still images (PICT) or audio files (AIFF).

Three types of media are used in producing videos:

**Digital Media**  Computers can read and process digital media files without converting them. Most electronic cameras and audio-recording equipment on the market save images and sound in a digital format. Many digital video cameras can be connected to a computer with IEEE-1394 ports and cable known as *Firewire*. Firewire transports both video and audio channels to the computer so the digital information can be captured. (For the purposes of this chapter, I will be referring to the digital video format.)

**Analog Media**  Film and conventional tape formats (both video and audio) are examples of analog media. To be used in the digital world, analog information must be converted to a digital form in a process called *digitizing*. If you want to edit analog video, you will need to add a digitizing card to your computer. Contact your computer manufacturer for details on how to upgrade your system.

**Type**  Adobe Premiere and other NLE systems have limited text generators, so editors have turned to Photoshop to create title graphics. True Type fonts and PostScript fonts will enhance the overall look of the end product.

## Understanding Pixels and Video Aspect Ratio

*Pixels* are the foundation of the digital image. In Photoshop, you can vary the resolution of an image, affecting its size and quality. Once you enter the digital video realm, however, the pixel *aspect ratio* has a set number for width and height and a constant resolution of 72 dpi.

Video pixels come in two shapes. In Photoshop and standard analog video (once it has been digitized), the pixels are square (Figure 26.2, left). In digital video, created with a digital video camera, the pixels are rectangular (Figure 26.2, right).

There are two video frame aspect ratios. The most commonly used frame aspect ratio is 4:3 (4 width by 3 height). Notice that the image is squeezed. Widescreen video formats (anamorphic) have a frame aspect ratio of 16:9 (16 width by 9 height). This is also the format of HDTV (high-definition television) and PAL, the European video format standard. PAL is quickly becoming the standard format for digital videos that are transferred to film.

Figure 26.2

Square pixel image created in Photoshop on a 640×480-pixel canvas, which is the analog 4:3 frame aspect ratio (left). Rectangular pixel image from a digital video camera that is 720×480 pixels, which is the standard 4:3 frame aspect ratio in digital video (right).

Table 26.1 shows the dimensions of NTSC (National Television Standards Committee), digitized video, digital video, widescreen, and PAL.

| FORMAT | SQUARE PIXEL PHOTOSHOP | RECTANGULAR PIXEL |
|---|---|---|
| NTSC 4:3 analog | 640×480 | N/A |
| NTSC 4:3 digital | 720×534 | 720×480 |
| NTSC 16:9 anamorphic | 864×540 | 720×480 |
| PAL 4:3 | 768×576 | 720×576 |

The environment of the video frame has a consistent frame ratio with a specific number of pixels, regardless of the size of the television monitor that it plays on (see Figure 26.3). That relationship is 4 wide by 3 deep. Both a frame ratio with 720×480 rectangular pixels in a digital video format and the same 4:3 frame ratio for analog video with 640×480 square pixels have a resolution of 72 dpi.

> If you're capturing your video through a capture card (not through Firewire), you will be importing your Photoshop images into a square pixel environment, so you won't have to be concerned about converting Photoshop images to the rectangular pixel environment of digital video.

## Preparing Photoshop Images for Digital Video

Now, how about that home video you're planning to show at your next family gathering? You want your family members to be sitting on the edge of their seats instead of looking for their "great escape." This section shows you how to prepare an opening title sequence that will draw your audience in and let them know that this experience will not be an repeat of Aunt Marge's video marathon.

Figure 26.3

720×480 rectangular 4:3 frame ratio (left) 640×480 square pixel 4:3 frame ratio (right)

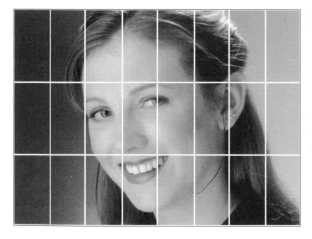

The plan is to make an opening sequence for a vacation video. First, you'll select a background image to use as a base for layers of small images of various shapes floating across the screen. These floating images will precede the title, which will also move into place and then fade away.

1.  Open `sunset.psd` in the `Ch26` folder on the *Photoshop 7 Savvy* CD.

2.  Choose the Crop tool . In the Options bar, set the width to 640 px, the height to 480 px ppi.

3.  Drag the marquee in the sunset image (Figure 26.4). Click the check mark to commit the crop.

4.  Save the file in PSD format. Now your image is ready to import into your NLE software.

> If you save your Photoshop image in a 640×480 frame size at a resolution of 72 dpi, it will fit into your Adobe Premiere, digital video (DV), or analog project without distorting the Photoshop image.

Figure 26.4

**The image with the crop marquee**

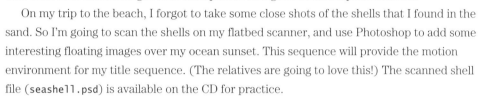

If your image is layered, when you import it to Adobe Premiere, you will get a dialog box (see Figure 26.5) with the options for Merged Layers or Layer 1. To select your full frame image, select Merged Layers.

Figure 26.5

**Choose the Merged Layers option.**

## Floating and Layered Images

We've just prepared and imported a sunset background image for a video project, and now we want to add some images with random shapes that will "float" over the background image. This time we'll create images with transparent backgrounds and alpha channels.

On my trip to the beach, I forgot to take some close shots of the shells that I found in the sand. So I'm going to scan the shells on my flatbed scanner, and use Photoshop to add some interesting floating images over my ocean sunset. This sequence will provide the motion environment for my title sequence. (The relatives are going to love this!) The scanned shell file (`seashell.psd`) is available on the CD for practice.

Figure 26.6

**The scanned shell**

After scanning the shells at 72 ppi directly into Photoshop (File → Import) and saving them in PSD format, I want to make the area around the shell transparent:

1. Duplicate the document by choosing Image → Duplicate. Name the document **Seashell**.

2. Choose Layer New → Layer From Background.

3. Select the part of the shell you want to use with the Lasso tool (see Figure 26.6).

4. Inverse the selection using Select → Inverse.

5. Press Delete (Mac) or Backspace (Win). The image should look like Figure 26.7.

6. Make any changes you want to the image, but keep the background transparent. Save the image as a Photoshop document.

Figure 26.7

**The shell with a transparent background**

Repeat this process until you have saved all of the various images you want to float across your background image in the movie. For this demo, I prepared six shell images and imported them into Adobe Premiere. When you import the image into Adobe Premiere, select the layer (see Figure 26.5 earlier in this chapter) from the Choose Layer dialog box because you want to maintain the transparent background. Adobe Premiere automatically creates an alpha channel to maintain the transparency. (Again, you can use `seashell.psd` for practice.)

When you import still images into Adobe Premiere or any other NLE system, they are given a set number of frames, or seconds of screen time; they do not import as just a single frame. The length of the imported still image is unimportant because any still image can be stretched to fill any amount of time that you desire. In Adobe Premiere, the default time element for imported still images is 5 seconds. You can easily change that by placing your cursor over the edge of the image in the timeline, then click and drag the image to the desired length.

> In Adobe Premiere, the images with transparency need to be used in Video Tracks 2 and above. Placing transparent images in Video Track 1 will ignore the transparency and display a white background; it will distort your image if it is not in the 4:3 frame aspect ratio.

Figure 26.8 is an example of what the Adobe Premiere screen looks like in the Sunset on the Beach project. Bin 1, in the upper-left quadrant, contains all of the still images we have imported into the program. The timeline on the bottom half of the screen shows how the images are layered and placed in a time relationship. The Monitor field in the upper-right quadrant shows the frame where the edit line is positioned on the timeline. Also, there are four video tracks in this sequence with four floating shells above the sunset.

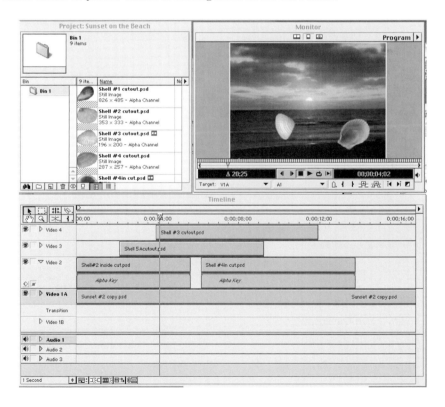

Figure 26.8

**The Adobe Premiere interface showing the beach project**

## Titles for Digital Video

Once you assemble the background for the opening sequence, you can add the title. The sunset and the shells used in the opening sequence came from a fun winter vacation, so our title will be "Keep Clam, Life's a Beach."

1. Press ⌘/Ctrl-N to create a new document. For the size, enter 640×480 pixels with a resolution of 72 dpi. For the mode, choose RGB Color, and for the contents, choose Transparent (see Figure 26.9). Remember that this is the frame size of video with square pixels.

Figure 26.9

The New document window with specifications for the title document

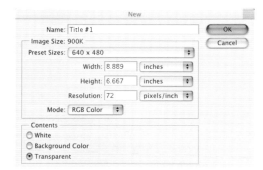

2. Select the Type tool. In the Options bar, set the font and size that you want. (The example font is Sand and the size is 100pt.)

Figure 26.10

The Title Safe/Action Safe grid for an NTSC 640×480 frame

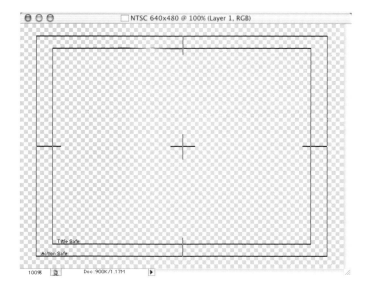

When preparing titles for video, your titles should stay within the Title Safe and Action Safe grid for the NTSC 640×480 video frame (see Figure 26.10). Keep in mind the relationship to the frame when you prepare titles in Photoshop that will be imported into an NLE project. The Title Safe and Action Safe grid is the area within the frame where you can be sure that the information will be seen on any video monitor or television set.

3. Type the title and select a color for it, as shown in Figure 26.11.

4. Apply layer styles to the title. Figure 26.12 shows the layer window with the effects that have been applied to the title; in this case, the title has been beveled and embossed.

Figure 26.11

**The title**

Figure 26.12

**The title with the Bevel and Emboss layer styles applied**

5. Next you need to discard your background so that your title effects will be maintained when you import them into Adobe Premiere. Target the background and drag it to the trash icon in the Layers palette (Figure 26.13).

6. Save the document as a Photoshop file (PSD). Import the image into Adobe Premiere. To maintain the transparency, in the Layer Selection dialog box, select "Life's a Beach" from the Choose A Layer pull-down menu.

7. Add the title to the timeline, add motion effects, render, and play. Figure 26.14 is an example of the NLE timeline with the tile over our sunset.

8. Since the "Keep Clam" text will behave differently on-screen, you'll need to repeat the process. This time make a separate document and type **Keep Clam**. I used 72 Brush Script for the font and applied a Bevel and Emboss Layer Style.

9. Play the "Life's a Beach" QuickTime movie on the CD to see the motion effects that were used to make all of the still images in this exercise appear to be motion video.

Figure 26.13

**The merged title with the layer mask in the Layers palette**

Figure 26.14

**The Premiere interface with all of the elements**

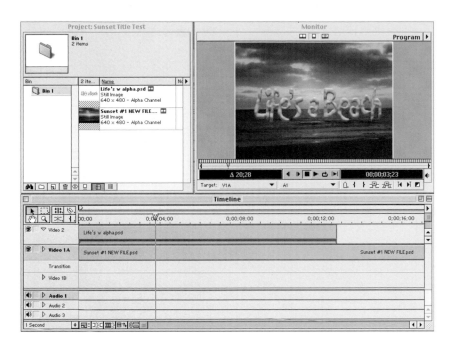

# Appendices

This section of the book *provides descriptions and explanations of Photoshop's many components. It will expand and clarify some of the concepts presented in the main body of the book. You can use the appendices to reference information that is indispensable to the digital imaging process. You will find definitions for some of the more technical aspects of the program, like file formats and blending modes, and enhanced tool descriptions, an index of keyboard shortcuts, and a glossary of terms related to the world of digital images.*

**APPENDIX A** ■ Tool Descriptions

**APPENDIX B** ■ File Formats

**APPENDIX C** ■ Blending Modes

**APPENDIX D** ■ Quick Keys

**GLOSSARY**

# Tool Descriptions

*Photoshop's tools are found* on the Tool palette (Figure A.1). Some tools are grouped into sets, such as the Blur, Sharpen, and Smudge tools, and only one of the tools from a group appears on the Tool palette.

To choose a tool, click its icon on the Tool palette. To select a tool that is not currently displayed, press and hold down the mouse button over the tool that appears in the same position in the Tool palette, and select the tool from the pop-up list.

Figure A.1

**Adobe Photoshop 7 Tools**

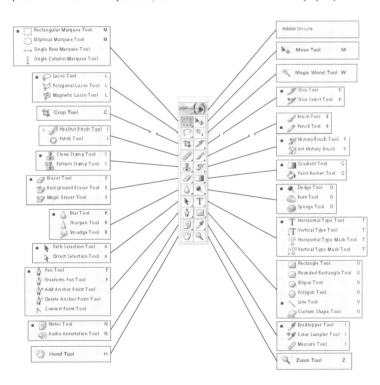

To select a tool quickly, press its shortcut key (the shortcut letter or Shift plus the letter, depending on your preference settings). For grouped sets of tools, pressing the shortcut key repeatedly cycles through the tools in the group.

This appendix describes the tools in Photoshop's Tool palette, in alphabetical order. For each tool, you will find a brief description of its function and usage, as well as a list of its options and the other tools that share its position in the Tool palette.

Some tools are exclusive to a specific part of the program: the Extract dialog, the Liquify dialog, or ImageReady. These tools are included in this list, with a note about where they're used.

## Add Anchor Point ▶

Adds anchor points to existing paths. To use it, click the Add Anchor Point tool; then click the path. You can add anchor points to the middle of a segment, but you can only add segments to the endpoints of an open path. See Chapter 9 for more information.

**Shares Position with**  Pen, Freeform Pen, Delete Anchor Point, and Convert Point

## Airbrush ✍

Simulates painting with an airbrush. (Found on the Options bar for the Brush, Clone, Pattern Stamp, Eraser, Sponge, Burn, and Dodge tools.) To use it, select the Airbrush in the Options bar for any of the tools listed, and the tool's image-editing function will be performed as if done with an airbrush. See Chapter 10 for more information.

**Options**  Brush, Mode, Opacity, Flow, and the Brush Palette options

## Art History Brush ✍

Allows you to apply a variety of painterly effects to an existing image, history state or snapshot. To use it, Click the Art History Brush tool or press Y, click the column next to a state or snapshot in the History palette, and drag in the image. When you paint with the Art History Brush, color is deposited rapidly in several directions. See Chapter 10 for more information.

**Options**  Brush, Mode, Opacity, Style, Area, and Tolerance

**Shares Position with**  History Brush

## Audio Annotation ◀))

Adds an audio annotation to an image (requires a microphone attached to the computer). To use it, click the Audio Annotation tool or press N; then click where you want the audio annotation icon (a speaker icon) to appear. Record the message, using the Record and Stop buttons in the dialog box that appears. To play back the audio annotation, double-click the speaker icon. See Chapter 4 for more information.

**Options**  Author, Color, and Clear All

**Shares Position with**  Notes

# Background Eraser

Erases the background elements in an image, making the pixels on the layer transparent. To use it, click the Background Eraser tool or press E; then drag through an area to erase it. See Chapter 10 for more information.

**Options**  Brush, Limits, Tolerance, Protect Foreground Color, Sampling, Brush Palette options

**Shares Position with**

Eraser and Magic Eraser

# Bloat

Expands an area in all directions simultaneously. (Found in the Filter → Liquify dialog box.) To use it, place your cursor over an area, click, and hold the mouse. Drag to affect adjacent areas. See Chapter 20 for more information.

**Options**  Brush Size, Brush Pressure, and Turbulent Jitter. Holding down the Option/Alt key reverses the effect.

# Blur

Softens an area by decreasing the relative contrast of adjacent pixels. To use it, click the Blur tool or press R, and then drag through an area to blur it. See Chapter 10 for more information.

**Options**  Brush, Mode, Use All Layers, and the Brush Palette options

**Shares Position with**  Sharpen and Smudge

# Brush

Applies strokes of color. Click Brush tool or press B, click in the image, and drag to apply the selected color. To create a straight stroke, click where you want it to begin, hold down the Shift key, and click where you want it to end. See Chapter 10 for more information.

**Options**  Brush, Color Blending Modes, Opacity, Flow, Airbrush, and Brush Palette options

**Shares Position with**  Pencil

# Burn 🔥

Darkens an area by lowering the brightness values of pixels. To use it, click the Burn tool or press O, and drag over the portion of the image you wish to darken. See Chapter 10 for more information.

**Options** Brush, Range, Exposure, and the Brush Palette options

**Shares Position with** Dodge and Sponge

# Cleanup 🖉

Makes the extraction mask transparent or semitransparent or restores opacity to the mask. (Found in the Filter → Extract dialog box.) You must be in preview mode to use the Cleanup tool. Select the Cleanup tool icon or press C. Click and drag over the area that you want to make transparent. To restore opacity, press the Option/Alt key while dragging. See Chapter 21 for more information.

**Options** Brush Size and Extraction Smoothness

# Clone Stamp 🖋

Copies (samples) an area of an image and paints with the sample. To use it, click the Clone Stamp tool or press S, place the pointer over the area to sample, hold down the Option/Alt key, and click. Release and reposition the cursor where you want to paint, and then drag over the area to paint with the sample. See Chapter 10 for more information.

**Options** Brush, Mode, Opacity, Flow, Airbrush, Aligned, and Use All Layers, plus Brush Palette options

**Shares Position with** Pattern Stamp

# Color Sampler 🖊

Marks areas of an image for before-and-after comparisons of color adjustments. To use it, click the Color Sampler tool or press I, place the cursor on the area to sample, and click. The cursor leaves a marker, and the Info palette expands to display the data for that particular marker. You can sample up to four colors and record the information in the Info palette. See Chapter 16 for more information.

**Options** Sample Size and Clear

**Shares Position with** Eyedropper and Measure

# Convert Point 🖉

In a path, changes a corner point to a curve or a curve to a corner point. To use it, select the Convert Point tool, click an anchor point, drag out the direction handles until the desired curve is achieved, and release the mouse button. See Chapter 9 for more information.

**Shares Position with** Pen, Freeform Pen, Add Anchor Point, and Delete Anchor Point

# Crop 🔲

Crops an image to a selected area. To use it, click the Crop tool or press C, drag through an area in the image to define the bounding box, and then click the Commit (check mark) button in the Options bar or press the Return or Enter key. You can also double-click inside the cropping area to commit your crop. To adjust the crop before committing it, drag the bounding box handles, move the bounding box by placing the cursor inside its boundaries and dragging, or move the mouse just outside any of the corner selection handles until the cursor changes to the curved rotation icon and rotate the crop. See Chapter 13 for more information.

**Options** Width, Height, Resolution, Front Image, Clear, Delete, Hide, Shield Cropped Area, Color, Opacity, and Perspective

# Custom Shape 🖉

Generates custom shapes. To use it, click the Custom Shape tool or press U, choose a shape from the Options bar Shape menu, click in the image, and drag until the shape is the size and proportion you want. To draw from the center of the shape, hold down the Option/Alt key as you drag. See Chapter 9 for more information.

**Options** Shape Layer, Path, Fill Pixels, Shape Library, Create New Shape Layer, Add, Subtract, Intersect, Exclude, Layer Properties, Style Library, Color, plus Unconstrained, Defined Proportions, Defined Size, Fixed Size, and From Center under Custom Shape options

**Shares Position with** Rectangle, Rounded Rectangle, Ellipse, Polygon, and Line

# Delete Anchor Point 🖉

Removes anchor points from existing paths. To use it, click the Delete Anchor Point tool, and then click the anchor point you want to remove. The two segments connected by the point join into one. See Chapter 9 for more information.

**Shares Position with** Pen, Freeform Pen, Add Anchor Point, and Convert Point

# Direct Selection

Selects and moves individual anchor points and segments in a path. To use it, click the Direct Selection tool or press A, click a segment or anchor point to select it, and drag. Dragging an anchor point repositions it. Dragging a segment reshapes it. See Chapter 9 for more information.

**Shares Position with** Path Selection

# Dodge

Lightens specific areas of an image by increasing the brightness values of pixels. To use it, click the Dodge tool or press O; then drag over the area you wish to lighten. See Chapter 10 for more information.

**Options** Brush, Range, Exposure, Airbrush, plus Brush Palette options

**Shares Position with** Burn and Sponge

# Edge Highlighter

Highlights the edges of an area to be extracted. (Found in the Filter → Extract dialog box.) To use, click and drag around the edges of the area to be extracted. See Chapter 19 for more information.

**Options** Brush Size, Color, Smart Highlighting, Show/Conceal Highlight

# Edge Touchup

Cleans the edges of an extracted area. (Found in the Filter → Extract dialog box.) You must be in Preview mode to use the Edge Touchup tool. Select the tool icon or press T. Click and drag over the edge of the extraction. Press ⌘-Option/Ctrl-Alt and drag to change the position of the edge. See Chapter 19 for more information.

**Options** Brush Size and Extraction Smoothness

# Ellipse

Draws a circular or elliptical shape. Click the tool or press U, click in the image, and drag to size the ellipse. To constrain the shape to a circle, hold down the Shift key as you drag. To draw from the center of the shape, hold down the Option/Alt key as you drag. See Chapter 9 for more information.

**Options** Shape Layer, Path, Fill Pixels, Shape Library, Create New Shape Layer, Add, Subtract, Intersect, Exclude, Layer Properties, Style Library, and Color; plus Unconstrained, Defined Proportions, Defined Size, Fixed Size, and From Center under Ellipse options

**Shares Position with** Rectangle, Rounded Rectangle, Polygon, Line, and Custom Shape

# Elliptical Marquee ⬭

Selects elliptical or circular portions of an image. To use it, click the Elliptical Marquee tool or press M, click in the image, and drag in any direction to produce an elliptical or circular selection. To constrain the selection area to a circle, hold down the Shift key as you drag. To originate the marquee from its center, place your cursor in the center of the area and hold down the Option/Alt key as you drag. See Chapter 6 for more information.

**Options**  New Selection, Add to Selection, Subtract from Selection, Intersect Selection, Feather, Anti-aliased, Style (Normal, Fixed Aspect Ratio, and Fixed Size), Width and Height

**Shares Position with**  Rectangular Marquee, Single Row Marquee, and Single Column Marquee

# Eraser ⬛

When working on the Background, replaces the area with the background color. When erasing to a layer, replaces the layer content with transparency (or background color if Transparency is Locked). To use it, click the Eraser tool or press E, and then drag over the area you wish to remove. See Chapter 10 for more information.

**Options**  Brush, Mode, Opacity, Flow, Airbrush, and Erase to History, plus Brush Palette options

**Shares Position with**  Background Eraser and Magic Eraser

# Eyedropper ⬛

Specifies the foreground or background color by sampling directly from an image. To use it, click the Eyedropper tool or press I; then click or drag in the image to select a foreground color. To sample a background color, hold down the Option/Alt key as you click. See Chapter 16 for more information.

**Options**  Sample Size

**Shares Position with**  Color Sampler and Measure

# Freeform Pen ⬛

Draws a freeform line that converts itself to a path when the mouse is released. To use it, click the Freeform Pen tool or press P, place the cursor in the image, click, and drag to draw a path. When you release the mouse, the path is produced. See Chapter 9 for more information.

**Options**  Under Shape Layers: Magnetic, New Layer, Add, Subtract, Intersect, Exclude, Style, Color. Under Paths: Magnetic, Add Subtract, Intersect, and Exclude.

**Shares Position with**  Pen, Add Anchor Point, Convert Point, and Delete Anchor Point

# Freeze

Protects areas of the image from the effects of the Liquify tools and commands. (Found in the Filter → Liquify dialog box.) To use it, select the Freeze icon or press F; then click (or click and drag) the mouse to deposit masking color. See Chapter 20 for more information.

**Options** Brush Size, Brush Pressure, and Color

# Gradient

Blends multiple colors into each other or into transparency over a specified distance. To use it, click the Gradient tool or press G, click the image where you want the gradient to start, and drag in the desired direction. Release the mouse where you want the gradient to end. You will fill a selection if one is active, or the entire Background or layer if no selection is active. See Chapter 10 for more information.

**Options** Linear Gradient, Radial Gradient, Angle Gradient, Reflected Gradient, Diamond Gradient, Gradient Editor, Mode, Opacity, Transparency, Reverse, and Dither

**Shares Position with** Paint Bucket

# Hand

Pans across the image when the image exceeds the size of the image window. To use it, click the Hand tool or press H, click the image, and drag to move the image around. See Chapter 4 for more information.

# Healing Brush

Copies (samples) an area of an image and paints with the sample, and then blends the sample into the surrounding area. To use it, click the Healing Brush tool or press J, place the pointer over the area to sample, hold down the Option/Alt key, and click. Release and reposition the cursor where you want to paint, and then drag over the area to paint and blend with the sample. See Chapter 10 and 19 for more information.

**Options** Brush, Mode, Source: Sampled or Pattern, Pattern Library, and Aligned

**Shares Position with** Patch

# History Brush

Restores a portion of an image to a former state. To use, click the History Brush tool or press Y, click the column next to a state or snapshot in the History palette, and drag in the image. See Chapters 10 and 11 for more information.

**Options** Brush, Mode, Opacity, Flow, Airbrush, plus Brush Palette options

**Shares Position with** Art History Brush

# Horizontal Type T

Creates horizontal type generated from installed fonts. To use, click the Type tool or press T, click the point in the image where you want the text to appear, and enter the text from the keyboard. When you enter type in Photoshop using the Type tool, a new layer is automatically created. See Chapter 8 for more information.

**Options**  Text orientation, Font, Style, Size, Anti-Aliasing Method, Left Align, Center Align, Right Align, Color, Warp Text, and Show Character and Paragraph Palettes, and Cancel/ Commit To Edit buttons

# Horizontal Type Mask T

Creates horizontal type selection outlines generated from installed fonts. To use, click the Type tool or press T, click the point in the image where you want the text to appear, and enter the text from the keyboard. Text will be entered in the form of selection marquees, which you can use to cut type from existing layers or to paste visual elements into the type. See Chapter 8 for more information.

**Options**  Text orientation, Font, Style, Size, Anti-Aliasing Method, Left Align, Center Align, Right Align, Color, Warp Text, and Show Character and Paragraph Palettes, and Cancel/ Commit to edit buttons.

# Image Map

Defines areas on the image to make interactive. (Found in ImageReady only.) To use, click and drag to define a rectangle or ellipse. Click and release to deposit a point. Move the mouse to define a side. Click to establish the next point. See Chapter 25 for more information.

**Options**  Rectangle, Ellipse, Polygon, and Image Map Selection tools

# Lasso

Makes a freeform selection. To use, click the Lasso tool or press L, click the edge of the area you want to select, and drag to surround the area with the selection border. Close the marquee by dragging the cursor to the starting point, or release the mouse to close the selection with a straight line. See Chapter 6 for more information.

**Options**  New Selection, Add To Selection, Subtract From Selection, Intersect With Selection, Feather, and Anti-Aliased

**Shares Position with**  Polygonal Lasso and Magnetic Lasso

# Line ◥

Draws a line. To use, click the Line tool or press **U** and drag in the image to create a line. To draw in only multiples of 45-degree angles, hold down the Shift key as you drag. See Chapter 9 for more information.

**Options**  Add To, Subtract From, Intersect With, Exclude Overlapping Area, and Weight, plus Arrowheads: Start, End, Width, Length, and Concavity

**Shares Position with**  Rectangle, Rounded Rectangle, Ellipse, Polygon, and Custom Shape

# Magic Eraser ◨

Erases all pixels of colors similar to the selected color. When working on the Background, replaces the area with the background color. When erasing to a layer, replaces the layer content with transparency (or background color if Transparency is Locked). To use, click the Magic Eraser tool or press E; then click an area in the image that contains the color you want to erase. All similar colors in the image will be erased. See Chapter 10 for more information.

**Options**  Tolerance, Anti-Aliased, Contiguous, Use All Layers, and Opacity

**Shares Position with**  Eraser and Background Eraser

# Magic Wand ◨

Selects areas of an image that are similar in color. To use, click the Magic Wand tool or press W, place your cursor in the area to be selected, and click. Adjacent pixels of similar color will be included in the selection. See Chapter 6 for more information.

**Options**  New Selection, Add To Selection, Subtract From Selection, Intersect With Selection, Tolerance, Anti-Aliased, Contiguous, and Use All Layers

# Magnetic Lasso ◨

Makes selections based on the contrast values of pixels. To use, click the Magnetic Lasso tool or press L, click in the image, and drag. The Magnetic Lasso deposits a path that is attracted to areas of the most contrast. Release the mouse, and the path becomes a selection. See Chapter 6 for more information.

**Options**  New Selection, Add To Selection, Subtract From Selection, Intersect With Selection, Feather, Anti-Aliased, Width, Edge Contrast, Frequency, and Stylus Pressure.

**Shares Position with**  Lasso and Polygonal Lasso

# Measure

Measures the distance between two points. To use, click the Measure tool or press I, and drag from the starting point to the ending point. To measure in only multiples of 45-degree angles, hold down the Shift key as you drag. The distance between the two points appears in the Info palette. See Chapter 4 for more information.

**Shares Position with**  Eyedropper and Color Sampler

# Move

Moves, rotates, or scales a layered element or a selected element. To use, click the Move tool or press M, and then drag the element to move or transform it. To constrain proportions in transformation operations, press the Shift key as you drag. To make a copy of the element instead of moving it, hold down the Option/Alt key as you drag. See Chapter 13 for more information.

**Options**  Auto Select Layer, Show Bounding Box, and Alignment and Distribution

# Notes

Adds textual notes to an image. To use, click the Notes tool or press N, click in the area where you want the note icon to appear, and type your note in the window that appears. After you've entered the text, click the Close button (in the upper-left corner) in the note window. To read the note, double-click the note icon. See Chapter 4 for more information.

**Options**  Author, Font, Size, Color, and Clear All

**Shares Position with**  Audio Annotation

# Paint Bucket

Fills an area with color. To use, click the Paint Bucket tool or press G, place your cursor on the area you want to fill, and click. See Chapter 10 for more information.

**Options**  Fill, Mode, Opacity, Tolerance, Contiguous, Anti-Aliased, Use All Layers, and Pattern

**Shares Position with**  Gradient

# Patch

Blends a source selection or pattern into a targeted area. To use, click the Patch tool or press J. If you are patching with a selection from an image, click Patch → Source from the Options bar and make a freeform selection. Click Destination and drag the selection to the area to be repaired. The selection will be blended into the patch area. If you are patching with a pattern, select Patch → Destination, and outline the desired patch. Use the pull-down menu to choose a pattern and click the Use Pattern button. A patterned patch will be placed in the selected area. See Chapter 10 for more information.

**Options**  Source, Destination, and Use Pattern

**Shares Position with**  Healing Brush

# Path Selection

Selects and moves the path as a unit. To use, click the Path Selection tool or press A; then click to select all of the anchor points and segments of a path. To reposition a path, drag it with the Path Selection tool. To duplicate a path, drag and drop it with the Path Selection tool while holding down the Option/Alt key. To add paths to a selection, hold down the Shift key and click the paths to add. See Chapter 9 for more information.

**Options**  Show Bounding Box, Add, Subtract, Intersect, Exclude, Combine, Align, and Distribute

**Shares Position with**  Direct Selection

# Pattern Stamp

Paints an area with a repeating pattern. To use, click the Pattern Stamp tool or press S, select a pattern from the Options bar, and click and drag to paint with the pattern. See Chapter 10 for more information.

**Options**  Brush, Mode, Opacity, Flow, Airbrush, Pattern, Aligned, Impressionist, and Brush Palette Options

**Shares Position with**  Clone Stamp

# Pen

Draws straight lines or smooth curves. To use, click the Pen tool or press P. To draw a straight path, click to place the first anchor point, release the mouse button, and then continue to click and release. To draw a curve, click and drag. Without releasing the mouse button, drag the handle to form the curve. To finish drawing an open path, click the Pen tool or hold down the ⌘/Ctrl key and click outside the path. To create a closed path (a shape), place the cursor over the first anchor point and click. See Chapter 9 for more information.

**Options**  Under Shape Layers: Auto Add/Delete, New Layer, Add, Subtract, Intersect, Exclude, Style, Color. Under Paths: Auto Add/Delete, Add, Subtract, Intersect, Exclude.

**Shares Position with**  Freeform Pen, Add Anchor Point, Convert Point, and Delete Anchor Point

# Pencil ✎

Produces an aliased or hard-edged stroke. To use, click the Pencil tool or press B, click in the image, and drag to create the stroke. To create a straight stroke, click where you want it to begin, hold down the Shift key, and click where you want it to end. See Chapter 10 for more information.

**Options**  Brush, Mode, Opacity, and Auto-Erase

**Shares Position with**  Brush

# Polygon ⬭

Draws a polygonal shape. To use, click the Polygon tool or press U, click in the image, and drag until the shape is the size and proportion you want. To draw from the center of the shape, hold down the Option/Alt key as you drag. See Chapter 9 for more information.

**Options**  Add To, Subtract From, Intersect With, Exclude Overlapping Area, and Sides, plus Radius, Smooth Corners, Indents Sides By, and Smooth Indents under Polygon Options

**Shares Position with**  Rectangle, Rounded Rectangle, Ellipse, Line, and Custom Shape

# Polygonal Lasso ⬠

Creates straight-edged selection borders. To use, click the Polygonal Lasso tool or press L; then click and release the mouse. Reposition the mouse to the next corner of the polygon, and click and release again. Repeat the process until the area is surrounded. Close the marquee by clicking the starting point again. See Chapter 6 for more information.

**Options**  New Selection, Add To Selection, Subtract From Selection, Intersect With Selection, Feather, and Anti-Aliased

**Shares Position with**  Lasso and Magnetic Lasso

# Pucker ▦

Contracts an area in all directions simultaneously. (Found in the Filter → Liquify dialog box.) To use, select the Pucker icon or press P, place your cursor over an area, and click and hold the mouse. Drag to affect adjacent areas. Press the Option/Alt key to reverse the effect. See Chapter 18 for more information.

**Options**  Brush Size, Brush Pressure, and Turbulent Jitter

# Reconstruct

Restores portions of the image that have been Liquified. (Found in the Filter → Liquify dialog box.) To use, select the Reconstruct icon or press E, place your cursor over an area, click and hold the mouse. Drag to affect adjacent areas. See Chapter 18 for more information.

**Options**  Brush Size, Brush Pressure, and Turbulent Jitter

# Rectangle

Draws a rectangular shape. To use, click the Rectangle tool or press U, click in the image, and drag to size the rectangle. To constrain the shape to a square, hold down the Shift key as you drag. To draw from the center of the shape, hold down the Option/Alt key as you drag. See Chapter 9 for more information.

**Options**  Add To, Subtract From, Intersect, and Exclude Overlapping Shape Area, plus Unconstrained, Square, Fixed Size, Proportional, From Center, and Snap To Pixels under Rectangle Options

**Shares Position with**  Rounded Rectangle, Ellipse, Polygon, Line, and Custom Shape

# Rectangular Marquee

Selects rectangular or square portions of an image. To use, click the Rectangular Marquee tool or press M, click in the image, and drag in any direction to select a rectangular area. To constrain the selection area to a square, hold down the Shift key as you drag. To originate the marquee from its center, place your cursor in the center of the area and hold down the Option/Alt key as you drag. See Chapter 6 for more information.

**Options**  New Selection, Add To Selection, Subtract From Selection, Intersect With Selection, Feather, Anti-Aliased, and Style, plus Width and Height if Constrained Aspect Ratio or Fixed Size are chosen as the Style

**Shares Position with**  Elliptical Marquee, Single Column Marquee, and Single Row Marquee

# Reflection

Moves the center areas to the outside edge of the brush as you drag. (Found in the Liquify dialog box.) To use, select the Reflection icon or press M. Click and drag. See Chapter 18 for more information.

**Options**  Brush Size, Brush Pressure, and Turbulent Jitter

# Rounded Rectangle 🔲

Draws a rectangular shape with rounded corners. To use, click the Rounded Rectangle tool or press U, click in the image, and drag to size the rectangle. To constrain the shape to a square, hold down the Shift key as you drag. To draw from the center of the shape, hold down the Option/Alt key as you drag. See Chapter 9 for more information.

**Options**  Add To, Subtract From, Intersect, Exclude Overlapping Area, and Radius, plus Unconstrained, Square, Fixed Size, Proportional, From Center, and Snap To Pixels in the Rounded Rectangle Options

**Shares Position with**  Rectangle, Ellipse, Polygon, Line, and Custom Shape

# Sharpen △

Increases the relative contrast values of adjacent pixels, creating the effect of a sharper focus. To use, click the Sharpen tool or press R, and then drag over an area to sharpen it. As you drag over an area, the pixels randomly change color. The more you drag, the more diverse the colors of the adjacent pixels become. See Chapter 10 for more information.

**Options**  Brush, Mode, Pressure, and Use All Layers, plus Brush Palette options

**Shares Position with**  Blur and Smudge

# Shift Pixels 🔳

Moves pixels perpendicular to the direction of the movement of the mouse. (Found in the Filter → Liquify dialog box.) To use, select the Shift Pixels icon or press S. Click and drag to the left to shift pixels down, to the right to shift pixels up, upward to shift them to the right, or downward to shift them to the left. Pressing the Option/Alt key reverses the direction of the shift. See Chapter 20 for more information.

**Options**  Brush Size, Brush Pressure, and Turbulent Jitter

# Single Column Marquee 🔳

Selects a single vertical column of pixels. To use, click the Single Column Marquee tool, and then click in the image. A selection marquee appears around a single column of adjacent pixels that runs vertically across the entire image. See Chapter 6 for more information.

**Options**  New Selection, Add To Selection, Subtract From Selection, Intersect With Selection, and Feather

**Shares Position with**  Rectangular Marquee, Elliptical Marquee, and Single Row Marquee

## Single Row Marquee

Selects a single horizontal row of pixels. To use, click the Single Row Marquee tool; then click in the image. A selection marquee appears around a single, continuous row of adjacent pixels that runs horizontally across the entire image. See Chapter 6 for more information.

**Options** New Selection, Add To Selection, Subtract From Selection, Intersect With Selection, and Feather

**Shares Position with** Rectangular Marquee, Elliptical Marquee, and Single Column Marquee

## Slice

Divides an image into slices, which can be saved as individual files. To use, click the Slice tool or press K; then click and drag over the area that you want to make a slice. To constrain the slice to square, hold down the Shift key as you drag. To draw the slice from the center, hold down the Option/Alt key as you drag. See Chapter 25 for more information.

**Options** Normal, Fixed Aspect Ratio, and Fixed Size, plus Height, Width, Show Slice Numbers, and Line Color when Fixed Aspect Ratio or Fixed Size is selected.

**Shares Position with** Slice Select

## Slice Select

Selects a slice in the image. To use, click the Slice Select tool or press K, and then click the slice you wish to select. You can add slices to the selection by Shift-clicking. See Chapter 25 for more information.

**Options** Bring To Front, Bring Forward, Send Backward, Send To Back, Promote To User Slice, plus a Slice Options button that opens a dialog box with options for setting Slice Type, Name, URL, Target, Message Text, Alt Tag, and Dimensions.

**Shares Position with** Slice

## Smudge

Moves one area of color into another while blending and mixing the colors as they are moved, simulating charcoal or pastel effects. To use, click the Smudge tool or press R, and then drag to paint with the tool. See Chapter 10 for more information.

**Options** Brush, Mode, Pressure, Use All Layers, and Finger Painting, plus Brush Palette options

**Shares Position with** Blur and Sharpen

# Sponge 🖊

Enhances or diminishes color intensity by changing the saturation or levels of gray. To use, click the Sponge tool or press O; then drag through the area that you wish to affect. See Chapter 10 for more information.

**Options** Brush, Saturate, Desaturate, Flow, Airbrush, and Brush Palette options

**Shares Position with** Dodge and Burn

# Thaw 🖊

Unfreezes areas that have been frozen. (Found in the Filter → Liquify dialog box.) To use, select the Thaw icon or press T, and then click or click and drag. See Chapter 20 for more information.

**Options** Brush Size, Brush Pressure, and Turbulent Jitter

# Twirl Clockwise ≋

Spins pixels in a clockwise motion. (Found in the Filter → Liquify dialog box.) To use, select the Twirl Clockwise icon or Press R. Click or click and drag to affect the pixels. The longer the tool is held in position, the greater the effect. See Chapter 20 for more information.

**Options** Brush Size, Brush Pressure, and Turbulent Jitter

# Twirl Counterclockwise 🅢

Spins pixels in a counterclockwise motion. (Found in the Filter → Liquify dialog box.) To use, select the Twirl Counterclockwise icon or Press L. Click or click and drag to affect the pixels. The longer the tool is held in position, the greater the effect. See Chapter 20 for more information.

**Options** Brush Size, Brush Pressure, and Turbulent Jitter

# Vertical Type ⊺

Creates vertical type generated from installed fonts. To use, click the Type tool or press T, click the point in the image where you want the text to appear, and enter the text from the keyboard. When you enter type in Photoshop using the Type tool, a new layer is automatically created. See Chapter 8 for more information.

**Options** Text orientation, Font, Style, Size, Anti-Aliasing Method, Left Align, Center Align, Right Align, Color, Warp Text, and Show Character and Paragraph Palettes, and Cancel/ Commit to edit buttons.

## Vertical Type Mask 🔳

Creates vertical type selection outlines generated from installed fonts. To use, click the Type tool or press T, click the point in the image where you want the text to appear, and enter the text from the keyboard. Text will be entered in the form of selection marquees, which can be used to cut type from existing layers or for pasting visual elements into the type. See Chapter 8 for more information.

**Options**  Text orientation, Font, Style, Size, Anti-Aliasing Method, Left Align, Center Align, Right Align, Color, Warp Text, and Show Character and Paragraph Palettes, and Cancel/Commit to edit buttons.

## Warp 🔳

Pushes pixels forward as you drag. (Found in the Filter → Liquify dialog box.) To use, select the Warp icon, or Press W. Click and drag. See Chapter 20 for more information.

**Options**  Brush Size, Brush Pressure, and Turbulent Jitter

## Zoom 🔳

Enlarges or reduces the size of the displayed image. To use, click the tool or press Z; then click the area you want to enlarge. Each time you click, the zoom increases, to a maximum view magnification of 1600%. To reduce the size of the displayed image, click with the Option/Alt key held down. (The tool will have a minus sign to indicate that it is in reduction mode.) To restore the display to 100% view, double-click the Zoom tool. See Chapter 4 for more information.

**Options**  Resize Window To Fit, Ignore Palettes, Actual Pixels, Fit On Screen, and Print Size

# File Formats

*Photoshop 7 can open* and save image files in a variety of file formats. The number of supported file formats can be further extended with the addition of plug-ins that attach to the Import and Export submenus.

## File Compression Methods

Because graphics files are usually quite large, most graphic file formats use compression to reduce the size of the file when it is saved. There are two categories of compression: lossy and lossless.

**Lossy** compression schemes create smaller files but can affect image quality. When the image is decompressed, it is not identical to the original. Usually, colors have been blended, averaged, or estimated in the decompressed version.

**Lossless** compression schemes preserve image detail. When the image is decompressed, it is identical to the original version.

Some image file formats have built-in compression methods, so that when you save a file, the compression is handled automatically. Other formats, such as JPEG and TIFF, have optional compression that you control through a dialog box when you save the file.

Photoshop supports the following types of compression:

**CCITT** (International Telegraph and Telekeyed Consultative Committee) is a lossless compression technique for black-and-white PDF and PostScript images.

**JPEG** (Joint Photographic Experts Group) is a lossy compression method used for JPEG, PDF, TIFF, and PostScript formats. It is typically used to prepare files for the Web or to archive images to read-only media.

**LZW** (Lempel Ziv Welch) is a lossless compression method supported by TIFF, PDF, GIF, and PostScript formats. It is typically used to prepare files for the Web or for use in desktop-publishing programs.

**RLE** (Run Length Encoding) is a lossless compression method supported by TIFF, BMP, and TGA formats.

**ZIP** is a lossless compression method supported by PDF and TIFF files.

# Supported Image File Formats

Photoshop 7 opens and saves to the following file formats:

| | | | |
|---|---|---|---|
| AVI | BMP | DCS 1.0 and 2.0 | EPS PICT Preview |
| EPS TIFF Preview | Generic EPS | Filmstrip | GIF |
| JPEG | Kodak Photo CD | PCX | Photoshop PDF |
| Generic PDF | Photoshop 2.0 | PICT | PICT Resource |
| PIXAR | PNG | PSD | Raw |
| Scitex CT | TGA | TIFF | WBMP |

These file formats and the Photoshop options for them are described in the following sections.

## AVI (Audio Video Interleaved)

The AVI format is the standard Windows format for audio and video data.

## BMP (Microsoft Bitmap Format)

BMP is the native format for Microsoft Paint, the generic graphics program included with Windows. BMP supports 32-bit color and RLE compression. You can open and save BMP files in RGB, Indexed, Grayscale, and Bitmap color modes.

## DCS 1.0 and 2.0 (Desktop Color Separation)

The DCS format, also known as a Five-File EPS, is designed to separate the cyan, magenta, yellow, and black color information. Before saving to this format, be sure to convert the color mode to CMYK. This format is often used in desktop-publishing programs like QuarkXPress, Adobe PageMaker, and Adobe InDesign.

The DCS formats create five files, one for each of the four process-color channels and a separate file as a low-resolution composite preview to be placed in the desktop-publishing program. You can print the low-res image from the desktop-publishing application as a proof. This saves processing time and streamlines workflow. When you print to film, the four process-color files are used to create the high-resolution output version. The preview and the separated files must all remain in the same folder.

You can choose to save a file in DCS 1.0 or DCS 2.0 format. DCS 2.0 also supports grayscale images with spot color. Both formats allow you to save the four separate color channels and a composite image that is placed in your desktop-publishing program.

In the DCS Format dialog box, which appears when you choose to save an image in DCS 1.0 or 2.0, you can choose from a variety of options for file inclusion, preview formats, and encoding methods. You also have the Include Halftone Screen and Include Transfer Function options, which offer the same settings that are available for EPS files (described in the next section).

## EPS (Encapsulated PostScript)

EPS files often contain vector graphic elements generated by PostScript illustration programs such as Illustrator, FreeHand, and CorelDRAW. You can open and save EPS files in CMYK, RGB, Lab, Indexed, Grayscale, Duotone, and Bitmap color modes. EPS does not support alpha channels, but it does support clipping paths.

When you *open* an EPS file in Photoshop, it becomes rasterized (Photoshop converts the vector art into pixels). Photoshop displays the Rasterize Generic EPS dialog box, which lets you specify the size and resolution of the image and the mode to which you want it converted. Because the vector image is resolution-independent, you can specify any dimension without compromising its quality. You can also choose the Anti-Alias option, which will slightly blur the pixels between vector objects when they are rendered.

When you open a vector EPS file in Photoshop, areas that contain no information—the white pasteboard in the illustration program—become transparent.

You can *place* an EPS image in an existing Photoshop document by choosing File → Place. The image is displayed on a separate layer and can be sized, rotated, or positioned. If the vector image contains an imported raster image that has been placed into it, you should enter the resolution of the imported image and leave the suggested dimensions unchanged to maintain the quality of the imported image.

You may want to save your document as an EPS file when you intend to use it in a desktop-publishing program like QuarkXPress or an illustration program like Adobe Illustrator, particularly if you plan to print it on a PostScript printer. When you save your file in EPS format, it is saved in two parts: the PostScript code and the on-screen preview. In the EPS Options dialog box, which appears when you choose to save a file in EPS format, you can set the following options:

**Preview** For Macintosh platforms, you can choose to save as 1-bit Macintosh for a black-and-white preview (the smallest file), 8-bit Macintosh for a 256-color PICT preview, or a Macintosh JPEG for a 24-bit color preview with JPEG compression. For Windows platforms or Macintosh-to-Windows transfers, you can save the preview as a 1-bit (black-and-white) or 8-bit (256-color) TIFF.

**Encoding** Your choices are Binary, ASCII, or JPEG. When saving the image for use in an illustration or desktop-publishing program, select Binary, sometimes called Huffman Encoding, to compress the file. Some programs and older printers do not recognize binary encoding, in which case you'll need to save the document in ASCII encoding, which produces a larger file. Choose JPEG if you want to use this compression method to compress the file. (See the "File Compression Methods" section earlier in this appendix for more information about JPEG compression.)

**Include Halftone Screen**  You can include a halftone screen in the EPS document if you saved one in Page Setup.

**Include Transfer Function**  This option controls the brightness and contrast settings on your printer (selected in the Page Setup).

**Transparent Whites**  Displays white areas as transparent. This option is available only for images in Bitmap mode.

**PostScript Color Management**  Choose this option if you are printing to a PostScript Level 2 or 3 printer. It converts the file's data to the printer's color space.

**Include Vector Data**  If there are unrendered type layers or vector shape layers on an image, check this box to preserve them.

**Image Interpolation**  Check this box to include the interpolation method in the file should it be scaled in a destination program. It is a PostScript RIP–level calculation and output function and not application specific. It anti-aliases the printed appearance of a low-resolution image.

## EPS TIFF/PICT Preview

These formats let you open images saved in file formats that create previews but that are not supported by Adobe Photoshop (such as QuarkXPress). An opened preview image can be edited and used like any other low-resolution file. EPS PICT Preview is available only in MacOS.

The EPS TIFF and EPS PICT formats were more relevant for use in earlier versions of Photoshop. The current version of Photoshop includes rasterization features for opening files that include vector data.

## Filmstrip (QuickTime Movies)

Filmstrips that have been saved as QuickTime movies in Adobe Premiere can be edited frame by frame in Photoshop (each frame can be edited individually or as a group). When you open the file in Photoshop, each frame is separated by a gray bar, with the frame number appearing on the right and the time code appearing on the left. Filmstrip works only with RGB images.

When you are working with a Filmstrip file in Photoshop, do not change its size or add canvas to it. Resizing prevents you from saving the changes to Filmstrip mode.

## GIF (Graphics Interchange Format)

The primary GIF format, also called GIF87a, supports 256 colors, but does not support transparency or animation. GIF89a, the later GIF version, does support transparency and animation, making it a popular Web format. GIF format uses LZW compression, making it lossless within the confines of the Indexed 256-color mode.

## IFF (Amiga Graphic File Format)

Graphics files generated by Amiga (a personal graphic arts workstation introduced in the 1980s by Commodore Computer) still exist. Photoshop lets you open and save these files in IFF (Interchange File Format). You can open and save IFF files in RGB, Indexed, Grayscale, and Bitmap color modes.

## JPEG (Joint Photographic Experts Group)

JPEG format is primarily used for two purposes: to compress files and to save files for use on the Web. You can open and save JPEG files in RGB, CMYK, and Grayscale color modes.

As explained earlier in this appendix, JPEG is a lossy compression mode, which means that it loses information to make the file smaller. The amount of data that is lost depends on the settings you choose when you save a file in JPEG format.

> Avoid opening a JPEG file, editing it, and saving it back to the JPEG format. Photoshop recompresses the image each time you save it; therefore the quality will diminish with each open-and-save cycle. A better approach is to work in the native Photoshop format (PSD) until the image is complete. Archive the final version to a read-only CD as a JPEG at maximum quality to get the most compression with a minimum loss of quality.

When you choose to save a file in JPEG format, the JPEG Options dialog box appears. This dialog box is divided into three sections:

**Image Options** This section offers either a drop-down list or a slider for choosing a compression setting. The list includes Low, Medium, High, and Maximum settings. The slider offers 12 numerical settings. The more the file is compressed, the less space it consumes on your hard disk and the lower its quality.

**Format Options** The three radio buttons control how the image downloads to a Web browser. The Baseline Standard setting displays the image all at once, only when all of the data has been received from the modem into RAM. (If the image is large, the site visitor may need to wait quite some time to see anything on the screen.) The Baseline Optimized setting loads the image in strips, from top to bottom, as the data is received. The Progressive setting gradually resolves the image as it loads, depending on the number of scans you choose (3, 4, or 5).

**Size** The numbers at the bottom of the dialog box display the file size and the download time. For comparison, you can choose a modem speed from the drop-down list to recalculate the information for the selected speed.

## Kodak Photo CD

You can open Kodak Photo CD format images in Photoshop. Photoshop does not, however, save to the Photo CD format.

Kodak Photo CD, images have a default resolution of 72 pixels per inch, which can be changed. The smallest option, 64×96, is a little over 1.3×0.8 inches and is 18 KB. The largest, 3072×2048, is just over 42×28 inches and is 18 MB. A Pro version of the Photo CD contains one additional image size of 6144×4096 pixels.

## PCX (PC Paintbrush Format)

PCX is the native format for PC Paintbrush, the Windows paint program. It supports 24-bit color. You can open and save PCX in RGB, Indexed, Grayscale, and Bitmap color modes.

## PDF (Portable Document Format)

PDF is the format Adobe Acrobat uses to produce cross-platform, electronic documents for on-screen viewing. You can save both raster and vector art to PDF format. PDF files look like electronic versions of desktop-published documents, complete with formatted text and graphics. They are ideal for transport over the Internet because their file sizes are relatively small. In order to view PDF files, you need a copy of Acrobat Reader, which Adobe distributes for free.

When you open, in Photoshop, a PDF file saved from an application like Adobe Illustrator or Adobe Acrobat, it becomes rasterized. You can edit PDF documents in Photoshop and browse through page thumbnails (provided that the previews were originally saved with the document). PDF supports RGB, CMYK, Indexed, Grayscale, Lab, and Bitmap color modes.

## Photoshop 2.0

Photoshop 2.0 format is backward compatible on Macintosh Photoshop versions 2.0 and 2.5, which do not support layers. Saving an image in Photoshop 2.0 format eliminates layers and other attributes of later versions of the program. Before converting a file to Photoshop 2.0 format, you may want to duplicate it or rename the file when you save it.

## PICT (Macintosh Picture)

PICT is the native Macintosh image format. It is used extensively in desktop-publishing applications and for transferring files across platforms. PICT can support bitmaps and object-oriented images, can compress files, and works particularly well on images with large areas of color, such as black-and-white alpha channels.

You can open and save PICT files in RGB (with one alpha channel), Indexed, Grayscale, and Bitmap (without alpha channels) color modes. You can save grayscale images in bit depths of 2, 4, and 8 bits. RGB images can be saved in 16 or 32 bits.

If you have QuickTime installed on your Macintosh, you can choose between four JPEG compression levels. However, if you want to compress your file this way, it is better to save it as a JPEG, unless you need backward compatibility with an older Macintosh system.

## PICT Resource (Special Macintosh Format)

PICT Resource files are special Macintosh files. You can import a PICT Resource file into Photoshop, and you can save a file in PICT Resource format. PICT Resource format supports RGB (with one alpha channel), Indexed, Grayscale, and Bitmap (without alpha channels) color modes.

To open a PICT Resource image, choose File → Import → PICT Resource and select the Scrapbook file in the System folder. When the PICT Resource dialog box appears, choose Preview to browse forward or backward in the Scrapbook. When you locate and select the PICT Resource file you wish to open, click OK.

One reason to save a file in PICT Resource format is to create a custom splash screen for your Macintosh. The resource fork of your MacOS system file contains the splash screen image that welcomes you when you boot up your Macintosh. You can save an image in PICT Resource format to the System folder to create your own splash screen to greet you every time you launch your computer. To save an image as a splash screen, follow these steps:

1. Create an image at the pixel dimensions of your monitor (see the Monitors information in the Display Control Panel for these dimensions).

2. Choose Image → Image Size and make sure that the resolution is set to 72 ppi.

3. Choose File → Save → Format → PICT Resource. Name the image StartupScreen and save it to your System folder.

4. In the PICT Resource dialog box, enter the name SCRN. Select None for compression and click OK. Enter 0 for the Resource ID and choose between 16 or 32 bits for the image size.

## PIXAR (3-D Animation Workstation Format)

PIXAR is the 3-D animation workstation used to create feature-length animated movies (like *Shrek, Monsters, Inc.,* or *Ice Age*). Photoshop can open images saved to PIXAR format and save images for use on a PIXAR workstation. PIXAR format supports RGB and Grayscale color modes (with one alpha channel).

## PNG (Portable Network Graphic)

In part, PNG was developed in response to two aspects of the GIF format: Patent issues surrounded GIF's LZW compression method, and 256 colors were too limiting to many digital graphic designers and end users. PNG supports transparency, 16 million colors, and in many instances can compress files more efficiently than GIF. Although it was not supported by older Web browsers, the rapid changes in Web sophistication have made this format increasingly popular.

PNG uses a non-patented lossless compression method known as *deflation*. The format supports RGB and Grayscale color modes (with one alpha channel). When you choose to save a file in PNG format, the PNG Options dialog box opens. In this dialog box, you can choose Adam 7 to interlace the file, so that the image will resolve in increasing detail as it loads into the browser. You can also choose to compress the image using the following filters:

- The None option uses no filter compression and is recommended for grayscale and bitmap images.
- The Sub filter compresses images with horizontal patterns or gradients.
- The Up filter compresses images with vertical patterns or gradients.
- The Average filter compresses low-level noise by averaging the RGB values of adjacent pixels.
- The Paeth filter compresses low-level noise by reassigning the color values of adjacent areas.
- The Adaptive option applies the most appropriate filter to the image.

Adobe recommends that you choose the Adaptive option if you are unsure of which filter to apply.

## PSD (Photoshop Format)

PSD is the native Photoshop format. It supports all the capabilities that the program has to offer. Photoshop opens and saves PSD files more quickly than files in other formats. PSD is backward compatible with Photoshop versions 3, 4, 5, and 5.5. This means that you can open a Photoshop 6 document in Photoshop 3 (although you will lose some of the attributes that the earlier version does not support, like the ability to run Actions, create spot color channels, use vector-based shapes and type, and all of the other cool features supported by the Photoshop 6).

Photoshop's native format is now compatible with several other programs in varying degrees. Adobe AfterEffects and Adobe ImageReady will open a layered PSD file. Corel's

Painter and PHOTO-PAINT and Jasc's Paint Shop Pro can import PSD files with layers. Adobe Illustrator gives you the option of converting layers to objects. Macromedia Free-Hand can open Photoshop files and supports layers to a limited extent. Adobe InDesign can place Photoshop files; however, it does not support Photoshop layers.

Adobe PageMaker and QuarkXPress are the last holdouts of professional mainstream publishing software that don't open or place native Photoshop files. To use an image in a PSD file in Quark, you will need to flatten it (eliminate its layers) and convert it to TIFF, EPS, or another compatible format.

> It's a good idea to check your destination application and version for the degree of compatibility.

## Raw Format

Images generated on mainframe computers cannot be saved in any of the common image formats that are used for publishing. The Raw format is used to transfer files of unknown origin between platforms and applications. It is stripped-down binary code that describes color information about each pixel.

You can open and save Raw files in CMYK, RGB, and Grayscale color modes with alpha channels and multichannel, and in Indexed, Lab, and Duotone color modes without alpha channels.

When you open a Raw document, the Raw dialog box appears, which allows you to assign values that control how the image information will be structured. Fill in the Raw dialog box fields as follows:

- In the Width and Height fields, enter the dimensions of the document. (Swap reverses width and height.)

- In the Count field, enter the number of color channels in the image. For example, if the image is CMYK, enter a value of 4.

- In the Depth field, enter the number of bits per channel.

- For the Byte Order, choose PC or Mac for 16-bit images.

The Interleaved check box controls the sequence in which the color information is described. The pixels are described in bytes in a particular order. Checking the Interleaved box describes the color information pixel by pixel. For example, for an RGB image, the code sequentially describes the red, green, and blue values of each pixel at a time. If the Interleaved box is unchecked, the code describes the information channel by channel. In the case of an RGB image, the code first describes all of the red, then the green, and then the blue values of the entire document in sequence.

The Header field indicates how much information in the header that Photoshop can ignore. The Retain Header When Saving option tells Photoshop to retain the header information in the code if its value is greater than zero.

You can click the Guess button to have Photoshop guess at the values of the information, but you need to know either the width or height or the header information.

You might want to save a file as a Raw document to prepare it for a mainframe or another type of computer that doesn't support other common formats. When you choose to save a file in Raw format, the Raw Options dialog box appears. In the File Type field, enter the four-character code, such as TIFF or PICT, if you are using the file on a Macintosh. For the File Creator setting, use the default 8BIM code for Photoshop. In the Header field, enter the size of the header in bytes. For the Save Channels In setting, choose Interleaved Order or Non-interleaved Order.

## Scitex CT

Scitex CT format saves files for use on the Scitex continuous-tone, color-processing computer and image-scanning systems. It is used primarily for high-end image processing for full-color output to film color separations. This format supports RGB, CMYK, and Grayscale color modes with no alpha channels.

## TGA (Targa)

TGA, or Targa, format is designed for MS-DOS color applications running with a TrueVision video board for compositing images onto live video. Targa supports 32-bit RGB, Indexed, and Grayscale color modes.

## TIFF (Tagged Image File Format)

TIFF format is a standard for images that will be placed in desktop-publishing programs. It can be neatly transported across platforms and compressed to reduce file size.

You can open and save TIFF files in RGB, CMYK (with alpha channels), Grayscale, Lab, Indexed, and Bitmap (without alpha channels) color modes. TIFF format can support a total of 24 channels in a document. If you want to reduce the file size, choose Save A Copy, select TIFF as the format, and check the Exclude Alpha Channels box.

Photoshop can save layers in TIFF format, but if the image is opened in another program, the layers will appear flattened. TIFF format can also save annotations and can now save vector data, but only Photoshop can read it as vector; other software uses the flat raster version held in the file.

When you save an image in TIFF format, the TIFF Options dialog box appears. This dialog box offers the following options:

**Image Compression**  Choose between LZW, ZIP, or JPEG compression. (See the "File Compression Methods" section at the beginning of this appendix.) Note that many service bureaus request that you do not choose LZW compression when saving a file for placement in a desktop-publishing program if you are going to print it on a high-resolution imagesetter. A TIFF image that has been compressed with LZW compression takes longer to process and print. It also can cause errors in older raster image processors. When in doubt, contact your service bureau.

**Byte Order**  Choose Mac or PC, depending on the platform you are working on or to prepare a file to work on a different platform.

**Image Pyramid**  Saves the image cache with the file, allowing for faster rendering on screen.

**Transparency**  Select this box if the image contains transparent elements that you want to save.

**Layer Compression**  RLE or ZIP compression of layered data is available, or you can choose to discard the layers and save a copy of the document.

## WBMP (Wireless Bitmap)

This new format is used for images destined for mobile devices, such as cell phones. WBMP supports 1-bit color, or only black and white pixels. To change color or grayscale pixel values to black or white, use the Dither Algorithm menu to determine the method: Diffusion, Pattern, or No Dither. Diffusion dither applies a random pattern that is usually less noticeable than Pattern dither, but it may cause seams to appear across slice borders. To erase any seams, link the slices; this diffuses the dither pattern across all linked slices.

You can specify a Dither percentage to control the amount of dithering that is applied to the image. To vary the Dither percentage across an image, use masks from Type layers, Shape layers, and alpha channels. This technique produces high-quality results in the key areas of your image—and without giving up file size.

# Blending Modes

*The blending mode* you select for a painting or image-editing tool or command controls how the color you are applying with the tool blends with the existing color in the area where you are working. The Mode menu on the Options bar (and repeated at the top of the Layers palette and within the Fill, Apply Image, Calculations, and Fade commands) offers these 27 blending modes.

| Mode | Description |
|---|---|
| Add | Available in the Apply Image and Calculations dialog boxes. Adds the brightness value of each pixel in the source image to the aligned pixel in the target image, divides the difference by the scale, then adds the offset value. The Add mode lightens the image. Here's the formula: (Target + Source) ÷ Scale + Offset = Brightness value. |
| Behind | Available only with the painting tools. Applies the action of the selected tool to just the transparent portion of the layer (provided that the Preserve Transparency setting is not in effect). |
| Clear | Fills an area or draws a line (created with the Line tool, Paint Bucket, Fill command, or Stroke command) with transparent pixels. |
| Color | Blends the color being applied with the original color, using the original color's luminance value and the applied color's hue and saturation values (so the original levels of gray are maintained). |
| Color Burn | Looks at each channel's color information and darkens the original color to reflect the color being applied with the selected tool. Blending with white produces no change. |
| Color Dodge | Brightens the original color to reflect the color being applied. Looks at the color information in each channel, and brightens the base color to reflect the blend color by decreasing the contrast. Blending with black produces no change. |

| Mode | Description |
|---|---|
| Darken | Colors the area affected by the selected tool with the darkest color (either the original color or the color being applied by the selected tool). |
| Difference | Blends the original and applied colors by subtracting the color values of the one that is less bright from those of the brighter color. Blending with white inverts the base color values; blending with black produces no change. |
| Dissolve | "Dissolves" the applied color into the original color by replacing the pixels with either the original color or the color being applied, based on the opacity of the pixels in the area. (Opacity is set using the Opacity slider on the Options bar.) |
| Exclusion | Works much like the Difference mode, but the resulting contrast is not as great. Blending with white inverts the base color values; blending with black produces no change. |
| Hard Light | Produces an effect similar to casting a glaring light on the area affected by the selected tool. Depending on the color applied, this mode either lightens or darkens the area. Applying a color that is less than 50% gray lightens the affected area, as with the Screen mode. Applying a color that is more than 50% gray darkens the area, as with the Multiply mode. |
| Hue | Blends the colors using the original color's luminance and saturation values and the applied color's hue value. |
| Lighten | Colors the area affected by the selected tool with the lightest color (either the original color or the color being applied by the selected tool). |
| Linear Burn | Industrial-strength burn pushes the darkest colors in the image to black. Looks at the color information in each channel and darkens the base color to reflect the blend color by decreasing the brightness. Blending with white produces no change. |
| Linear Dodge | Industrial-strength dodge pushes the lightest colors in the image to white. Looks at the color information in each channel and brightens the base color to reflect the blend color by increasing the brightness. Blending with black produces no change. |
| Linear Light | Hyper-saturates the layer. Burns or dodges the colors by decreasing or increasing the brightness, depending on the blend color. If the blend color (light source) is lighter than 50% gray, the image is lightened by increasing the brightness. If the blend color is darker than 50% gray, the image is darkened by decreasing the brightness. |

| Mode | Description |
|------|-------------|
| Luminosity | Blends the colors using the original color's hue and saturation values and the applied color's luminance value. |
| Multiply | Blends the colors by multiplying the values of the original color by those of the applied color, producing a darker color. |
| Normal | Applies the color used by the selected tool to the affected area, which is the default mode. In a layer blend at 100% opacity, any portion of the top layer that is not transparent simply blocks out the pixels in the layers below. This mode appears as Threshold for Bitmap and Indexed color images. |
| Overlay | Overlays the original color with the applied color, blending to produce a lighter color (like the Screen mode) or a darker color (like the Multiply mode), depending on the original color. |
| Pin Light | "Softer" than Soft Light, this mode often has a graying action that can offer subtle shading effects. Replaces the colors, depending on the blend color. If the blend color (light source) is lighter than 50% gray, pixels darker than the blend color are replaced, and pixels lighter than the blend color do not change. If the blend color is darker than 50% gray, pixels lighter than the blend color are replaced, and pixels darker than the blend color do not change. This is useful for adding special effects to an image. |
| Saturation | Blends the colors using the original color's hue and luminance values and the applied color's saturation value. |
| Screen | Blends the colors by multiplying the inverse values of the original color by the applied color, producing a lighter color. Blending with black has no effect; blending with white produces white. |
| Soft Light | Produces an effect similar to bathing the affected area in a soft light. Depending on the color applied, this mode either lightens or darkens the area. Applying a color that is less than 50% gray lightens the affected area, as with the Color Dodge mode. Applying a color that is more than 50% gray darkens the area, as with the Color Burn mode. |
| Subtract | Available in the Apply Image and Calculations dialog boxes. Subtracts the brightness value of each pixel in the source image from the aligned pixel in the target image, divides the difference by the scale, then adds the offset value. The Subtract mode darkens the image. Here's the formula: (Target − Source) ÷ Scale + Offset = Brightness value. |

| Mode | Description |
|------|-------------|
| Threshold | Applies the color used by the selected tool to the affected area, which is the default mode for Bitmap or Indexed color images. This mode appears as Normal for other types of images. |
| Vivid Light | Harsher than Hard Light, this blending mode can create highly saturated effects or obliterate detail with high contrasts. Burns or dodges the colors by increasing or decreasing the contrast, depending on the blend color. If the blend color (light source) is lighter than 50% gray, the image is lightened by decreasing the contrast. If the blend color is darker than 50% gray, the image is darkened by increasing the contrast. |

# Quick Keys

*Photoshop 7 offers* keyboard shortcuts for many program operations. This appendix lists the more commonly used shortcuts, organized as follows:

- Display
- Document
- Tools
- Scrolling
- Image editing
- Type
- Layers
- Filmstrip editing
- Channels
- Palettes

Many of Photoshop's commands are the same as ImageReady's. Key commands that are exclusive to either program are noted.

# Display

| ACTION | MACINTOSH | WINDOWS |
|---|---|---|
| Set default colors | D | D |
| Set Display mode options | F | F |
| Jump to ImageReady/Photoshop | Shift-⌘-M | Shift-Ctrl-M |
| Switch to Quick Mask/Standard mode | Q | Q |
| Switch background and foreground color | X | X |
| Zoom in | ⌘-+ (plus sign) | Ctrl- + (plus sign) |
| Zoom out | ⌘- – (minus sign) | Ctrl- – (minus sign) |
| Show/hide open palettes, Tool palette, and Options bar | Tab | Tab |
| Show/hide open palettes | Shift-Tab | Shift-Tab |
| Show Preferences dialog box | ⌘-K | Ctrl-K |
| Show/hide Brush palette | F5 | F5 |
| Show/hide Color palette | F6 | F6 |
| Show/hide Layers palette | F7 | F7 |
| Show/hide Info palette | F8 | F8? |
| Show/hide Actions palette | F9 | F9? |
| Fit on-screen | ⌘-0 | Ctrl-0 |
| Actual pixels | ⌘-Option-0 | Ctrl-Alt-0 |
| Gamut Warning (Photoshop) | Shift-⌘-Y | Shift-Ctrl-Y |
| Show proof colors (Photoshop) | ⌘-Y | Ctrl-Y |
| Toggle standard/precise cursor | Caps Lock | Caps Lock |
| Launch browser for preview (ImageReady) | ⌘-Option-P | Ctrl-Alt-P |
| Show rulers | ⌘-R | Ctrl-R |

# Document

| ACTION | MACINTOSH | WINDOWS |
|---|---|---|
| New | ⌘-N | Ctrl-N |
| Open | ⌘-O | Ctrl-O |
| Browse | Shift-⌘-O | Shift-Ctrl-O |
| Close | ⌘-W | Ctrl-W |
| Close All | ⌘-Shift-W | Ctrl-Shift-W |
| Page Setup | Shift-⌘-P | Shift-Ctrl-P |
| Print With Preview | ⌘-P | Ctrl-P |
| Print | ⌘-Option-P | Ctrl-Alt-P |
| Print One Copy | Option-Shift-⌘-P | Alt-Shift-Ctrl-P |
| Quit/Exit | ⌘-Q | Ctrl-Q |
| Save File | ⌘-S | Ctrl-S |
| Save Optimized (ImageReady) | ⌘-Option-S | Ctrl-Alt-S |
| Save Optimized As (ImageReady) | Shift-⌘-Option-S | Shift-Ctrl-Alt-S |
| Save For Web (Photoshop) | Shift-⌘-Option-S | Shift-Ctrl-Alt-S |
| File Info (ImageReady) | Shift-⌘-K | Shift-Ctrl-K |

# Tools

| TOOL | KEY |
|------|-----|
| Rectangular Marquee/Elliptical Marquee | M |
| Lasso/Polygonal Lasso/Magnetic Lasso | L |
| Crop | C |
| Healing Brush/Patch Tool | J |
| Clone Stamp/Pattern Stamp | S |
| Eraser/Background Eraser/Magic Eraser | E |
| Blur/Sharpen/Smudge | R |
| Path Selection/Direct Selection | A |
| Pen/Freeform Pen | P |
| Notes/Audio Annotation | N |
| Hand | H |
| Move | V |
| Magic Wand | W |
| Slice/Slice Select | K |
| Brush/Pencil | B |
| History Brush/Art History Brush | Y |
| Gradient/Paint Bucket | G |
| Dodge/Burn/Sponge | O |
| Horizontal Type/Vertical Type/Horizontal Type Mask/Vertical Type Mask | T |
| Rectangle/Rounded Rectangle/Ellipse/Polygon/Line/Custom Shape | U |
| Eyedropper/Color Sampler/Measure | I |
| Zoom | Z |

Table D.3

**Quick Keys for Tools**

# Scrolling

| ACTION | MACINTOSH | WINDOWS |
|--------|-----------|---------|
| Scroll up | Control-K | PgUp |
| Scroll up slightly | Shift-Control-K | Shift-PgUp |
| Scroll down | Control-L | PgDn |
| Scroll down slightly | Shift-Control-L | Shift-PgDn |
| Scroll left | ⌘-Control-K | Ctrl-PgUp |
| Scroll left slightly | Shift-⌘-Control-K | Shift-Ctrl-PgUp |
| Scroll right | ⌘-Control-L | Ctrl-PgDn |
| Scroll right slightly | Shift-⌘-Control-L | Shift-Ctrl-PgDn |

Table D.4

**Quick Keys for Scrolling**

# Image Editing

| ACTION | MACINTOSH | WINDOWS |
|---|---|---|
| Undo | ⌘-Z | Ctrl-Z |
| Redo (toggle) | ⌘-Z | Ctrl-Z |
| Deselect | ⌘-D | Ctrl-D |
| Reselect | Shift-⌘-D | Shift-Ctrl-D |
| Select all | ⌘-A | Ctrl-A |
| Inverse selection | Shift-⌘-I | Shift-Ctrl-I |
| Extras (Selection Edges, Grid, Slices) | ⌘-H | Ctrl-H |
| Copy to Clipboard | ⌘-C | Ctrl-C |
| Copy merged layers | Shift-⌘-C | Shift-Ctrl-C |
| Paste | ⌘-V | Ctrl-V |
| Paste into selection | Shift-⌘-V | Shift-Ctrl-V |
| Cancel operation | ⌘-period | Esc |
| Step forward | Shift-⌘-Z | Shift-Ctrl-Z |
| Step backward | ⌘-Option-Z | Ctrl-Alt-Z |
| Feather | ⌘-Option-D | Ctrl-Alt-D |
| Free transform | ⌘-T | Ctrl-T |
| Transform again | Shift-⌘-T | Shift-Ctrl-T |
| Extract (Photoshop) | ⌘-Option-X | Ctrl-Alt-X |
| Liquify | Shift-⌘-X | Shift-Ctrl-X |
| Pattern Maker | Option-Shift-⌘-X | Alt-Shift-Ctrl-X |
| Show Color Settings dialog box (Photoshop) | Shift-⌘-K | Shift-Ctrl-K |
| Show Fill dialog box | Shift-Delete | Shift-Backspace |
| Fill with the foreground color | Option-Delete | Alt-Backspace |
| Apply foreground color fill to areas with pixels | Shift-Option-Delete | Shift-Alt-Backspace |
| Fill with background color | ⌘-Delete | Ctrl-Backspace |
| Fill with background color with preserve transparency | Shift-⌘-Delete | Shift-Ctrl-Backspace |
| Reapply filter with changed options | ⌘-Option-F | Ctrl-Alt-F |
| Fade | Shift-⌘-F | Shift-Ctrl-F |
| Add to selection with selection tool | Shift-drag | Shift-drag |
| Subtract from selection with selection tool | Option-drag | Alt-drag |
| Duplicate selection contents with selection tool | ⌘-Option-drag | Ctrl-Alt-drag |
| Duplicate selection contents with the Move tool | Option-drag | Alt-drag |
| Change opacity of selected painting tool | Type a number between 0 and 100 | Type a number between 0 and 100 |

# Type

| ACTION | MACINTOSH | WINDOWS |
|---|---|---|
| Increase selected type size in 2-point increments | Shift-⌘-> | Shift-Ctrl-> |
| Decrease selected type size in 2-point increments | Shift-⌘-< | Shift-Ctrl-< |
| Increase selected type size in 10-point increments | Shift-⌘-Option-> | Shift-Ctrl-Alt-> |
| Decrease selected type size in 10-point increments | Shift-⌘-Option-< | Shift-Ctrl-Alt-< |
| Increase selected type tracking/kerning in 20–em space increments | Option- → | Alt- → |
| Decrease selected type tracking/kerning in 20–em space increments | Option- ← | Alt- ← |
| Increase selected type tracking/kerning in 100–em space increments | ⌘-Option- → | Ctrl-Alt- → |
| Decrease selected type tracking/kerning in 100–em space increments | ⌘-Option- ← | Alt-Ctrl- ← |
| Increase selected type baseline shift in 2-point increments | Shift-Option-↑ | Shift-Alt-↑ |
| Decrease selected type baseline shift in 2-point increments | Shift-Option-↓ | Shift-Alt-↓ |
| Increase selected type baseline shift in 10-point increments | Shift-⌘-Option-↑ | Shift-Ctrl-Alt-↑ |
| Decrease selected type baseline shift in 10-point increments | Shift-⌘-Option-↓ | Shift-Ctrl-Alt-↓ |
| Align left | ⌘-Shift-L | Ctrl-Shift-L |
| Align right | ⌘-Shift-R | Ctrl-Shift-R |
| Align center | ⌘-Shift-C | Ctrl-Shift-C |
| Decrease/increase leading by 10 points | ⌘-Option-↑ or ⌘-Option-↓ | Ctrl-Alt-↑ or Ctrl-Alt-↓ |
| Decrease/increase leading by 2 points | Option-↑ or Option-↓ | Alt-↑ or Alt-↓ |

Table D.6

**Quick Keys for Type Operations**

# Layers

| ACTION | MACINTOSH | WINDOWS |
|---|---|---|
| Bring layer to front | Shift-⌘-] | Shift-Ctrl-] |
| Bring layer forward | ⌘-] | Ctrl-] |
| Send layer backward | ⌘-[ | Ctrl-[ |
| Send layer to back | Shift-⌘-[ | Shift-Ctrl-[ |
| Make new layer | Shift-⌘-N | Shift-Ctrl-N |
| Make new layer via copy | ⌘-J | Ctrl-J |
| Make new layer via cut | Shift-⌘-J | Shift-Ctrl-J |
| Group layer with previous | ⌘-G | Ctrl-G |
| Ungroup | Shift-⌘-G | Shift-Ctrl-G |
| Merge layers down | ⌘-E | Ctrl-E |
| Merge visible layers | Shift-⌘-E | Shift-Ctrl-E |
| Select contents of layer | ⌘-click layer | Ctrl-click layer |
| Merge visible layers to a targeted layer | Shift-Option-⌘-E | Shift-Alt-Ctrl-E |

Table D.7

**Quick Keys for Layer Operations**

# Filmstrip Editing

| ACTION | MACINTOSH | WINDOWS |
|---|---|---|
| Scroll up one frame | Shift-PgUp | Shift-PgUp |
| Scroll down one frame | Shift-PgDn | Shift-PgDn |
| Move a selection one frame up | Shift-↑ | Shift-↑ |
| Move a selection one frame down | Shift-↓ | Shift-↓ |
| Clone a selection up or down | Shift-Option | Shift-Alt |

# Channels

| ACTION | MACINTOSH | WINDOWS |
|---|---|---|
| Load composite as selection | ⌘-Option-~ | Ctrl-Alt-~ |
| Load layer mask as selection | ⌘-Opt-\ | Ctrl-Alt-\ |
| Load selection channel 1–9 | ⌘-Option-1–9 | Ctrl-Alt-1–9 |
| Select channel 1–9 | ⌘-1–9 | Ctrl-1–9 |
| Select composite channel | ⌘-~ | Ctrl-~ |
| Select layer mask (channel) | ⌘-\ | Ctrl-\ |
| Toggle channel/Rubylith view | ~ | ~ |
| Toggle layer mask as Rubylith | \ | \ |

# Palettes

| ACTION | MACINTOSH | WINDOWS |
|---|---|---|
| Show/hide Actions palette | F9 | F9 |
| Show/hide all palettes | Tab | Tab |
| Show/hide Color palette | F6 | F6 |
| Show/hide Info palette | F8 | F8 |
| Show/hide Layers palette | F7 | F7 |
| Show/hide toolbar and palettes | Shift-Tab | Shift-Tab |
| Show options/Brushes palette | Return | Enter |

# Glossary

**Action** A Photoshop script that automates a single operation or a sequence of operations. Photoshop comes with default Actions, and you can create and save custom Actions to a file. When you need a particular Action or Action sequence, you can play it and apply its operations to any image by pressing a function key.

**Actions palette** The Photoshop palette that contains controls for recording and playing back Actions.

**additive primary colors** Red, green, and blue, which are used to create all other colors when direct, or transmitted, light is used (for example, on a computer monitor). When pure red, green, and blue are superimposed on one another, they create white.

**Adjustment layer** In Photoshop, a separate layer containing the mathematical data for an adjustment operation applied to an image. You can reedit the Adjustment layer at any time during the imaging process.

**Adobe Gamma calibration package** A package that includes Adobe Gamma software, the Gamma Wizard, and ICC (International Color Consortium) color profiles for some RGB devices. You can use the Gamma software to calibrate your monitor.

**alpha channel** An 8-bit, grayscale representation of an image. Alpha channels are selections that have been stored for later use. The values of gray can represent tonality, color, opacity, or semitransparency. Image formats that support alpha channels include Photoshop (PSD), Photoshop 2.0, Photoshop PDF, PICT, PICT Resource, PIXAR, Raw, Targa, TIFF, and Photoshop.

**analog** Signals made up of continuously varying wave forms.

**anti-alias** A process that adds a 2- or 3-pixel border around an edge that blends into the adjacent color to create a small transition zone. Without the anti-alias, an image would look stair-stepped and not have smooth transitions between colors. The width of an anti-alias is determined by the resolution of the image; you have no control over its size.

**artifact** An unintentional image element produced in error by an imaging device or inaccurate software. Dirty optics are one common reason for artifacts.

**aspect ratio** The height-to-width ratio of a selection, an image, or—in the case of digital video—a frame.

**Background** In Photoshop, the area behind layers. The contents of all layers float on top of the Background. Unlike a layer, the Background is opaque and cannot support transparency. If the document contains more than one layer, the Background is always at the bottom of the stack and cannot be moved or placed in a higher position. When new layers are added to the document, their content always appears in front of the Background.

**baseline** An imaginary line on which the bottom of most textual characters are placed. Some characters, such as *g* and *y*, have descenders that extend below the baseline.

**baseline shift** The movement of the baseline of a character horizontally or vertically from its default starting position. Unlike leading, which affects all of the characters in a paragraph, baseline shift affects individual characters.

**batch Action** An Action that will be applied to all of the images in a folder automatically, also known as *batch processing*. You can batch-process a group of images within a folder or from a different source, such as a digital camera or scanner with a document feeder.

**Bezier curves** Lines and shapes composed of mathematically defined points and segments. Bezier curves are used in vector graphics.

**bit depth** Refers to the amount of information per color channel. Photoshop can read images with 16 bits of information per channel, such as a 48-bit RGB or a 64-bit CMYK color image. Even though images with higher bit depths contain more color information, they are displayed on the monitor at the bit-depth capability of the computer's video card, which is 24 bits in most cases.

**Bitmap mode** A Photoshop mode that displays and converts images that are composed of pixels, each containing 1 bit of information. The pixels are either black or white. Bitmap images are used to create line art and digital halftones. Bitmap image file sizes are smaller than grayscale images, which contain 8 bits per pixel, or color images, which contain 24 bits per pixel. Bitmapped images do not support layers, alpha channels, filters, or any operations involving color.

**black point** The darkest pixel in the shadow areas of an image. In Photoshop, you can set this point in the Levels and Curves dialog boxes.

**blending mode**  A preprogrammed color formula that determines how the pixels in an image are affected by painting or image-editing and overlay operations. In Photoshop, the Mode menu on the Options bar offers a choice several blending modes.

**brightness**  The relative lightness or darkness of a color, measured from 0 to 100 percent. Brightness is also referred to as *value*. Colors with low brightness values are dark; colors with high brightness values are light.

**burn**  A technique used by photographers in the darkroom to underexpose or darken areas of an image. Photoshop's Burn tool darkens by lowering the brightness values of pixels as you move the tool over the image.

**calibrated monitor**  The foundation from which all other color settings are determined. You can use a calibration device or the Adobe Gamma calibration package to calibrate your monitor.

**calibration bars**  The grayscale or color indicators that appear on printed output. When you print a CMYK color separation, the calibration bars appear only on the black plate. On a color image, the calibration bars are the color swatches printed at the sides of the image.

**canvas**  In Photoshop, the surface on which your image resides.

**capture**  Specific to digital video, the transferal of video information via Firewire to a computer environment for nonlinear editing.

**channel**  Analogous to a plate in the printing process, the foundation of an image. Some image types have only one channel, while other types have several channels. An image can have up to 24 channels. See also *color channels*.

**Channel Mixer**  A Photoshop feature that allows you to adjust the color information of each channel. You can establish color values on a specific channel as a mixture of any or all of the color channels' brightness values.

**Channels palette**  The Photoshop palette that allows you to work with an image's color information, or channels, and create alpha channels.

**Character palette**  The Photoshop palette that contains settings for type, such as size, tracking, kerning, and leading.

**chroma**  See *saturation*.

**CIE (Commission Internationale d'Eclairage)**  An international organization of scientists who work with matters relating to color and lighting. The organization is also called the International Commission on Illumination.

**clipping group**  Layers grouped together to create effects. In order to join two layers into a clipping group, the image on the bottom layer must be surrounded by transparency. When a layer is clipped, it fills the shape of the image on the layer below it so that it acts as a mask to clip the layer immediately above it.

**clipping path**  A path designed to be used as a mask in other applications. In Photoshop, the Clipping Paths option in the Paths Palette menu allows you to create a path that will knock out the area outside the path when it is opened in another program. The interior portion of the path will be displayed, and the area outside the path will be transparent.

**cloning**  In Photoshop and other image-editing programs, a feature that allows you to copy a part of an image and use that copy to replace another part of the image. Cloning is accomplished with the Clone Stamp and Pattern Stamp tools.

**CMYK**  The colors used in process printing. Each color plate contains tiny dots of cyan, magenta, yellow, or black (CMYK). The densities of the colored dots on each plate influence the surrounding colors when the eye mixes them together.

**CMYK color mode**  A color mode that produces a full range of color by printing tiny dots of cyan, magenta, yellow, and black ink. Because the colored dots are so small, the eye mixes them together. The relative densities of groups of colored dots produce variations in color and tonality. CMYK is referred to as a *subtractive* color system.

**CMYK image**  A four-channel image containing a cyan, magenta, yellow, and black channel. A CMYK image is generally used to print color separations.

**CODEC**  An acronym for the compression/decompression process. Reducing storage requirements and the data rate required to retrieve video from a disk for decompression and playback.

**color channels**  Color information from an image. The number of color channels depends on the image's color mode. For example, Photoshop configures the information for an RGB image into three color channels (for the red, green, and blue components) plus a composite RGB channel, which displays the entire image in full color. The computer processes the information in each channel as an independent grayscale image. Each pixel is assigned a specific numeric gray value, where black equals 0 and white equals 255. Each color channel is actually an 8-bit grayscale image that supports 256 shades of gray.

**color correction**  Changing the colors of pixels in an image—including adjusting brightness, contrast, midlevel grays, hue, and saturation—to achieve optimum printed results.

**color depth** Refers to the number of shades that an imaging device can capture at once. The more bits there are per pixel, the more hues you can represent. The most common color depth, 8 bits per color, can produce 256 shades of each hue.

**color management module (CMM)** The color management engine used by software to convert colors. The Adobe engine is ACE (Adobe Color Engine). Others you might encounter include Agfa, Apple ColorSync, Apple, Heidelberg, Imation, Kodak, Microsoft, and X-Rite.

**color management policies** Policies that determine how Photoshop deals with color profiles when opening RGB, CMYK, or Grayscale files.

**color mapping** Operations that can radically alter existing colors in an image. Color mapping provides the means to alter the basic characteristics of color while maintaining the image's detail.

**color mode or model** A system of displaying or printing color. Photoshop supports the HSB color model and RGB, CMYK, Lab, Indexed, Duotone, Grayscale, Multichannel, and Bitmap color modes.

**color separation (process)** An image that has been separated into the four process colors: cyan, magenta, yellow, and black (CMYK). The image is then printed on four separate plates, one for each of the process colors.

**color space** The colors produced by a specific device, such as a printer or monitor. Photoshop 7 allows you to edit and store an image with a color space other than that of your monitor. The image is embedded with an ICC (International Color Consortium) profile that describes the working color space. The image can then move from one computer to another with its profile, and it can be displayed on two different monitors and appear the same.

**colorize** To convert gray pixels to colored pixels. Before a black-and-white image can be colorized in Photoshop, you must change its mode from Grayscale to a mode that supports color (RGB, CMYK, or Lab). By colorizing, you apply color to the image without affecting the lightness relationships of the individual pixels, thereby maintaining the image's detail.

**continuous-tone image** An image containing gradient tones from black to white.

**contrast** The tonal gradation between the highlights, midtones, and shadows in an image.

**crop** To select part of an image and discard the unselected areas.

**crop marks** The marks that are printed near the edges of an image to indicate where the image is to be trimmed.

**Curves** A Photoshop color-adjustment tool that allows you to lighten, darken, add contrast, and solarize images.

**densitometer** An instrument used by print shops and service bureaus to measure the tonal density of printed halftones.

**density** The ability of an object to stop or absorb light. The less the light is reflected or transmitted by an object, the higher its density.

**density range** The range from the smallest highlight dot that a press can print to the largest shadow dot it can print.

**digital video (DV)** The configuration of video into a pixel-based media that can be interpreted and displayed on a computer monitor.

**digitize** Converting analog image or video information to a digital format.

**digitizer board** A special-purpose computer card that transforms video signals into image data. Image sources for this technology include television signals and the output from VCRs and traditional analog video cameras. Digitizer video boards are also called *frame grabbers*, because they receive the frames sent by the video image sources.

**distort** To stretch a selection or layer contents along either of its axes. Unlike skewing, distortion is not restricted to a single border at a time.

**dither** A method of distributing pixels to extend the visual range of color on-screen, such as producing the effect of shades of gray on a black-and-white display or more colors on an 8-bit color display. By making adjacent pixels different colors, dithering gives the illusion of a third color.

**dodge** A technique used by photographers in the darkroom to overexpose or lighten specific areas of an image. In Photoshop, the Dodge tool performs a similar function by increasing the brightness values of pixels as you paint with it.

**dot gain** A phenomenon in printing that causes dots to print larger due to the absorbency of the paper they are printed on. Dot gain creates darker tones or colors. Dot gain is reflected in an increase in the density of light reflected by an image.

**dots per inch (dpi)** The measurement of the number of dots produced by a printer that defines the tonal elements of a halftone dot or stochastic screen. The dpi determines the resolution of printed output.

**Droplet** A mini application that contains Actions. A Droplet can sit on the desktop or be saved to a disk file. You can apply an operation to a file or group of files by dragging the file or folder onto the Droplet's icon.

**drum scanner**  A type of scanner that uses a spinning drum. The image is taped to a drum that spins very rapidly while the scanner's sensors record its color and tonality information.

**Duotone**  An image that uses two inks. Duotone can add a wider tonal range in a grayscale image by using more than one shade of ink to fill in the gaps. Duotone curves let you control the density of each shade in the highlights, midtones, and shadows. Photoshop creates Duotones by applying the various curves that you've defined to a single image.

**Duotone mode**  A Photoshop mode that displays Duotones, which are images that have been separated into two spot colors. Duotone mode also supports Monotone (images with one color), Tritones (images with three colors), and Quadtones (images with four colors). The Duotone Mode color information is contained on one color channel. Photoshop displays a preview that is an RGB simulation of the ink combinations.

**DV**  See *digital video*.

**emulsion**  The photosensitive layer on a piece of film, paper, or plate.

**equalization**  A technique for distributing image data across a greater range of pixel values. Typical equalization techniques include gamma correction and adaptive histogram equalization.

**EQ (equalization)**  Specific to digital video, the altering of the frequency/amplitude response of a sound source or a sound system.

**fade-out rate**  The rate at which the Photoshop Paintbrush and Airbrush tools fade out as you paint with them to simulate an actual brush stroke.

**feather**  A process that creates a gradual transition between the inside and the outside of image borders. When you apply an effect to a feathered selection, it diminishes and becomes more transparent, producing a softening or blurring effect. Feathering gradually blends colored pixels into each other and eliminates hard edges. Feathering differs from anti-aliasing in that you can determine the size of the soft edge in pixels.

**feather edge**  The area along the border of a selection that is partially affected by changes you make to the selection.

**fill**  To paint a selected area with a gray shade, a color, or a pattern.

**Fill layer**  A Photoshop 7 method for filling an area. Fill layers combine the action of the Fill command with the flexibility of layers. You can create Fill layers with colors, gradients, or patterns.

**filter**  A software method for applying effects to images. With filters, you can adjust focus, eliminate unwanted artifacts, alter or create complex selection masks, and apply a wide range of artistic effects.

**Firewire**  A cable that allows the capture of DV (digital video) images and audio via an IEEE 1394 port.

**flatbed scanner**  A type of scanner that reads a line of an image at a time, recording it as a series of samples, or pixels, by bouncing light off the area it needs to digitize. The scanner directs the bounced light to a series of detectors that convert color and intensity into digital levels.

**floating selection**  In Photoshop, a selection that has been moved or pasted on an image or converted to a floating selection using the Float command in the Select menu. The selection floats above the pixels in the underlying image until it is deselected, and it can be moved without affecting the underlying image.

**font**  The style or appearance of a complete set of characters. The four main categories of fonts are serif, sans serif, cursive, and display or decorative.

**font obliqueness**  Refers to whether the characters in a font lean, as does italic style type.

**font weight**  Refers to the thickness or heaviness of the characters in a font.

**frame grabber**  See *digitizer board*.

**full-color image**  An image that uses 24-bit color. A full-color image uses three 8-bit primary color channels—for red, green, and blue—each containing 256 colors. These three channels produce a potential of 16.7 million colors ($256^3 = 16,777,216$). Photo-realistic images that consist of smooth gradations and subtle tonal variations require full color to be properly displayed.

**gamma**  A measurement of midtone brightness for a monitor. The gamma value defines the slope of that curve halfway between black and white. Gamma values range from 1.0 to about 2.5. The Macintosh has traditionally used a gamma of 1.8, which is relatively flat compared to television. Windows PCs use a 2.2 gamma value, which has more contrast and is more saturated.

**gamut** The range of viewable and printable colors for a particular color model, such as RGB (used for monitors) or CMYK (used for printing). When a color cannot be displayed or printed, Photoshop can warn you that the color is "out of gamut." In terms of color working spaces, the gamut of a monitor is a triangular space with its corners in the red, green, and blue areas of an industry-standard color gamut chart. The gamut chart plots the device's available colors compared to the gamut of colors that humans can see.

**GIF87a and GIF89a** The Graphics Interchange Formats (GIFs), used for Web applications and for saving animations produced in ImageReady. GIF is a *lossless-compression* format that compresses the image through reduction of the available colors. GIF87a does not support transparency. GIF89a is used to omit the visibility of selected colors on a Web browser.

**gradient** Variations of color that subtly blend into one another. Photoshop gradients blend multiple colors into each other or into transparency over a specified distance.

**gradient fill**
A fill that displays a gradual transition from the foreground color to the background color. In Photoshop, gradient fills are added with the Gradient tool or a Gradient Fill layer.

**gray-component replacement (GCR)** An operation that removes a mixture of cyan, magenta, and yellow, and replaces them with black. GCR is generally more extreme and uses more black than undercolor removal (UCR).

**grayscale image** An image that use an 8-bit system, in which any pixel can be one of 256 shades of gray. Each pixel contains 8 bits of information. Each bit can either be on (black) or off (white), which produces 256 possible combinations.

**Grayscale mode** A Photoshop color mode that displays black-and-white images. A grayscale image is composed of one channel consisting of up to 256 levels of gray, with 8 bits of color information per pixel. Each pixel has a brightness value between 0 (black) to 255 (white). Grayscale pixels may also be measured in percentages of black ink, from 0 percent (white) to 100 percent (black). When color images are converted to Grayscale mode, their hue and saturation information is discarded and their brightness (or luminosity) values remain.

**grid** In Photoshop, a series of equally spaced horizontal and vertical lines that create a visual matrix. A grid helps you see the global relations between aligned elements on a page. Grids do not print.

**GUI (graphical user interface)** A software program's way of interacting with users. The GUI (pronounced "gooey") of Photoshop lets you perform virtual operations that mimic real-world tasks like painting, compositing, or filtering.

**guide** In Photoshop, a horizontal or vertical line that can be positioned anywhere on the image's surface. Guides do not print.

**halftone** The reproduction of a continuous-tone image, which is made by using a screen that breaks the image into various-sized dots. The resolution, or number of lines per inch (lpi), of a halftone depends on the printer's capabilities. The tonal densities of an image are determined by the size of the dots. The larger the dot, the more ink deposited, and the darker the area appears. When you send an image to a printer, Photoshop, in tandem with the printer driver software, automatically converts the tonal information contained in pixels into dot-density information that the printer uses to construct the image.

**halftone screen** Refers to the dot density of a printed image, measured in lines per inch (lpi). A halftone screen, also called *screen frequency*, is a grid of dots.

**highlight** The lightest part of an image, represented on a digital image by pixels with high numeric values or on a halftone by the smallest dots or the absence of dots.

**histogram** A graph of the brightness values of an image. The more lines the histogram has, the more tonal values are present in the image. The length of a line represents the relative quantity of pixels of a particular brightness. The taller the line, the more pixels of a particular tonal range the image will contain. Histograms are displayed in Photoshop's Levels and Threshold dialog boxes.

**History palette** The Photoshop palette that records all of the changes that you make to an image during a session, as a series of individual states. You can use the History palette to revert to former versions of an image and to create special effects. The History palette also works in conjunction with the History Brush and Art History Brush tools.

**hotspot** In an image map, an area that links to another Web page or URL.

**HSB color model** A color model that uses hue, saturation, and brightness characteristics to define each color.

**HTML (Hypertext Markup Language)** The programming language used to create Web pages.

**hue** The color of light that is reflected from an opaque object or transmitted through a transparent one. Hue in Photoshop is measured by its position on a color wheel, from 0 to 360 degrees.

**ICC** See *International Color Consortium.*

**image caching** A mechanism that accelerates screen redrawing during the editing process.

**image link** A link on a Web page activated by clicking an image.

**image map** An image on a Web page that has multiple links to another Web page or URL. Each link is called a hotspot. Image maps let you define circular, polygonal, or rectangular areas as links.

**image size** The physical size and resolution of an image. The size of an image specifies the exact number of pixels that compose a picture.

**ImageReady** A companion program to Photoshop, used to create dynamic Web graphics.

**Indexed color image** A single-channel image, with 8 bits of color information per pixel. The index is a color lookup table containing up to 256 colors.

**Indexed color mode** A color mode that uses a maximum of 256 colors to display full-color images. When you convert an image color to Indexed mode, Photoshop stores the color information as a color lookup table. You can then use a specific palette to display the image to match the colors as closely as possible to the original. Because it contains fewer colors, Indexed color mode creates smaller file sizes than the other color modes produce.

**Info palette** The Photoshop palette that shows information about the current image. By default, the Info palette displays Actual Color and CMYK fields, the $x$ and $y$ coordinates of the position of the cursor, and the height and width of the selection. This palette can display values in many different modes, including Web, HSB, Lab, Total Ink, and Opacity.

**interlacing** A technique used to display a GIF image progressively on a Web page.

**International Color Consortium (ICC)** An organization that sets standards for color management systems and components.

**interpolation** In Photoshop, the setting for how the program resamples, or sizes, images.

**inverse** In Photoshop, to reverse the selection; that is, to change the selected area to the portion that you did not select with a selection tool.

**invert** To remap the brightness values of a channel to its opposite value. When you invert a channel, the white pixels with a value of 255 become black with a value of 0. Dark gray pixels in the channel with a value of 20, for example, will be remapped to a value of 235.

**JPEG (Joint Photographic Experts Group)** A *lossy-compression* file format that supports 24-bit color and is used to preserve the tonal variations in photographs. JPEG compresses file size by selectively discarding data. JPEG compression can degrade sharp detail in images and is not recommended for images with type or solid areas of color. JPEG does not support transparency. When you save an image as a JPEG, transparency is replaced by the matte color. (See also *matting.*)

**kerning** The space between two individual characters in text.

**knockout** An area that prevents ink from printing on part of an image, so that the spot color can print directly on the paper. Knockouts keep a spot color from overprinting another spot color or a portion of the underlying image.

**Lab color mode** A color mode that is device-independent. Lab color consists of three channels: a luminance or lightness channel (L), a green–red component (a), and a blue–yellow component (b). Lab can be used to adjust an image's luminance and color independently of each other.

**labels** A Photoshop printing option that prints the document and channel name on the image.

**layer** A software feature that allows you to isolate image elements so that you can work on each one individually. You can also rearrange the positions of layers, allowing parts of an image to appear in front of other parts. Earlier versions of Photoshop supported 99 layers; Photoshop 7 supports an unlimited number.

**layer mask** A mask that conceals an area from view. When you apply a layer mask to an image, you control the transparency of a particular part of the layer.

**Layers palette** The Photoshop palette that contains controls for working with layers, including creating and deleting layers, reordering layers, merging layers, and many other layer-related functions.

**layer set** A Photoshop 7 layer-management tool. Layer sets let you consolidate contiguous layers into a folder on the Layers palette. By highlighting the folder, you can apply certain operations to the layers as a group. For example, the layers in a layer set can be can simultaneously hidden, displayed, moved, or repositioned.

**layer styles** Predefined Photoshop 7 effects, such as drop shadows, neon glowing edges, and deep embossing. Layer styles apply their effects to the edges of the layer. Because they may be translucent or soft-edged, the colors of the underlying layer can be seen through the effects.

**leading**  The typographic term to describe vertical spacing between lines, measured from baseline to baseline.

**Levels**  A Photoshop tool that allows you to adjust an image's tonal range. When you perform a Levels adjustment, you are actually reassigning pixel values.

**ligature**  A set of two characters that is designed to replace certain character combinations, such as fl and fi, to avoid spacing conflicts.

**linear gradient**  A gradient that is projected from one point to another in a straight line.

**lines per inch (lpi)**  A measurement of the resolution of a halftone screen.

**Liquify**  A Photoshop feature that allows you to distort pixels and transform areas of an image using a special set of distortion and transformation tools.

**lossless compression**  An image-compression scheme that preserves image detail. When the image is decompressed, it is identical to the original version.

**lossy compression**  An image-compression scheme that creates smaller files but can affect image quality. When decompressed, the image produced is not identical to the original. Usually, colors have been blended, averaged, or estimated in the decompressed version.

**lpi**  See *lines per inch*.

**margin-style background**  A background that is configured so that the image repeats vertically but not horizontally. This type of background appears as a continuous design down the depth of the page. It is a common visual element that helps unify the design of a Web page.

**mask**  An element that isolates and protects portions of an image. A masked area is not affected by image editing such as color changes or applied filters. Masks are stored as 8-bit grayscale channels and can be edited with Photoshop tools.

**matting**  Filling or blending transparent pixels with a matte color. Matting can be used with GIF, PNG, and JPEG files. It is typically used to set transparent image areas to the background color of a Web page.

**midtone**  A tonal range of brightness values located approximately halfway between white and black.

**moiré pattern**  An undesirable pattern in color printing, resulting from incorrect screen angles of overprinting halftones. Moiré patterns can be minimized with the use of proper screen angles.

**monitor profile**  A description of a monitor's characteristics used by Photoshop to display images correctly on that monitor. One way to create a monitor profile is to make a visual calibration of your monitor using Adobe Gamma and then save the resulting information as a color profile.

**monitor resolution**  The number of pixels that occupy a linear inch of your monitor screen. The resolution for most Macintosh RGB monitors is 72 ppi. Most Windows VGA monitors have a resolution of 96 ppi.

**monospaced type**  Type in which all of the characters are the same horizontal width.

**Multichannel mode**  A Photoshop mode that allows you to view the spot-color channels in color separations. The number of channels in a Multichannel document depends on the number of channels in the source image before it was converted. Each channel in a Multichannel document contains 256 levels of gray. Multichannel mode will convert RGB to cyan, magenta, and yellow spot color channels, and CMYK into CMYK spot color channels.

**Navigator palette**  The Photoshop palette that shows a map of the current image displayed as a thumbnail. It indicates the exact location of what appears in the image window relative to the entire image and provides features for scrolling and zooming.

**noise**  In an image, pixels with randomly distributed color values. Noise is primarily a result of digitizing technology. Noise in digital photographs tends to be the product of low-light conditions.

**nonlinear editing (NLE)**  The random access of video storage.

**NTSC (North American Television Standards Committee) system**  The video standard for television used in North and South America and many Asian countries.

**object-oriented software**  Vector-based illustration applications (such as Adobe Illustrator, Macromedia FreeHand, and CorelDRAW) and page-layout programs (such as QuarkXPress, Adobe PageMaker, and Adobe InDesign). Vector-based illustration software is appropriate for creating graphics such as charts, graphs, maps, cartoons, architectural plans, and other images that require hard edges and smooth blends. Vector-based page-layout software is suitable for creating books, pamphlets, brochures, flyers, and other documents that combine images and text. Photoshop is *raster-based software*, rather than vector-based illustration software; it does not print object-oriented graphics as vectors.

**one-quarter tone** A tonal value located approximately halfway between the highlight and midtone.

**optimization** In Photoshop and ImageReady, features that put images in the best possible form for Web applications, such as the file format, color-reduction method, and matting settings. In Photoshop, optimization settings are available in the Save For Web dialog box. In ImageReady, these settings are on the Optimize palette.

**Optimize palette** The ImageReady palette that contains controls for optimizing images for Web applications.

**Options bar** In Photoshop, the area that contains settings for tools. When you select a tool in the Tool palette, the Options bar changes to reflect the options available for the selected tool.

**overprint colors**
Two or more inks that are printed one on top of the other.

**PAL (Phase Alternation Line) system** The video standard for television used in Western Europe, Australia, Japan, and other countries.

**PANTONE** A brand name of spot color inks. The PANTONE Matching System is a group of inks used to print spot colors. PANTONE inks are solid colors used to print solid or tinted areas. The PANTONE system is recognized all over the world.

**Paragraph palette** The Photoshop palette that contains settings that apply to entire text paragraphs, such as alignment and hyphenation.

**path** A vector object that mathematically defines a specific area on an image. Vector objects are composed of anchor points and line segments known as *Bezier curves*. Paths enable you to create straight lines and curves with precision. If a path's two endpoints are joined, it encloses a shape. A path can be filled with color, stroked with an outline, or stored in the Paths palette or the Shape library for later use. A path also can be converted into a selection.

**Paths palette** The Photoshop palette that contains controls for working paths, including creating deleting paths, filling paths, stroking paths, and saving work paths.

**perspective** In Photoshop, a transformation that squeezes or stretches one edge of a selection, slanting the two adjacent sides either in or out. This produces an image that mimics the way you perceive a picture slanted at a distance.

**pixel** An individual square of colored light, which is the smallest editable unit in a digital image. The pixels (short for *picture elements*) in a digital image are usually so small that, when seen, the colors blend into what appears to be a *continuous-tone* image.

**pixels per inch (ppi)** The number of pixels that can be displayed per inch, usually used to refer to pixel resolution from a scanned image or on a monitor.

**plug-in** A modular mini program or filter, usually developed by a third-party vendor, that adds functions to Photoshop.

**PNG-8** A lossless-compression file format that supports 256 colors and transparency. PNG-8 is not supported by older Web browsers.

**PNG-24** A lossless file format that supports 24-bit color, transparency, and matting. PNG-24 combines the attributes of JPEG and GIF. PNG-24 is not supported by older Web browsers.

**point** A measurement system for type. There are traditionally about 72 points in 1 inch.

**ppi** See *pixels per inch*.

**preferences** In Photoshop, settings that affect the appearance and behavior of the program, which are stored in the preferences file.

**Preset Manager** A library of palettes that can be used by Photoshop. As you add or delete items from the palettes, the currently loaded palette in the Preset Manager displays the changes. You can save the new palette and load any of the palettes on the system.

**printer resolution** The number of dots that can be printed per linear inch, measured in dots per inch (dpi). These dots compose larger halftone dots on a halftone screen or stochastic (random pattern) dots on an ink-jet printer.

**process color** The four color pigments used in color printing: cyan, magenta, yellow, and black (CMYK).

**progressive JPEG file** A file that displays a low-resolution version of the image while the full image is downloading.

**Proof Colors** A Photoshop 7 control that allows the on-screen preview to simulate a variety of reproduction processes without converting the file to the final color space. This feature takes the place of the Preview In CMYK feature in earlier Photoshop versions.

**Quadtone** An image that has been separated into four spot colors.

**Quick Mask mode** A Photoshop mode that allows you to edit a selection as a mask. This mode provides an efficient method of making a temporary mask using the paint tools. Quick Masks can be converted into selections or stored as alpha channels in the Channels palette for later use.

**radial gradient** A gradient that is projected from a center point outward in all directions.

**random access memory (RAM)** The part of the computer's memory that stores information temporarily while the computer is on.

**raster image** An image that consists of a grid of pixels. Raster images are also called *bitmaps*. The file sizes of raster images are usually quite large compared to other types of computer-generated documents, because information needs to be stored for every pixel in the entire document. See also *raster-based software*.

**raster image processor (RIP)** Software on a computer or a device inside an imagesetter or PostScript printer that interprets a vector curve by connecting a series of straight-line segments.

**raster-based software** Photoshop and other programs that create raster images. Raster-based software is best suited for editing, manipulating, and compositing scanned images, images from digital cameras and Photo CDs, continuous-tone photographs, realistic illustrations, and other graphics that require subtle blends, soft edges, shadow effects, and artistic filter effects like Impressionist or watercolor.

**rasterize** Converting vector information into pixel-based information. For example, you can rasterize type so that you can apply filters and other effects that do not work on vector-based type. Rasterized type cannot be edited as individual characters and appears at the same resolution as the document.

**red eye** An effect from flash photography that appears to make a person's eyes glow red.

**registration mark** A mark that appears on a printed image, generally for color separations, to help in aligning the printing plates.

**rendering intents** Settings established by the International Color Consortium (ICC) under which color conversions can be made. Rendering intents cause the color of an image to be modified while it is being moved into a new color space. The four rendering intents are Perceptual, Saturation, Relative Colorimetric, and Absolute Colorimetric.

**resample** To change the size or resolution of an image. Resampling down discards pixel information in an image; resampling up adds pixel information through interpolation.

**resolution** The number of units that occupy a linear inch of an image, measured in pixels per inch (ppi) on an image or monitor or dots per inch (dpi) on a printer. The resolution of an image determines how large it will appear and how the pixels are distributed over its length and width. Resolution also determines the amount of detail that an image contains. High resolutions produce better quality but larger image file sizes. Resolution can also refer to the number of bits per pixel.

**resolution-independent image** An image that automatically conforms to the highest resolution of the output device on which it is printed.

**RGB color mode** A color mode that represents the three colors—red, green, and blue—used by devices such as scanners or monitors to display color. Each range of color is separated into three separate entities called *color channels*. Each color channel can produce 256 different values, for a total of 16,777,216 possible colors in the entire RGB gamut. RGB is referred to as an *additive* color model. Each pixel contains three brightness values for red, green, and blue that range from 0 (black) to 255 (white). When all three values are at the maximum, the effect is complete white.

**RGB image** A three-channel image that contains a red, a green, and a blue channel.

**rollover** A mini animation that is activated by mouse behavior. Rollovers add interactivity to a Web page. Rollovers depend on layers for their behavior. You designate a rollover on an image by changing the visibility of a layer's content.

**safe action** A defined area for video display that indicates the space where the video action will be displayed on standard television screens.

**safe title** A defined area for video display that indicates the space where the image is not distorted or cropped by the curve of standard television screens.

**saturation** The intensity of a color. Saturation, or *chroma*, is determined by the percentage of the hue in proportion to gray, from 0 to 100 percent. Zero-percent saturation means that the color is entirely gray.

**scanner** An electronic device that digitizes and converts photographs, slides, paper images, or other two-dimensional images into pixels.

**scratch disk** An area of memory that Photoshop uses as a source of virtual memory to process images when the program requires more memory than the allocated amount.

**screen angles** The angles at which the halftone screens are placed in relation to one another.

**screen frequency** The density of dots on the halftone screen, commonly measured in lines per inch (lpi). Also known as *screen ruling*.

**SECAM (Sequential Color and Memory) system** A video standard for television used in some European and Asian countries.

**shadow** The darkest part of an image, represented on a digital image by pixels with low numeric values or on a halftone by the smallest or absence of dots.

**skew** To slant a selection along one axis, either vertical or horizontal. The degree of slant affects how pitched the final image appears.

**slice** To cut an image into pieces, saving the individual parts as image files and writing an HTML document that reassembles the slices on the screen. Slicing increases the efficiency of displaying images with a Web browser by decreasing the download time. Slices also allow you to define rectangular areas as links to other Web pages or URLs.

**SMPTE-C** A movie industry standard, compliant with the Society of Motion Picture and Television Engineers standards for motion picture illuminants.

**snapshot** In Photoshop, a saved image's state. By default, when the image is opened, the History palette displays a snapshot of the image as it appeared when it was last saved. You can save the current image to a snapshot to preserve that state.

**soft proof** An on-screen document that appears as close as possible to what the image will look like if printed to a specific device. Image formats that allow you to embed a soft proof profile in the saved document are Photoshop EPS, Photoshop PDF, and Photoshop DCS 1.0 and 2.0.

**splash screen** A screen that appears when you first load a program. For example, the default Photoshop 7 splash screen indicates the components that are loading and program-specific data, such as the registered owner's name and the program's serial number.

**spot color** Ink used in a print job in addition to black or process colors. Each spot color requires a plate of its own. Spot colors are printed in the order in which they appear in the Channels palette. Spot color channels are independent of the color mode of the image, which means that they are not blended with the other channels in a Grayscale, RGB, or CMYK image. Spot color channels are also independent of layers, which means that you cannot apply spot colors to individual layers. Image formats that support spot color are Photoshop (PSD), Photoshop PDF, TIFF, and Photoshop DCS 2.0.

**sRGB color space** A color space designed for corporate computer monitors and images intended for Web applications. sRGB is the default color working space in Photoshop 7 but other color spaces are available.

**state** In Photoshop's History palette, a stored version of an image. Each time you perform an operation, the History palette produces a state with the name of the operation or tool that was used. The higher the state appears in the stack, the earlier in the process the state was made.

**stroking** Outlining a selection border with a color. In Photoshop, strokes can vary in width and relative position on the selection border.

**subtractive primary colors** Cyan, magenta, and yellow, which are the printing inks that theoretically absorb all color and produce black. Because pigments subtract light components from the white light in the environment, they reduce its intensity, making it less bright than unfiltered light. Subtractive colorants reduce the amount of light reflected back at the viewer.

**timeline** The window that provides a schematic view of your program including all video, audio, and superimposed video tracks in nonlinear editing programs like Adobe Premier.

**tolerance** A parameter of the Magic Wand and Paint Bucket tools that specifies the color range of the pixels to be selected.

**Tool palette** In Photoshop, the area that contains icons for tools, also called the Toolbox. Some of the tool icons expand to provide access to tools that are not visible, bringing the entire number of tools to 50, plus paint swatches, Quick Mask icons, view modes, and the Jump To command. The Tool palette is a floating palette that you can move or hide.

**tool tip** A GUI identifier that appears when you hover your cursor over a screen element and wait a few seconds. Photoshop includes tool tips for the tools on the Tool palette, as well as for many of its operations accessible from other palettes, the Options bar, dialog boxes, and windows.

**tracking** The global space between selected groups of characters in text.

**transparency scanner** A type of scanner that passes light through the emulsions on a piece of negative film or a color slide. A transparency scanner's dynamic range determines its ability to distinguish color variations.

**trap**  A technique used in preparing images for printing color separations. Misalignments or shifting during printing can result in gaps in images. A trap is an overlap that prevents such gaps from appearing along the edges of objects in an image.

**Tritone**  An image that has been separated into three spot colors.

**tweening**  From "in betweening," a method for adding transitions between frames in animations.

**undercolor removal (UCR)**  The process of reducing the cyan, magenta, and yellow inks from the darkest neutral shadow areas in an image, and replacing them with black.

**Unsharp Mask (USM)**  A mask that exaggerates the transition between areas of most contrast, while leaving areas of minimum contrast unaffected. It can help increase the contrast of an image and fool the eye into thinking fuzzy areas of the image are in focus.

**value**  See *brightness*.

**vector graphics**  Images that are composed of lines and objects that define their shapes. The objects created in vector-based software are made from *Bezier curves*, which are composed of mathematically defined points and segments. Vector images take up less space on a disk than raster images of comparable dimensions. See also *object-oriented software*.

**virtual memory**  The memory space that is separate from the main memory (physical random access memory, or RAM) in a computer, such as hard-disk space. Virtual memory helps to increase the amount of memory available to work on large documents.

**wallpaper tiles**  A background that is configured so that the image is displayed as repeating tiles.

**Web colors**  Colors that are browser-safe, meaning that all Web browsers can display them uniformly. Photoshop's Web-Safe Colors feature lets you choose colors that will not radically change when viewed on other monitors of the same quality and calibration as the one on which you are working.

**white point**  The lightest pixel in the highlight area of an image. In Photoshop, you can set this point in the Levels and Curves dialog boxes.

**work path**  In Photoshop, a temporary element that records changes as you draw new sections of a path.

# Index

**Note to the Reader:** Throughout this index **boldfaced** page numbers indicate primary discussions of a topic. *Italicized* page numbers indicate illustrations.

# Get Savvy™

# Soluti👁ns™ FROM SYBEX®

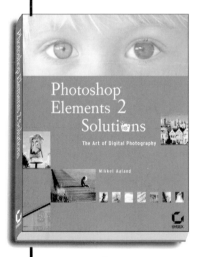

## ABOUT SYBEX

Sybex has been part of the personal computer revolution from the very beginning. We were founded in 1976 by Dr. Rodnay Zaks, an early innovator of the microprocessor era and the company's president to this day. Dr. Zaks was involved in the ARPAnet and developed the first published industrial application of a microcomputer system: an urban traffic control system.

While lecturing on a variety of technical topics in the mid-1970s, Dr. Zaks realized there wasn't much available in the way of accessible documentation for engineers, programmers, and businesses. Starting with books based on his own lectures, he launched Sybex simultaneously in his adopted home of Berkeley, California, and in his original home of Paris, France.

Over the years, Sybex has been an innovator in many fields of computer publishing, documenting the first word processors in the early 1980s and the rise of the Internet in the early 1990s. In the late 1980s, Sybex began publishing our first desktop publishing and graphics books. As early adopters ourselves, we began desktop publishing our books in-house at the same time.

Now, in our third decade, we publish dozens of books each year on topics related to graphics, web design, digital photography, and digital video. We also continue to explore new technologies and over the last few years have been among the first to publish on topics like Maya and Photoshop Elements.

With each book, our goal remains the same: to provide clear, readable, skill-building information, written by the best authors in the field—experts who know their topics as well as they know their audience.

## **ABOUT** THE AUTHOR

Steve Romaniello is an artist, educator, and writer. He began his career in graphics in 1980 as a production artist and typesetter; soon he was promoted to designer and then art director. In 1982, he became a partner in Armory Park Design Group. Three years later he founded Congress Street Design, a full-service design firm. In 1987, at the beginning of the digital revolution in graphics technology, he purchased his first graphics computer. Romaniello accepted a faculty position in 1990 in the Advertising Art program at Pima Community College in Tucson, Arizona, with the intention of developing a state-of-the-art digital graphics program. He served as chair of the renamed Communication Graphics department for eight years.

Romaniello has developed curriculum and training materials for many of the mainstream graphics programs, and has offered seminars at the Maine Photographic Workshops in Rockport, Maine; the League for Innovation; and National Business Media. A certified instructor in Adobe Photoshop and an authorized trainer in QuarkXPress, he currently teaches digital art at Pima Community College. He is the coauthor of *Mastering Adobe GoLive 4* and the author of *Mastering Photoshop 6*, both published by Sybex. His column, "The Digital Eye," appears monthly in *Digital Graphics* magazine. Romaniello is the founder of GlobalEye Systems, a company that offers seminars and onsite training and consulting throughout the country. He lives in Tucson, Arizona, with his wife Rebecca and daughter Leah.